KT-118-850

ATLAS
OF
MAN

ATLAS OF MAN

Marshall Cavendish

Editor	John Gaisford
Art Editor	Steve Leaning
Assistant Editor	Lynette Singer
Executive Editor	Richard Carlisle
Principal Advisor	André Singer

CONTRIBUTING CONSULTANTS

John Beattie	Linacre College, Oxford
Jonathan Benthall	Director, Royal Anthropological Institute
Don Brothwell	Institute of Archaeology, London University
Ken Brown	Dept. of Anthropology, Manchester University
Neville Colclough	Dept. of Social Anthropology, Kent University
C. von Fürer-Haimendorf	School of Oriental and African Studies, London
Brian Hook	Dept. of Chinese Studies, Leeds University
Stephen Hugh-Jones	Dept. of Anthropology, Cambridge University
Caroline Humphrey	Scott Polar Research Institute, Cambridge
Richard Lawless	Centre for Middle Eastern & Islamic Studies, Durham
Diana Martin	Institute of Social Anthropology, Oxford University
Malcolm McLeod	Keeper of Ethnography, British Museum
Anthony Milner	Dept. of S.E. Asian Studies, Kent University
André Singer	Royal Society for Asian Affairs
Andrew Strathern	Dept. of Anthropology, London University
James Wilson	British & European Studies Group, London

THE MAPS

Main Colour Maps	John Thompson Associates
Cartographic Typographer	Catherine Lawrence
Colour Diagram Maps	Roy Flooks
Black and White Maps	Eugene Fleury

Title photograph: The Hindu temple of Besakih, on the slopes of Bali's sacred Mount Agung

Typesetting	Gee & Watson, Horsfall & Sons
Reproduction and Assembly	Paramount Litho

Published by Marshall Cavendish Books Limited
58 Old Compton Street, London W1V 5PA
© Marshall Cavendish Limited, 1978, 1981
First published in 1978
This volume published 1981
Printed in Spain by Sopena-Print Export,
Barcelona, Madrid
This volume published 1981
ISBN 0 85685 445 X

Contents

H.R.H. THE PRINCE OF WALES

Preface

In my capacity as Patron of The Royal Anthropological Institute I was delighted to have been asked to contribute something towards this ambitious book. I say ambitious because it cannot have been an easy task to assemble a body of consultant anthropologists and then to ask them to write a description of the different peoples of the world (this atlas covers more than 400 in total) with each entry covering the main characteristics of a society in no more than 100 to 500 words! When I think of the acres of print dealing with just *one* society, which I read at Cambridge, I can imagine how difficult it must have been to compress so much information into a short space.

With the world rapidly becoming a smaller place and with increasing numbers of people being able to travel to remote parts of it there is a very real need for easily accessible and readable information of a non-specialized kind. It strikes me that ignorance of each other as human beings, as tribes or as races has been one of the root causes of all past conflicts between mankind. The more that can be done to increase the spread of knowledge, and thereby understanding and tolerance, the more likely are we to be able to co-exist with each other and resist the machinations of those unscrupulous politicians who tend to exploit ignorance.

It is imperative, too, that we understand the basic elements of Western society – what is often referred to as "the civilized world" – so that we can perceive the effect, at a sufficiently early stage, of "Westernization" on the more remote peoples of the world and decide whether it is the sort of effect that *should* be made upon them. There is little doubt that the constant pressure of Westernization has seriously threatened, and is still threatening, the traditions and structures of a considerable number of the societies described in this atlas. The consequent rapid changes tend to cause appalling problems and yet it seems no-one ever learns from past experience or mistakes. I suppose it is hardly surprising when so many of us live in advanced technological societies and are deluded into thinking that this represents civilization at its best, in contrast with the "uncivilized" existence of so-called primitive peoples. Industrialization has many advantages, but one of its disadvantages is that it tends to blind us to the natural world around us. By this I mean that we have become ignorant of the natural forces which have shaped the social structures and habits of "primitive" peoples and from this stems intolerance and prejudice.

I sincerely hope that this atlas will contribute something towards the knowledge we have of each other as human beings and that it will be enjoyed and used as a convenient source of the kind of information which up to now has been lacking in a single publication.

Charles

Part 1

The World of Man

In the 100,000 years since *Homo sapiens* began to evolve into modern man, human society has been reflected in a multitude of different cultures and civilizations. Modern communications have reduced the separation which used to exist between geographically remote peoples, and the impact of Western industrialized societies has reached almost every corner of the globe. Although the effect of this has been to create more cultural uniformity, there are still enormous variations in the way people live in different parts of the world. This book provides information, both general and specific, about the main groups of people living in the world today.

Part One, the World of Man, is a background to themes recurring throughout the book, a wider context in which the information about individual societies can be placed. It describes the factors that shape and influence all human societies, so that the reader may appreciate and understand the underlying unity of even the most apparently diverse cultures. Beginning with an outline of man's evolution and history, this section discusses the universal features of social organization, kinship, politics, language, religion, ritual and economics, and ends with a consideration of the impact of industrialization and its possible implications for the future of mankind.

Opposite: The world as it was known to Europeans in the late 16th century

Evolution

Nearly 4,000,000,000 people inhabit the earth today. All are derived from a common stock, and all are members of the same species, *Homo sapiens*, yet in physical appearance and in culture they exhibit an extraordinary variety. Biologists, concerned mainly with physical characteristics, have in the past attempted to classify regional variations by dividing mankind into categories known as 'races', based on features such as skin colour, physique, hair and facial structure. None of these schemes, however, has fully coped with the complexity of the situation, and popular usage has confused biological with social characteristics to misleading and often damaging effect. Anthropologists, concerned more with cultural variations, either avoid such terminology altogether or use it merely to indicate major groupings such as Negroid, Mongoloid or Caucasoid.

Groups of people living together in particular environments, whether in rural or in urban settings, tend to have distinctive cultural features, the most obviously cohesive of which is language. Thus the Ainu can be distinguished from the Japanese, the Eskimos from the Amerindians, the Lapps from the Swedes. Yet even here, precise distinctions are difficult to draw and, conversely, relationships between different peoples are often hard to establish, especially as migrations resulting from increasing population pressures during the past few thousand years have taken many groups from their original homelands. Neither anthropology nor biology can alone explain such a complex mosaic of different societies. Cultural and biological factors are inextricably mixed in the evolution of mankind, a process so complex and so gradual that we must combine information from fields as diverse as modern genetics and palaeontology—the study of fossils—to grasp even the bare outlines.

The Genetic Heritage

Physical characteristics are passed from parents to children by the action of genes—bio-chemical units contained within the nucleus of each cell in the human body. The combination of inherited genes is unique in every individual, accounting for numerous minor variations, but any group of people has a limited quantity of genes (known as a gene pool) available to pass on to later generations. Where a community lives undisturbed by outsiders for a long period, distinctive physical features may emerge through selective in-breeding.

The influence on later generations of a restricted gene pool, when a group is separated from a larger society through migration or environmental conditions, is known as founder effect. The physical characteristics of the Amerindians, for example, are markedly different from those of Asiatic peoples, who are their closest relatives. The gene pool of the nomadic groups who first entered America was modified only slightly by later arrivals such as the Eskimos, and thus evolved in almost total isolation.

Mankind has been forced to adapt to a wide range of ecological conditions. The genetic make-up of human groups can be influenced by environment, when physical characteristics useful for specific conditions are favoured and developed. Probably the most striking examples of genetic adaptation are found in the varying proportions of the body—mountain dwellers, for example, show a widespread tendency to be barrel-chested, as an adaptive response to the need for large lungs in conditions where the air is thinner.

Other groups have adapted to extremes of heat and cold. The Dinka people of Sudan are extremely tall, with straight, narrow bodies and long, thin limbs: the average height is well over six feet. In contrast, Eskimos are short and stocky, with a thick layer of fat. The large surface area of a Dinka's body allows heat to be radiated extremely efficiently, while an Eskimo's conserves heat, since the radiating surface is far smaller. The colour of human skin is also an adaptive feature, for dark skin (with a high melanin content in the outermost layers) protects the body from intense sunlight and ultra-violet rays, believed to cause cancer of the skin.

Similarly, the human face has been influenced by the environment. The Evenki of Siberia and other Mongoloid peoples have flat faces, reducing the surface area—and therefore heat loss—to a minimum. The region around the eyes is well padded with fat, which reduces the visible part of the eye to a distinctive slit. The fatty tissue covers the nasal sinuses and protects the eyeball from severe cold and the retina from snow-glare. Fatty pads around the nose provide added insulation and warm the air on its way to the lungs.

Early Migrations

These genetic adaptations took thousands of years to develop; indeed the evolutionary line leading to *Homo sapiens* himself dates back to beyond 5,000,000 years ago. Modern man became fully established only in the Upper Pleistocene, a geological phase of some 100,000 years in duration which ended in about 8,000 BC. During this period of repeated glaciation broken by milder intervals, other human varieties occupied much of Europe (Neanderthal), southern Africa (Rhodesian) and South-East Asia (Solo). It seems likely that our direct ancestors emerged along a geographical belt free of ice, covering much of southern Asia and perhaps extending into north-east Africa.

The early development of the species remains uncertain, but our ancestors had almost certainly begun separating into smaller groups and exploring new areas by about 40,000 years ago. This expansion probably resulted from the constant quest for food—by following herds of large game such as mammoths, reindeer, bison and horses, and gathering wild vegetable crops—as well as from natural curiosity. Glaciation had reduced sea-levels, exposing land bridges by which nomadic groups crossed from Siberia to Alaska, and from mainland South-East Asia into Java. Well before 10,000 years ago, the species must have been divided into geographically separate tribes and even nations.

Human groups were already developing physical as well as cultural differences. Archaeological sites in Europe provide evidence that, as the ice withdrew at the end of the Pleistocene, the Neanderthals were replaced by people apparently little different in appearance from modern Europeans. In Africa, people with Negroid and Bushmanoid characteristics adapted to humid and arid environments had completely replaced Rhodesian man perhaps as early as 30,000 years ago. In central and eastern Asia, fossil remains probably indicate evolving Australian and southern Mongoloid characteristics, while evidence in America suggests that Amerindians were distinguishable, at least on a skeletal level, before 10,000 years ago.

By the end of the Pleistocene, it seems, *Homo sapiens* was already divided into a number of broad categories inhabiting widely varied terrain, adapting to different climates and food resources, and developing resistance to different diseases. Cultural distinctions had also emerged; it has been suggested, for example, that by 30,000 years ago there were already a number of major language groups, with perhaps 60 or more sub-divisions. As the different peoples gradually separated further, into independent tribal groups, thousands of dialects developed. Similarly, it appears from cave art, human burial practices and evidence of bear cults, that rituals and other forms of social behaviour were being elaborated, further emphasizing the differences between groups.

The Agricultural Revolution

Humans first began to settle in permanent communities some time around the end of the Pleistocene. After many thousands of years following a nomadic hunting-gathering economy, climatic changes and reductions in the herds of large game animals demanded a new means of subsistence. Some groups turned first to more specialized economies, hunting small game, fowling and fishing, and developed an elaborate technology with bone, wood and stone as materials. Others, in the Middle East, southern Asia, Europe and the Americas, began to domesticate animals or grow plants during the years between 8,000 and 3,000 BC.

At first the change would have involved the greater control and protection of wild animals such as sheep, goats and pigs, or the simple cultivation of wild grains. Probably only much later was there any intentional culling of undesirable elements in the livestock, selection of favourable grains for sowing and thus the beginnings of strain differentiation. Gradually the new economy demanded radical innovations in material culture—the improvement of containers, the invention of tethering or fencing, even perhaps the development of veterinary skills. Settlement in villages and then towns required better building techniques and allowed the production of heavy pottery, which would have been useless in a nomadic community. Such advances had occurred in parts of the Middle East by 8,000 BC and in the Far East at least as early as the fifth millennium BC.

A parallel development was the increasing exploitation of rocks and minerals. Some 6,000 years ago the Thracians were carving figurines from softer rocks such as marble and the Egyptians were mining and shaping even hard igneous rocks into sophisticated implements. Metal pins, beads and other objects probably 9,000 years old have been found in eastern Anatolia, and in the same region techniques of working gold, copper, meteoric iron and, to a far lesser extent, silver ores were gradually developed. Melting and annealing techniques, however, came much later, and bronze was not produced until the third millennium BC. Recent discoveries in Thailand suggest that metal-working began independently in South-East Asia at an early date.

Settled life, whether based on agriculture, livestock-herding or mixed farming, meant that particular skills could be recognized by the community as a whole. With the domestication of long-haired animals such as sheep, weaving had become a common occupation in the Middle East; skilled weavers, like potters, wood-carvers, basketmakers and others, could now become specialists, exchanging their produce for food and other necessities. Traders carried useful commodities such as fine-grained flints and the volcanic rock obsidian from region to region; even a luxury trade in turquoise and other semi-precious stones gradually developed. Religious and political leaders must also have acquired a privileged position: modelled heads at the early town of Jericho, which extended over some 10 acres and may have housed as many as 2,000 people, suggest an elaboration of rituals, and a military hierarchy related to defensive needs.

World History

The present distribution of peoples and cultures has been considerably influenced by the way in which early advances, such as the domestication of plants and the development of cities, spread out around the world. With the passage of time, innovations tended to move concentrically outwards from their centre of origin, but this did not occur in a precise geometrical pattern, because of irregular social and geographical conditions. As new groups were exposed to innovations, there were a variety of ways in which they could respond. The innovation might be accepted if people perceived that its use was beneficial. It might be rejected if it did not appear useful, or if it was socially unacceptable. Finally, there was the possibility that it would be adopted to meet more closely the needs of that society. To a large degree, each group's character is defined by the particular mixture of innovations it has accepted, rejected and adapted.

Archaeologists and anthropologists have attempted to trace the diffusion of many innovations, but the picture is complicated by the possible occurrence of two, or more, centres of independent origin. For example, it seems certain that man first domesticated plants in the Middle East, and probable that the Amerindians developed agriculture with no outside influence, but it is questionable whether knowledge of agriculture diffused to South-East Asia and West Africa or whether these were independent hearths of origin. Research is helping to clarify such matters, but definite answers are unlikely to be found, as much of the archaeological evidence, being of organic substances, has long since decomposed.

There are three main ways in which innovations spread through early human populations. The first and most obvious was by the actual migration of more advanced peoples into new area. Indigenous populations would copy or adopt objects and concepts from the newcomers, if they seemed sufficiently advantageous. A second means of dispersion was through trade, by both land and sea. As various groups developed the capacity to provide surplus goods, exchange became possible and societies sought to obtain those objects or crops which they could not produce themselves. Gradually a group might gain knowledge of new production techniques until eventually it could supply the articles for itself. Trading was greatly stimulated by the rise of élites in urbanized peoples and their demand for imported commodities.

A further mode of cultural diffusion was by conquest. Often a technologically superior society had the means to conquer a less developed group and to introduce or sometimes force its culture on to the vanquished. Conquest and warfare became increasingly important as people began to live in large groups; military classes developed, perhaps initially for defensive purposes, and saw in warfare an opportunity for exacting tribute from neighbouring groups, thus attaining greater political stability and control of the environment.

Settlers and Nomads

The earliest agriculturalists were probably located to the north of Mesopotamia. Their technique was probably to kill off a number of trees by slashing off the bark and then, when the leaves had fallen and sunlight could reach the forest floor, to plant seeds in the soft leaf mould around the trunks. As this method would allow only three or four crops to be raised on the same plot before soil fertility was diminished these early food-producing communities moved continually in search of new land. This accelerated the diffusion of both the knowledge of grain-growing and the seeds themselves, so that an increasing number of people in the Middle East gradually began to raise crops.

Shifting agriculture is suited only to a forested environment, however, and the early techniques had to be modified before cultivation could extend into non-forested areas. The peoples around the Tigris and Euphrates rivers were the first to respond to this challenge, gradually adapting farming methods to suit the flat alluvial plains on which they lived. Over the centuries they developed sophisticated irrigation techniques, which permitted yearly renewal of the soil's fertility with river silt. Furthermore, the construction and maintenance of canals and dykes required massed labour and strict social discipline, reflected in the growth of the first cities.

The open grasslands of the vast Eurasian steppe were similarly unsuited to shifting agriculture, but could support herds of animals. Consequently, the hunters of the steppe responded to the array of farming skills that reached them by accepting animal domestication and rejecting grain cultivation. A distinctive pastoral lifestyle evolved, based on cattle and horses in moister areas and sheep, goats and donkeys in dry areas. The emergence of pastoralism cannot be dated precisely, but it was probably not a common way of life until some time after 3,000 BC. Full adaptation to a nomadic life took thousands of years, however, and the technique of horse-riding was not fully mastered until around 1,000 BC.

Probably the most important agricultural development, however, was the invention of the plough, some time shortly before 3,000 BC. The plough altered and diversified the nature of human life immensely. It allowed farmers to become fully sedentary and made grain cultivation and animal husbandry dependent on each other, so that mixed farming became the dominant economy throughout the Middle East. The plough was used to till lands that had previously been cropped and, although yields were not as high as from virgin soil, a greater area could be cultivated, permitting higher overall production. The realization that fallowing allowed a certain degree of regeneration of soil fertility seems to have occurred fairly soon afterwards and, as a result of ploughing the same plots of soil time after time, a pattern of small rectangular fields appeared in the Middle East which can still be seen today.

The early farming communities were peaceable and egalitarian in character, but pastoralist groups retained the fierceness of hunters; their lifestyle required regular migrations and the leadership of a powerful chieftain. The interaction between farming and pastoral groups is prominent in the subsequent history of the Old World. Farming communities had the advantage of greater numbers, but pastoralists usually had superior military skills. The balance between the two fluctuated with developments in technology and social organization. The clashes between the different groups were often bloody and destructive, but served to stimulate mankind into a constant search for new tools and weapons, and an endless experiment with different ways of living.

Early Civilizations

The Sumerians, who settled in Mesopotamia, the land between the rivers Tigris and Euphrates, in about 5,000 BC, were among the first peoples to build large cities, irrigation canals and, dykes. A stratified social structure developed as a managerial class took control of the organization of labour. At the same time the increased levels of agricultural productivity permitted these early cities to support a small group of specialists who were not required to farm for their living, and this stimulated a large number of technical developments. By about 4,000 BC pictographic writing had been developed, and within a very limited period the Sumerians learned to make pottery, metal tools, wheeled vehicles, sailing vessels and monumental buildings. Eventually, however, competition between the cities over water rights led to a long period of political and military turmoil.

It seems probable that sea-borne traders from Sumer introduced irrigated agriculture to the Nile valley and, around 3,000 BC, the Egyptian civilization evolved by a process of imitating and adapting Sumerian inventions. The pharaohs held considerable power over their subjects by being able to control the Nile, which was the area's only transport artery. The Old Kingdom, which lasted for almost a thousand years, reached high levels of both technical and cultural achievement—notably, the development of the first calendar. Much less is known of the Indus civilization, which also emerged in the third millennium BC, but the major contact with Mesopotamia again seems to have been through sea-borne traders. Although the art style and script of the Indus peoples do not appear to be derived from Sumer, the stimulus to develop them probably arose from knowledge of the Sumerian skills. Indus civilization flourished from about 2,500 BC to 1,500 BC, when Aryan-speaking tribesmen invaded from the north and destroyed the two major cities of Mohenjo-daro and Harappa.

In the Mediterranean, Minoan culture seems to have developed through trading ties between Crete and Egypt. Further to the east, Malta appears to have been the origin of another high culture, that of the megalithic temple builders, whose structures dot the coastlands of Europe and Africa from Sweden to Morocco.

While these high civilizations were evolving, the pastoralists of the Eurasian steppe were refining the techniques of bronze-smelting. Armed with bronze weapons, the already warlike nomads were formidable and in the latter centuries of the third millennium BC overran most of western Europe, absorbing the pre-existing populations and introducing Indo-European languages. The greatest nomadic advances, however, came after 1,700 BC, with the invention of the light, horse-drawn war chariot, which had the advantages of increased mobility and firepower in battle. The Minoan and Indian civilizations were almost totally destroyed by Achaean and Aryan assaults. Mesopotamia and Egypt also suffered setbacks, but as their conquerors wished to enjoy civilized pleasures these societies were allowed to retain their structures and eventually overthrew the foreign rulers.

A major effect of the nomads' expansion seems to have been to stimulate, almost simultaneously, the evolution of Classical Greek, Indian and Chinese civilizations, based upon a military and aristocratic governance. These empires had turbulent, but relatively stable histories until another wave of nomadic advances occurred between 1,200 BC and 1,000 BC, when warriors armed with iron weapons occupied new territories. The Assyrians established a large empire, but most of the other tribal confederations were short-lived. A further period of expansion came between 800 BC and 600 BC, when riders from the steppes began to exploit their expertise at horse-riding with successful cavalry raids. The Scythians brought down the Assyrian state and returned to their lands laden with plunder.

Within half a century, however, a new Middle Eastern empire emerged under Cyrus the Persian. In the following decades the techniques by which the Persian Empire was maintained were refined. Regional administrators, deriving power from their offices rather than their persons, governed the provinces, while a substantial military force was kept at the capital, ready to quell any rebellion in outlying areas. It was around this time that monotheism first became established in the Middle East, with Judaism in Palestine and Zoroastrianism in Iran.

By 500 BC the major axis of a new Aryan civilization moved from the Indus to the Ganges, as iron tools allowed forested areas to be quickly cleared. Indian civilization developed along very different lines from the Middle Eastern societies which had initially stimulated its growth. A distinct cultural identity evolved, still recognizable in contemporary India, in which social organization was based upon a caste system and religious practices centred upon transcendentalism and asceticism.

Although the initial stages of Greek history closely resemble those of Indian history, as far as can be surmised, the product by about 500 BC was very different. The Greeks made the city state their prime basis of social organization and sought to explain the world and man by laws of nature, rather than mystic revelation. Pressure on the land encouraged emigration, and colonization hastened the diffusion of Greek culture and ethnic features. However, the productive energies channelled into the development of individual cities turned ultimately to civil strife between them, crippling the empire.

Chinese civilization had its origins in the valley of the Yellow river (Huang Ho) but little is known of its early history. Some scholars have argued that it had no connections with the civilizations of western Eurasia, but it seems quite likely that nomadic charioteers may have moved eastward into central Asia, occupying the oases, and that some two centuries later their descendants reached the Yellow river. The Shang dynasty held power until 1,051 BC when it was overthrown by the Chou. In 771 BC the Chou's capital was overrun by nomads, central authority was paralysed and the age of 'warring states' began, with local princes vying for power. A rapid expansion of Chinese culture occurred as refugees from the wars moved into new areas.

Social and cultural evolution occurred at a much slower pace in the areas peripheral to the four major Eurasian civilizations. Sub-Saharan Africa was virtually cut off from the rest of the world and its early history remains unclear. Egyptian influence went south into Nubia, but does not seem to have extended any further. Amerindians, moving south through the two continents, did not fully people South America until about 3,000 BC and, although comparatively dense populations were developing in Central America and Peru, by 500 BC the Aztec, Maya and Inca cultures were still in their infancy. In South-East Asia it seems likely that the Dongson people of southern China had sailed to and colonized Borneo and the Philippines, and that the original dark-skinned Australoid inhabitants were being driven into mountain and swamp areas.

Four Centres of Empire

During the early history of mankind the Middle East enjoyed predominance in the world, but as the cultures of Europe (Greece), India and China assumed their own distinctive shapes they became increasingly independent. By 500 BC, the four major civilizations were roughly equal to each other, and remained so for nearly 2,000 years. Contacts between urban centres increased during this period and cross-cultural borrowing was a major stimulus to innovation.

The Greeks managed to throw off Persian overlordship in 480 BC. Under Athenian rule a golden age followed, with drama, philosophy, science, rhetoric, architecture and sculpture reaching new peaks of expression. However, war again broke out among the Greek cities, which were eventually conquered by an army under Philip of Macedon. His son, Alexander the Great, set out to conquer the world, leading an army as far as north-west India and back to Greece before his sudden death in 323 BC. Meanwhile Rome, whose political career had begun in 509 BC as the centre of a federation of Italian cities, was steadily growing in military and economic power. The Romans eventually controlled an empire extending from Britain to the Holy Land, and their influence in Europe was pervasive, but much of Roman culture was an adaptation and development of the Greeks' achievement.

In India the Mauryan dynasty, founded after Alexander's withdrawal, occupied most of the sub-continent by the time of Asoka (274-236 BC). Shortly after his death it was fragmented by invaders, who were driven concertina-fashion across central Asia when the Chinese occupied Inner Mongolia, displacing nomadic groups. Another great Indian empire—the Gupta—was formed in the 4th century AD under Chandra-Gupta I and a classical age of Indian culture ensued. Traders introduced Indian ideas to China and Japan, while missionaries took Hinduism to Thailand, Malaya and the East Indies.

In the 4th and 5th centuries AD, there was a further wave of nomadic expansion throughout Eurasia when the Juan-Juan (Avars) occupied Manchuria and swept westwards to form the first Mongol empire. Central Asian groups such as the Huns and Vandals were forced into Europe, driving the Germanic tribes before them. Rome never recovered from this series of onslaughts, and only an emasculated empire survived. The states emerging from the nomad invasions tended to be short-lived, however, as the steppes men quickly adopted settled lifestyles and were overthrown by the people whom they had originally conquered. The Chinese managed to absorb their invaders and imperial unity was re-established in 589 AD. In India the Gupta empire was brought down by the raiding Epthalites (White Huns), a branch of the Juan-Juan Mongols. Only the heavy cavalry of a revived Persian empire managed to stand firm against the nomad horsemen.

The Persians eventually fell to Arab armies attacking from the south. The prophet Muhammad managed to unite the peoples of Arabia, who engaged in holy war to spread the world of Islam across the Middle East and North Africa. By 712 AD they had even occupied Spain. The speed of Muslim expansion slowed down in the 8th century due to internal divisions and in 744 AD the Abbasids overthrew the Ommayad dynasty, and moved the capital from Damascus to Baghdad. From 730 AD to 1200 AD Islamic cities were centres of learning. Scholars studied the works of Persians, Greeks and Indians, themselves adding to knowledge in the fields of medicine, chemistry, mathematics and astronomy.

During the years from 600 AD to 1000 AD, control of Europe was divided between the Frankish (German) empire of Charlemagne and the Byzantine successor to the Roman empire. European scholars—mainly monks—were content to treat the theories of Plato and Aristotle as ultimate truths. In the field of science, Europe fell well behind the other Old World civilizations, but a number of important advances did occur. The first was the invention of the heavy, mould-board plough, which allowed the expansion of the Celts, Germans and Slavs into areas of clay soil. Secondly the feudal system began to develop—the forerunner of the nation state—and finally there was a growth in inter-regional trade and a mercantile class began to develop.

In the Far East, the garden-style of cultivation was slowly spreading into the Yangtze valley. The Chinese empire, reunited under the Sui dynasty in 589, passed to the Tang in 618 and the central administrative system established at this time remained basically unchanged until 1912. Buddhism, which had reached China from India in the 1st century AD now passed to Japan, which was rapidly adopting the Chinese way of life. The Indians responded to Muslim pressures by withdrawing into Hindu traditions and the Buddhist cult practices known as Tantrism underwent vast elaboration. Gradually, Buddhism itself was absorbed into Hinduism or combined with it.

The Muslim world underwent further expansion in the early centuries of the second millennium AD, when the military energy of the Mongols (originally led by Ghengis Khan) and Turks was channelled into Islamifying Asia Minor, eastern Europe and southern Russia. The Ottoman Empire of the Turks became the most powerful state of the age and gained complete control of the Middle East with the capture of Constantinople, the Byzantine capital, in 1453. From the 10th century, Muslims expanded progressively into north India and, in the Far East, Mongols ruled China from 1190 to 1294, when the empire split up at the death of Kublai Khan.

Another major development in the period 1000-1500 was the growth of two new civilizations on the flanks of the Old World—those of northwestern Europe and Japan. Both developed rapidly, but the European civilization exhibited two unique features. The first was the commercial importance of basic commodities such as grain, herring, cloth and iron, which were transported in bulk. Trade in most other parts of the world centred almost entirely upon luxury items. The second feature was the mutability of European civilization: political, economic and technological developments were already beginning to accelerate. By 1500 both European and Japanese civilizations had reached a level comparable to the longer-established communities of the Old World. At the same time, the Russian state of Moscow was preparing to expand eastwards into Siberia, pushing back the Tatars who had inherited the Mongol conquests in the west.

In the New World, complex societies had been developed by the Aztecs, Maya and Incas. In South-East Asia, Tai tribes had occupied the area around the Mekong and adopted Buddhism, while the Malay peninsula and East Indies became the seats of Muslim régimes. The Polynesians, whose ancestors were probably of mainland Asian origin, had peopled the whole of Oceania by 600 AD, following the invention of the out-rigger canoe, which permitted safe sailing in open seas.

Sub-Saharan Africa remained very much isolated from the civilized world, but external influences did occur. Around 100 AD, Indonesian peoples colonized Madagascar, introducing crops that would later spread into central Africa. During the 5th and 6th centuries, Bantu-speaking peoples of the Congo began to expand southwards, using newly developed iron tools and cultivating crops of Indonesian origin by slash-and-burn agriculture. Centuries later a second wave of Bantu pastoralists moved south, and by 1500 the Bantu had reached the Zambezi river. In West Africa there were links with the Islamic world through trans-Saharan traders and from about 800 to 1500 AD several Muslim states arose in the sudanic regions.

The Dominance of the West

Around 1450 AD, Europeans began to make the cultural advances and geographical discoveries which would enable them to dominate the rest of the world. Determined to find their own routes to the East and destroy the Arab monopoly of trade in spices and silks, they made voyages across previously uncharted oceans. With the discovery of the Americas and their unimagined riches, attention focused upon exploration and within a relatively short period seafarers created a new cultural frontier along almost every habitable coast in the world, displacing indigenous peoples by force and fear.

Christian missionaries, fired with enthusiasm by the religio-political upheavals of the Reformation and Counter-Reformation, followed in the footsteps of explorers and soldiers. All were confident that the peoples whom they conquered could only benefit from contact with European civilization. The earliest and some of the most dramatic consequences of this process of colonization occurred in the Americas. Within a few decades of contact with the *conquistadores*, the Aztec and Inca Empires had collapsed. Introduced diseases such as smallpox and measles caused a terrible decline in the indigenous population of both continents, and with immigration increasing over the following centuries, Indians were reduced to a small minority. Meanwhile the slave trade further transformed the American population: for 300 years, West Africa was exploited as a source of labour for the plantations of the West Indies and North America, and thousands of men, women and children were transported across the Atlantic.

As the forces of Christendom advanced beyond the borders of Europe, the three great Muslim empires contracted. The Ottoman Turks posed a major threat to the European states throughout the 15th and 16th centuries, but in the 1690s their last serious challenge came to an end. Their power, like that of the Moguls in India and the Safavids in Persia, began to disintegrate. The Moguls in particular succumbed to economic and then political domination, mainly by the British. In the Far East the Manchu dynasty managed to maintain control over China, Outer Mongolia, Tibet and part of Turkestan until the 19th century.

Wherever the Europeans became established during the 16th and 17th centuries—in the Americas, West Indies, India and East Indies— they took ideas developed during the Renaissance. Scholars had welcomed the argument that all theories concerning the nature of the world should be tested by experiment. Following the invention of the printing press in the 15th century, this radical materialism had been disseminated throughout Europe. In the 16th century it formed the basis of a scientific revolution which would have far-reaching effects, not only on the way people looked at the world, but also on technology and agricul-

tural methods. The consequent improvements encouraged the industrial revolution, fuelled by profits from investment in conquered lands.

As first Britain and then the other European countries began to industrialize in the 18th and 19th centuries, a new impetus was given to the process of colonization. States competed with each other for control of countries which could provide food and raw materials, and markets for manufactured goods. Gaining control of another country's economy did not always involve annexation: the Chinese and Japanese régimes remained intact, while kow-towing to the Europeans. Indo-China, Burma, New Guinea, the Philippines and Africa had a very different fate.

Some areas of Africa—particularly the south and east—attracted European immigrants. Since the 18th century, the rapid growth in Europe's population—made possible by improvements in agriculture and medicine—had caused large-scale migration. North and South America, Australia, New Zealand and Siberia were all countries with only a small indigenous population and apparently ample space for newcomers. In the United States, railways opened up the interior and further encouraged the development of agriculture and industry. In all western nations, industrialization resulted in a mass movement of population to the towns and, as the old family networks broke down, central governments began to extend their control over people's lives.

Coinciding with this development was the growth of nationalism. In the 19th century this was largely confined to Europe, where the belief that a state's boundaries should be determined by geography, history and language led, for example, to the unification of Italy and Germany. In the late 19th and 20th centuries, the conviction that religion could also form the basis of national ties produced revolutionary movements amongst Christians in the Ottoman Empire and Muslims in Dutch Indonesia. In India, Muslims refused to remain as a minority in a Hindu state and demanded the creation of Pakistan: more than 10,000,000 people crossed the new border in the migrationary movements of 1947. Similarly, Zionists believed that a common history and religion provided a strong

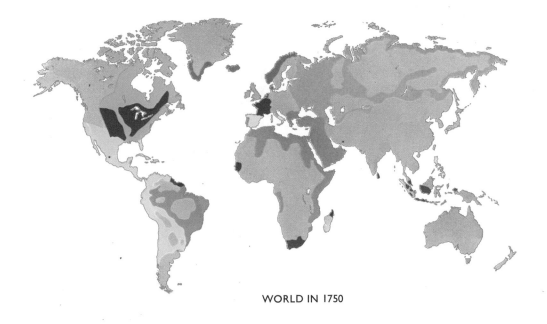

WORLD IN 1750

Spanish
Portuguese
British
Dutch
French
Russian
Danish
Arab and Turkish

foundation for a new Jewish state and years of agitation resulted in the creation of Israel in 1947. Anti-colonialism provided the inspiration for nationalist movements in Indo-China against the French, in India against the British and in Africa against all European imperialist powers. In South America it strengthened a resolve to resist the US stranglehold on the continent's economies.

Only in the Soviet Union and China (both still agricultural societies at the end of the 19th century) did empires remain intact. In the 20th century these two land-based empires veered away from the western imperial powers by adopting communism. The landed aristocracies were overthrown by revolutionary parties who formed strong central governments, which redistributed land, established communes and, particularly in the Soviet Union, embarked on programmes of rapid industrialization. By the end of the Second World War the Soviet Union had become a super-power, controlling new communist governments in Eastern Europe. In China the transformation was delayed until the 1940s, when the communists finally defeated an American-backed nationalist government. In the next two decades the Americans continued to give support in South-East Asia to states trying to resist the communist challenge, but in the 1970s they admitted defeat in Indo-China.

Outside the communist bloc, the United States continues to dominate the world economy. The Third World countries—largely in the southern hemisphere, where both agriculture and industry are under-developed—continue to suffer the after-effects of colonization. Often dependent on one or two cash crops, whose price fluctuates greatly, they cannot accumulate sufficient capital to compete with the long-established industrial powers who find them ready markets for their manufactured goods. Division between north and south, and the competition between communism and capitalism, are two of the main features of the late 20th century world.

Social Organization

Homo sapiens is basically a social animal; humans everywhere must maintain some co-operative relations with their fellow men in order to survive. This inescapable dependence is as important in modern industrialized societies as it is in the smaller-scale cultures described by anthropologists. Many animals also have complex societies, but the relationships involved in human social organization, unlike those of animal societies, can only be adequately understood by reference to shared ideas and beliefs.

The way in which members of human societies perceive their relationships is a crucial factor in their operation; the capacity for abstract thought and the development of language are fundamental to all human societies. Indeed, it is because human culture including language, has to be learnt that human children take so long to reach adulthood; they must be taught the rules, how and what to think as well as how to behave. Once taught, the rules must be obeyed, at least sufficiently to avoid total social breakdown.

Institutions aimed at securing conformity thus form part of all social organizations. The law is the most important of such coercive institutions, at least in those societies possessing formal civil and criminal codes. In others a range of sanctions, usually involving penalties of varying severity, may serve to sustain a measure of conformity. Even in societies lacking formal law, such sanctions as the fear of retaliation by an injured party (such as the feuds of the Jivaro Indians in Ecuador and Peru) or the withdrawal of essential economic co-operation may be extremely effective. Religious belief may also embody powerful sanctions, and public opinion can be an effective force for conformity, especially in communities where everyone is well-known to everyone else.

Social Categories

The fundamental principle of all human social organization is that different kinds or classes of people should be distinguished. How we categorize our fellow humans determines how we treat them and expect to be treated by them, so to understand the different kinds of social organization described by historians and ethnographers we must try to recognize the different kinds of social categories, and ways of thinking about people, that are involved.

For all practical purposes, a few basic classifications seem to be universal. Everywhere females are socially (as well as biologically) distinguished from males, children from adults, and so on. Kinship is recognized everywhere, although the ways in which kin are classified may differ greatly from one culture to another. Some distinctions of class and status are made, formally or informally, in all societies, and have important implications for social action.

The extent to which social categories and the types of social organization associated with them may differ from one culture to another is remarkable. Thus in most human societies throughout history a distinct category of political head or ruler has been recognized; but in many others, even today, this is not so. Among the tribes of the Amazon basin the role of headman is loosely defined and carries no authority, and the Nuer of the Sudan do not even acknowledge the concept of a leader or chief. Evidently a difference such as this must considerably affect the ways in which social order is perceived and maintained.

A second basic principle of social organization is that of group membership. In most societies until recent times (and in many even now) everyone has had to be a member of a mutually co-operating group—for example, a village or a hunting band—merely in order to survive. In the precarious conditions of many small-scale societies living at or near subsistence level, such group membership necessarily involves a high degree of corporate identity and responsibility. Such a group may or may not have a leader, but the maintenance of order within the group, and of its solidarity against outsiders, will probably be among the major concerns of its members.

Groups vary in scale, in the nature of their organization and in the scope of their interests. Members may own some common property—for example, a totemic animal, as with some Aborigine clans, or agricultural lands, or grazing rights. They may simply meet for recreation, as with a dramatic society or a cricket team. Furthermore, people may belong to several different groups, with different rights and duties in each, or to groups within groups. The Qashqai of Iran, who are pastoral nomads, belong as individuals to a *beyleh*, or camp group, which is part of a *borkuh*, migrating together and sharing the same pastureland. A larger group still is the *tireh*, under a headman who owes allegiance to the leader of a *taifeh*, the major political unit. Six *taifeh* in voluntary association compose the Qashqai people.

Kinship and Marriage

Some form of family grouping is a basic unit of social organization almost everywhere, but particularly in small-scale societies kin relationships may be all-important. These may be perceived in terms of the nuclear or elementary family—a parent or parents and children—or of a much larger unit, for example, a group of brothers with their wives, children and perhaps other relatives and dependents. In many societies still larger groups are needed, whose members can be mobilized for heavier agricultural tasks and for warfare.

One means of using kinship to form strong and effective social groups is the principle of unilineal descent. People who are, or believe themselves to be, descended from a single ancestor, either through the male line (patrilineal) or, less commonly, the female (matrilineal), form a distinct group or association. In this way, depending on how far back the common ancestor is traced, groups can be formed containing hundreds or even thousands of people. Units of this kind still form the core of political organization in many parts of the world, with order being maintained between and within communities by a kind of balance among the component sections. Such societies often lack any kind of specialized political authority.

Kinship may confer social identity and status even in the western industrialized nations—for example, among the European aristocracy. Almost everywhere, moreover, it is important for the control of property or of economic rights, and particularly for their transmission from generation to generation. Yet matrilineal systems do not imply matriarchy; even when inheritance is through the female line, the control and administration of property generally reside with men.

Marital links are an important part of social organization in many societies, although the forms of marriage vary enormously throughout the world. In most industrialized nations, marriage is regarded as an emotional contract between individuals, prohibited only between close kin. In traditional cultures, however, it is of greater concern to the community, and group membership frequently determines or limits the choice of partners. In some cases, prohibition may extend to all the members of a lineage, band or village, forcing marriages to be contracted exogamously (outside the group). In others, marriages must be arranged endogamously (within the group), as in India, where they are forbidden between members of different castes.

The choice of partner is often made on economic grounds, and in patrilineal societies the contract may be sealed by the payment of bridewealth in recognition of the benefits accruing to the husband. Marriage may also be politically important: the exchange of wives between groups creates and perpetuates bonds and is frequently used for making alliances. Among the Yanomamo of northern Brazil, wives are exchanged at the culmination of peacemaking efforts and this generally precludes further hostilities.

Systems of Authority

Other relatively simple systems of social organization include those based on age. In some East African societies, boys are admitted into an age set, usually through painful initiation rites, at or before puberty. Recruitment to a particular set is closed after a few years. As they grow older, the sets thus formed move as a group through a series of age grades, the junior grades being responsible for the harder physical tasks, including war, while the elders are accorded a certain amount of authority in decision-making and the adjudication of disputes.

In most human societies, however, a higher degree of specialized political leadership has developed. This has usually involved both the emergence of a greater measure of centralization of authority and, with improved communications and advancing literacy, more wide-ranging and complex forms of political organization and bureaucracy. The difference between centralized and uncentralized societies, however, is very much one of emphasis. In smaller-scale societies, a lineage-based type of social organization may co-exist with kingship or chiefship, and both be overlapped by an age grade system.

There is no single explanation for the emergence of centralized policies, but in individual cases the historical process may throw light on the subsequent form. Some states, for example, have been created by conquest: in many instances a small group of outsiders have taken over and imposed their own rule upon previously uncentralized communities. This has often resulted in socially stratified communities, with the conquerors and their descendants maintaining a status superior to that of their subjects. Elsewhere centralization has been brought about by rapid social and economic change. Thus a leader whose traditional significance was primarily religious rather than political may have used his position to acquire or to increase his secular power. Alternatively, a member or members of one of the component groups in a segmentary society may emerge as the first among equals.

A major factor in all of these developments is likely to be the growth of patron-client relationships. As new kinds of material goods become available (guns, for example, or horses, as in parts of West Africa), able and ambitious individuals may use their economic status to build up powerful followings. They may thus emerge as leaders or chiefs, or at least as 'big men' of power and influence, as in present-day Melanesia. With centralization comes growth of officialdom, for any state, traditional or modern, must provide both for the maintenance of the central power and for some form of territorial government. The former may involve an elaborate court organization and a proliferation of palace officials, both secular and ritual; the latter usually demands a cadre of regional authorities, among whom power delegated from the centre is dispersed, usually with some safeguards.

With the spread of western technology, most societies must sooner or later move from relatively simple and small-scale traditional forms to the more complex structures of the modern industrialized state. Two broad and connected trends may be noticed. First, with increasing specialization in many fields, social classifications, and the kinds of behaviour they imply, become increasingly determined by what people do (by their technical or professional skills, for example), rather than by what they are—that is, by their predetermined status in such systems as kinship or a traditional class structure. Relationships based on status tend to give way to relationships based on contract. The second trend is towards a growing individualism, itself associated with increasing specialization combined with the acceleration of communications and advancing literacy.

In most communities these factors have brought an immense broadening in the range and scope of social and economic relationships, with a corresponding decrease in the importance to everyone of their traditional commitments to small, cohesive social groups. For most people today, loyalty to the little community of family, lineage or petty chiefship has largely been replaced by multiple and often competing commitments to a variety of widely dispersed associations, from the state downwards. The difficult problems of loyalty and personal identity caused by participation in such complex organizations are part of the price we pay for their advantages.

Language/Communication

Communication is the exchange of messages; whether by touch, gesture or utterance. It is a universal activity in the animal world, yet although the variety of methods is enormous only man has developed the sophistication of speech. The possession of verbal language is a feature common to all human societies; it is fundamental to the development of culture and constitutes one of the crucial differences between man and the higher primates. All children are born with the capacity for speech, but language is learnt through contact with other speakers; there is a critical period for this process, and it has so far been impossible to teach speech to anyone who has not acquired it by the age of eight years.

Verbal language makes many things easier and some things possible; without it communication is laborious and the discussion of distant times and places inconceivable. It has even been suggested that some thought processes cannot take place without the medium of language. Through it information gained by one person can be shared with others; and an individual can learn the accumulated knowledge of preceding generations without having to repeat their experiences. The acceleration of human knowledge stems from the ability of each generation to start where the previous one left off.

Language allows practical matters of co-operation, teaching and organization to proceed more efficiently, but the crucial importance of verbal language is its potential for abstraction and generalization. In particular, it makes possible the transmission of history, planning, speculation and imagination. Explanation, reasoning and the manipulation of abstract concepts are everyday experiences for language users, all of whom, without necessarily being aware of it, use the complicated rules and conventions of their language with each utterance they make. Because languages are governed by rules, or grammar, anyone using them can create new statements which will be perfectly understandable to other speakers of that language. Language can be thus used with great precision, but because of its essentially symbolic nature, it is also capable of considerable ambiguity. This possibility of layers of meaning gives rise to metaphor and humour, poetry and literature.

Language is such a complex phenomenon that other aspects of human communication are often overlooked. When people are face to face they use much more than their voices to impart messages. Usually these non-verbal signals reinforce the spoken word, but they can directly contradict it, to the confusion of the receiver. Non-verbal communication consists of facial expression, gesture, and the positioning and minute movement of the body. It is governed by rules which are learnt during childhood but which are rarely spelled out; most people are unaware of the constant stream of messages sent out through body language, but research has indicated that their meaning is clear to others sharing the same culture. Because this sort of language is less overt than speech, the differences arising between cultures are often overlooked. Nonetheless there is considerable variation in the meanings of body movements from one culture to another, and serious misunderstandings can arise when non-verbal signals are either ignored or misinterpreted.

Languages of the World

There seems to be no way of establishing whether the thousands of languages currently in use have a common origin or arose spontaneously in different parts of the world. It does seem reasonably clear, however, that some languages are quite closely related and derive from the same original or protolanguage. During the 19th century considerable effort was directed towards comparative philology in an effort to trace the relationships between the various languages and to set up a sort of family tree; no satisfactory resolution has ever been reached. There has also been much debate on the best way of analysing and comparing languages; currently a system of measuring grammar and sound equivalencies is being used to show the relation of members of language families. Languages appear to change according to systematic rules; by discovering and applying these it is possible to trace related languages back to a starting point.

About 11 separate language families can be distinguished. By far the largest is the Indo-European group, whose speakers constitute almost half the world's population. Indo-European is believed to have originated in central Europe as long ago as 5,000 BC, and to have been broken up by migration into Indo-Iranian, Balto-Slavic, Italo-Celtic and Germanic groups. Further sub-divisions then occurred to produce what we know as separate languages today; and the Italo-Celtic and Germanic languages, being those of the chief industrializing nations of the West, have had a profound effect on other parts of the world.

Not all Europeans speak languages derived from the Indo-European family. Ural-Altaic families are also represented and the Basques, sandwiched between French and Spanish speakers, have an unrelated language whose only affinities lie with the geographically remote Caucasian group. The most important language families of the rest of the world include Sino-Tibetan, Hamito-Semitic, Bantu, Malayo-Melanesian and Japanese. Some languages

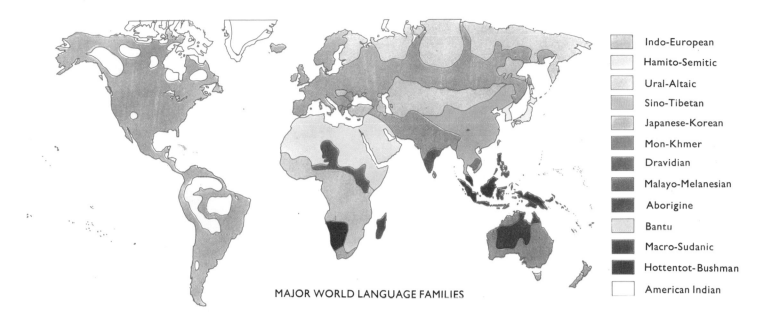

MAJOR WORLD LANGUAGE FAMILIES

- Indo-European
- Hamito-Semitic
- Ural-Altaic
- Sino-Tibetan
- Japanese-Korean
- Mon-Khmer
- Dravidian
- Malayo-Melanesian
- Aborigine
- Bantu
- Macro-Sudanic
- Hottentot-Bushman
- American Indian

spoken by small numbers of people constitute separate families: Bushman, Hottentot and Australian Aborigine seem to be unconnected with any other languages. American Indian languages once numbered more than 1,500, and even those still surviving show remarkable diversity. Until all these families can be shown to have some sort of relationship it is impossible to use linguistic evidence to reveal the direction of the larger migrations of peoples across the earth. Archaeology tells us that the American Indians crossed from Asia to Alaska, but this is not borne out by any relationship between the relevant languages.

Although there are a great number of different spoken languages, they all operate according to broadly similar principles. If this were not so, translation would be impossible. No language is more advanced or developed than another; all fulfil the current needs of the people who use them and all are capable of expansion to meet new needs. The vocabulary of English, for example, is considerably larger than that of Mursi, because of the complications of western technology, but there is nothing to prevent the Mursi vocabulary reaching similar proportions. Vocabulary reflects the particular interests and concerns of a culture—the Nuer of Sudan, whose culture revolves around cattle herding, can describe a cow in one of several hundred possible ways, and the Eskimos subdivide our category 'snow' into numerous descriptive terms.

A language embodies much of the world view of the people who speak it; it is a classifying operation in which experience is categorized and labelled. Once this has taken place a certain amount of rigidity is inevitable, and it has been suggested that the cultural restraints which a language places upon perception impose distinctive patterns of thought upon its speakers. To some extent, however, the differences in conceptualization may be more apparent than real; it may simply be a question of alternative methods of formulation. Nonetheless, there are considerable differences in the structure of languages; one of the most striking to English-speakers is that of the Hopi Indians of the American south-west. Hopi language has no verb tenses,

and events cannot be placed upon an objectified time-scale; instead verbs have built into them 'validity forms' to indicate the degree of certainty or immediacy and 'aspects' which denote the expected duration. Navajo Indians modify their verbs to take account of the object to which the action is directed. Thus the verb 'cut' would vary its form in order to reflect whether the object was soft, thick, rigid, et cetera.

Despite these divergences, there is no barrier to speakers of one language learning to express their meaning in another, even if they do have to adopt a new way of going about it. It is this fact of translatability which more than anything suggests that the patterning which language imposes upon experience is not a final determinant of modes of thought. Language is not inflexible; it responds to and reflects change in a society, and innovation is readily accommodated. The rate of change can be quite rapid, and operates over space as well as time. Just as we can no longer understand Middle English without effort, a rural English dialect may well be unintelligible to an American.

Change can take place among isolated groups, who over time evolve words and usages peculiarly their own; more spectacular changes occur when different languages come into contact and borrowing adds something to both. Loan words indicate the introduction of new ideas and inventions, and are strongly linked to trade and military domination. The English words 'veal' and 'beef' date from the Norman conquest, when numerous French words were assimilated into the language; similarly, the names of imported items such as pyjamas (Persian) often reflect the country of origin.

Writing and Printing

Although language is a pre-requisite of all human culture, its recording in written form is an added refinement. Writing permits communication through time and space: we can read words written many years before our birth or many miles from where we live. The restraints of personal interaction which govern spoken language are removed and the spread of knowledge increases accordingly. The accumulated knowledge and experience of an entire culture can be recorded in an accessible form.

It is not known for certain when writing first appeared. The earliest script was probably in the form of pictographs—sequences of pictures each of which represented a specific object or action. Such writing was used by the Egyptians as early as 3,000 BC, and signs and symbols were gradually added to represent things which could not easily be depicted. Eventually symbols representing sounds were developed to clarify other parts of the script. Although this hieroglyphic method is capable of transmitting complex messages, it is extremely cumbersome: users need a knowledge of several thousand characters once a reasonable degree of refinement has been attained and symbols have replaced the more basic communicating power of pictographs. Nonetheless, such writing systems can be enduring, as is demonstrated by Chinese script, the earliest examples of which date from 1500 BC. Chinese characters represent words or part-words, and there are some 8,000 in current use. Japanese writing, which was learnt from the Chinese during the 5th century, incorporates some signs denoting syllables to make a more flexible system.

The breakthrough to a more efficient writing system came with the symbolization of sounds instead of words. The number of sounds in any language is relatively small and thus much easier to handle; an alphabet dealing with sounds only can be arranged to reflect the spoken word quite precisely.

Not all languages have their own script, and those that do were not all put into written form by the original speakers. Yet cultural survival can be severely threatened by the lack of writing; many languages have died out without being recorded, and non-literate societies are among those most vulnerable to the onslaughts of industrialized society. When this happens, not only is the language itself lost but with it valuable oral traditions and lore—dramatic, poetic, mythical and factual knowledge—all of which can be lost irretrievably with the death of the last member of the society.

Although writing opens up possibilities for the storing and dissemination of knowledge and experience, its potential is not fully realized when the ability to read and write is restricted. The teaching of these skills is time-consuming and expensive, especially with complicated scripts such as Chinese, and in the past literacy was largely confined to certain privileged classes. Without wide distribution of the written word, moreover, the use of literacy is inevitably limited and until the 15th century, when paper manufacture and the printing press were developed in Europe, large-scale production of books was out of the question.

Even with this new technology, literacy was not general in Europe until industrialization was well under way and mass compulsory education was introduced. Illiteracy is a severe handicap to full participation in industrial society; yet according to a United Nations survey, two out of every five adults in the world today are unable to read or write. The spread of western culture has made universal literacy possible, but it has also made it essential.

The Mass Media

With recent developments in media technology, mass communication is no longer limited to the printed word. Radio and television now reach huge audiences, and illiteracy is no barrier to the reception of their messages. The speed of radio and television far outstrips that of newspapers or books and events can be known all over the world almost as soon as they occur. The impact is immediate and the images are powerful; there is an enormous potential for education, but also for propaganda. So influential can mass communications be that in many countries they are controlled by the state and, like newspapers and books, subject to censorship.

Recently fears have been expressed that the transmission of western culture through television and radio will result in world-wide cultural uniformity. Such fears need not be justified; the media can just as well relay important aspects of other cultures and in many cases they are being used to do just this. There has even been some regeneration of oral culture through the use of radio; in Somalia, for example, bards are now experiencing a revival of popularity, and elsewhere traditional cultures are holding their own against imported programmes.

Religion/Ritual

It is not surprising that systems of belief and religious practices vary widely from culture to culture when the societies themselves show so many different forms of organization and livelihood. Although we do not know when human groups first began to develop ideas of the supernatural, there are indications of a belief in an afterlife and of what could be interpreted as 'religious' activities among early human groups: for example, 60,000 years ago Neanderthal man took trouble to bury his dead and also covered their corpses with flowers. While evidence such as this is illuminating, however, the exact definition of religion is difficult to make. At times anthropologists have tried to view it in terms of the contrast between two spheres of action and belief: the sacred and the profane. At others they have been more concerned to suggest the probable path of its evolution; thus Sir James Frazer saw it as a stage in man's intellectual progression from belief in magic to the development of science. Such evolutionary theories are now out of fashion for not only are they unprovable but they do not help elucidate the inter-relationships between social forms and religious practices and beliefs.

For individuals, religious beliefs and practices may have many functions: they can help explain and justify the way the world, as well as society, is organized and also explain the apparently random incidence of misfortune and illness. In some circumstances they can also overcome an individual's isolation from his fellow men or provide a channel whereby he can escape from a lowly social position and achieve standing among the community. Nonetheless these functions must be related to the overall form of the religion and to the type of society with which it is associated. Crucial to this is the degree to which beliefs and practices are institutionalized and the extent to which there are specialists who control the operation of religious rituals. It is clear that there is a considerable formal difference between those religions in small-scale societies which involve a professional priesthood and those which do not.

As societies become more settled and complex it becomes possible for a more or less full-time priesthood to develop and for special buildings to be set apart for the housing and worship of gods. How-

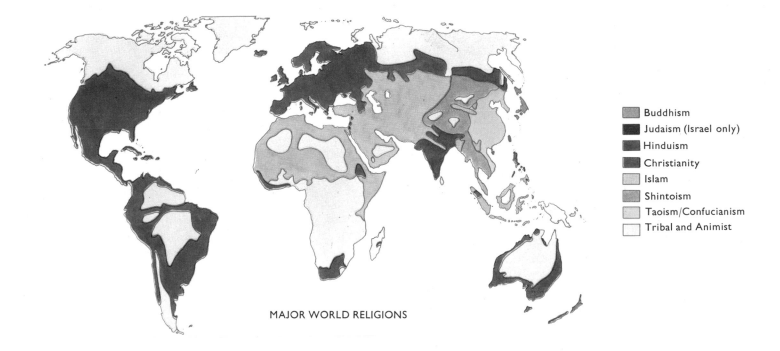

Buddhism
Judaism (Israel only)
Hinduism
Christianity
Islam
Shintoism
Taoism/Confucianism
Tribal and Animist

MAJOR WORLD RELIGIONS

ever, even nomadic and hunting and gathering groups may have part-time specialists who are thought to be able to help their fellow men communicate with the non-human world and its powers. These people, often referred to as shamans, can enter into trance states, which are seen as demonstrating their possession by a god or their entry into the other world, and in these they are supposed to be able to foresee the future, discover the causes of illness and misfortune or see what is happening at places far away.

In more developed societies religion may also become involved in state power: the role of kings in most societies is one which is considered to be somehow holy. The king is thought to be nearer God than other humans and special rituals are performed to imbue him with spiritual power. In some societies, such as the Shilluk of southern Sudan, the king's physical and moral state is believed to be closely connected with the prosperity and success of the whole community. Such 'divine kings' are, it is said, slain once they become weak or aged. In other cases the state may attempt to impose an official religion, or the religious authorities offer their support to the state's rulers; any refusal to subscribe to the official religion is seen as treasonable and the weight of belief is used to justify and sanction the existing political system.

It is usual in most religions for there to be some explanation, not only of the world as it now exists and for what occurs in it, but of how it came into being. In some groups, such as the Australian Aborigines, the beginnings of the world and the creation of men are conceived as happening in a special period of time, the dreamtime, which has now passed away for ever. In other groups the beginnings of man's life in society are traced back in myth to a specific act which led to a severance of the previously harmonious relations with the Creator. Thus among many African groups there are myths of how God was annoyed by the incessant pounding of food by woman, or by the inquisitiveness of man, and so broke the link between heaven and earth. Communion with God can therefore only be

achieved on a brief and insecure basis; by prayers, by offerings or libations or while in some extraordinary state, or by communal acts in which everyday preoccupations and individualism are firmly set aside. Religious rites may thus do much to emphasize and strengthen the common obligations of men living in society with their fellows.

From time to time new types of religious cults arise promising their followers that the world as it is known and constituted will soon come to an end and a new heaven and a new earth will come into being. These millennarian movements are often associated with groups which are suffering periods of great change and deprivation, although the new revelation on which they are founded may, in due course, become institutionalized as the group grows in strength and success. In parts of the Pacific so-called 'cargo cults' have been reported in the days since white contact: the prophets of these cults promise their followers a new moral order in which indigenous peoples will no longer be subservient to white colonialists and in which they will have unlimited access to the goods, or 'cargo', of the whites, which is one of their most striking attributes in native eyes. Such movements seem to be caused in part by the overthrow of the local conceptual, economic and political order by Europeans without the substitution of any new order.

The World Religions
The development of a uniform, or even a rigid, pattern of religion within a group is greatly aided by the introduction of writing. Although religious rites and formulae in small-scale societies often contain archaic forms and are supposed to be immutable in order to be effective, it is probable that these do in fact change and are adjusted as society changes. Once writing is introduced sacred texts and the procedures of ritual may become more or less fixed and a special class can develop charged with interpreting these texts and seeing that they are strictly adhered to. In this way a rigidity is introduced into religious life and change can only come about with

considerable upheaval and schism. The texts themselves may also provide members of society with a consciousness of their own past by giving them a fixed base-line from which they can measure previously imperceptible changes.

It is also of great significance that the spread and eventual dominance of such religions as Islam and Christianity depends to a considerable extent on their possession of a basic written text which is concerned to cover all the main aspects of a believer's life. The emphasis on the central position of written texts in religion is most clearly seen in Judaism but is also apparent in both Christianity and Islam, two great religions which in origin owe something to preceding Jewish writings, practices and beliefs. The existence of their sacred texts allows a uniformity of belief and ritual to be achieved and maintained to a degree which is difficult or impossible without such virtually immutable foundations for religious activity. Nevertheless, all such major religions show adaptations to particular regions and cultures and they also demonstrate substantial changes through time. Within each, separatist or reforming sects arise and in new circumstances the basic tenets and texts of the faith are reinterpreted.

In Judaism the continuing relationship between God and his chosen people is recounted, explored and commented upon in the sacred writings: the Torah, comprising the writings attributed to Moses, subsequent prophetic writings, the psalms and much of the Old Testament; and in the two Talmuds, in which the commentaries, interpretations and decisions of successive rabbis are given. The enduring quality of the Jewish community and its emphasis on the understanding and extrapolation of sacred texts at home and at the synagogue is most striking: despite the Jews' movement from their homeland and their subsequent persecution, often at the hands of European Christian groups, they kept their distinction as a community. This has been achieved while major new schools of interpretation such as the mystic Kabbala movement, from the 13th century, or the 18th century Hasidic movement, with its strongly traditional emphasis, have arisen in response to outside pressures and changes.

In some ways it is possible to see early Christianity as one of the Jewish reinterpretations and reformations: the importance of Judaism and the general situation of Jews under Roman dominance to the development of Christianity is clear. However, it must also be remembered that the new religion took up Hellenistic influences. While Judaism was the religion of an exclusive group, which deliberately avoided marriage with outsiders, Christianity, with its emphasis on baptism, inclusion and missionary activity, had a much greater opportunity to spread into new areas and throughout all classes of society. Its great success tied it in with systems of political authority and, after 313 AD, it became the official religion of the Roman Empire.

Political and economic changes consequent upon the break up of the Roman Empire had much to do with the separation of the Eastern and Roman Catholic Churches and there was also a strong political element in the rise of Protestantism in the 16th and 17th centuries. The early Church had grown through the development of separate, monastic communities as well as through popular conversion, the converts staying within the world; but the Reformation saw the ending of monasticism and the development of new forms of belief which some have interpreted as more compatible with emerging capitalism. Similarly, Christian missionary activity followed closely on European expansion into the rest of the world and the establishment of white colonial rule. In many cases, indigenous people were more or less forced to abandon their traditional religions in favour of Christianity.

This desire to convert others to one's own religion and to do battle against those who hold other beliefs is also strong in Islam, where the *jihad* or holy war against unbelievers is considered of great importance, although in some interpretations it is seen more as a spiritual than a coercive physical process. At some stages in Islamic history the *jihad* has been almost as important as the 'five pillars' of Islam: the confession of faith, communal prayer, alms-giving, fasting and the pilgrimage to Mecca. In the centuries after Muhammad, born about 570 AD in Mecca, received his vision, Islam spread rapidly across much of the Middle East. After the flight (*hijira*) to Medina, the new revelation of Muhammad, in which earlier Jewish and Christian prophets were given an honoured place, had rapid successes. The *jihad* took Islam across North Africa and later into sudanic Africa, the whole of the Middle East came under the domination of Muslim Arabs and the new faith eventually reached India and central Asia. Today it is still important in Malaysia and Indonesia.

Like Judaism and Christianity, Islam is a religion of the book and all Muslims learn the Koran—often knowing its key passages by heart. The contact between man and God is direct and, while teachers may help clarify the text, there is no separate priesthood in Islam. Because of this and the emphasis on communal prayer (especially at the mosque on Friday) Islam effects a pervasive influence on the societies in which it is found, a feature supported by the development of Islamic law, which deals with nearly all aspects of life in society. It has thus proved adaptable to many different types of cultures, whose members are united in terms of common practices and a common holy text.

It is a matter of debate whether Buddhism should be considered as being a religion of the same broad sort as Christianity, Islam and Judaism, because it has no central deity. Buddhists accept the original revelation of the Buddha, the Enlightened One, born in India sometime between 600 and 400 BC. The Buddha taught that man suffers because of his attachment to the world and the people and things in it. By practising moral restraint, contemplation and meditation, the self could become separated from the world and reach *Nirvana*, a state of self-extinction. This, once achieved, removed man from the otherwise endless cycle of death and rebirth.

Buddhism is thus at base a religion which enjoins a detachment from the sensations of the world, but since its earliest days it has assumed many different local forms and schools in Asia. In the centuries following the Buddha's teaching, Indian Buddhism was spread by missionaries throughout the Asian world, undergoing inevitable changes. Traditionally the varieties of Buddhism have been divided into three main groups: Theravada, mostly in South-East Asia, Mahayana in Nepal, China, Sikkim, Japan and Korea, and Tantrayana in Tibet,

Mongolia and Siberia.

Theravada is in many ways a continuation of the ancient Indian schools and has a more or less fixed body of texts and teaching and has long been the established religion of various states in the area. Most of these are built on separate functions for laymen and monks, who work to gain contact with *dharma*, the truth, and who serve to legitimate the ruler who agrees to follow *dharma*. Mahayana Buddhism is far more diffuse and involves a complex fusion of many schools and sects, and in it monks have far less prestige than in the older form of the religion. Tantric Buddhism, often linked with the theocracy of Tibetan Lamaism, includes esoteric magical elements, while the Japanese development of Zen Buddhism lays emphasis on inner intuitive knowledge. This form has recently received considerable attention in the West.

Mythology

Much of mythology is ostensibly concerned to explain or narrate the origins of the world and the past history of particular groups within it. At times these myths are closely connected with religious rituals and therefore they may become the more or less esoteric knowledge of priests. Myths may have many functions and the way these operate is closely connected with how myths are transmitted, recited and owned by those who know them. For many years it was debated whether religious rites were an enactment of myths or whether myths derived from, and existed to explain rituals.

In recent years attention has shifted to attempts to identify the underlying structure of myths. Those involved in this study argue that myths are devices whereby man attempts, in a disguised way, to deal with basic conceptual problems arising from his life in society and to try to answer the contradictions these may pose. Where many religious rituals are concerned to stress the need for ideal behaviour and for the integration or re-integration of the individual into society, myths may serve to explore and answer fundamental paradoxes about human existence.

Ancestor Worship

Beliefs and rituals concerned with ancestors are found in many societies where descent groups form an important part of the social and political system. It must be understood that these beliefs are different from those which are concerned with the dead or with ghosts of the dead. An ancestor is not simply a dead person, or some spiritual element derived from such a person, but is someone who occupied a position of jural and political authority during his or her lifetime and whose descendants carried out the rituals required to elevate him to full ancestral status. Such ancestors are thought to take a continuing interest in the activities of their descendants, to warn and advise them in dreams or visions and to inflict misfortunes and sickness on them for breaches of morality or in order to have sacrifices made to them. Usually each named ancestor is commemorated and represented by some physical object: perhaps parts of his skeleton, perhaps a wooden effigy, tablet or stool.

These things are usually in the care of the ancestor's successor and prayers and offerings are made at them to the ancestor. Indeed the successor's role is closely bound up with this right to approach the ancestors of his group: it is an important aspect of his authority and helps him control those under him who have no right of direct approach. In this sense ancestor worship can be viewed as an extension of the system of political leadership and control and descent group ownership of resources within society. It must also be realized that ancestor worship or propitiation can exist side by side with belief in other spiritual powers: in many societies it is believed that a creator god and lesser gods or powers also affect the affairs of men. In such cases it is usual for the different beings to be envisaged as causing different types of event and being able to offer different sorts of help to mankind.

Rites of Passage

A person's life in society can be interpreted as a series of more or less formalized roles which he or she occupies at different stages of life. It is usual for transitions from one role or another to be ritualized in most small-scale societies and this practice is also found in some areas of life in complex, industrialized societies. The rituals are performed in order to make clear that the person's old role and position in life has been abandoned and a new one assumed. These rites of passage or transition have a common underlying structure which was first analyzed by the anthropologist Arnold van Gennep around the turn of the century. In essence they consist of three basic parts or elements: a ritual by which a person is separated from an existing role, a central intermediary or interstitial period in which the person is, as it were, held in suspense from any direct involvement in society, and a rite by which he or she is re-integrated into society in a new role. The degree to which each of these three elements is emphasized and elaborated varies from society to society and according to the importance of the transition, nevertheless each of the elements and the overall sequence can be identified in all rites of passage.

Such rites are often linked more or less closely with important stages in an individual's biological existence and especially with birth, physical maturity and, finally, death. The ritual serves to stress and make clear to the individual the fact that an old role has been discarded and a new one assumed and publicly demonstrate this to other members of the society. The association between the rites and the biological events need not be exact: for example, it is usual in many societies for a baby to be admitted formally to society a week or so after its actual birth. It is only when it has demonstrated, as it were, a potential for continuing life in the group that members of society accept it into their company.

Many rites of passage centre around the change from youth to physical maturity and the potential this provides for individuals to become full members of their society. While physical maturity in girls can be linked directly with the beginnings of menstruation, the signs of physical maturity in males are less dramatic and definite. This may in part explain the fact that rites of passage initiating males into adulthood tend to be less closely tied to their physical changes (although there are many other factors involved). Indeed it is clear that in many societies the stages of social life and the stages of physical growth, maturity and decline may be considerably out of step and, as among some Nuba people of southern Sudan, men at the height of their physical powers may find that they are moved out of positions of responsibility in society and more or less retired.

Perhaps the most spectacular and best known rites of passage are those connected with the initiation of youths into manhood and especially those initiation rites practised in certain parts of Africa. In many African societies youths are initiated in groups rather than singly. The initiation rite first takes the maturing boys away from their parents and kinsfolk. Once separated, they usually enter into a period of seclusion, during which they live in the forest or bush away from normal human settlements. During this period they may be treated as being morally as well as physically outside society and normal rules and behaviour are suspended for them: they may be forced to eat foods which are ordinarily despised or forbidden, allowed sexual and other forms of license, and be treated almost as wild beasts. During this time they may also be instructed in the esoteric knowledge they will need for adulthood and be subjected to trials and ordeals. After this stage they are formally re-admitted to society in their new roles as adults, after which they are expected to assume adult responsibilities and such adult rights as that of being free to marry and procreate.

Many initiation rituals also involve physical mutilation and hardship: this is usually seen as a way of testing a candidate's fitness for the next stage of life. Among the Nuer, for example, adolescent boys have two of their teeth prised out and six deep gashes cut across their foreheads. Among other groups, tattooing, circumcision and scarifications are used. The pain and physical shock involved in these operations as well as in other ordeals has the function of separating all previous experience, in former roles, from all subsequent experience. In addition it helps bind initiates together through their common suffering and give them an irremovable mark of their new status. If the mutilation is inflicted on a visible part of their body, it serves to show their status to other people.

Other rites of passage are less dramatic and painful, but they can occur at all major turning points in an individual's social life: marriage, parenthood, accession to high office or, in some cases, expulsion from the social group. Nor do these rites cease with death. When people die it is necessary for their roles, possessions and duties to be re-allocated among their successors. The rites of passage by which this is done, and in which the corpse is disposed of and the spirit moved into the next world, may be long and complex. Burial is usually separated from the rituals concerned with the disposal of the social personality although in some societies, such as our own, the two are generally combined. In all societies the changes which are necessitated by a person's death are given formal expression, and the introduction of new individuals into the roles occupied by the deceased exhibits the underlying pattern of rites of passage.

Witchcraft and Sorcery

The strong emphasis on sharing and internal co-operation which is found in many small-scale societies is reflected in beliefs about witchcraft and sorcery. Although these beliefs show a considerable range of variation from group to group, the witch or sorcerer is usually seen as a person who has some-how become possessed of special powers which enable him or her to harm or help other members of the group. These special powers are generally feared and regarded as unnatural: the witch is someone within society but who is not fully committed to the ordinary ways of life and the basic values which most people feel they ought to respect. Witchcraft powers may be obtained in several different ways: in some cultures they are thought to be inherited from one or other parent; they may then lie dormant until activated by the possessor's anger or malice. In other cases it is thought that they may be purchased from, or given by, other witches, or that the recipient may be infected with them without knowing about it until later.

Each society has its own concept of the witch, but this nearly always involves an expression of the idea that the witch somehow contradicts or opposes the basic values on which social life is built in that group. Thus witches are thought to commit incest, murder their kin, kill the children they should nurture, consort with wild animals in the bush instead of with other humans within the village, or to fly naked through the night. In some societies it is believed they can walk upside down, a method of progression which can only be seen by other witches and those who have the power to combat them. In many cases accusations and confessions of witchcraft can be interpreted as attempts by individuals to deal with situations with which they can no longer cope. These situations are therefore regarded as being due to the activities of witches rather than to more abstract and impersonal forces.

Cults to combat witches, that is to protect the community against the betrayers in its midst and to identify and neutralize them, arise from time to time and enjoy brief but spectacular successes. They spread rapidly and widely and at their shrines suspected witches are accused, tested and sometimes confess. Often these cults seem to be ways of dealing with the problems and disruption caused by rapid social change and especially change brought about by western contact. The failures and miseries due to the breakdown of the old order are ascribed to the increasing activities of witches, and the new cults and medicines are imported to combat these. For a while they succeed in re-introducing harmony and co-operation but, as the root causes remain unaltered, their success is usually brief and they die away, only to be replaced by similar movements which flourish and then fail for the same reason. The spread of such cults in modern Africa has also been encouraged by the fact that the ordeals used to identify witches, formerly controlled by indigenous political authorities, were forbidden by colonial authorities. The way was thus open for the introduction of new ways of witch-finding.

Traditional Economies

Agriculture has been described as the basis of civilization. Neither cities nor any large concentrations of population would be possible without agriculture, and the industrialization which provides much of the world with its livelihood could not have taken place. In technologically advanced societies such as the United States and Western Europe, mechanized farming with fertilizers and pesticides achieves massive yields with a

WORLD LAND USE

Commercial agriculture
Subsistence agriculture
Shifting cultivation
Hunting, gathering, fishing
Nomadic herding
No economic activity

minimum of human labour. In these societies, although a great number of people are involved in processing, distributing, importing or exporting foodstuffs, less than 10 per cent of the population is directly engaged in food production.

The impact of commercial food production on the Third World has been immense. In Nigeria, for example, the traditional independence of many rural households has given way to a reliance on cash incomes derived from the sale of cocoa, ground-nuts and other commodities exported to the industrialized nations. Although a shrewd bargainer, the Yoruba or Hausa farmer has no control over the prices he receives for such crops, since these are determined by world market conditions. Protective agrarian policies like that of the European Economic Community keep Third World farmers subject to constant fluctuations in demand. From a position where most produced their entire food requirements, more Third World countries become net importers with every year that passes.

With a world population of more than 3,700,000,000, and less than 10 per cent of the earth's surface cultivable, the pressures on the available land are increasing and those small-scale societies whose economies required the use of large areas are rapidly disappearing. Hunter-gatherers, for example, were once widespread and relatively self-sufficient; today many hunters in central Brazil and on the Gran Chaco of northern Argentina have been deprived of their land by settled populations. Compelled to adopt shifting cultivation and to keep domestic animals, groups such as the Bororo in the Amazon basin now grow maize, manioc and rice to supplement their diet. Nonetheless, in the marginal areas of desert, mountain, forest and grassland, where mechanized agriculture remains costly or unviable, many peoples still subsist by traditional methods of food production.

Hunting-gathering

A recent American review suggested that there are only about 70 societies today where more than 75 per cent of subsistence is dependent upon the gathering of wild plants and berries, the hunting of wild animals or fishing. All of these groups live in marginal areas, either where no alternative agricultural economy is possible, or where communications are so bad that pressures from modern society have been slow in reaching them. The hunting-gathering groups are mainly to be found in the desert fringes of Australia, southern Africa and North America; in the forests of Asia, South America and central Africa; and in the frozen wastes of Siberia, the far north of America and the Arctic.

Seasonal change and the movements of wild animals have usually required hunting-gathering groups other than certain fishing communities to be partially nomadic. The limited resources of marginal lands and the constraints of the nomadic existence have kept population densities low: the only cross-cultural surveys available give average density estimates of approximately one person per 20 square miles, with most residence groups having fewer than 100 persons. By contrast, the Kwakiutl Indians of America's north-west coast, with plentiful supplies of salmon and other fish, and of deer, elk and mountain goats, reached a population density of one person per square mile.

Although hunting-gathering provides a viable way of life in areas where other means of subsistence are difficult or impossible, it is often precarious. Drought can cause widespread starvation, and a change in animal migration patterns can have disastrous consequences for the hunters whose lives depend on them. Nonetheless, anthropologists have described hunter-gatherers as the original 'affluent societies'. Some detailed studies, including two on the Hadza of Tanzania and the Kung Bushmen of the Kalahari, revealed that these people spent on average only about 20 hours per week in search of food. Their dietary intakes were well above the minimum requirement and much of the week could be devoted to other pursuits.

In remote parts of central and northern Australia, Aborigines still lead an almost exclusively hunting and gathering existence. Their cultures developed in isolation from any agricultural peoples for 20,000 years: their only social contact was with Melanesians and Indonesians in the north

25

until the arrival of European settlers in 1788. For this reason it is particularly interesting that their social organization should be so highly developed and that their perception of land, people, animals and plants, and the relationships between them, is so complex.

Hunting, gathering and fishing normally demand a high level of skill that is transmitted from one generation to the next only by extensive training. Co-operation is often essential within a group wider than the immediate family, and most hunting-gathering groups have a flexible membership. The Mbuti Pygmies, for example, often hunt with nets and need enough people in each group to drive animals into the nets and to kill them when trapped. As with practically all other hunting-gathering societies, the meat is shared among all members of the group, yet there are rarely figures of authority to enforce such communal behaviour.

In the absence of material possessions, inheritance is of little consequence. Even ownership of territory is rare, and this in the 20th century has made survival for the hunter-gatherer very difficult, as settled populations have claimed more and more of their land. Some groups, like the Guayakí of Paraguay, have resisted these encroachments on their resources, but they have rarely had the support of national laws and have been forced to adapt or retreat. Without rigid legislation to protect them, only those groups that can survive in areas unwanted by agriculturalists or developers retain much of their traditional lifestyle; but even they are being steadily seduced from their hunting-gathering economy by the industrial societies surrounding them.

Pastoral Nomadism

Pastoral societies are those in which a sizeable proportion of the subsistence economy is based on the herding of animals. The category includes groups as diverse as the steppe nomads of central Asia and the transhumant herders of Switzerland. The nomadic lifestyle, which involves extensive movement from one grazing area to another, has always caused concern to the sedentary authorities, and the pressures of modern society are today as intense and effective against pastoral nomadism as they are against hunting-gathering.

As a distinct way of life, nomadism developed in the Old World, where five main zones can be identified. The Arabian camel is well adapted to the desert and semi-desert regions of the Sahara, East Africa, Arabia, Iran and Baluchistan. Cattle are suited to the lush savanna grasslands of central Africa and also to the sudanic belt, while sheep and goats are kept on the fringes of the arid deserts and savannas. Sheep are the main herding animals in the more temperate mountain and valley regions of south-west Asia and the Mediterranean borderlands. In the more extreme continental climate of the central Asian steppe, the nomads traditionally favoured the horse, but also raised Bactrian camels, sheep, goats and often cattle. Finally, in the sub-Arctic tundra regions of northern Eurasia, where the ground remains frozen the whole year round, only reindeer can be herded.

Nomadism can therefore be viable in extremes of both heat and cold. Conditions fundamentally unfavourable to nomadism are found only in humid and forest regions where disease, insects and lack of suitable pasture make life intolerable for the animals. Nonetheless, nomads must everywhere respond to variations in terrain and climate in order to provide the best possible conditions for their animals. The patterns of movement, dispersal and congregation depend in arid regions on the poverty and size of the grazing areas, and in better watered regions on the distances between seasonal pastures. Migrations of people and animals take a regular form from year to year, usually involving a change in altitude, and as much in response to changes in rainfall as to changes in temperature.

The nomads' attitude to their animals derives partly from economic dependence and partly from their value in ceremony and ritual. Cattle- and camel-herding nomads, who depend heavily on their animals for both purposes and market little of the produce, tend to be especially devoted to them. Even in the case of sheep- and goat-herding nomads, it is the camels and horses, used only for transport purposes, which are tended with most devotion.

The solitude of the herding life, the insecurity of the pastoral economy, the nomads' mobility and history of martial superiority, are reflected in the values they attach to independence, fortitude, honour, generosity and hospitality. Yet the nomads also have characteristic vices, and their contempt for the farming peasantry is reciprocated with some justification in many parts of the world.

Pastoral nomadism has nearly always been practised in conjunction with sedentary society, for nomads need many of the products of town and village. They may exchange animals or their produce for grain (often a staple food), dates, a variety of manufactured goods and animal fodder. If political conditions are favourable, they may extract their needs from settled communities in the form of tribute or 'protection money', or simply by raiding. Many nomads themselves cultivate crops: they may have winter villages which they leave after a spring harvest to take their herds to summer pastures, before returning to plough and plant again in the autumn. Alternatively, a single village community may combine settled agriculture with nomadic pastoralism, individuals specializing in either role.

Most nomadic pastoralists exploit marginal lands of little use to anyone else, and in many cases they make major contributions to their national economies. However, in less accessible regions their mobility enables them to evade laws, taxes, conscription and even health and education facilities which central authorities wish to impose on them. Their reluctance to accept the dominance of settled society is resented by governments intent on economic and political integration, many of whom therefore want to end the nomads' wandering lifestyle and make them become farmers.

The most humane and, in the long term, beneficial method of achieving this transition has been firstly to help the nomads establish settled areas with watering and fodder facilities, and then to improve their breeding techniques, their management of pastures and their marketing procedures.

Agriculture

To plant, tend and reap any type of crop requires a certain amount of time to be spent repeatedly in the vicinity of the cultivated area. Thus agriculture must always have encouraged people to establish permanent bases, even if they used them only at intervals. In turn, stability of domicile encourages the acquisition and storage of surplus goods, and it has often been suggested that the domestication of grains and the adaptation to settled farming was crucial for the elaboration of material culture. Plant cultivation undoubtedly formed the basis of an economic and social revolution, yet the time spent on food gathering in small-scale agricultural communities is as great, if not greater, than in hunting-gathering and pastoral societies.

Agriculture is commonly divided into two main categories: shifting cultivation, or horticulture, and settled, or complex, agriculture. According to a recent estimate, some 50,000,000 people subsist by shifting cultivation and approximately 700,000,000 by settled agriculture. The latter have at their disposal about 570,000,000 acres of land; the former have some 265,000,000 acres in their total resources, but cultivate only about one-fifth in any particular year.

Shifting cultivation is restricted mainly to the tropics and sub-tropics, where the rich humus collected beneath the shelter of forest or jungle can support crops for only a limited period. The easiest way of removing trees and bushes felled to gain cultivable land is to burn them; moreover, the ashes provide valuable fertilizer for the soil. For this reason, this method of clearing is also known as slash-and-burn cultivation.

Humus can easily be damaged by ploughing, so the exclusive use of manual labour applied with a digging-stick or light hoe is characteristic of shifting cultivation. But the feature which has given this method its name is the necessity of abandoning a plot after two or three years when its fertility begins to decline. Farmers then move on to another area and repeat the process of clearing and burning. This may be done either haphazardly, or in a regular cycle which provides fallow periods long enough to preserve the fertility of all the land in the possession of a particular group.

In the long term, it is likely that shifting cultivation will become an obsolete and unimportant farming technique. Yet even in today's world of rapid changes, the total development of all areas of the tropics in which shifting cultivation continues will not be accomplished within a short time. Where all the level and easily cultivable land has been occupied by more powerful populations, the weaker groups often have no choice but to till steeply sloping surfaces. Many have come to regard the hill country as their preferred environment and are not easily persuaded to change, even when offered level land for plough cultivation.

Currently, shifting cultivation is still a pioneering system, employed on the frontier settlements of forested landscapes. Yet it is practised by the seeker of quick profits, unmindful of ecological damage and future problems, as well as by the careful occupant concerned about the long term. In many parts of the world the interests of the shifting cultivator and those concerned with the intensive exploitation or even preservation of forests are therefore antagonistic.

Colonial governments as well as the governments of the Third World states have tended to stabilize mobile agricultural populations in the pursuit of greater control over land and forest resources. Where increased pressure on the land, caused by population growth, upsets the traditional cycle of forest clearance, shifting cultivation can certainly be harmful to vegetation and to soil fertility. Where local populations possess adequate land, however, their shift cycles are usually ecologically sound and constructive.

Land that is kept permanently under cultivation has to be dug regularly and cleared of weeds, and the fertility of the soil must be preserved by a system of crop rotation or the application of fertilizers. Steeply sloping land, though suitable for periodic slash-and-burn cultivation, can be tilled year after year only if the hill sides are transformed into a series of level terraces. For this reason terracing, often combined with irrigation from mountain streams, is a common method of turning rugged tracts of land into valuable fields.

On land not permanently flooded, grasses compete with grain crops and under arid conditions the surface of dry land hardens so much that turning the soil by hand puts an enormous strain on labour resources. In this situation the plough, drawn by oxen, or more rarely by horses, mules or camels, has proved invaluable. The full mechanization of agriculture, however, has so far proved better adapted to the heavy, loess soils of the middle latitudes—in North America, Europe, the Soviet Union, South Africa and Australia—than to tropical conditions.

Intensive, permanent agriculture without the use of the plough or draught animals normally requires artificial irrigation. This obviates the need for regular turning of the top-soil and helps to keep down the growth of weeds and grasses. In parts of tropical Asia, such as Bengal, Thailand, Burma and Vietnam, large alluvial plains yield two rice harvests per year. Such intensive cultivation is only possible with fertile soils, using dykes and irrigation canals and all sources of manure.

The advantage of settled over shifting agriculture is that a higher density of population can be supported and land can be used more intensively. Those who expect to live in the same locality for generations tend to plant not only crops to be harvested within months, but also trees which will bear fruit or provide timber after many years. The Apa Tanis of the eastern Himalayas, for example, who are wet-rice cultivators, also have extensive groves of fruit trees, bamboo and pines. The last are grown as building materials and firewood, and anyone who fells a pine tree is expected to plant a sapling to preserve his family's timber supply.

The major disadvantage is that societies relying on complex, settled agriculture are rarely self-sufficient. Where hunter-gatherers, pastoralists and shifting cultivators generally live in small groups and are able to provide most of their food requirements with a minimum of exchange, the large populations engaged in settled agriculture tend to develop complex dependencies on their neighbours. In many parts of the world they are now compelled to specialize, in order to produce the cash crops demanded by urban populations.

Trade and Traders

The large surpluses produced by complex agriculture allows extensive trading between nations, but all societies today have some relations of exchange with other groups. Even pastoralists like the Masai of East Africa, who once lived solely by the produce of their cattle, now trade with agriculturalists for grains; similarly, meat forms a staple part of the cultivators' diet. Other commodities, including metal goods and textiles, may be bought from townspeople, who are in turn dependent on the rural food producers.

Exchanges are frequently made at markets, where the various demands of neighbouring groups can all be supplied in one place. The adoption of money as the medium of exchange in situations where the direct transfer of goods was previously used has coincided with greater specialization, and occurs where barter has become too unwieldy. Even market trading is often formalized, with prohibitions regarding sex or social status. At Darfur in Sudan, it is considered immodest for women to sell millet beer in the market, even though the beer itself is in great demand. By contrast, the Nupe women of northern Nigeria do all the market trading and gain considerable economic power as a result.

The distribution of goods need not be the most important function of the market. In ancient Rome, the market place was literally a meeting place—the *forum*—where people gathered to exchange news and debate politics, and the same is true of many smaller-scale societies today. For the Tiv of Nigeria the market is a place where courts can be convened and disputes settled in public.

The exchange of goods and food at a local level is often based on a system of reciprocal obligations, through kinsfolk or friends, and cannot be considered a purely economic process. Although trade is generally regarded as a means of filling gaps in home production in return for domestic surplus, it can also be used for establishing and maintaining relationships, facilitating inter-group marriage and increasing or preserving status and power. The *kula* in Melanesia, a highly ritualized exchange of shell necklaces for shell bracelets between men living on the various islands, creates strong partnerships that enhance both their economic and their political well-being.

Most local trade can operate through the traditional mechanism of the market, but some mountain and pastoral peoples have no direct links with agriculturalists and their dependence on certain imported goods has made outside traders vital to their economies. The Kirghiz nomads in the Pamir range of the Himalayas live above the crop line and rely on Pashtun traders from lowland Afghanistan to bring grains, vegetables and other goods. Several groups have specialized in such trading: until recently, Tibetan traders crossed into Kashmir with salt to exchange for grains and cash, and the Otavalo of Ecuador still travel far across South America with their woven goods.

On a larger scale, trade between nations has always been subject to fluctuations in demand, the availability of transport and the control of supply sources. Throughout history, empires have grown wealthy through control of trade, cities have sprung up along trading routes and urban centres have determined prices paid in local markets. The colonization by Europeans of vast areas of the world was motivated by their desire to monopolize supplies, especially when industrialization accelerated home demand and brought vastly improved transport facilities. The effects of 19th century imperialism in particular are still being felt by the developing nations of the Third World. Indeed the economic power exerted by the West today is frequently described as 'neo-colonialism'.

Impact of Industry

The industrial revolution which took place in Europe and North America during the late 18th and 19th centuries has by now radically changed the way of life of nearly all the peoples of the world. There are still a few tribal groups, for instance in the rain forests of Brazil, who are almost untouched by modern trade and depend on their own labour and natural resources for food, clothing and shelter, so that all producers and consumers are familiar with each other as kinsmen and neighbours. Such self-contained societies will soon no longer exist at all. Even the Nagas of Assam, for instance, who still live by traditional techniques of shifting cultivation, are now accustomed to such commodities as electric torches, matches, metal pots and bicycles. Though these are at present paid for by subsidy from India, it is inevitable that the Nagas will soon develop trading relations of some kind with other regions.

The change from such traditional ways of life is sometimes relatively smooth, when the central government is sympathetic and local entrepreneurs exploit opportunities for trade or tourism; or when (as in the case of some nomadic peoples) the indigenous way of life is well suited to difficult geographical conditions. In other cases, perhaps the majority, there is a painful phase of dispersal and poverty.

In principle, industrial techniques can be recombined in so many different ways that it is unwarranted to think of any technological changes as irreversible (except in one or two special cases such as the invention of the nuclear bomb, which obviously demands the maintenance of an international system of political and technical safeguards). It is easy to imagine future scientific inventions triggering off social and economic changes in quite unforeseen ways. Historically, however, the impact of mechanization, systematic merchandising and accelerated communications has had irreversible effects in that many economic and social systems have been destroyed and will never be revived—though they may be mourned and some at least of their distinctive cultural heritage invariably survives into the new context.

Only about 10 per cent of the world's land surface is at present cultivated, but a majority of the world's population still lives in rural or semi-rural conditions. In the advanced economies, agriculture comes to be regarded as just another industry. All over the world, traditional farming techniques are being transformed through the introduction of machinery, agrochemicals, irrigation and new strains of cereal. Unwanted side-effects frequently intervene, such as the development of resistant strains of insect in response to pesticides; but this is the rule with nearly all technological innovations.

Mineral extraction has a particularly sharp impact on customary ways of life, but can also bring sudden industrial prosperity. In Australia and elsewhere, valuable mineral deposits may be discovered under land traditionally occupied by aboriginal peoples, and the question of legal title to the land becomes crucial. Such conflicts are not confined to extractive industries, nor to countries colonized by Europeans. Timber companies in Indonesia have a similar impact on tiny close-knit jungle communities.

Many Third World governments have set out to

copy western industrialization, sometimes for reasons of prestige. There is now a trend towards developing patterns of technology more appropriate to local conditions. Industrial progress in general seems to be irresistible because of the pressures of expanding population. It also brings many benefits, especially in increasing the number of options open to individuals. However, there is no inevitable unilinear process of 'modernization'.

The World Economy

The population of China, some 850,000,000, outnumbers that of the Soviet Union, the United States and the European Economic Community all added together. China, however, like some of the other communist countries, has preferred to develop domestic industries rather than international trade, and at present counts for relatively little in terms of the world economy as it is usually perceived. The same is true to a lesser extent of India, with 650,000,000 people, of whom some 70 per cent depend on agriculture, although India has some important intercontinental exports such as cotton, jute and tea, as well as an industrial sector which has to import technology. The essentially rural character of India is expected to survive into 2,000 AD.

Considered in terms of gross national product (GNP), the world economy is dominated by the United States, the Soviet Union and Western Europe, together with Japan, Canada, South Africa, Australia and New Zealand—all wealthy mechanized nations with extensive trading links. Apart from the production of food, these industrial societies are dependent on two basic factors: the supply of energy, and the production of iron and steel. Western Europeans and North Americans tend to be wasteful of food and energy in a way which strikes many analysts as wildly improvident, and their economies rely on the manufacture of consumer goods such as motor-cars and household machinery. They are characterized also by the extensive manufacture of armaments on the one hand, and on the other hand, of seeming frivolities such as cosmetics and pet-food.

Control of these economies rests in a number of large financial and political conurbations, employing many people in administration and in service and information industries (the 'tertiary sector'), who have to be supported by workers in primary production and in processing and manufacture (the 'secondary sector'). Western economies have faced a prolonged crisis for much of the 1970s, owing to a combination of recession and inflation.

When economists and politicians speak of depression or recovery in the world economy, they make use of indices such as sales of motor-cars and lorries, unemployment, housing starts, and investment by government and industry. They assume that any changes in the western way of life should happen in a gradual and orderly way, not merely because such analysis is what their public expects, but also more reflectively because any sudden sharp fall in the material standard of living would have unfavourable repercussions for democratic institutions. Illiberal political régimes might emerge during a period of economic protectionism, if countries tried to shield themselves from recession in this way.

The viewpoint of commentators in the Third World is very different, and often resentful in tone.

The GNP per head per year in India and most of Africa is 30 or 40 times less than that in Sweden or the United States. Admittedly, the GNP is a crude measure; but in such a context the recent economic embarrassments of Britain or Italy seem trivial. Even in countries with high growth rates such as Brazil and Mexico, about 40 per cent of the people live at subsistence level.

The so-called 'development gap' may be reduced to some extent by current increases in the prices of raw materials, foodstuffs and fuels. However, the boom in oil prices has resulted most conspicuously in a new form of economic colonialism by some wealthy Arab states. Many of the less developed countries are oil-importers themselves, and their own raw material exports are subject to violent fluctuations in the world's commodity markets.

Analysts of the development gap may be broadly divided into liberals and Marxists. Liberals see world trade as fundamentally beneficial, and argue that economic growth in the Third World will ensue from education, technical and financial aid, better planning, and so forth. Marxists argue that capitalism is the chief factor inhibiting growth in the Third World, and that only by revolution, whether regional or worldwide, will the scandal of world poverty be ended. They are less perturbed than are western liberals by the dangers of Stalinism, because many governments in the Third World are already totalitarian and militaristic.

Population Growth

Between 1850 and 1970 the world population rose from 1,200,000,000 to 3,700,000,000. The current global rate of world increase is about 2 per cent a year, compared to 0.5 per cent in 1750-1900 and 0.8 per cent in 1900-1950. More than 80 per cent of this increase takes place in the Third World. Thomas Malthus argued at the beginning of the 19th century that increases in food production would never be able to keep pace with increases in population. Since the late 1950s similar pessimism has been fairly common because a simple extrapolation of the current growth-curve results in enormous figures over a period of only a few decades. Some writers have evoked fears of widespread famines, massive pollution, dictatorship and mental disturbances—all as a result of excessive population.

During the 1960s it was often claimed that the United Kingdom had a problem of over-population, as had been argued in the 19th century. More recently, in the 1940s, it was under-population that seemed to be the problem—both in Britain and in other European countries. Now, in the mid-1970s, no more is heard of Britain's over-population problem, since the birth-rate is static or falling. In fact, the United Kingdom, like many other industrial countries, is populated very unevenly. In the sense that it depends to a great extent on imported food, Britain can be said to be over-populated; but if its economy were suddenly converted to become self-supporting in food, many food-exporting countries would suffer.

With very fast-growing populations, the birth rate itself can become a force for social change or a political issue. One of the most controversial policies of Indira Gandhi in India was her compulsory sterilization campaign. However, population growth or decline is primarily an index of social and economic changes. The reason for the rise in the

Solid red indicates greatest density

High density – fast growth

High density – moderate growth

Low density – fast growth

Low density – moderate growth

Sparsely populated

WORLD POPULATION

Third World population growth rate to 2-3 per cent is that there has been little if any overall decrease in the birth rate to match the decline in the death rate due to better living conditions and medical technology. In Western Europe, North America and Japan, the birth rate has declined for several reasons. For example, many people left farming for industry and cities; health facilities were improved so that it was no longer necessary to have many children to ensure the survival of a few as economic security; women came to be employed in industrial and service sectors of the economy. A similar pattern has been identified in the most recent industrialization of Singapore, Hong Kong and Taiwan.

Campaigns to reduce birth rates in countries such as India and Kenya through western contraceptive technology have so far been ineffective, and were indeed misguided in so far as techniques of fertility control already exist in most traditional societies. The real problem is that the benefits of economic development do not 'trickle down' into poor rural areas, and that many of the people concerned have no desire to limit their families. The exceptional situation in Sri Lanka, where the birth rate actually is declining, may be due to lack of employment and other symptoms of economic stagnation—as in some parts of 19th century Hungary, where the only way to preserve the standard of living was to have one heir to whom the total property could be passed, and where a special moral code developed to sanction this norm.

A genuine demographic transition in the Third World is only likely to occur when a majority of people are in a position to make plans for their own lives, and for the lives of their children. This has been achieved to a considerable extent in China, through an anti-natalist campaign integrated with political propaganda at all levels; free family planning services integrated with the health care system; security for old age; and the development of opportunities for women. It remains uncertain which other countries will succeed like China in assimilating self-interest to communal goals, or will even try. Yet without some reduction in the rate of population growth, the problems of the Third World are likely to have repercussions elsewhere.

Labour Migration

In the United States, Japan and England, more than 70 per cent of the population live in or around cities. In Kenya the proportion is as low as 10 per cent. Worldwide, the proportion continues to increase, but very unevenly (about 12 per cent over the last quarter-century in India, as opposed to 65 per cent over the same period in Brazil). Poverty, exploitation and lack of land are the three most pressing reasons that lead people to migrate. Apart from the symbolic value of urban life as a stepping-stone to the opportunities of civilization, they may be enticed by offers of employment from industrial concerns that need cheap labour. The pattern is classical and the conflict of motivation in migrants has been explored in many novels and films.

Networks of interaction between the new city-dwellers and their former villages often persist, and may result in a shared prosperity. Other migrants end up in wretched slums or shanty-towns. Some analysts have seen progressive elements in the squatter-settlements of Rio de Janeiro or Lima—in Peru, for example, some of these 'young towns' have become permanent settlements developed by the government. Elsewhere, so long as squatters live under constant threat of official eviction, they invest in movables instead of in permanent housing.

A consideration of specific societies shows the difficulty of generalizing about urban migration. A recent study of a Spanish Basque village shows that although its peasant farmers are moving increasingly to cities, they are leaving farms which are profitable. Now, in exchange for unremitting manual work, they get regular paid holidays. They usually get an education before leaving the farms, so that they can get skilled or white-collar work. When their farm-lands are sold they often invest the proceeds in local industry.

Larger-scale migrations across nations and continents have been widespread for centuries, for a great variety of reasons. Particularly important in the Mediterranean region over recent years has been short-term labour migration to German, Swiss and French cities, where the migrant (usually male) uses his income to meet traditional family obligations, such as dowries and expensive gifts. He often lives in a segregated barracks, and has limited legal rights in his country of employment. In the last few years, for instance, at least 200,000 foreign workers, or 6 per cent of the labour force, have been obliged to leave Switzerland, keeping national unemployment artificially low.

Longer-term migration to such countries as the United States and Britain results at best in an invigorating variety of cultural traditions, but at worst in severe conflict between ethnic groups. The United States, for all its immense economic thrust and democratic ideals, is even now suffering from the repercussions of the old slavery system. As for in England, the growth of the West Indian population in some of the big cities has resulted in comparable problems of race relations.

Marked awareness of ethnic differences has affected every known society's economic dealings as well as its cultural tone. The prejudices ensuing from migration and forced co-existence in Northern Ireland and the Middle East are very violent without the admixture of marked biological differences. In Japan, 3 per cent of the population—the *eta* or *burakumin*—are hereditary outcasts, but differ little if at all from the majority of Japanese in appearance. Social scientists disagree as to whether perception of the biological differences between 'white' and 'black' acts as a more powerful force for antagonism than the perception of differences in culture, rank, or economic power.

Health and Wealth

True well-being cannot be studied comparatively. It is impossible to measure the well-being of an assembly line worker, prosperous but bearing all the pressures and anxieties of urban-industrial life, against that of a villager living at subsistence level, whose traditional belief system enables him to make sense of hardship and suffering. Nonetheless, literary romantics have always sentimentalized about the lost paradise of primitive, 'face-to-face' societies; and there is an important element of truth in the myth. Some peoples do in fact cling tenaciously to traditional lifestyles, or accept change only with reluctance.

Certain historians have reached the world-weary conclusion that the benefits of all social innovations tend to be cancelled out, sooner or later, by drawbacks—though the beneficiaries and the sufferers are not always the same people. The most intense illustrations of this are the notorious slum-cities of Inner Calcutta in India and Soweto in South Africa. In a world where today 1,200,000,000 people lack access to safe drinking water or health care, 700,000,000 do not have enough food, and 250,000,000 urban dwellers are inadequately housed, it is impossible to be satisfied with the notion of world economic progress. Small economic communities left to themselves managed to co-adapt mutually with their natural environment.

Even parts of the world that are prosperous suffer increasingly from environmental pollution, from social disorders such as violent crime, and from the bodily ills of industrial civilization such as cancer and arteriosclerotic heart disease. The triumphs of medical technology in eradicating malaria or polio, curing rare diseases and making chronic ones tolerable, are balanced by the artificial prolongation of painful old age, by the unwanted side-effects of many drugs, and by the dangers of over-population. The paradoxes seem endless. The West's suicidal consumption of heroin and tobacco gives an honest livelihood to cultivators in poor countries. Valued technologies such as coal-mining, and transport by road and air, have cost innumerable lives. Nuclear energy offers to save us from economic collapse when fossil fuels are exhausted, but with the certainty that when unforeseen disaster does strike it will be on a massive scale.

Some objective progress has certainly been made in the Third World since 1950. For example, life expectancy, though still 30 per cent lower than in the industrialized countries, has increased during this period from about 40 to 50 years. There has also been overall economic growth, though it has not helped the poorest. Recent thinking by development analysts has tended to back away from a policy of maximizing economic growth, towards the priority of meeting the basic human needs of the poorest. Furthermore, social scientists are for the first time beginning to consider the role of women in production and reproduction.

World Resources

Operating Manual for Spaceship Earth was the title chosen by Buckminster Fuller for a book about the problem of world resources. His position, and that of America's Hudson Institute, may be summed up as one of trust in mankind's technological inventiveness. The opposite position, sometimes combined with mystical or anti-scientific leanings, contends that nature sets limits to human capacities. These arguments represent long-established western traditions of thought, one viewing man as despot over nature and the other viewing man as steward of and collaborator with nature.

This long-standing debate has been given new urgency by the widespread realization that many of those resources upon which the industrialized world economy rests are indeed exhaustible. The fossil fuels—oil, gas and coal—supply some 90 per cent of world energy requirements, yet only coal exists in sufficient quantities to last more than a few decades at current rates of increased use. When all the fossil fuels are exhausted, science will probably find alternative workable sources of energy, whether through dangerous nuclear technology or through safe (but at present inefficient) methods using the sun, waves or wind. A more serious problem may be food supplies. Experts disagree as to how serious the long-term outlook is, but it is generally agreed that the growth rate in the world's population will have to level out soon.

It is hard for us to weigh the rival claims of experts, with their abstract, systematic knowledge. It is equally difficult to decide what members of the industrialized world can do as individuals to alleviate the problem of world resources. Enlightened citizens influenced by the conservation movement are buying smaller cars (or travelling by bicycle), eating less food, and re-using old envelopes. Yet the richer countries are also warned by economists that they must be able to accept a sharp rise in imports from the Third World, and for this to happen there must actually be an increase in consumption. It is doubtful whether a drastic impoverishment of the West would accelerate economic development in the Third World; and without such development, it is likely that world population will indeed come to outstrip food resources.

31

Part 2

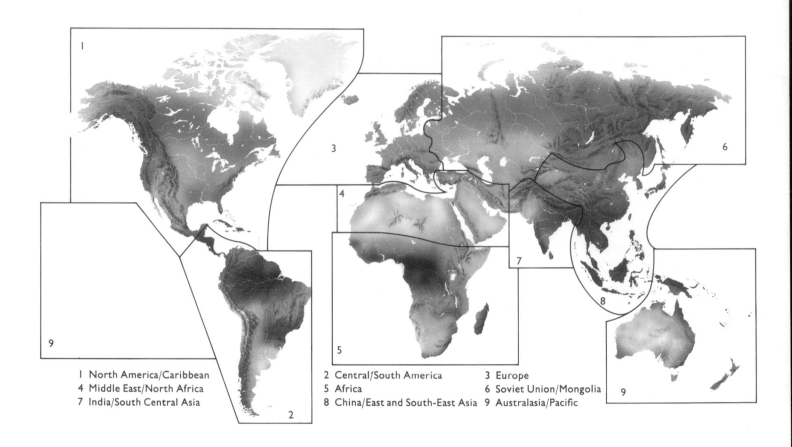

1 North America/Caribbean
4 Middle East/North Africa
7 India/South Central Asia

2 Central/South America
5 Africa
8 China/East and South-East Asia

3 Europe
6 Soviet Union/Mongolia
9 Australasia/Pacific

People/Countries of the World

The main body of the Atlas is divided into nine sections, corresponding to the geographical divisions illustrated on the facing page. Each section begins with an introduction to the historical, geographic and cultural characteristics of the region, illustrated with appropriate maps. Then individual entries describe the countries and main groups of people living within the region, and on each double page there is a map showing their location. If a tribe or ethnic group occupies a wider but still definable territory, a supplementary map appears in the margin. Similar 'thumbnail' maps illustrate other aspects of interest, such as the extent of former kingdoms, or the historical expansion of now-dominant peoples. Other maps, in colour, show larger-scale details of significant areas. Under each entry are noted societies either related to or in close contact with the one under discussion. A comprehensive index is provided at the end of the book, as well as a glossary of unfamiliar terms.

Population figures are included at the beginning of each entry. For nations these are dated and refer to a census or an official estimate. For tribes and ethnic groups the figures are estimates and their main purpose is to give some idea of orders of magnitude, rather than precise head-counts.

North America/Caribbean

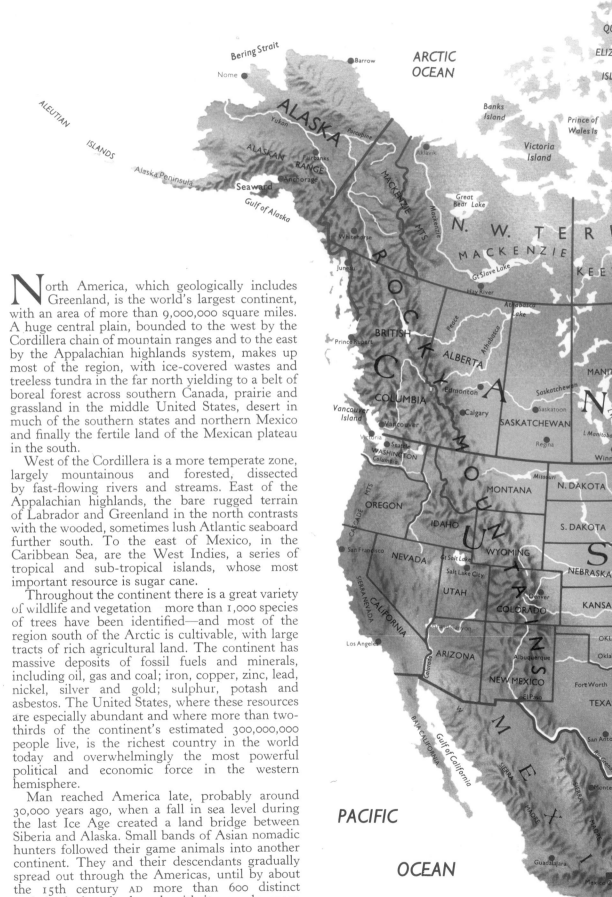

VEGETATION

Ice
Permanent ice field

Tundra
Moss and lichen

Conifer Forest
Pine, spruce, larch

Broadleaf Forest
Deciduous

Temperate
Arable, broadleaf, grass

Mediterranean
Citrus, olive, agave

Subtropical
Dry and wet evergreen

Tropical
'Selva'

Prairie
Long grass

Savanna
Grass and scrub

Semi Desert
Cactus, sparse shrub and grass

Desert
No vegetation

Marsh and Swamp

Salt
Salt lake, marsh

■ **Capital Cities**
• **Major Towns**
• **Towns**
Small town village
— **Country Borders**
— **Borders**
Provinces, states

North America, which geologically includes Greenland, is the world's largest continent, with an area of more than 9,000,000 square miles. A huge central plain, bounded to the west by the Cordillera chain of mountain ranges and to the east by the Appalachian highlands system, makes up most of the region, with ice-covered wastes and treeless tundra in the far north yielding to a belt of boreal forest across southern Canada, prairie and grassland in the middle United States, desert in much of the southern states and northern Mexico and finally the fertile land of the Mexican plateau in the south.

West of the Cordillera is a more temperate zone, largely mountainous and forested, dissected by fast-flowing rivers and streams. East of the Appalachian highlands, the bare rugged terrain of Labrador and Greenland in the north contrasts with the wooded, sometimes lush Atlantic seaboard further south. To the east of Mexico, in the Caribbean Sea, are the West Indies, a series of tropical and sub-tropical islands, whose most important resource is sugar cane.

Throughout the continent there is a great variety of wildlife and vegetation—more than 1,000 species of trees have been identified—and most of the region south of the Arctic is cultivable, with large tracts of rich agricultural land. The continent has massive deposits of fossil fuels and minerals, including oil, gas and coal; iron, copper, zinc, lead, nickel, silver and gold; sulphur, potash and asbestos. The United States, where these resources are especially abundant and where more than two-thirds of the continent's estimated 300,000,000 people live, is the richest country in the world today and overwhelmingly the most powerful political and economic force in the western hemisphere.

Man reached America late, probably around 30,000 years ago, when a fall in sea level during the last Ice Age created a land bridge between Siberia and Alaska. Small bands of Asian nomadic hunters followed their game animals into another continent. They and their descendants gradually spread out through the Americas, until by about the 15th century AD more than 600 distinct societies had evolved, each with its own language and way of life, and together numbering perhaps 30,000,000 people. About two-thirds of the total population probably lived in Mexico, where a highly sophisticated agriculture had been developed —nearly half of all foods cultivated in the world

Projection: Bonne

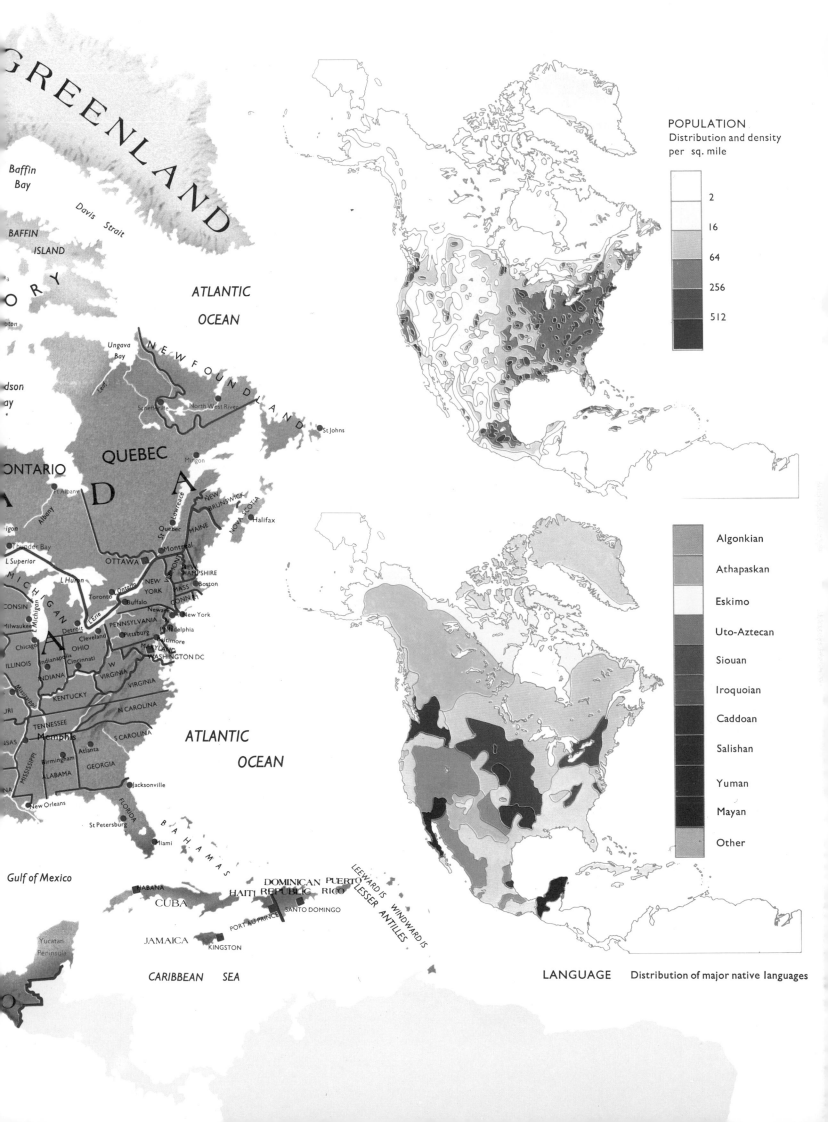

GREENLAND

Baffin
Bay

Davis Strait

BAFFIN
ISLAND

ATLANTIC
OCEAN

NEWFOUNDLAND

Ungava
Bay

Schefferville   North West River

St Johns

QUEBEC

Mingon

ONTARIO

Ft Albany

Albany

NEW
BRUNSWICK

NOVA SCOTIA

Halifax

St Lawrence

Quebec   MAINE

Thunder Bay

Montreal

L Superior

OTTAWA

NEW
HAMPSHIRE

L Huron

MICHIGAN

Ontario

NEW
YORK

MASS

Toronto   Buffalo

CONN

WISCONSIN

L Erie

Newark   New York

L Michigan

Detroit   PENNSYLVANIA

Milwaukee

Cleveland

Philadelphia

Chicago

Pittsburg   Baltimore

ILLINOIS

INDIANA

Indianapolis

Cincinnati

OHIO

W
VIRGINIA

MARYLAND

WASHINGTON DC

KENTUCKY

VIRGINIA

N CAROLINA

TENNESSEE

Memphis

ATLANTIC

OCEAN

MISSISSIPPI

ALABAMA

Birmingham   Atlanta

S CAROLINA

GEORGIA

Jacksonville

New Orleans

FLORIDA

St Petersburg

BAHAMAS

Miami

Gulf of Mexico

HABANA

DOMINICAN   PUERTO
REPUBLIC   RICO

CUBA

HAITI

LEEWARD IS
LESSER ANTILLES

WINDWARD IS

SANTO DOMINGO

PORT AU PRINCE

JAMAICA

KINGSTON

Yucatan
Peninsula

CARIBBEAN   SEA

POPULATION
Distribution and density
per sq. mile

2
16
64
256
512

Algonkian
Athapaskan
Eskimo
Uto-Aztecan
Siouan
Iroquoian
Caddoan
Salishan
Yuman
Mayan
Other

LANGUAGE   Distribution of major native languages

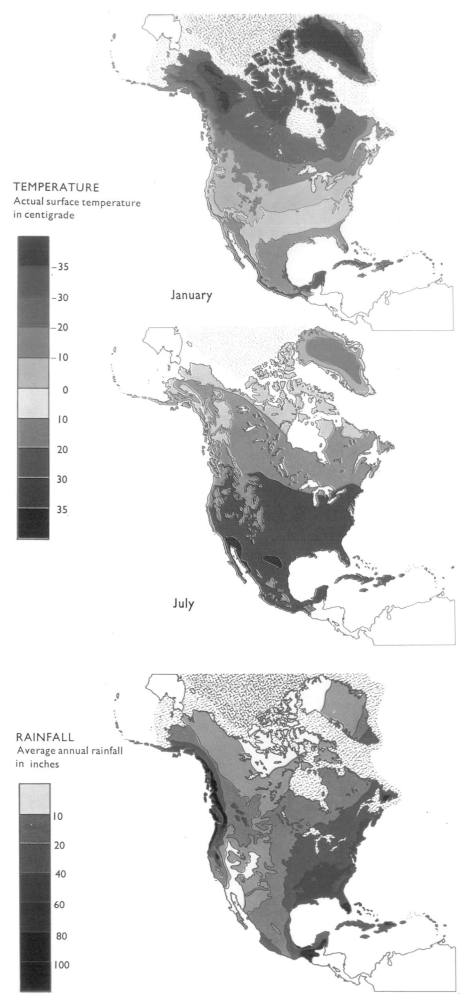

TEMPERATURE
Actual surface temperature
in centigrade

-35
-30
-20
-10
0
10
20
30
35

January

July

RAINFALL
Average annual rainfall
in inches

10
20
40
60
80
100

today were first grown by American Indians—
allowing populous permanent settlements and the
rise of large-scale, organized civilizations such as
the Mayan and the Aztec.

Farming spread northwards to the south-west
United States, along the Atlantic seaboard as far as
Maine and to parts of the plains and prairies.
Elsewhere, fishing, food gathering and hunting
were the main means of subsistence and people
generally lived in small bands of at most a few
hundred, moving seasonally through defined
territories, or — along much of the bountiful
Pacific coast — building semi-permanent villages
and subsisting through the winter on surplus
produce. In the far north the Eskimos, who arrived
from Siberia by boat only about 4,000 years ago,
evolved an enormously efficient Arctic culture,
based on hunting sea mammals, and spread east as
far as Greenland.

Despite all these differences many native peoples
shared certain characteristics: self-sufficient economies which exploited all available renewable
resources with enormous skill; a close, often
mystical identification with their land, which they
frequently regarded quite literally as a mother and
treated with great reverence; and a deeply religious
attitude which saw life's main object not in terms
of progress or the attainment of individual fulfil-
ment, but following a cycle of activities, repeated
every year, which was ordained by a deity or culture
hero and which kept mankind in harmony with
the whole of creation.

Norse seamen reached Greenland, where they
established a colony, and Canada by about the
11th century, but America was not effectively
'discovered' until Columbus' Atlantic crossing in
1492. Europe at that time was in a state of turmoil,
with a rapidly growing population, emerging nation
states competing for power and trade, and a mood
of mounting religious fervour. After their long
isolation from the rest of the world, the American
natives were neither physically nor culturally
prepared for the sudden contact. The single-
minded ruthlessness of white men seeking wealth,
power, land, slaves and converts was almost
incomprehensible to them, and alien diseases
against which they had no resistance massively
depleted their populations.

The Spanish first took the West Indies, whose
inhabitants were virtually exterminated within a
century, then conquered Mexico. There the
Indians, enslaved in gold and silver mines and on
conquistador estates, fell in their millions, but
sufficient numbers survived to mix gradually with
the Europeans and produce the mestizos who form
most of the population today. Further north,
English, French and Dutch traders established
little colonies to exchange European goods for furs
and other Indian produce; after the natives had
been decimated and demoralized by illness, their
land was generally settled and the survivors
massacred or driven further inland.

The colonists, most of them English, included
utopians, religious refugees—most notably the
Pilgrim Fathers who landed in New England in
1620—and gentlemen adventurers such as the
founders of Jamestown, Virginia, in 1607. The
combination of self-righteousness, Puritanism and
commercial considerations created a local system
of values that has dominated later development of
the area. The population tended to concentrate in

ports such as Montreal, on the St Lawrence, and New Amsterdam (later New York) and Boston on the Atlantic coast, and a flourishing maritime trade developed. At the same time, thousands of slaves were brought from Africa to work tobacco-growing estates in and around Virginia and sugar cane plantations in the West Indies, which had been divided among the four colonial powers.

The white population grew rapidly, expanding into more and more Indian land, until by the second half of the 18th century there were some 1,500,000 British subjects in 13 colonies along the Atlantic seaboard. After a long series of colonial wars Britain also controlled Canada, where the white population was predominantly of French ancestry, language and culture. Danes, meanwhile, had re-established a colony in Greenland and started intermarrying with Eskimos to form the present population, while Spain was expanding into California, Florida and the south-west, with the customary brutality but without extensive settlement.

The American revolution of 1776, when the 13 British colonies combined to form an independent nation, was crucially important for the subsequent development of the whole continent. Although Mexico gained independence in 1821 and Canada achieved home rule in 1867, only the people of the United States made a complete, conscious break with the Old World, which they regarded as decadent, morally compromised and constricted by archaic political traditions.

The US constitution, framed in accordance with the newest European thought, guaranteed private property, individual liberty, freedom of speech and a balance of power between the various branches and levels of government. Still deeply Protestant by religion and temperament, and with a profound faith in the virtues of industry, thrift, sobriety and self-reliance, Americans envisaged a just, free and prosperous society that would serve as a model for the rest of the world. To the west lay seemingly unlimited land which could be tamed to support a great new civilization. With enormous confidence, Americans opened their doors to the poor and oppressed of the Old World and began a relentless drive across the continent.

Between 1820 and 1920 some 35,000,000 immigrants entered the United States. To begin with they were mostly British and German; later came the Irish, escaping from the appalling famine that followed the potato blight in the 1840s; refugees, such as Poles and Slovaks from the rambling, semi-feudal empires of eastern Europe; Italians, Greeks and others from the impoverished Mediterranean countries; Jews from many places, most notably Russia, where they faced persecution; and numerous others. Some groups, such as the Italians and the Irish, were financially, culturally or linguistically ill-equipped for the fiercely competitive free enterprise system and the strongly Protestant ethos. Tending to remain in their own national communities in eastern cities, they formed a source of cheap labour for the rapid industrialization of America.

Others, especially those with money, went to join the swelling flood of people following the frontier in search of land. Huge areas were bought or won from other countries: in 1803 the Louisiana Purchase from France added a vast territory centring on the Mississippi river; then Florida,

California and the south-west were gained from Spain and Mexico; and Alaska was acquired from Russia.

New cities sprang up every decade, first along waterways and around the Great Lakes, where Cleveland, Chicago and Detroit became thriving centres, and then on the routes of the railways that snaked across the country. In this dynamic mood of national self-assurance, the Indians who occupied most of the land were scarcely considered; they were forced by trickery, corruption or violence to relinquish ever-increasing areas of their territory and then shunted out of sight on to reservations. The Indian population was devastated; in California, for example, it fell from about 150,000 in 1850 to less than 20,000 in 1890.

By the end of the 19th century, the whole continent had been conquered and North America had taken on roughly its present shape, with the United States and Canada—where there had been less immigration and a less reckless territorial expansion—extending from the Atlantic to the Pacific, and a reduced Mexico lying south of the Rio Grande. Of predominantly European ancestry, the population also contained substantial minorities descended wholly or partly from black slaves and pre-Columbian peoples.

During the 20th century there has been an astonishing rate of economic growth in much of North America. Today the United States, with a generally high standard of housing, a 99 per cent adult literacy rate and nearly a third of its population engaged in full-time education, has in material terms the highest standard of living in the world, and Canada is not far behind. The concentration of industry in cities such as Detroit, centre of car manufacture, and Pittsburgh, where steel is produced, means that more than 75 per cent of all Canadians and Americans are now urban dwellers. Of these, more than half live in the suburbs, enjoying a vast range of consumer goods, entertainment and other services.

The United States dominates both its neighbours —goods exported to Mexico, for example, represent only about 3.9 per cent of US exports but 66.6 per cent of Mexican imports—and, through massive investment, many other parts of the world, particularly Latin America. Even in Canada, however, where the population of only about 23,000,000 is concentrated along the southern border, there is increasing hostility to US influence on culture and the economy. Nonetheless, most Canadians seem happy to enjoy the conveniences of an American-style way of life.

In Mexico too, where there have been some attempts to improve conditions for the poor by land reforms and other measures since the revolution of 1910-20, there is a now growing desire to find a modern identity overshadowed neither by the Spanish cultural roots of the élite nor by the economic power of the United States. Although the overwhelming majority of the population is Roman Catholic and Spanish-speaking, there are sizeable Indian minorities and a growing interest in the heritage of the pre-Columbian civilizations. Many islands of the West Indies, following the lead of Castro's Cuba and the newly independent socialist Jamaica, are also trying to create a new place for themselves free from the colonial past and the present economic dominance of the advanced industrial nations.

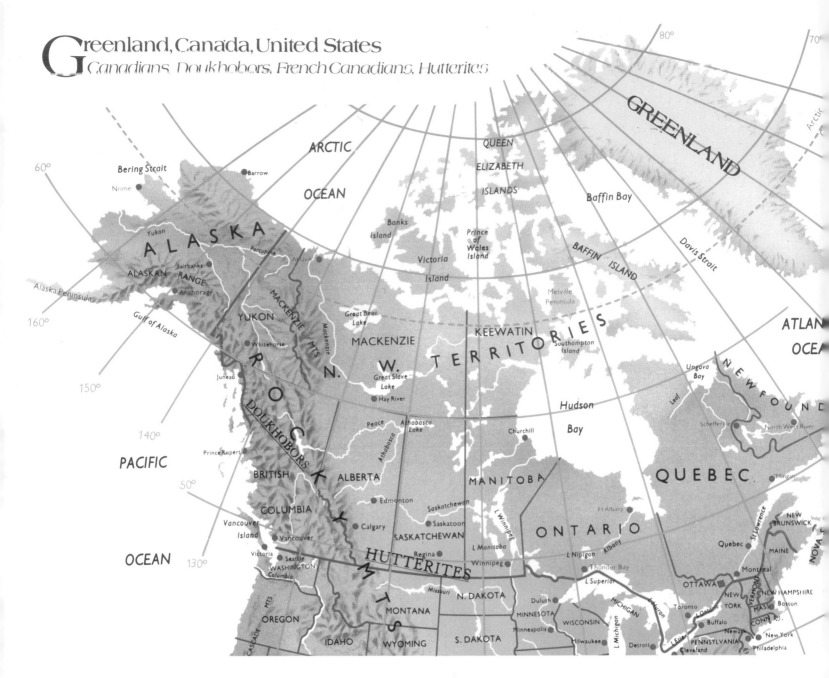

**French Possessions
before 1763**

Greenland

pop: 51,000

The world's largest island, Greenland is a province of the kingdom of Denmark. Lying mostly within the Arctic circle, the land is almost entirely covered by ice, and permanent settlement is confined to the coastal fringe. Eskimos form the majority (40,000) of the population, but pure-blooded groups are now found only in the far north near Thule and on the east coast. Danish settlement began in 1721 but European influence was slight until immigration increased in the 1950s and 1960s.

Greenland's economy is now based on fishing (cod, shrimp and salmon), which has replaced the overworked seal trade. Some animal husbandry takes place in the milder southwest and rich mineral resources are now being exploited.

Canadians

pop: 23,314,000 (1977)

The second largest country in the world after the Soviet Union, most of Canada is inhospitable to human settlement because of its mountainous terrain and Arctic climate. Indeed 90 per cent of the population inhabits a 200-mile belt along the US border.

Canadians are a mixture of several different ethnic and cultural groups. Approximately 45 per cent came originally from the British Isles, 30 per cent from France and 25 per cent from elsewhere in Europe. The Eskimo and Indian minorities form only about 1 per cent of the total population. The non-French immigrants have tended to assimilate into the British-Canadian culture, and in 1971 59 per cent of the nation claimed English as their first language, as against 28 per cent who claimed French.

Economic interests also divide the nation: while the poor maritime provinces are heavily dependent on central government, the prosperous eastern provinces of Ontario and Quebec display a common tendency towards regional autonomy. In addition there is a profound mistrust of the city dwellers on the part of Canada's prairie provinces. Improved communications, while unifying Canadian territory, also serve to link the country to the United States, whose culture threatens to dominate the whole northern continent.

The Arctic climate and rugged terrain of the far north have so far delayed the extraction of rich natural resources of copper, zinc and iron ore. There is strong resistance amongst Canadians against encouraging already large US corporate investment, but plans for the first

exploitation of vast natural gas fields in Alaska and the Yukon gained momentum during the bitter early months of 1977.

Doukhobors
pop: 20,000

A non-conformist Christian sect, the Doukhobors—whose name means 'spirit fighters'—originated in the Ukraine during the 18th century. After years of persecution, they emigrated to Canada at the turn of the 20th century. The sect divided into three colonies, which differ in creed and economic organization, but all Doukhobors are both pacifists and vegetarians. Traditional lifestyle is most strongly preserved in British Columbia.

Austerity pervades Doukhobor society. Religious practice is devoid of external apparatus and ceremony of any kind, including marriage and baptism. Revelation rather than instruction is the guiding principle. Illiteracy is encouraged, and secular education eschewed.

French Canadians
pop: 5,000,000

The territory of New France, comprising rather more than the present-day provinces of Quebec and New Brunswick, was ceded to Britain in the treaty of Paris in 1763. Even today, 80 per cent of Quebec's 6,000,000 population are of French ethnic origin, and nearly all speak French as their mother tongue.

Outside the cities, and in Montreal's old quarter, French and Catholic traditions are preserved in daily life and holy day festivals. But for the most part traditional French Canadian society, based on agriculture, with the farm and the parish as its basic institutions, has given way to urbanization and industrialization. Although most farmland is still owned and tilled by French people, the majority of Québecois are employed in industries owned by English speakers.

The 1950s and 1960s saw the beginnings of a separatist movement (Québec Libre), under the banner of French-language preservation. The separatists pointed to the ills of Quebec's industrial society as the direct result of exploitation by English-speaking business-men. By 1978, more and more Québecois supported demands for the exclusive use of French in business, and independence from Canada was in prospect.

Hutterites
pop: 17,500

An Anabaptist sect dating from the 16th century and originally based in Moravia and Slovakia, the Hutterites emigrated to the United States in 1874. Today they have farms in the Canadian provinces of Manitoba, Saskatchewan and Alberta as well as the American states of Montana and Dakota, where they practise communal living and agriculture under a rigorous religious discipline.

Subordination of the individual to the community under the guidance of God binds Hutterites in a way of life in which violence, crime and anti-social behaviour are virtually unknown. The absence of television, radio and cinema, and the avoidance of luxuries allow them to preserve their independence from American culture. This, while strengthening internal economy, tends to alienate Hutterites from their neighbours. Women have no decision-making powers in the community government.

Hutterite farmers
tend a sick cow

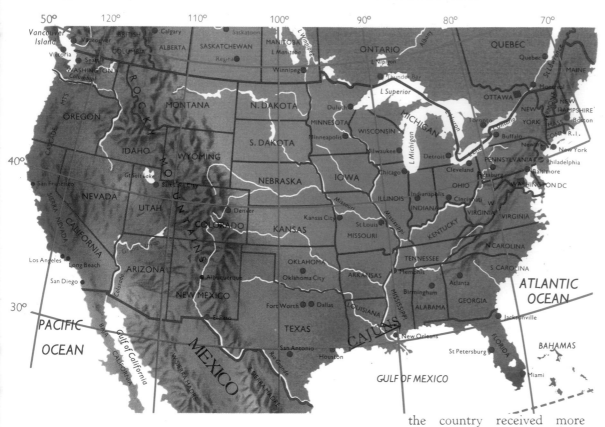

Expansion of United States

1. United States in 1783
2. Louisiana, 1803
3. North Dakota, 1818
4. Florida, 1819
5. Texas, 1845
6. California, 1848
7. Oregon, 1846
8. Alaska, 1867

Amish

pop: 66,000

The Amish are members of a protestant sect which broke off from the Mennonites while still based in Switzerland at the end of the 17th century. They emigrated to America soon afterwards and are now scattered throughout the United States and Canada, but the majority live in small, self-sufficient communities in the states of Pennsylvania, Ohio and Indiana. Their lifestyle is rigid and puritanical in its doctrines.

The most conservative groups are unaided by any form of modern technology, but others make use of electricity and the motor car. All live by farming, but women make clothes by hand and run small cottage industries. Education is religious, advocating love of fellow-men and the practice of thrift.

Americans

pop: 215,966,000 (1977)

The world's leading country in economic development and in living standards, the United States of America displays a remarkable degree of national homogeneity in view of its diverse ethnic and racial composition. In less than two centuries, between 1776 and 1921,

the country received more than 35,000,000 immigrants from all over the world. Yet each ethnic group, while maintaining strong cultural traditions, has largely aspired to integration within America's English-based society. At the same time, mass production and mass communications have promoted a broad uniformity of material culture.

A kind of 'ethnic hierarchy' has traditionally stretched from the white Anglo-Saxon community, originally centred on the New England states, down through other European groups to the Chinese of the west coast and the black descendants of African slaves brought to work the southern plantations. In recent years, Puerto Ricans and illegal Mexican immigrants have to some extent replaced Black Americans as the lowest in this social ladder. Meanwhile the indigenous Indian groups are confined to reservations or at best partially assimilated into white society.

Many of the problems facing Americans derive from the very pace of industrial development. In less than 100 years, the country has been transformed from a rural to an industrial nation, with major densities of population in vast city areas. More than 30,000,000 people live in an almost unbroken megalopolis

on the Atlantic seaboard stretching from southern Maine to central Virginia. Chicago, Detroit and Los Angeles are also centres of vast conurbations.

There, despite the United States' unparalleled wealth, the economic system has so far proved incapable of providing full employment or even eradicating poverty. In 1971, 25,600,000 people had incomes below the poverty line assessed by government statisticians. Decaying inner cities, poor housing and ghetto areas breed violence, which the more affluent avoid by moving to the outer suburbs.

For the majority of Americans, living standards are higher than anywhere else in the world, most notably in diet, education and housing. High incomes and ready access to transport—most Americans own at least one car—have encouraged exceptional mobility, for the country is served by extensive highway systems. Moreover, Americans of all ages have increasing opportunities to travel abroad. Their growing awareness of belonging to a global community has contributed to a changing assessment of American culture.

Black Americans

pop: 23,900,000

For Black Americans more than any other minority group, the duality of integrated Americanism and ethnic consciousness is especially acute. From one point of view, their history can be seen as a slow process of emancipation, from the abyss of slavery in the colonial era, through the promise of equality in the constitution, to the reforms made after the civil war and finally to gradual desegregation in the southern states today.

On the other hand, 200 years of oppression and a growing urge to re-establish pride in African origins have produced an assertion of black culture which clashes violently with the notion of the Americanized negro. The confirmation of a distinctive black culture has been manifested most strongly in blues, jazz and soul music.

Typically in America, even the black community ranges over a wide spectrum from the very rich to the abysmally poor.

Around 70 per cent of Black Americans now live in the northern states in a settlement pattern typified by Chicago. The city's outer zone houses the highest percentage of blacks in professional jobs, married and owning their own houses. The inner zone contains the highest number of illiterates and unemployed; the largest proportion of female-headed households; the highest rate of illegitimate births, desertions and charity cases. Crime rates in the ghettos are high, housing is appalling and education inadequate. For the inhabitants of the ghettos of Watts or Harlem, the prospects of equality, either social or economic, seem faint indeed.

Mormons
pop: 3,000,000

The Mormon faith—the Church of Jesus Christ of Latter-Day Saints—has spread throughout the world, but its centre is a self-sufficient society based on Salt Lake City in the state of Utah. Despite a history of conflict with the US government, the Mormon lifestyle seems to reflect the American dream both in its patriarchal-capitalist political structure and in its belief that clean living, patriotism and fearing God brings material reward and comfort.

The Church was founded in 1830 by Joseph Smith, and led to Utah by Brigham Young in in 1897. Polygyny, long the most controversial aspect of Morman society, was renounced by the Church 13 years later. Religious discipline is firm but tolerant. All Mormon males over the age of 12 are expected to join the priesthood; Sunday school is faithfully attended by everyone; coffee, tobacco and liquor are forbidden; health and recreation are emphasized and education is particularly valued. The *Book of Mormon* proclaims free will and the need for effort to achieve salvation.

Cajuns
pop: 500,000

The Cajuns occupy the bayous of southern Louisiana and the marshlands along the Missis-sippi, with a lifestyle more French than American—in some communities English is hardly spoken at all. They are descended from refugees forced to leave French Canada in the 18th century, who met a less than hospitable reception from the aristocratic Creoles of Louisiana. Their history is one of isolation, originally social and economic but later reinforced by racial discrimination: during the 19th century they interbred with both Negroes and Indians.

Today the Cajun economy prospers on a rural and maritime basis. The marshland is an ideal fishing base. Louisiana is one of America's top shrimp-producing areas and most of the catch is gathered by Cajun boats. Other types of fishing, sugar cultivation and fur-trapping supplement their economy.

Cajun tradition is most obvious at celebrations like the Mardi Gras when, in a festival of masks, costumes, eating and drinking, the whole community comes alive in a vigorous assertion of an independent culture.

Student parade at the University of Wyoming

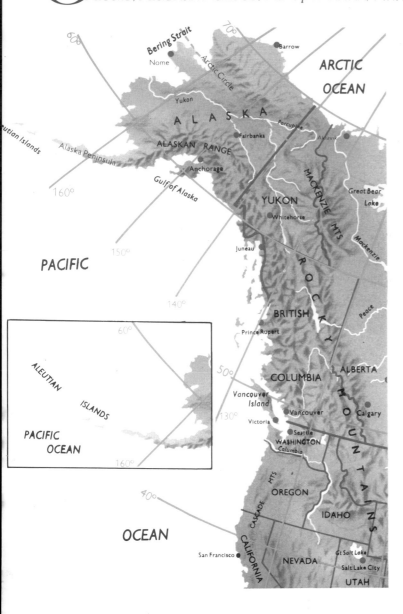

Aleuts

pop: 2,300

At the beginning of the 18th century there were perhaps 24,000 Aleuts, distributed among some 70 islands that stretch in a chain from Alaska across the north Pacific. Their economy, like that of the Eskimos, was based largely on seals, sea-lions, whales and other sea mammals, which were hunted from kayaks and which provided for most material needs: meat, skins for clothing and boat coverings, intestines for waterproofing *parka* coats, flippers for boot soles, blubber for oil. Contact with North-West Indians led the islanders to adopt basketry and carved wooden hats; there was also some social stratification.

Russian fur traders reached the Aleuts about 1750 and subjected them to a régime of en-

Distribution of Athapaskan-Speakers

slavement, robbery, rape and murder which, together with alien diseases, reduced their population by about 90 per cent and largely obliterated their original culture. Survivors today usually work in commercial fishing, canning, sealing or other operations, and European influences, notably the Russian Orthodox Church, are widespread.

Alaskan Natives

pop: 70,000

The native people of Alaska are divided among some four main groups. The Eskimos, who constitute substantially more than half the total, live mainly along the Arctic and Bering Sea coasts and originally lived, like their relatives in Siberia, Canada and Greenland, primarily by hunting sea mammals and fishing. The Aleuts of the Aleutian archipelago were racially and economically similar, but in a long period of isolation had evolved a different language and culture. The Athapaskans of the interior lived mostly like their relations in Canada. Finally, the tribes of the west coast–Tlingit, Haida and Tsimshian–shared the North-West Indian culture.

There was some interchange among these groups, which produced unusual cultural variation. The Eskimos, for example, introduced the dog-sled and clothing styles to the Athapaskan Kutchin. The most influential peoples, however, were the coastal Indians, elements of whose more organized society were found among the Aleuts, neighbouring Athapaskan bands and the Eskimos immediately north of them.

First Russian and then American traders, missionaries and fortune hunters disastrously affected the Alaskan Natives, depleting particularly the Aleuts and some Eskimos by brutality and disease, although some interior peoples were not contacted until the early 20th century. In 1973, in a unique settlement, Alaskan Natives received not reservations but 40,000,000 acres (11 per cent of the state) in fee simple and $962,500,000 compensation. In the next century it will be seen if this approach helps them to adapt to new pressures more adequately than the reservation.

Athapaskans

pop: 35,000

Apart from Eskimos and some coastal Indians, all the peoples aboriginally living in America north of the 56th parallel were Athapaskan speakers. They are thought to have been late arrivals to the continent, moving from Siberia 5–6,000 years ago, and before white contact they seem to have been pushing south, the Navajos and Apaches migrating to the southwestern United States, the Sarcis settling on the plains, and groups such as Hupa and Mattole reaching the Pacific coast.

The northern Athapaskans, including Ahtena, Koyukon, Kutchin, Tanana, Tanaina, Ingalik, Han and Nabesna in the north-west, and Tutchone, Hare, Kaska, Tahltan, Sekani, Carrier, Beaver, Slave, Dogrib, Yellowknife and Chipewyan in the Canadian interior—subsisted mainly by hunting moose, caribou, musk oxen, bear, and other game, supplemented by wild plants. The climate was harsh and variable, causing periods of great scarcity.

Most Athapaskans lived in small, simply organized bands of a few families. Among certain groups, including the Kutchin, women were treated harshly—some mothers killed girl babies to spare them later suffering—and the old were often abandoned or killed when they became a hindrance. Leadership was informal, but shamans, mediating with an often fearful world of spirits and ghosts, were respected and witches were much feared.

Many Athapaskans were largely unaffected by Europeans, except insofar as they became fur trappers, until the 20th century; but exploitation of mineral and energy resources in their territory is rapidly bringing them into contact with the dominant white culture and threatening their own traditional economies, languages and beliefs.

North-West Indians

pop: 54,500

The north-west Pacific coast, from southern Alaska to northern California, has a generally more temperate climate than most of North America. Ab-

originally it was densely populated: in the north were Tlingit, Haida, Tsimshian and Bella Coola. Further south were Kwakiutl, Nootka, Makah, Quileute, Puyallup, Nisqually, Klallam, Chehaus, Lummi, Snohomish, Snoqualmi, Swinomish, Muckleshoot, Chinook, Coos and Takelma.

The North-West Indians gathered wild plants and berries and hunted variously sea mammals, bear, wild goat and other game. The basis of their economy, however, was fish, particularly salmon, which was so plentiful along the coast and rivers that it enabled them to build up huge surpluses of food and remain year-long in permanent villages, where they developed a culture as complex as those of agricultural peoples. Slaves sometimes comprised 30 per cent of the population.

The chiefs, who had great authority but little coercive power, inherited their office and came generally from noble families. They demonstrated their position in the *potlatch* ('giving') where the quantity of possessions they gave away or destroyed—including slaves —demonstrated their status. Carved wooden posts—totem poles—stood outside the nobles' long plank houses showing their ancestry, clan membership and events of which they

were proud. Competition for rank was intense and sometimes led to warfare or even suicide. Religion was highly organized, with spirits and dances belonging to each clan.

The North-West Indians were disastrously reduced by European diseases and thought to be dying out, but today their numbers are increasing. In the United States they are fighting for recognition of their treaty fishing rights, while in British Columbia they are demanding settlements of land claims which will give them a base on which to create a future for their children.

Kwakiutl

pop: 2,900

The Wakashan Kwakiutl originally occupied some 20 communities with a total population of perhaps 10–20,000. Each village was divided into descent groups, called *numima*, every member of which had a specific rank. The *numima* controlled specific territories and fishing grounds where its members worked, and lower-ranking families were expected to pass on surpluses to the highest-ranking, who then demonstrated their wealth by holding ceremonial feasts, or *potlatch*.

The members of a rival *numima* or village would be in-

vited, and the *potlatch*-giver would distribute food and presents to his guests, singing and proclaiming his own fame, wealth and courage. The rivals then had to hold a return *potlatch*, and give away more or accept an inferior position. The *potlatch*, although given by the head of a *numima* or a village, affected the relative standing of the group as a whole.

The hierarchical principle extended into religion. Each *numima* had a number of guardian spirits with whom it enjoyed a special and hereditary relationship. Certain dances, songs, costumes and names associated with these beings were regarded as personal property, and the most spectacular and powerful of them were accumulated by the nobility.

With the arrival of the white man, trade goods increased the Indians' wealth and disease devastated their population, so that more and more was distributed among fewer and fewer people. *Potlatch* was banned in the 1920s, but elements of the old values are still evident today. Commercial fishing, clam-digging and logging are replacing traditional pursuits, and many Kwakiutl beliefs and customs are weakening, despite efforts to preserve wood-carving, dancing and other aspects of the culture.

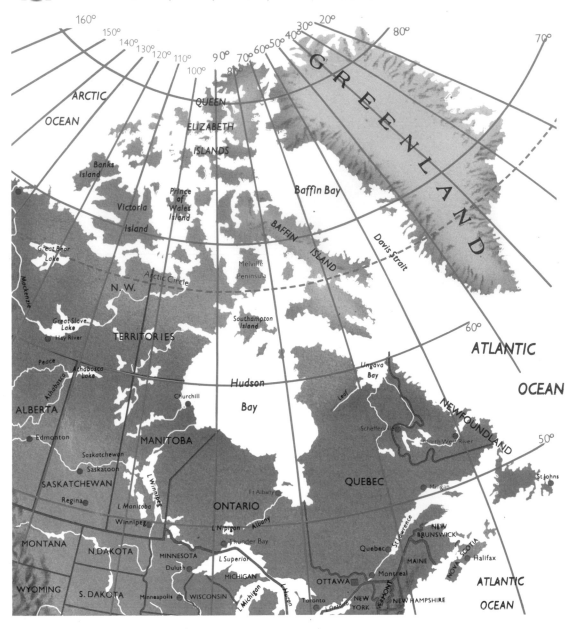

Eskimos

pop: 62,000

The aboriginal culture of the Eskimos (or Inuit, meaning people, in their own language) was one of the most materially sophisticated and best adapted in the world. It evolved gradually, over some 7,000 years, as the Eskimos' ancestors spread east from the Bering Strait, and by the 18th century, despite many regional variations, it was remarkably homogeneous through the 3,000 miles or so from Siberia to Greenland.

The Eskimo economy was based essentially on hunting. Except in Alaska, where fish predominated, and among the Caribou Eskimo north-west of Hudson's Bay, who lived inland all year and depended primarily on caribou, most Eski-

Distribution of Eskimos

mos subsisted by taking sea mammals—particularly seal—which were caught through air holes and on the ice during winter and from kayaks in the spring and early summer. In addition to meat, sea mammals provided blubber for oil, which was burnt in a stone lamp (pottery in parts of Alaska); bones and tusks for harpoons, spears, toggles, ice-chisels, sled shoes, thimbles, needles, toys, amulets and other objects; skins for waterproof clothing, boat coverings, harness, ropes and housing; translucent gut for windows; sinews for thread and many other necessities.

Through most of North America the Eskimos moved inland in the summer from their settlements on the coast or islands to hunt the caribou, which annually migrated north

on to the tundra. In Greenland, the Polar Eskimos of the far north depended very little on land animals, although they netted birds and gathered berries in summer.

The Eskimos lived in small groups of families, 50–100 strong, and usually built winter houses, which were often subterranean, from driftwood, earth sods, or—in Greenland—logs. For summer trips inland, bands usually split up into smaller groups and lived in sealskin or caribou skin tents.

There were numerous technological variations, but social life was fairly similar in most of the area. Shamans were concerned with curing diseases and interceded with a supernatural world potent with innumerable and often dangerous beings and forces. They had some influence, but there was no system of authority. Those who were successful in the hunt provided for all those in need, and various arrangements—including wife-lending and exchange—strengthened ties of friendship. Eskimos were expected to be cheerful, amenable and uncomplaining, although jealousies and frictions sometimes erupted in murder, feud and fears of witchcraft.

The Eskimos today are probably most traditional in parts of the Canadian Arctic, but everywhere they are under pressure to surrender their old way of life and the land on which it was based and enter the larger society growing up around them. At the same time, political consciousness is growing, and with it the determination to preserve much that is good in their own traditions.

Chipewyans

pop: 5,000

The Chipewyans are the largest and most easterly Athapaskan group in the Canadian interior, and originally occupied the biggest area. They lived in bands of varying size—usually a few families—and subsisted primarily by hunting caribou, which they followed north on to the barren lands in the summer. Women ranked lower than in any other tribe and were often treated as little more than draught animals, and old people were often abandoned.

There was no formal leader-

Eskimo hunter shooting seals, Greenland

ship, but shamans and men who had successful dreams or visions of the hunt often acquired prestige. Religious belief was vague, concentrating on a host of spirits who might be mollified or antagonized. The dead were thought to travel towards an island in a stone boat which would sink if the occupants were evil.

About 90 per cent of the Chipewyan died in an 18th century smallpox epidemic. Today their population has recovered somewhat, but dependence on trade goods and welfare has eroded their traditional way of life and left them largely demoralized.

Ojibwa
pop: 97,000

The Ojibwa, or Chippewa, originally occupied a large area of southern Canada centering around the north shore of Lake Superior. Like the Cree, their Algonkian neighbours and relatives, they were predominantly migratory people who subsisted by hunting, fishing and food gathering, but their closest social ties were with the Potawatomi and Ottawa, who lived to the south.

The basic political unit of Ojibwa life was the band, consisting of perhaps 3–400 people, usually under a hereditary leader, who moved seasonally to exploit a variety of food sources: maple syrup, wild berries and rice, fish, small game and moose. There were a number of exogamous totemic clans, usually patrilineal, which extended throughout the Ojibwa and created some national cohesiveness, but there was no institutionalized tribal organization. Ojibwa religion, based on a secret Grand Medicine Society, was highly structured, with four grades of members and an important annual festival, the *Midewiwin*. It involved a dualistic concept of the universe, with supreme good and evil beings and lesser spirits whose aid could be obtained by medicine men or by vision quests. Witchcraft was very much feared.

Today Ojibwa communities, scattered through Michigan, North Dakota, Wisconsin, Minnesota and adjoining parts of Canada, vary greatly. In some, food gathering is still practised and language and beliefs remain relatively strong.

Cree
pop: 67,000

Aboriginally the Algonkian Cree occupied an area from western Quebec to western Manitoba, but with the arrival of white fur traders and European goods they pushed further west in the search for pelts and game, displacing or absorbing other groups, and today their communities stretch from Quebec to Alberta. Some bands also moved on to the plains and became bison hunters, and about 1,800 of their descendants now live in Montana.

Apart from the plains, the Crees' homeland was mainly forested and they subsisted by hunting and gathering in bands. The most highly prized game were woodland caribou, moose, bear and beaver, but in winter many bands were forced to live on hares, which they caught in willow bark snares. The breeding cycle of hares produces periodic decreases, during which the Cree might face starvation and some would resort to cannibalism, which was feared and utterly abhorred. Perhaps the most persistent figures in Cree mythology are *windigos*, human cannibals transformed by their act into supernatural giants.

Two disastrous smallpox epidemics in the 18th and 19th centuries drastically reduced the Cree population, and they have never recovered their power. Today, like other Indians, they are caught between their traditional world and the white man's, often demoralized and in great poverty.

45

Indian Culture Areas

- Plateau
- California
- Great Basin

Plateau Indians

pop: 34,500

The North American plateau, between the Rocky and Cascade mountains, is a high area of forested mountains, streams and rivers, valleys, canyons and bare volcanic regions. Aboriginally it contained many different peoples, including Shuswap, Lilooet, Thompson Indians and Chilcotin in the north; Kalispel, Coeur d'Alène, Colville, Sanpoil, Spokan, Cowlitz, Palouses and Kutenai in the centre; and Nez Perce, Flathead, Cayuse, Wallawalla, Umatilla, Yakima, Klikitat, Molala, Klamath and Modoc.

Salmon, which were netted, speared or trapped in weirs during their annual runs up the rivers, were the staple diet for most of the Indians. Gathering and hunting were also important. Most groups lived in semi-permanent villages, alternating between semi-subterranean or well-sheltered buildings, sometimes extended into longhouses during the winter, and rough rush or bark-covered huts in summer.

Each village was generally autonomous, with leaders selected on merit—although a few communities had hereditary chiefs. There was little tribal identity, although villages sometimes combined for hunting, warfare, or other purposes. At puberty boys would be sent on a vision quest, during which they would acquire the aid of one or more spirit beings, and those with especially strong spirits might become shamans and practise curing and healing.

The speed and force of white settlement in the 19th century disrupted the tribes and their populations fell, but some, such as the Yakima, still fight to retain much of their culture.

Nez Perces

pop: 2,500

The Penutian Nez Perces were one of the many hunting, fishing and gathering peoples in the largely forested country of the Columbia river. For most of the year they lived in small semi-permanent settlements, usually consisting of semi-subterranean houses occupied by one or more families, and often located close to one of the many streams and rivers crossing the area. Fish, particularly salmon, which were trapped, netted or speared on their annual run, were the most important food source, but the Indians also hunted wapiti, deer, bear, moose and other game and gathered wild plants.

Each village acknowledged a headman, chosen for wisdom, ability or past achievement, who usually served for life. He had no coercive power and generally acted as a guide and advisor, settling disputes and overseeing the life of the community. The different villages would sometimes co-operate in common enterprises such as trade or hunting under a single leader, but there was no tribal organization.

Around puberty, boys were sent on a vision quest, seeking a *weyekin* or guardian spirit, who would help them in later life and mediate between the individual and the populous supernatural world. Men with powerful *weyekin* and religious authority became *tiwets*, or shamans, from among whom leaders were often chosen.

In the 18th century the Nez Perces, like many neighbours, acquired the horse and started to venture east on to the plains for hunting trips. By 1805, when the Lewis and Clarke expedition encountered them, they had adopted *tipis*, feather war-bonnets and other plains characteristics, and had become expert horse breeders. Although the hunting parties would leave home for long periods they always returned ultimately to their villages.

During the troubled opening of the west in the mid-19th century the Nez Perces prided themselves on their friendship with the white man, but eventually a number of traditional bands were plunged into war by refusing to accept a treaty, following the discovery of gold in their land. The treaty was signed by Christianized chiefs in 1863 and effectively reduced their reservation from 4,688 to 781 square miles. After a heroic war in 1877, in which they repeatedly defeated the US army, the bands were captured and exiled to Oklahoma. Eventually they were allowed to go to the Colville reservation in Washington where their descendants still live. The bulk of the Nez Perces are on the remains of their original Idaho reservation.

Yurok

pop: 1,000

Before white contact the Algonkian Yurok were one of a group of north-west Californian peoples—including also Hupa, Tolowa and others—who lived by harvesting salmon, lampreys, seafood, acorns and other foods. There were more than 50 Yurok settlements, consisting of gabled timber houses built round a square or octagonal pit, with a total population of perhaps 2,500–3,000 extending along the lower Klamath river and the coast.

The Yurok and their neighbours had less social and religious organization than almost any other North American Indians but, like the peoples of the north-west Pacific coast, they were deeply preoccupied with personal property. Wealth, which was the only means of acquiring prominence, was measured in dentalium shells, worked obsidian, woodpecker scalps and other valuables, and there was an elaborate and exact system of payment, ranging from bride-wealth to recompense for insult, destruction of property and murder, which varied according to rank and which formed the foundations of social stability. Failure to observe it led to disgrace, feud and ultimately the breakdown of the community.

Yurok mythology was largely concerned with culture heroes and with stories about the *Wage*, a race who inhabited the earth before man. Shamans, usually women, gained strength by taking into themselves the 'pains' which caused illness in other people, and magic was widely practised. Fine basketry was produced, and a great variety of beautiful utensils were carved from elk-horn, wood and other materials.

Although they were disastrously affected by disease, brutality and loss of land after the arrival of Europeans, the Yurok were less devastated than most other Californian groups and some of their traditional culture still survives.

Californian Indians
pop: 15,000

Pre-Columbian California was one of the most densely-populated and culturally diverse areas of North America, with more than 105 distinct native societies, speaking languages of six different parent stocks and totalling perhaps 350–400,000 people. Along the coast, in the north there were groups such as Tolowa, Hupa, Mattole, Yurok and Wiyot, all of whom are usually classified as belonging to the north-west coast cultural area. Further south were Pomo, Costanoans, Salinans, Chumash, Gabrielino, Luiseno and Diegueno. Baja California, culturally part of northern Mexico, was inhabited by Cochimi, Waicuri, Pericu and others. In the northern interior were Achomawis and Atsugewis, culturally similar to the neighbouring Great Basin bands, and Karoks, Shasta and Yana; in the centre were Yukis, Patwin, Maidu, Miwok, Wintun and Yokut; while in the south were Serrano, Cahuilla and—around the border with Arizona—Yuman speakers of the south-west culture area.

The mild climate of California and the profusion of different kinds of food enabled the large population to be supported without agriculture. Oak-trees grew in abundance in much of the area, and acorns provided a staple part of the diet. They were collected in large conical baskets, shelled, dried and stored; when needed, they were pounded into meal, from which the acid was leached out, and made into gruel or bread. Different peoples also variously collected seeds, fruit, nuts, roots, berries, plants and shellfish, hunted elk, deer and smaller game, and caught birds, reptiles, insects and fish. Most groups inhabited defined, and usually mutually respected, territory through which they moved during the spring and summer, returning to more permanent settlements in winter.

Many peoples lived in bands of 100 or so individuals, consisting of a few extended families under a headman, but there were also larger, more organized groups. The Yokuts, for example, had a total population of about 50,000 divided into some 50 tribelets, each with a single main village and several transient ones, and a number of patrilineally-inherited offices. In some villages, throughout the area, there were clans as well as secret societies training young people in supernatural matters and organizing ceremonies, often in circular earthen lodges.

The Indians of California were decimated by disease and brutally persecuted by both Spaniards and—especially during the gold rush—Americans. Many groups were wiped out and the population fell from perhaps 100,000 in 1853 to under 20,000 in 1906. Today, few peoples remain, and many of the survivors are virtually landless, although some try to preserve their traditions.

Great Basin Indians
pop: 12,500

The Great Basin, comprising most of Utah and Nevada and parts of neighbouring states, is one of the driest and barest regions in North America. The peoples who lived there aboriginally included Utes in the south-east, Shoshoni in the north-east, Paiutes and Gosiutes in the south and centre and Chemehuevis, Paviotsos, Monos, Kawiisus and Panamints in the west. Washoes, Achomawis and Atsugewis also lived along the western edge.

The Great Basin peoples usually practised no agriculture and subsisted primarily by harvesting wild plants such as grass and pine nuts. Using their knowledge of what would be ripe at a particular season and altitude, they moved from place to place, sometimes supplementing their diet with insects, small animals and birds and fish. They lived in small extended family units of 25–30 people, coming together into larger bands during the winter. There was no formal political or religious organization, though there were shamans whose main function was curing, and people of profound wisdom, called 'talkers', were turned to for advice.

Some groups on the periphery of the area enjoyed a more prosperous way of life. A few Washoes and a band of Paiutes practised agriculture; the Utes of the Colorado mountains lived in bigger settlements and traded with other tribes; some of the Shoshone, having acquired the horse from the white man, became bison hunters, and their relatives, the Comanche left the region altogether for the plains.

Their timidity and small numbers made the Great Basin Indians especially vulnerable to white invaders, who shot them for sport while crossing the area *en route* for California. Today, they live largely on barren reservations with little economic potential, and are generally very poor. Many of them still speak their own language.

Papagos/Pimas
pop: 18,000

The Papagos and Pimas of southern Arizona are related Uto-Aztecan peoples whose aboriginal way of life was based on extensive cultivation and, especially among the semi-nomadic Papagos, food gathering. Both groups lived in villages made up of patrilineal extended families. Papago communities were largely autonomous, but the Pima village headmen elected a single tribal leader. An annual rainmaking ceremony was the most important religious celebration. In both peoples there was a strong taboo against killing. Recently water has been diverted from their already arid lands and they are among the poorest native Americans, but their language and much of their traditional culture remains.

47

United States
South-West Indians, Navajos, Apaches, Pueblos

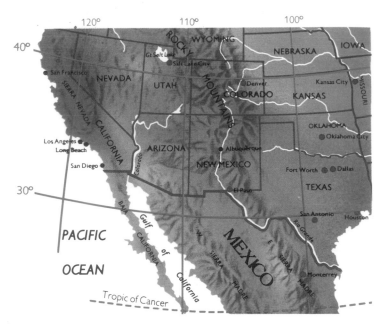

**South-West
Culture Area**

South-West Indians
pop: 204,000

The south-west culture area of the United States, comprising Arizona, most of New Mexico, and parts of Utah, Colorado and Texas, runs from a high plateau in the north to low desert in the south. Except where it is crossed by the Colorado, the Rio Grande and other rivers, the land is largely arid, and until the United States won the south-west from Mexico in the middle of the 19th century few white settlers were attracted to the region. Consequently, native cultures have been less disrupted than elsewhere and today the area has the largest Indian population in the United States.

There is great cultural diversity. Major groups include the Navajos and Apaches, who arrived in the south-west 700–1,000 years ago after a long migration from the Canadian north, and the Pueblos, Papagos and Pimas, whose cultures are all descended from ancient desert farming civilizations.

Among the smaller tribes are the Mohaves, Cocopas, Maricopas and Yumas of the lower Colorado river, believed to be among the most ancient inhabitants of the area. They lived by farming, fishing and hunting and practised a unique culture based on the absolute significance of dreams. The Chemehuevis followed a similar way of life. Further north were the Yavapais, Walapais and Havasupais, who were fundamentally hunter-gatherers

like the neighbouring Great Basin bands, but who were also influenced to varying degrees by agriculturalists.

Navajos
pop: 140,000

The Athapaskan Navajos are the largest tribe in the United States, most of whom live on a 24,000 square mile reservation in Arizona, New Mexico and Utah. Their large numbers and the comparative isolation of many of their communities, together with a remarkable capacity to acquire new skills and adapt to changed conditions, have given them perhaps the most flourishing Indian culture in North America today.

The Navajos are divided into 60 or so matrilineal clans, with strong taboos against a man marrying into either of his parents' clans, but the natural social unit of everyday life is a local community. The community, which covers a specific area and may elect its own headman, is made up of a number of 'outfits' comprising two or more matrilineal extended families that co-operate in economic and ceremonial activities. Today, there is a 75-member tribal council set up to deal with the US government and the outside world.

At the heart of Navajo existence is a complex religious system. The most important deity is Changing Woman, who created man, taught him to harmonize creation and continues to help him: the other 'holy people', as gods and spirits are called, have both good and evil potential. They must be coerced to aid 'earth surface people', who include human beings and ghosts.

Witches, sorcerers and wizards are much feared; the kinds of harm, principally illness, which they can cause is minutely classified, and most Navajo ceremonies, which are difficult and elaborate and may last up to nine days, are concerned with curing such ailments. There is no organized priesthood, but Navajo shamans—called 'chanters'—have to acquire an immense body of lore, involving singing, painting and the use of holy objects.

Today, Navajo land is badly eroded and many Navajos are among the poorest North Am-

erican Indians. This is despite attempts to exploit mineral and fossil resources on the reservation, to develop tourism, and to increase income from sale of the blankets and silverwork for which the tribe is famous. Mixed farming remains the basic means of subsistence.

Apaches
pop: 16,800

The Apaches, originally Athapaskan migrants from northern Canada, were primarily hunter-gatherers, living in matrilineal family clusters without strong tribal identity. There were considerable local variations, many resulting from the influence of other Indians. The western Apaches and the Jicarillas practised some agriculture; the Jicarillas, the Mescaleros and the Lipans showed traits of plains culture; and in the east the Kiowa-Apaches joined the bison-hunting Kiowas of the plains. Most Apaches observed

an annual cycle of sacred ceremonies, in which the puberty rite was especially important, and worshipped spirit beings, such as the mountain spirits, who profoundly affected human affairs. Today traditional culture is generally stronger in the west.

Pueblos

pop: 35,000

Some 400 years after white contact, the Pueblo Indians, living in 20 distinct tribal communities in New Mexico and Arizona, preserve their pre-Columbian way of life to a greater extent than any other major Indian group in the United States.

The Pueblos' traditional livelihood—the cultivation of corn, squash, beans, gourds, cotton and other crops—involves a highly sophisticated system of desert farming, including extensive irrigation. Unlike most other south-west-

ern Indians, who were always moving in search of food, the Pueblos were enabled by their agricultural skill to live in permanent villages, often built on steep-sided *mesas* for defence. Approached by an entrance in the roof, the houses are arranged around central communal plazas in which the vitally important social and ceremonial events take place.

The Pueblos' complex political and social organization is founded on both an awareness of the interdependence of people living and working in harsh conditions, and on a highly developed religious system. Relations between the individual, the community and the world of gods and spirits are part of a single cosmic order, and keeping them in harmony is the prime object of human life.

Civil authority is exercised by officers of the dozen or so religious societies, each of which has a special function,

such as healing or rainmaking, and responsibility for particular celebrations in the annual calendar of ceremonies, which are crucial for the well-being of the group and the universe. Limitations on the membership of the societies ensure that they can only operate when all the clans are involved.

The centre of each religious society's life is the *kiva*, a semi-subterranean chamber where meetings are held and rites performed. At some public ceremonies dancers put on masks to impersonate *kachinas*, or gods, and it is not until his initiation rite in his society's *kiva* that a boy officially knows that the performers are human.

Today some Pueblos—most notably the traditional Hopi—are more conservative than others, but developers and bureaucrats put increasing pressures on even the most withdrawn communities, and disputes over water threaten the basis of Pueblo farming.

Inside a Navajo house, Arizona

49

Indian Culture Areas

- ■ Prairies
- ■ Plains
- ■ East

Plains Indians

pop: 108,500

Plains Indian culture, the last major flowering of native American civilization, was brought about by the arrival of the Europeans. Before Columbus the flat, open grassland of the great plains was sparsely populated by semi-agricultural groups such as Wichita and Osages. But as white colonists pushed the Indians west, many other peoples were forced into the area, where the horses and guns introduced by Europeans enabled them to live as nomadic hunters.

The Plains Indians, including the Blackfoot, Assiniboine, Crow, Teton and Yankton Dakota, Cheyenne, Arapaho, Pawnee, Kiowa, Kiowa-Apache and Comanche, subsisted almost entirely by hunting bison, which provided nearly all their material needs: meat for food; skins for clothing, shields, ropes, harness, and *tipis*; stomachs and intestines for cooking pots and water bags; bones, horns and hoofs for toys, utensils and religious objects.

Bands of perhaps 100 people would hunt alone for most of the year, coming together for annual celebrations such as the sun dance, at which tribal unity would be re-established and supernatural help and har-

mony sought. Around puberty, boys would be sent on a vision quest in which, after days of isolation and fasting, they were visited by a spirit being, often in the shape of an animal, who would give them protection, special skills and personal rituals to follow.

Tribal organization was generally fairly loose, and leadership informal. Individuals who distinguished themselves by religious and prophetic powers or physical courage might gain prestige and attract a following. Most tribes had soldier societies which conducted raids and policed hunts to ensure an equitable distribution of meat. At tribal gatherings, warriors would 'count coup', which involved publicly reciting their exploits.

Some Plains Indians were never militarily defeated by the US Army and the government conquered them only by destroying their livelihood, the bison. Although the economic basis of their traditional life has gone, some Plains Indians preserve their language and many of their beliefs and ceremonies. In Oklahoma, however, where the reservation system was abolished early in the 20th century, tribal identity is waning.

Cheyenne

pop: 7,000

Like many other Plains Indians, the Algonkian Cheyenne were woodland farmers and hunters driven on to the plains by white expansion in the 17th century. They then adopted the life of mounted nomads, subsisting almost entirely by hunting the bison. They crossed the Missouri river and after much wandering divided into a northern group, based in the upper basin of the North Platte river, and a southern group along the upper Arkansas river.

In most aspects Cheyenne

life was typical of the area, but they had an unusually highly-organized tribal structure. A tribal council of 40 chiefs met during annual ceremonies, when all the bands were assembled, to decide common policies and adjudicate in disputes. Five council members were priestly chiefs, who outranked the others, and one of these, called sweet medicine chief after the tribe's culture hero, presided and manipulated the sacred arrows, the Cheyenne's most awesome religious objects. If a murder or some other transgression had been committed, an arrow renewal ceremony was needed to cleanse the whole tribe.

Today the northern Cheyenne have retained many beliefs and traditions, although like the neighbouring Crow reservation their land is threatened by a massive coal-mining scheme. The southern Cheyenne are settled with a group of Arapahos in Oklahoma.

Dakota

pop: 60,000

The Dakota, known as Sioux to the white man, are the descendants of three distinct farming and hunting tribes pushed west from around Lake Superior in the 17th century. Some 60,000 now live on reservations in North and South Dakota, Minnesota and Nebraska, but many more live elsewhere in the United States.

The most easterly group is the Santee, whose migration stopped in Minnesota and who continued to hunt and farm like their ancestors. In the centre are the Yankton and Yanktonai, who settled in the eastern Dakotas, where they also farmed but became primarily hunters. Furthest west are the Teton, the most numerous, who hunted on the plains.

Like other Plains Indians, the Teton Dakota depended almost entirely on the bison, which they hunted with the horse and gun, for their food, shelter and clothing. Some wild roots and berries were also used for food and decoration, but agriculture was completely abandoned. Bands of around 100 people hunted independently for most of the year and then congregated together for such annual celebrations as the sun dance, at which cere-monies, songs and dances were performed to ensure the renew-al of the seasonal cycle of life.

During the sun dance young men would undergo sacrificial acts of self-torture and mutila-tion in which they sometimes experienced supernatural vis-ions and demonstrated the two qualities most exalted by the Dakota: physical courage and religious power. Around pu-berty, boys would leave the band to seek a vision of their own spirit guardian and men-tor, and would then return to take their place in the group. Tribal organization was in-formal, although older men noted for their wisdom and spiritual abilities might be ack-nowledged as peace chiefs, and younger warriors could attract a following as war chiefs.

With the destruction of the bison the Dakota were driven on to reservations where, in general, they have not adapted easily to American life. Some communities, such as the Og-lala Pine Ridge reservation, are split between 'traditionals' who maintain their language, philosophy and religion, and—often mixed-blood—'progres-sives' who try to encourage Americanization.

Eastern Indians
pop: 200,000

The eastern United States ori-ginally contained a great num-ber and diversity of native peoples. Several language stocks were represented—prin-cipally Algonkian in the north and centre, Muskogean and Caddoan in the south, and Iroquoian and Siouan distri-buted throughout the area.

The Atlantic coastline was densely populated. In the north, the Micmac, Penobscot and Passamaquoddy lived mainly by fishing and hunting. Further south, stretching to the Carolinas, was a series of settled agricultural peoples who sometimes formed local con-federacies for mutual defence and co-operation. Among these were the Massachusetts, Wampanoag, Narragansett, Pequot, Mahican, Mohegan, Delaware, Powhatan, Tusca-rora and Catawba. In the deep south were larger farming nations, including the Creek, Choctaw, Chickasaw, Natchez

and Cherokee. Further inland the Five Iroquois Nations and the Huron lived in settled agri-cultural communities, formed powerful confederacies and dominated much of the north. South and west were smaller groups, who also depended to varying degrees on agriculture, including the Menominee, Sauk and Fox, Potawatomi, Peoria, Kickapoo, Miami, Shawnee, Winnebago, Qapaw, Tunica, Caddo and Waco.

Bearing the first brunt of European contact, Eastern In-dians were massively reduced by alien diseases and usually dispossessed to make way for settlement. Some, such as the Five Nations, had enough mili-tary power to retain some of their land and identity, but the survivors of most were driven into isolated commun-ities where they were largely forgotten. Recently, however, descendants of the Passama-quoddy, Wampanoag and others have been emerging to demand recognition and rights as Indians.

Iroquois
pop: 41,000

The League of Six (originally Five) Nations, known collect-ively as the Iroquois, is the only one of several Iroquoian groups including the Huron, Neutral, Erie, Tobacco and Costenoga, to survive in large numbers.

The League was first est-ablished in about 1570 by Deganawida, a Huron prophet, who travelled to the Mohawk, Oneida, Seneca, Onondaga and Cayuga of present-day upper state New York, and persuaded them to end their differences.

The Iroquois lived in wood-en longhouses, each of which contained several nuclear families called 'firesides'. The firesides were organized into matrilineages, owachira, two or more of which formed a clan. The female heads of the owa-chira exercised great power, selecting the men who served as chiefs and as tribal and clan officers. The matrilineages controlled the fields and the women farmed while the men hunted and conducted warfare.

The Iroquois celebrated a series of annual festivals, cul-minating in a mid-winter cere-mony. Religion, as with most

American Indians, was very important and there were sev-eral medicine societies. The Iroquois believed that all people and objects have a spiritual potential, *orenda*, which could be used to combat evil and disharmony; to maintain the *orenda* of the group as a whole the Five Nations adopted sur-vivors of defeated peoples into their own community.

The League was joined about 1715 by the Tuscarora, a southern Iroquoian tribe dispossessed by colonists. It continued as a powerful force, destroying or subjugating In-dians threatening its interests —including the Hurons and other Iroquoians—and con-taining the Europeans, until the American revolution. It then split into two factions, and with US independence its power was broken. Some Iro-quois went to Canada, where about half the Six Nations live today. Despite efforts to assimi-late them a traditional faction has always proudly proclaimed Iroquois sovereignty.

Creek
pop: 18,000

At the time of white contact there were perhaps 18,000 Creeks, living in some 50 towns in modern Georgia and Alabama. Like other groups in the area, their way of life was based on farming but was unusually complex, both social-ly and politically.

About 31 Creek towns were 'white', which meant they ad-ministered civil functions and provided principal chiefs of the confederation; the rest were 'red' and provided war leader-ship. Every year the Creeks celebrated a number of festi-vals, most importantly the green corn dance at which the new corn was eaten and offen-ces were forgiven.

After the arrival of Euro-peans the Creeks, Choctaws, Chickasaws, Seminoles and Cherokees quickly adopted many aspects of white culture and became renowned as the Five Civilized Tribes. In the 1830s they were moved west to Oklahoma where, after many further assaults on their iden-tity, they remain today. Their former organization is now broken, but their language and some traditions are still intact.

Mexicans

pop: 63,192,000

Mexico, with a mosaic of tropical zones, deserts, humid primeval forests and inaccessible hill regions, is the largest Spanish-speaking country in the world. The composition of population is complex: there are numerous Indian groups, speaking some 50 indigenous languages, and a small upper class of pure Spanish blood, but 80 per cent of all Mexicans are mestizos of mixed Indian and Spanish descent.

Several major civilizations emerged in Mexico before the arrival of the Spanish: the Olmec (1st–5th century AD) in the tropical lowlands of the Gulf coast; the Teotihuacan (1st–9th century AD) on the central plateau; the Toltec in the central highlands (9th–12th century AD); and most notably the Mayan in Yucatán (3rd millennium BC to the conquest) and the Aztec, which enjoyed unprecedented power and luxury from 1376 until 1521, when Cortés' expeditionary force initiated 300 years of colonial rule in Mexico.

After the conquest, many Indians were put to work on plantations and in the silver mines, but other communities were only marginally affected by the change of rulers. Today the most important numerically are the Nahuatl-speaking tribes, who inhabit the region extending from Culiacán to the Guatemalan border. Other major groups include the Otomi, the Tarascan, the Zapotec and the Mixtec.

In religious life, however, change has been all-pervasive. Catholicism, spread by the Spanish friars, was integrated quickly and subtly with Indian beliefs. Architecture and painting became a rich blend of indigenous and European elements, and religious ceremonies still combine Christian iconography with the fantastic symbolism of Indian mythology.

The great majority of Mexicans are peasant cultivators, living in villages and growing maize, wheat and barley, as well as potatoes, vegetables and many kinds of fruit. Sugar, coffee and cotton are important cash crops. Maize remains the staple food, eaten by Mexicans of all classes in the form of *tortillas*. In the more prosperous villages and towns, turkey is eaten on feast days.

The cultural and economic gap between the villagers and the bourgeois élite remains enormous, despite the revolution of 1910, which was largely fuelled by rural discontent. The civil war which followed resulted in the replacement of one dictatorship by another, and land reforms were delayed until the 1930s. In modern Mexico the availability of cheap domestic labour still permits ostentatious luxury for a tiny urban élite.

Tarahumara

pop: 100,000

The Tarahumara are survivors of the North American Apache. Their culture combines North and South American traditions, with little Spanish influence on account of the region's inaccessibility and infertile soil. Tarahumara live in extended family groups, each owning its own *rancho* or windowless log cabin, fields in the upland valleys and plots in the warmer canyons which are sheltered during winter. Maize and beans are their staple diet, supplemented by hunting and food-gathering.

The people are physically handsome, stocky and agile (their name for themselves is *raramun*, or fleet-footed). Traditional dress for men is the loin-cloth; for women, full-length skirts. Self-governed through elected *gobernadors*, the tribe's social life is characterized by co-operation. *Tesguinadas* are work projects shared by community members to aid a particular family—the 'reward' is *tesguina* (beer). Religion is nominally Catholic but rooted in North American traditions.

Yaqui

pop: 6,000

The fertile lands of the Uto-Aztecan Yaqui, with their substantial silver lodes, have interested colonizing Europeans since 1519. After four centuries of colonization, the Yaqui are faced with the alternatives of exile in Arizona or Mexicanization on home reservations centred around eight *pueblos* ranged along the Yaqui river. Each village has a Mexican garrison in residence, originally installed to prevent military co-operation among the Yaqui settlements. Today the Mexican presence relates mainly to district government and legal administration where the Yaqui's own judicial system has been delimited—for example, in murder and property disputes.

Catholic dogma has been absorbed into Yaqui mythology alongside witchcraft and plant animism. Although the lay-priests (*maestros*) dominate political and religious life there are several other cults. Ceremonies take the form of dance, music and allegorical drama, as in the symbolic battles between Christ and Rome, staged on Holy Saturday. Yaqui religion extends to a mystical relationship with the environment—particularly plant and animal life, giving rise to such cults as deer dancers and *pascolas* (animal mimers). Beyond this, there is general agreement on a wide variety of phenomena, although most Yaqui have no coherent knowledge of occult traditions.

Under severe economic and political pressure, the moral cohesion of Yaqui life is fast disintegrating. Adults in the reservation lands take little notice of their infants, and child care is the province of the teenagers. Marriage is taken seriously only by the Catholic cult members and

Aztec Empire

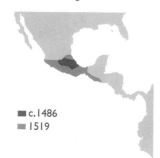

■ c.1486
■ 1519

those who wish to take advantage of the associated tax relief. Unless the people can develop effective cultivation of their remaining lands, the best they can expect is subsistence-level labour for the big Mexican and American agricultural combines along the coast.

Huastec

pop: 70,000
Originally part of the Maya group, the Huastec parted from their kinsmen long before the classical period of Mayan civilization, settling in a large area in the north. After the Spanish conquest most of their lands were expropriated, and they are now restricted to a small region of eastern Mexico. The process of Mexicanization, particularly through education, has gradually eroded their original culture.

The lush vegetation of their land provides an abundance of fruits for which there is no external demand. Coffee, henequen and sugar are the main cash crops, but most Huastec subsist by slash-and-burn cultivation of maize and beans. The men plant, weed and harvest communally, but both plots and yields are individually owned. Farmyard animals including turkeys, chicken, horses and cattle are raised, and many families also keep bee-hives.

Huichol

pop: 10,000
The Uto-Aztecan Huichol, or Vixarica, have preserved a life-style, language and system of religious beliefs which show less Spanish influence than those of other Mexican Indians. This is mainly the result of their retreat during the 16th century into the western Sierra Madre, where today most of the Huichol live in five self-governing *communades*. The most important social unit is the extended family household (*rancheria*). Although certain Christian ceremonies including Holy Week have become established in the ritual calendar, less than half the Huichol speak any Spanish.

Like the related Cora, the Huichol cultivate maize by the slash-and-burn method but harvests barely reach subsist-ence level. The National Indian Institute has introduced mechanization in some areas but the Huichol may not be able to reconcile such aggressive techniques with their concept of the soil as a divinity, personified as the Earth Mother. For the Huichol, all material phenomena are imbued with a life force, or soul, which requires spiritual and even physical nurturing.

Peyote is eaten to achieve a state of ecstasy in which confrontation with the ancestral deities is possible. Each year small parties of the most devout Huichol make a pilgrimage to a sacred place in the high desert of San Luis Potosí. The pilgrimage, which is arduous physically as well as psychologically, is both a vision quest and an initiating rite for Huichol youth.

Zapotec Indians in Juchitán

Nahua

pop: 1,000,000

The language of the Aztecs survives with the Nahua tribes of central Mexico—in the states of San Luis Potosí, Hidalgo, Puebla, Guerrero and Veracruz. The Nahua constitute Mexico's largest indigenous population, many of whom live in simple adobe villages, growing a staple diet of maize, chillies and beans. The degree of Mexicanization varies according to the proximity of villages to major towns and cities, as does the number of mixed-blood mestizo peoples in the Nahua community. These latter are usually to be found working in the commercial and service areas of village society.

Work in the fields is often conducted on a co-operative basis in community-owned fields, or *milpas*. Harvesting is carried out by both men and women. Markets are held once or twice a week and are great social occasions during which all manner of specialized products, including medicinal herbs, bark paintings and straw sandals, are sold.

The other important events in Nahua villages are the fiestas. Ostensibly Catholic celebrations, many of them date back to Aztec times. The whole community is involved in extensive preparation of elaborate foods and the building of the *castille*—a huge tower of fireworks, often incorporating models of animals or a tableau of the local patron saint.

Zapotec

pop: 300,000

Inhabiting the state of Oaxaca in southern Mexico, the majority of Zapotec are subsistence farmers, supplementing agricultural produce with hunting and fishing. Specialization by sex, education and location is highly developed and efficient, but labour is increasingly lost through migration to the cities.

Family responsibilities are acquired gradually during childhood. Marriage is at the age of 8–20 for girls and 12–22 for boys. Marriage by capture is widespread as it avoids the payment of bridewealth. Generally a newly-wed couple lives with the husband's family until the first child is born. In the mountains monogamy is the rule, but valley men sometimes support several women simultaneously.

Religion is a blend of Catholic and indigenous rituals. Increase rituals, designed to guarantee a good harvest, include rain ceremonies, corn ceremonies and ceremonies honouring the master of the mountains. Death rites are more festive than mournful, to ease the transition of the departed to the next world, and soften the blow felt by the living. When an unmarried man dies, a wedding feast is held before the funeral.

Lacandón

pop: 250

The inaccessibility of the area of jungle in southern Mexico which constitutes Lacandón territory has preserved a culture virtually unaffected by European influence. With the mysterious collapse of Mayan civilization, the Lacandón became heirs to the crumbling ruins, the memorial of that society. Today they survive by slash-and-burn maize cultivation, hunting, fishing and fruit gathering—the main crops include maize, cassava, sweet potatoes, pimentos, beans, tomatoes and bananas.

The tribe is ostensibly divided into 10 clans and these are further reduced to *caribals* consisting of one or two extended families. As a rule, Lacandón villages consist of a cluster of four or five houses hidden deep in the forest. Houses are built of four upright poles with thatched roofs and no walls. The village temple is similarly designed but better cared for.

Lacandón religion is Mayan in origin and, though simplified, still embodies a pantheon of 15 major gods, each of which controls other minor deities or spirits. Mensabak, the god of rain, must be

placated at all costs, as too much rain can easily spoil the harvest. Like the Mayan, the Lacandón world-view is fatalistic, acknowledging an impending cataclysm, when herds of jaguars will pour out of the forests and assume control.

Tzotzil

pop: 120,000

The Tzotzil are survivors of the Mayan peoples. The population is spread thinly throughout Mexico but remains centred in 24 communities in the state of Chiapas. The Tzotzil engage primarily in shifting cultivation, growing a variety of crops including maize, wheat, potatoes, coffee, sugar cane and citrus fruits. Cattle and sheep are bred, and most homesteads raise chickens.

Tzotzil townships are presided over by a small number of temporary office-holders. Each individual is born into a patrilineage and receives two surnames, one Indian and one Spanish. Particular lineages maintain their wealth and prestige over several generations. Religious festivals are a rich hybrid of Catholic and pre-Columbian rituals, supervised by a hierarchy of officials.

In the face of an expanding population and infringements on Tzotzil land rights, families are forced to migrate to the fast vanishing lowland jungles. State programmes of social and economic development do little to assuage their resentment at exploitation by middlemen and usurers, who control both the marketing of cash crops and the rent of alienated land.

Tzotzil village in the Chiapas highlands

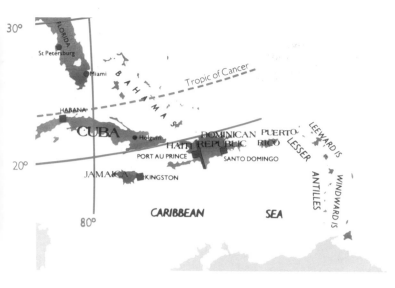

West Indians

pop: 24,470,000

The West Indies consist of three main island groups: the Bahamas, the Greater Antilles and the Lesser Antilles. All are vulnerable to the annual danger of hurricanes. There are three main ethnic groupings: the African, the European and a small element from China and the sub-continent of India. Pre-Columbian Amerindians (Arawaks, Caribs and Tanala) were rapidly wiped out after the Spanish conquest by overwork, dispossession of land, warfare and disease. A few hundred Caribs survive on the island of Dominica.

During the 17th century England, France and the Netherlands displaced Spain from the Lesser Antilles and Jamaica. As sugar and tobacco plantations flourished, the European colonists needed more and more labour: at first, the indentured labour of white criminals, political prisoners and vagabonds imported from Europe. Descendants of these peoples constitute the 'poor whites' of the Caribbean.

Next the vast and lucrative structure of plantation slavery began. Black slaves, skilled at tropical cultivation, were drawn from an area of West Africa bounded by Senegal to the north and Angola to the south. Transportation, work and living conditions were often brutal—rationalized by white masters in terms of the 'animal behaviour' of black peoples. The disappearance of African culture was almost immediate, due to the separa-

photograph: Schoolgirls in Roseau, the Dominican capital

tion of families and tribes. Today, traces of African rituals can be found most strongly in extant magical cults, notably voodoo in Haiti and *quimboiseur* sorcery in both Martinique and Guadeloupe.

Abolition of slavery (1834 in the British Caribbean; 1848 in French territories) initiated a new wave of indentured labour, predominantly Asian, Chinese, Portuguese from Madeira and the Azores, and Lebanese. Their society is characterized by endogamy and a rapid development away from rural labouring into commerce.

The most severe social problems endemic throughout the West Indies are over-population — only slightly alleviated by emigration (Jamaicans to Britain, Puerto Ricans to America) — and sporadic racial conflicts. Island governments are faced with the huge problem of salvaging economies ravaged for centuries by foreign exploitation.

Cubans

pop: 9,567,000

Apart from a brief period of English rule in 1763, Cuba remained in Spanish hands from the conquest until 1898. The island's bountiful yield of sugar, tobacco and fruit, and a strategic position off the coast of Florida, have kept it prominent in world affairs.

When Spain was forced to grant autonomy to Cuba, the United States declared war on Spain, won and with the Platt Amendment initiated 60 years of intervention and commercial exploitation. From then until the revolution in 1959, heads of state were virtually puppets of the US government.

In 1958, there were 500,000 unemployed out of a population of 6,000,000; 5,000,000 lived in *bahios*—huts without light, water or sewerage. In rural areas there were no schools or hospitals; illiteracy was as high as 43 per cent. The revolution led by Fidel Castro, a Cuban lawyer, initiated a period of immense change. In response to the two-fold problem of habitual corruption in government and almost total economic dependence on the United States, a programme of agrarian and urban reform was begun. Over a period of 10

years this drastically reduced illiteracy, the crime rate, racial discrimination and rents. The *bahios* have disappeared; tenants buy their property through rent. All Cubans are entitled to free medical care.

Industrialization, under the supervision of Che Guevara, was slow and difficult, due to the exodus of technicians, skilled workers and foreign capital in 1959. American trade embargoes began the same year and by 1962 had become a blockade. However, the oil-refining (with Soviet assistance) and fishing industries have developed; sugar production doubled in 10 years.

Life in rural areas has been largely unchanged, since the grinding routine of sugar cultivation continues. Beans, rice and bananas remain the staple foods. The countryside has, however, received an influx from the towns, for a deliberate campaign to depopulate the urban centres, especially Havana, was launched in the early 1960s.

Like other West Indians, Cubans are of mixed descent. Perhaps one-third are black or mulatto, the rest white. Since 1900 there has been little evidence of racial friction, and waves of immigration since 1900—of Spaniards, Jamaicans and Haitians—if anything have diminished tension. In the past, however, parents often encouraged their children to marry a partner of lighter skin.

Haitians

pop: 4,682,000

Haiti constitutes the western third of the island of Hispaniola, which was once France's richest colony. In 1791 it was seized and defended by rebel black slaves under Toussaint L'Ouverture—later captured by the French. Since then, the history of Haiti (split from the Dominican Republic in the 1840s) has been one of violence and racial hatred. A 5 per cent French-speaking mulatto élite rules in conspicuous affluence, while the predominantly agricultural population suffers conditions of poverty, overcrowding, unemployment, appalling medical facilities and 80 per cent illiteracy. Despite rich deposits of bauxite, iron, manganese,

56

coal and silver, *per capita* income is the lowest in the western hemisphere.

Cultural life, however, remains rich. Artistic, especially musical, skills thrive in the Lent festivals or *Rara*, and accompany each stage in the cultivation of the staple crops —maize, beans, manioc and yams. Music is equally important in voodoo, a synthesis of tribal African and Catholic rituals which united the first slave rebellions, but has since been used to repressive effect by the government. In co-operative work parties (*combite*), again accompanied by music, neighbours and friends take turns to help one another at crucial periods in the farming year.

Puerto Ricans
pop: 3,112,000

Intermarriage between the Spanish and negro inhabitants of Puerto Rico has resulted in a large mulatto majority. Control of the island passed from Spain to the United States after the Spanish-American war, and Puerto Ricans have held US citizenship since 1917. Being the richest Latin American country but also the poorest US territory creates a cultural schizophrenia which pervades life on the island.

Conspicuous American wealth (US companies control the tobacco, sugar and tourist industries) highlights the extreme poverty of the shanty towns (*barrios*), which proliferate around the cities, especially San Juan, the capital. These are populated by dispossessed rural families in an unstable atmosphere of violence and alcoholism.

Since 1952, when Puerto Rico became a commonwealth with its own government and constitution, some social and economic progress has been made. The construction of many new factories combined with large investment in education and health departments has relieved poverty and disease, and considerably reduced illiteracy. Overcrowding remains a serious problem— population densities are as high as 766 per square mile— and the only escape is emigration to New York, where Puerto Ricans face enormous cultural difficulties.

Central/South America

The physical environment of Central and South America is dominated by mountains. One range forms the backbone of Central America, ending close to where the Panama isthmus joins the South American mainland. The Andean chain stretches down almost the entire western side of South America from northern Colombia to southern Chile. In both ranges there are a large number of active volcanoes. East of the Andes, the major river systems of the Orinoco, the Amazon and the Paraguay-Paraná-Plata, flow into the Atlantic Ocean, covering roughly two-thirds of the entire continent. The Amazon basin, a huge alluvial plain, is bordered by the Andes to the west, by the Brazilian Mato Grosso highlands to the south and by the Guiana highlands to the north. South of the Amazon, between the Andes and the Brazilian highlands, there are interior plains lying below 1,000 feet which extend southwards towards Argentina.

The climate of this vast region varies with altitude and latitude. The high peaks of the Andes, many of them close to the equator, are permanently under snow. The Guianas, the Amazon basin and the Atlantic coast of Brazil all receive high rainfall. Eastern Patagonia and the Mato Grosso are much drier, as is the semi-arid north-east of Brazil which is subject to serious droughts. In Peru and Chile, the narrow coastal strip which lies in the shadow of the Andes has virtually no rain at all. Northwards into Colombia, and in southern Chile, the west coast is very humid with rainfall reaching a peak in the Chocó area of Colombia and Panama. The temperature is relatively constant in the forested areas, but is subject to extreme fluctuation in the mountains.

This highly varied physical environment is reflected in the vegetation. The most humid areas, notably the Amazon basin, are covered in immense expanses of tropical rain forest. Further south, in Chile, dense temperate forests occur and where there is a marked dry season, as in the Paraguayan Chaco, tropical deciduous forests are found. In the driest parts, these forests take the form of *caatinga*, a type of vegetation resistant to drought. There are also true deserts, notably on the coast of Peru and northern Chile. In the Andean region, the vegetation changes with altitude from humid tropical forest at the base, through sub-tropical and temperate zones, to the bleak *puna* of the high Andes and the humid *paramo* of Colombia.

The first Americans were Mongoloid peoples who are presumed to have crossed from Siberia to Alaska in the area of the Bering Strait and from there spread down into South America across the Central American land-bridge. The earliest firm date for man in South America is around 12,000 BC., but other evidence could be taken to suggest a much earlier arrival. Although South American Indians share basic Mongloid features, they display great variation in physical type, the result of successive waves either of one or of many different stocks. The first inhabitants were hunter-gatherers, but in the Andes and in northern Central America, these people discovered agriculture, developed high civilizations and established large cities.

At the time the first Europeans arrived, the Indians of South America spoke a vast number of mutually unintelligible languages. Although many of these survive today, only Quechua and Aymara, used throughout highland Peru and Bolivia, and Guaraní, one of the national languages of Paraguay, are of significance in contemporary South America. To the north, the Mayan languages are widely spoken by the peasant Indian populations of highland Guatemala. Elsewhere, the remaining languages are either used only by small groups of Indians or have been partially or totally replaced by Spanish, Portuguese and to a lesser extent by French, Dutch and English, the languages of the different nations that colonized the region. Apart from their great diversity, the Indian languages are notable for their patchwork distribution, evidence of extensive migrations in prehistoric times.

With the exception of the Mayan civilization, focused on great ceremonial centres in the lowland regions of Yucatán,, Belize, Honduras and Guatemala, the development of Indian society reached its peak in the mountainous regions of South America. By a series of conquests over neighbouring peoples, who were then absorbed into a single state, the Inca empire expanded outwards from its capital, Cuzco, in the Peruvian Andes. Unified by a complex administrative system and a network of roads, it was based upon elaborate systems of irrigation and terracing that integrated the productivity of different ecological zones. At the time of the Spanish conquest the empire extended from northern Ecuador down to Chile and across Bolivia to the Argentine frontier. Further north, in Colombia, there were the smaller chiefdoms of the Tairona and Chibcha, but in the low-lying areas of forest and savanna, the Indians remained fragmented into numerous small tribal groups, with scattered bands of hunter-gatherers principally in the extreme south of the continent.

Despite the contrast between the state systems in the highlands and tribal organization in the forests, the Indians shared a number of basic cultural features, especially with regard to religion and mythology. All attached religious importance

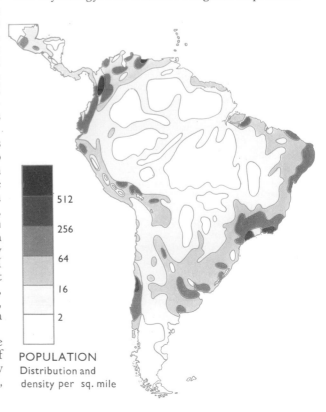

512

256

64

16

2

POPULATION
Distribution and
density per sq. mile

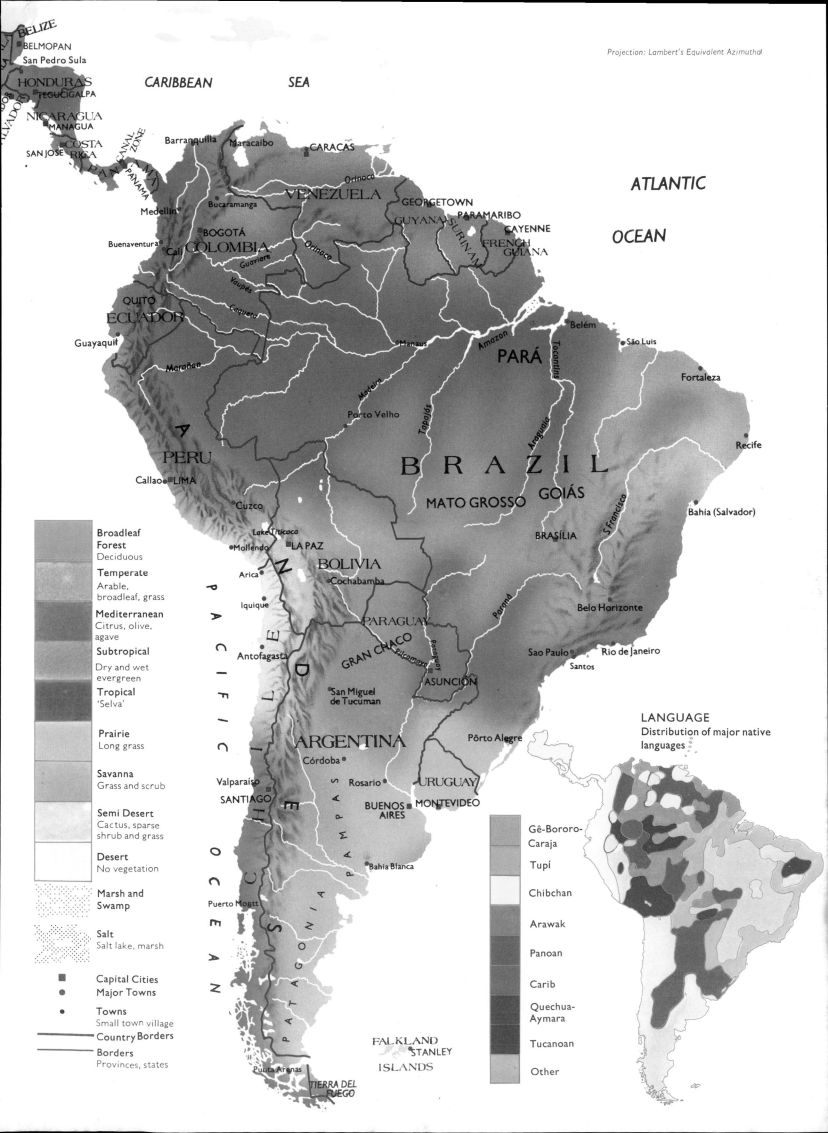

Projection: Lambert's Equivalent Azimuthal

CARIBBEAN   SEA

ATLANTIC

OCEAN

BELIZE
BELMOPAN
San Pedro Sula
HONDURAS
TEGUCIGALPA
NICARAGUA
MANAGUA
COSTA RICA
SAN JOSE
PANAMA
CANAL ZONE

Barranquilla   Maracaibo   CARACAS
Medellin   VENEZUELA   GEORGETOWN   PARAMARIBO
Bucaramanga   Orinoco   GUYANA   SURINAM   CAYENNE
Buenaventura   BOGOTÁ   FRENCH GUIANA
Cali   COLOMBIA   Orinoco
Guaviare
Vaupés
QUITO   Caquetá
ECUADOR
Guayaquil   Belém   São Luis
Marañon   Manaus   Amazon   PARÁ   Fortaleza
Madeira   Tocantins
Porto Velho   Tapajós   Recife
PERU   B R A Z I L
Callao   LIMA   MATO GROSSO   GOIÁS   Bahia (Salvador)
Cuzco   BRASÍLIA   S Francisco
Lake Titicaca
Mollendo   LA PAZ   Belo Horizonte
Arica   BOLIVIA   Paraná
Cochabamba
Iquique   Paraguay
PARAGUAY   Sao Paulo   Rio de Janeiro
Antofagasta   GRAN CHACO   Pilcomayo   Santos
San Miguel   ASUNCIÓN
de Tucuman   Pôrto Alegre
ARGENTINA   URUGUAY
Córdoba
Valparaíso   Rosario   MONTEVIDEO
SANTIAGO   BUENOS AIRES
Bahia Blanca
PAMPAS
Puerto Montt   PATAGONIA

PACIFIC   OCEAN
A N D E S
C H I L E

FALKLAND
STANLEY
ISLANDS
Punta Arenas
TIERRA DEL FUEGO

Broadleaf Forest
Deciduous

Temperate
Arable, broadleaf, grass

Mediterranean
Citrus, olive, agave

Subtropical
Dry and wet evergreen

Tropical
'Selva'

Prairie
Long grass

Savanna
Grass and scrub

Semi Desert
Cactus, sparse shrub and grass

Desert
No vegetation

Marsh and Swamp

Salt
Salt lake, marsh

■ **Capital Cities**
● **Major Towns**
• **Towns**
Small town village

— **Country Borders**
— **Borders**
Provinces, states

LANGUAGE
Distribution of major native languages

Gê-Bororo-Caraja
Tupí
Chibchan
Arawak
Panoan
Carib
Quechua-Aymara
Tucanoan
Other

to the sun and moon and to predatory animals such as the eagle, jaguar and anaconda. Today, these aboriginal religions survive only in marginal areas, for the vast majority of South Americans are Catholic, a legacy of the Spanish and Portuguese conquests with their heavy emphasis on religious conversion. Amongst the survivors of the indigenous civilizations, this Catholicism has been grafted on to the aboriginal religion to produce a syncretic mixture. In addition, the ecstatic religious cults of Umbanda and Candomblé in Brazil display strong elements of African religions, brought over by Negro slaves.

The conquest of the developed civilizations of Central and South America was rapid and total. Between 1492, when Columbus reached America, and 1550, the Spaniards conquered virtually the whole of Central America and the western portion of South America. The unexplored territories of South America were divided between Spain and Portugal according to the treaty of Tordesillas in 1494, the Spaniards taking the lands to the west of an imaginary line, the Portuguese the lands to the east.

Starting from Central America and urged on by rumours of Inca gold, the Spanish *conquistadores* pushed southwards into Peru. After the capture and murder of the Inca ruler Atahualpa, resistance crumbled and Cuzco fell in 1533. Other conquests followed rapidly and the cities of Quito in Ecuador, Lima in Peru, Buenos Aires in Argentina, Asunción in Paraguay, Bogotá in Colombia, Santiago in Chile and Sucre, Potosí and La Paz in Bolivia were founded in quick succession. These cities, each one isolated from the rest by mountains, forests and inhospitable plains, were an extension of the urban settlement pattern of Spain, a pattern that remains characteristic of contemporary South America. As regional economic and political centres, each with its own local character derived from differing Indian cultures, they eventually gave rise to different nation states.

Though the Spanish authorities made efforts to protect the Indians, who were regarded as subjects of the Crown, essential for the exploitation of their rich lands and for a supply of women, they suffered terribly. Quickly reduced in numbers by massacres and new diseases, they experienced serious famines and were forced to work as slaves in the mines that fed the Spanish economy. The Spanish operated a system of indirect rule, grafting their administration on to the existing states and replacing the old rulers with captains subject to the king. Outside the Spanish zone, the conquest of the lowland tribal peoples was piecemeal, brutal and slow. When the Spanish conquest was complete, the Portuguese, now competing with the French and Dutch, had only a few settlements on the Brazilian coast; and this coastal orientation of Brazilian society persists today.

The economy of Spanish America was based largely on the mining of precious metals, with Spain jealously guarding its trading monopoly. Immigration was limited to Spanish citizens, who interbred with the Indians to produce a mestizo population. Only *peninsulares*, persons born in Spain, were given positions of authroity; Indians, mestizos and *criollos* (people of Spanish blood born in the Americas) were usually excluded from political affairs. The Brazilian economy was dominated by sugar production on large estates using slaves imported from Africa, who interbred with both the Indians and their colonial masters to produce the modern Brazilian population. The tradition of large estates, characteristic of colonial times, persists throughout Central and South America. Meanwhile, the interior of Brazil was gradually opened up by *bandeirantes*, armed bands of slave-raiders who progressively pushed back the frontiers with the Spanish possessions.

In the early 19th century, with Napoleon's invasion of the Iberian peninsula, the links of Spain and Portugal with their American colonies were radically altered. This, combined with friction

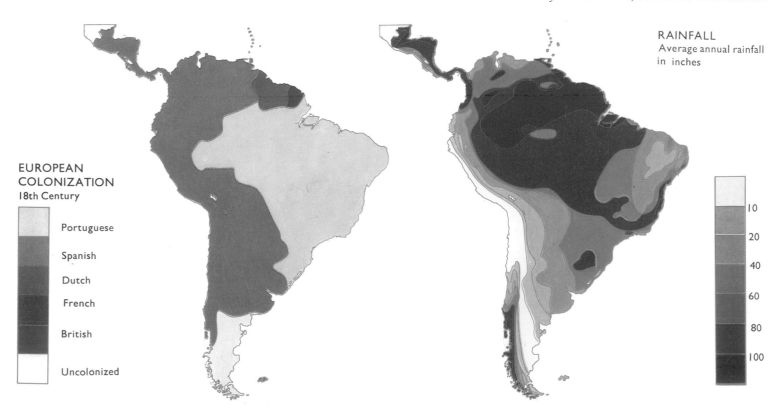

EUROPEAN
COLONIZATION
18th Century

Portuguese

Spanish

Dutch

French

British

Uncolonized

RAINFALL
Average annual rainfall
in inches

10
20
40
60
80
100

between the ruling élite and those excluded from government, produced a series of revolutionary movements which culminated in independence for all of Latin America (including Mexico)—first for the Spanish possessions and later for Brazil. Each population cluster produced its own revolutionary leaders who expressed different local aspirations. In spite of efforts to unify the liberated territories, geographical isolation and differing regional interests led to the fragmentation of the Spanish possessions into today's independent republics.

After liberation there followed a period of economic disorder and social and political chaos. Political instability led to the rise of *caudillos*, military strongmen, and to conflicts of interest between town and country. The legacy of the *caudillos* is enshrined in the constitutions of many Latin American states, which give extraordinary political powers to their presidents, making them legalized dictators. While the old *caudillos* depended upon the support of wealthy landowners, however, the modern rulers of countries such as Brazil, Argentina and Bolivia also rely on support from industrial workers in the cities.

With independence, Latin America was opened up to foreign trade, investment and immigration. In the latter half of the 19th century, with the aid of European and North American capital, the region underwent an economic transformation, exploiting the vast natural resources to export raw materials and food to the metropolitan centres of Europe and America. At the same time, immigrants from Spain, Italy, Germany and Portugal entered South America to become an important element of the population in countries such as Argentina, Uruguay, Chile and Brazil.

Many of the countries became dependent on the export of one or two commodities such as coffee, cotton, oil, bananas, sugar, tin, copper and nitrates, a situation that is still characteristic of most Latin American republics, making them vulnerable to price fluctuations on the international market. At the same time, the power and wealth of a small, landowning élite increased enormously so that today, despite programmes of land reform, cultivated land tends to be concentrated in the hands of a tiny minority. These factors, together with the fact that the strategic products on which each country must rely tend to be produced in fairly restricted areas, by relatively few enterprises employing a small proportion of the total labour force, result in lopsided economies that benefit only a small urban élite.

Today, after a long period of relative isolation, many Latin American countries—notably Brazil—are assuming an increasingly important role in the world. Many of the old problems remain, however, and are made worse by rapid industrialization and a massive increase in population. Advances in living standards are still concentrated in urban districts and the benefits of development go almost exclusively to the city-dwelling élite. The gap between rich and poor is increasing, with a huge mass of rural peasantry remaining illiterate, undernourished and isolated from the mainstream of national life. Political instability goes hand in hand with the oppressive military dictatorships that dominate the southern half of the continent.

Although a massive road building programme has diminished the problems of geographic isolation, it has also facilitated the migration of the peasantry from the countryside to the cities, causing huge urban slums and rural stagnation. Modern cities such as Rio de Janeiro, Lima and Bogotá are surrounded by sprawling shanty towns, whose inhabitants suffer chronic unemployment, lack of sanitation and totally inadequate medical facilities. The Indians of the highlands form the lowest strata of society, looked down upon by rural mestizos and urban whites. With the opening of the Amazon basin for mining and the creation of huge cattle ranches, the remaining tribal Indians are being decimated by disease and their lands expropriated by land-hungry settlers.

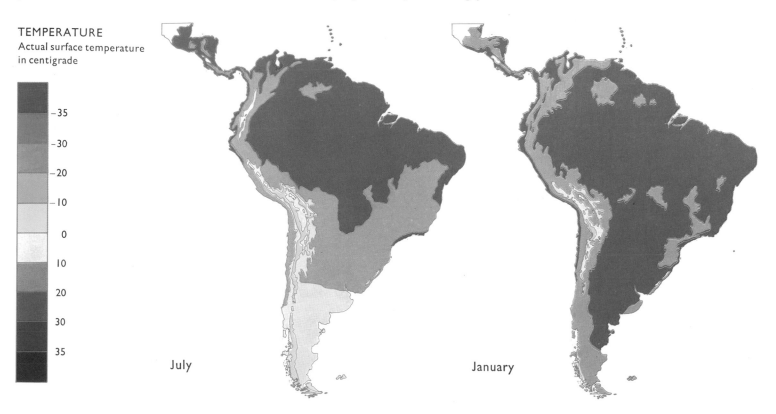

TEMPERATURE
Actual surface temperature in centigrade

-35
-30
-20
-10
0
10
20
30
35

July

January

Guatemala

pop: 6,099,000 (1977)
Guatemala is a predominantly agricultural country whose coastal plains on both the Atlantic and Pacific are filled with plantations of bananas, cotton and sugar. The population is heavily concentrated in the central highlands, where land reform attempts have not succeeded in altering the inequitable pattern of ownership.

Coffee is grown on the lower slopes; higher up, the Quichi, Man, Cakchiquel and Ketchi Indians, descendants of the Maya, live at subsistence level. The large mestizo population is concentrated in the provincial towns, supplying labour for shops, offices, industry and the newly excavated nickel mines.

Maya

pop: 2,000,000
The present day Maya are the descendants of one of the most impressive and mysterious Central American civilizations, which from 300–900 AD produced the foremost mathematicians and astronomers of the contemporary world. They created a magnificent architecture, apparently without knowledge of the wheel, and must somehow have produced sufficient surplus food for the builders without the invention of the plough.

Indians speaking the Mayan languages today inhabit an area of more than 100,000 square miles, from the northern coast of the Yucatán peninsula to the highlands of Guatemala and Honduras, closely corresponding to the territory of the old Mayan civilization. There are 15 distinct dialects spoken today, the most important of which is the classical Mayan of Yucatán. The others are Lacandón, Ketchi, Pokomay, Tzotzil, Tojolabel, Tzutuhil, Aguacatec, Chorti, Quichi, Chuli, Urpantec, Cakchiquel, Ixcl and Man, and each group maintains its language with considerable determination.

Most of the present Maya are farmers, cultivating the land in much the same way as their forefathers. The staple crops are maize and beans, tended by women on fields cleared by the men. Some livestock is generally kept, usually chickens and pigs. The highland villages consist of oval huts thatched with grass, surrounded by patches of cleared fields. Kinship ties remain important in the organization of work, which is often co-operative. Some Maya have craft skills: pottery and fabrics find a ready market with tourists and can provide a valuable cash supplement to their agricultural produce.

Mayan groups have had great difficulty in retaining the ownership of their land, and have been forced further and further into the less fertile uplands in order to safeguard their independence. In Guatemala much of their land has been taken over for coffee plantations, and when this happens the Maya are reduced to becoming unskilled labourers. One practice has been to allow the Maya to clear a plot of land for their own subsistence in return for labour on the plantations.

Belize

pop: 145,000
A heavily forested country divided between virtually uninhabited highland plateau in the north and rolling lowland plains in the south, Belize is Britain's last remaining colonial possession in South America. Most of the population is mestizo or mulatto, with some Black Caribs along the southern coast; some 40 per cent live in Belize City, the former capital. The Maya are the main Indian group.

Shifting cultivation of maize, beans and upland rice is practised in forest clearings (*milpa*) by about half the population. Sugar, tobacco and citrus fruits are the main cash crops, while chicle gum and mahogany are the major exports. Belize depends upon Britain to avoid incorporation into neighbouring Guatemala.

Honduras

pop: 2,872,000
Honduras is a predominantly mestizo country. About 80 per cent of its people are of mixed Indian and European descent, and only the Black Caribs form a distinct group. Much of Honduras is undeveloped land; banana plantations are the only large-scale agricultural concerns.

The Black Caribs are settled in a band around the Caribbean coast; remnants of the Mosquito and Sumo Indians are found in the east; and some Chorti, descendants of the Maya, also survive. There are a number of pure-blood Amerindians but their lifestyle is so similar to that of the mestizos that they are often hard to distinguish.

Black Caribs

pop: not available
The Black Caribs, or Garif as they are sometimes known, are descendants of the Caribs (the original inhabitants of the Caribbean) and some of the first African slaves to arrive on the island of St Vincent in the 16th and 17th centuries. The slaves had either escaped from nearby islands or were captured by the then-dominant Caribs. Their descendants adopted the Carib language and way of life, becoming known as the Black Caribs to distinguish them from the pure, or Yellow, Caribs.

From their original home on St Vincent, the Black Caribs were exiled to the coast of Central America for participating in independence struggles. Only a few remained on St Vincent, their numbers further reduced by a series of natural disasters. Today Black Caribs are to be found along the east coast of Belize, Honduras and Nicaragua, where their strong cultural identity makes them a distinctive group.

Mayan Civilization
7th century AD

The culture of the Black Caribs represents a mixture of many elements: Carib, African, French, English and Spanish. Despite their conversion to Christianity, shamanism plays an important part in their beliefs and its prevalence emphasizes the place of Carib traditions in their culture. The African influence is expressed in the form of possession rites, which are used to communicate with the spirits of ancestors.

Two other important elements of Carib culture are apparent in the daily life of the Black Caribs: the dependence upon the sea for much of their livelihood, and the communal organization of labour. Work is divided between the sexes, with the men fishing and clearing the forest for gardens while the women plant and harvest the crops. The Black Caribs have also retained the Carib kinship structure.

El Salvador
pop: 4,195,000

More prosperous than some of its neighbours, El Salvador shares with the other Central American countries a dependence upon plantation agriculture. Ownership of the acres of coffee and banana plantations, however, is confined to a small élite. The population density is high; 80 per cent are mestizo and there are some Europeans and Amerindians. The latter are sometimes hard to distinguish from their mestizo neighbours, except some Lenca who hunt and fish in the uplands.

Nicaragua
pop: 2,263,000

Nicaragua is the largest of the Central American republics, and is divided by the central highlands into Pacific and Caribbean regions. The arrival of the Spanish in the 1500s caused a violent disruption of the Indian population, who now constitute only 4 per cent of Nicaraguans.

The vast majority are mestizo, with some Zambos (Indian-Negroes) and a tiny white élite. More than half the population live in towns, where poverty, disease and overcrowding are prevalent. Surviving Indians include the Monimbo and the Subtavia in the Pacific zone, and the Mosquito in the Caribbean region.

Religious procession, Guatemala

now dependent on the external economy.

With an increase in animal herding many Guaymi have become wage labourers on the ranches, while for those remaining farmers there are difficulties over land. The ever increasing land shortage means that even with modern crops the Guaymi cannot survive without relying on hunting trips into the wilder regions. There is still a considerable amount of trading among the Guaymi and their neighbours, but there has been a decline in the manufacture of pottery and cloth, once valuable items.

Panama

pop: 1,745,000

Panama occupies a strategic position as the narrowest section of the isthmus linking North and South America. It is bisected by the canal zone, a strip of American land controlling the Panama canal. The population is relatively homogeneous, but there is a Jamaican community, and some indigenous Indians, including the Cuna, Noanama and Guaymi.

The economy is primarily agricultural, with bananas the only significant export. If Panama regains control of the enormously important canal zone in 1999, as is now proposed, its chances of prosperity would be increased.

Cuna

pop: 30,000

The Cuna Indians live on the shores of the Caribbean Sea, in two coastal areas of Colombia and Panama. A group of 20,000 live on the San Blas Islands, commuting to their mainland gardens by boat, while smaller enclaves are found around the Gulf of Urabá, in Colombia, where there is a Cuna reserve. Like the Noanama, with whom they share many cultural characteristics, the Cuna spend most of their time in, on or by the water. They use canoes, sailing boats and increasingly motor boats to fish and to travel, frequently making the three or four day trip between the Colombian and Panamanian settlements.

The Cuna live in extended family units, with the men moving to their bride's house-

hold after marriage. Each household cultivates a garden for bananas, maize and fruits, while protein is supplied by fish, caught in great numbers by a variety of methods in both sea and freshwater. Most settlements have a chief and two lesser chiefs, whose main job is to co-ordinate households and liaise with outsiders. Consequently they are chosen for their command of Spanish and their ability to win respect. They hold regular settlement meetings at which plans are made and grievances and problems aired and settled. Chiefs are respected, as are the shamans, or *nele*, who have a special relationship with the spirit world. The *nele* is a curer but, like all those who wield supernatural power, he may use it for evil purposes so he is simul-

Costa Rica

pop: 2,041,000

The most prosperous of the Central American countries, Costa Rica owes its success to the extensive coffee plantations created after independence from Spain in 1821. Few Costa Ricans share in this wealth, however, as the majority of the population do not own land. About 90 per cent of the people are mestizo, the remainder being of African descent or Amerindian.

The largest surviving Indian group are the Guaymi, Chibcha-speakers who are found in the tropical forest to the north of the country and in the Pacific uplands to the south.

Guaymi

pop: not available

In the Caribbean lowlands of Panama and Costa Rica live the remnants of a large group of Chibcha-speaking Indians. They include the Bribri, the Cabecar, the Changuena, the Guetar, the Rama and the Guaymi, who are the largest and best known, having expanded into the depopulated lands around them after the Spanish conquest.

Traditionally the Guaymi were farmers organized into chiefdoms, living in an almost constant state of war for territory, slaves and sacrificial victims. Today the large fortified dwellings have been replaced with smaller houses and the nuclear family is the basic economic unit; the slaves have vanished and the Indians are

PANAMA CANAL

tancously respected and re-garded with suspicion.

The Cuna are excellent craftsmen and have a strong artistic sense. They are most famous for their highly decorative *molas* or appliqué blouses and these are often bought by tourists. The men are also skilled carvers. They make stools from single blocks of wood, as well as spindle shafts and weaving tools, carved cooking utensils and the small *nuskana* figurines used in curing ceremonies.

The Cuna people have managed to keep their distinctive culture intact through a very gradual absorption of outside elements. But the isolation upon which their survival has depended is now threatened. For a long time the forests and swamps of the isthmus of

Panama have been a barrier to overland travel between Central and South America. However, it is now likely that the final section of the Pan-American Highway will be driven through the area where the Cuna live, and there is little doubt that their distinctive way of life will be eroded.

Guajiro
pop: 50,000

There are few Amerindian groups as large and prosperous as the Arawak-speaking Guajiro, who now live in the desert interior of the Guajiro peninsula of Colombia and Venezuela. They owe their success to the adaptability with which they met the threat of the invading Spanish 400 years ago. At that time the Guajiro were following a hunter-gatherer way of life in the more fertile and temperate south, although coastal groups collected seafood. All retreated before the Spanish into the desert, having exchanged their coastal pearling skills for animals, the care of which they learned from African slaves. They developed a successful pastoralist economy and now lead a seminomadic life, moving in search of grazing and water, sometimes digging salt and gypsum for cash, and occasionally smuggling across the border.

The Guajiro are divided into 30 *casta*, matrilineal kinship groupings which are each associated with defined territories. A man's property is inherited by his sister's son, as is political leadership. A large bridewealth of cattle is now paid on marriage and animals are also used as compensation for injury. Guajiro women grow patches of fast-growing corn near the semi-permanent rainy season camps; they spin and weave, using wild cotton rather than wool.

Kogi
pop: 2,000

The Arhuacan Kogi are a remnant of the Tairona, a people of highly developed culture who were among the first South American Indians to come into contact with the Spanish. In the ensuing hostilities the Tairona were forced to retreat into inaccessible mountain val-leys where they cut themselves off from European contact. The present-day survivors can be divided into three main groups: the Kogi, the Ika and the Saha, who are neighbours and similar in culture.

The Kogi live on the eastern slopes of the Sierra Nevada. They cultivate individually owned fields at different altitudes, migrating between them and returning to their villages periodically. Potatoes, beans, manioc, plantains and coca are the staples, and sugar cane is grown as a cash crop. In the villages men and women have separate houses and are not permitted to enter each other's dwellings.

Women may not use coca, the symbol of male adulthood, but do participate in some of the rituals which are central to the strongly developed religious life of the Kogi. Led by the *mama*, or priest, rituals are conducted at the birth, initiation and death of each individual. The universe is pictured in the form of an egg with nine layers, whose centre is the Sierra Nevada. The conical roof of the men's ceremonial house symbolizes both universe and mountains, all of which are in the womb of the mother—the supreme goddess.

The coherence of their beliefs and their geographical isolation have enabled the Kogi consciously to reject all but the most utilitarian aspects of European culture.

Motilones
pop: 2,800

The name Motilone refers to two distinct tribes whose home is the Sierra de Perija along the frontiers of Venezuela and Colombia. The largest tribe is the Yuko, Carib-speakers living in the northern section; only about 800 of the Chibcha-speaking Bari still survive. Although the Yuko and the Bari differ in language, clothing, houses and pottery, they share the same way of life as forest hunters and gatherers and shifting cultivators. Both groups suffered badly from contact with outsiders when oil was first discovered, and their lands remain threatened by cattle ranchers and other settlers. Venezuela has recently established a Yuko reserve.

photograph:
Yuko Motilone mother
and child, Venezuela

65

Colombia, Venezuela, Ecuador, Peru
Llaneros, Guambiano, Otavalo, Jivaro

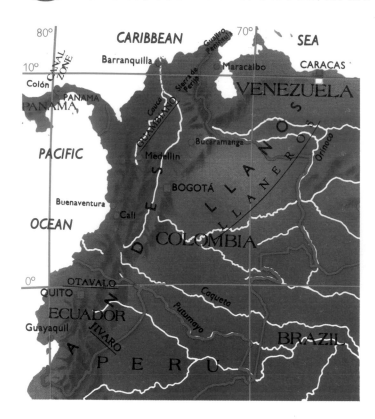

Colombia
pop: 24,541,000

Despite the fact that Colombia is broken by not one range of Andean mountains but three, the population density is one of the highest in South America, 46 per square mile. This population is largely of mixed origin: about 45 per cent are mestizo and a further 20 per cent are descended from African slaves and either white settlers or Amerindians.

However, many distinctive groups remain and Colombia is by no means culturally homogeneous. The Cuna pursue their marine lifestyle around the Gulf of Urabá; the Guajiro subsist in the desert of the Guajiro peninsula; the Kogi live to the south of them on the slopes of the Sierra Nevada; the Motilones live in the Sierra Perija on the border with Venezuela, with the Guambiano and Paez to the south; and the Coastal and Caribbean Negroes constitute a recognizable sub-group around the coast.

The pressure on land caused by increasing population and expanding plantations for crops such as coffee, the leading export, has resulted in migration to the cities and the eastern plains. The economically successful eastward expansion of agriculture poses a serious problem for the lowland Indians still living there. Indian groups include the Guahibo, Tikuna, Vaupés Indians, Baniwa, Witoto and Cuiva.

Llaneros
pop: not available

The Llanos is a vast plain lying to the south of the central highlands of Venezuela and spreading across the border into Colombia. It consists of poor, infertile soils and miles of thin pasture, with an uncomfortable climate and an unhealthy abundance of insects. Since the arrival of Spanish settlers the plains have been used as the centre of the cattle farming industry, which is important to the economy of both countries. During the 1920s and 1930s, cattle ranching expanded, and the number of cowboys or Llaneros grew with it.

The cowboys lead a hard and uncomfortable life, and are subject to strict discipline within the hierarchical structure of the ranches. They have a reputation for toughness; cattle rustling and banditry used to be common and Llaneros formed the core of the army which won independence for Venezuela. During the expansion of the ranches the Llaneros came into frequent contact with Indians, particularly the Guahibo. Atrocities were reported, and many other encounters ended in death and injury to the Indians.

Guambiano
pop: 15,000

Of the three great Indian nations of 16th century Colombia, the Pubenses, Paez and Guambiano, only the remnants of the Paez and Guambiano still survive, living on 57 reservations in the hills above the Cauca valley. The degree of acculturation varies, but unlike the Paez the Guambiano retain their own Chibcha language.

There have been harsh battles over the Guambiano's right to their land. The reservations are controlled by a governing council which allocates specific areas to each family, but the land itself is the communal property of the whole group. The Guambiano practise subsistence agriculture, growing maize, potatoes, wheat and beans. They raise a few animals for cash.

Reservation income is low; some Indians supplement it by wage labour or by selling craft goods to tourists. During 400 years of contact the Guambiano have resisted assimilation into Colombian society. Their religion and traditional medicine are not revealed to white visitors for fear that they will lose their power, and the Guambiano are now joining forces with the various Paez groups of the Cauca.

Ecuador
pop: 7,133,000

One of the smaller South American countries, Ecuador is dominated by the volcanic peaks of the Andes. Formerly, the highlands of the Sierra constituted the most important region, with a string of towns along the central valley. Half the population, among them the Otavalo Indians, still live there but the failure of land reforms has been accompanied by a drift in emphasis to the coastal lowlands, where the Coastal Negroes and mestizos predominate.

Recently oil has been found on the eastern side of the Andes, and its exploitation theatens the Jivaro and other jungle Indians who live there.

Otavalo

pop: 34,000

The Otavalo live in an Andean valley about 70 miles north of Quito, but they can be seen all over the continent and sometimes as far afield as Mexico and California. The reason for their travels is the sale of their woven goods, which has made them the most prosperous Indians in Ecuador. The demand for their weaving is so great that some groups now use mechanical looms and synthetic dyes.

The Otavalo have not always lived in their present home: in the 15th century the land was occupied by the Cara, of whom only archaeological traces remain. The Cara were defeated by Inca invaders who replaced them with a subject people from Lake Titicaca. These people, the Otavalo, adopted the language and much of the culture of the Incas and now consider themselves to be of Inca descent. Around the valley are dotted villages and smallholdings where the Otavalo keep pigs, chickens, ducks, goats and sheep, and grow staple vegetables. The wool from the sheep is spun and woven and subsequently taken to many different markets.

Like many of the Quechua Indians in Ecuador the Otavalo celebrate fiestas. They are nominally Catholic but their fiestas are a mixture of Christian and Inca elements, with drinking, feasting, dancing and processions. In the fiesta of San Juan a mock battle takes place, and in others there are dramatic horseback displays.

The blending of Catholic and Inca ritual in these festivals is an example of the way in which the Otavalo have adopted aspects of the dominant culture without losing their own cultural identity. Many Ecuadorian Indians have abandoned their traditional way of life and left the villages in search of work in the cities of Quito and Guayaquil, but the Otavalo by becoming economically self-sufficient have been able to exercise more choice.

Jivaro

pop: 20,000

The Jivaro, or Shuara, inhabit the tropical lowlands to the east of the Andes, on the edge of the forests of the Amazon basin. They are the largest of a group of Jivaroan-speakers in the area: the Achuara, Huambisa, and Aguaruna are similar in culture and language. They are all slash-and-burn cultivators, hunting and fishing for protein. Their houses, for 1 - 3 families, are separated by at least half a mile.

Most Jivaro are permanently engaged in feuding, which is the means by which disputes are settled within the tribe. Although this involves killing, head trophies are not taken among fellow tribesmen: raiding for heads is carried out only against neighbouring tribes.

The Jivaro's purpose in head hunting and shrinking the captured head is related to their concept of existence, the supernatural and the soul. Killing confers invulnerability and even immortality upon a man by providing him with a special type of soul, which cannot be acquired by any other means.

Another type of soul can escape from the body of a murdered enemy in order to seek revenge on the killer; to prevent this from happening the head is removed and shrunk to trap the revenge soul and render it harmless. The head is taken back to the head-taker's house, where subsequently it plays an important role in ritual feasting. At the end of the ritual the soul is expelled from the head and it is then of no further significance.

Contact with settlers has meant that headhunting is declining, although the Jivaro continue to feud, and retain their complex supernatural belief system.

Planting potatoes near Cayambe, Ecuador

67

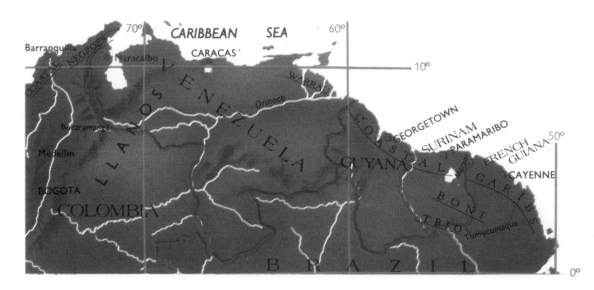

Venezuela

pop: 12,366,000

The pattern of Venezuela's population distribution is common in South America—three-quarters of the people live in overcrowded conditions in towns while most of the land is sparsely inhabited. Many of the town dwellers are unemployed: Venezuela is industrializing on the basis of its oil deposits, yet few Venezuelans possess the skills in current demand. However, town life is preferred to that of the interior, where settlers share the subsistence economy of the Indians.

The majority of the population is mestizo, with African, mulatto and European minorities. The Indians of Venezuela have fared better than in other parts of South America. Their land is subject to more stringent legal safeguards and most have retained rights to their territory. The Panare, Piaroa and Yanomamo are fairly isolated from contact, while the Motilones and Guajiro maintain their cultural identity despite years of interaction. Other Indian groups include the Guahibo, Baniwa and Warrau.

Coastal Negroes

pop: not available.

Along the coastal strip stretching from Ecuador to Venezuela there are substantial numbers of black settlers, descended from West Africans brought as slaves to work on the plantations during the 16th and 17th centuries. They are known as Coastal Negroes, and although their way of life varies across this large geographical area they share many cultural characteristics and constitute a distinctive social grouping.

They differ from the Black Caribs in their resistance to Indian influence: they remain apart from Indian communities and have often supplanted them. In Colombia and Ecuador, Indians such as the Noanama, Embera and Cavapa are now being displaced, and in the Pacific lowlands, especially in Colombia, the Coastal Negroes dominate the population.

Culturally, Coastal Negroes combine African and Spanish features: their religion is nominally Catholic, but there are strong elements of African spirit belief contained within it. Their economy is varied: some live entirely by subsistence farming, while others have smaller gardens tended by women when the men travel in search of wage labour.

Warrau

pop: 7–10,000

The Warrau of the Orinoco delta present an unusual combination of features which makes it difficult to classify them among the types of societies found in South America. They live on the marshy land of the delta in multi-family houses; in the more swampy regions these houses are elevated on platforms made of layers of tree trunks covered with clay. Warrau society is matrilineal and matrilocal.

Although there is some agriculture with the growing of plantains and manioc, the Warrau hunt, gather and fish for much of their food. They depend particularly upon the Mauritia palm, making use of nearly every part of the plant. Unusually for a hunter-gatherer group with marginal agriculture, the religious life of the Warrau centres on a supreme being and involves temples, idols and priests. Shamans, who are curers and often headmen, are separate from the priests of the temples.

Guyana

pop: 818,000

The first of the Guianas to achieve independence, Guyana is left with the legacy of colonial rule. Sugar is still the leading export, with bauxite and rice becoming increasingly important. African slaves were brought to Guyana to work on the extensive sugar plantations, and after the abolition of slavery many remained in the country. Their place on the plantations, however, was taken by a new workforce brought from India and the East, and more than half the population is now Asian. Descendants of the Africans make up most of the other half, with a few Akawayo, Trio and other Amerindians.

Surinam

pop: 431,000 (1977)

Very few of Surinam's native population survive today. First African and then Asian labourers were imported by the Dutch colonists and now make up about 95 per cent of the country's inhabitants. The sugar plantations are still economically vital, although bauxite is increasingly important.

Ethnic identity among the Surinam groups remains strong, with little integration between African and Asian communities. There are some Coastal Carib and Trio Indians and a distinctive group of Bush Negroes, the Boni, who are descended from escaped slaves and who live in isolated villages in the jungle.

French Guiana

pop: 55,000

The smallest of the Guianas, French Guiana still has not achieved independence. In common with Surinam and

Guyana, it has experienced a form of colonization resulting in an influx of foreign labour, virtually replacing the indigenous peoples. Most of the land was given over to plantations, worked by imported African slaves. About 45 per cent of the present population is descended from these slaves, and the remainder are of mixed descent, mestizo and mulatto. There are a few Europeans, and some surviving Indians including the Wayana and Oyampi.

Coastal Caribs
pop: 2,000
Near the coasts of Surinam, Guyana, French Guiana and Brazil live groups of Caribs whose way of life revolves around their proximity to water. They are mainly to be found on the lower reaches of the Barama and Maroni rivers, where they interact with both Europeans and the Bush Negroes who live deeper in the forest.

The coastal strip itself is mainly uninhabited mangrove dunes; further inland there is swamp with some shrubs and vegetation, but it is only where the land dries to savanna and forest that the Indians build their villages, accessible only from the river. Each cluster of houses lies along the river bank, and transport is by canoe. Gardens are cleared behind the village for manioc cultivation, but fish forms an important part of the diet. A variety of fishing methods are used, ranging from bow and arrow to traps and poison, and the surplus is sold to provide cash income.

Despite long contact with settlers and missionaries the Coastal Caribs have been remarkably resistant to change. Their population is beginning to increase and although they are involved in the larger national economy they are still able to subsist independently when they wish.

Trio
pop: 1,500
Along the watershed between the northern tributaries of the Amazon and the rivers flowing to the northern coast is an area inhabited by numerous small tribes. Typical of them are the Trio, Carib-speakers who live across the borders of Surinam and Brazil. Traditionally they lived away from the main waterways, tending manioc gardens and relying upon forest game; their villages were small, averaging about 30 people.

Contact first occurred through trade, and it was by this means that the Trio also contracted European diseases to which they had no resistance. By 1950 their population had declined to such an extent that it looked as if they were following the classic route towards extinction. In the last 15 years, however, the trend has been reversed and the Trio are one of the few Amazon basin tribes whose population is actually increasing. This change is due to the efforts of missionaries who arrived in the area in 1960. The Trio were attracted to the missions by the prospect of trade, and received along with imported goods valuable medical care which sharply cut the mortality rate.

This development was not without its effects on Trio culture. The small forest villages have been abandoned in favour of large new settlements near airstrips and mission stations, and missionary influence has halted many traditional activities. Despite this the Trio are less acculturated than their circumstances would indicate.

Many of the other Guiana Carib groups have fared worse than the Trio; the Makiritare (Yequana) are still quite isolated, as are the Piaroa, but their trading partners the Akawayo have had to abandon their gardens for wage labouring and are heavily dependent on European trade goods and food. The Wai-Wai have suffered severe depopulation in Guyana and Brazil.

Land encroachment is a threat to the Trio as to all other South American Indians. In 1968 a 10,000 square mile reservation, the Tumucumaque Park, was created for them, but a projected road comes very close to their land.

Boni
pop: 1,000
Among the forests of Surinam and French Guiana, along the coast and inland on the tributaries of the Maroni river, live groups of people known as Bush Negroes. They are the descendants of African slaves who revolted and fled from the plantations into the interior during the 19th century. The various Bush Negro tribes are the result of different revolts and include the Djuka, the Paramaka and the Boni, who originated from the last revolt in 1772.

The tropical forest environment into which the Boni escaped was alien to the way of life they had previously known. In order to survive they had to turn to the Indians of the interior for help, and the result of this was twofold: a strong dependency on the Amerindians, and the adoption of many of their subsistence techniques.

Perhaps the most important feature of Boni life, and one which distinguishes them from the Amerindians, is their settlement in more or less permanent villages, some of which are more than 150 years old. The population of a village can vary between 60 and 160, usually forming a single matrilineage, known as a *lo*, all of whose members trace their descent from a common ancestress— an African characteristic.

Although the members of a *lo* must marry an outsider, neither men nor women leave their village on marriage. For each *lo* the village is a sacred site, and its members are held to it by certain ritual and economic ties. The *lo* is the corporate landowning group and it is through membership of the *lo* that a Boni man or woman has a right to land. This right reverts to the *lo* after an individual's death.

Contact with neighbouring Indians, especially the Trio, led to complex trading partnerships in which the Boni did most of the travelling, and they still retain their grip on the river transport system, using dugout canoes now powered by outboard motors. Although the Boni, like the other Bush Negroes, borrowed extensively from the Indians, they have now begun to develop a material culture peculiarly their own. This takes the form of wood carving and decorating and many everyday objects such as combs, spoons and canoe paddles are beautifully produced.

Venezuela, Peru, Brazil
Piaroa, Yanomamo, Baniwa, Vaupés Indians, Witoto, Tikuna

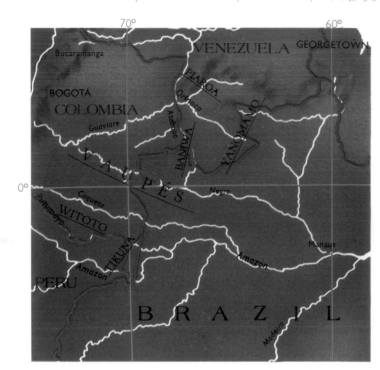

Piaroa
pop: 3–4,000

The Piaroa live along the tributaries of the Orinoco river in Venezuela. They are hunters and cultivators, peaceful people with more in common with Guiana Caribs such as the Trio than with their Makiritare neighbours. However, the rate of outside contact has accelerated over the last 10 years and the erosion of their culture has already begun.

The Piaroa build large communal houses, *itso'de*, housing up to 60 people, several of which form a territory under the protection of one of about 12 powerful shamans. Shamans protect their people, gardens and the surrounding jungle through control of supernatural forces and beings; they supervise the nightly ritual in which the men take hallucinogenic drugs and chant in order to ward off sorcery, and continue their ritual preparations while the other men hunt.

During the dry season, from December to February, the Piaroa lead a nomadic life, leaving their houses in small groups to visit relatives within their own and other territories. Hunting, fishing and collecting become considerably more important during this period of wandering. The Piaroa are skilled blowgun hunters and are famous for the quality of their curare and fish poisons.

Yanomamo
pop: 15,000

The Yanomamo are one of the last large South American Indian tribes living relatively undisturbed on their own lands. They occupy about 30,000 square miles of southern Venezuela and northern Brazil, an area of forested, mountainous country.

The Yanomamo language is distinct from the major linguistic families of South America and is unintelligible to their Carib and Arawak neighbours. Several dialect groups have so far been identified, but all Yanomamo groups share a ceremonial language, which differs from everyday speech and is used by men on public occasions.

Yanomamo differ from other lowland Indians in their means of subsistence. Their staple crop is plantain, which supplies more than 70 per cent of their food, and garden produce is supplemented by hunting, fishing and gathering in the forest. Hallucinogenic drugs are taken by the men, who prepare them either from cultivated plants or the bark of forest trees.

One feature of Yanomamo life which has attracted much attention is their propensity for warfare. This is not uniform throughout the region: the highest incidence occurs in the central villages. Hostilities take the form of raiding, warriors from one village stealthily approaching another for a dawn attack. The objective is to kill and then escape without casualties, preferably kidnapping a woman or child as well. Reasons given for mounting such a raid include revenge and the shortage of women.

Where raiding is intense, certain related features can be seen. The *shabono*, or circular communal house, is entirely enclosed and protected from surprise attack; gardens are larger to provide a surplus for the entertainment and occasional support of allies, and the role of the aggressive male warrior is heavily emphasized. Individuals and groups strive to project an image of invulnerable strength in order to discourage potential attackers, but if these tactics fail a whole village can be forced to flee to escape annihilation. On the outer edge of Yanomamo territory, where there is less fighting, these features are either absent or much reduced.

Baniwa
pop: 2–5,000

The Baniwa group of Indians are found on the borders of Colombia, Brazil and Venezuela, centring around the Atabapo river. There are several sub-groups, including the Baré on the Casiquiare, the Piapoco on the Guaviare and the Curipaco on the Guaina river in Colombia. The Baniwa belong to the Arawak-speaking tribes who are distributed throughout the Amazon basin; the largest groups are the Campa of Peru and the Terena of the southern Mato Grosso. The Piro of Peru are also Arawak, as are the Waura, Mehinaku and Yawalapiti of Brazil.

The Baniwa are slash-and-burn agriculturalists, supplementing their manioc staple with fish and some game. They once lived in communal houses and are skilled at crafts including the manufacture of carved wooden benches, traditionally for village use but now often sold for cash. In the past there were frequent festivals with ritual and dancing; now many of the groups have been assimilated into local settler communities and their cultural features lost.

Vaupés Indians
pop: 14,000

The Vaupés region of Colombia and Brazil is the home of as many as 40 groups of forest Indians. They are divided into a large number of small, named groups, each of which speaks its own language and has certain distinctive cultural features. However, nearly all these languages belong to the same eastern Tukanoan family, and in general their societies show close similarities. Among the most important Tukanoan groups are the Tukano, Cubeo, Desana, Wanano, Pira-Tapuyo, Barasana and Bará. Non-Tukanoan groups include the linguistically isolated Makú.

Among the Vaupés Indians, language is used to signify group membership and common ancestry and is important in the arrangement of marriages. Generally, people who speak the same language are regarded as being related to each other as brother and sister, and cannot marry. As a result a married couple will normally speak different languages. Children speak the language of their father, although able to understand that of their mother.

The main focus of Vaupés life is the river. Houses and villages are usually built along the major watercourses, and most travel is by canoe. Fishing is an important activity, but the bulk of the food comes from agriculture.

The semi-nomadic Makú live in the forest areas between the rivers. These Indians live a life markedly different from that of their more sedentary neighbours. They are expert hunters and much of their diet comes from meat and other forest produce. The Makú have often been regarded as slaves of the river Indians, but in reality the relationship seems to be more complex. The Makú supply meat and occasional labour in exchange for agricultural produce and western trade goods.

Almost all the Vaupés Indians have been in contact with Europeans since about 1900. First rubber prospectors and later missionaries entered the area and caused severe disruption to Indian life. Now the rubber trade is no longer significant and there are no means for the Indians to obtain the goods which they have grown to need, yet mission schools fight against a return to a more traditional way of life.

Witoto
pop: 2,100

The name Witoto is commonly used to refer to all the Indians living between the Caqueta and Putumayo rivers in Colombia. These Indians, including the Bora, Muinane, Ocaina and Witoto proper, suffered terribly at the hands of rubber collectors during the rubber boom at the turn of the century. Once very numerous, they experienced severe depopulation and physical displacement; some of them now live in Peru.

Although still heavily involved with traders, the remaining groups of Witoto retain many aspects of their old culture. Communities consist of about 100 people who may live in a single house, the interior of which is divided into nuclear family compartments. This household is the basic socio-political unit, an exogamous patrilineal group with its own decision-making headman and council. Subsistence is by shifting cultivation of manioc, and the Witoto now keep chickens and pigs.

In the past the Witoto did not make intoxicating drinks, but were familiar with the use of coca. Periodically there are large gatherings for festivals and rituals with much dancing and remarkable displays of body painting, masks and barkcloth costumes, accompanied by the music of carved drums, Pan-pipes and flutes. As with the Bora and Muinane, however, the elaboration of these festivals has declined with the Witoto's fortunes.

Tikuna
pop: 1,000–1,500

The Tikuna, or Tukana, live along tributaries of the Amazon, on the borders of Colombia and Peru. There are few other Indians in this part of the Amazon basin, but traders and settlers have been in the area for many years, and the Tikuna have become quite thoroughly acculturated. They still practise agriculture and rely heavily on fishing, but their main effort is directed towards the extraction and lumber industries of the region, for which they provide much of the labour.

The Tikuna population merges at some points with that of the neighbouring Caboclos, who have a similar lifestyle and share the same problems of economic hardship. During the messianic movements which occurred amongst the Tikuna during the early 1970s many Caboclos participated in the cult activities, causing concern among the white settlers. The Tikuna face increasing difficulties over their land, much of which they have already lost to settlers. Recently they have begun to move away from the tributaries towards the main stream of the Amazon and engage more freely in trade and Caboclo life.

A Makiritare carves a canoe paddle, Venezuela

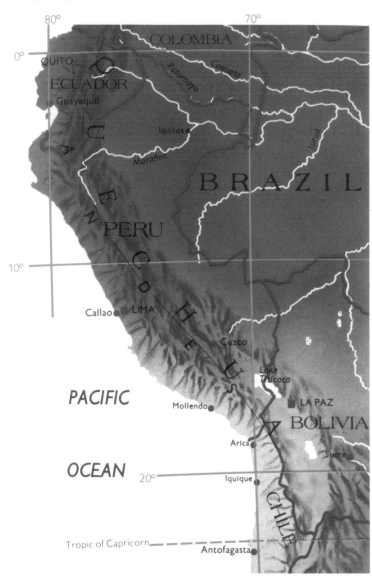

Inca Empire

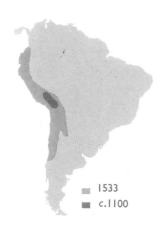

▆ 1533
▆ c.1100

Quechua

pop: 3,000,000

Before the arrival of the Spanish in South America, the Inca Empire extended from Quito in the north through present day Ecuador, Peru and Bolivia to northern Chile. Today there remain only two enduring legacies of Inca rule, their magnificent architecture and their unwritten language, Quechua, which has given its name to the descendants of their subjects.

Since the conquest, intermarriage between indigenous and Iberian peoples has blurred the ethnic boundaries to such an extent that there is considerable overlap between the Indian and mestizo population. Nevertheless in practice a clear distinction exists between mestizo and Indian groups, marked chiefly by language and lifestyle rather than physical characteristics.

The mestizos, or Cholos, speak both Quechua and Spanish, are predominantly urban, and constitute a sort of middle stratum between the European élite and the poverty-stricken Quechua. They are becoming more important as they take up the role of a skilled workforce in their newly industrializing countries.

The Indians usually speak Quechua and live mainly in the Andean highlands, supplementing their traditional subsistence farming with cash cropping and wage labour. They live in isolated communities based on the pre-Inca *ayllu*. Often a group owns fields at different altitudes and can grow potatoes, maize and coca as well as keeping sheep, llamas and alpacas for wool to weave into shawls and ponchos. Religious life is a combination of pre-Columbian and Catholic beliefs: Pachamama, the spirit of the fertility of the earth, is associated with the Virgin Mary and both are invoked in ceremonies and festivals.

The variation among different groups of Quechua stems both from their pre-Columbian cultures, and the degree to which they have remained aloof from European contact. The Morochucos of Peru, reputed to be descendants of the

Quechua Indians at
Chincheros market, Peru

first *conquistadores*, live in an isolated highland valley where they are distinguished by their skill at riding and breeding horses, the legacy of that contact. The Chipaya are culturally similar to the Quechua, but their language is Uru. Although they live on the Bolivian altiplano in close proximity to the Aymara, they are different, in both language and culture, from their neighbours.

All of the Quechua have suffered poverty and hardship at the hands of their colonizers. Recently some effort has been made to redress the balance with reforms in land tenure, education and local politics.

Peru

pop: 16,027,000

The Andes run the length of Peru, taking up the bulk of the land and dividing the country into three distinct regions. The highlands themselves used to be the most important area and are still the home of many Quechua. In the 20th century there has been a steady migration to the coastal cities from the harsh life of peonage in the Sierra, but recent land reforms have begun to reverse that trend. Inefficient *haciendas* have been removed from their absentee landlords to become productive co-operatives owned

and run by highland Indians.

The narrow coastal strip has become the centre of urban life. Rapid industrialization attracted both Indians and mestizos, or Cholos, to the towns but there is not enough work or housing for unskilled labourers.

Half of Peru's population are Indian, the majority being Quechua speakers, but to the east of the Andes in the lowland forests live Tikuna, Amahuaca, Jivaro and Campa Indians. The eastern lowlands are sparsely populated and, before the discovery of oil, the Indians there were relatively isolated from contact with farmers and settlers.

73

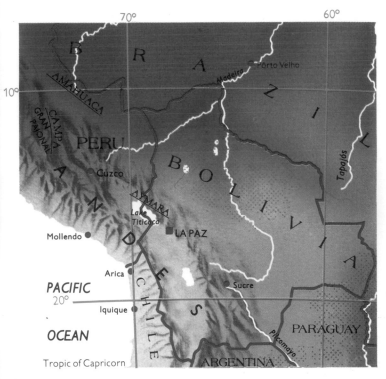

tals through the use of *aya-huasca*, a hallucinogenic drug taken during healing ceremonies, night-long rituals of chanting and singing which take place every few weeks.

Campa
pop: 25,000

The Campa live in one of the most inaccessible parts of Peru, the Gran Pajonal. Protected by mountains, thick forest and unnavigable rivers, they remained relatively isolated from settlers until the Obteni colonization project in 1945. Now only about 2,500 Campa still follow the traditional way of life, among the sub-groups of the Machiguenga and the Piro.

The location of Campa territory, half-way between the Andes and the Amazon basin, is reflected in their culture. As a mountain people the Campa have much in common with the Indians of the high Andes, but their language links them with the vast Arawak-speaking group of Amerindians who inhabit the forests of the Amazon basin as far east as the Xingu.

The Campa practise shifting cultivation, clearing gardens to grow cassava, plantains and sugar cane as well as coca, a mild narcotic of which most Campa are regular users. Hunting is important, as meat is the main source of protein, and part of the complex of Campa spirit beliefs refers to the 'owner of animals', a supernatural being who controls the availability of game.

Villages consist of clusters of extended family groups living in open-sided houses. Campa do not sleep in hammocks; this, like their use of coca, distinguishes them from other Arawak Indians. Village decisions are made communally, although there is a leader whose major role used to be the organization of war parties.

The traditional Campa way of life is well adapted to their survival in the difficult environment of the Peruvian montaña. However, every isolated group needs to have access to a large area and, with the acceleration of economic development since the Second World War, the territory of the Campa has been encroached upon increasingly. This not only makes their economic sur-

vival difficult, but also disrupts their social organization. Depopulation has so reduced the numbers of the isolated groups that they have become almost unworkable both as economic and family units.

Many Campa now provide cheap labour for the destruction of the very environment upon which some of their people still depend for their livelihood. Unless positive steps are taken to create a reserve of the Campa land, more and more will leave their traditional culture behind them to join the already large reservoir of poor, unskilled Campa wage-labourers.

Bolivia
pop: 5,624,000

The landscape of Bolivia varies from Andean peaks in the west to tropical forest and scrub in the east. Tin is the most important mineral resource. Of the mixed population, almost 70 per cent are Amerindian. The Andean highlands are still the home of numerous Quechua-speakers; their neighbours the Aymara and the Chipaya speak different languages but share their subsistence lifestyle, while the travelling Kallawaya are quite distinct. There are forest Indians, such as the Siriono, in the eastern lowlands. Apart from 250,000 Europeans, the remainder of the population are Cholos of mixed Indian and Spanish descent.

Aymara
pop: 1,250,000

High above the dense forests of the Amazon basin, surrounded by the peaks of the Andes, lies a wide barren plateau, the altiplano, and a huge inland sea, Lake Titicaca, the highest lake in the world. The shores of this lake and the plains that surround it are the homeland of the Aymara. The majority live in Bolivia, while half a million are scattered on the western side, in Peru.

Where they came from and how they arrived in this desolate region is unknown. In their villages they live in houses similar to those of the workers of Inca times, and live on what they can grow from the arid soil. Few Aymara can afford meat and the main source of

Amahuaca
pop: 500

The small group of surviving Amahuaca live deep in the forested montaña at the Peruvian headwaters of the Amazon. Contact was sporadic until the end of the 19th century when rubber prospectors decimated them with violence and disease, driving them from their riverside villages into the forest.

Throughout the area are distributed other groups of Panoan-speaking Indians similarly affected by contact, including the Cashinahua, Marinahua, Chosinahua, Yaminahua and Sharanahua, and the larger Conibo-Shipibo group. Before contact, hostilities existed between most of these groups, with raiding for women a frequent occurrence. Even now the more remote settlements are well protected from surprise attack and the shortage of women, precipitated jointly by the practices of female infanticide and polygyny, is still reflected in the extreme youth of many Amahuaca brides.

The economy rests on cultivation of cassava, maize, plantains and fruit, with considerable importance placed on hunting and meat-eating. The spirit world figures prominently in Amahuaca life, but can only be contacted by mor-

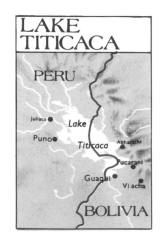

Campa village on the
Gran Pajonal, Peru

protein is fish from Lake Titicaca caught from reed boats. The climate is harsh, the diet poor and the work hard. To ease their condition the Aymara use coca, a mild narcotic which numbs against hunger and cold and produces a sense of well-being.

A maize beer, *chicha*, is consumed in large quantities during fiestas, when the reciprocal relationships which bind the community are reinforced by feasting and drinking. Although these fiestas fall on Catholic holidays, the religious outlook of the Aymara is strictly practical, and old beliefs are incorporated with the new into a religion which is far from orthodox Catholicism. For curing, the Aymara rely upon the Kallawaya, a neighbouring group of Indians from the east of the lake, who travel amongst them to diagnose sickness and to sell the benefits of their herbal knowledge.

A feature of Aymara society is the prominence of the *compradrazgo* ties of ritual kinship. At each child's baptism the parents choose another couple who agree to fulfil a number of ritual and economic obligations and act as godparents. Further *compradrazgo* ties are added at marriage, and the links between families ramify throughout the society.

The Aymara remain subsistence farmers, and only coca is produced in sufficient quantities for commercial export. Where they have migrated to the towns or the mines to supplement an inadequate income, their strong family ties have been loosened and many have turned to alcohol. Success in the towns is almost impossible, as everywhere positions of authority are held by Europeans or the Cholos of mixed blood who increasingly occupy the middle ranks. The Aymara, along with other Indians in the area, remain on the bottom rung of the ladder.

75

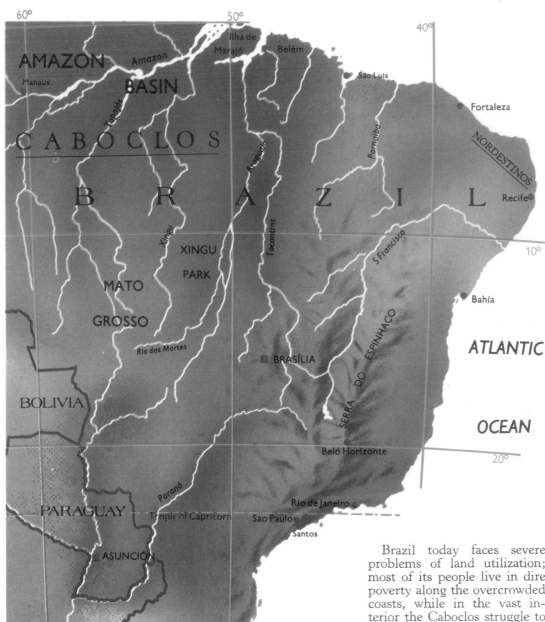

Brazil

pop: 111,666,000

Brazil is the fifth largest country in the world. Its inhabitants range from the very rich to the destitute and, although life expectancy is only 55 years, a high birth rate ensures a growing population, the majority of which is concentrated in the coastal regions.

The wealth of Brazil came originally from sugar plantations, with subsequent booms in rubber, coffee and now minerals; labour was imported from Africa and later Asia. Of the present population, 60 per cent are of European descent, 30 per cent of African descent and the rest Amerindian and mestizo.

Brazil today faces severe problems of land utilization; most of its people live in dire poverty along the overcrowded coasts, while in the vast interior the Caboclos struggle to survive on their smallholdings. Land speculation is rife and Indians and settlers have been dispossessed to accommodate development schemes.

The greed which has characterized the post-contact history of Brazil has resulted in the near total destruction of the Amerindian population; those remaining are afforded little protection from land encroachment. Surviving groups include Xingu Indians, Shavante, Mundurucu, Suruí, Bororo, Atroari, Kayapo, Yanomamo and Nambiquara.

Nordestinos

pop: 32,000,000

The north-east of Brazil, including the notorious 'polygon of drought', is one of the most poverty-stricken regions of the western hemisphere. Its inhabitants make up approximately one-third of Brazil's population; they are a mixture of three peoples—African, Amerindian and European (mainly Portuguese).

Portuguese colonists founded the first cities on the coastal strip and established large sugar plantations using local Indians as labour. The Indians soon died or ran away and were replaced by African slaves; today the sugar refineries are still owned by a handful of families and the direct descendants of slaves continue to work the sugar cane fields.

Just inland from the coastal strip lies the only area where small and middle-sized farms exist. This region supplies meat and cereals for the coastal towns. Further inland still is the region mostly affected by the brief and uneven rainfall, and here the land is divided into huge cattle ranches with tiny subsistence farms dotted amongst them. The racial characteristics of the population reflect the varying history of the regions. The preponderance of Africans is more marked near the coast, while Indian influence prevails further inland.

The interior was known until recent years for the incidence of messianic movements, a series of which occurred from the late 16th century onwards; some believers still wait for the return of a saviour. The urban poor increasingly participate in possession cults, dancing and feasting, with an amalgam of Catholic, African and Indian beliefs.

The north-east as a whole is beleaguered by problems which are primarily man-made and centre on the distribution of land. Most Nordestinos suffer from malnutrition to some degree and nearly all are pitifully poor. One of the root causes is the distorted agrarian structure in which great estates exist side by side with tiny holdings and over 50 per cent of the land is owned by 3 per cent of rural landowners. About 20,000 of the coastal dwellers are Jangadeiros (raft fishermen).

Nearly all rural Nordestinos lead a tenuous economic existence with no reserves, and the droughts of the interior are made far more destructive by this fact. Because they have no alternative, people from the region have, in times of crisis, been forced to migrate in large numbers to other parts of the country, notably Amazonia.

Caboclos
pop: not available

The term Caboclo refers to the non-Indian poor living in the backlands, the interior of the Amazon basin. Caboclos are generally the descendants of Portuguese settlers and Indians, who have evolved a distinctive culture in the isolation of the forests.

When the Portuguese first penetrated the basin they brought profound changes to the Amerindian societies there. Many remained in the interior and took Indian wives, establishing the first Caboclo population; with the subsequent development of the extractive industries this population grew and absorbed many of the acculturated Indians drifting towards a westernized way of life. Rubber collection during the boom of the late 19th century was the basis for the growth of Caboclo numbers and the establishment of a characteristic culture.

Just as the Caboclos themselves are the result of intermarriage, their language and culture are a product of mixtures and adaptations. Lingua Geral is a Tupi-based language adopted as a *lingua franca* by Jesuit missionaries who took it throughout the Amazon basin. It combines Portuguese and Tupi elements and provides a common language for all Caboclos. Likewise their way of life was originally European, adapted through contact with the Indians to allow maximum exploitation of a tropical forest environment.

Most Caboclos clear the forest to grow manioc, and have copied Indian methods of hunting and fishing. Many are also involved in trade and are enmeshed in a credit system which extends across the country and does much to maintain the Caboclos in poverty and dependence; this system began with rubber collection and extended to other extractive industries. A network of traders supply credit for essential items to individual collectors, who then are committed to selling their products exclusively to one particular trader.

Now that the Amazon basin is being opened up to road transport and development the Caboclos, as well as the Indians, face disruption and change. Already the emphasis is shifting from water transport to trucks and cars and the Caboclos must reconcile themselves to the new circumstances.

Shanty-town women in Rio de Janeiro, Brazil

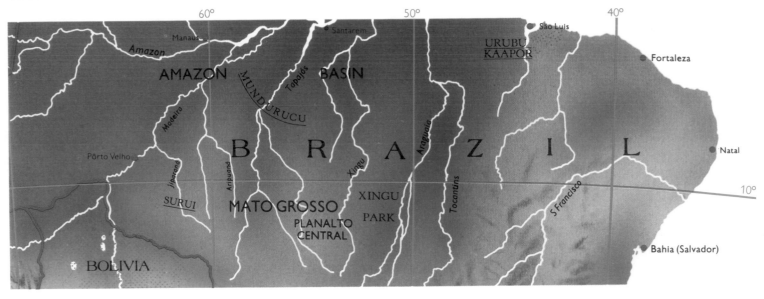

Suruí

pop: 1,500–6,000

The Suruí, a large group of uncontacted and recently contacted Tupi-speaking Indians, live between the Jiparaná and Aripuanã rivers of the northern Mato Grosso. About 60 of the contacted Suruí live around the Indian post at Sete de Setembro; the others make up possibly 80 settlements in the surrounding jungle. They are also known as the Cintas Largas, a term loosely applied to the unadministered Indians of this area.

The history of contact has not been happy: the Suruí were the victims of one of the most serious atrocities reported to the 1967 Brazilian parliamentary commission of inquiry. Gangs of rubber extractors were guilty of shooting, dynamiting and sadistic murder during systematic attempts to rid the area of Indians. After the first peaceful approaches in 1968–9 there was an epidemic of influenza which resulted in many deaths, and now the Suruí are suffering from severe depopulation and gradual encroachment on their land by settlers arriving by the new road. Suruí culture is short-lived when brought into sudden contact with the outside world.

Mundurucu

pop: 1,500–3,000

The Mundurucu live in scattered groups in the area of the lower Tapajós river; there may still be some uncontacted groups in the savanna region. Acculturated Mundurucu are found along the river banks. Like many other Tupi-speakers in Brazil some of the Mundurucu have been assimilated into the Caboclo population. They are not currently suffering undue pressure on their land, and numbers are slowly increasing.

There have ·been considerable changes in Mundurucu life since the contact period at the end of the 18th century. Then they covered a large area and had a reputation for fierce fighting and headhunting. They rapidly formed a relationship with the settlers and progressed from fighting to trading in rubber and farinha. Now only the more remote Mundurucu live by hunting and gardening. Their villages are characterized by large men's houses, rigid sexual division of labour and a strong emphasis on communal work. The collection of rubber is a solitary task; in order to pursue it, most Mundurucu have left their villages and set up nuclear family units near their rubber trees.

Xingu Indians

pop: 1,500

The Xingu Park occupies 11,500 square miles of the northern Mato Grosso, in the transitional area between the savanna of the Planalto Central and the rain forests of the Amazon basin. The upper Xingu was the home of Indian tribes long before the creation of the park in 1961. When the Villas Boas brothers, Orlando, Leonardo and Claudio, first arrived in the area 11 tribes were already living in close proximity and reasonable harmony. For many years the brothers worked to protect the Indians, whose land and very existence were threatened by encroaching settlers.

The Xingu Park was the culmination of these efforts, a barrier to outsiders and speculators, behind which the Indians could adapt to the inevitability of contact at a pace which gave them some hope of success. Threatened Indian groups from outside the region have subsequently been moved within its boundaries, presenting considerable challenges to the peace and stability of Xingu life.

All the major linguistic families of lowland South America are represented: The Kayabi, Aweti, Kamayura and Juruna are Tupi; the Yawalapití, Waura and Mehinaku are Arawak; the Kalapalo, Kuikuru, Matipu and Txicao are Carib; and the Suya, Kreen-Akrore and Txukuhamae are Gê. The Trumai speak an unrelated language.

Although some of the tribes now sharing the park were once enemies, outbreaks of fighting are rare. There is a surprising degree of cultural uniformity; the *maloca*, or large communal house, is characteristic, and the groups share a rich mythology and a religious life marked by frequent intertribal festivals and ceremonies. Large gatherings for both ritual and social purposes are a regular part of

Xingu Park

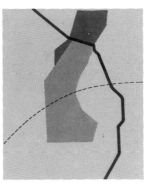

■ Northern area of park, lost after 1968

— Highway 080

-- Projected Highway 242

life; there is music and dancing and special attention is paid to the ornate and varied body painting which many of the groups adopt.

Trading has become an important bond between the Xingu tribes and intermarriage fosters and reflects the growing sense of unity. Problems still beset the park, however. In 1968 the BR 80 road cut through the middle of the protected land, and now the fertile northern part of the park has been withdrawn and sold to ranchers. More Indians crowd into diminished lands and find it increasingly difficult to maintain their livelihood without going outside to work on neighbouring ranches.

Urubu-Kaapor
pop: 500

The Urubu-Kaapor are the group most similar in culture to the Tupinamba, once among the more infamous South American tribes. The Tupinamba were in the direct path of arriving settlers and rapidly suffered the effects of disease and colonization: their coastal villages eventually broke up and the survivors fled to the interior. Tupinamba culture was effectively destroyed, but similar Tupi groups in more favourable locations—including the Urubu-Kaapor, who live on the eastern edge of the tropical forest—have fared better.

The Tupi-speaking tribes have long been famous for hostile relations with others and for their custom of eating their enemies. Some, such as the Mundurucu, were not cannibals but took the heads of their victims as part of the ritual of war, but for both the Tupinamba and the Urubu-Kaapor the killing and eating of enemies had both religious and social significance.

The presence of Europeans meant the end of this type of organized warfare, although the Urubu-Kaapor still fight with the Guajajas, wandering Tupis who sometimes hunt in Urubu areas. Cannibalism has not occurred for many years. With these profound changes Urubu society has encountered the sort of problems which may have played a part in the breakdown of Tupinamba culture. Both societies placed particular

emphasis on the concept of the warrior, as the only acceptable role for an adult man; now the Urubu have adapted their system of ideas and behaviour.

The Tupinamba experienced a series of messianic movements during the decline of their culture, believing in the existence of a perfect life which could be entered after the performance of complicated rituals. The Urubu have not responded in this way but remain with a lifestyle broadly similar to their previous one; they plant manioc and hunt, and live in large villages of households arranged around a central plaza. They have shamans and observe the important rituals surrounding

birth, death and puberty.

The Urubu-Kaapor are also well-known for their skill in making feather and bead ornaments. These were formerly worn on ceremonial occasions and conformed to prescribed conventions of colour and design. Everyday ornaments include ear-pendants and wristlets of blue and red feathers, but only adult men, for example, wore yellow, red and black head-dresses. These decorations identified the wearers as true Urubu-Kaapor and were worn only by them; now a surplus is produced to new designs, to satisfy outside demand and provide the Urubu with a source of cash income.

Yawalapití dancers in Brazil's Xingu Park

79

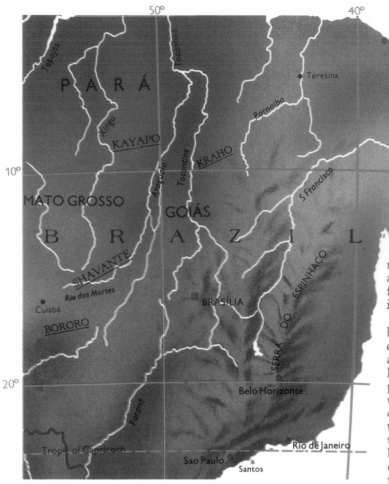

Kayapo

pop: 2,000

The Kayapo Indians live in the state of Pará in north-eastern Brazil, roughly between the Araguaia and the Xingu rivers. They belong to the Gê group of tribes who are spread all over central Brazil, speaking a similar language and sharing many cultural characteristics. The Gê group includes the Shavante, Sherente, Apinaye and Timbira.

The Kayapo themselves are further sub-divided into named communities, each the result of political splits of the original division into northern and southern Kayapo. These subgroups include the Xikrin, Gorotire, Kuben-Kragn-Kegn, Txukahamae and Kokraimoro.

All Kayapo are cultivators, clearing the forest to grow manioc, maize and sweet potatoe. Hunting supplements the garden produce, and there is a fishing season. Their huts are thatched with palm leaves and, unlike most Amazon tribes, the Kayapo sleep on mats on the floor. The villages are ar-ranged in a circle with the huts around the edge; paths radiate from the circle to the surrounding forest and gardens.

The members of each village belong to one of two groups, each of which has its own chief and lives in one half of the village circle. The groups are politically competitive and line up against each other for dances, rituals and games. In the middle of the village stands the men's house, which is forbidden to women. It is the centre of male social life and the place where all political decisions are taken and plans made for the future.

The most distinctive Kayapo decoration, applied to a baby's skin on the very first day of its life, is that of painted body patterns. Since they make neither pottery nor sculpture, this is their sole outlet for artistic expression, and the designs often have magical and ritual significance.

The Kayapo are currently experiencing a population decline. The Xikrin group, for example, have fallen below 100, and many of the others are dropping to dangerously low figures. There are plans to create a Kayapo reserve which, if implemented, may prevent further encroachment.

Kraho

pop: 600

Between the Amazon jungle and north-east Brazil lies a region of empty savanna known as the Campo. Many of this rather desolate country's Indian inhabitants, having survived an initial period of warfare, are today relatively undisturbed by white settlers. They are known collectively as the eastern Timbira, and consist of the Kraho, the Canela and the Apinaye. The Timbira belong to the Gê family of tribes which includes the Krikati, Gavioes, Shavante and Kayapo, all of whom speak variants of the Gê language.

The Kraho live by manioc cultivation, hunting and gathering. Like many of the Gê they are fast runners and often simply run down animals when hunting. Villages are circular, with the houses spread around the perimeter. Unlike many Amazon Indians, the Kraho sleep on the ground, rather than in hammocks. Paths to each house radiate from the centre, which is the site for all public activities, including council meetings, ceremonies and, recently, football matches. Traditional log races still take place around the edge of the villages; heavy buriti palm logs are carried on the shoulders of the young men, each representing one of the two moieties into which the villages are divided.

The presence of missionaries has had little effect on the Kraho beliefs and rituals. A new political structure has been imposed with the presence nearby of a government agent, and a police force has been recruited, but the only repercussions have been the effects of new incomes on the distribution of wealth.

The Kraho have successfully retained the essentials of their culture, and the conservatism which has so far kept their society intact may safeguard their survival in the future. The Kraho travel as far as Brasília to trade and make representations to the government. Their land is now a reserve, but game is being depleted and there is a continual threat of invasion by ranchers.

Shavante

pop: 2,000

The Shavante once lived in their thousands on the upland plains of northern Goiás; now they are confined to small reserves north of the Rio das Mortes.

The Shavante belong to the central Gê group of Indians. All Gê tribes have broadly similar cultural characteristics and language, and the Shavante have much in common with the

Kraho, Kayapo and Canela. The Sherente were probably once part of the Shavante; it seems likely that the two groups were separated when fighting with settlers took place in the 1840s. There was little contact for many years and feelings of mutual suspicion developed.

The Shavante had a reputation for fighting; they were once at war with the Tapirape to the north and they regarded the Bororo and Karaja as enemies. They resisted the entry of settlers and missionaries into their area and thus protected their way of life until about 30 years ago. Their bellicosity and wanderings have since been curtailed.

Like many South American Indians, the Shavante have had their land sold from under them to speculators and have been confined to smaller and smaller areas. Until a few years ago they were semi-nomadic, leaving their villages and gardens to go on treks through the forest, taking up to three months to follow one of their pre-determined routes, and hunting and gathering as they went. Their present narrow confines make this impossible.

Traditional Shavante life was rich in ritual, of which much has survived. Villages are divided into two moieties and this characterizes their social, religious and political life and is reflected in their ceremonies and games. Men are dominant in public life; they are divided into age grades and live in a bachelors' hut during the years before initiation. Then they emerge to live with the family of their bride and begin to take part in the political life of the community. Mature men hold a council each evening, a debating session at which decisions are made and political battles decided, and it is here that youthful training comes to fruition.

The modern life of many of the Shavante includes learning western skills in a rapid acculturation process. Despite the changes, the Shavante population is increasing and the men's councils are gaining effectiveness in defending Indian rights to their remaining lands.

Bororo
pop: 500–1,000

Once an extensive Indian group, the Bororo now live in smaller numbers in a reduced area of the southern Mato Grosso. Through 200 years of contact they have maintained their culture, despite severe depopulation and missionary opposition. Once more reliant on hunting and gathering, they now practise intensive agriculture as a result of encroachment on their land by settlers. By the mid-1970s their future was uncertain, and their land continues to shrink.

There are many cultural similarities between the Bororo and other Gê speaking peoples. One of these is the circular shape of their villages, which can also be seen amongst their northern neighbours the Kayapo, as well as being a feature of the Shavante and the Apinaye. This circular layout reflects the organization of Bororo society, composed of moieties, clans and lineages, and thus plays an essential part in all aspects of Bororo life.

Kayapo women and children, Brazil

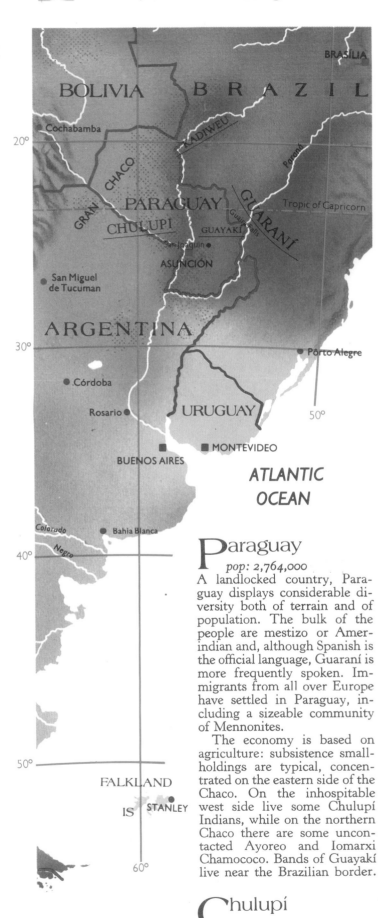

ATLANTIC
OCEAN

Paraguay
pop: 2,764,000

A landlocked country, Paraguay displays considerable diversity both of terrain and of population. The bulk of the people are mestizo or Amerindian and, although Spanish is the official language, Guaraní is more frequently spoken. Immigrants from all over Europe have settled in Paraguay, including a sizeable community of Mennonites.

The economy is based on agriculture: subsistence smallholdings are typical, concentrated on the eastern side of the Chaco. On the inhospitable west side live some Chulupí Indians, while on the northern Chaco there are some uncontacted Ayoreo and Iomarxi Chamococo. Bands of Guayakí live near the Brazilian border.

Chulupí
pop: 12,300

Although Paraguay is dominated by Guaraní-speakers, there are large numbers of other Indians living on the Chaco and overflowing into neighbouring Argentina, Bolivia and Brazil. In addition to the Chulupí, or Ashluslay, these include the Matacoan Choroti, the Mascoi (Lengua) and the Toba, who are Guaicuran speakers. The Chaco is a generally arid and inhospitable region, discouraging settlers until quite recent times, but once ranchers and missionaries arrived the process of acculturation was rapid. Now few Indians retain their native culture, except for some in the north-west who are being steadily pushed off their land.

The Chulupí were originally hunters and gatherers, doing some farming to supplement wild produce; they moved in matrilineal bands of up to 100 people. When ranches began to spread over the Chaco, game became scarce and the migratory paths were blocked.

Some Chulupí then acquired horses and animals and remain independent, but many now work as wage labourers on the ranches. Some migrated to sugar plantations in search of work. The religious life of the Indians has also been disrupted, but the Toba retain their shamans and belief in a spirit world despite the efforts of the missionaries in whose care many of them live.

Kadiweu
pop: 200

The Kadiweu, of Brazil are the descendants of the once-powerful Guaicurú, who at the end of the 18th century were successful sheep and cattle herders dominating the Gran Chaco. They had acquired horses from the Spanish and quickly became skilled horsemen, riding into battle against colonizers and neighbouring Indians alike. One such neighbouring group was the Guaná, settled agriculturalists whom the Guaicurú used as servants and food producers in return for military protection.

As the pace of colonization increased the Guaicurú succumbed to violence and disease, their numbers dropping sharply until they capitulated and agreed to move to the Bodoquena reserve on the Mato Grosso. The survivors are the present-day Kadiweu, who now live on the reserve in considerable poverty. Most of their land is leased by the government to cattle ranchers, while the Kadiweu struggle for subsistence, retaining little of their traditional art or skills.

In contrast, the once servile Guaná have increased in numbers, and their descendants, the Terena, now occupy six reserves. Although they have retained their language (Arawak) and elements of their culture the Terena also speak Portuguese and support themselves by working on nearby cattle ranches.

Guayakí
pop: 450

The Guayakí, or Aché, are one of the last groups of hunter-gatherers surviving in South America; they live in eastern Paraguay near the Brazilian border, scattered over several areas to the west of the Guaira Falls. Of all Indians, the hunter-gatherers have had the most severe problems since the European settlement of South America. They need large areas of fertile, game-bearing land to support them and competition has become intense.

In Paraguay, the Guayakí have seen much of the forest cleared by cattle ranchers and woodcutters, This, coupled with disease and physical assault, has caused a drastic decline in the Indian population. Some Guayakí bands still manage to live by hunting and gathering, despite land shortage and the danger of attack, but about 100 have been moved to a colony west of San Joaquin. Very few have survived in their new environment. Although the stated aim was to provide a protected reserve for the Guayakí to adapt to sedentary agriculture, recent reports indicate that death, disease, malnutrition and poverty have been the main result.

Those groups remaining outside the colony hunt and gather over shrinking territory. Led by a headman, and rarely exceeding 30 people, Guayakí rely entirely on the produce of the forest. The men make daily expeditions in search of food; as well as hunting, they gather honey, larvae and palm pith.

The sexual division of labour among the Guayakí thus differs from the normal Amazonian pattern, in which gathering is a female domain. Guayakí women are confined to cooking, child care, basketry and pottery, as well as carrying the band's possesions. The separation of male and female spheres is symbolized by the association of men with bows and women with baskets, objects which are taboo to the opposite sex.

Guaraní
pop: 20,000

The Guaraní are a large group of Indians who, although mainly concentrated in Paraguay, are also found in Argentina and Brazil. Their language is related to that of the Tupi family of tribes, who have migrated over much of South America and include the Tupinamba and Urubu-Kaapor, the Mundurucu, the Suruí and some of the Xingu Park Indians.

Since the arrival of European settlers the life of the Guaraní has changed radically. In Paraguay there was much intermarriage between Spanish and Guaraní, and although the descendants of these unions kept Guaraní as their language, their culture became distinctly Hispanic. Thus, despite the prevalence of the Guaraní language among the Paraguayan peasantry, it would be misleading to think of them as Guaraní Indians.

The true Guaraní consist of several dialect groups, including the Chiripa, the Nandeva, the Kaiwa, the Mbya and the Pai-Tavyera. In addition there are small groups of Guayakí in eastern Paraguay. They are at varying stages of acculturation; wandering bands of Mbya remain isolated from contact, but many semi-nomadic groups and a number of sedentary communities derive their livelihood from a combination of wage labour and cultivation.

Mobility is still characteristic of the Guaraní, although circumstances may often prevent this. The most common living pattern is a group of four or five extended families travelling and living together, the men dividing their time between working for wages and hunting, sometimes clearing a patch of land for the women to cultivate.

Many of the Guaraní came under the influence of Jesuit missionaries at an early stage of contact, but their own religious system proved very resistant to change. Although there is often a veneer of Catholicism, the strong mysticism of original Guaraní culture is still distinctive. Shamans are priests and curers, seers and politicians, and are immersed in rituals and supernatural communications. For most Guaraní, religion is part of everyday life and takes up considerable time and energy; they believe in transcending the ordinary world to reach a better one, and this has been a factor in the frequent messianic movements which have occurred since their conquest. In the course of these an entire community, led by its shaman, begins to migrate towards the coast in pursuit of a perfect existence in a 'Land Without Evil'. The failure of these various movements is generally attributed to mistakes in the observance of rituals.

Uruguay
pop: 2,788,000

Virtually no trace of the original inhabitants of Uruguay remains in this European-dominated country: only 8 per cent of the population are Amerindian or mestizo. The rest are immigrants from Italy and Spain who arrived during the economic boom of the late 19th and early 20th centuries. The wealth of Uruguay lay in beef, with cattle ranches covering almost the entire country; today ineffective management by the handful of landowners has brought severe economic and political problems. The bulk of the population live in towns, half of them in the capital, Montevideo, but cattle are still the main source of wealth.

Southern Gê
pop: 2,000

The southern Gê represent the third branch of the Gê-speaking peoples of Brazil. Within this widespread family of tribes there are as many differences as similarities, a fact which prevents the consideration of the northern, central and southern Gê as homogeneous entities. The central Gê, for example the Shavante, and the northern Gê, including the Kayapo and Timbira, have most similarity; the southern Gê have least in common with the other groups.

There are two southern Gê tribes, the Kaingang and the Aweikoma. Both have been badly affected by contact and the Aweikoma now face extinction. Their home in southern Brazil was penetrated during the 19th century by soldiers and disease; this combination, along with the intense pressure on their land by coffee-planters, rapidly reduced their population and resulted in their adoption of European clothes and trade goods on the small reservations they now occupy.

Some of their traditional culture still survives. The Kaingang have a system of patrilineal descent, with each group divided into a pair of exogamous moieties, Kanyero and Kame. During rituals both men and women paint themselves with the symbol of their moiety, each of which is associated with aspects of the natural world, in a typically Gê style of classification.

The Aweikoma are one of the very few societies in which women can have more than one husband. This occurs in one of two ways: either a husband accepts his wife's lover as a hunting companion, in which case they pool their game and live as co-husbands in the same hut; or an ageing husband invites a younger man to become his wife's co-husband, thereby augmenting the family's supply of food.

Another feature of Aweikoma culture absent among the Kaingang is the pinewood lip-plate which Aweikoma males used to wear in their lower lips. At birth Aweikoma children were not regarded as either male or female; their sexual character was determined only after they had undergone the appropriate birth ritual, in which boys had their first lip-plates inserted and girls received a cut below the left knee.

The last time the birth ritual was performed was in the 1930s and since then many more customs have fallen into disuse. Unlike their northern and central cousins the southern Gê were too accessible to outside contact to endure for very long and today even the last relics of their once flourishing culture are fast disappearing.

Distribution of
Gê-Speakers

■ Southern Gê
■ Northern and Central Gê

83

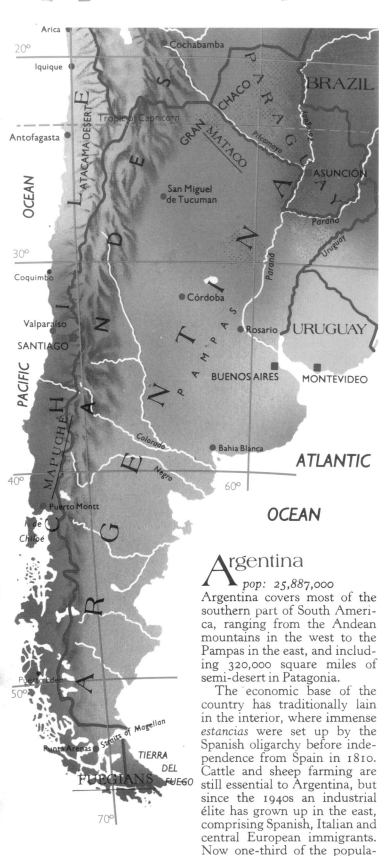

colonization; there is almost no mestizo population. A few Fuegians survive in the southern islands, and some 50 Tehuelche remain in Patagonia. More numerous Guaraní live near the Paraguayan border, while the Chulupí and other groups are found on the northern Chaco.

Argentina
pop: 25,887,000

Argentina covers most of the southern part of South America, ranging from the Andean mountains in the west to the Pampas in the east, and including 320,000 square miles of semi-desert in Patagonia.

The economic base of the country has traditionally lain in the interior, where immense *estancias* were set up by the Spanish oligarchy before independence from Spain in 1810. Cattle and sheep farming are still essential to Argentina, but since the 1940s an industrial élite has grown up in the east, comprising Spanish, Italian and central European immigrants. Now one-third of the population lives in and around the capital Buenos Aires, and the most recent immigrants, mestizos from Paraguay, Bolivia and the Argentinian interior, suffer chronic unemployment and poverty.

Almost all the Indians in Argentina died during its

Mataco
pop: 12,000

The Gran Chaco is an extensive area of savanna, mixed with forest and scrub. The western part is the home of the Mataco, who traditionally hunted, gathered and fished between the Rio Pilcomayo and Rio Bermejo. Settlement of this area by outsiders was neither stable nor continuous until the beginning of the 20th century, but its effect upon the ecological balance of the existing system has been so extreme that few Mataco are able to continue their former way of life. Those who still maintain some independence live mostly in the north-east, and even these groups rely to some extent on casual labour.

Most Mataco migrate in search of work; there are some settled rural communities where agriculture and sheep- and goat-rearing offer hope of autonomy, but the majority are dependent on work in timber and sugar mills and odd jobs on the fringes of towns and villages. This work is very badly paid and offers no escape from poverty and hardship.

About half of the Mataco have been converted to Christianity by evangelical Protestant missions. There are communities of converts living at the missions, where they receive protection and some economic assistance in return for the abandonment of their cultural practices and beliefs.

Chile
pop: 10,543,000

Some 3,000 miles long and only 100 miles wide, Chile stretches from the tropics almost to Antarctica. Most of the population is concentrated along the axis formed by the central valley, but the greatest wealth lies in the wastes of the Atacama desert to the north—where nitrate and copper pro-

vide Chile's most important exports. The majority of Chileans today are mestizos of mixed European and Amerindian descent. Only 2 per cent of the population is Indian, consisting largely of Mapuche and a few surviving Fuegians.

Mapuche
pop: 500,000

The Mapuche Indians of south central Chile are one of the most fiercely independent Indian societies in South America; they were defeated and pacified as late as 1882, and now farm territory in the foothills of the Andes. Archaeological evidence shows that they were cultivators and llama herders for centuries before the arrival of the Spaniards. During the following 300 years there was bitter fighting between settlers and Indians in which the Mapuche were frequently victorious. Eventually many thousands crossed the Andes into Argentina where they constitute a sizeable population today; others went into hiding

to the south of their former homelands. By 1882 the struggle was over and in 1884 their territory was divided into reservations on which they were legally bound to live.

Within the protective framework of reservation status the Mapuche managed to retain their native language, their religion and a social organization which rested on patrilineal descent, inheritance of land and succession to the office or status of one's father. Mapuche men never married women from their own reservation; women moved to their husband's household upon marriage, and men stayed on the reservation of their birth. Each reservation had a chief who was the lineage elder and wielded political and economic power. During the public ceremonies for funerals and festivals he was also the ritual chief, but the shaman, or supernatural curer, was usually a woman. She struggled against evil spirits on behalf of her sick clients, and often gained considerable wealth and prestige.

In 1960, however, the reservation system was abolished by Chile's national congress and the Mapuché were legally transformed into small landowners. Those who continue to live in the reservation area hold on to their customs tenaciously, while those who have left reservation land try to blend into the mestizo population of lower-class workers in the cities. But since 1960 there have been significant changes in the Chilean government. Following the military coup in 1973 reports suggest that many Mapuché have been killed by government troops and once again they are struggling to hold on to their land.

Fuegians
pop: 100

The Fuegians were the original inhabitants of the cold and inhospitable islands at the southern tip of Argentina and Chile. Some lived on the Chilean coast but, despite the harshness of the environment, several groups of Indians lived in

Tierra del Fuego, including the coastal Alacaluf, Chono and Yahgan, who were known as the Canoe Indians, and the Ona and Haush, who hunted in the interior. The northern lands of the Ona were taken over by sheep ranchers at the end of the 19th century and the Indians were taken to missions, where only a few survived.

The Canoe Indians fared slightly better, but since their removal the most southerly islands are uninhabited. The cold there is extreme; yet the Alacaluf, Chona and Yahgan lived on seafood and birds and went almost naked in below-freezing temperatures. They were found to have a physiological adaptation which gave them a higher metabolic rate and enabled them to withstand even the cold of the sea. The few Alacaluf who survived the effects of contact are based around the Chilean settlement of Puerto Eden. They have retained their language and some of their material culture, notably their canoes and their skin tent dwellings.

Cowboys on an Andean ranch, Chile

Europe

Europe, the smallest continent apart from Australasia, is both physically and culturally the least clearly defined. To the east it merges imperceptibly into the steppes of Asia; the Mediterranean countries which form its conventional southern boundary have as much in common in terms of climate, ecology and shared values and institutions with North Africa and the Middle East as with the transalpine region to the north; even the Atlantic, the least ambiguous of natural frontiers, has lost much of its former significance. The overseas expansion of the maritime powers of western Europe, from the late 15th century onwards, led to the creation of common linguistic and cultural traditions between Europe and the Americas at least as strong as those shared amongst the European nations themselves.

In climate, topography and mineral and energy resources, Europe occupies a privileged position. Its peninsular configuration, relief and location on the western side of the Eurasian land mass maximize the beneficial effects of the Gulf Stream. Thus, despite its wide latitudinal spread, Europe has few arid or polar zones and affords a range of physical environments favourable to human settlement and exploitation. Its long, indented coastline, wide continental shelves and easily navigable inland seas and river systems have stimulated maritime activities and, together with open frontiers to the east and south, have ensured a constant and mainly fruitful interchange of population, ideas and commodities with other, non-European, cultures.

Within this generally favourable habitat, however, there are marked regional variations in climate and the distribution of resources which have profoundly influenced the history of European development. Early neolithic farmers and traders settled in all the temperate regions of Europe, and especially on the grasslands and readily cultivable loess soils of western and eastern Europe. Yet it was the Mediterranean, with its easy navigation and tideless seas, hot dry summers and mild wet winters, and thin, easily-cleared, evergreen forest which provided them with their most suitable ecological niche. Crete, with a rich agricultural hinterland and trade links with Egypt and the Middle East, was already a flourishing urban centre by the third millennium BC. Through Crete the urban traditions of the Fertile Crescent passed first to the Greek mainland and then through Italy and Rome to the rest of Europe.

Throughout the prehistoric period, the colder environment of northern and central Europe was sparsely settled or left to aboriginal hunting and herding peoples. It was only with the Germanic migrations of the 12th and 13th centuries that much of eastern Europe was intensively settled and urbanized; and the colonization of central and northern Scandinavia was not completed until the 19th century.

Interregional differences were equally important during the industrial revolution. Although the presence of iron and coal deposits was only one factor in the complex causal sequence which brought large-scale factory technology to north-west Europe, their virtual absence in the south proved a formidable obstacle to early industrialization. Despite the high technology alternatives of the 20th century, the Mediterranean regions have never fully overcome this disadvantage.

With 34 nation states—26 before the breakup of the Austro-Hungarian Empire and Tsarist Russia after the First World War—and with between 40 and 50 distinct languages, Europe projects an image of increasing territorial fragmentation and ethnic complexity. Yet its major linguistic groups—Celtic, Germanic, Romance and Slav—are all of

VEGETATION

Ice
Permanent ice field

Tundra
Moss and lichen

Conifer Forest
Pine, spruce, larch

Broadleaf Forest
Deciduous

Temperate
Arable, broadleaf, grass

Mediterranean
Citrus, olive, agave

■ Capital Cities

● Major Towns

• Towns
Small town village

── Country Borders

── Borders
Provinces, states

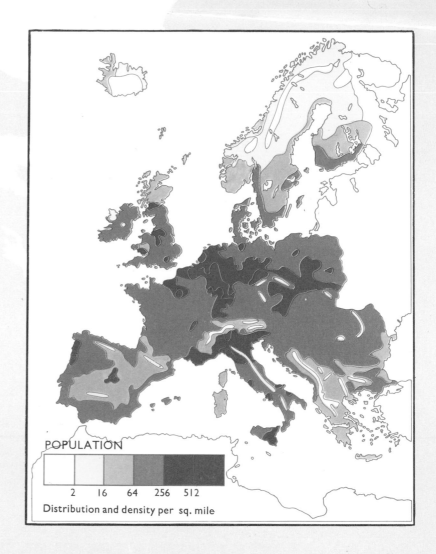

POPULATION

2	16	64	256	512

Distribution and density per sq. mile

Indo-European origin; the main exceptions are either aboriginal survivals (Basque) or cultural imports from Asia (Finnish, Magyar).

In part, this diversity stems from a long sequence of migration, conquest, settlement and cultural absorption which began in prehistoric times with the colonization of Europe by Indo-European speaking peoples from Asia Minor. This process gathered momentum with the Germanic and Slavonic migrations which followed the fall of Rome, and was virtually completed with the occupation of the Danube plain by invading Magyar nomads in the 10th and 11th centuries. The variety is also partly the product of centuries of dynastic struggles and alliances between the European powers. Even more important, however, were the concerted efforts in the 19th and 20th centuries to realign the linguistic and political maps of Europe to satisfy the nationalistic aspirations of minority groups.

Between 1830 and the end of the First World War no fewer than 15 European peoples gained political independence, most of them at the congress of Versailles in 1919. This congress formally recognized the principle of self-determination—the right to self-government for peoples of the same language and culture. Unfortunately, however, the application of the principle created a legacy of frustrated nationalist expectations which has bedevilled European politics ever since.

The ethnic fragmentation of the Balkans proved particularly intractable, with the newly-founded nation states of Yugoslavia and Czechoslovakia containing almost as many discontented ethnic minorities as the Austro-Hungarian empire they

Projection: Bonne

succeeded. Furthermore, the fact that it was only the territories of the vanquished powers that were partitioned became the main pretext and a contributary cause of the Second World War. Today, despite widespread recognition of the need for supranational integration, there are few states which are not troubled by insistent demands for separation or regional autonomy from highly articulate ethnic minorities—Basques, Bretons, Catalans, Croats, Scots, Walloons or Welsh.

Nurtured on separate traditions of national education and value systems, most Europeans are more conscious of the things which divide them than the customs, values and assumptions they hold in common. Their perception of these differences has been heightened by sharp linguistic barriers—particularly the lack of a modern *lingua franca*—and the nationalist wars which ravaged the continent in the first half of the 20th century. Yet, important though these differences are, they obscure a more subtle and deep-seated unity based on a shared historical tradition and a surprisingly broad similarity in social, economic and political institutions.

Among the many historical forces which have shaped the European experience, probably the most significant are the legacy of the classical world, Christianity and the scientific and industrial revolutions. The role of the Roman Empire in transmitting the technology and high culture of the wider Mediterranean to the rest of Europe can hardly be overestimated. Under its tutelage, European peoples had their first experience of shared governmental and legal institutions; their first and only *lingua franca;* their first universal religion; their first common trading empire. The advance of Roman military and civil technology beyond the Alps opened the way for the spread of that most distinctive of Mediterranean institutions, the city. This, with its internal structure of literate élites, clergy, merchants and craftsmen was to remain the repository of European high culture after the fall of Rome.

With the collapse of the Roman Empire,

Christianity became the main force for European integration. Based on former imperial towns, the medieval church began its protracted mission of pagan conversion. Throughout the Middle Ages, it was the standard bearer of classical urban traditions, the only effective custodian of literacy and scholarship, patron of the arts and arbiter of aesthetics and morals. Its organization of opposition to Islam during the crusades rekindled a real if temporary sense of unity among the Christian nations of Europe. After the Reformation, the Church's impact on society seemed increasingly divisive, but its basic task of promoting a standardized faith and cosmology among the peoples of Europe had already been achieved.

Before the 16th century, there was little difference in economy or technology between Europe and any of the world's other major agricultural civilizations; some three centuries later, Europe had clearly outstripped all rivals. By any of the standard measures of economic development—capital investment, volume of trade, *per capita* income, specialized labour and entrepreneurial skills, technological innovation—Europe was far ahead: its imperial hegemony encompassed all the other continents, and its capitalist political economies were distinctly different from anything that had gone before.

Such dramatic changes—consequences of the scientific and industrial revolutions—had a profound impact on Europe's internal structure, paradoxically both uniting and dividing it. The delineation of basic methods of scientific discovery and proof led to a cumulative expansion of western science and technology, and the emergence of a culturally quite distinctive mode of thought and explanation. Its main beneficiaries, Europe's intellectual élite, came to share a common set of scientific paradigms and a common, genuinely supranational, mode of understanding and ordering the natural universe. But, as formal education became a more specialized and increasingly prized resource, the gap between Europe's educated and non-educated classes grew wider; and with the

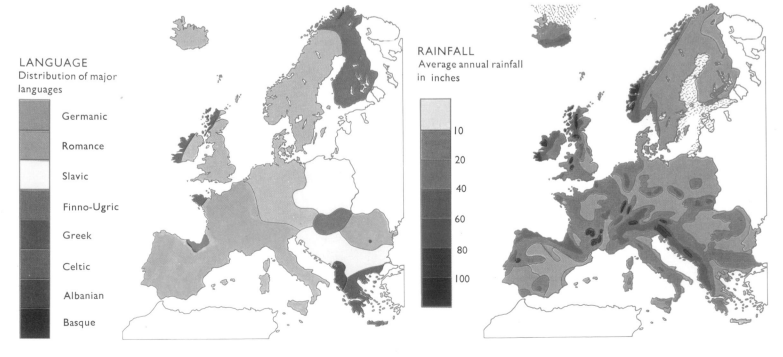

LANGUAGE
Distribution of major languages

- Germanic
- Romance
- Slavic
- Finno-Ugric
- Greek
- Celtic
- Albanian
- Basque

RAINFALL
Average annual rainfall in inches

- 10
- 20
- 40
- 60
- 80
- 100

advent of large-scale industrial technology it widened further still.

Industrialization produced two main divisions: the first, stratification by social class within the core industrial societies of western, northern and eastern Europe; the second, a growing economic and social disparity between the industrial heartlands and the mainly peasant-based agricultural regions of the Mediterranean, parts of central Europe and the north-western fringes.

All the capitalist and mixed economies of north-west Europe show marked class differences which, despite the growing political influence of trade unions and left-wing parties, have proved surprisingly resilient. These divisions derive partly from a complex division of labour, in which the rewards accruing to different occupational skills are primarily determined by market scarcity and partly from ownership of property, which, despite frequent attempts at redistribution through taxation and death duties, is still concentrated in remarkably few hands. Rates of social mobility—especially élite mobility, the best indicator of equality of opportunity—are uniformly low; and the undoubted improvement in general living standards and welfare provision of the post-war era owes at least as much to rapid economic expansion as to conscious political efforts to reduce inequalities.

In the absence of private property, and with the distribution of income and other benefits firmly in the control of state planners officially committed to the ideology of a classless society, the command economies of central and eastern Europe present a more egalitarian image. Rates of mobility are higher and the line between manual and non-manual workers—the major divide in the class systems of the capitalist economies—is much less firmly drawn. But even here, income differentials and privileges—the allocation of special housing, party cars, holidays and so forth—are enjoyed by party officials and the intelligentsia. These and, above all, increased opportunities to pass them on to their children, have enabled socialist dissidents

to talk of the emergence of a new class. Furthermore, recent attempts to improve productivity in the more heavily industrialized socialist societies such as Czechoslovakia by 'increasing the pay differentials of skilled workers and technocrats lend support to the contention that industrialism everywhere leads to a similar pattern of stratification.

Since the industrial revolution, peasant and pastoralist communities have grown steadily more isolated from the mainstream of European economic life. At the end of the 18th century, the split between urban and rural populations was about 20-80; today the proportions are reversed. Over the last century, many millions of peasants have forsaken the land for ever; and those who remain face the prospect of either becoming commercial smallholders or making periodic forays as temporary migrants into the industrial economies which surround them. Increasingly, Europe's peasant communities are turning into villages of passage, where people are born, grow up, marry and die, but from which they are absent for the greater part of their adult working lives.

This decline stems mainly from economic causes. The spread of capitalism into the countryside, population increase, the enclosure of grazing lands and the mechanization of agriculture all threatened the viability of peasant smallholdings. Domestic and rural crafts were virtually destroyed by industrial competition. In the 20th century land reform and collectivization schemes—in so far as they have succeeded at all—have generally hastened the transformation of peasants into commercial farmers or agricultural wage labourers.

Above all, the higher living standards offered by urban industrial employment have compelled peasants to re-evaluate their traditional modes of livelihood, which they have generally found wanting. In recent years, at least, the most resounding lamentations for the near demise of European peasant societies have come from the urban middle classes, very rarely from peasants themselves, who are only too aware of the misery and hardships of the world they have all but lost.

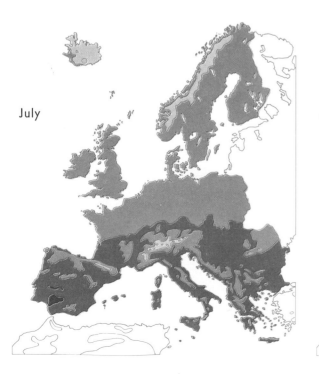

July

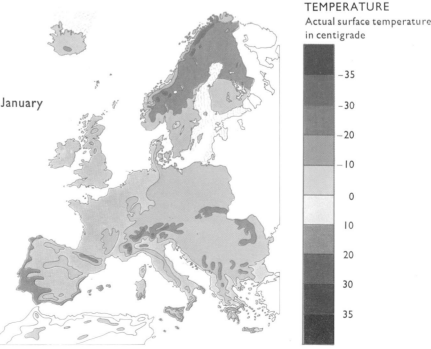

January

TEMPERATURE

Actual surface temperature in centigrade

- −35
- −30
- −20
- −10
- 0
- 10
- 20
- 30
- 35

Celts
pop: 2,000,000

In many ways the term Celt refers more to an ancient than to a modern population group. It is a classification based primarily on language—in ancient times peoples speaking Celtic tongues, the westernmost group of the Indo-European languages, spread very widely over western, central and northern Europe. On the western continental fringes, in Scotland, Ireland, Wales and Brittany, there are some 2,000,000 people who still speak Celtic languages and retain elements of traditional Celtic culture.

Celtic kingdoms survived in Cornwall until the 10th century, and in the less anglicized western part of Ireland an extensive folklore—poems, songs and myths—testifies to the continuing strength of Celtic traditions. Today the Irish language is in danger of extinction, although it is enthusiastically fostered by the government. Gaelic Scotland remained remote from English society as late as the 20th century, and it

was only in the 1950s that the ancient custom of waulking, the chanting of traditional verse by women while shrinking tweeds, finally died out. Very few people in Scotland speak Gaelic today.

The Welsh language is still spoken by some 700,000 people and its use for official documents has been greatly extended since 1966, when it was first recognized by the British government. Folk festivals called *eisteddfods* are held annually throughout Wales, sustaining musical and poetic traditions. Elsewhere, however, Celtic culture is disintegrating, although in Cornwall and Brittany concerted attempts to revive the ancient languages have formed the basis of regional separatist movements.

Irish
pop: 4,848,000

Divided between Eire (*pop: 3,167,000*) and the six counties of the north (*pop: 1,681, 000*), the political condition of modern Ireland reflects a long history of English rule. Ireland never became part of the Roman Empire, but Christianity, the Latin language and the art of writing were introduced to the Gaelic Celts in the 5th century AD. Viking, Norman and English invaders were restricted to the east coast and gradually assimilated into the Gaelic community.

The reign of the Stuarts in England during the early 17th century saw a deliberate policy of Anglicization for Ireland. Irish rebellions brought cruel repression, confiscation of land and settlement by English, Scots and Welsh protestants. The two north-eastern counties of Antrim and Down were settled with a large number of soldiers in order to maintain a permanent garrison.

The struggle for independence continued, despite a high level of emigration, particularly to North America, and repeated failures of the potato crop on which Ireland's rural population subsisted. The Easter Rising of 1916 came as a prelude to guerrilla warfare and finally the partition of Ireland in 1921. The north, with a Protestant majority in only two of the six counties, remained part of the United Kingdom.

Eire is still closely bound to England, which provides more than half its imports, and takes two-thirds of its exports. Agriculture remains the basis of the economy, employing a quarter of the workforce and operated mainly by family farms. Livestock and dairy products are most important, but cereals are grown in the east and southeast. Industry is actively encouraged by the government.

Northern Ireland has a more developed industrial base, especially around the port of Belfast. Since 1969, however, the economy has been devastated by fighting between the Catholic and Protestant communities, despite military intervention and direct rule by Britain. The Catholic Provisional IRA (Irish Republican Army) seeks the reunification of Ireland, a prospect fiercely resisted by the Protestant community and with little appeal for the government of Eire so long as sectarian differences remain unresolved.

Scots
pop: 5,044,000

The Scots were originally a Celtic people, who came from Ireland in the 5th century. The kingdom of Alba, which had been established by the mid-9th century, included most of lowland Scotland and all the highlands not controlled by Norsemen. Norman families such as the Bruces, Stewarts and Comyns settled in the lowlands 300 years later. A deep division gradually developed between the Gaelic-speaking highlanders and the English-speakers of the lowlands.

English institutions gained a foothold in Scotland in the early Middle Ages and the two kingdoms were finally joined in 1707. However, a number of distinctions remain: Scotland adopted Roman law in place of common law; and Presbyterian influence has been marked since the 16th century, contributing to the high traditions of education in Scotland.

Scotland experienced the full force of the industrial revolution in the 19th century and, while peasant farming continues in a few remote areas, the population is today heavily concentrated in the industrial central lowland region. Centuries

of economic depression have resulted in large-scale emigration, particularly from the highlands. This is often blamed on commercial exploitation from England and, with the discovery of oil off the Scottish coast, demands for independence are gathering momentum.

Welsh
pop: 2,802,000

The Welsh were originally Celtic-speaking peoples forced into the mountainous peninsula by the Romans and later the Saxons. Political unification remained incomplete until Owain Glyndwr's rebellion against the English in the early 15th century. In 1536 Wales was forcibly united with England and experienced a long period of economic, political and cultural assimilation. The Welsh gentry in particular were rapidly Anglicized.

Industrialization had a massive impact in the late-19th century, as the rural population migrated to urban centres in south and north-east Wales. The south Wales coalfield employed 200,000 workers by 1911, and urbanization was accompanied by the rise of militant trade unionism. During the depression of the 1920s, 20 per cent of the Welsh population was forced to emigrate, mostly to England. The Welsh are still among the first to suffer the effects of recession in the British economy.

Resentment of the English is still an important factor in Welsh consciousness. The Welsh language, which was not recognized for official purposes until 1966, has become the focus of a revival in Welsh culture and growing demands for political autonomy.

English
pop: 46,516,000

The English have long been the dominant nationality in the British Isles. They are the most numerous, with 83 per cent of the population of the United Kingdom, and they inhabit the more favoured lowland part of the island which has an equable climate, numerous river valleys and fertile soils.

Germanic tribes invaded the island and settled in the 5th century, with the collapse of the Roman Empire. The Norman conquest in 1066 initiated a rapid transformation of Anglo-Saxon society into an unusually pure feudal system. Peasants were tied to the land, with formal obligations to their lord. In the medieval period the country became rich through the export of wool and developed many of its characteristic institutions, such as common law and parliament.

The English were the first people to feel the full effects of industrialization and a total transformation took place in the 19th century, utterly destroying the old peasant society. For almost a hundred years, Britain was 'the workshop of the world', exporting machinery and processed goods to all quarters of the globe. At the same time, a vast imperial expansion occurred, building on the existing empire which already included India, the West Indies, Canada, Australia and New Zealand. Colonialism in the tropics aimed largely at securing monopoly markets and supplies of raw materials. With the dissolution of the empire after the Second World War, Britain has received migrants from many former colonies, particularly from southern Asia and the West Indies.

With almost 900 people to the square mile, the English are one of the most densely concentrated populations in the world and, with 80 per cent living in towns, are also one of the most urbanized. Agriculture employs only 3 per cent of the workforce and rural dwellers, with the exception of some in remote highland parishes, lead an essentially urban type of life.

British trawlermen in the North Sea

Iceland, Scandinavia
Icelanders, Norwegians, Swedes, Finns, Lapps, Danes

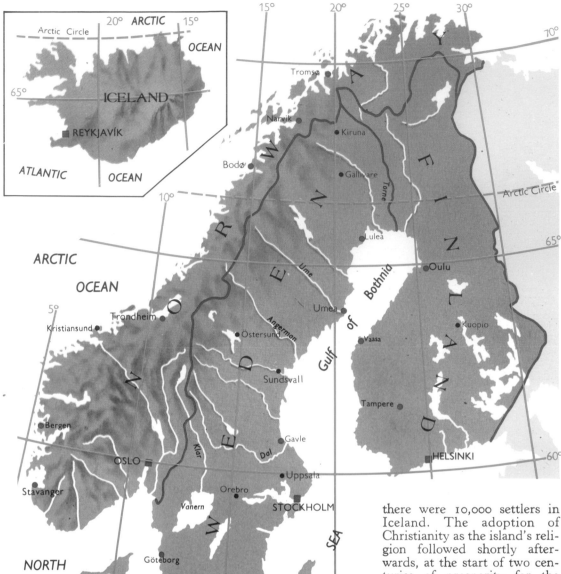

live in the scattered homesteads which housed nearly all Icelanders in 1900. Even their location on the fault line of the mid-Atlantic ridge has been beneficial: most modern houses are heated by steam or water from hot springs and geysers.

Norwegians
pop: 4,037,000

Norway occupies the western part of the Scandinavian peninsula; one-third of its 125,000 square miles lies within the Arctic circle and most of the land is too harsh and mountainous to be brought under cultivation. The sea is the most valuable natural resource, providing both a food supply and an opportunity for the development of a merchant shipping fleet. Recently it has also yielded oil, a welcome source of wealth and a stimulus to Norwegian industry.

Formerly under Danish and Swedish rule, Norway has been independent since 1905. Regional differences account for the existence of two official languages: Bokmal is closer to Danish, while Landsmal is based on regional dialects. Norwegians remain strongly influenced by Norse traditions and Lutheran Christianity, but the isolated subsistence of the rural peasant has been replaced by a more urban orientation.

In the north of Norway live about 20,000 Lapps occupying one of the five traditional regions of the country. In the Pasvik valley the reindeer-herding Lapps have encountered considerable difficulties, because the Soviet frontier denies them access to their traditional grazing areas. Others have abandoned their distinctive culture to integrate with the southern Norwegians.

Swedes
pop: 8,326,000

Sweden is the fourth largest country in Europe, extending for a thousand miles from north to south on the eastern side of Scandinavia. One-seventh of the country is taken up by the Norrbotten, a sparsely inhabited frontier region, but in the mountainous and heavily forested central area the climate is surprisingly mild, while the southern agricultural penin-

Icelanders
pop: 221,000

One of the most active volcanic regions of the world, Iceland is normally considered part of Europe, although the nearest landmass is Greenland, 180 miles to the north-west. It was first settled in the 9th century, largely from Norway but also from the British Isles, since when its population has remained both stable and homogeneous. The Icelandic language is related to Old Norse.

By 930 AD, when the first meeting of the Althing, or national assembly, took place, there were 10,000 settlers in Iceland. The adoption of Christianity as the island's religion followed shortly afterwards, at the start of two centuries of prosperity for the mixed farming and fishing economy. This was the time when many of the sagas were recorded; the art of writing was introduced by the Church.

From 1262 to 1944, Iceland was subjected to rule first by Norway and then by Denmark. Until the early 20th century, this era was characterized by severe economic depression and increasing emigration, but the growth of the fishing industry signalled an improvement in the island's fortunes. By the 1970s, however, over-fishing by large trawlers seriously threatened Iceland's stocks, and foreign vessels were banned within a 50-mile radius.

On the basis of the fishing industry and hydro-electric power, Icelanders have achieved some economic diversification. More than half the population now lives in the south-west, which includes the capital Reykjavik, and only 20 per cent

sula, Skåne, resembles Denmark. The Swedes are overwhelmingly Protestant in religion and share a common culture, in which a belief in equality and individual expression is an important component.

Sweden won independence from Denmark in the 16th century and by 1700 an important Swedish empire had developed, but a period of decline followed: by 1900 Sweden was among the poorest countries in Europe. Since then a remarkable transformation has taken place, which has given Swedes the highest standard of living in Europe. Building on their resources of iron ore, hydro-electric power and timber, as well as their tradition of neutrality, Swedes have created an economy in which 45 per cent of the population is engaged in industries such as metallurgy and engineering.

Nearly three-quarters of all Swedes live in the southern provinces, where the principal cities are concentrated. Recent development has been a model of industrial modernization, social democracy and stable government. Sweden expends a high proportion of the national wealth on social services and education, seeking to ensure maximum equality of opportunity to its younger generation. Maintaining an army is the next major expense.

Finns
pop: 4,738,000

Finland is one of the most northerly states in the world, with one-third of its area lying within the Arctic circle. The population is concentrated in the south-west coastal area, which is also the site of the capital, Helsinki. Natural vegetation consists almost entirely of coniferous forest and the Finns have traditionally made their living by combining forestry with farming and fishing.

Until the 1930s only one-sixth of the population was urban, but in recent years industrialization, at first based on timber and hydro-electric power, has developed and diversified. Now more than half the Finns live in towns and Finland has a solid reputation for the design and manufacture of furniture, textiles, metal and glassware.

Until 1809, when it was taken over by Russia, Finland was part of Sweden and a small but declining number of Finns still speak Swedish. Independence from Russia was achieved in 1917, and Finland now maintains a strict neutrality in its buffer position between the Soviet bloc and Scandinavia.

The major religion of Finland is Christianity, with some 90 per cent of the population belonging to the Evangelical Lutheran Church. A minority belong to the Finnish Orthodox Church, granted autonomy by the Russian Orthodox Church in 1920.

In the extreme north of the country live about 3,000 Lapp speakers, whose language belongs to the north Lapp dialect group. They are the survivors of nomadic and semi-nomadic hunters, gatherers and reindeer herders, but are now largely integrated into the culture and economy of northern Finland.

Lapps
pop: 35,000

The Lapps, or Samer, occupy a region in the extreme north of Scandinavia, more than 15,000 square miles in area. Much of the land lies within the Arctic circle and is characterized by treeless tundra, but some Lapps live as far south as 62°N, where the main vegetation is coniferous forest.

The Lapps probably came from the region of Lake Onega in Russia, moving westwards about 10,000 years ago. The Lappish language, of which several mutually unintelligible dialects are spoken, is related to Finnish and it seems probable that the Lapps were the original inhabitants of Finland. Today the majority, about 20,000, live in Norway. There are 10,000 in Sweden, some 3,000 in Finland, and 2,000 in the Soviet Union.

Traditional Lapp society was organized as a loose association of families. The Lapps had no chiefs or central political authority, but they combined readily in large hunting groups to capture the migrating reindeer, whose habits they well understood. Gradually they began to domesticate the herds and developed their husbandry to a very high degree.

In the forests, Lapps live in permanent settlements with year-round pasture, but some 50 per cent of all Lapps live along the coast, fishing, trapping and farming. Nomadic herding is now restricted to about 10 per cent of the population, whose routes are controlled by the national governments. Herds average 500 animals and the longest journey is 220 miles, much of it covered at night when the snow is hard. The Lapps are suffering severely from industrialization: land has been taken for mining and hydro-electric schemes, and new roads have disrupted the migratory routes.

Danes
pop: 5,079,000

Denmark is a small country consisting of the Jutland peninsula, which extends northwards from the north European plain, and more than 500 islands. The capital, Copenhagen, is located on the largest of these islands. The Danes have had strong links in the past with both the German lands and Scandinavia; their own state first developed in Roman times, uniting populations from Sweden, Finland and the north European plain. The kingdom became powerful during the Middle Ages and, by the Union of Kalmar (1397), Denmark gained control of the entire Scandinavian area. Greenland and the Faeroe Islands still remain part of the Danish kingdom.

Danish peasants were bound to the land until 1788, living in large villages and growing mainly grains on a common field rotation system. Today most farms are small, averaging between 25 and 150 acres, and nearly all are freehold. There is a considerable degree of co-operative enterprise and, although the glacial soils are not generally very fertile, yields per acre are high. Dairy farming has become increasingly important, but more than half the cultivable land is still devoted to cereal production.

Movement into the towns and modern specialist industry developed towards the end of the 19th century. Industry now employs more than twice as many people as agriculture, and cement, ships and porcelain are important exports.

Danish Kingdom at Union of Kalmar, 1397

France, Belgium, Holland, Luxembourg
French, Belgians, Dutch, Luxembourgers

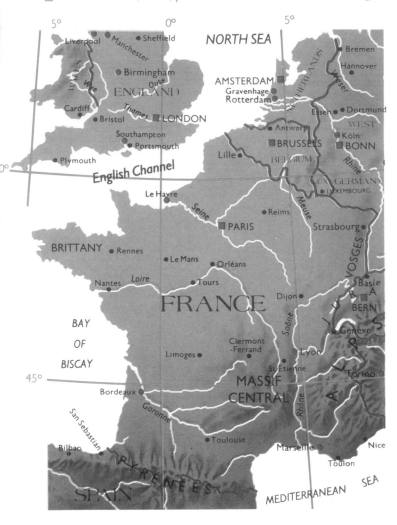

Ethnic divisions of Belgium

- Flemings
- Walloons

French
pop: 53,096,000

France, at 213,000 square miles, is the largest country in Europe and one of the least crowded. Enclosed to the south and south-east by the Pyrenees and Alps, only the eastern frontier is open to easy population movement, a factor which contributed to the early development of national unity. A strong French kingdom centred around Paris began to emerge from the 10th century, and from the reign of Philip Augustus, who ascended the throne in 1180, dates the tradition of strong administrative centralism that is still characteristic of France today.

Local variations, however, are striking. It is a long way both in distance and in culture from Paris, the fourth largest metropolis in the world, to a peasant village in the Massif Central. Several regional languages, including Breton, Basque, Provençal, Corse, Flemish and Alsatian, persist and have formed the basis of separatist movements. A more uniform culture is now spreading over France as a result of mass communication.

Like Britain, France built a large colonial empire, which eventually caused serious political tensions. Defeat in Vietnam in 1954 was followed by a long war in Algeria, from which France withdrew in 1962. A sizeable minority of immigrants from the former colonial territories, including many from tropical Africa, now live as citizens in France.

French industrial development was slow, dominated at first by the small family firm. As late as 1901 only 41 per cent of the population lived in towns of 2,000 or more (the proportion was around 70 per cent in 1971) and they were mainly concentrated in Paris. France is still the greatest agricultural producer in western Europe, with 40 per cent of land under cultivation in 1971.

An inter-war period of stagnating birth rate and economic decline, combined with much political experiment and a great cultural flowering, ended with the crushing military defeat by Germany in 1940. The immense upsurge since then, both economic and demographic, has not occurred without tension. Whole new areas of cities have developed almost overnight, sometimes as shanty towns or clusters of high-rise buildings, and the technocratic middle class has benefited much more from economic progress than has the working class. Since 1945, the efforts of the left wing to achieve national political power have only been resisted with severe strain.

Belgians
pop: 9,826,000

Surrounded by France, Luxembourg, West Germany and the Netherlands, Belgium is a small, densely-populated country covering only 11,781 square miles. It is a meeting place of Latin and Germanic culture and language, and indeed Belgium itself is divided along these lines.

In the region roughly to the north of a line drawn below Brussels live the Flemings, whose language is related to Dutch, and who traditionally occupied the plain of Flanders in small, family farms. In the south and east of the country, where Belgian industry first developed around the coalfields, live the Walloons, French-speakers who until recently dominated the country

through superior numbers and economic power. Now more than half of the population are Flemings, and post-war development has brought increased prosperity to the north.

Religion further divides the two groups. The Flemings extend the influence of the Catholic church to the running of schools, hospitals, trade unions and other institutions, but elsewhere in Belgium their organization is secular.

Brussels is one of the few parts of the country where the groups overlap. Both languages are spoken there, while in other towns and cities bilingualism operates only in theory. Despite independence from the Netherlands since 1830, Belgium is less a unified nation than an internal alliance, tolerated for its economic and political advantages. However, membership of the European Economic Community, whose headquarters are in their capital, has forced Belgians into increasing participation in international affairs.

Dutch
pop: 13,868,000

One-third of the Netherlands lies below sea level, and much of the land has been reclaimed from the sea using a complex system of dykes. The rivers Rhine, Maas and Scheldt enter the North Sea in a broad composite delta, where the Dutch have created a considerable commercial, maritime and industrial economy.

The population is similar ethnically to those found throughout the North Sea basin, and the Dutch language is close to German. Nationhood began to develop in the early Middle Ages, with the establishment of co-operative bodies to reclaim sandy or marshy land, and in the 16th century the Netherlands freed itself from Spanish domination. A division between Calvinism and Catholicism still marks political life, and is reflected in provincial borders.

During the 19th century, building on the transit trade of the Rhine delta, industry was developed at considerable speed. In recent years a great urban horse-shoe, the Randstad, housing more than 4,000,000 people, has linked Amsterdam with Rotterdam. A belt of open land has been preserved in the centre of this region, where a specialist agriculture still employs 18 per cent of the population.

Despite large-scale emigration, encouraged by the government, the Netherlands is one of the world's most densely populated states. Free immigration from Ambon in the Moluccas and Surinam in South America—the legacy of Dutch colonialism—has created a sizeable coloured minority. The demands of immigrant South Moluccans for independence from Indonesia, formerly a Dutch colony, have brought a new bitterness into domestic political life.

Luxembourgers
pop: 361,000

Luxembourg is the smallest fully independent state in Europe, at 999 square miles. The survivor of a much larger feudal state, it has been a grand duchy since 1867. Today the area is a meeting place of French and German culture; nonetheless, Luxembourgers have a strong sense of national identity and their own language, Letzeburgisch.

The land is mainly hilly, with fertile soils in the south (the Gutland or Bon Pays) which are intensively farmed. Local ores, an extension of the huge ironfield of Lorraine, form the basis of an important iron and steel industry. The country is also popular with international organizations and tourists.

Cattle market in the Loire valley, France

Dutch houseboat-owner, Amsterdam

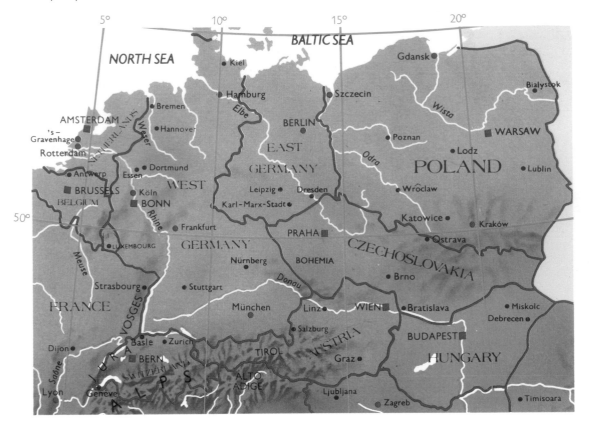

Germans
pop: 78,368,000

It is difficult to define the historical boundaries of German nationality or culture, since Germans have at various times lived throughout the north European plain. The term 'German' entered Roman literature in the second century BC, around which time Germanic peoples began a major expansion from what is now northern West Germany into the whole North Sea basin.

Complex migrations after the fall of Rome produced several distinct population groups (*Volksstämme*) and, until the 19th century, Germany remained a bewildering patchwork of kingdoms, duchies, princedoms and prince-bishoprics. Nonetheless, a common German culture did emerge, given notable expression in the flood of German music and a literary language of great expressiveness and strength.

The emergence of a national state was delayed in the 19th century by the struggle for leadership between Austria and Prussia and this, together with the inclusion in the new state of many Poles and the exclusion of many Germans, was later a source of tensions. East Germany still has a minority of 250,000 Sorbs, descendants of Slavic settlers. With unification, however, Germany embarked upon an intensive industrial revolution. In 1866 two-thirds of the German workforce depended on the land for a living; 50 years later the proportion was one-third, and Germany had replaced Britain as Europe's leading industrial power.

During the Second World War, German capital equipment was almost totally destroyed by bombing and the country was divided and reduced in size. Since then an 'economic miracle'(*Wirtschaftswunder*) has taken place in both Germanies. The Democratic Republic (East Germany), although poorer in natural resources than the Federal Republic, has become the world's seventh greatest industrial power; West Germany is now the third.

The Federal Republic of Germany, (*pop: 61,590,000*) enjoyed an average economic growth rate of 7.9 per cent during the 1960s and has an integrated regional system of production. An almost continuous megalopolis stretches along the rivers Rhine and Main, incorporating the old cities of Essen, Düsseldorf, Cologne, Bonn and Frankfurt. The now divided former capital, Berlin, landlocked in East Germany, is something of a backwater in the West German context, but remains a source of international friction.

The German Democratic Republic (*pop: 16,778,000*) is heavily industrialized in the south but predominantly rural in the north. Shipbuilding has been developed on the Baltic coast to counter this imbalance and agriculture has been mechanized. Villages have been transformed by the establishment of co-operative and collective units: private farms and individual houses alike have given way to modern community centres, with separate housing, work, education and leisure facilities.

Swiss
pop: 6,415,000

Switzerland is a mountainous country at the heart of Europe, where German, French and Italian culture meet. Nationhood has developed gradually and piecemeal since 1291, when three Germanic communities around Lake Lucerne (the Vierwaldstätter See) declared an 'everlasting confederation' independent of the Holy Roman Empire. Over the centuries they were joined by neighbouring communities, and a strong sense of regional loyalty persists. The country is divided into 22 cantons, but since 1848 a federal constitution has been in operation and a modern industrial society has developed, which is noted for cohesion and even conformity.

Most Swiss are at least bilingual, but some 75 per cent of the population speak German as a first language, 20 per cent French and 4 per cent Italian. In 1938 Romansch, a dialect spoken by only 1 per cent of the population, was made the fourth official language of Switzerland.

The task of building a united society has itself contributed to Swiss progress. A tradition of tolerance for refugees has brought many people with skills into the country, while a policy of determined neutrality has promoted the development of banking and international organizations. With few mineral resources, Swiss industrial success is based on skill and technical excellence: most notably, in watchmaking and

Linguistic divisions of Switzerland

- German speakers
- French speakers
- Italian speakers
- Romansch speakers

precision engineering. Only 4 per cent of the population is now in agriculture. Switzerland also derives much income from tourism and insurance services.

Switzerland enjoyed a financial boom after the 1950s, and although this slowed down in the mid-1970s, the country faces problems mainly associated with prosperity. Nearly half the population now live in the four big cities of the central plateau—Zürich, Basle, Geneva and Bern. Villages around the lakes in central Switzerland have tended to merge into each other in an uncontrolled fashion and environmental problems may become pressing.

Austrians
pop: 7,524,000

The present republic of Austria was established in 1919. Some 70 per cent of the land is mountainous, and the bulk of the population lives in the eastern lowlands. Control of the Danube, one of Europe's major trading routes, gave Austria

significant economic advantages in the past.

The nucleus of the modern Austrian state developed after 800 AD as the Ostmark, the eastern frontier region of the Holy Roman Empire, which it eventually came to dominate. Under the Hapsburg dynasty, which ruled for 700 years, Austria controlled a multinational empire in central and eastern Europe and in the 19th century competed with Prussia for the role of leading German state. With the disintegration of the empire in the First World War Austria's weakness was evident and in 1938 it was annexed by the Nazis. Today, straddling the border of East and West, Austria is studiously neutral.

The country is divided into three major regions: the high Alps of western Austria; upper Austria, which is sub-alpine and richly wooded in parts; and lower Austria, which stretches into the Hungarian plain and is the centre of most agriculture and industry. Al-

though there are regional dialects, all Austrians speak the German language.

The population is overwhelmingly Catholic and urbanized; nearly half now live in towns of more than 10,000 people, and Vienna holds one-fifth of the entire population. Only in the Tirol and Salzburg areas has rural depopulation been slight; industry there is limited, but tourism gives a considerable boost to the local economies.

Since the Second World War, Austrian politics have been dominated by the conservative People's Party and the the moderate Socialist Party, often working in unison. Relations between labour and management have been relatively stable, and continuous economic growth with full employment was achieved throughout the 1950s and 1960s. Austria's prosperity is based mainly on industry and trade, with timber, iron and steel accounting for a quarter of all exports.

Tuba players in Ulm, south Germany

97

Poland, Czechoslovakia
Slavs, Poles, Czechoslovaks

BALTIC SEA

Slavs
pop: 260,000,000

The Slavs inhabit much of eastern Europe and the western part of the Soviet Union. They are divided into three main groups, according to language: the eastern Slavs—Russians, Ukrainians and Belorussians; the western Slavs—Poles, Czechs, Slovaks and Sorbs (Wends); and the southern Slavs—Slovenes, Croats, Serbs and Montenegrins.

The Slavs probably originated in the area between the Oder and Dnepr rivers, and subsequently spread to the Balkans, central and eastern Europe and northern Asia. Languages within the group are clearly related and some are mutually understandable. All are now established as the main language either of independent states or of autonomous parts of states in the areas affected by Slav influence.

In most areas the traditional Slavic culture has been abandoned, with only elements such as the *zadrugas*, extended family agricultural and dwelling units, surviving. Slav religion was rich in ritual and involved numerous deities and spirits; some aspects of this belief system persist in folk-lore.

Poles
pop: 34,566,000

The Poles belong to the western group of Slavs and are closely related to the Czechs

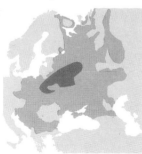

Slav Expansion

■ Slav distribution 200 BC-200 AD
▨ Present distribution of Slavs

and Slovaks. Apart from some mountainous areas in the south, Poland lies entirely within the vast north European plain; the name means 'field country'. The boundaries have often moved as Poland's relationships with its neighbours have changed, but the centre of the country today corresponds closely to that of the original Polish state, founded 1,000 years ago.

In the later Middle Ages, Poland became a major power, with very large territories, but by the 18th century it was surrounded by aggressive, tightly-organized autocratic states. The first partition of Poland between Russia, Prussia and Austria took place in 1772. Poland became independent again in 1918 and almost immediately won large territorial gains from Russia, only to fall under Soviet domination after 1945. Society in Poland in the inter-war period was overwhelmingly rural, organized in a close network of settled agricultural communities, with a powerful landed nobility.

In the 1945 settlement Poland was shifted to the west, losing 40 per cent of its agricultural land but gaining the important industrial region of Silesia. The country is now highly industrialized, with more than 50 per cent of the population living in towns. Development has been concentrated on heavy industry and improvements in the standard of living have been slow.

Poland is sufficiently powerful economically to be treated with respect by the Soviet Union, which does not in practice interfere in domestic affairs. Uniquely for a Soviet-bloc country, 85 per cent of land is privately owned and there are many private businesses in the industrial sector. The government can be forced to be responsive by a well-organized workforce, as was demonstrated by industrial strife during the early 1970s.

Czechoslovaks
pop: 14,989,000

There are two main peoples in Czechoslovakia, the Czechs and Slovaks, who have maintained a precarious unity since the state was formed in 1918. Both are descended from Slavic

tribes who moved into the area in the 5th and 6th centuries AD; their customs are similar and their languages are mutually understandable.

The Czechs, who inhabit mainly the fertile plateau of Bohemia, outnumber the Slovaks by two to one and in modern times have attained a much higher degree of prosperity. Regional differences are gradually disappearing, however, while tensions between the majority peoples and the various national minorities, especially the Germans, are now much diminished. Some Magyars, Ruthenes and Germans still speak their own languages in Czechoslovakia.

The history of the region is one of constant struggle between the Slavs and Germans. There was a major Germanic migration into the country from the 11th century onwards and the first of all German universities was founded in Prague in 1348. From the 17th century onwards native culture was heavily repressed by a German ruling class, but during the 19th century vigorous and successful attempts were made to revive Czech culture and language. At the same time Bohemia became the main industrial region of the Austro-Hungarian empire and peasants flocked into the growing towns. Owing to the lack of a native upper class, a relatively egalitarian society was created, with values of education and frugality widely dispersed among the population.

The collapse of the Austro-Hungarian empire in the First World War gave Czechoslovakia a long period of independence before the brutal Nazi conquest of 1938. At the end of the war, it came under Soviet hegemony, and since 1945 industry has continued a steady and impressive growth, now employing nearly half of the working population. The chemical and metallurgical sectors have grown fast, and industry, especially leather processing, has spread into Slovakia, which now accounts for 20 per cent of industrial production. The agricultural sector, dominated by extensive collective farms, is prosperous. In 1968, a reformist government was overthrown by invading Soviet forces.

photograph:
Cafe at night, Czechoslovakia

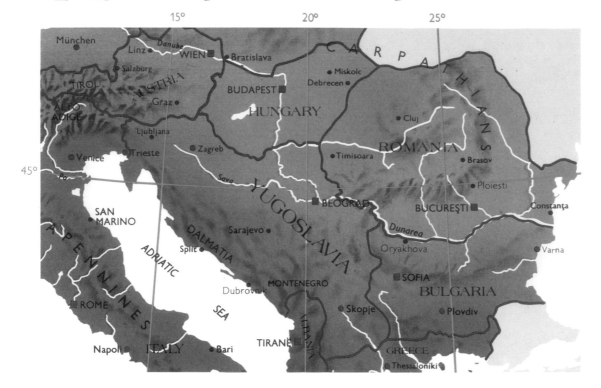

Yugoslavs

pop: 21,650,000

Apart from the Danube valley in the north-east and the valley of the Vardar in the south, Yugoslavia is a mainly mountainous country. The ancient inhabitants of the area were the Illyrians, who are thought to have been the ancestors of the Albanians, and from the 6th to 8th centuries AD there was a massive incursion of Slavs, who all spoke closely related tongues.

Over the following centuries political circumstances and changing cultural affiliations tended to divide these peoples into various embryo nationalities, and in the early modern period the Austrian and Turkish empires divided the area between them. In the 19th century the Serbs, who live in what is now eastern Yugoslavia, won a measure of independence from Turkey, and after the disintegration of the old empires in 1918 a 'kingdom of the southern Slavs' was formed. The boundaries of this state have been substantially maintained under the communist administration which emerged from the Second World War.

There are six major and 18 minor ethnic groupings among the Yugoslavs; two alphabets, the Latin and Cyrillic; three major languages, Serbo-Croat, Slovene and Macedonian; and three important religions, the Roman Catholic, Greek Orthodox and Islamic. The two major ethnic groups are the Serbs and the Croats, who speak dialects of a common language but are culturally very distinct, the Croats being Roman Catholic and westward-oriented, and the Serbs Orthodox and self-consciously Slav.

Economic differences tend to be divisive. There was a high annual growth rate in the 1960s but this has mainly benefited the more developed northern regions: on average a Croat is about five times more wealthy than a Macedonian. The government, however, has made vigorous attempts to diminish social tensions, and an ambitious programme of decentralization has been mounted.

Yugoslavia practises a markedly experimental form of communism, in which workers' councils play an important role and state control is minimal. About 80 per cent of the national income now comes from the social and co-operative sector, and more than 1,000,000 jobs have been created in industry since the war.

Hungarians

pop: 10,634,000

The Hungarians occupy the low-lying central portions of the Danube basin, with some higher ground to the north. The date traditionally given for their arrival in these lands is 896 AD, but they had probably been migrating westwards from the steppe lands north of the Black Sea for several centuries before that. Many Slavs and Germans arrived during the medieval and modern periods. The Hungarian language, Magyar, is unrelated to any other European language except perhaps Finnish.

In 1910 two-thirds of all Hungarians earned their living from the land. Traditional Hungarian society, which survived until the communist period, was rural and hierarchical; the development of commercial life was left largely to foreigners. Indeed, urban settlement was not characteristic of Hungary, and in the Alfold, or great plain, a type of village as large as many towns, but without urban functions, was more common.

More than half the population is now urbanized, with more than 2,000,000 people in Greater Budapest alone. Industry contributes some 60 per cent of the national income, but emphasis has been on heavy engineering. Hungary's dependence on imported minerals has been alleviated by the discovery of bauxite deposits.

Communist rule has not encouraged popular participation in politics. The Soviet repression of a Hungarian rebellion in 1956 had the effect of turning many people away from politics, often to the pursuit of higher living standards. Frustrations are frequently expressed in an indiscriminate dislike of everything Russian.

Further social tension has accompanied the emergence of a privileged class—functionaries, civil servants, managers and those allowed by the government to work in the small but profitable private sector. Industrial workers sometimes feel that their part in making the economy prosper has not been adequately rewarded.

Romanians

pop: 21,555,000

With extremely varied topography, Romania is roughly the same size as West Germany, but much less heavily populated. Despite a complex and turbulent history, Romanians have strong cultural unity and

a deep sense of nationhood. The Emperor Trajan incorporated the region into the Roman Empire in 106 AD. The Romans called the province Dacia, and the ancient peoples from whom the Romanians trace their descent were known as Dacians or Vlachs. During the Dark Ages there were many Slav admixtures to the Dacio-Roman population, but the survival of the Romanian language, which is based on Latin with Slav and Turkish loan words, proves an element of cultural continuity.

In the Middle Ages two principalities developed, Moldavia and Wallachia, which won independence and unity under French 'protection' in 1856. Romania suffered a marked reduction in territory after the Second World War, when coming under Soviet hegemony. Today, although the Romanians are perhaps the most rigid of the satellite countries in their internal policies, they are also the most insubordinate in their attitude towards the Soviet Union.

The national population is 85 per cent Romanian, but Hungarians form 10 per cent of the population in Transylvania, the northern part of Romania, and there are also small minorities of Germans, Jews and Gypsies. Two-thirds of the population are still in agriculture, but Romania gains half its income from mining and manufacturing. It is Europe's largest producer of oil and the world's eighth largest wheat producer.

Bulgarians
pop: 8,795,000

The word *bulgar* means 'a man of mixed blood', and Bulgarian ethnicity is complex. The Bulgars were a tribe of Turkic origin who moved into the Danube basin in the 7th century AD, but they were quickly absorbed into the older Slav and ancient Thracian populations, with whom they founded the first Bulgarian state in 681 AD. Over the next centuries there were many Asiatic admixtures to the population, and many Turks were absorbed between the 14th and 19th centuries, when Bulgaria was part of the Ottoman Empire. Today the Turks are the most substantial national minority although there has been a tendency for them to emigrate home; the Gypsies are the most numerous of several other minorities.

Occupying the fertile Danube basin, Bulgaria has long been subject to imperial contact. Byzantine and Ottoman influences were most important in earlier centuries; in modern times the dominant cultural influence has been that of Russia, under whose 'protection' Bulgaria became an independent state in 1878. Since 1945 the country has been firmly within the Soviet orbit.

The topography of Bulgaria is varied, with broken mountain ranges and intermittent plains, but nearly half the land is under cultivation; wheat is the principal crop. Before the Second World War agriculture was peasant-based, but collectivization has improved rural living standards and agricultural production. Industry has developed more rapidly than in any other Balkan country since the war, but the emphasis has been on heavy engineering and consumer industry has been relatively neglected.

Street scene in Sofia, the Bulgarian capital

Montenegrins

pop: 541,000

Montenegro forms the southwestern part of Yugoslavia, to the north of Albania, and consists mainly of elevated ridges. It forms part of the larger Serb cultural area and Serbo-Croat is the language spoken, but while the Serbs were defeated by the Turks at Kosovo (1389), Montenegro remained independent of the Turkish empire. In the 19th century it emerged as a Balkan kingdom, but was forcibly annexed to the new Yugoslavia in 1918.

In recent years the Montenegrins have been markedly hostile to the communist government ruling from Belgrade. Primarily agriculturalists, their main activity is now livestock breeding and some staple foods are imported. There are few towns in the area and a rich rural culture has survived. The chief town is Titograd, with a population of 22,000.

Albanians

pop: 2,499,000

The modern Albanians may be descended from the Illyrians, an Indo-European people who moved into the area in the first millennium BC, although there have been later Slav admixtures to the population. The Albanian language is not related to any other spoken in Europe. In the past, settlement was in remote mountain pockets and Albanian nationhood is largely a product of the 20th century. The country has been independent since 1912 and a fairly homogeneous society has developed; 98 per cent of the people are Albanian in nationality and language, but they are divided by religion into Muslim, Roman Catholic and Greek Orthodox.

In the past there were two main groups of Albanians. The Tosks, who lived in the southern, more lowland area, were tenant workers on the large feudal estates of Muslim Turkish landowners. The mountain dwelling Ghegs of the north, however, were one of the few tribal peoples surviving in Europe at the start of the 20th century. Society was organized around the patrilineal clan and the extended family, and was regulated by a fierce code of honour. The blood-feud was so common that families sometimes had to live under siege conditions and a distinctive type of fortified house (*kulla*) was evolved. The household (*shpi*) was the basic social unit; families as large as 100 members sometimes lived together under the parental roof.

Industrial development, which stems from modern communist rule, is very recent. In 1939 only 15 per cent of the population lived in towns and there were no railways until 1948. However, Albania is rich in mineral resources, and by the mid-1960s industry already accounted for one half of the national income. New towns such as Tirane and Durres are burgeoning, and large collective farms have been developed on the coastal swamps. Despite strong links with China from the 1960s, Albania's leaders show a fierce determination to retain independent control of their country's development.

Gypsies

pop: 5,000,000

Alone among modern nomadic or semi-nomadic peoples, the Gypsies are dispersed worldwide and interact fully with urban and industrial society. Their origin was long in dispute, but in the late 19th century the identification of their language, Romani, with an archaic dialect of Sanskrit, established that they were largely of Indian origin.

Medieval records suggest that they began to migrate westwards as early as the 10th century; they are first mentioned in Cretan records in 1252 and they had moved as far as Paris by 1427. Initially, representing themselves as Christian pilgrims returned from Egypt, they were well received by local populations. However, owing to their efforts to support themselves by horse-dealing, tinkering, entertaining and begging, they came to be regarded as thieves and vagabonds and severe persecution began from about 1500.

Methods of dealing with the Gypsies have differed widely in various European countries. In 1572 they were banished from Venice, Milan and Parma; but in Russia, Catherine the Great attempted to assimilate

them as serfs. In 1725 Frederick William I of Prussia ordered all Gypsies over the age of 18 to be hanged, irrespective of sex (in parts of the Austro-Hungarian empire at the same period female Gypsies were merely shorn of an ear). More recently, Hitler organized the murder of 500,000 Gypsies.

Over the last two decades many organizations have been set up to represent the Gypsies, one of which, called Romanistan, agitates for a national homeland. The first international congress of Gypsies met at Orpington, England in 1972. In recent years the Catholic Church has taken a positive interest in the welfare of Gypsies, especially in Spain,

and this has led to some weakening of traditional Gypsy culture. In general, however, their sense of identity and community have remained strong.

Gypsies are widely dispersed throughout Europe, North Africa and North America; more than a million live in the Soviet Union. They are organized in four great tribes, subdivided into lineages whose members trace common patrilineal descent from a founding ancestor. Lineage members, although widely scattered, come together to defend common interests. Monogamous marriage within the lineage or between members of friendly lineages is generally preferred. Although there are new Gypsy churches,

religion is in general a form of ancestor worship. Social life is marked by elaborate ritual restrictions, almost total lack of routine, love of fun and celebration, and a feeling of alienation from the foreigners or *payos* who surround them.

Some Gypsies, especially the Spanish Gitanos, no longer speak pure Romani; many now live in flats or carpeted caves. With increasing sedentarization and the Gypsies' reluctance to deal with national authorities, attempts to estimate the population are difficult. The problem is exacerbated because other itinerant peoples, speaking a variety of argots, are frequently confused with the Gypsies themselves.

Gypsies travelling through the Balkans

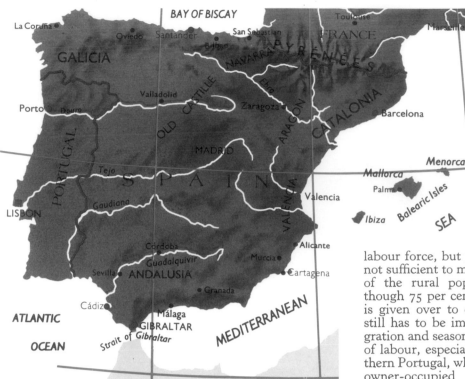

try led eventually to the election of a moderate socialist government. Like Spain, Portugal is now applying for membership of the European Economic Community.

Spaniards

pop: 36,161,000

Spain is the third largest European country, occupying most of the Iberian peninsula. The central region is a semi-arid upland plateau, but on the fringes of the country, especially in the north, are richer lowlands. The Spanish are ethnically very mixed, the country having suffered many invasions over the centuries, and regional loyalties are strong. Some 200,000 Gypsies still lead a nomadic life, and are found mostly in Andalusia.

Spain came under Arab domination in the 8th century and it was 500 years before the north became free of Muslim rule, in the early Middle Ages. Liberation elsewhere was delayed, but Granada was finally annexed to the Spanish crown in 1492 and Spain entered on an era of massive colonial expansion in Central and South America. Most of these imperial possessions were lost during the 19th century, following Napoleon's invasion of the Iberian peninsula, but Spanish remains the official language throughout much of Latin America.

Despite regional variations, there is a distinctively Spanish culture. Sociability and finesse of manners are valued by all classes. The Mediterranean morality of honour and shame, seen most clearly in the man's duty to protect his family and the emphasis on sexual modesty in women, is deeply ingrained. Roman Catholicism and the survival of popular events such as the fiesta and the bull-fight further strengthen Spanish cultural identity.

Drought, salinity, erosion and excessive monoculture have caused major problems for agriculture and until recently Spain was a very poor country. In the north the isolated farm is the traditional economic unit, in the centre the agricultural village and in the south the great estate. The 'stabilization' plan of 1959 marked the beginning of very

Portuguese

pop: 9,587,000

The Portuguese are a homogeneous and culturally united people, whose language is spoken with very few regional variations. Portugal was the first of the European nation states, being consolidated into one political unit during the 12th century, and although not markedly isolated from Spain (all the major rivers of the country rise in Spain), it fell only briefly under Spanish rule, between 1580 and 1640. During this long period of independence, it has developed a rich and distinctive culture, of which the unique Manueline style of architecture is perhaps the most famous aspect.

Portugal was both the first and last of the European states to maintain an overseas empire. The first voyages of discovery left from Lisbon during the 14th century; Portuguese rule in southern Africa ended abruptly and chaotically in 1973.

Meanwhile the country had become peripheral to world affairs and increasingly impoverished. It has the highest illiteracy rate and the lowest standard of living in western Europe, and very many villages are still without electricity and running water. Agriculture employs about 25 per cent of the labour force, but production is not sufficient to meet the needs of the rural population. Although 75 per cent of the land is given over to cereals, grain still has to be imported. Emigration and seasonal movement of labour, especially from northern Portugal, where the small owner-occupied farm rather than the large estate has been traditional, continued to increase in the 1960s. Between 1960 and 1970 more than a million people left the country to work elsewhere.

For such a small country Portugal has surprisingly wide variations in landscape and economy, and many cultural distinctions remain. In the northern provinces of Minho, Trásos Montes and the Beiras traces of medieval village community organization can still be found. Religious festivals (*romarias*) often last several days and include singing, dancing and bull-fights in which, unlike those in Spain, the bull is not killed.

The quasi-fascist régime which ruled Portugal from 1928 to 1974 maintained stability at the cost of stagnation. Industrial development was slow until the 1960s and even now industry consists mainly of food processing, textiles and construction. It is concentrated in the two main cities, Lisbon and Porto, which together house about 40 per cent of the population.

The revolution that broke out on April 25th, 1974, followed a long period of social and economic unrest, but was precipitated by dissatisfaction among army officers with the conduct of Portugal's colonial affairs. A period of intense politicization within the coun-

rapid industrial expansion, directed by the state holding company and the five major banks of Spain, but this centralized authority did not disperse the new prosperity, and one-third of Spanish firms are still found within 20 miles of Barcelona. Outside Catalonia, Madrid and the Basque country, industry is found only in isolated patches.

The death of General Franco in 1975 ended a Fascist dictatorship that had lasted nearly 30 years. Social tensions have since been given free expression, with the Communist Party restored to full legality and the release of political prisoners. Regional autonomy, granted to Catalonia in 1977, may also be extended to the Basque country.

Galicians
pop: 2,600,000

A hilly region in the extreme north-west corner of Spain, Galicia is one of the poorest parts of the country. Two-thirds of the population still derive their living from the land. Vigo is an important fishing port, but industry is otherwise confined largely to food processing.

Galicia was an area of Celtic and later of Visigothic settlement and during the early Middle Ages strong Galicician kingdoms flourished; the people remain distinctive and have their own language, Gallego, from which modern Portuguese originated. Now spoken mainly in rural areas, Gallego was once the foremost literary language of the Iberian peninsula and there are attempts to revive it in Galician intellectual circles.

Basques
pop: 1,500,000

The Basques occupy an area of about 3,000 square miles in the inner corner of the Bay of Biscay, from Bayonne in southern France to Bilbao in northern Spain. The greater part of the Basque region is in Spain, between the Cantabrians and the Pyrenees, and it is here that Basque nationhood is most strongly developed, with an active separatist movement and a standard of living that is twice the Spanish average. The French Basques, by contrast, inhabit one of the most underdeveloped rural areas of France and there is heavy emigration to other parts of the country.

The Basques are one of the more culturally distinct groups in Europe, but their ethnic origin is still a matter of debate. Their language, Basque, is of considerable complexity and unrelated to any other European tongue. They were already established as a distinct people when the Romans completed the conquest of the Iberian peninsula in 19 BC, and retained some independence even during the Roman period. In the Middle Ages they came under the jurisdiction of the kings of Castile but were able to retain many local privileges (*fueros*). During the short-lived republican régime (1931–36) they were granted regional autonomy; this was withdrawn by the Fascists under General Franco, but now seems likely to be restored by Spain's social democratic government.

The mountainous terrain has contributed to isolation from Spain, yet Basque country lies on the main highway between Spain and the rest of Europe. Agriculture has always been fairly poor, but the Basques developed a maritime economy and by the 15th century had a virtual monopoly of the European whaling trade. Since the late 19th century an industrial revolution, based on hydroelectric power, has taken place in the Spanish region: in the biggest town, Bilbao, with a population of 370,000, there are now blast furnaces, steel mills, shipyards and heavy engineering works.

In the rural areas traditional life survives with many distinct regional features. The isolated Basque farmhouse (*basseria*), built around a single ground-floor room with an open space to allow carts in, is the basic economic unit of rural society. It houses an extended family who work co-operatively, and is passed intact from one generation to the next.

Catalans
pop: 5,125,000

Present-day Catalonia consists officially of four provinces of north-west Spain, between the Mediterranean and the Pyrenees, but the area in which Catalan is spoken is considerably greater than this. Centred on Barcelona, it is the most industrialized part of Spain, with extremely articulate working and middle classes. Separatist demands are persistent and well-supported and the continuing strength of the Catalan language is an index of their intensity. However, the sense of ethnic identity is founded less on distinctive cultural traits than on the consciousness of a common historic, economic and political experience.

Catalonia was the first area of Spain to free itself from Muslim domination, and a Catalan state flourished during the 13th and 14th centuries, claiming colonies as far away as the Balkans. Since the later 19th century industrial growth has been rapid; in 1818 Barcelona had only 83,000 inhabitants but by 1975 this had grown to almost 4,000,000. Regional autonomy, granted by the Republican régime in 1932, but withdrawn by the Fascists under General Franco, was restored to Catalonia in 1977.

Andalusians
pop: 6,000,000

Andalusia includes most of Spain south of the Sierra Morena, which since 1833 has been divided into the eight provinces of Almería, Cadíz, Córdoba, Huelva, Jaén, Málaga, Seville and Granada. During the 5th century AD it was occupied by the Vandals, and in 711 was invaded from Tangier by Tarik ibn Ziyad. Before their expulsion in the 15th century the Arabs built magnificent palaces and fortresses, including the Alhambra at Granada and Andalusian Spanish retains many Arabic words.

Arab influence is still seen in Andalusian life. In this dry, mountainous region, villagers work terraced small-holdings irrigated by Muslim systems of channels and water wheels; among the many crops, almonds, apricots and sugar cane were introduced by the Arabs. Ranches for stock rearing are found on the coastal plains. This century the Sierra Morena has become an important mining region, and tourism is hightly developed along the Costa del Sol.

Corsicans

pop: 219,000

With its granitic soils, mountainous interior and widespead covering of *maquis* scrub, Corsica is separated from Sardinia to the south by a narrow strait. Although most Corsicans speak Corse, a dialect of Italian, French is the official language. The island has been part of France since 1768 and is one of its poorest administrative *départements*. The traditional subsistence economy was based on animal husbandry and agriculture, with cereals, chestnuts, olives and grapes the most important crops.

Despite frequent foreign invasions, Corsica remained essentially isolated until the First World War. Most of the indigenous population retreated long ago into the valleys between the two mountain ranges, where they lived in autonomous village groups which held land collectively. Domestic exchange was based on barter and payment in kind, and village affairs were regulated by a body of customary law well adapted to the environment.

Within the villages, the basic social unit was the extended family. Emphasis on the values of family honour and independence was reflected in the use of *vendetta* and the feud for settling disputes and maintaining order in the absence of any central authority. As individual families grew stronger, however, the collective landholding tended to break down into a system of private holdings and patronage.

During the 20th century agriculture has become increasingly uncompetitive and imports are increasing, while a steady rate of emigration keeps the population in decline. However, the coastal lowlands were finally cleared of malaria by 1952, and there more specialist agriculture is developing, along with tourism. Industry remains very underdeveloped.

Sards

pop: 1,495,000

Sardinia lies 120 miles to the west of central Italy, and is separated from Corsica to the north by a narrow strait. It has a degree of administrative autonomy from Italy and its culture differs from that of the mainland in several respects. Although Italian is the common language, the dialects spoken are as close to Latin as to modern Italian, while the distinctive history of Sardinia, which was a province first of the Byzantine Empire and later of Spain, has reinforced its individuality.

Sardinia was incorporated into the newly-founded Italian state in 1861, but until comparatively recently government control of the mountainous interior was tenuous and ineffective. Banditry—an archaic form of peasant protest—was endemic in the Barbagia until well after the Second World War; and in the mixed peasant and pastoralist communities of the interior feuding and sheep rustling (*abigeato*) were important mechanisms of social control.

Since 1950 the Italian government has made conscientious efforts to develop the island, and several economic plans have been put into operation. Some economic diversification has taken place, but Cagliari, with a population of 220,000, remains the only important industrial and commercial centre. For the great majority of Sard peasants and shepherds emigration to mainland north Italy and Common Market countries has proved the only viable way of improving living standards.

Italians

pop: 56,410,000

Italy is a land of marked regional contrast. Ethnic minorities proper—Albanian communities in the south, French-speaking enclaves in Piedmont, Germans in the Alto Adige—constitute only a tiny fraction of the population, but even amongst the Italian-speaking, overwhelmingly Catholic majority, there are striking differences in dialect, diet, codes of behaviour and living standards. The product of long centuries of economic and political fragmentation between the breakdown of the Roman Empire and the unification of Italy in 1861, these have been only partially eroded by the introduction of standardized national education programmes and, more recently, by the impact of the mass media.

By far the most important of these differences is the social and economic disparity between north and south. Until well after the Second World War the Italian south, with its mixture of large, absentee-owned, cereal estates and fragmented peasant plots, was one of the poorest and most underdeveloped regions in Europe. The contrast between the 'two Italies' was heightened by the rapid industrial expansion of northern Italy in the 1950s and early 1960s, particularly in the triangle of Turin, Genoa and Milan. Since 1950 the Italian government has actively sought to develop the southern economy, but their overall objective of achieving economic parity between north and south has not been achieved.

Italy's rapid transformation into a modern industrial state has produced a series of problems. The northern industrial cities, overwhelmed by the influx of migrants and rapid, largely uncontrolled, industrial growth, suffer from pollution, overcrowding and the near breakdown of social and welfare services. Bureaucratic inefficiency and a patronage-

based political and administrative system (*sotto governo*) have led to widespread corruption and the dissipation of scarce development resources. Growing social tensions and an upsurge in political violence threaten the delicate balance of centre and left wing government parties on which the Italian policy-making system has come to depend

Sicilians
pop: 5,000,000

Sicily is the largest island in the Mediterranean and is the third most populous of the regions of Italy. At one point it is separated by only two miles from the southern tip of the Italian mainland. Yet its cultural heritage is one of the most complex in Europe: there are native Sicilian, Greek, Carthaginian, Norman, Albanian, Spanish, Italian, Arab and Berber elements in the population. Although Italian is the main language, there are some surviving Albanian and Greek dialects.

The structural characteristics of Sicilian society are not greatly different from those of the southern Italian mainland as a whole, but its remoteness from cultural and political centres has given its values and institutions a sharp and distinctive edge. Thus, the Mafia, best known of Sicilian institutions, is effectively confined to western Sicily, although the conditions which produced it—the introduction of capitalism into 19th century rural society—and the values that support it—*omertà* (manliness), distrust of the state, and the belief that an honourable man should settle personal disputes without recourse to the law—are common throughout southern Italy.

Half the labour force is in agriculture; a wide area is cultivated but productivity is low, due mainly to the dominance of large inefficient estates. Until 1945 industry was limited to fruit processing and sulphur mining. The discovery of oil and gas deposits in the 1950s gave a modest boost to the economy and as a result of government intervention parts of the southern and eastern seaboard are now partially industrialized.

Harvest picnic, southern Italy

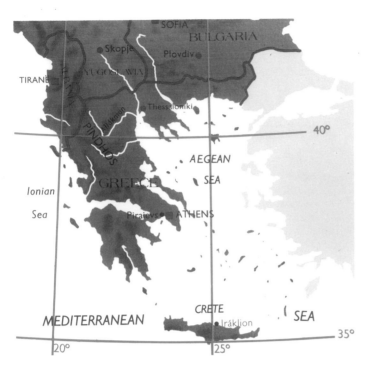

Macedonia

Macedonians

pop: 3,370,000

Macedonia extends from the Nestos river in the south-central Balkans to the west Rhodope mountains and is divided politically between Greece, Yugoslavia and Bulgaria. The area is mountainous, with some fertile basins, and agriculture is the mainstay of the economy. The principal city, Salonika in Greece, has most of the industry in the region.

Macedonia was an important kingdom in the ancient world, and has a distinctive Slavic language akin to Bulgarian. A Macedonian independence movement gained considerable strength at the beginning of the 20th century, but an attempted uprising in 1903 was brutally suppressed by the Turks. In the inter-war period Turks, Greeks, Vlachs, Jews, Gypsies, Albanians and Bulgarians also inhabited the region, but mass population exchanges have simplified the situation since the Second World War.

Greeks

pop: 9,123,000

The Greeks occupy the southern part of the Balkan peninsula and numerous islands, which comprise about a quarter of the national territory. Only 26 per cent of the land surface is cultivable, but the popula-

tion has always been predominantly agricultural. Since the Second World War the peasant economy has begun to collapse in the face of rapid urbanization and industrialization.

The roots of Greek culture lie in the villages, where particular emphasis is placed on the social virtues of honour and shame. In theory, these apply equally to both men and women, but in practice honour is the term applied to ideal masculine behaviour, shame to that of women.

A man derives honour from protecting his family, in both economic and moral terms. In the traditional areas, this involves acts of physical courage and moral endurance, but in districts which are more influenced by modern values, the demands of honour tend to be channelled into the pursuit of prosperity. To some extent, honour also conditions men to vanity and self-assertion.

For women, the values of shame are centred on sexual modesty, demanding chastity in unmarried girls and total fidelity in married women. Sexual shame is the keystone of a woman's moral and social personality, and all other qualities tend to be judged by its presence or absence. Marriages are still arranged in village society, for love matches could endanger the family interest.

Villagers regard the family on earth as a reflection of the heavenly family, and it is within the home that their religious values are most clearly seen. Hospitality is a cardinal virtue: guests and strangers, once under the protection of the house, are treated with extreme generosity. Between villagers, however, there is a spirit of intense competition — envy, jealousy, suspicion and quarrels are common.

In recent years, emigration from the villages has damaged the rural economies and challenged the traditional sense of purpose. Many single men now work abroad, principally in Germany and Canada, or simply move to the towns. Similarly, women are drawn to men who will take them away from the rural life. Greater Athens alone now holds 20 per cent of the population.

Since Greece achieved independence in 1830, after 400

years of Turkish occupation, the country has increasingly been involved in world events. Arguments with Turkey continue to be bitter, particularly with regard to Cyprus and the exploitation of oil reserves beneath the Aegean Sea. Nonetheless, internal arguments between the left and right, exacerbated in the past by the involvement of the monarchy, dominate political attitudes.

Cretans

pop: 500,000

Extending over 3,189 square miles, Crete is the largest of the Greek islands. Its geographical position was fundamental to its importance in history, and since the Minoan civilization which flourished there around 2000 BC, the island has come under Arab, Venetian, Turkish and Greek domination. In the Second World War it was occupied by German forces.

Agriculture plays an important role in the Cretan economy; the existing industry is centred on the processing of agricultural produce, particularly olives, grapes and animal products. However, only about 30 per cent of the total area can be used for farming, as severe deforestation and soil erosion have occurred in the uplands.

Farms are generally small and family-run without much mechanical assistance. The rural population forms a pattern of villages, from which the inhabitants must travel to their surrounding fields. The Cretan system of land inheritance tends to result in the splitting of fields into small, separated lots which make mechanized farming methods difficult to implement. An exception to this is the Mesarás plain, where more favourable soil and rainfall contribute to the economic prosperity of the region.

Most Cretans belong to a separate branch of the Greek Orthodox Church, and participate in its festivals and ritual. Priests were the only native leaders under Turkish rule, and retain some of their former status. There are innumerable wayside shrines and chapels, but many elements of Cretan Christianity show elements of an older paganism, and folklore abounds in the more remote parts of the island.

photograph:
Villagers in Thessaly, Greece

Middle East/North Africa

ATLANTIC OCEAN

MEDITERRA

Straits of Gibraltar
Tangier
RABAT
Casablanca
ALGIER
TUNIS

Marrakech
HAUT ATLAS
Mt Toubkal
TRIPOLI

MOROCCO
TUNISIA

Tarfaya
ALGERIA
Ghudāmis

Ain Salah
LIE
Marzuq

HAGGAR

MAURITANIA
SAHARA

NOUAKCHOTT

Senegal

VEGETATION

Conifer Forest
Pine, spruce, larch

Broadleaf Forest
Deciduous

Temperate
Arable, broadleaf grass

Mediterranean
Citrus, olive, agave

Subtropical
Dry and wet evergreen

Tropical
'Selva'

Steppe
Short grass

Savanna
Grass and scrub

Semi Desert
Cactus, sparse shrub and grass

Desert
No vegetation

Marsh and Swamp

Salt
Salt lake, marsh

■ Capital Cities
● Major Towns
• Towns
Small town village

━━ Country Borders

━━ Borders
Provinces, states

The Middle East and North Africa present a harsh physical environment and, with the exception of huge oil reserves, very limited natural resources. Most of the land is virtually uninhabitable, With vast areas of desert in the south and immense fold mountains to the north in Turkey, Iraq and Iran. In the west, the Atlas mountains range from Morocco to Tunisia, falling away considerably towards the east. Landscapes elsewhere are mostly wide and open, broken only by the uplands of western Syria and Lebanon, the mountains of western Arabia and Yemen, and Egypt's eastern highlands. The most important rivers are the Nile and the Tigris-Euphrates systems; many others have insufficient volume to break through to the sea, and end in salt basins or swamps.

The climate is characterized by long, intensely hot and almost totally dry summers, and a winter that is stormy at times, calm at others, with heavy rain in the northern and western hills. From early June to mid-October cloud cover is scarce and temperatures over 55°C are not uncommon—far hotter than at the equator. Parts of the region have rain only once in several years, with much of the Sahara, inner Arabia and eastern Iran practically rainless. Winter temperatures are mild near the coasts, but sharp cold can prevail inland; in the north and east conditions are bitter with snow lying for three months or more in highland areas.

Despite its aridity, the region has a rich plant life. In the cooler areas of high rainfall—chiefly the hills of the centre and the north—there were once extensive woodlands, but centuries of woodcutting reduced much of this to scrub, and recovery was often prevented by goats grazing unrestricted. The deserts to the south have practically no vegetation: in the driest parts there are sand formations in the form of ridges and dunes, often crescent-shaped and as much as several hundred miles in length, or else irregular seas of sand. On the desert fringes, however, plants are more numerous and there is a gradual transition to steppe conditions—permanent clumps of low bushes and a flush of grass in winter and spring.

Despite the many obstacles to permanent settlement, some of the most significant human advances have been made in the Middle East. Agriculture was first developed here, and the first cities emerged in the river valleys of Mesopotamia and Egypt. The great empires of the Persians, Arabs and the Ottoman Turks were founded on the Fertile Crescent formed by the Tigris-Euphrates and the eastern Mediterranean seaboard, and three of the world's major religions—Judaism, Christianity and Islam—were born in the Middle East.

Arabic became the main language of the whole region following the rise of Islam in the 7th century AD. Within 100 years, Bedouin warriors had conquered the entire region, most of Spain and parts of central Asia. Earlier languages such as Aramaic virtually disappeared. Today the Arabic of the press and literature is an extremely constant international language, intelligible and substantially the same from Morocco to Iraq. There are considerable differences in the spoken language as a result of loan words from other languages and regional variations in pronunciation, but a common

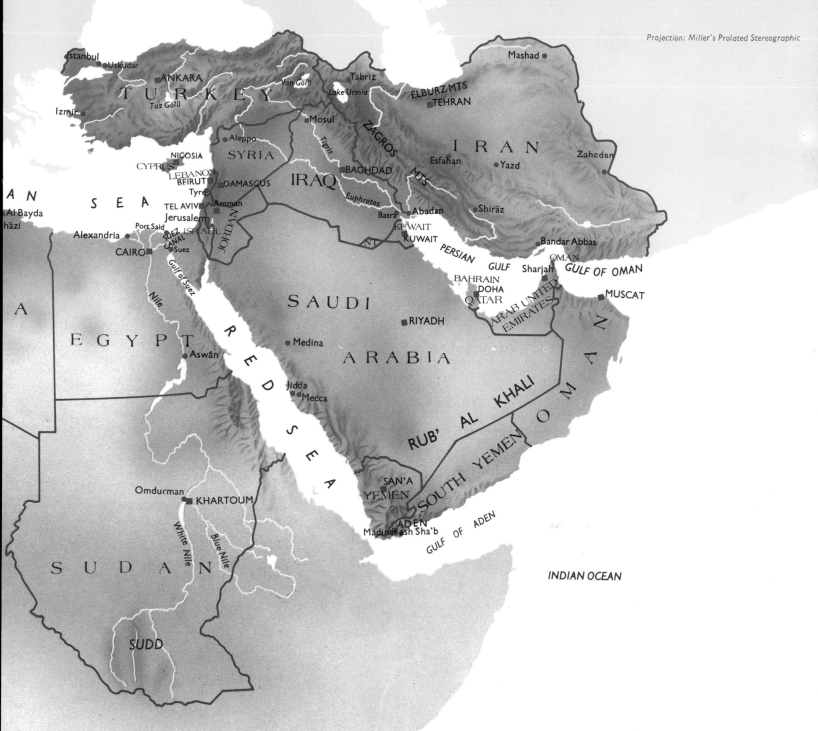

Projection: Miller's Prolated Stereographic

colloquial form based on current press usage serves as a *lingua franca* among literate people.

The dominance of Arabic is, however, by no means complete, and the process of Arabization failed to penetrate the mountainous zones in the north and the west. Turkish, the language of the Ottoman conquerors, is spoken in Asia Minor, and important Turkish-speaking minorities are also found in Iran. The third major language group of the Middle East is Iranian, which forms a part of the wider Indo-European group and is used in the north-eastern part of the region. Finally, Berber dialects survive in the mountains and hills of Morocco and eastern Algeria.

The Arab conquests also resulted in the Islamization of the region. The religion of the conquerors spread quickly and, although divisions have appeared over the centuries, orthodox Sunni Islam remains the dominant religion. The Shi'i sect, the most important minority within Islam, is the official state religion only in Iran, but the

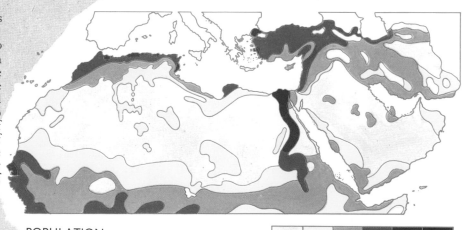

POPULATION
Distribution and density per sq. mile

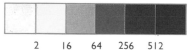

2   16   64   256   512

Shi'i represent about half the population of Iraq and considerable numbers are found in southern Lebanon and Bahrain. Further divisions within the Shi'i community led to the emergence of a number of distinct sects, notably the Zaidis, the majority group in North Yemen, the Ismailis in north-west Syria, parts of Iran and Oman, and the Druze, concentrated in southern Lebanon, south-west Syria and northern Israel.

Both Christians and Jews as 'people of the book' had a recognized place in Islamic society, forming strong urban minorities, while Christian communities also survived in mountainous areas. The Christians belong to many different sects, as a result of past heresies and schisms and because a part of each sect later decided to recognize the Pope's authority. They include the Greek Orthodox, Assyrians and Syrian Orthodox, mainly in the Fertile Crescent; the Copts, almost all confined to Egypt and the Armenians, scattered throughout the region; together with the unionate churches in communion with Rome—the Maronites of Lebanon, Greek Catholics, Chaldeans and Armenian Catholics. With the creation of the state of Israel in 1948 there was a mass exodus of Jews from Arab countries, but sizeable Jewish minorities survive in Turkey and Iran.

In the 15th century, Asia Minor was invaded by the Ottoman Turks, a group of Mongol nomads. By 1566 they had expanded their territory to include the whole of Turkey and all the Islamic lands west of Iran apart from Morocco. Each subject people was categorized as a *millet*, or religious community, and accorded autonomy over its internal affairs. By the 19th century, European powers were vying for influence, and the Ottoman Empire was partitioned after the First World War between Britain, France and Italy. Independence for much of the region came only after 1945.

The states which emerged were artificial creations and, in spite of strong efforts by the new governments, a sense of popular loyalty to the state has developed very slowly. The habit of associating politics with religion still persists. Until the outbreak of civil war in 1975 party politics and the structure of government in Lebanon were organized on a religious basis, and sectarian differences continue to influence political developments. In Saudi Arabia the political authority of the ruler traditionally derives from his alliance with the Wahhabi movement, a puritan Islamic sect which arose in the 18th century. In contrast, the power of the religious establishment in Turkey was swept away, after the First World War and the religious orders suppressed to create a strong secular republic.

The three main ecological groupings of the Middle East and North Africa are the nomads *(badawin)*, settled cultivators *(hadhar)* and the townspeople. Each has a distinctive way of life and operates in a different setting, although traditionally they were mutually dependent and each contributed to the support of the other two communities.

The nomads were never numerous, and have suffered a dramatic decline since the mid-19th century; today they represent less than five per cent of the total population. They are the stockbreeders of the region, using the vast desert, steppe and mountain pastures for grazing their herds of camels, sheep and goats. As mobility is essential for this way of life, the tribes have few possessions other than a tent of coarse goat or camel hair. Although the nomads were feared and respected as warriors and sometimes engaged in raiding, especially in periods of weak central government, relations with the villagers and townspeople were usually peaceful. Today, however, central governments are stronger and there is no political place for the nomads in the new nation states.

Between half and three-quarters of the population are cultivators, living in small, compact villages with few amenities beyond the mosque, bath-house and a few shops. Most homes are meagrely furnished one-storey structures of mud-brick or stone, which the family sometimes shares with its animals. Straw mats or blankets spread on the floor, together with a few cooking utensils, make up most of the villagers' possessions. Until recent years life had changed little for centuries: poor health, high infant mortality rates, illiteracy, oppressive forms of tenancy, crippling debts through high interest rates and extremely low standards of living were widespread.

Today, though many villagers still live near the margin of subsistence, ther are some signs of improvement. In most countries land reclamation and irrigation schemes are expanding the cultivated area and permit more intensive cropping. Foodstuffs, particularly wheat and barley, remain the most important crops, but the cultivation of cash crops such as cotton, vegetables and fruit has greatly increased. Fertilizers, insecticides and improved equipment are enabling the villagers to achieve much higher yields. As a result of the break-up of multi-village estates many cultivators have become smallholders and new co-operatives provide technical advice, credit and marketing facilities.

Most villages remain unhealthy and depressing places, though a growing number now have piped water and some at least also have electricity. Far more rural schools exist than ever before, though many more are still needed. Through the influence of the mass media, especially the transistor radio, the villagers' horizons are beginning to expand beyond their own small communities after centuries of isolation. Many aspects of rural life are therefore changing, yet much remains unchanged.

The Middle East and North Africa have had a long and venerable tradition of urban life, based on trading activity, administrative control and religious

LANGUAGE
Distribution of major languages

Arabic   Berber   Turkish   Iranian   Kurdish   Balochi   Hebrew   Other

associations. At the height of the medieval period cities such as Cairo, Baghdad and Damascus outshone all their European rivals in the development and sophistication of their intellectual and artistic life. The commercial area, known as the bazaar or *suq*, was a labyrinth of narrow streets and alley ways, lined with artisans' workshops and merchants' stalls. Residential areas emphasized privacy and security: houses presented few openings to the outside, and the bare, solid exterior walls were devoid of ornamentation. The citizens were grouped by religious sect or ethnic community, and it was common for Jews, Armenians, Greeks and other Europeans, and the various Muslim sects to occupy distinct areas within the city.

The last two decades, however, have seen a steep rise in the number of town dwellers, and in most countries at least one-third of the population is now urbanized. Istanbul, Ankara, Tehran, Alexandria, Cairo, Damascus and Baghdad each have more than a million inhabitants and the Greater Cairo region, with a population approaching 8,000,000, is one of the world's major conurbations. The centre of gravity of urban life has moved from the old city, or *medina*, to the central business district of the modern city. Almost everywhere the urban élites have moved out of the traditional quarters into the new suburbs, and the older quarters have been occupied by rural migrants. In varying degrees the *medinas* have fallen into disrepair and in some cases deep decay.

The growth of many of these cities owes much to migration from villages in the surrounding countryside, as in the case of Baghdad, or to immigration from other parts of the region, as in the main towns of the Gulf states. Nevertheless, natural increase is an important factor in urban growth. Mortality rates are much lower than in rural areas as a result of better working and housing conditions, enormous improvements in sanitation and hygiene, and a marked concentration of medical facilities in the cities. Indeed the gulf which has always separated town from country has been greatly accentuated in recent years, because the urban dweller has been the main beneficiary of modern social and economic development.

The rapid increase in urban population has led to serious housing shortages. Shanty towns—also known as squatter settlements or *bidonvilles*—have proliferated on the outskirts of many cities, sometimes penetrating right into the heart of the urban area. These makeshift homes are built with reeds, sun-dried mudbricks or stone and sometimes new materials such as tin; they provide at least minimal shelter. Shanty towns are rarely in line with the overall pattern of urban expansion, however, and high population densities and the lack of basic services bring severe health risks and social problems. Consequently squatter settlements are generally regarded as undesirable by the urban authorities.

Today, with some two-thirds of the world's known oil reserves, the Middle East and North Africa are undergoing rapid modernization, yet the effect on particular communities varies tremendously. In some areas the way of life has changed little since Biblical times and, although isolation is declining with improved communications, one can still find groups of people with traditions, language, religion and ethnic origin radically different from those of near neighbours.

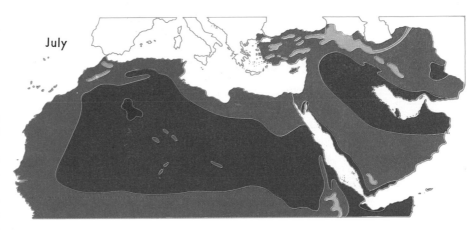

July

TEMPERATURE
Actual surface temperature in centigrade

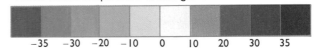

−35 −30 −20 −10 0 10 20 30 35

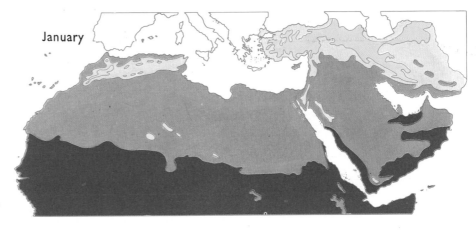

January

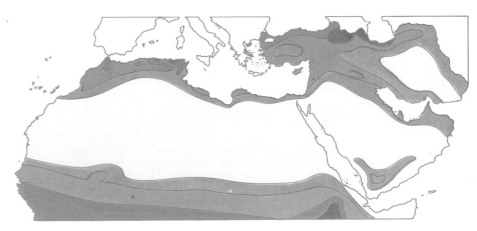

RAINFALL
Average annual rainfall in inches

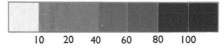

10 20 40 60 80 100

Western Sahara, Mauritania, Morocco
West Saharans, Mauritanians, Moroccans, Berbers

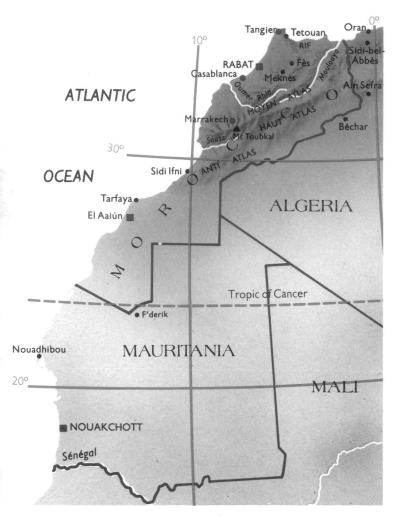

West Saharans
pop: 117,000

The land recently known as Spanish Sahara is almost entirely barren desert. The Saharans who occupy it are descended from the Sanhaja Berbers, who were the earliest inhabitants of the area, but they have intermarried with later Arab immigrants and also with freed Negro slaves. These people did not intermingle with sedentary populations and their nomadic traditions have remained largely intact. It was only with the help of the French that Spain finally succeeded in 'pacifying' the interior in 1934. Colonial rule ended in 1974, with the territory divided between Morocco and Mauritania.

There are dozens of different tribes. On the coast live the Imraguen fishermen; inland and to the south are the warlike Ulad Delim. By far the biggest tribe is the Reguibat, who have spread over into Algeria, Mali, Mauritania and Morocco. They provide the core of the Polis-ario independence movement. Many Saharans settled on the coast or near the phosphate mines during Spanish rule, but are returning to the desert to escape the armies of their powerful neighbours.

Mauritanians
pop: 1,371,000

Mauritania, with an area of 397,953 square miles, is composed almost entirely of desert. The population, which is 75 per cent Moors, also includes some Fulani pastoralists, and minorities of Toucouleur, Soninke and Wolof agriculturalists along the Senegal river.

The first ancestors of the Moors are said to have been Berbers who came to Mauritania with the Almoravid chieftain, Abu Bakr ibn Umar. Other Moors claim descent from Moroccan and Algerian invaders of the 12th and 13th centuries. A third influx started in the 15th century, led by Hassan of the Beni Mgil tribe. Legend has it that the newly-arrived Hassani people fought the established inhabitants for control of the country. The Hassani won and in consequence became the dominant tribe, holding temporal power. The defeated tribes, known as Zawiya, remained the second most influential group, controlling the country's economic resources and serving as the nation's spiritual guardians. The noble Hassani and Zawiya groups were served by a number of tributary tribes.

European commercial interests in Mauritania began in the 18th century and in the early 20th century France took control of the country. The French 'pacification' forced many Hassani to take up livestock-rearing and commerce, although the political authority of their emirs was strengthened.

The majority of the population remain nomadic and make their living from herding. In the north only camels, sheep and goats can be raised, but cattle, mainly African zebu, are kept in the Sahel. A terrible drought hit Mauritania in the early 1970s; many people died and most of the country's livestock perished or were driven to neighbouring countries for slaughter. Many pastoralists may never return to their former occupations.

Since independence in 1960 the exploitation of Mauritania's iron ore and copper deposits has introduced a small but extremely profitable modern sector into the economy. Although the mines offer few employment opportunities they provide the government with revenues with which to improve livestock production and expand the area of irrigated agriculture. However, the war against Polisario for control of the southern half of the former territory of Spanish Sahara is proving increasingly costly.

Moroccans
pop: 18,090,000

Morocco is the most westerly of the Maghreb nations of northern Africa, separated from Europe by the Straits of Gibraltar. It has recently attempted to occupy part of the former Spanish Sahara. In 1978 it was still involved in a costly war against the forces of Polisario, the independence movement of Western Sahara.

Most of Morocco's population are settled agriculturalists, but in the extreme south of the country, on the edge of the Sahara, there are a number of camel herding groups who are almost entirely nomadic. The Arab conquest of the 7th and 8th centuries converted the indigenous Berber peoples to Islam, but Arabization occurred at a slow pace for there were few Arab settlers.

Berber power reached its zenith in the 11th and 12th centuries with the flowering of the Almoravid and Almohad Islamic dynasties on Moroccan soil; at their peak these empires controlled the whole of the Maghreb and much of Spain. In the mid-13th century the Almohad dynasty crumbled and the country underwent a series of divisions between successive dynasties and principalities. The present ruling dynasty, the 'Alawis, came to power in the 17th century.

In the 19th century Spain, France and Germany became interested in Morocco and in the early part of this century Spain and France colonized the country. There was violent nationalist resistance to coloniz-

ation right through to independence in 1956. In the subsequent struggles for power between the political parties, the palace and the army, the palace has maintained control.

In contemporary Morocco there is a sharp contrast between the traditional and modern sectors of society. Agriculture is the focus of traditional society, which tends to be organized on a tribal basis. Communities are more or less self-sufficient and subsist on their own cereals, vegetables, fruit and livestock.

Pressure on the land and rural unemployment have forced many Moroccans to migrate to the towns in recent years. There has been a rapid growth in shanty towns, which surround the major cities, and there is little prospect of improvement. Morocco's most valuable mineral resource is phosphate, which cannot provide sufficient capital to modernize agriculture or stimulate the growth of industry.

Berbers
pop: 10,000,000

The Berbers are scattered throughout the inhospitable mountain and desert areas of northern Africa. Their origins are unknown, but it is thought that they once inhabited the whole of this vast region. They trace their history back to their conversion to Islam, by the Arabs, in the 8th century. When the Arabs came, the Berbers lost the fertile lowlands and were banished to the mountain ranges of the Atlas, the Rif and the Aurès and into the depths of the Sahara, where groups such as the Sanhaja Berbers had already evolved a nomadic way of life.

The Berbers have a common language and culture, although their life style varies widely with each region, according to local conditions and climate. The language is complex, with a number of dialects that are mutually incomprehensible. Many Berbers have learnt Arabic as a second language.

The Shluh, who inhabit the Atlas and Anti-Atlas ranges of Morocco, and the Rifians of the mountains further north, are mainly settled agriculturalists. Every possible patch of ground is cultivated with the aid of terracing and extensive irrigation. In the Moyen Atlas mountains, the home of the Imazighen tribes, winters are longer and harder, and livestock raising is more important.

The Imazighen practise transhumance, but still maintain villages. A small number always stay behind to guard the collective granaries.

To the south of the Atlas mountains, the land becomes increasingly arid and the tribes are nomadic, relying on their herds of camels, sheep and goats and trading their products for cereals and fruit from more fertile areas. The most famous of these nomads are the Tuareg, who formerly moved throughout the Sahara.

Berber social organization remains mostly local and tribal. For sedentary agriculturalists, life centres on the village, consisting of 10-15 extended families with their own council; the canton made up of three or four villages; the tribe and the confederation. The latter were only of real importance in the past, for inter-tribal warfare and feuding. The nomads' most important grouping is the faction, composed of *duwars*, or groups of tents, in a specific area. This is both a political and fighting unit, with a council made up of the heads of important families. In many Berber areas, hereditary holy men play an important role as arbitrators and conciliators.

Berber women carrying water, Tunisia

Distribution of Berbers

115

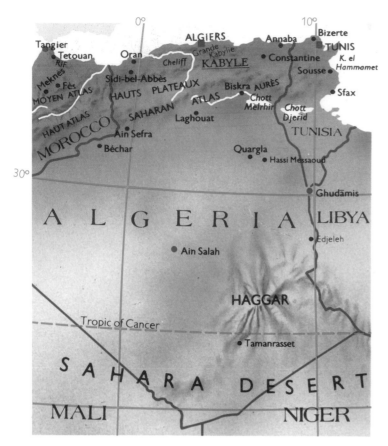

Distribution of Tuareg

Algerians

pop: 17,558,000

Algeria is the largest of the Maghreb states of north-west Africa, but much of it is waterless desert. The Algerians are of mainly Berber origin, but most of them speak Arabic and the town-dwellers have an Arab lifestyle. Despite the variety of groups that make up the population the people display a remarkable degree of unity, as there are no closed communities and Islam provides a unifying influence. In the mountains of the Grande Kabylie, however, the main language is still Berber, and the people follow a more traditional way of life.

In 1830 the French occupied Algiers and gradually extended their rule throughout Algeria. French settlers took over the better agricultural lands and organized large farms. During the 1950s, there was a bitter war between the Algerian National Liberation Front (NLF) and France and by the time independence was achieved in 1962 most of the *pieds-noirs* European settlers (almost 1,000,000) had abandoned their holdings.

Most Algerians make their living from agriculture and population is concentrated in the fertile and well-watered coastal areas. Wheat, vines, olives and citrus fruits are grown, but the Algerian peasants have found it difficult to manage the large farms left by the French. In these fertile areas the people live in permanent villages.

In drier regions, Algerians have a semi-nomadic lifestyle, living for a few months of the year in stone or clay houses near the land they cultivate, and for the rest of the year following their flocks. The Sahara and high plateau regions can support only a scant population of fully nomadic pastoralists who raise goats, sheep and camels.

Although Algerians are not traditionally town-dwellers, there has been large-scale migration to urban areas in recent years, as the government has promoted rapid industrialization, exploiting the nation's oil and gas revenues. Employment has not kept pace with urban growth, however, and large numbers of Algerians live in poverty on the outskirts of the towns. There is a considerable degree of labour migration to France, both temporary and permanent.

Kabyle

pop: 2,000,000

Of the Berber-speaking peoples of Algeria the Kabyle are the most important in number and influence. They occupy a mountainous region to the east of Algiers known as Grande Kabylie. Because of the ruggedness of their lands they have remained relatively isolated from outside contacts.

The villages in which they live are built high in the mountains. In the past, an assembly, or *jema*, composed of the heads of families, ruled the village and administered justice. Alliances between villages tended to have a chequerboard pattern, so that neighbours were enemies, while neighbours-but-one were allies. Kabyle lands are now overpopulated and suffer from severe soil erosion. Olives and figs are the major crops, and most of the cereals eaten are imported.

Despite the solidarity of the Kabyle community, emigration has become a way of life and they now form a major group in the national capital. In recent decades a growing number of Kabyle men have gone to France to work.

Tuareg

pop: 500,000

The Tuareg inhabit a vast area of the west-central Sahara and the Sahel – in modern political terms, southern Algeria, much of Niger, northern Mali and south-west Libya. Before the arrival of the Europeans, most Tuareg were nomadic stock-breeders with large herds of camels, cattle, sheep and goats. With the exception of the nobility, all Tuareg engaged in caravan trading, exchanging livestock for dates and millet. Until the late 19th century, caravans crossed the Sahara bringing gold, ivory and slaves from West Africa to the Mediterranean, while south-bound caravans carried salt, and Arab and European goods.

The Tuareg fall into seven main groups or political units, with only the two northern-most groups living in true desert country. The other groups, known as the southern Tuareg, live in the Sahel. The major class division is between nobles and vassals; and in most Tuareg groups there are tribes of *marabuts*, the religious class founded after the introduction of Islam. There was also a large class of Negro slaves, or *iklan*, who were obtained from the south or taken from caravans travelling north. However, the independent governments of the region have taken firm action to abolish slavery.

The arrival of the French at the beginning of this century profoundly changed the Tuareg economy. Raiding was suppressed, the trans-Saharan caravan trade declined in the face of competition from sea and rail transport, and the imposition of political boundaries and customs duties made even the trade in Saharan salt less viable. Although many Tuareg remain nomadic, government restrictions and regulations have caused others to settle permanently, despite their contempt for agriculture. The disastrous drought of the

early 1970 s drove thousands of Tuareg south into Niger and Nigeria, and many of these have since turned to farming.

Tunisians

pop: 5,975,000

Tunisia is the smallest of the Maghreb countries of northeastern Africa. The people are basically of Berber origin, but there have been many external influences—Phoenician, Roman, Arab and Turkish. During the 18th and 19th centuries, Europeans became interested in Tunisia and in 1881 the French occupied the country. The settlers took over much of the better agricultural land and were bitterly resented by · the Tunisians. Fighting between nationalists and the colonial government continued until independence in 1955.

Most Tunisians make their livelihood from agriculture, but the pattern of rural life varies with the land. In the Tell and along the coast, the people grow barley and wheat, and maintain citrus and olive groves. The Sahel produces large quantities of olive oil for export, but pressure on the land is becoming a problem. The farmers of the central parts of the country are semi-nomadic, cultivating cereal crops but migrating to the uplands with their sheep and goats during the hot summer months. To the south, the land becomes drier and a fully nomadic economy is practised.

An increasing number of Tunisians are moving to urban areas in search of industrial employment. The country has vast phosphate deposits, as well as iron, lead and zinc ores, but industrial development can only occur at a slow pace and some traditional social structures may continue. The government is seeking foreign investment for industrialization and encouraging the southern tribes to adopt a sedentary lifestyle, by sinking wells around which vines and olives can be grown.

Tuareg women at a desert well, Niger

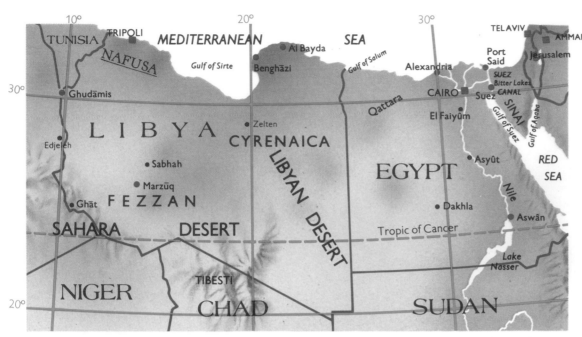

Libyans
pop: 2,599,000

In a land that is mostly desert, Libyan society has undergone rapid transition in the last 20 years as oil revenues have changed it from one of the poorest to one of the richest nations of the world. The population is predominantly Arab, but the early settlers were a mixture of Greeks and Berbers, who practised sedentary agriculture wherever the land was suitable.

Arab invaders arrived during the 7th century and were followed by further waves culminating in the 11th-century occupation by Bedouin Arabs. The latter group put an end to the arable and orchard farming system and nomadic pastoralism became the main economic activity. Areas with higher rainfall were used for dry-season pasture, and the inland scrub was foraged at other times of year.

Italy occupied Libya in 1911, seizing land for the settlement of Italian colonists. The colonial government undermined the indigenous social structures by defeating tribal resistance led by the Sanusiyah religious order. In 1940 war stopped the planned integration of Libya into the Italian state and, after a brief period of British administration, Libya became independent in 1951.

The oil revenues which have flowed into the country have brought immense changes. An industrialization programme based on the manufacture of petro-chemicals and construction materials has produced many jobs. Much of the rural population has moved to the cities and oilfields in search of high wages. The government has attempted to offset the attraction of towns by channelling a large proportion of investment into rural housing, schools, hospitals and roads. In consequence, many rural dwellers have abandoned agriculture and are employed in construction and services.

Libya is now one of the most urbanized countries of the Middle East and North Africa. More than half the population lives in villages and towns of more than 5,000 people; of all urban dwellers, two-thirds are citizens of Tripoli and Benghazi, where shanty towns are growing. Rural depopulation is most evident in the Fezzan and the Jebel Nafusa. Only a tiny fraction of the land surface is now cultivated.

Nafusa
pop: 40,000

The Nafusa are the only sizeable Berber group in northern Libya; they live in the mountainous Jebel Nafusa region. Over the centuries the Nafusa have evolved a rural economy well suited to their semi-arid environment. Everywhere they use their limited resources to the best advantage, building dams and terraces for the cultivation of crops. The olive, fig and palm are their main sources of food, but in better-watered areas they plant wheat and barley and graze their sheep and goats.

The Nafusa are distinguished from their Arabized neighbours by their language and religious sect. They belong to the Ibadi sect of Islam, which they originally adopted in defiance of their orthodox Arab conquerors. There are a few mixed villages, but most Nafusa live apart from the Arabized inhabitants of the Jebel. Their own villages are strongly nucleated, built for defence and difficult to reach. Fortified communal granaries are the dominant feature of most villages, although many are now in ruins. Flat-roofed stone houses cluster around the granaries, and underground dwellings carved into the limestone are also common.

In the past Nafusa men sought work in neighbouring Tunisia, regularly returning home with whatever money they had saved. Today, the process of modernization in the Jebel has begun, but the pace of change is still slow and many of the young men seek employment in the towns.

Egyptians
pop: 38,533,000

Egypt has a coastline on both the Mediterranean and Red Seas, in the extreme north-east corner of the African continent. In this vast land, only the areas around the river Nile are inhabited, as most of the country is barren desert.

The 7th century witnessed the first of several waves of Arab conquest. Most of the population converted to Islam, which remains the official religion. In the 19th century, Muhammad Ali, who established Egypt's autonomy within the Ottoman Empire, led Egypt into a series of wars with nearby countries. Eventually there came British occupation which ended in large scale civil disorder and a military coup, followed by a war with Israel, Britain and France for control of the Suez Canal. In recent years there have been two additional wars with Israel, military involvement in the Yemen and skirmishes with Libya.

The majority of Egypt's people (about 56 per cent) are peasants, *fellaheen;* the lands they cultivate are some of the most densely populated in the world. Their compact villages of mud huts are built on infertile rocky outcrops and may have from 1,000 to 5,000 inhabitants. Social life centres around the extended family and marriage is usually to a close relative.

The *fellaheen* grow mainly maize and millet for subsistence and cotton as a cash crop. Despite new dams as at Aswan, the operation of irrigation schemes for around the year cropping, the use of fertilizers and recent land reforms, the *fellaheen* have a very low level of subsistence and their life is extremely hard.

Many *fellaheen* have moved to the cities where conditions are little better: despite expansion in the textile, chemical, cement and food industries, there is a high rate of unemployment. Apart from a wealthy urban élite, most town-dwellers live in poverty.

Copts
pop: 3,000,000

The Copts are Egyptian Christians who live throughout the habitable areas of the republic. They are the direct descendants of the ancient Egyptians.

Christianity was established in Egypt during the 2nd century AD, and the number of converts increased when the country's Roman oppressors became Christian. In the 5th century, with virtually the whole of Egypt Christianized, the Coptic church withdrew from the Orthodox church. This was because the Copts adopted the belief of Monophysitism—that Christ was entirely a god and never a man.

During the 1920s the Copts united with their Muslim compatriots in support of Saad Zaghlul's nationalist movement. There were tensions later when Nasser's socializing policies led to some Copts losing wealth they had amassed during British rule. Today there is very little to distinguish the Copts from other Egyptians, although in towns they tend to congregate in the same suburbs.

Sudan
Sudanese, Ja'aliyyin, Kababish, Baggara, Homr

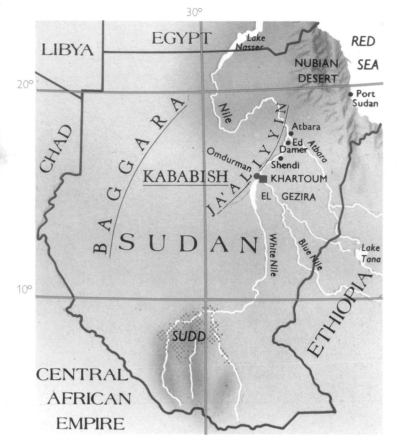

Ethnic division of Sudan

- Arabs
- Negroes

Sudanese

pop: 18,428,000

Sudan occupies the central and upper Nile basin of north-east Africa. Although parts of the country are arid most of the land has savanna vegetation, which is thicker in the south where rainfall is higher.

The peoples of the Sudan are mainly agriculturalists and comprise a number of different tribal groups. In the north these are of Semitic descent and have their origin in the Arab conquests. Both Nilotes and Negroes live in the south.

Most of the population subsist on crops of millet and maize and grow cotton as a cash crop. The characteristic method of cultivation in many areas is known as *hariq* and entails burning the grassy and weedy ground before planting. Around Gezira there has been a successful, large-scale irrigation scheme for growing cotton, which forms the bulk of the Sudan's exports. In drier areas nomadic peoples such as the Baggara breed cattle and the Kababish raise camels and goats. The authorities are trying to exert more control over these groups, who graze large areas but pay little tax.

Sudan's recent history has been turbulent and the success of development plans will depend on whether or not the northern and southern people can be permanently reconciled. The southerners, who are partly Christianized, feel that the country is dominated by the Muslim northerners and have frequently resorted to armed rebellion.

Ja'aliyyin

pop: 1,500,000

Ja'aliyyin is the name given to a group of Arab tribes distributed over northern and central Sudan. Most of these people live close to the banks of the Nile. Shendi, with a population of 16,000, is the main tribal centre and was an important market for several caravan routes. Road and rail transport, however, have reduced the income from camel porterage.

The Ja'aliyyin claim descent from Muhammad's uncle and they have a reputation for manliness, bravery and generosity. Their last king, Mek Nimr, gained a distinctive position in Sudanese history for his resistance to the Ottoman Empire in the early 19th century. Later the Ja'aliyyin split into two distinct factions, one centred on Shendi and ruled by the Nimrab family, and the other at Metrama led by the Sa'adab family.

Despite heavy migration to the cities and modern influences, the Ja'aliyyin retain their tribal solidarity and ethnic identity. They can usually be recognized by distinctive H- or T-shaped scars cut into their cheeks. Exogamous marriage is opposed and polygyny is still practised by the wealthy, although men will not have more than four wives at one time, in accordance with the Islamic law.

The father has authority over his wives and children, whose marriages he controls. Elders are highly respected, and their arbitration is essential in family disputes. Mutual aid, or *kadah*, is important at times such as circumcision, marriage and funerals. When someone dies, the family is provided with food by neighbours and relatives who will also share the funeral expenses.

Today, the Ja'aliyyin make their livelihoods in a variety of ways. Those who live in the tribal area have a mixed economy, herding cattle, camels, sheep and goats and cultivating millet. A second group, who live to the east of the Nile between Shendi and Atbara, are semi-nomadic. They have no regular seasonal cycle of movement, but graze their animals over short distances within the circuit of their wells. The third and increasingly important group are those who have gone to live in cities and towns. They constitute the bulk of the Sudanese urban population and form the merchant class of entrepreneurs, shopkeepers, contractors, pedlars and lorry-owners.

Kababish

pop: 100,000

The home of the Arab camel nomads called Kababish lies due west of Khartoum, the capital of Sudan. Their arid lands are unsuitable for cultivation, but provide good grazing for camels, goats and desert sheep. Three historic caravan routes run through the area and for centuries the Kababish have acted as guides and suppliers of animals to merchants crossing their territory. In the 18th and 19th century the Kababish were a loose confederation of tribes of diverse origins, but at the beginning of the 20th century the first paramount chief, Shaikh Ali at-Tom, welded them into a cohesive political unit.

Except during the dry season when they settle at watering centres known as *damar*, the Kababish move about with their animals in small, family groups. During the annual migration, however the livestock are herded *en masse*, as this permits the animals to be moved with greater speed over large distances. Millet is the staple diet of the Kababish and is purchased by regularly selling animals.

A man's ideal is to be head of his own household, have many sons and dependants, and own a large herd. Material possessions are cumbersome for the nomads and the family tent, which is owned by the

woman, will have little inside it. The Kababish value their independence and nomadic existence far above the comforts of urban life, but some members of the chiefly family are playing an increasingly important role in Sudan's political and economical life.

Baggara
pop: 800,000

Baggara is a collective name applied by the Sudanese to several nomadic cattle-owning tribes living in the dry savanna belt between the Nile and the border with Chad. The tribes are culturally similar: all speak Arabic and follow the Islamic faith. They are of Arab origin but inter-marriage with Negro slaves has darkened skin colouration, and lighter skins are considered prestigious.

The Baggara's annual migration begins in December when grazing becomes poor and they move southwards in search of water. The following months are hard until the rains

come in April. June sees the first move north completed as the Baggara arrive at the most permanent of their camps. The women and children settle to cultivate millet while the men take the cattle further north. In November and December they return; the crop is harvested, the cattle eat the stubble and the group moves south again.

On marriage, the husband pays a bridewealth of cattle to his wife's kin. She must be a virgin and this is ensured by infibulation (the sewing up of the vulva) at an early age. Once married, women are forced to **work hard, performing all the domestic chores, milking the cows and moving the tents.**
Relations between the government and the Baggara have never been good, since the tribes graze large areas but pay little tax. The authorities now insist that children should be educated in boarding schools, but this has been resisted, for pastoral techniques can only be learned by

long and patient experience, and the parents fear that their children will abandon the nomadic life.

Homr
pop: 55,000

The Homr are the largest of the Baggara tribes of the Sudan, and live almost exclusively by nomadic cattle herding. Social organization is patrilineal, based on two main lineages, the 'Ajaira and the Felaita, but the *surra*, or camp group, is the important unit for everyday life. Each *surra* is composed of extended families linked by a common ancestor some five generations back. Marriage within the *surra* is favoured.

A man's quality is determined by his success with cattle, which in turn determines his prestige and influence in other areas of life. Wealth attracts not only wives, but dependents and the masculine values of courage and vengefulness are balanced by loyalty and generosity.

Ja'aliyyin trader,
Khartoum

121

Yemenites

pop: 8,555,000

The Yemenites occupy a mountainous but fertile land in the south-western corner of the Arabian peninsula. The earliest settlers probably came from north-eastern Africa, but there was later large-scale Semitic immigration. By the 7th century BC the prosperous civilization of Saba had emerged but the area came under Persian rule in the 6th century AD. There then followed a long period of imperial control as power passed through the hands of the Arabs, Turks, Egyptians, Dutch, Portuguese and British. Independence for most of the region was achieved in 1934, but the protectorate of Aden remained in British hands until 1967, an important entrepôt centre on the Red Sea.

A consequence of the Yemen's history has been the formation of a stratified society. The first layer are the wealthy and educated élite who claim descent from the prophet Muhammad; second are the Qahtani, who trace their ancestry to the pre-Islamic civilizations – mostly tribesmen, they form the majority of the rural population and belong to a Shi'i sect of Islam; third are the townsmen, the majority of whom are Sunni Muslims; fourth are the former slaves, who are usually of African descent.

There is a tradition of friction between the people of the towns and those in rural areas. The highland Qahtani tribesmen, who grow grains, vegetables and mocha coffee, are fiercely independent and have their own customs, laws and courts.

The civil war between royalists and republicans which broke out in 1962 was the result of many different tensions between the country's social groups. In 1970 it was ended by mutual agreement and North Yemen was established as the Yemeni Arab Republic. With few physical resources and limited agricultural potential, development depends heavily on foreign aid.

The People's Republic of South Yemen, the former Aden protectorate, came into existence in 1967 and was at war with its neighbour until 1972. It has a population of some 1,764,000 (1977), who are generally very poor. The cease-fire agreement announced that the two Yemeni states would merge within a year, but since then formal unification has been postponed indefinitely.

Hadrami

pop: not available

The Hadramawt forms part of the People's Republic of South Yemen. It lies inland from the coast, a vast, dry plateau broken only by a system of *wadis* and deep valleys. About half the Hadrami live in the scattered towns built by the *wadis* or in the port of Al Mukalla and nearby fishing villages. The rest are semi-nomadic, growing crops when there is enough rain and moving in search of pasture for their sheep, goats and camels during the frequent droughts. In past centuries the Hadrami built up a thriving trade with Africa, the Far East and other Arab countries. Today there are Hadrami colonies in all the major ports of the Indian Ocean.

In the 19th century the Qa'ity and Kathiri sultans ruled the Hadramawt but their power was largely confined to the cities and villages. The lands in between were controlled by warring nomadic tribes. The sultans gained control over the tribal areas after 1937 with the help of British military support. Under colonial rule the Hadramawt existed as two separate protectorates until 1967 when the sultans were deposed in an independent South Yemen.

Although all Hadrami speak the same Arabic dialect and are Muslims, there has always been antagonism between the townspeople and the nomads. The towns are walled and built on steep slopes for protection. Houses are made of mud and are often several stories high. Outside the town lie the fields of millet and date palms.

The nomadic tribesmen are essentially egalitarian but in the towns a stratified society has evolved, based on lineages. There are three main strata, the highest of which is the *Sadah*, who claim direct descent from the prophet Muhammad. As well as being the religious leaders of the community they have usually held political power and even today dominate city councils and monopolize government jobs. Second are the *Mashaikh* (scholars) and *Gabail* (tribesmen), who are both mostly farmers. The former have a religious status in the community, while the latter are respected for their fighting prowess. Finally come the *Masakin*, who usually work as carpenters, masons, smiths or servants.

Traditional Hadrami society was held together by a complicated web of ties between families of different strata, formed for political or economic reasons. The British reinforced the class system by investing administrative power in the hands of the *Sadah*. It is not yet clear whether this hierarchical structure central to Hadrami society will survive under a government dedicated to egalitarian ideals.

Omani

pop: 525,000

Oman forms the south-east corner of the Arabian peninsula and its strategic position has brought a close association with Britain for many years. In the north and south are mountainous regions where agriculture is possible, but these are separated by a large, sparsely inhabited desert plain.

A number of peoples have settled the area and the Omani

claim descent from Arab tribes of both northern and southern Arabia. The coastal people were renowned for their seafaring and had links with both India and Africa. From the 6th to the 16th century, the region was dominated by the Persians. Ibadism, a sect of Islam, has its deepest roots in Oman and it was an Omani tribe, the Azd, who spread Islam to Persia.

On the coast, many people make their living by fishing, while in the mountainous areas grain and vegetables are grown by skilful irrigation methods. Around 30,000 Bedouin range the arid plains with their herds of camel and goats.

A period of rapid transition has begun in recent years, following the discovery of oil. Revenues are being spent on construction and the provision of education and health services, and the drift of population to the towns can be expected to increase. Since Sultan Qabus bin-Said deposed his father in 1970 there has been a relaxation of traditional attitudes, freeing of slaves, release of prisoners, emphasis on economic development and controlled modernization.

Muscati

pop: 2,000,000

Muscat, the capital of Oman, has a fine, natural harbour and was for many centuries the chief port of Arabia. The Muscati made their living from pearling, fishing, sea-faring and trading. In winter, with the north-east monsoon, Arab vessels sailed down the African coast as far as Zanzibar, using the south-west monsoon to return in summer with cargoes of ivory, beeswax, tortoise-shell and slaves. In the 19th century, the Omani sultanate was divided, with one capital in Muscat and one in Zanzibar.

In 1964, a revolution on the island overthrew the sultan and many Zanzibari of Omani origin have returned to Muscat, where the last decade has brought many changes. Since 1970 traditional society has been liberalized and oil revenues are being used to transform the capital into a large, modern city, with an international airport and a deepwater harbour at Mina Aqbus.

Arabs

pop: 40,000,000

The Arabs occupy a broad band of territory stretching across the Middle East and North Africa, from Iraq to Morocco. They are of Semitic origin, but much of the unity of the Arab world centres on a common language, Arabic, and a common religion, Islam.

The original Arabs were nomadic and semi-nomadic tribes. The first really powerful Arab community appeared in Medina under Muhammad, the prophet of Islam, in the 7th century AD. Unified by religion, Arab groups set off on a trail of conquest. Within a century, successive waves spread across Persia and into India and through North Africa and Spain into France. Eventually their power dwindled, but most of the lands they conquered were irreversibly changed by Islamic culture.

Based on five 'pillars', Islam requires practical observances which remain constant throughout the Arab world. These are the declaration of faith in Allah (*shahadah*); the performance of the daily prayers (*salat*); giving alms (*zakat*); fasting between dawn and dusk during the holy month of Ramadan; and the pilgrimage to Mecca (*hajj*).

Muslims must also obey the *shari'ah*, a body of law governing all aspects of daily life, including marriage, divorce, inheritance, taxation, duties of and to rulers, the treatment of slaves and infidels, and the conduct of war. These regulations are based on the Koran, the holy book of Islam, and on the *hadith*, traditions of Muhammad's life and sayings.

Arab life in rural areas has until recently been organized tribally, with a *shaikh* at the head of each tribe or village. Marriages within the lineage, often to a close relative, are preferred. In the Arabian peninsula, women are still veiled and have few rights, but elsewhere they have more freedom.

The first confrontations between European colonialism and the Arabs came in the 16th century. The Arabs suffered successive defeats and, with the fall of the Ottoman Empire after the First World War, all Arab lands were colonized. The growth of Arab nationalism followed as the peoples of the Middle East and North Africa created political movements and won independence.

Saudi Arabians

pop: 7,517,000

The Saudi Arabians are today a dominant force not only in the Arabian peninsula but in most of the Middle East and North Africa. When the Arab Empire disintegrated in the Middle Ages, control of the peninsula passed through various hands until the early 18th century, when Wahha-

Arab Empire by 945 AD

bism spread through the Najd and into the Hijaz. This aimed to restore Islam to its earlier undefiled form. Arabia then came under the control of the Ottoman Empire, and unity was delayed until 1926 when Ibn Saud, the Sultan of Najd, became the King of the Hijaz. Since then, the isolated and poor country he ruled has been revolutionized by a flood of oil revenues.

Many Saudis have moved into the towns in search of work, but there are large areas where life still follows traditional patterns. In the arid regions the Bedouin base their lives on the camel and the date palm, roaming far from their wells in search of forage during the cool season. In the moister areas, such as the Azir mountains, sedentary peoples grow grain and other crops.

Despite a programme of rapid industrialization and development along western lines, Saudi Arabia maintains a puritan Islamic orthodoxy. Alcohol is prohibited, the sexes are rigidly segregated and public entertainments are discouraged. Political centralism has increased and the government is trying to make the nomadic Bedouin adopt a sedentary lifestyle.

Gulf Arabs
pop: 2,500,000

The Arabs of the Persian Gulf share a common language, religion and culture, and it is only in recent years that their governments have drawn up international boundaries. Apart from Saudi Arabia, the Gulf states today include Kuwait, Bahrain, Qatar and the United Arab Emirates.

These lands are almost entirely desert and were used only by nomads until Arab tribes settled around the freshwater springs on the coast. There they lived by fishing and pearling and during the 19th century some of their settlements developed into important trading centres.

The immense oil revenues which have accrued to the Gulf states since the Second World War have brought considerable changes; much of the population, and many foreign immigrants, have moved into the new, western-style cities. Massive national infrastructures have been developed within a few years and large-scale education, social welfare and industrial programmes have been implemented.

Bedouin
pop: 4-6,000,000

The Bedouin are pastoral nomads who live in the vast tracts of semi-desert and desert of the Middle East and North Africa. Although they represent less than one-tenth of the area's total population, they utilize nine-tenths of the land.

They are probably descended from farmers and traders who gradually adopted a nomadic lifestyle between the times of Christ and Muhammad. Among them tribes of 'noble' ancestry trace descent back to either the Qaysi of northern Arabia or the Yamani of southern Arabia. There are a number of lower status Bedouin tribes with no specific claims of lineage, whose members often work as blacksmiths, artisans and entertainers for the 'noble' tribes. Despite this hierarchy, Bedouin society is essentially informal, and a lowly tribesman can approach a *shaikh* on a personal basis.

Bedouin live off the milk and, occasionally, the meat of their animals. During the rainy season grasses spring up in marginal regions and the herds are grazed far from the better-watered dry season pastures. The tribesmen sell animals during their journeys in order to buy cotton clothes and foods such as wheat, dates and coffee.

Many aspects of Bedouin life are common to all Muslim societies, but the tribes are renowned for their hospitality to strangers, who are always lavishly entertained. Individualism and bravery have been bred by the harsh conditions, and from an early age a boy must be capable of fending for himself. Women are allowed more freedom than their counterparts in the towns.

Traditional Bedouin values include contempt for settled life and wage labour, but in recent years many tribesmen have gone to live in the towns and cities, and some now occupy offices of national importance. Others have become truckers, machinists and skilled workers in the oilfields. The governments of the various countries in which they live are bringing increasing pressure on the tribes to settle.

Bedouin camp in the Rub'al Khāli, Arabia

Cyprus, Lebanon, Israel, Jordan
Cypriots, Lebanese, Israelis, Palestinians, Jordanians

Cypriots

pop: 650,000

The third largest island in the Mediterranean, Cyprus is also the most highly cultivated area in the Middle East, with a rich and highly varied agriculture. About half of the population live in some 600 prosperous villages, but the six main towns are growing rapidly; the capital, Nicosia, is the largest. Mining and industry are both well developed by the standards of the region and tourism brings a substantial income.

Cyprus was colonized by Greeks in Mycenean times (c. 1200 BC) and although it has subsequently been ruled by many invading peoples, a strong Greek Orthodox culture has survived; 78 per cent of the population are Greeks. The Muslim Turks held the island from 1570 to 1878 and a Turkish population became established during that period. The two communities are separated by language and religion, but the Turks were, until recently, scattered over much of the island and more than 100 villages were mixed. Within the villages, however, segregation always existed and intermarriage was rare.

Britain acquired the island in 1878 and kept control through 80 years of nationalist agitation until 1960, when Cyprus became an independent sovereign republic. Fighting between Greeks and Turks became serious in 1963, partly due to Turkish suspicion of the EOKA movement for union with mainland Greece. A right-wing coup by Greek army officers in 1974 precipitated an invasion from Turkey, since which the island has been divided.

Lebanese

pop: 2,454,000

Lebanon is a small, mountainous country, unique among the Arab nations in having Christianity as an official religion. The Lebanese are a Semitic people descended from Phoenicians, Hebrews, Arameans and Arabs. In ancient times they were ruled by the Egyptians but power later passed to the Romans and Christianity was introduced. In the 7th century came the Arab invasion of the Fertile Crescent; although much of the population was converted to Islam, the Maronites and Druze in the mountains resisted Muslim influence.

During the centuries of Ottoman rule, the Maronites were placed under the jurisdiction of local Druze emirs. Throughout the 19th century, relations between the Maronites and Druze deteriorated and in 1860 the Druze killed a large number of Maronites. This provoked French intervention and in 1864 Mount Lebanon became an autonomous region. In 1926 an enlarged Lebanon became an independent state.

Around 40 per cent of Lebanon's population is employed in agriculture, the chief crops being wheat, barley, olives and fruit. The land is heavily populated, but improved agricultural methods give high yields. Much of the country's wealth, however, comes from financial and trading activities. Lebanon has the most convenient ports for lands to the east and Tripoli has become the major oil pipeline terminal for the region. Most Middle Eastern and international banks operate from Beirut and large revenues have accrued from this.

Slightly more than half of Lebanon's population is said to be Christian and the remainder Muslim, but a census has not been held for many years and the proportions are by now probably reversed. In an attempt to balance power between the two groups the president has always been a Maronite Christian, and the prime minister a Muslim. Since most administrative power lies with the president, Muslims feel that they are denied equal participation in national affairs. Religious tensions have been strong throughout the country's recent history–in 1958, US marines were landed at Beirut when open rebellion broke out against the government.

A form of peace returned to the nation, but in the 1970s tensions rose again, partly aggravated by the influx of Palestinian refugees, and in 1975 a civil war began. Beirut was devastated and Christian and Muslim groups killed each other throughout the country. Frequent calls for cease-fire were never answered and in 1976 Syria sent in a large number of troops, crushing the Palestinian guerrilla groups who had supported the Muslim forces and leaving the Maronites in control of the country's political institutions.

Israelis

pop: 3,545,000

Israeli society has undergone dramatic changes since the state's foundation. in 1948, when Jewish settlers took control of the British mandated territory of Palestine. The country lies on the Mediterranean, and is surrounded by the Arab states of Syria, Jordan, Egypt and Lebanon.

The original home of the Jews was in Palestine, but after the Romans sacked Jerusalem in 70 AD the Jewish people scattered throughout the world. In the 19th century Jewish nationalism developed and with it Zionism – the idea of mass immigration back to the Holy Land. Jews from central and eastern Europe came to Palestine and saw in the Balfour Declaration of 1917 and the establishment of the British mandate after the First World War the promise of a Jewish national home. By the end of the Second World War, they were sufficiently powerful to dominate the indigenous Arab

Cyprus

Turkish sector to north

population. Since the 1948 Arab-Israeli War there has been continuous tension and three more wars with neighbouring Arab states.

Israel's population today is made up of a variety of differing elements, for immigrants have come from 102 countries and represent many language groups. The Ashkenazim, of western origin, tend to be the best-educated and hold most key political and administrative positions. The oriental Jews, or Sephardim, find it harder to adjust to Israel's western-style development and the majority are in the country's lower social classes. Marriage between Ashkenazim and Sephardim is still fairly rare.

Some 86 per cent of the population live in towns and work in the many industries that have been developed in recent decades. In the rural areas, settlement has been influenced by social aims. The kibbutz is a collective agricultural settlement in which all property is owned in common and needs are provided for on an egalitarian basis. Children usually live away from parents in separate children's homes, but the family unit remains strong and parents and children are together whenever possible. Another form of agricultural settlement is the *moshav*, where each family owns its land, but produce is sold and supplies bought through co-operatives.

Palestinians
pop: 3,500,000
Before the First World War, Palestine was part of the Ottoman Empire, with a population of around 700,000. The majority of its people were Muslims of mixed Arab origin, but about a quarter were Christian. There was a Jewish minority of around 85,000.

Most Palestinians were rural dwellers and grew grains and vegetables in the more fertile regions of the land. Some 7 per cent were Bedouin, in the northern Negev desert. The remainder were town dwellers engaged in business, commerce and the professions.

During the First World War the British drove the Turks out of the area and in 1917 the Foreign Secretary, Arthur Balfour,

issued his famous declaration that the British government viewed with favour 'the establishment in Palestine of a national home for the Jewish people'. Throughout the British mandate, from 1922 to 1948, the Palestinians opposed the constant stream of Jewish immigration, but never presented a combined front.

The United Nations voted in 1947 to partition Palestine between Arabs and Jews. In May 1948 the British withdrew and the Jews proclaimed the state of Israel in the areas allocated them by the United Nations. Bitter fighting ensued when the armies of the Arab League crossed the Jordanian border, which resulted in more than 700,000 Palestinians fleeing the area and the Israelis occupying new territory.

The largest number of refugees fled to that area of Palestine which in 1948 became the West Bank region of Jordan, while others moved into the Gaza Strip, Lebanon and Syria. The Six Day War of 1967 caused further displacements and ended with Israeli occupation of the West Bank and the Gaza Strip. The Palestinians who remain in Israel are isolated from the Jewish majority, and there are now well over 2,000,000 refugees.

Responsibility for their welfare is in the hands of UNRWA (the United Nations Relief and Works Agency), which has established camps, provides health and education services and dispenses rations. Conditions in the camps vary; usually they are overcrowded and amenities are minimal, but their very existence has been a major factor in preserving and encouraging a Palestinian identity. Some refugees, who have found employment in towns, have been assimilated by the host communities.

Militant Palestinian organizations have undertaken a series of guerrilla exploits to draw world attention to their aspirations and rights as a people. Relations with host countries have sometimes been strained. In 1970 King Hussein used the full force of his army to crush Palestinian guerrillas in Jordan. More recently, Syrian troops moved against guerrillas supporting the Muslims in Lebanon. However,

in recent years the Palestinian political movements have gained increasing support and international recognition.

Jordanians
pop: 2,833,000
The kingdom of Jordan has borders with Syria, Iraq and Saudi Arabia; to the west the Jordan river forms a temporary armistice line dividing it from Israel. Much of the country is desert, but in the west the land is fertile and mountainous.

The Jordanians are of mixed ancestry. In early Biblical times the west was inhabited by a number of Semitic tribes; Bedouin occupied the desert areas. By the 4th century BC the Greek invasion had brought a large number of Greek settlers. Control then passed to the Romans, but after 636 AD Arabs from the peninsula fused with earlier ethnic groups, introducing both their language and the religion of Islam.

In 1921 the country came under British mandate. Independence as Transjordan followed in 1946, and much of the eastern part of Palestine was taken over during the 1948 Arab-Israeli War, when the state was renamed Jordan. Hostility with Israel continued and in 1967 the Israelis occupied a large portion of Jordanian Palestine, which they still control.

The western mountains maintain a prosperous, sedentary population. Villagers grow wheat, barley and maize, and have orchards of apples, apricots, peaches and olives. Cultivation methods remain traditional, for machinery cannot be used on the narrow, hilly terraces. East of the mountains is a rolling plain, some 25 miles wide, where wheat and barley are grown by mechanized techniques.

Further east still the rainfall decreases and only the Bedouin inhabit the arid limestone hills. During the moister winter and spring months they graze their camel herds in the deserts, but in summer, when the grass dries up, they return to the edge of the cultivated area where their animals forage the stubble fields after harvest. In recent years government control has virtually halted intertribal warfare.

Israeli Expansion

■ Borders proposed by United Nations, 1947

■ Borders of Israel, established 1949

■ Greatest extent of occupied territory, 1970

Turkey, Syria
Turks, Syrians, Alawites, Druze

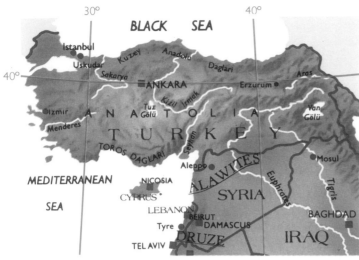

Ottoman Empire
*c.*1680

Turks

pop: 41,516,000

Forming a bridge between Europe and Asia, Turkey's location has been of prime importance in its history, culture and politics. Anatolia's early settlers were a mixture of Caucasoid peoples: the Turks themselves, who are descended from the Huns of central Asia, did not arrive until the 11th century. The Seljuk dynasty established the first Turkish state in Anatolia, but later fell to the Mongol Ottomans, who were soon absorbed by the Turkish population. The Ottoman Empire, which at its peak included most of the Middle East and North Africa, was dismembered after the First World War, and the present republic of Turkey was established in 1923.

Despite the many differing groups which made up the Turkish people, the population has become remarkably homogeneous in physical and cultural terms. The only sizeable minority are the Kurds, who retain their own culture and strongly resist government interference. A large proportion of the Turkish population are agriculturalists living in settled villages. Grain crops, vegetables, sheep and goats provide personal subsistence, with sugar beet, cotton and tobacco grown as cash crops. The rural areas have experienced a rapid population expansion in the last few decades and, despite subdivision of plots and the cultivation of previously unused lands, there is a severe lack of employment.

In recent years thousands of peasants have moved to the cities, building shacks, or *geçekondu*, on the outskirts. Almost two-thirds of the population of Ankara now live in such settlements. Many of these people are unable to find work and their only alternative is to join the many Turkish migrant workers in the north European countries. Those able to get contracts to work overseas usually send most of their wages home to family and village. Many migrant labourers suffer from severe loneliness and families often break up when the father goes abroad to work. There are now more than a million Turks employed in northern Europe, developing a sub-culture of their own.

Almost the entire population of Turkey is Muslim, but in sweeping reforms in the 1920s Islamic education was stopped, women unveiled, Koranic law replaced by European law and the relationship between the state and religion disentangled. More recently governments have made concessions to Islam to win the votes of the devout and religion is playing a greater role in politics.

Syrians

pop: 7,722,000

Syria has occupied a prominent place in the history of the Middle East because of its trans-continental position between Turkey and Iraq. The modern state has been shorn of frontier lands, which now belong to Lebanon, Israel and Jordan, but it still holds a strip of the Mediterranean coast.

The Syrians' ancestors were among the earliest civilized people of the Mediterranean basin but the kingdoms they formed were never unified. Their city-states were controlled by a series of empires – Sumerian, Egyptian, Hittite, Persian, Greek and Roman – all of which have left some mark on the culture and ethnicity of modern Syria.

In the 7th century a wave of conquerors from the Arabian peninsula brought the religion of Islam. Syria fell and Damascus became the seat of the ruling Umayyad dynasty for a century. Control over the country passed through Persian, Egyptian, Turkish and French hands before independence in the 1930s. The first 20 years of independence were marked by violent political upheaval. Parliamentary experiments were followed by coups and counter-coups, all producing governments of varying military and civilian proportions. In recent years though, the Ba'thist régimes have brought a degree of political stability.

Syria's population is formed of many ethnic and religious groups: Arabs, Kurds and Turkmen, among whom there are Sunni and Shi'i Muslims, Druze, Alawites and Christians. The lives of the Muslims are based on similar principles to those of most Arab groups, but other religious minorities vary greatly in their customs and social organization.

Until recently the landowners, the feudal chiefs and merchants were the most powerful and cohesive political groups, but since the Second

World War a new element, the intelligentsia (teachers and doctors, lawyers and army officers), has challenged their authority.

About 60 per cent of Syrians earn their living from agriculture. Wheat, barley and cotton are the chief crops, but fruit, vegetables, tobacco and livestock are also important. Much of the country is naturally fertile, with the river systems providing water for irrigation, but antiquated farming methods, inefficient land reform and variations in natural rainfall keep production far below potential. The damming of the Euphrates and a redistribution of land ownership have begun to encourage some expansion of agriculture.

The proportion of Syrians involved in industry and trade is growing steadily. The extractive industries of oil, gas, phosphates and metals are most important, but textile production and food processing have both developed. The 1973 war with Israel resulted in the destruction of much of Syria's industry and infrastructure, but the Arab oil states provided capital for reconstruction.

Alawites

pop: 900,000

The Alawites, occasionally known as the Nusayri, are a Shi'i Muslim sect who occupy the mountainous Jebel Ansariye region of north-west Syria. By avoiding intermarriage with other Muslim groups, they have maintained a distinct physical appearance as well as their own traditions. They recognize the festival of Christmas and some of their rituals, such as fertility ceremonies, have pagan origins.

The Alawites have survived persecution by the Crusaders and later by the Turks. At other times they have warred with their neighbours and even amongst themselves. Under French rule, their cultural autonomy was encouraged and they were administered as an individual state, with Latakia, on the Mediterranean coast, as the capital. Later this state became part of the Syrian Arab Republic.

Alawites have played a prominent role in the nation's political life, supporting the Ba'th Party, maintaining a dominant position in the armed forces, and providing the most recent president. The majority of the Alawites, however, remain agriculturalists, cultivating grains, cotton and tobacco, and breeding silk-worms.

Druze

pop: 300,000

The Druze are distinguished from their neighbours by their religion. One of their basic tenets is that their beliefs must be kept secret from outsiders, and this has given them a reputation as a taciturn people.

Today they occupy mountainous areas in southern Lebanon, south-western Syria and northern Israel. Their ethnic origins are obscure, but the development of their religion dates back to 1019 AD, when Ismail Darazi, a supporter of the last Egyptian caliph, fled to Lebanon. The religion, which was named after him, is based on belief in one god who is continually reincarnated on earth.

The Druze developed a village-based mixed farming society, recognizing both village and local leaders. In the 16th and 17th centuries, internal disputes resulted in the defeated factions migrating to south-western Syria. Today wheat grown by the Druze contributes greatly to the Syrian economy and Syrian law recognizes their particular customs.

The Druze believe in a hierarchy of spiritual beings and their social structure, while allowing equal status to men and women, reflects this. At the top are the *ajawid*, or elders, who represent only 2 per cent of the population. They are drawn from the *uqqal*, or knowledgeable ones, who number about 13 per cent of the Druze. The remaining 85 per cent are the *juhhal*, or ignorant ones, who must be at least 40 years old before they can become *uqqal*.

photograph:
Druze village near the
Golan Heights, Syria

wool). The different orders each follow the teachings of one man, using a variety of ritual exercises to reach one end: unity with god. Turkey's Maulavi or Whirling Dervishes are renowned for their dances; the scattered Qadiri Dervishes reach such an ecstatic state in their rituals that they are capable of skewering their flesh and eating glass, apparently without pain.

Each Dervish order is led by a *shaikh* or *pir* who claims spiritual descent from the original founder, and whose absolute authority must be recognized by the total submission of the initiate. The number of Dervishes is declining as the younger generations of the Middle East reject the disciplines of the mystic tradition. In many countries the religious establishment has branded the practices of the orders as unorthodox.

Kurds

pop: 9,000,000

Kurdistan covers a vast area of mountains from the Taurus and Pontic ranges in Turkey, to the Zagros in Iran. It is the homeland of the fourth largest language group in the Middle East and straddles five countries. About half live in Turkey, while most of the remainder are in Iran and Iraq, and a few in the Soviet Union and Syria. The Kurds have lived in this rugged area for centuries; perhaps the most famous Kurd was Saladin, who fought against Richard Coeur de Léon in the Third Crusade.

In the late 19th century, Shaikh Ubaidally of Oramar tried unsuccessfully to establish an autonomous Kurdish state within the Ottoman Empire. In 1920 the Treaty of Sèvres included a draft scheme for a Kurdish state which, although it was never ratified, has not been forgotten. In all three countries where there are significant Kurdish populations – Turkey, Iran and Iraq – there has been unrest since the First World War.

Turkey has dealt with this unrest by repression; Iran has been somewhat gentler. In Iraq, however, the nomadic Kurds have been more or less in continuous revolt for the last half century. Mullah Mustafa Barzani emerged as a forceful leader during the 1940s and has since waged a number of campaigns against the Iraqi government.

The vast majority of Kurds outside Iraq farm in the mountain valleys and lowland plains. They grow wheat, rye, barley, peas, beans, rice and tobacco. Houses are built of mud bricks with a roof of boards covered with earth. Kurds owe allegiance both to their family group and to the tribe as a whole; men carry weapons at all times. Women enjoy a more privileged position than in most Muslim societies and do not wear a veil; where there are schools, it is quite usual for Kurdish families to send girls as well as boys. In the past, there have even been instances of women heading tribes.

A number of Kurds now live in large cities and there is inevitably a contrast between these people and the mountain Kurds who still acknowledge the authority of tribal leaders. Among the urbanized Kurds there are doctors, lawyers, civil servants and even cabinet ministers. Yet during the last uprising, which finally collapsed in the spring of 1975, many of these city Kurds joined their kinsmen fighting in the hills.

Dervishes

pop: not available

The name Dervish is applied to the followers of a number of mystical Islamic orders found throughout the Middle East. Their traditions date back to the early Muslim ascetics known as Sufis, after their woollen robes (*suf* is Arabic for

Iraqis

pop: 11,577,000

Iraq was known to the classical world as Mesopotamia, the 'land between the rivers', for both the Tigris and the Euphrates flow through the country. Near them are the sites of the world's earliest cities. This fertile land has undergone many conquests, but the most important was the Arab invasion of the 7th century, spreading the new religion of Islam. For several centuries the caliphs, the successors to the prophet Muhammad, ruled the Muslim world from Baghdad.

In the mid-13th century, there was a brief period of Mongol rule, and Iraq then became part of the Ottoman Empire. It remained so until after the First World War, and full independence was delayed until 1932. A revolution in 1958 deposed King Feisal and Iraq was declared a republic. Since that date there have been several coups, and various constitutions, but the army has held power at all times.

Despite a variety of peoples, languages and even religions, time has gradually brought a sense of national identity. Arabs constitute the main part of the population, but there are also groups with Mongol,

Distribution of Kurds

Turkish, Turkmen, Armenian and Circassian ancestry.

The largest minority group are the Kurds, who constitute some 20 per cent of the population and inhabit a mountainous area in the north-east. They practise some agriculture, but are primarily pastoral nomads. For almost half a century the Kurds have been in more or less continuous revolt against the government.

Religious loyalties run across Iraq's ethnic and linguistic divisions. Islam plays a central part in daily life, particularly in rural areas. However, the Muslims, who make up 90 per cent of the population, are split between the two branches of their faith, Sunni and Shi'i, and this has caused friction for centuries.

Agriculture supports about 70 per cent of the people. In the north it relies on rainfall, but there are large-scale irrigation projects in the south. Dates are the main cash crop, but wheat, barley, linseed, beans, millet and rice are also grown. Since the revolution, land-ownership has moved

from tribal chiefs to co-operative associations and productivity has improved.

By far the most important export is oil. Iraq is a member of the Organization of Petroleum Exporting Countries (OPEC), and recent increases in oil revenues have enabled the government to begin rapid industrial development and modernization of agriculture. The opportunities for urban employment have attracted more people to the towns than can be accommodated. In the cities, western influence is plain, but in rural areas traditional values are still strong.

Marsh Arabs

pop: 50,000

The Marsh Arabs, or *ma'dan*, inhabit a vast area of marshland in southern Iraq, where the Tigris and Euphrates rivers meet. The inaccessibility of the marshland made it a refuge for defeated tribes and persecuted minorities. They have intermarried for centuries but are of diverse origins: Arab, Iranian and Negro. Arabic is

the main language, and the Marsh Arabs have retained the values of their desert ancestors: they offer hospitality in the same manner as the Bedouin and status is conferred by lineage rather than wealth.

A typical marsh village consists of low houses made of reeds standing on damp, man-made islands; canoes provide transport. The *ma'dan* can be divided into two occupational groups: water buffalo breeders and those who fish and make mats. The former are nomadic and move according to their animals' needs; the latter are settled, but keep buffalo for their milk and dung. Although the marshmen have a contempt for commerce and trade, they must sell mats in order to buy essential imports.

In recent years there has been a drift of population from this area to the cities and oilfields. The government now exerts more control over the marshes and a money economy is being introduced. There is a possibility that in the future much of the marshland will be drained.

Ma'dan boatmen in the marshes, southern Iraq

Iran
Iranians, Bakhtiari, Qashqai, Baluch

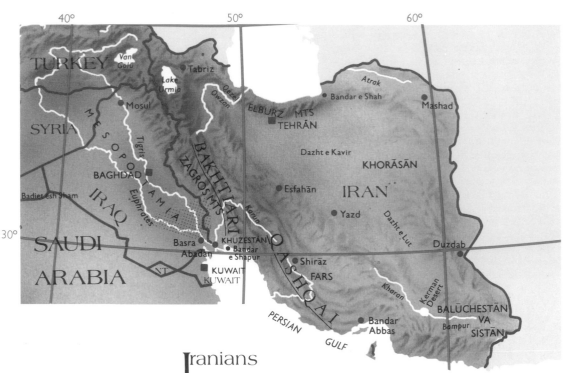

Iranians

pop: 34,455,000

When large bands of Aryan tribesmen migrated from the southern steppes of Russia to settle east of the Euphrates valley, about 2,000 years before the birth of Christ, they laid the basis of the first Persian Empire. Their successors conquered Ethiopia, Egypt and India, but were eventually defeated by the Greeks.

The Arab conquest of Persia in the 7th century AD had a more lasting effect than that of the Greeks, despite later invasions by Mongols and Turks. Arabic never replaced the Persian languages, however, of which Farsi is now the most important. The Saffavids in the 16th century created a second Persian Empire and formally adopted the Shi'i branch of Islam. They were followed by a succession of dynasties, of which the latest started in 1925.

In the fertile, lower-lying parts of the country the primary means of livelihood has been share-cropping on the estates of great landlords. If the peasant's only contribution is labour he is only entitled to one-fifth of the produce he grows – if he provides tools or animals he will receive more. Peasants supplement this income by raising goats for wool, milk, yoghurt and cheese, keeping chickens and selling carpets woven by the women and children of the household. Land reforms in recent years have attempted to give the peasants a fairer share of their produce.

The way of life in the mountain areas is considerably different from that of the plains villagers. In the Zagros ranges live pastoral nomads such as the Qashqai, Bakhtiari and Lur. These people graze their sheep and goats in the foothills of the mountains in winter and in summer move them up to the higher pastures. Other nomadic and semi-nomadic groups include Kurds and Turkmen in the north, and Baluch in the east.

Iran has witnessed many changes since the Second World War. In the fertile areas that border the Caspian Sea, fishing and rice cultivation are being replaced by cotton farming based on factory farm methods. As a result of oil revenues, a western-style bureaucracy and education system have been introduced. The cities have been rapidly developed and Tehran is beginning to suffer from traffic congestion and air pollution.

Bakhtiari

pop: 500,000

The Bakhtiari live in the Zagros mountains of western Iran; they are mostly nomadic, herding sheep and goats. They also cultivate a few crops, such as wheat and barley, at their winter quarters in Khuzestan province. There are a variety of tribes in this rugged area, with diverse ethnic origins and a tradition of hostility. Central government has never had much control over the mountain tribesmen, who traditionally dominated the settled villagers with whom they came into contact.

The Bakhtiari are divided into a number of sub-tribes known as *taifeh*. *Taifeh* members regard themselves as being the descendants of a distant ancestor and therefore as kinsmen. The *taifeh* is subdivided into other units, down to the level of a camp group, or *mal*, which usually consists of 4-10 tents. Marriage between members of different *taifeh* is rare, and often blood feuds between sub-tribes may persist for generations.

Although some Bakhtiari have adopted a settled mode of existence in recent decades, life for many of the tribes still revolves around the annual migrations. Each *taifeh* has its own traditional summer and winter quarters, and the distance each group must travel varies greatly.

The winter pastures dry up in late spring and the sheep and goats must then be moved to the higher summer pastures. This may entail a journey of 250 miles over the mountains. The spring migration is fairly leisurely: the animals graze on the lower slopes and are gradually taken higher. In the autumn, however, both food and water are scarce and the nomads must return to their winter quarters as quickly as possible. The severe weather conditions and difficult terrain can cause high mortality amongst the animals and bad luck can wipe out a family's entire wealth and livelihood.

During the migrations the men herd and protect the flocks and raise the tents; when camp settles, the women do all the work of cooking, milking animals and fetching water. Although the Bakhtiari are Muslims, the women have more freedom than their settled counterparts.

The economic condition of the Bakhtiari is varied. Those with poor grazing eke out a miserable existence, but those with better lands can live quite comfortably and possess sizeable flocks. Government policy has encouraged many of the tribe to give up the hardships of migration, take on a sedentary life and receive medical services and education.

Qashqai

pop: 150,000

The Qashqai occupy an area in the south of Iran, in the provinces of Fars and Esfahan. Although they are commonly considered pastoral nomads, a large number have traditionally been engaged in irrigated agriculture. Six sub-groups or *taifeh* make up the whole tribe and each of these has a leader. The *taifeh* is subdivided into smaller units down to the level of the *beyleh*, a camp group of 6-10 tents.

During the winter the nomads live in the lowlands to the south of the Zagros mountains, where they graze their animals and cultivate grains and vegetables. As pasture becomes scarce in spring, they migrate north to higher ground. The Qashqai's journeys are taxing, but not as spectacular as those of tribes such as the Bakhtiari. Work is divided sexually: men do jobs such as setting up tents and herding, the women undertake domestic chores like cooking and weaving.

Until recently the Qashqai had considerable influence in the provincial capital of Shiraz, but the government now favours tribes with more sedentary interests. Attempts to make the Qashqai settle have met with little success, although some men have gone to urban centres as wage labourers. Education is now available in the form of mobile tents, with teachers recruited from the tribe itself.

Baluch

pop: 1,000,000

The Baluch inhabit a vast mountainous area divided between Iran, Pakistan and Afghanistan; they have their own language. Although economies vary with each community, Baluch generally rely on a mixture of nomadic pastoralism and settled agriculture. They keep a variety of animals and grow wheat, barley, vegetables and fruit.

Small agricultural plots, shared by up to 10 people, ensure that the nomads never move far from their territory. These plots must be tended regularly by the owners, or they forfeit their claim to the produce. The northern plateaux of Baluchistan provide good spring pastures for sheep and goats, but to the south rain is uncertain and the date palm is the most reliable means of subsistence.

As well as a network of kinship and marriage ties, which ensures freedom of movement and good relations over a wide area, the Baluch share a common system of social and political behaviour. Baluch society is hierarchical, and everyone knows his place, both in the tribe and in the regional hierarchy. Marriages are arranged at an early age and follow Islamic rites. The families agree on a bride-wealth paid in sheep and goats. After marriage, women perform domestic chores, while the men herd the flocks and tend the small plots.

Baluchistan has long been isolated, but now all three governments are beginning to develop their areas with roads and agricultural schemes.

Baluchistan

photograph:
Morning prayer in the
Blue Mosque, Esfahān

Africa

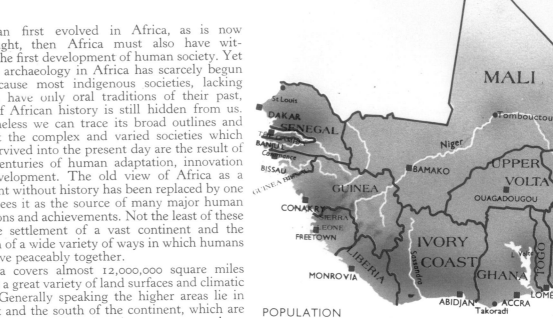

If man first evolved in Africa, as is now thought, then Africa must also have witnessed the first development of human society. Yet because archaeology in Africa has scarcely begun and because most indigenous societies, lacking literacy, have only oral traditions of their past, much of African history is still hidden from us. Nevertheless we can trace its broad outlines and see that the complex and varied societies which have survived into the present day are the result of many centuries of human adaptation, innovation and development. The old view of Africa as a continent without history has been replaced by one which sees it as the source of many major human inventions and achievements. Not the least of these was the settlement of a vast continent and the creation of a wide variety of ways in which humans could live peaceably together.

Africa covers almost 12,000,000 square miles and has a great variety of land surfaces and climatic zones. Generally speaking the higher areas lie in the east and the south of the continent, which are drained by several major river systems such as those of the Nile, Zaire (formerly Congo), Zambesi and Volta, recently dammed to create the world's largest man-made lake. A series of rift valleys runs for more than 3,000 miles down the eastern side of the continent. The passage from one climatic region to another tends to be gradual but, with such a large land mass, there are startling contrasts: the great deserts of the Sahara in the north and the Kalahari in the south can support few people, but elsewhere the tropical savanna of the plateaux and the lush equatorial rain forests are densely populated. At the southern tip of the continent a Mediterranean type of climate and vegetation prevails.

It is likely that the original inhabitants of Africa were people of small stature, physically similar to the Bushmen (San) and Pygmies of today. They lived by hunting and gathering, using simple wood, horn and stone tools and weapons and almost certainly leading a semi-nomadic existence. This mode of life was easier in the past when parts of the continent, such as the area which is now the Sahara, were far more fertile. Even now a few groups of people continue to live in this way; most, like the Bushmen of the Kalahari desert and the Hadza of Tanzania, have managed to survive only by exploiting areas which are unsuitable for use by their agricultural or pastoralist neighbours. While economies of the latter sorts can support large, centralized political systems, African hunters and gatherers tend to live in small loosely-structured groups without formal systems of leadership and government, moving about the large territories which enable them to survive years of drought and scarcity.

Today Africans of the Bushmen physical type survive only in the south and the continent is dominated by agricultural and pastoral populations of a larger and more robust physical character. Whatever their ultimate origin these people had already begun to expand through much of Africa more than 5,000 years ago. Some time after this expansion began two crucial innovations occurred which profoundly influenced the subsequent history of Africa: the spread of agriculture and the introduction of iron working. These ultimately allowed the growth of large populations, the

VEGETATION

- **Conifer Forest** Pine, spruce, larch
- **Broadleaf Forest** Deciduous
- **Temperate** Arable, broadleaf, grass
- **Mediterranean** Citrus, olive, agave
- **Subtropical** Dry and wet evergreen
- **Tropical** 'Selva'
- **Prairie** Long grass
- **Savanna** Grass and scrub
- **Semi Desert** Cactus, sparse shrub and grass
- **Desert** No vegetation
- **Marsh and Swamp**
- **Salt** Salt lake, marsh

- ■ **Capital Cities**
- ⋮ **Major Towns**
- • **Towns** Small town village
- —— **Country Borders**
- —— **Borders** Provinces, states

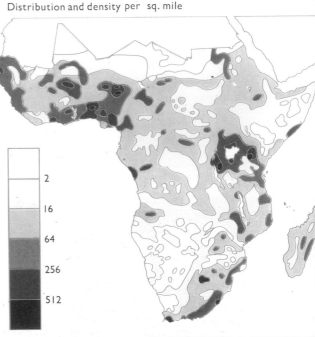

POPULATION
Distribution and density per sq. mile

	2
	16
	64
	256
	512

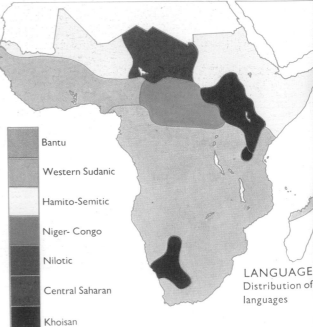

- Bantu
- Western Sudanic
- Hamito-Semitic
- Niger-Congo
- Nilotic
- Central Saharan
- Khoisan

LANGUAGE
Distribution of languages

NIGER

Agades

CHAD

L. Chad

N'DJAMENE

Kano

GERIA

Benue

CAMEROON

YAOUNDÉ

BATA

EQUATORIAL GUINEA

LIBREVILLE

Port Gentil

GABON

CONGO

BRAZZAVILLE

KINSHASA

Boma

Kwango

LUANDA

Lobito

ANGOLA

Nova Lisboa

Kunene

OCEAN

ATLANTIC

Walvis Bay

NAMIBIA

WINDHOEK

BOTSWANA

GABORONE

PRETORIA

Johannesburg

Vaal

Orange

SOUTH

Kimberley

Bloemfontein

AFRICA

Cape Town

East London

Port Elizabeth

CENTRAL

AFRICAN EMPIRE

BANGUI

Ubangi

Bomu

Uele

Zaire (Congo)

CONGO

Kisangani

BASIN

ZAIRE

Congo

Kasai

Ilebo

Lualaba

Luvua

Kamina

L. Mweru

Kalemie

Kigoma

TANZANIA

Kafue

ZAMBIA

Lubumbashi

LUSAKA

Livingstone

Victoria Falls

SALISBURY

ZIMBABWE

Bulawayo

Beira

MOZAMBIQUE

Zambezi

LILONGWE

Zomba

MALAWI

L. Nyasa (Malawi)

Ruvuma

Mtwara

Rufiji

L. Rukwa

DAR ES SALAAM

Zanzibar

Mozambique

Mozambique Channel

Majunga

Tamatave

TANANARIVE

MADAGASCAR

MAPUTO

MBABANE

SWAZILAND

MASERU

LESOTHO

Durban

SUDAN

Omdurman

KHARTOUM

El Obeid

White Nile

Blue Nile

Nile

Port Sudan

RED

SEA

Asmara

ADDIS ABABA

ETHIOPA

L. Abaya

Shebelle

DJIBOUTI

DJIBOUTI

GULF OF ADEN

SOMALI REPUBLIC

INDIAN

OCEAN

MOGADISHU

Juba

L. Rudolf

UGANDA

L. Albert

L. Kyoga

KAMPALA

L. Edward

L. Kivu

KIGALI

RWANDA

BUJUMBURA

L. Victoria

KENYA

NAIROBI

Tana

Lake Tanganyika

Projection: Miller's Prolated Stereographic

TEMPERATURE

Actual surface temperature
in centigrade

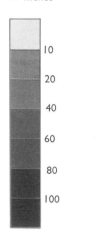

- −35
- −30
- −20
- −10
- 0
- 10
- 20
- 30
- 35

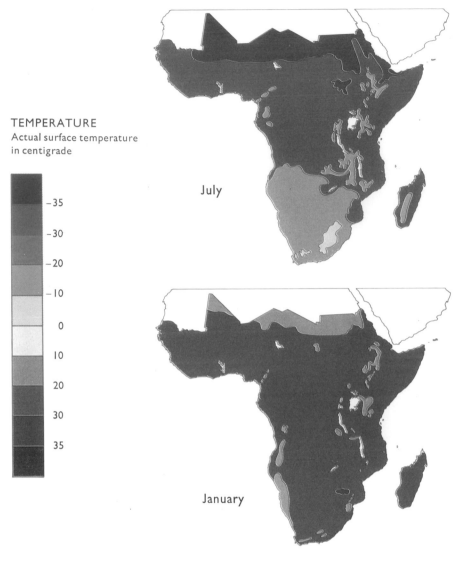

July

January

RAINFALL

Average annual rainfall
in inches

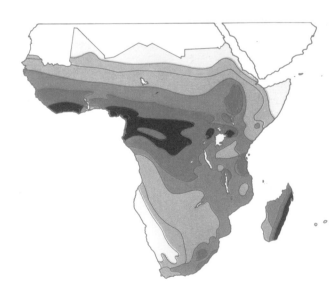

- 10
- 20
- 40
- 60
- 80
- 100

exploitation of new areas and the development of more elaborate systems of government.

The technique of iron smelting probably reached sub-Saharan Africa from Meroë in Sudan in the first millennium BC. The history of African agriculture is still not fully established: some crops seem to have diffused from Egypt; others, such as certain types of yam and grain, may have been domesticated within Africa; others still were brought by Europeans from the Americas. In East Africa a variety of banana introduced from Indonesia made a major contribution to the farming economy. The plough was not used in sub-Saharan Africa before white settlement and all crops were cultivated by hand using simple digging sticks and hoes, usually with each family farming for itself.

The use of iron tools and of iron weapons seems to be one of the key factors which led to the expansion of Bantu-speaking groups into central and southern Africa. This expansion probably began around 500 BC, possibly starting from the Nigeria-Cameroon region. Thousands of years of population movement, new crops and adaptation to a variety of environments have created a patchwork of different societies right across Africa. Even now there are more than 700 distinct languages within the four major families into which African languages are divided and in many areas people with very distinct histories, languages and modes of livelihood live next to each other.

New crops, tools and weapons, and an increase in trading between different areas, favoured the growth of population which, in places, led to the development of more elaborate political systems. Although many African societies, for example the Masai and Nuer, were organized in descent groups well into the present century and had no institutions of chiefship, centralized states are recorded from sub-Saharan Africa as early as the 8th century. The first of these, Ghana, may have existed before this date: like later states such as Songhai and Kanem-Bornu its existence probably owed a lot to trans-Saharan trade links along which African gold and other products passed to the Mediterranean and Islamic worlds. In east and central Africa states appeared shortly afterwards. An important feature of the history of East Africa is the incursion of cattle-keeping groups from the north, some of which may have destroyed earlier centralized systems among the agriculturalist inhabitants of the area, while others seemed to have helped the establishment of centralized and stratified systems. In this connection the histories of the Ganda and of the Hutu and Tutsi groups are particularly interesting.

In most areas major movements of population and consequent political upheavals were still under way when colonial rule was forced on the Africans. The comparatively simple technology Europeans encountered caused them to overlook the distinctive African achievements in other areas and especially in the field of social control. In many African societies there is a great awareness of the problems of living together, the need to respect the rights of others and the importance of sharing. In some groups, such as the Nyakusa of southern Africa, sharing and good companionship are thought to be the most basic of social virtues, while in most other societies there are numerous mechanisms whereby adults and children are reminded of the need to live in amity with other members of their community. Proverbs and stories, riddles and jokes, the use of ridicule and the precepts taught in initiation rites all serve to bind the community together in a network of co-operation and exchange.

More direct methods of social control vary greatly. Among such semi-nomadic groups as the Mbuti Pygmies or the Hadza, disputes are usually settled by those involved going to join different groups, while in kingdoms like those of the Fon, Ashanti or Mossi disputes may be taken further and further up the hierarchy of office holders for judgement. In some East African societies the tasks of defence, arbitration and judgement are given to particular ranks within the age-sets into which the society is divided. Adults of roughly the same age are placed together in these age-sets, which cut across the ties and responsibilities of kinship.

Systems of belief and religious practices vary widely, but there are some common features. In many societies in which descent groups form an important part of the social and political system, ancestors are revered and their spirits consulted. Many groups also believe in a creator god, although he is often thought to take little interest in the day to day affairs of men and appeals are made to lesser deities. The strong African emphasis on fairness and sharing is reflected in beliefs about witches and sorcerers—humans who have somehow become possessed of special powers, which enable them to help or harm other members of their own group. The ability to take unfair advantage is thus regarded as unnatural, or inhuman.

The history of Africa in recent centuries is largely the history of European contact. At first this was limited to trading, and few whites stayed long in Africa. Yet even this limited contact had profound effects which reached far into the interior. In West Africa the old trans-Saharan trade patterns were disrupted and more and more trade shifted towards the coast. European goods were imported and firearms, the most important of these, helped the growth of states such as that of the Ashanti of Ghana.

For these goods, cloth, metal, arms and trinkets, Africans payed a heavy price in slaves and the consequent disruption of their societies. Every year thousands of Africans were shipped across the Atlantic, often under appalling conditions. Many died on the long voyage and those who survived lived on under harsh and restricted conditions with almost no rights; nevertheless many groups retained elements of their African heritage.

In Africa the effect of the slave trade was far-reaching: strong groups raided weaker ones for slaves to sell, and the movement of peoples, some fleeing for safety, and the disruption of old patterns of trade and alliances reached way beyond the coast. With the ending of the slave trade in the first half of the 19th century Europeans sought new trade opportunities, exploiting goods such as palm oil, rubber and cocoa. The continent then became an area of competition between the European powers, and force and deceit were used to seize vast territories from their indigenous rulers. To develop and control these new lands large numbers of Europeans moved into Africa.

The colonial period led to the commercial exploitation of many of the natural resources of Africa, the rapid and almost uncontrolled growth of new cities, the destruction of traditional political

boundaries and the introduction of Christianity. At the same time there was an almost complete failure by most Europeans to understand and respect the traditional cultures and beliefs of the Africans. In some areas missionaries, often supported by the colonial authorities, tried forcibly to eradicate traditional religious activities. Sculptures and masks, used in rituals, were seized and destroyed and many practices were outlawed. Well-established closed (secret) societes, responsible for education or the maintenance of law and order, were forbidden by the white authorities who considered them a threat to their rule, and in most areas attempts were made to reduce polygamy.

Where no chiefs existed the colonial governments imposed them; where they already existed the authorities tried to incorporate them into their new system of over-rule. Gradually the work of some administrators, anthropologists, and the efforts of Africans themselves began to demonstrate that native culture, with its own morality and values, was worthy of respect and that many customs, when seen in their full context, made sense. It is only now, when most of these have undergone profound change, that they are receiving the attention they deserve.

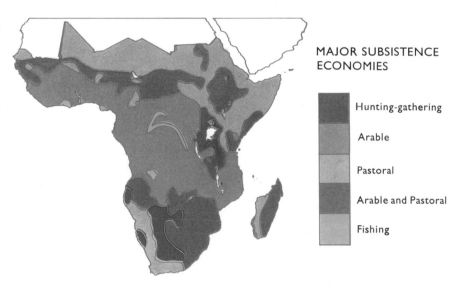

MAJOR SUBSISTENCE ECONOMIES

- Hunting-gathering
- Arable
- Pastoral
- Arable and Pastoral
- Fishing

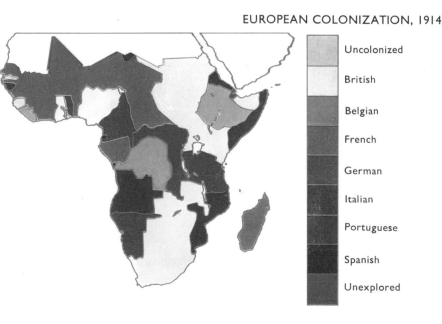

EUROPEAN COLONIZATION, 1914

- Uncolonized
- British
- Belgian
- French
- German
- Italian
- Portuguese
- Spanish
- Unexplored

migrating to the towns. French is the official language.

Gambia
pop: 544,000

A narrow strip of land surrounded by Senegal, Gambia is Africa's smallest country and consists of marshy valley and low sandy savanna plain, on either side of the Gambia river. Brikama, Kerewan, Georgetown and the capital port Banjul (formerly Bathurst) are the major towns. The official language is English. Mande speaking peoples form the majority of the population—in addition to a large group of Malinke, they include Serahule traders, Dyula rice growers and the Wolof; there are also some Fulani. Senegalese migrants do seasonal farmwork, helping produce groundnuts, the major cash crop, rice and cotton.

Senegal
pop: 5,174,000

Africa's westernmost state, Senegal consists of lowland savanna, dissected by river valleys in the south, merging into uplands in the south-east and semi-desert in the north-west. Major towns include the new oil-refining centre at Cayar, the major port and capital Dakar, St Louis and Kaolack.

Despite some industrialization and mineral resources including phosphates, agriculture employs most of the population. Groundnuts provide the majority of export revenues, but the government has recently attempted to extend the cultivation of cotton and develop market gardening.

Major ethnic groups divide linguistically into West Atlantic, Fulfulde and Mande speaking peoples, many with traditions of strictly organized, hierarchical societies. The Islamic Wolof, who form about one-third of the population, are mainly agriculturalists; the southern Serer are cultivators and cattle breeders; the Fulani, traditionally pastoralist, are now increasingly becoming settled cultivators; and the Dyula specialize in growing rice. The Toucouleur, rulers of ancient Tekrour and the earliest Islamic converts, are primarily agriculturalists although increasing numbers are

Kingdom of Tekrour,
c.1200 AD

Wolof
pop: 1,500,000

Senegal's largest ethnic group, the Wolof occupy the savanna plains near the coast, between the Senegal and Gambia rivers. Like their neighbours the Serer, they are mainly agriculturalists, growing the staples millet and sorghum, with groundnuts as a cash crop. Many also own cattle, which are often entrusted to Fulani herdsmen. Wolof also work in the urban centres of Dakar and St Louis as traders, craftsmen, teachers and civil servants.

The Wolof probably developed from a mixture of incoming peoples and indigenous inhabitants during the 11th century. Gradually expanding towards the south, they have taken over many new regions and recently sought better land for their farming activities in Gambia's Cassamance region.

A clear system of social ranking still exists in rural areas, dividing the Wolof into three main strata. The freeborn class traditionally included those of royal lineages, those who held regional office, titles or electoral power, and other independent Wolof. Slaves were ranked according to their owner's status, and those born in the household were considered superior to those captured or purchased. It is still rare for freeborn women to

marry men of slave origin. Smiths, leatherworkers and musicians made up the despised craftsman class.

The Wolof live in large villages consisting of a series of fenced-off compounds which house extended family groups. Polygyny is permitted, although most men have only one wife—chiefs and headmen often have several. Divorce is frequent and relatively simple for men; women have to instigate court proceedings.

Guinea-Bissau
pop: 518,000

Guinea-Bissau's swampy coastal region is backed by lowland rain forest, where the rural population grow rice, cassava, maize and groundnuts. Bissau, the capital, Bolama and Catcheu are the main towns. Major ethnic groups include the Balente, Pepel, Mandjak, Fulani and Malinke; there are also a sizeable number of Cape Verde creoles, whose patois has become a *lingua franca*. Guinea-Bissau won independence from Portugal in 1974, but Portuguese remains the official language.

Guinea
pop: 4,584,000

Guinea's coastline is fringed with mangrove swamps, backed by a plain. Further inland, the steeply rising Fouta Djallon runs into grassland to the north and forest in the south. Coffee, bananas, pineapples and palm products are the main exports.

Major ethnic groups include the Fulani, Malinke and Susu. Some Fulani still raise cattle in the Fouta Djallon; elsewhere staple crops include rice, millet, maize and cassava. Guinea possesses vast bauxite deposits, but their exploitation is still in its infancy. The official language is French.

Sierra Leone
pop: 2,810,000

Rain forest and swampland spread up the river valleys from Sierra Leone's coastal plain, with wooded savanna plateau inland. Major towns include Pepel, Kenema, Bo and Freetown, settled originally by slaves freed *en route* to the Americas. A Freetown

élite have monopolized political and professional positions.

The main ethnic groups include the Mende and Temne, traditional rivals, the Limba, Kuranko, Susa and Sherbro. There are small Kru, Vai, Fulani and Lebanese minorities. Despite rapid urbanization, and mineral wealth including diamonds, iron ore and bauxite, four-fifths of the population are still engaged in agriculture, growing the staple rice and cash crops including cocoa, coffee, ginger and kola nuts. The official language is English.

Mende
pop: 1,000,000

The equatorial rain forest of central and eastern Sierra Leone, and the western corner of Liberia, is the homeland of the agriculturalist Mende people. Since independence, they have dominated political office in Sierra Leone and have been drawn increasingly into urban administration.

Mende wealth was formerly based on the barter and exchange of slaves for commodities such as salt and cattle. An important source of bridewealth, slaves were for a long period the only cultivators in Mende society. Now practising shifting hoe agriculture, the Mende grow a variety of staple and cash crops, including upland rice and palm produce.

Although the Mende were a strong military force in the 18th and 19th centuries, they never formed a unified nation state. They divided into independent, warring chiefdoms, based on towns. The Mende are still divided into about 60 chiefdoms, consisting of several sub-chiefdoms based on towns and their surrounding villages. Headmen are the oldest patrilineal descendants of each settlement's founder.

Social organization was, and still is, dependent on 'secret' societies with specialized community functions, most of which are publicly known. The control of these societies over Mende moral conduct is based on the belief that leaders possess powerful supernatural medicines and have knowledge of rituals, signs and symbols.

Mental illness is thought to result from offences against the Njayei society, when individuals have either trespassed on its sacred bush, or seen the ritually unpurified body of an important member. The cure is by initiation and therapy, including the prescription of various herbs and leaves administered by ritual sprinkling, poultices and potions.

The principal societies are Poro for men and Sande for the women, which confer on initiates the right to procreate. Boys have to undergo severe tests at puberty and are given vocational and moral training by the Poro. At their final initiation ceremony supplications are made to dead society members. Sande girls are taught rituals and practices appropriate for marriage and for motherhood.

Divided into local chapters, the Poro, with its officials masked as spirits, provided the intimidation and mystical sanction necessary for the secular power of the chieftaincy. Sometimes taking priority, the Poro council discussed both external and internal affairs, and decided important legal cases in secret tribunals.

With strong traditions of ancestor worship, the Mende also believe in the existence of certain spirits or genii, with human and supernatural characteristics, contact with whom is dangerous but possibly fortunate. However, westernization has curtailed religious and secret society activities. The Sande has altered considerably and the Poro initiation has become a fee-paying rite.

Liberia
pop: 1,554,000

The republic of Liberia was established in 1847 by black settlers, predominantly emancipated and escaped slaves from the United States. These Americo-Liberians, whose transportation was arranged by the philanthropic American Colonization Society, purchased land to found coastal settlements—Harper, Greenville, Buchanan, Robertsport and Monrovia, the capital.

Considering themselves civilized Americans and introducing Christianity, they maintained relations of colonial dominance over the indigenous peoples. Despite intermarriage and government policies of unification, their descendants still form a politico legal élite and dominate Liberian economic life. English is the official language.

Most of the indigenous ethnic groups have links with related peoples in neighbouring countries. Occupying about half the territory and forming a quarter of the population are the Kru-speaking Bassa, De, Grebo, Krahn and the mariner Kru. Others include the Gola, Kpelle, Grebo and Vai, who developed their own written language during the 19th century.

A division exists between the interior, where the majority engage in subsistence agriculture, and the coastal cash economy. Rubber has been a major export since 1926 and the government has maintained free enterprise.

Kru
pop: 85,000

The Kru had probably reached their present home on the south coast of Liberia by the 16th century, migrating from somewhere near the source of the Niger river. Since the 18th century, they have provided deck hands for foreign ships, and were even protected from the slave trade by special agreements. Their knowledge of safe anchorages and watering places makes them invaluable pilots. Ashore, they work as lightermen, dock hands and warehousemen.

On land, social organization was based on township clusters, clans and age sets. Each township was independent, under the ultimate authority of its own chief, or *koloba*, and clan elders, or *pantons*. Kru towns were sometimes linked by dialect and migration traditions to form sub-tribes, or *dako*. These now form part of Liberia's administrative system.

The Kru have resisted incorporation with the Americo-Liberian élite, although some hold positions in the civil service, government and professions. Since 1930, many Kru have left their homeland to settle in Monrovia or in Freetown, Sierra Leone, where wage-employment is possible. Known as *kpafoka*, they have developed tribal-based corporations under Kru governors.

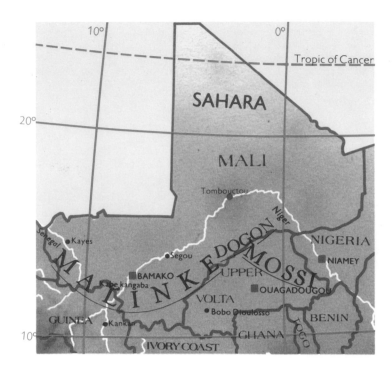

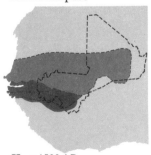

Mali Empire

- ◼ c.1500 AD
- ◼ c.1300 AD
- ---- Present borders of Mali

Malinke
pop: 1,500,000

An area extending across nine West African nations, bounded by Gambia in the west, Upper Volta in the east, the northern desert margins of Mali and the southern forests of Ivory Coast, is populated by the Mande, a network of linguistically and culturally related peoples. The largest groups are the Malinke and their Bambara neighbours.

In the Middle Ages the Malinke ruled the vast trading empire of Mali, established by Sundiata, the 'lion king', in the 13th century. They trace their expansion from its centre, the small mountainous area around Kangaba on the Niger river, where iron and gold deposits provided early wealth and financed wide-ranging conquest.

The tightly-knit social system of the Malinke is a complex organization with both clan and caste aspects. The *dyamu*, or patrilineage, whose members share common prohibitions and obligations, has integrated the Mande-speaking world. The *namakala* or craft group system embraces patrilineages traditionally associated with specific crafts or professions, such as iron-, gold- and silversmithing and leatherwork. Individuals with the same patrilineal craft name traditionally accord each other hospitality when they meet.

Malinke bards, or *dyeli*, belong to an important 'guild', which maintains ritual solidarity by gathering every seven years at Kangaba for secret ceremonies. The *dyeli*, many of whom specialize in playing such intruments as the elaborate 21-string harp-lute or *kora*, have preserved ancient lore and musical traditions through their recitations and songs.

Living in compounds of either the older style thatched, cylindrical houses, or square buildings roofed with corrugated iron, the Malinke are mainly agriculturalists growing a wide range of staple and cash crops. They also keep cattle, which they did not milk until the practice was introduced by Fulani herdsmen. Their trading traditions have continued, however; the Dyula people, part-Malinke and part-Bambara in origin, remain important traders in many West African nations, speaking their own language, a Mande dialect.

Mali
pop: 5,815,000 (1977)

With savanna in the south and barren sandstone plains and desert in the north, Mali is divided by the Niger bend, providing a fertile central region. The main towns are Bamako, the capital, Sikasso, Ségou, Mopti and the inland port of Kabara (near ancient Tombouctou). Major ethnic groups include the Malinke, Bambara, Sarakole, Songhai, Dogon and Senoufo, with nomadic Moors and Tuareg in the north. After livestock breeding, subsistence agriculture is the main economic activity; maize, millet and sorghum are the staple crops. The official language is French.

Dogon
pop: 250,000

The arid, rocky plateau land of the Bandiagara escarpment in eastern Mali near the border with Upper Volta is the remote homeland of the Dogon. Subsistence agriculturalists, they grow a variety of staples, including maize, millet and shallots. Surplus produce is traded in markets with Fulani pastoralists and other groups for meat, fish, salt and some imported goods.

Many aspects of Dogon social and economic organization are linked to an elaborate and intricate cosmology. The Dogon explain the structure of their universe and the interrelationships of their physical and social worlds in a complex tapestry of myths. Symbol and reality correspond and co-exist: social life reflects the working of the universe, which conversely depends on the proper ordering of society. Only a few wise men, however, have deep knowledge of all the myths.

One of the least complex part-myths concerns the original creation of life in the universe. A small cultivated seed called *kize-uzi*, the little thing, symbolizes the origin of life. Beginning as an internal vibration—a series of seven pulses which are envisaged as expanding in a revolving spiral—*kize-uzi* broke its sheath and grew to reach the ends of the universe.

Decorative motifs on Dogon houses are often interpreted as representing such vibrations, which are sometimes held to symbolize the perpetual alternation of opposites—high–low, right–left, odd–even, male–female. Similarly, each individual is considered the product of the same seven vibrations and the whole of creation is conceived as a cosmic egg, or *aduniotal*, in which the smallest part implies the whole. These principles, recurring with others in more complex myths, are said to permeate all aspects of Dogon society and culture.

The Dogon live in exogamous, patrilineal groups, inheriting totems through the male line. Widespread marriage exchanges are practised; marriage with the daughter of a maternal uncle is preferred and mythically sanctioned. Dogon districts are controlled by powerful, spiritual leaders, or *hogon*. Although the *hogon* of Arou is considered most important, there is no central system of authority and rule.

Upper Volta
pop: 6,300,000 (1977)

The large plateau of Upper Volta, with poor, coarse soil, is cut by the wooded valleys of the Black, Red and White Voltas and their tributaries. Ouagadougou, the traditional trade centre and capital of the Mossi empire, Bobo Diou-

lasso, Koudougou and Fada N'Gourma are the largest towns. The More-speaking Mossi form half the population, which also includes Yarse traders, Fulani, Senoufo and Dyula. The official language is French. Livestock is important to the economy, which is largely based on subsistence cultivation of maize, sorghum, millet and rice, with cotton and groundnuts grown for cash. Labour migration to neighbouring Ghana, Ivory Coast and Gabon is common.

Mossi
pop: 2,000,000

The arid, semi-desert region of Upper Volta is the homeland of the Mossi, predominantly subsistence agriculturalists. Owing to the conditions, more than 500,000 migrants, many permanent, now work in the cocoa and coffee plantations, mines and factories of Ivory Coast and Ghana. However, the rural economy has not benefited from labour migra-

tion, since families have lost their able-bodied young men, who are rarely able to save what they earn abroad.

According to one tradition the Mossi chieftainship derived from the more southerly states Mamprusi and Dagomba. The first Mossi king, or *naba*, conquered surrounding areas and created a network of interconnected royal houses, founding an enduring lineage of chiefs. By the 15th century, the Mossi state was established as a prosperous centre on the trans-Saharan caravan routes, its chiefs obtaining revenue through taxing market transactions. Many Yarse traders, Muslims of Mande origin, settled and introduced their religion to the Mossi.

Mossi society traditionally divides into three interdependent social estates: royalty, who claim patrilineal descent from the first *naba*; commoners, descendants of the founder's cavalrymen and local women; and the original indigenous inhabitants, who retain ritual

power as earth custodians, or *tensoba*. Different economic specializations are also recognized and often associated with distinct ethnic identities.

Plagued by droughts, barren soils, high population density and lack of alternative employment, the Mossi are forced to practise shifting cultivation on lands viable for only 3–5 years. The slow but continuous population movement created by shifting agriculture has led to the merging of many culturally and linguistically diverse ethnic groups into cohesive local communities, which have increasingly recognized a common Mossi cultural identity.

The role of Mossi chiefs was redefined by the French colonial administration, who used them to recruit forced labour and collect taxes. Consequently the chiefs became increasingly resented and were displaced by an educated élite. The election of chiefs above village level was prohibited in 1965, but informally the system has remained strong.

Masked dancers at a Dogon funeral, Mali

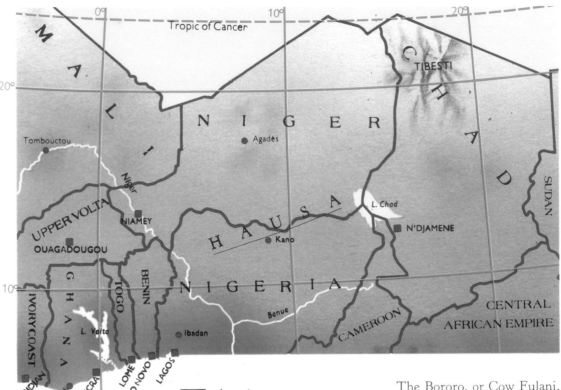

the south where the greater part of the population lives. The major ethnic groups in the north include the Tuareg and the nomadic Teda, and in the south the Kanuri, Hausa, Zerma and Songhai.

Niger achieved independence in 1960, but economically the country still relies heavily on France. Peanuts and livestock are the principal sources of revenue, but mining for uranium began in 1971. French is the official language.

Hausa

pop: 9,000,000

The Hausa live mainly in cities in the open savanna and semi-desert bushland of north-west Nigeria and southern Niger; their grammatically simple, composite language is estimated to be spoken by nearly 40,000,000 people. Practising intensive hoe cultivation, the Hausa grow a wide variety of staples and cash crops, including maize, rice, cotton and groundnuts. Rural labour is organized under a co-operative system, *gandu*, controlled by family heads, who provide their sons with seeds, equipment and land in return for their work on the *gandu* lands. Wealthy Hausa may also keep cattle, often tended by Fulani herdsmen. Trading is an important dry season activity, and local produce is exchanged in weekly markets.

According to legend the Hausa originated when a young nobleman slew a snake which was oppressing the town of Daura. Taking the title of *Makas-serki*, the snake-killer, he married the local queen, and their sons became the chiefs or *serki* of the seven original Hausa cities. Kano, the largest, was certainly established by the mid-11th century. The Hausa city states gradually extended their domination over outlying villages, but were never united into a large unit. Relations between them were always highly competitive, particularly during the period of slave raiding. Islam, introduced by Malinke traders from the west, was dominant in the main cities and courts by 1500, although its strength varied over the years. The religion was eventually firmly established by Uthman dan Fodio's

Distribution of Fulani

Fulani

pop: 6,000,000

The Fulani, originally nomadic pastoralists who led their cattle herds into areas not used by surrounding cultivators, are now distributed throughout western sudanic Africa from Senegal to the Central African Empire. Major concentrations, with different Fulfulde dialects, are found in Nigeria and Niger, Senegal and Mali, Guinea and Cameroon. The Fulani are physically striking for their skin is paler than that of their neighbours and they have straight hair, thin lips and narrow noses. It is possible that they are of mixed Negroid and Caucasoid origin and began to spread across West Africa from Senegal during the 11th century.

From the 14th century onwards, the Fulani increasingly became Muslims, spreading the Islamic faith through evangelism and conquest. The most important Fulani *jihad*, or holy war, was led by Uthman dan Fodio, titling himself *Serkin Musulmi*, commander of the faithful. In the early 19th century, he conquered the Hausa and established an empire of emirates right across northern Nigeria and neighbouring countries. The current Fulani rulers and aristocrats in Hausa towns are often members of his clan, the Toroobe.

The Bororo, or Cow Fulani, living in the borderlands between Nigeria and Niger, still live exclusively by nomadic pastoralism. They move seasonally with their herds and come to town only for dances and trading. The Bororo despise agricultural work and their lives revolve around concern for cattle, family and pride in personal appearance. Considered primitive and uncivilized by their settled neighbours, they are treated with guarded tolerance.

In addition to the town-dwelling ruling class, who have often forgotten their native language and whose herds are maintained by other Fulani, there are also communities of settled middle-class Fulani in a wide variety of occupations. Many others adopted agriculture long ago, living in permanent villages and practising mixed subsistence farming. Permanent grazing lands free from pests have now been established on the Jos plateau; household heads often work the farm while sons tend the herds. The Fulani still supply most of Nigeria's beef and cattle hides.

Niger

pop: 4,792,000

Desert in northern Niger gives way to a marginal region where nomadic pastoralists raise cattle, and a cultivated zone in

photograph:
Bororo youths perform a courtship dance, Niger

jihad, or holy war, in the early 19th century, when Hausa rulers were replaced by Fulani conquerors. Fulani emirs still administer many northern Nigerian states, but they no longer speak their native Fulfulde and have intermarried with the Hausa.

In contrast to the more egalitarian rural areas, Hausa cities have a high degree of social stratification. Each level of the social structure has special forms of etiquette. The city hierarchy is traditionally headed by the royal families and official nobility, followed by a class consisting of Muslim intellectuals, lawyers, teachers, preachers and scribes. High government officials and professional men with non-Islamic qualifications overlap with these, and are followed by wealthy long-distance traders. Below them are lesser traders and the numerous highly skilled Hausa craftsmen.

Chad
pop: 4,155,000

A vast, landlocked state, Chad consists of savanna grassland and woods in the wetter southern area, giving way to a semi-arid central lowland region and a hot arid northern desert area. Natural borders are formed by the eastern highlands and the northern mountains. Chad's major towns are Sahr, Moundou and the capital N'Djamena in the south, and Faya-Largeau in the north.

Rumours of mineral discoveries have yet to be substantiated. The economy is mainly agricultural: the staple crops are cassava, millet, maize and rice, with cotton grown for export in the south. Lake Chad provides large quantities of fish, but stock breeding has been badly affected by drought and rebellion in recent years.

Major ethnic groups include the Kanuri, the pastoral Fulani and their Hausa neighbours, the Buduma and Kuri around Lake Chad, the Arabized Kanembu and Tunjur, and the Kotoko descendants of the ancient Sao peoples. The southern-dwelling Sara have dominated the civil service, army and gendarmerie. Islam predominates in the north, Christianity in the south. French is the official language.

143

Sudan
Shilluk, Nuer, Dinka

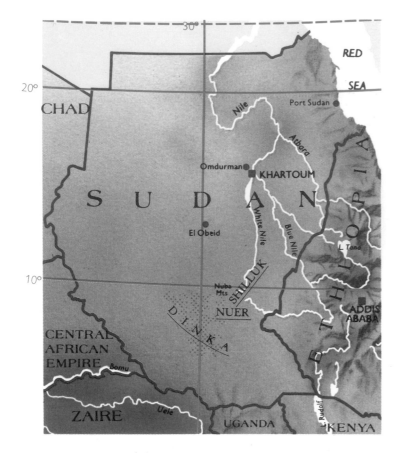

Ethnic divisions of Sudan

■ Arabs
■ Negroes

Sudan
pop: 18,428,000

The name Sudan is derived from the Arabic word for black, for the country has long been a meeting place between Arabs from the north and east, and Africans from the south. From the 14th to the 19th century the Negroid peoples west of the Nile retreated towards the Nubian mountains and the volcanic massif of Jebel Marra, as Arab pastoralists pushed their way south; but at Sennar on the Blue Nile the Fung African sultanate persisted for 300 years.

Sudan achieved independence from Britain and Egypt in 1956, but was in a perpetual state of civil war until 1972. The main cause of unrest was the deep fear among the southern Negroid people that the Arabs would impose their culture on the south, as well as asserting political dominance. Religious difference was another source of friction, for many southerners are Christian. The official language is Arabic.

The peoples of Sudan belong to four major linguistic groups: Arabic, Nilotic, Nilo-Hamitic and the eastern Sudanese group, which includes the Azande and the Moru-Madi. In general, the Arabic speakers are found in the north of the country; they include the Nubians, who trace their ancestry back to the ancient Nubian kingdom, and the Beja pastoralists. The Nilotes of the southern Sudan, including the Nuer, the Dinka and the Shilluk, are first and foremost cattle herders, whose lives revolve around the needs of their animals. The Nilo-Hamites, including the Bari, the Lotuko, the Taposa and the Murle, are also pastoralists.

Only 10 per cent of Sudan's population live in towns. The largest urban centres are the complex of Khartoum, the capital, and Omdurman, at the confluence of the Blue and White Niles, and Port Sudan on the Red Sea. The national economy is based on agriculture and depends on the waters of the Nile for irrigation and the annual floods. Cassava, rice, groundnuts, maize and millet are the main food crops. The most important cultivated area is Gezira, the triangle of land between the two Niles, producing nearly all the cotton which forms Sudan's principal export. Several dams have been constructed and other irrigation schemes are being introduced. Sudan has considerable mineral resources, including asbestos, chromite, iron ore, gold, gypsum and manganese.

Shilluk
pop: 100,000

The Nilotic Shilluk inhabit the flat flood plains of the White Nile in southern Sudan. Like their neighbours to the south, the Nuer and the Dinka, they regard themselves primarily as cattle herders, but they also keep sheep and goats and grow maize, sesame, beans, pumpkins and tobacco. The staple food crop is millet, which is made into a thick porridge. Millet stalks are often used to build enclosures round the conical mud houses of Shilluk villages.

Reality and religious myth are intertwined in the Shilluk's legends of their origin. Their mythical founder, Nyikang, came from the south, and the peoples he conquered became the Shilluk. In his exploits and character, Nyikang encom-passes many important aspects of society for the Shilluk and they perceive their world through him. Most importantly he enters the body of the Shilluk divine king, the *reth*, at his coronation. The king is required to be in a state of ritual purity and physical perfection, because he is a symbol of the spiritual and material well-being of the nation. It is said that if he became senile or sick he could be killed. The *reth* probably had little direct political power, but acted mainly as a religious focus for the nation and as a peacemaker in times of dispute. The *reth* is now part of the Sudanese government system.

Nuer
pop: 300,000

The tall, Nilotic Nuer live in southern Sudan, neighbouring on the Dinka, whom they raided in the past, and the Shilluk. Nuer economic life

and social organization revolve around their cattle, which provide them with a basic milk and meat diet, supplemented during the dry season by fishing, hunting and some gathering. The central part of Nuer country, around Lake No, is mostly uninhabitable from about May to September because of flooding, so villages are built on patches of sandy ground higher up; they consist of scattered homesteads which often suffer water shortages during the dry season. The cattle are grazed on the plains during the dry season, and driven back into the hills when the rains begin.

Nuer social organization is based on patrilineal descent, providing kin groups of varying size which form and re-form according to the needs of the occasion. At initiation, boys receive six horizontal cuts across the forehead, which mark them permanently as Nuer; they are also given cattle and become members of an age set, uniting the group across kinship ties. When a man marries he is given more cattle by his father, and sons will try to herd together even after their father's death. Although there are no chiefs in whom political power is vested, major disputes are settled by the 'leopard skin chiefs', who have spiritual authority.

Dinka
pop: 500,000

From the highlands which separate Zaire and Sudan, a network of rivers flows north into the White Nile and the papyrus swamps of the Sudd. The Nilotic Dinka people, who live among these rivers, are pastoralists who have adapted to the yearly cycle of rainy and dry seasons.

Permanent villages are built above the flood level and the women and old men remain in them throughout the year, cultivating the millet which is the Dinka's staple diet. Crops are planted when the light rain begins in spring. Later on, heavier rain causes the rivers to flood and the cattle are taken into the savanna pastures. Men and cattle return for the harvest in October and, as the floods recede, the cattle are moved to the lower valleys.

Cattle represent wealth to the Dinka, but they also have social and religious significance. They are given as bridewealth and as compensation for murder. At initiation, each young man is given a special ox; he takes his adult name from the colour and shape of this animal.

Nhialic is the supreme being of Dinka religion. In each group a 'master of the fishing spear' acts as priest and peacemaker. If he grows old and feeble he may be buried alive at his own request, to show that man can still remain in control of his own destiny.

Evening in the Shilluk royal village, Sudan

Ethiopia

pop: 29,044,000

The mountain plateaux which dominate Ethiopia are divided by the rift valley and its chain of lakes into a western block and a lower eastern block. To the south and west are lowlands and the Danakil depression, which is more than 300 feet below sea level. Ethiopia has had a distinct identity for more than 2,000 years, but many people have mingled in the area, creating a complex pattern of cultures.

More than 100 languages and their dialects are spoken in Ethiopia: the three major language groups are Cushitic, Semitic and Nilotic. The nomadic Galla and Somali of the east are Cushitic speakers whose territory is claimed by neighbouring Somalia. The languages spoken by the Amhara ruling group and the Tigre are Semitic: Amharic, now the official language, has been an important unifying factor in Ethiopian nationalism, along with the Coptic Church.

Addis Ababa and Asmara are both large cities, but the population is predominantly rural. Coffee and cotton are the main cash crops, with maize, millet and other grains, and ensete, a plantain, the main food crops. Cattle are numerous, and their hides and skins are exported.

Amhara

pop: 5,000,000

The high plateau north of Addis Ababa is the home of the Amhara people, the dominant group in modern Ethiopia. According to legend, their kingdom was founded by Menelik, son of Solomon and Sheba; with the exception of the Zagwe dynasty, all Ethiopia's emperors have traced descent back to Solomon. The kingdom's influence was at its height in the 2nd-9th centuries.

Before 1975, when the emperor was overthrown and rural land nationalized, huge estates were owned by a few hereditary landowners; tenant farmers and clients owed labour or taxes. Agriculture is unmechanized: the unfenced plateau fields are cultivated with the plough rather than the hoe, which is used in the south of the country. On higher lands the Amhara grow the indigenous grain *teff*, barley, beans and lentils; on lower ground, maize and millet are favoured. Animal dung is taken for fuel in the houses and fertilizers are rarely used; the soil is impoverished and erosion is a serious problem.

Villages are spread out, for the Amhara prefer to live at some distance from their neighbours. Houses are traditionally round and thatched, often with an upper storey; chickens and small livestock are brought in at night to keep them from predators. The focal point of Amhara social life is the rural market: people travel for miles to exchange news, to sell any surplus agricultural produce and to buy household goods.

The Amhara recognize three types of marriage: *qurban*, church marriage, which cannot be dissolved even after death; *semyana*, a civil contract; and *damoz*, a temporary marriage in which a man hires a woman to satisfy his sexual and domestic needs for a short period. Formerly a father would choose the marriage partner for his children.

Afars

pop: 110,000

The Afars inhabit the rough triangle of the Danakil desert, between the high Ethiopian escarpment and the shores of the Red Sea. Temperatures can reach 50°C in the direct sun; there is no rain for three-quarters of the year and even the large river Awash falters and dries up in the shallow saline lakes. Some Afars live in Djibouti with the Somali Issas, but the majority are in Ethiopia, where they are represented in parliament by the Sultan of Aussa, their most powerful leader. Government influence on the Afars is tenuous.

The Afars, who speak a Cushitic language, are Muslims with strong traditions of loyalty to their clans and hospitality towards guests. Bravery is the most honoured quality of manhood. Afar boys are circumcised during adolescence, when their bearing also influences chances of a future marriage. Girls undergo infibulation and clitorodectomy. Formerly they would only marry a man who could prove that he had killed, by displaying his enemy's dried genitalia.

Most of the year is spent moving through the desert in search of pasture, but in the rainy season from November to February the Afars climb to higher ground to avoid the floods and mosquitoes. Houses, *ari*, consist of mats over a framework of supple sticks which are erected and dismantled by the women. Women also look after the sheep, goats and cows being milked; men herd the other cattle, camels, horses and donkeys.

Djibouti

pop: 150,000

Djibouti, formerly the French Territory of the Afars and Issas, became independent in 1977. An arid country in the horn of Africa, it is populated by equal numbers of the Somali Issas and the Afars. Animal skins are exported, but the country's revenues come mainly from the capital and port, Djibouti, which handles Ethiopian exports.

Both Issas and Afars are Muslim, speak similar languages and—outside the city—

live as pastoral nomads, herding flocks of sheep, goats and cattle. The Issas are divided into three groups, the Abgals, the Dalols and the Wardiqs, under a supreme *ougaz* (chief). They are more urbanized than the Afars and desire political union with Somalia.

Somalia

pop: 3,265,000

The Somali Democratic Republic lies in the extreme east of the African continent. Most of the country is covered by flat grassy plains, but in the north a mountain escarpment slopes sharply down to an arid coastal plain. The Juba and Shebelle, south of the capital Mogadishu, are the country's only permanent rivers; in drought years the Shebelle often does not reach the sea.

There are small areas of subsistence cultivation in the north, but the land between the rivers is the most productive area for agriculture: bananas grown here provide one of Somalia's chief exports. Sor-

ghum, millet, beans and maize are also grown on irrigated land and along the rivers. A traditional export is the gum frankincense, collected from wild *Boswellia* trees.

Somalia is inhabited almost solely by the Muslim Somali, although there is a small Arab minority. A further 2,000,000 Somali live across the national borders, in Kenya, Ethiopia and Djibouti. The stated aim of the Somali government, to unite all Somali people in one country by extending the present boundaries, has caused considerable friction with these countries. Ethiopia in particular has experienced severe pressures on the eastern Ogaden region.

Most of the Somali have been nomadic pastoralists since time immemorial. Their lifestyle depends on mobility, so family units are small, usually consisting of a man, his wives and their children, with perhaps one or two older dependents. Houses, owned by each wife, are made of woven mats draped over a framework of

branches of the *galol* tree. Each homestead is built with an encircling barricade of thorns and the sheep and goats are driven inside the fence each night for protection against enemies and predators.

Camels are herded separately from the rest of the stock, as they can go without water for long periods and range further. The camels of several kinsmen are usually herded together by the young boys of the clan. Descent groups, reckoned patrilineally, are the main form of social organization and when fights break out, for example over water or stock, the support of kinsmen is automatic.

Prolonged droughts in 1974 were some of the worst in living memory. In Somalia, 18,000 people died and the country's best export resource, its livestock, was seriously depleted. As a result, the government has attempted to settle many nomads in fishing villages on the Red Sea, thus breaking the Somalis' dependence on their herds, and ultimately on the unreliable rainfall.

Konso threshing millet, eastern Ethiopia

Distribution of Somali

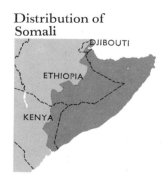

Liberia, Ivory Coast, Ghana, Togo, Benin
Dan, Ashanti, Gonja, Fon

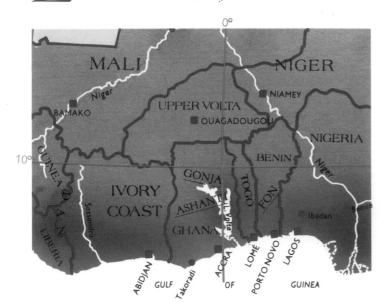

Dan
pop: 100,000

The Dan inhabit an area on the border of Liberia and Ivory Coast. Their gently undulating land ranges from tropical forest in the south to savanna in the north. According to their traditions they were driven south from the sudanic region by Muslim warriors with superior weapons and horses, who halted when they reached the forest zone and tsetse flies destroyed their mounts.

The Dan have adapted to the highly variable soils and climatic conditions of their present lands by developing a complex but flexible agricultural system. Rice, their major crop with at least 40 distinct varieties, is planted on newly cleared fields for the first two or three years; sorghum, millet and maize are added during the third year when the rice yield declines. These crops, with longer roots that penetrate the still fertile lower soil levels, are also grown in the fourth year, but subsequently replaced by manioc and yams, which finally exhaust the soil. Left fallow for 4-10 years, the land is then re-used in the same cycle. Most of the year is taken up with agriculture: forest clearing begins in February and crops are harvested between late July and November, when most of the markets are held.

With no traditions of large-scale political authority, Dan villages are autonomous, each with its own headman and council of elders to hear legal cases and settle disputes. Villages contain patrilineal rela-

tions, and inheritance, succession and names pass through the male line. Marriage involves the payment of bride-wealth, women leaving their natal homes to reside with their husbands; polygyny is now rare. Villages typically consist of up to 300 circular houses, with conical palm-thatch roofs and painted walls, clustered closely together.

Both boys and girls are initiated at puberty, undergoing circumcision and clitorodectomy respectively. Taught Dan traditions and respect for their elders, they are then admitted into 'closed' adult societies. The Gbasa society for men and the Togba for women fulfil educational functions and maintain standards of moral, social and ritual conduct.

Ivory Coast
pop: 7,045,000

Ivory Coast consists mainly of woodland, with savanna in the north, bordered by the forested Guinea highlands in the west. Major ethnic groups include the Agni, Baulé, and Senoufo, and the Malinke and Dyula in the north-west. Coffee, cocoa, cotton, pineapples, rubber and timber are processed by local industries for export. The 300 mile coastline has been navigable since the opening of the Vridi canal and a deep-water harbour in Abidjan, vastly improving communications. However, industrialization has encouraged migration to the main towns, and some 22 per cent of the population is now urban. The official language is French.

Ghana
pop: 10,281,000

Ghana's low sandy coastline meets a broad area of rain forest, cut by many streams. Further north this forest gives way to increasingly dry savanna scrub and grassland. The area has some mineral resources: gold, diamonds and manganese are important exports.

Agriculture varies regionally, with small-scale farming supplementing fishing on the coast, and subsistence cultivation and cattle breeding in the north. The fertile forest region provides valuable timber resources and the major cash and

export crop, cocoa. Major cities, including Tamale, Kumasi, and the ports of Tema, Sekondi-Takoradi and the capital Accra, house about one-third of the population. To offset the drift of population to the towns and food shortages due to overworking of farmland in some areas, the government has encouraged staple production, increasing rice and maize crops.

Major groups include Akan speakers (mainly Fanti and Ashanti), the Ga and Ewe of the south and south-east, and the Dagomba, Gonja and Lobi in the north. The Ashanti, rulers of a large forest kingdom, fought the British in a long series of wars before they finally came under British rule at the end of the last century. English remains Ghana's official language.

Ashanti
pop: 1,000,000

The Ashanti homeland is in Ghana's hot wet forest zone, north of the coastal region, and consists of fertile plain rising to plateau. Like their related Akan-speaking neighbours, the Ashanti are mainly agriculturalists cultivating several staples and vegetables. Their most important cash crop is cocoa, upon which the whole Ghanaian economy is highly dependent.

The origins of the Ashanti people are obscure, but by the early 18th century their kingdom was a powerful independent state, founded on the lucrative gold and slave trades and ruled from Kumasi by the *Asantehene*, the Ashanti king. The kingdom was eventually annexed as a British crown colony in 1901, following a long series of wars. The present state is a confederation, with every district or 'nation' having its own chief under the *Asantehene*. As a symbol of the kingship the Ashanti have a famous golden stool, which is believed to embody the soul of the whole Ashanti nation.

The Ashanti believe that every individual consists of two elements: blood from his mother and spirit from his father. Social identity is derived from the source of the stronger element—the *abusua*, or matrilineal clan, a group consisting of the descendants

of a common ancestress, through which Ashanti inherit property, most offices and residence rights. Paternal descent is recognized through the *ntoro*, or patrilineal clan, a division associated with moral and ritual obligations.

Women are barred from lineage leadership, owing to menstrual taboos and the danger of contaminating sacred objects. However, the 'queen mother', or female head, has considerable influence, advising on matters of importance and nominating candidates for vacant clan positions.

Stages of the life cycle, such as childbirth and puberty, are socially and ritually acknowledged. Women in late pregnancy were formerly cared for by their matrilineal kin, and newborn children are still not considered fully human until eight days old, when their fathers bring gifts and name them—before this, such infants are regarded as ghost children. On the occasion of their first menstruation, girls receive gifts and congratulations, are ritually cleansed and are 'set free' to have children.

Gonja
pop: 100,000

The Gonja, subsistence agriculturalists like their Dagomba and Mossi neighbours, occupy an infertile region of sparsely populated open savanna to the north of Ghana's man-made Lake Volta. In the 17th century a Gonja kingdom was founded on an enduring alliance between invading Mande warriors from the north and Muslim advisers and traders. The towns, where many Gonja still live, became major centres on the caravan trading routes.

Rural Gonja live in compounds, or *langto*, consisting of members of several closely related domestic groups, under the authority of a compound head. Territorial divisions, capital towns and outlying villages are ruled by local chiefs claiming patrilineal descent from NdeWura Jakpa, the leader of the original Mande warriors. The paramount chief, or *Yagbum Wura*, is selected rotationally from the major divisions, his position remaining a symbol of unity.

Divided into three social estates—ruling families, Muslim groups and commoners, or *nyamase*—Gonja families are formally identified by appropriate greetings, but are not tightly closed groups. Intermarriage, child fostering, frequent divorce and women's retirement to their natal home maintain strong kinship ties across social boundaries. The strongest kinship bond in Gonja, between the children of the same woman, ties brothers and sisters even when estate allegiances are different.

Togo
pop: 2,304,000

Togo's narrow coastal strip gives way to red soil plateau, crossed diagonally by the Togo mountains, and savanna grassland. There are approximately 30 ethnic groups, of which the largest is the Ewe, who live in the south; the Kabre, Kotokoli and Basari occupy the north of the country. French is the official language. Only 13 per cent of the population live in the main towns, Lomé, Sokodé and Palimé; the rest are engaged in agriculture, producing cocoa, coffee and palm nuts for export. Phosphates are the main mineral resource.

Benin
pop: 3,235,000

From rain forest on the coast, Benin's fertile clay plains rise to mountains, then fall away to savanna in the north. The over-populated coastal towns include Cotonou, Porto Novo, the capital, and the old slave-trading centre Ouidah. Major ethnic groups include the Fon, Adja, Samba, Ewe and Yoruba in the south, and Hausa and Fulani in the north. Most are subsistence farmers, growing cassava, maize, millet, rice and yams; industry is scarcely developed. The official language of Benin (formerly Dahomey) is French.

Fon
pop: 900,000

Humid equatorial rain forest, broken by savanna towards the coast, covers the homeland of the Fon, once famous for their powerful monarchy. They are mainly agriculturalists, growing a variety of food and cash crops and herding livestock; some Fon also engage in fishing. In recent years increasing numbers have been drawn into business in urban areas and into the administration of Benin (formerly Dahomey).

Ewe-speakers, the Fon live in compact towns and villages, divided into quarters and compounds composed of groups tracing descent from a common male ancestor. Inheritance and succession are patrilineal, and cross-cousin marriages, usually between local groups, are encouraged; polygyny is permitted. Each compound contains shrines to a variety of deities, rising in importance from personal and family gods and spirits to those of the descent group and the nation.

The Fon kingdom was founded in the early 17th century by a warrior band from the interior province of Arda. This group conquered the region around Abomey, which was extended by powerful monarchs in the 18th and 19th centuries. With direct access to Europeans on the coast, the kingdom prospered by controlling the slave trade. In 1894 the French destroyed its strict military and administrative organization.

With a strictly organized standing army, which may have included the famous female regiment, the 'Amazons', the Fon state was characterized by its hierarchical administration. The *muiga* fulfilled the role of commander-in-chief, prime minister and chief executioner. Ministers, always commoners appointed and dismissed by the king, had clearly defined responsibilities, and each official had a female equivalent who took formal precedence at court functions.

The principles of succession, hierarchical separation and male-female balance, apparent in the traditional political organization, have parallels in Fon religion and cosmology. The female creator god Mawu is thought to have given the other gods, her sons, their special powers and spheres of operation. Of these Sagbata and Xevioso, the earth and thunder gods, are considered the most important. Each major cult is further sub-divided into a ranked system of lesser deities descended from these three.

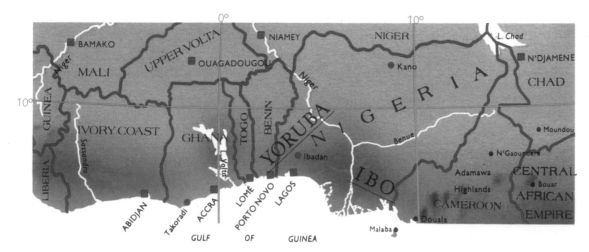

Nigeria

pop: 65,628,000

With a quarter of the population of sub-Saharan Africa, Nigeria shows an immense cultural and regional variety. Although the Niger-Benue river system has served as a trading route for centuries, the country was only united under a single administration in 1914. The present boundaries were drawn shortly before Nigeria became independent of Britain in 1963.

Nigerians comprise some 300 distinct ethnic groups, speaking almost as many different languages. In the north, most of the population are Muslim, in the south they are Christian—but traditional beliefs persist everywhere. The dominant groups are the Hausa and settled Fulani in the north, the Yoruba in the south-west and the Ibo in the south-east. The bitter civil war of 1967–70 resulted from the Ibo's attempt to secede from the republic. Other major groups include the nomadic Fulani in the north, the Kanuri near Lake Chad, and the Ibibio, Ijo, Edo and Tiv in the south. English is the official language.

Most of the population are engaged in agriculture, which provides nearly half of all exports, but the country's economic prospects have been transformed by industrialization and Nigeria now has a major influence on African politics.

Oil, natural gas, coal, tin and columbite are Nigeria's most important minerals, with oil accounting for 90 per cent of the country's export revenues in 1977. All the major industrial centres, oilfields and sea-ports are concentrated in the south.

Yoruba

pop: 7,000,000

The Yoruba occupy the rain forest and savanna lands of south-western Nigeria and the neighbouring republic of Benin. Together with the Fulani, Hausa and Ibo, they constitute Nigeria's dominant ethnic groups. Mostly agriculturalists practising fallow bush rotation, they cultivate a wide variety of staples, vegetables and cash crops, which include palm oil and cocoa. Despite the displacement of traditional deities by Christianity and Islam, they have maintained rich oral and dramatic traditions.

The Yoruba are traditionally urban dwellers, grouped in large compounds of patrilineal relations around a central palace and market. Most towns were surrounded by walls and ramparts. Kingship is held by the descendants of the town's founder. Following a complex installation ceremony, which symbolized the new king's assumption of supernatural powers and his withdrawal from commitments to the royal family, the Yoruba *oba* formerly remained hidden from public view, only appearing heavily veiled at important annual ceremonies.

With considerable wealth, many wives and a strong force of palace slaves, the *oba*'s ritual power was balanced by the political power of his council of chiefs. Choosing the king and submitting their decisions to him, the chiefs, appointed for life, were wealthy traders and agriculturalists, often members of the town's constituent commoner families. Under British colonial rule, kings were designated 'native authorities' and held responsible for town government. Many increased their secular power and most remain highly revered.

Yoruba today form the main population of Lagos as well as Ibadan, their capital, and many are employed in urban occupations. Migrants to the cities, regardless of wealth and occupation, normally maintain strong links with their original birthplace and are still identified by the name of their community. Migrants from small towns and villages often belong to improvement unions, mutual aid associations linking kin and marriage relatives, which help with urban problems and provide assistance for development of the home area. Larger Yoruba towns frequently have political pressure groups concerned with civic issues.

Ibo

pop: 4,000,000

Most of the Ibo live in the densely forested area between the river Niger in the west and the Cross river in the east: a tableland which rises northwards from the mangrove swamps of the vast Niger delta. Although the soil is poor, restricting the crops that can be grown, the forests are densely populated and it is thought that the Ibo have lived in their present surroundings at least since the 9th century.

Contact with Europeans first came in the mid-15th century, when Portuguese traders reached the area. Slaving grew to horrific proportions: in the last quarter of the 18th century, it is estimated that 16,000 Ibo were sold each year at the port of Bonny alone. Despite this pressure, the Ibo never evolved any political organization above the level of the village or village group, and villages remained determinedly egalitarian.

The arrival of missionaries in the 1850s was a crucial element in European penetration of Ibo territory, and the Ibo were quick to exploit the educational impetus provided by the early bush schools. Today the Ibo have probably the highest literacy rate in black Africa.

Although the wealth Nigeria

has drawn in oil revenues has meant that many Ibo have become caught up in western technology and lifestyles, rural communities continue very much in traditional ways. The village economy is still based on subsistence hoe agriculture, the staple crops being yams and manioc. Ibo men are responsible for cultivating the yams; the women are allotted their own plots, on which they grow maize, beans, manioc and coco yams, as well as melons, okra, pumpkins and beans.

Since Ibo women always marry outside their villages, they rarely own land, but male children are responsible for a part of their father's land and inherit a share of it when he dies. Most Ibo groups are patrilineal, although in some areas a system of double descent exists, and both sexes are ordered into age sets. Men, and to a lesser extent women, also join title societies as a way of increasing their status.

In 1967 the former Eastern Region, dominated by the Ibo, seceded from Nigeria, proclaiming itself the republic of Biafra. In the ensuing civil war many Ibo died in battle or from starvation caused by disruption of food supplies. Since their surrender, the federal government has made efforts to reconcile the Ibo with their former enemies, notably the Hausa and the Fulani. The war itself helped to unite the various Ibo-speaking groups.

A fishing festival near Sokoto, Nigeria

151

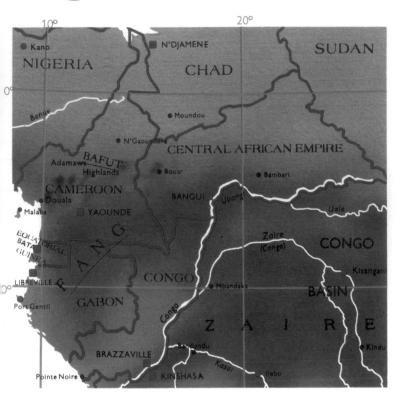

Bakoko, and small groups of indigenous Baguielli and Babinga Pygmies. In the north live pastoralists including the Sao, Kanuri, and the politically dominant Fulani. The official languages are English and French.

Bafut
pop: 20,000

The town of Bafut lies in a valley in the Bamenda highlands, to the north of Cameroon's rainforested coastal plain. The centre of the Bafut kingdom, the town is divided into 26 wards, each consisting of several family compounds. Nearly all the Bafut live within the town limits, surrounded by a patchwork of small fields.

Like their related Tikar neighbours, the Bafut migrated southwards more than 300 years ago, to escape slave raiders. They have retained a vestige of independence as well as many traditions. Their rulers, the *fon*, who were once worshipped as god-kings, retain considerable political and religious authority. Two days of the eight-day Bafut week are rest days in their honour.

Successors are selected on merit exclusively from the royal lineage. They undergo elaborate installation rituals, including symbolic stoning by the people, before being raised to sacred, untouchable status. Inheriting his father's many wives, the new *fon* also gains access to the sacred *achum* shrine, where he may retire to seek the counsel of his father's spirit, thought to reside in a shallow stone symbolizing the dead man's head.

Pygmies
pop: 150,000

Known since Egyptian times, Pygmy hunters and gatherers are widely scattered across the great equatorial forests of central Africa from Congo as far as the borders of East Africa. Among the least assimilated of the major groups are the Mbuti of the Ituri forest in north-eastern Zaire, who number approximately 35,000.

The Mbuti live in small bands, composed of up to 30 households, within their own large defined areas of territory. The bands constantly change

Cameroon
pop: 6,588,000

The thick equatorial rain forest of Cameroon's coastal and southern lowlands gives way to a fertile plateau and volcanic highlands in the north-west, with open savanna and semi-desert in the extreme northern lowlands. The main cities are the port of Douala, the interior capital Yaoundé, the railway terminus N'Gaoundéré, Bamenda and Garoua.

Agriculture, forestry and fishing employ approximately 85 per cent of the population. Major exports are cocoa, coffee, bananas, rubber, palm produce, cotton and timber. Poor communications have delayed development of mineral resources, particularly bauxite.

With more than 100 ethnic groups, Cameroon is the home of many small kingdoms and chiefdoms, including those of the Bafut, the Kom and the Bulu, who led resistance to colonialism. The largest group, the Bamileke, with strong traditions of ancestor worship including the keeping of skulls, inhabit the densely populated western plateau and highland slopes, with the Bamoun and other small Bantu-speaking groups. Southern forest and hill dwelling groups include the Bete, Fang, Bassa and

Distribution of Pygmies

size and composition according to the availability of game and vegetable resources. It is easier to define the 'family' as an economic than a biological unit among the Mbuti; kinship terms and behaviour are used towards all band members.

A sexual division of labour exists, with women engaged in gathering activities and men hunting. Skilled in the use of bow and arrow, hunting nets, javelins and traps, the Mbuti, like other hunters and gatherers, spend only a small part of their day in the quest for food. The remainder is spent making and repairing weapons, and in communal song, dance and story-telling.

Although they are skilful at exploiting the resources of the forest, the Mbuti rely on settled Negro agriculturalists, including the Bira, Ltsi and Ndaka, for metal and cloth. These are obtained by trading forest products and by working as labourers from time to time. By supplying the villagers, the Mbuti, who call themselves *bamiki*, or children of the forest, are able to protect their home from intrusion.

The Mbuti perform essential ritual roles for the villagers, in whose *nkumbi* circumcision

initiation Mbuti boys also participate. Through the Mbuti presence, the villagers come to terms with what they conceive as the hostile and powerful spiritual forces of the surrounding forest.

Central African E.

pop: 2,500,000

Mostly high plateau with savanna woodland, the Central African Empire is covered by dense rain forest in the southwest. The main towns are the capital port of Bangui, on the Ubangi river, and the agricultural and mining centre, Berbérati. Major ethnic groups include the **Baya,** Banda, Azande, Yakoma, Banziri and Buraka. Most of the population are subsistence agriculturalists, growing cassava, maize, millet, rice and sorghum; coffee, cotton, tobacco and rubber are produced for cash. Diamonds and uranium are the most valuable exports. The official language is French.

Equatorial Guinea

pop: 327,000

A former Spanish colony, Equatorial Guinea consists of two separate provinces. Rio Muni is a sparsely settled coastal enclave with a rain forested plateau. The largest of several ethnic groups, all subsisting by agriculture, is the Bantu-speaking Fang. The indigenous inhabitants of the fertile, volcanic island of Macias Nguema Biyoga (formerly Fernando Po) are the Bubi. Cocoa, coffee and timber are the main exports.

Fang

pop: 220,000

The hot, humid, equatorial rain forest of Gabon, Equatorial Guinea and southern Cameroon is inhabited by the Bantu Fang, the largest ethnic group of the area. They migrated from the savanna plateau in the north-east throughout the 19th century, conquering indigenous peoples. Now, like the neighbouring Beti and Bulu groups, they are becoming increasingly urbanized.

In the past, the Fang lived in temporary, patrilineal villages, with each family a self-sufficient unit. Adult men cleared forest land for their wives to cultivate subsistence crops such as manioc, maize and groundnuts. During the last 50 years, however, cash-cropping and wage-labouring, particularly associated with cocoa plantations, has replaced subsistence agriculture. Villages have become permanent settlements and individuals have formal land rights.

The organization of Fang life was formerly based on a combination of village-cluster, clan, age set and 'secret' society. With a strongly patrilineal kinship system, children had little or no active contact with their mother's descent group. Marriage, forbidden with any member of either parent's patrilineage, traced back for three generations, was dependent on the payment of *nsuba*, or bridewealth. The largest portion of the *nsuba* was not paid until a wife had fulfilled her major duty of bearing a child; barrenness resulted in divorce and repayment. Only the wealtheist Fang now practice polygyny.

The Fang had firm beliefs in the human cause of sickness and misfortune, considering these to be the result of witchcraft. Witches, both male and female (who might be unconscious of their powers) were feared as 'leopard men'. They were believed to have gained their power through the sacrifice and ritual eating of a close relative. Witchcraft was countered by magicians, diviners and healers, including members of the *ngil* society who exorcised evil spirits, administered ordeals and executed proven witches. Many Fang still believe that death can be the result of witchcraft.

Gabon

pop: 557,000

Covered by dense equatorial forest, Gabon's narrow coastal plain gives way to plateau and mountains, intersected by deep river valleys. The main towns, Libreville, Port Gentil, Lambarené, Oyem and Franceville, house a quarter of the population. The largest ethnic groups, mostly Bantu agriculturalists, include the Fang, Aduma, Echira, Okande and Kota. Cassava is the staple crop; coffee, cocoa, palm oil and rice are grown for cash. Manganese, uranium and iron ore are important mineral resources, mainly exported. The official language is French.

photograph:
Pygmy hunting band,
Central African Empire

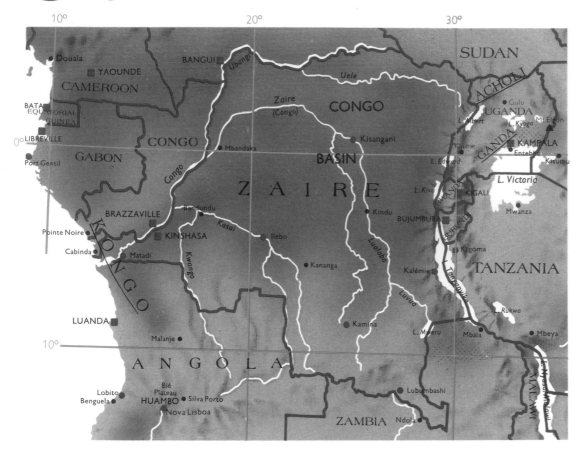

Congo

pop: 1,400,000

Congo's low-lying coastal plain rises inland to plateau and hills, with savanna grassland in the south. Rain forest and marshland surround the seasonally flooded and swampy valleys of the Zaire river and its tributaries in the north. Congo has varied mineral deposits, including copper, gold, tin, cassiterite and newly discovered phosphates. Some 40 per cent of the population lives in or around major towns.

Congo's major ethnic groups, all Bantu, include the Teke of the Bateke plateau and the Ubangi, who occupy the Zaire basin with the Sanga and Pygmy groups. The Kongo inhabit the southern region between Brazzaville and the coast. Following urbanization, intertribal contact has lessened the ancient rivalry between northern and southern peoples. The official language is French.

Kongo

pop: 4,000,000

The Kongo occupy a broad block of territory extending from Congo's coastal region along the Zaire estuary and its tributaries through Zaire to north-western Angola. More than a million Kongo reside in each of these three countries. Mostly agriculturalists, they cultivate a wide variety of staple and cash crops including maize, manioc, rice, vegetables, sugar cane, tobacco and hemp; many have been drawn into industry and commerce in Brazzaville and Kinshasa.

Probably established by the 14th century, on either side of the lower Zaire river, the Kongo kingdom was a strongly centralized state with developed legal institutions, ruled by a powerful 'divine' king, or *manicongo*, with his councillors. The ruler's economic power traditionally depended on trade in salt and palm oil.

Now a loose federation of autonomous tribes, Kongo group identity is based on common origin. Their villages, with an average of 300 people, consist of rectangular brick-built houses forming a grid pattern. Fishing and hunting are important economic activities, the latter being undertaken by a small group of men with specialist skills in each settlement. Although men assist with heavy tasks and grow some crops, the women are mainly responsible for agricultural production and gain economic independence through trading surplus produce at the weekly local market.

As the site of many initiation ceremonies and of the courts of justice, the market is the focal point of Kongo life. A rifle is ceremonially buried to denote the area's neutrality. In the past, severe penalties were imposed for breaches of marketplace rules—the death penalty could be imposed for fighting, theft or spreading scandal. Today the peace is maintained by a market chief.

Zaire

pop: 25,960,000

Equatorial forest covers much of Zaire, Africa's second largest country. The forests are the home of the indigenous Pygmies, whose language has been lost; they now speak the different languages of the peoples at the forest edge with whom they trade. The remainder of Zaire's population are Bantu speakers, although there are a few Nilotes in the northeast and Sudanese in the north. The largest groups are the Kongo, the Kwangu-Kwilu, the Mongo and the Luba, who carve wooden female figurines. French, Swahili and Lingala are the official languages. Staple crops are cassava, maize, millet, plantains and vegetables, grown in forest clearings. Cash crops include rubber, cocoa and palm oil. The timber industry is important, but the biggest world demand is for industrial diamonds from Kasai and copper and cobalt from Shaba.

Rwanda

pop: 4,397,000

Rwanda's landscape is generally rugged, with deeply cut valleys, and is dominated to the north by the Virunga volcanoes. The country is densely populated, with 84 per cent Hutu, 15 per cent Tutsi and 1 per cent Twa Pygmies. The groups are more balanced politically than in neighbouring Burundi. Kirundi and French are the official languages.

Kigali, the capital, has some industry, but Rwanda's economy is predominantly agricultural. The Hutu grow sweet

potatoes, cassava and maize, with bananas for food and beer; the Tutsi breed cattle. Coffee is the major cash crop and the minerals cassiterite and wolframite are also exported.

Burundi
pop: 3,897,000

The three major ethnic groups of Burundi are the Twa Pygmies, the Hutu and the Tutsi; all speak Kirundi. Although the Hutu are by far the most numerous, the Tutsi are the dominant group. French is an official language.

Burundi's capital, Bujumbura, is also a port on Lake Tanganyika and is separated by a mountain ridge from the plateau which forms most of the country. The economy is almost exclusively agricultural, with bananas, maize, beans and cassava grown for domestic use and coffee for export.

Hutu
pop: 7,000,000

In the pre-independence kingdoms of Burundi and Rwanda, the Hutu formed five-sixths of the population, yet were dominated both socially and economically by the Tutsi minority. During Belgian colonial rule, the Hutu were encouraged to question this inequality and they now control independent Rwanda. In Burundi, however, the Tutsi have maintained power by killing more than 100,000 Hutu.

Traditionally the Hutu were subsistence agriculturalists with only a few cattle, but poor soils and chronic overpopulation made their existence precarious. The highly-skilled Tutsi pastoralists, who entered Hutu lands some 400 years ago, infiltrated this economy through a system of clientage known as *buhake*. Hutu clients offered their services to Tutsi lords, *shebuja*, in return for military protection.

Before the introduction of medical services by Catholic missionaries, sickness was common among the Hutu and the mortality rate high, for they were constantly on the verge of famine. Even today they eat very little meat, never slaughtering their cattle for food and milking the cows only when they are feeding calves.

Males are pre-eminent in Hutu society. The labour of wives, daughters and even unmarried sons belongs automatically to the father of the household, who also owns certain rights to land or cattle. He nominates his successor before he dies and this choice can only be overruled by the lineage head of his kin group, or *inzu*. Members of an *inzu* trace their descent patrilineally to a common male ancestor about six generations back, and hold collective rituals.

Tutsi
pop: 1,347,000

The Nilo-Hamitic Tutsi pastoralists entered Rwanda and Burundi from the north in the 16th century, imposing their rule on the Hutu people. In 1962 Tutsi dominance was overthrown in Rwanda, but in neighbouring Burundi they savagely repressed a Hutu rebellion in 1972.

The Tutsi king, *mwami*, was supreme over Hutu and Tutsi, receiving tributes, gifts and service. His authority operated through three separate channels. Each district had a land chief whose responsibility was to settle disputes relating to cultivation or land; he also collected crops or grain. The cattle chief was of a similar rank and collected cattle, milk and butter as well as adjudicating in disputes over grazing or cattle ownership. Finally, all Tutsi belonged to a fighting regiment under the army chief.

The Tutsi used psychological means to help maintain their dominance, exaggerating the physical, temperamental and cultural differences between the two peoples. Tutsi generally have lighter skins and are taller and slimmer than the dark, stocky Hutu; these characteristics were held to demonstrate their innate superiority. The Tutsi also cultivated elaborate social manners and physical grace.

Uganda
pop: 12,148,000

Uganda is the most fertile country in East Africa and the population is mainly agriculturalist. The country produces nearly all its own food, with millet, sorghum, maize, cassava and bananas the main crops. Coffee, cotton, sugar, tea and tobacco are grown for export.

Only 7 per cent of the population live in the two biggest towns, Kampala the capital and the industrial town of Jinja. Most of the people are Bantu-speakers and the major groups are the Ganda, the Soga and the Nyoro. Others include the Nilotic Acholi, the Lango and the Karamojong. English and Swahili are official languages.

Acholi
pop: 225,000

The Acholi originated in the Nile region of the Sudan and migrated south; most Acholi now live in northern Uganda, with a minority in the Sudan. They resemble other Nilotic people like the Nuer and Dinka in their language and their tall slim physique. Unlike most Nilotes, however, they practise subsistence agriculture and keep only a few cattle.

The Acholi live in permanent villages, sub-divided into hearths called *o*. Allegiances are to the hearth rather than the village, and the different *o* compete against one another in hunting and at games.

Ganda
pop: 2,000,000

The Ganda live in Uganda on the north-west shores of Lake Victoria. Some work in the nearby capital city of Kampala, but the majority are farmers who grow cotton and coffee as cash crops and bananas and vegetables for their own food.

Most African agriculturalists pass down land within the family group, but the Ganda change villages every few years and buy and sell their land; a family usually settles down in one place only when the father becomes older. This means that families rarely live near their relatives or establish close contacts in a community. The family units alter over time because marriages often break down after a few years and there is a tradition of fostering some children with relatives. This system probably owes much to the high fertility of the area and to the fact that formerly there was no shortage of good land.

RWANDA/BURUNDI

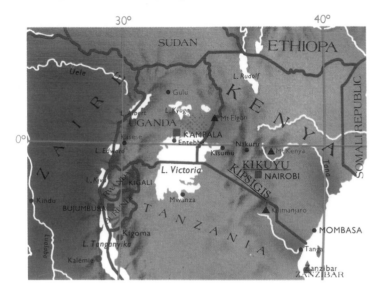

Distribution of Swahili

Distribution of Swahili

Kenya
pop: 14,113,000

Semi-desert in the north and north-east gives way to fertile grasslands in the south-western highlands and swamps and rain forest along the coast. The four main cities, Nairobi, Mombasa, Nakuru and Kisumu, house less than 10 per cent of the population, which is predominantly agriculturalist; some pastoralism continues in the north and in the arid lowlands of the rift valley. The major ethnic groups include the Kikuyu, Kamba, Luo, Luhya and the pastoralist Masai and Turkana. There are important Asian, European and Arab minorities. English and Swahili are the official languages.

Kikuyu
pop: 2,225,000

The high, ridged plateau between Nairobi and Mount Kenya is the homeland of the Kikuyu, Kenya's largest ethnic group. Like their close Bantu relatives the Kamba, they were intensive hoe cultivators before colonization, growing maize, beans, sweet potatoes and vegetables; many have since been drawn into industry and commerce. Today the Kikuyu dominate national politics and administration and are found throughout the country.

The structure of their society was deeply rooted in the land. The Kikuyu arrived from the north, acquiring ridge after ridge from the previous occupants, the Dorobo; lineages trace descent on the male side from the first settler of each ridge. Nine major clans and a number of sub-clans derived from these lineages, but the basic economic unit remained the domestic family homestead —a group of huts surrounded by a hedge or stockade.

In the countryside the importance of the family is still reflected in a powerful sense of communion with the ancestors. Procreation is a sacred duty, for if the line is broken, the ancestral spirits are condemned to wander. A man's prestige is increased by having children; at the same time, by taking several wives he is able to cultivate more land and thus increase his wealth.

Kikuyu men undergo a life-long series of initiations, with the four most important stages occurring at circumcision, marriage, fatherhood and the circumcision of the first son. In the past both boys and girls were circumcised in ceremonies held each year, and the shared experience of pain bound contemporaries together.

Europeans arrived in Kenya in the last decades of the 19th century, when Nairobi was just a small hamlet. By 1948 there were 20,000 white settlers and the Kikuyu had been restricted to a tribal reserve. Since their farming methods did not include crop rotation, the soil was rapidly exhausted and many young men were forced to seek day labour in the town.

When Kenya became independent in 1963, the Kikuyu dominance within the new government was out of all proportion to their numbers. Land alienated during colonial rule, however, was sold back to the Kikuyu at market prices so that while many wealthy men have acquired large estates the problem of urban unemployment and vagrancy remains severe.

Kipsigis
pop: 157,000

The Kipsigis are a cattle herding people today occupying some of Kenya's most fertile land; their centre, Kericho, is the country's major tea growing area. Since the Second World War there has been a steady trend towards agriculture, enclosing arable land and terracing the steeper slopes.

Together with the neighbouring Nandi, Keyo, Tugen, Marakwet, Endo and Pokot, the Nilotic Kipsigis probably migrated into their present lands from the north-east towards the end of the 18th century. These peoples are today all known as Kalenjin.

Social organization, oriented towards discipline for the young and respect for community opinion among elders, is based on village cluster, clan and age set. A group of perhaps 50 homesteads will all recognize a resident elder who, assisted by a council, dispenses justice on everyday matters.

Boys are circumcised and initiated into traditional lore at the age of 14–18. All those initiated within a period of about 15 years are expected to

treat each other as brothers. Girls undergo clitorodectomy rather earlier, and marriages are then arranged for them outside the clan. As wives they have their own homesteads with a vegetable garden, maize fields and a cattle pen.

Until they marry, boys herd the cattle, which are dispersed widely as a precaution against rinderpest disease and raiding. This is achieved either by lending the animals to friends or, for a man wealthy enough to have several wives, by distributing them amongst their homesteads.

The Kipsigis worship a single god, called Asis or Cheptalil, who is associated with the sun. For prayers and offerings each homestead has a shrine in which the supplicant faces east. Evil is thought to come from the envious or despondent non-reincarnated spirits of the dead.

Swahili
pop: 1,000,000

The Bantu Swahili have always lived in the narrow coastal strip of East Africa and on the offshore islands, Zanzibar, Pemba and Patta. From the 12th century onwards they founded small city states, based on Arab trade, with their own armies, coinages, written chronicles and mosques. In the 19th century they engaged in trade with Europeans, supplying ivory and slaves; they travelled far inland, spreading their language and customs. Today Swahili has been adopted as a national language in Kenya and Tanzania. It is also understood in parts of Mozambique, the Congo and Malawi.

The strong Arab influence on the Swahili is evident in their lifestyle. The women traditionally wear black *bouis bouis* which cover their bodies from head to foot. *Dhows* still sail with the monsoon winds to and from Arabia, and Islam has been adopted as the Swahili religion. Mosques are found even in small settlements. Agriculture and fishing have now replaced trade as the main economic activities.

Kamba women sorting sisal ropes, Kenya

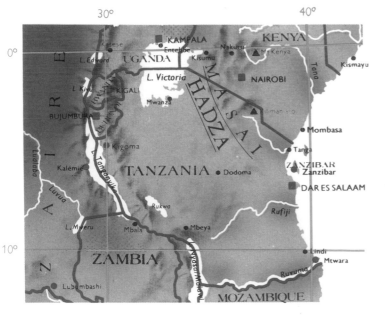

Masai
pop: 190,000

Equal numbers of the Nilotic Masai live in Kenya and Tanzania. They are descended from warrior groups who probably left the upper Nile in the 17th and 18th centuries and fought their way south to East Africa, where they established themselves in the grasslands.

Each adult man belongs to an age set with those of approximately his own age. Within each age set, all the members are considered equal and may speak at councils, but major affairs are regulated by the senior elders who are respected for their wisdom.

At the age of about 16, all the young men are circumcised and join the first age grade of *ilmurran* or warriors. These *moran*, as they are called, leave their homes and build huts in separate bachelor encampments called *manyatta*. The young men paint their bodies with ochre and have elaborate plaited hair styles; they are famed for their toughness, endurance and skill with weapons, especially their long spears. In the past the *moran* acted as the Masai army and were responsible for territorial defence and leading raids for cattle on neighbouring peoples such as the Kikuyu. Today they guard the cattle when they must be taken to pasture far from the village in the dry season and act as gatherers of news and information as they travel around their areas.

The women are circumcised after they have become physically mature and may not marry until the ceremony has been performed. After marriage a woman leaves her father's home for her husband's village, where she eventually builds a rectangular house for herself. A man may have several wives, for which his kin group pays bridewealth in the form of cattle. The wives' houses are placed in definite positions in relation to one another inside the thick thorn fence which encircles and protects the village. The first wife always has precedence, but each new wife is given exclusive milking rights over certain cows in her husband's herd. As her sons grow up, she allocates some of these cows to them; when they reach manhood and set up herds and families, they are entitled to these cattle and their progeny.

Masai believe that Ngai, the creator, made all the cattle in the world for them to live by, and cattle ownership is of central importance to their lifestyle. They also keep sheep, goats and donkeys, and all these animals are herded out to pasture in the morning and driven back inside the thorn fence at night. Until recently, when overgrazing became a problem and ranching schemes were instituted, the flexible herding system of the Masai allowed them to exploit efficiently all the territory they occupied.

The staple diet is cow's milk, which in the past was eked out with cow's blood during the dry seasons. This is rarely done today; the Masai prefer to buy grain or even to grow maize themselves. Meat is eaten at nearly all ceremonies, in case of illness and sometimes to celebrate the arrival of visitors.

Tanzania
pop: 15,772,000

Tanzania ranges from a humid, tropical coastline to a hot, barren interior. Dar es Salaam, the present capital, lies on a natural harbour just south of the clove islands of Zanzibar and Pemba, which are politically united with Tanzania. There are plans to move government offices to Dodoma, which is more centrally placed.

Tanzania has more than 120 distinct ethnic groups including the Sukuma, Nyamwezi, Ha, Makande, Gogo, Haya, Chagga and Hehe. There are also Sandawe and Hadza hunter-gatherers, and Masai pastoralists who cross the border with Kenya, but the majority are Bantu speakers. The Sukuma, who are the most numerous (1,400,000) live south of Lake Victoria and produce cotton for export, raise cattle and grow bananas and maize for their own food. Other concentrations of population occur on the shore of Lake Nyasa and on the foothills of Kilimanjaro.

Half of Tanzania's agricultural produce is still grown by subsistence farmers, who plant only as much cassava, sorghum, millet, maize, banana or coconut as they need. The country's financial resources are slight, due to fluctuations in the world market for sisal and coffee. The major political problem is to unite a poor and ethnically diverse country, yet to some extent the tribal divisions are an advantage, because no one group dominates the others. There is a further advantage in the legacy of slave and ivory traders, who penetrated far inland and took their language and culture with them, because the coastal Swahili is now understood everywhere and has become an official language, with English.

Hadza
pop: 1,000

The home of the Khoisan Hadza is an area of more than 1,000 square miles to the west and east of Lake Eyasi. Most of the country is bushland with rocky hillsides, but vegetation is thicker in the valley bottoms. The Hadza are distinguished from their neighbours both by their hunter-gatherer economy and by their click language, which is not related to any of the languages spoken by the peoples around them. In East Africa the Sandawe and the Dahalo also talk with click consonants, but there appears to be little connection between their language and the Hadza's.

Women and children do most of the collecting. A wide range of fruits and berries, roots and leaves are available

in the different seasons. Giant grey baobab trees are scaled by knocking wooden pegs into the trunks to make a ladder; the fruit is knocked down with sticks. The seeds and pulp are pounded into a highly nutritious porridge. Honey is one of their favourite foods; the Hadza are exceptionally skilled at finding bees' nests in the ground or in trees. Sometimes their attention is attracted by the small bird called the honey guide, which leads them to a nest by flying in front of them.

Hadza men spend much time gambling at their disc game *lukuchuko*, as well as hunting. The foreshaft and tips of their arrows are only poisoned when they are hunting big game such as buffalo, zebra, wildebeest or hartebeest, most of which live on the open plains. Poisons are distilled from the sap of *Adenium*, the desert rose, or the pods of *Strophanthus eminii*.

Hadza groups move camp every two or three weeks. There are no individual land rights, and theoretically anyone may travel anywhere. In practice, groups tend to stay in an area they know, where they are more efficient at exploiting the land's resources. Past attempts to settle the Hadza in one place have failed owing to their poor resistance to disease, but the Tanzanian government is continuing its efforts.

Masai warriors (ilmurran), Tanzania

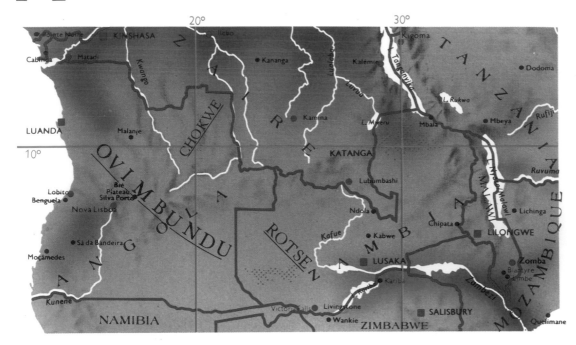

initiated into traditional knowledge at the age of 6–13. The transition to manhood is marked by elaborate ceremonies and a long period of seclusion in an initiation lodge, during which strict prohibitions must be observed. Women attempt to catch the initiates on their ceremonial return, but are prevented by the older men, thus severing symbolically the last links with childhood.

Ovimbundu
pop: 1,350,000

Once the most famous traders of Bantu Africa, the Ovimbundu occupy the Angolan plateau around Bié and Huambo; their language is Umbundu. They developed as a people in the 16th and 17th centuries, from a coalition of the Jaga (invading Lunda warriors from the Mwata Yamvo kingdom) and the indigenous population. Early contacts with Portuguese traders encouraged the Ovimbundu to act as middlemen.

Travelling deep into the continent, their caravans consisted of several thousand people under the leadership of *olofumbelo*, wealthy, elderly entrepreneurs. At first they exchanged Portuguese cloth, guns and rum for ivory, beeswax, and slaves for the Americas, but their greatest prosperity came from selling rubber during the late 19th century.

Efficient economic organization was facilitated by the Ovimbundu double-descent kinship system. Each individual inherited political, residential and land rights through a village patrilineal group, whose activities revolved around the men's dining-house, or *oluse*. Rights to movable property came through a dispersed matrilineal group. Although recruitment for trading expeditions was patrilineal, financial resources were provided matrilineally, thus ensuring a separation of village relations from the economic sphere of credit and trading wealth.

The collapse of the rubber market, the opening of the Benguela railway, an influx of European traders and Portuguese occupation, and finally a great famine in 1911 brought large-scale Ovimbundu trading to a halt. The distinctive nature of their kinship system disap-

Angola
pop: 6,148,000

Angola has a narrow coastal plain rising to highlands from which the land slopes to the valleys of the Zambezi and Zaire rivers; there is desert and scrub to the south. Major cities are Luanda, the capital, Lobito, Benguela and Sá da Bandeira (Lubango). The fight for independence from Portugal and subsequent civil war weakened the economy, depending on exports of coffee, oil, iron, copper and diamonds. Angola's peoples include the Ovimbundu, Bantu speakers and formerly great traders, the Lunda and Chokwe in the north and Hottentot and Bushmen groups in the south. The official language is Portuguese.

Chokwe
pop: 600,000

The Chokwe live in woodland savanna, broken by strips of rain forest, river swamp and marshland, in the Lunda district of north-east Angola. Their territory also extends into southern Zaire and northwest Zambia. The Chokwe developed as a distinct group from a combination of several indigenous peoples and Lunda conquerors moving into the area from the west, around the beginning of the 17th century. The Chokwe eventually subjugated the Lunda and, co-operating initially with neighbouring Ovimbundu middle-

men, they engaged in the ivory, wax, rubber and slave trades.

Hunting is an important activity in the north, where the villages are small, widely dispersed and often temporary The southern Chokwe live in larger, permanent settlements, practising hoe cultivation of several subsistence and cash crops including peanuts, millet and yams. Although women reside in their husbands' villages, the Chokwe trace descent matrilineally, with rights to property, land and political office inherited by a man's sisters' sons rather than his own children.

Since their single, omniscient creator god is considered remote and withdrawn, most Chokwe religious practice is concerned with the worship of ancestor and nature spirits. These spirits are believed to retain an active interest in everyday village life and, to ensure good fortune, they are represented by small carved statues and masks, to which offerings are given and supplications made. The Chokwe retain strong beliefs in the evil power of sorcery, though clearly distinguishing between natural and supernatural causes of illness and misfortune. A diviner, or ritual specialist, is consulted when witchcraft is suspected. By 'reading' a divination basket and questioning a rubbing board, the diviner will diagnose the cause of illness and prescribe a remedy.

Boys are circumcised and

Lunda Expansion, 17th century

peared and the nuclear family became their basic economic unit. Today most Ovimbundu live by shifting cultivation of cash crops including maize, tobacco, coffee and sisal, while many work in Lobito.

Zambia
pop: 5,099,000

The river Zambezi gives Zambia its name and forms most of the country's southern boundary; held back by a dam to form Lake Kariba, it also produces hydro-electric power shared with Zimbabwe (Rhodesia). Zambia's indigenous peoples speak six major Bantu languages; there are also European and Asian minorities and the official language is English. The largest ethnic group is the Bemba, mostly in the northeast; many Bemba men work in the towns of the copper belt including Ndola, Kabwe and Kitwe, which are the hub of Zambia's rich copper, lead and zinc mining industries. These minerals are the country's chief exports. There is little industry in the capital city, Lusaka, which is mainly an administrative centre.

Elsewhere, on the high plateau land and wooded savanna, Zambians grow food crops such as millet, maize, cassava and sweet potatoes by the slash-and-burn method, or *chitemene*. After crop production, when the ground is exhausted, it is left to regenerate and another area is cleared. However, *chitemene* is slowly giving way to modern methods which require less labour. Cash crops encouraged by the government include sugar, cotton and tobacco.

Rotse
pop: 410,000

The heartland of the Rotse or Lozi people is the flood plain of the river Zambezi in southwest Zambia. The flood plain extends for 100 miles along the river, but is rarely more than 25 miles wide. Here the sandy soil is enriched each year when the river floods, enabling the Rotse to grow sorghum, maize and other grains. They also fish and breed cattle.

The Rotse political system is one of numerous overlapping councils and offices. The hereditary king, or *litunga*, ruling from the north, shares power with both an elected prime minister and the *mulena mukwae*, the 'princess chief', who rules from the southern part of Rotseland. Each capital has a dry season and a flood season site. Although ultimate power lies with the *litunga*, he is advised by a complex series of councils representing a wide cross-section of the people.

The Rotse of the plain follow an annual routine, dictated by the cycle of the river. When the floods rise between February and July, they move to the higher savanna and forest, preceded by the king in his royal barge with a ceremonial procession. When the water drops, they return to the plain, but do not always reassemble in the same villages.

The Rotse who live on the higher ground produce items such as baskets, tobacco, ground nuts and honey as well as canoes, wooden dishes and drums. These are traded with the farmers and herders of the plains in return for meat, fish, sorghum, maize and other foodstuffs. In the past the Rotse were richer than neighbouring tribes like the Ila-Tonga, but they are now among the poorest people in modern Zambia. This makes it necessary for many men to work outside the province, in the nation's mines and industries.

Southern Chokwe homestead, Angola

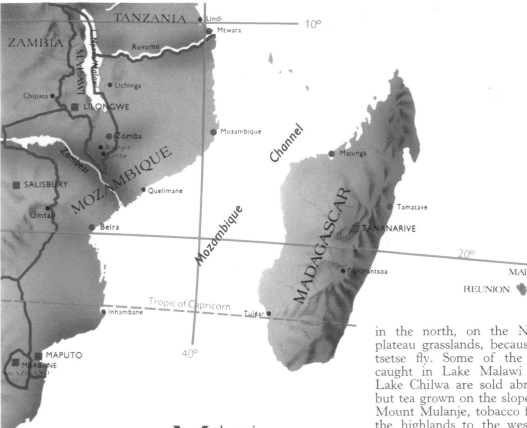

Malawi
pop: 5,245,000

The narrow country of Malawi lies along the western shore of Lake Malawi. Its earliest known history was turbulent: at the beginning of the 19th century, the principal tribal groups, the Chewa, the Nyanja, the Tonga and the Tumbaka, were disrupted first by Yao raiding down the Rovuma valley in search of slaves for Arab traders, and then by Nguni bands pushing north along Lake Malawi. Today the Chewa of the central highlands are the largest group. The main languages are Nyanja-Chewa, Tumbuka and English.

Population density is among the highest in Africa, concentrated on the shores of Lake Malawi, Lake Chilwa, around Lilongwe, the capital, and on the plateaux of the south near Zomba and Blantyre-Limbe. Many of the men go to Zimbabwe (Rhodesia), Zambia or South Africa to find work because Malawi has no large industries and the economy is based on village agriculture. Food crops including maize, cassava and millet are grown on a shifting cultivation system which has caused destruction of the natural forests.

There are few cattle except in the north, on the Nyika plateau grasslands, because of tsetse fly. Some of the fish caught in Lake Malawi and Lake Chilwa are sold abroad, but tea grown on the slopes of Mount Mulanje, tobacco from the highlands to the west of the river Shire, and cotton from the lower Shire valley are Malawi's major exports.

Mozambique
pop: 9,294,000

Mozambique has a coastline on the Indian Ocean of about 1,700 miles, with lagoons and a string of islands in the north. The river Zambezi, flowing south-east, has been dammed at Cabora Bassa to produce hydro-electric power. It meets the sea in an enormous delta covering 2,500 square miles, where stilt houses are built for safety during the floods, and the water is used for irrigating rice paddies.

The capital, Maputo (Lourenço Marques), and Beira are both ports and are the two largest towns in Mozambique. Both earn foreign exchange by handling imports and exports for landlocked Malawi and Zimbabwe (Rhodesia).

The people speak various Bantu languages and exhibit considerable cultural variety; in the north Islam is strong among the Yao and Makonde. The Makua and Shanga live along the coast, with the Tete, Nyanja, Ndau, Tswa, Nkuida and Nsengo in the west. To the south, the Tonga and Shona provide labour for the South African mines. Portuguese is the official language.

Agriculture is Mozambique's economic mainstay, but fluctuating rainfall makes crop production very unreliable. Groundnuts, sisal, cotton and cashews are grown for export. Quelimane in the north has the biggest coconut plantation in the world and exports copra. Inland, tea, cotton and sugar are cash crops; rice, wheat and maize are the staples.

Madagascar
pop: 7,812,000

With a wide range of climates, Madagascar has a similar diversity of peoples and cultures. The north-east monsoons bring high rainfall to the north and east coast; the central plateau has a temperate climate; semi-desert conditions prevail in the south-west.

Tananarive, the capital, and its port Tamatave are popula-

Zafimaniry village,
eastern Madagascar

tion centres, but most of the people live by agriculture in the north and on the central plateau. The most productive areas for rice cultivation are the valley bottoms, but it is also grown on hillsides cleared by slash-and-burn techniques. Many other fruits and grains are grown, and cattle are ranched extensively in the south-west. The island produces two-thirds of the world's vanilla, as well as cloves, but coffee is the major export crop. The only minerals are mica, graphite and coal.

Madagascar's population originates not only from the African mainland, but from Indonesia, Arabia and India. There are French and Taiwan Chinese minorities; French and Malagasy are the official languages. The Merina are the most numerous of the 18 different ethnic groups and show their Indonesian origin in their long straight hair and pale coppery skin, as well as in their language. Most Merina farm on the plateau, but others have become teachers, doctors and businessmen. In rural communities their red, two-storey houses are built with ritual orientation. All windows face the west, the kitchen is to the south and the father of the family sleeps in the north-east corner of the house—the side closest to the ancestral spirits.

The Betsimisaraka are more Negroid in appearance, yet are different in physique from East Africans. Their villages, all along the east coast, consist of one-room stilt houses with woven palm walls and palm thatches. The larger houses of clan heads are found at the north-east end of the different wards, again closest to the ancestors. Many villages have a carved pole about eight feet high, with two horns representing those of a bull. This post represents ancestors of the village and is surrounded by the skulls of sacrificed cattle.

Mauritius
pop: 900,000

A volcanic island almost ringed by a coral reef, Mauritius lies 500 miles east of Madagascar. Uninhabited in the 15th century, it was colonized by the French in 1715, after the Dutch had failed to establish any permanent settlement. The French introduced slaves from Africa and Madagascar to work on the sugar plantations and, after the abolition of slavery, Indian workers were also brought for this purpose.

Mauritian Indians are the largest ethnic group today, but are unpopular with creoles and Franco-Mauritians because of their trading success, particularly in the capital, Port Louis. Mauritian creole is the *lingua franca*; English and French are official languages. The lagoons are fished, and maize, cassava, tea and tobacco are grown, but the island's economy is still dependent on sugar exports.

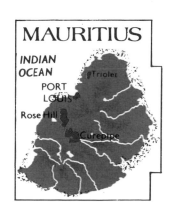

MAURITIUS

INDIAN OCEAN

Triolet

PORT LOUIS

Rose Hill

Curepipe

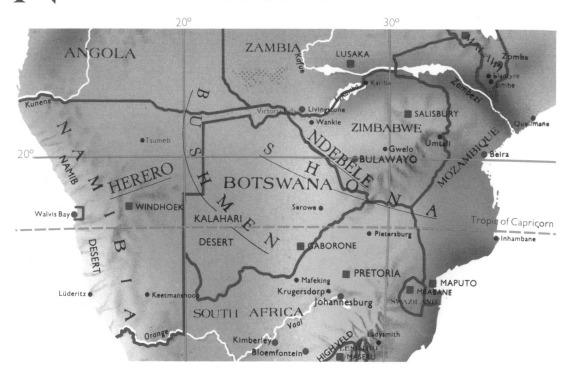

Namibia

pop: 929,000

The Namib desert, which fringes the west coast of Namibia, has remarkable animal life, but the only human inhabitants are at mining centres or fishing ports such as Walvis Bay—Namib means empty in the Nama language. Northeast of the desert, the largest ethnic groups, the Ovambo and the Kavango, practise mixed farming on a grassy plateau.

The other main groups, the Damara, the Herero and the Nama Hottentots, together with the majority of Europeans, live in the drier centre and south of the country, where industry is based on Windhoek, the capital. South African companies have continued to exploit deposits of diamonds, copper, lead and zinc despite a World Court ruling in 1971 that the South African administration was illegal. Independence for Namibia is now scheduled for 1979.

Herero

pop: 100,000

The Herero of Namibia have suffered even more than most African peoples from colonial rule. After rebelling against the Germans in 1904, 70,000 Herero were massacred out of a population of around 90,000. Many more died in the Kalahari desert, attempting to flee.

After the First World War, the territory was passed to South Africa under a League of Nations mandate; in 1971 the World Court ruled that South Africa's occupation was illegal. The Herero, now crowded in reserves at the centre of the country, are in the forefront of the struggle for independence.

The Herero lifestyle and social organization have been shattered by their experiences. Formerly they were primarily pastoralists, raising vast herds of longhorn cattle. Each Herero belonged to both a patrilineal and a matrilineal descent group. Today the chief occupation remains cattle farming, but many Herero have been forced to seek employment as labourers or servants.

Two tiny remnants of the tribe, the Himba and Tjimba in the north-west, avoided conflict with the colonial powers and retain the former lifestyle. Their culture is based entirely on ownership of cattle, and cultivation is considered a demeaning occupation: the staple food is soured milk. The Herero's Bantu language contains about a thousand words for distinguishing variations in their cattle.

Bushmen

pop: 20,000

The whole of southern Africa was probably once the home of the Khoisan Bushmen and Hottentots, who roamed over savanna and grassland and left rock paintings and engravings as marks of their culture. Today, owing to competition from other peoples, the largest group of Hottentots, the Nama, live in Namibia, while the Bushmen are confined to parts of Angola, Namibia and South Africa. Approximately half are in Botswana, in and around the fringes of the semi-desert Kalahari region. Bushmen on the Kalahari fringes often act as herdsmen for their neighbours, including the Bamangwato, and new boreholes in some regions of the Kalahari also bring the Bushmen into contact with other peoples. Under the impact of these cultures, their lifestyle is changing rapidly.

Bushmen probably split off from the Negroid stock very early. They are striking in appearance, because of their small stature and the large fat deposits in their buttocks, which serve as energy stores. These deposits are more marked in women than in men, decreasing in times of famine and also with age. Their skin is a pale, coppery colour and reflects more of the sunlight than the darker Negro skin; their hair grows in 'peppercorn' tufts; their eyes are slanted, sometimes with fat deposits in the eyelids. All this helps them survive in the difficult conditions of the Kalahari.

There are many different groups of Bushmen, but all speak languages of the Khoisan or click group, many of which are mutually unintelligible. Nearly a third of all Bushmen still practise a hunting and gathering economy, living in nomadic bands whose numbers fluctuate, decreasing in times of drought and increasing when conditions improve. Each band has a territory which may be several hundred square miles in area, with boundaries respected by adjacent bands. Within this territory they follow the herds of gemsbok, springbok, hartebeest, eland and wildebeest, which they hunt with bows and arrows. The arrows are small and do not inflict fatal wounds, but the tips are poisoned.

With superlative tracking ability, the Bushmen may follow their prey for days until it falls. When the kill is made,

they use almost every part of the carcass. Meat is eaten, and some is dried for future use; they drink the blood, and the rumen contents are squeezed to provide water. Bones are broken open for the marrow, and fragments taken to make arrowheads. The animal's hide provides cloaks for the women and loin-cloths for the men. Bushmen do not kill often; vegetables and fruits make up their staple diet. *Tsamma* melon is one of the few plants which yield water, which is sometimes stored in ostrich egg containers and buried underground to delay evaporation.

Botswana
pop: 720,000

Botswana is an arid country, consisting mainly of the Kalahari desert. The only major internal river, the Okavango, peters out in a series of large swamps and ephemeral lakes. With the exception of the Kalahari Bushmen, the indigenous people are mostly pastoralists and live in the east of the country, where the rainfall is slightly higher. Gabarone, the capital, is also in the east.

The Tswana, who are related to the Sotho further south, are the main ethnic group. Tswana sub-groups are the Bamangwato, the Bakwena, the Bangwaketse and the Batawana. Some 4,000 Europeans are involved in mining for diamonds, copper, nickel, coal, asbestos and manganese, which occur in the east. Many Tswana men migrate annually to work in South Africa. English is the official language.

Zimbabwe
pop: 6,648,000

The stone walls and towers of the ruined citadel of Zimbabwe, dating from about the 12th century AD, are a reminder of the country's ancient cultures. Between 1100 and 1800 the area was ruled by the Shona; European settlement in the country did not begin until the end of the 19th century, when Cecil Rhodes' pioneer column crossed the Limpopo. Outposts of the British South Africa Company were established in the high veld south of the Zambezi.

In 1978 Europeans form a governing minority of some 250,000, but are involved in a military struggle against African nationalists. More than 60 per cent of the black population are restricted to tribal reserves, overpopulated and overstocked, where food crops such as maize, millet and vegetables are grown. Ndebele and Shona peoples are the main ethnic groups, together with less numerous peoples such as the Tonga, Sena, Hlengwe, Venda and Sotho. English is the official language.

Agriculture and industry elsewhere are controlled by Europeans running large-scale enterprises. Tobacco, formerly the country's major export, has declined in importance since the white leaders declared themselves independent of Britain in 1965. Zimbabwe has major deposits of copper, gold, nickel, chrome and asbestos.

Ndebele
pop: 750,000

The Ndebele, or Matabele as Europeans called them, are a Nguni group, who fled to their present lands during the *Mfecane*, or 'Crushing', wars which accompanied the rise of the Zulu empire in southern Africa. They migrated northwards until they reached the granite hills and thickly wooded bush country of western Zimbabwe, then occupied by the Shona. With a few violent battles they took over a large territory, and continued to raid deep into Shona country when they needed women, cattle or food. Conflict with British settlers came at the end of the 19th century; the Ndebele army was decisively broken and tribal lands alienated to European farmers.

Ndebele boys are still trained to use traditional weapons—the assegai spear and the knobkerrie club. In the past these were also used for hunting, which provided most of the meat eaten by the Ndebele, although they also kept cattle and grew millet. Small family groups would hunt with trained dogs, and the kill was divided according to definite rules. Today, cattle are slaughtered for meat, which is then sometimes spiced and dried.

The descent system is patrilineal, and polygynous marriage is allowed. Female infidel-ity is socially unacceptable and often results in a heavy fine for the wife's father and her lover. Apart from its natural or 'little' mother, each child has a 'big' mother who acts as a surrogate if necessary. The emphasis on communal care is also seen in traditional breast feeding—infants are fed by all the mothers who are suckling children.

Today the Ndebele are integrated into the urban economy of Zimbabwe (Rhodesia) and work in mines and industries, as well as on large European farms. More than 20 per cent live in the crowded townships which surround the urban centres, but they retain close links with their homes in rural areas and many go back each weekend. A major source of political tension has been the government appointment of tribal chiefs, who formerly ruled by consent of the people.

Shona
pop: 4,000,000

The Shona comprise more than 75 per cent of the population of Zimbabwe and occupy large areas of Mozambique. They are also found in Botswana, South Africa and Zambia. They expanded east and south from the Zambezi in the 10th century, eventually reaching the Indian Ocean.

The Bantu Shona were principally cultivators who probably supplemented their diet by hunting and gathering. In addition to this, they began to mine gold, smelt iron and sell salt and ivory to neighbouring groups and traders on the coast. Such trading brought the various Shona groups into contact with the outside world and stimulated the growth of a series of independent states in the 12th–19th centuries.

When European settlement began much Shona land was taken for European farms and special Shona tribal areas were designated. Traditional life continued in the reserves, but with population growth and reliance on old agricultural methods, people were forced into the cities and mines to work. Subsequently the traditional authority of chiefs declined and under new political leaders the Shona have been active in the Zimbabwe independence struggle.

South Africa

pop: 28,591,000
European settlement in South Africa began in 1652, when the Dutch East India Company established a base at the Cape of Good Hope. The indigenous Hottentots and Bushmen were either employed or driven away. Britain took possession of the Cape in 1814, sparking off a rapid expansion of the colonized area.

To the north of the Great Fish river, the Bantu Sotho and Nguni occupied the high veld and the coastal plains respectively. In 1817, Shaka formed the Zulu nation from part of the Nguni and rapidly drove the other clans north and west in the *Mfecane*, or 'Crushing' wars.

In 1837, Boer descendants of the Dutch settlers marched north from the Cape to escape British rule. During the Great Trek they fought off Zulu attacks to establish the Orange Free State and the Transvaal. By 1902, however, the whole of South Africa was under British sovereignty. Full independence finally came in 1961.

The population of South Africa is now composed of four distinct groups: Africans (70 per cent), Europeans (17 per cent), Asians, and Coloureds—peoples of mixed descent. The largest of the African groups are the Bantu Zulus, Xhosa and Sotho. The Asians, mostly from India, are descendants of labourers brought to work on sugar plantations during the 19th century. The

Zulu Expansion, 19th century

 Zulu
Bantu groups dispersed in Mfecane wars
1. Swazi
2. Ndebele
3. Temba
4. Sotho
5. Xhosa
6. Shona

white minority dominates political and economic life, and since 1948 a policy of *apartheid*, or separate development, has segregated residential areas between white and black. Afrikaans and English are the official languages.

Of the African population, about half now live in Bantustans (African 'homelands', which have a measure of autonomy). None of these are economically independent, and many Africans work outside the Bantustans in factories and mines. Others work as servants and wage-earners in the cities. The white community occupies 86 per cent of the republic's land area.

South Africa produces a wide range of agricultural produce. Maize is the most important cereal, with oats, wheat, barley and sorghum; sugar and many fruits are also grown. Livestock, in particular sheep, are raised in vast numbers. Gold and diamonds, however, remain the country's most valuable resources; silver, uranium, asbestos, chrome, copper, and platinum are also mined.

Zulus
pop: 4,000,000

The Zulu empire was established at the start of the 19th century by Shaka, who united several Nguni clans to drive away or conquer many neighbouring groups. The rest of the century saw the Zulus increasingly in conflict with, and finally conquered by, colonizers from the south. The British annexed Natal in 1844 and in 1872, after ferocious resistance, the Zulus were finally brought under colonial administration.

The nation is now divided between the Bantustan of Kwazulu (Zululand), some small reserves in Natal and Zulu enclaves in towns such as Johannesburg, Krugersdorp and Durban. Many men leave their families regularly to work in the mines and factories. The Zulus have made a partial adaptation to urban conditions and have been prominent in expressions of militant black nationalism.

The basic unit of traditional Zulu society is the fenced *kraal* of a man and his family, with the houses of his wives and relations arranged around a central area for cattle and goats. Milk and meat are the principal foods, but women grow crops such as maize and sweet potatoes. Cattle are sacrificed on all important occasions, and this custom persists even in the townships, where white goats are sold for this purpose.

Clan relations remain important. Clansmen may not intermarry; they eat dairy food only at another clansman's house, and they seek assistance first from a clansman before turning to outsiders.

Lesotho
pop: 1,074,000

Situated in the very highest part of the Drakensberg range, Lesotho is completely surrounded by the republic of South Africa. Two-thirds of the country is rugged mountains and most of the inhabitants live on the lower land to the west, where the climate is warmer and drier. Apart from a small European and Asian minority, the population is overwhelmingly Sotho, a Bantu people united by their first ruler Moshoeshoe I, in the early 19th century. English and Sotho are the official languages.

Many of the men work in South Africa; women and girls cultivate the poor soils to produce staple crops of maize, sorghum and wheat. Young boys tend the cattle and goats, taking them regularly to the high mountain pastures.

Swaziland
pop: 518,000

The kingdom of Swaziland is one of the smallest states in Africa and is inhabited mainly by Swazis. The official languages are Swati and English. From the cool wet highveld in the west with the capital Mbabane, the country falls away gradually to the hot and drier lowveld with the Lebombo mountains to the east.

Most of the population lives in villages at the middle altitudes, where the soil is best for farming. Millet, rice and sorghum are the staple crops; citrus fruits, cotton and sugar are grown for cash. The country has valuable deposits of coal, asbestos and iron, tin and gold, but many men work as labourers in South Africa.

photograph:
Xhosa girl initiates, Transkei

photograph:
Afrikaner (Boer) farmer, South Africa

Soviet Union/Mongolia

The Soviet Union and Mongolia occupy most of northern Asia and parts of eastern Europe and central Asia. Covering an area of some 3,500,000 square miles, this vast region contains extremely varied environments, ranging from the fertile cornfields of southern Russia to Siberia's cold and swamp-ridden taiga forest and the dry, empty steppes of Mongolia and Kazakhstan. The peoples, language and cultures of these lands are equally diverse, yet in recent years an overlying unity has been created by the Soviet state.

European Russia, west of the Ural mountains, is a region of wide plains with large, slow rivers flowing south into the Black and Caspian Seas. The climate is extreme: the winter even in the south lasts up to six months and the variability of precipitation, temperature and pressure causes unpredictable snow and wind storms, droughts and floods. Yet today this is an area of relatively high agricultural production, with the Soviet Union's largest cities and its main industrial development. Most of the inhabitants are Slavs, the largest groups being the Russians, Ukrainians and Belorussians.

Some 2,000 years ago, the Slavs were an obscure people scattered thinly among the woods and marshlands of eastern central Europe, between the Vistula and Dnepr rivers and the Carpathian. From the 1st century AD they engulfed the indige-

nous Balts, ancestors of the Lithuanians and Latvians, who until then occupied a much larger area than they do today. In the 5th century the Slavs expanded and moved west into Germany, south into the Balkans and eastwards into the Ukrainian steppe.

The Slavs traded widely with Varangian merchants from Scandinavia and the Baltic, and a large number of towns grew up at strategic points along the rivers. Notable amongst these was Kiev, which during the 9th century became the capital of the first Russian state, Kiev Rus. In 988 AD its ruler adopted Byzantine Christianity, which remained Russia's official religion until 1917.

Regular attacks by nomads from the eastern steppe, however, culminated in the Mongol-Tatar conquest of 1237-40, which decisively broke Slav contact with western Europe. The conquered Russians were held in bondage for about 240 years by the Tatars, who ruled a vast empire indirectly by levying tribute. It was during this period that the small northern town of Moscow grew into the paramount Slav principality. By the end of the 15th century Muscovy was powerful enough to withhold tribute from the Tatars.

The great age of Russian expansion began with

Projection: Bonne

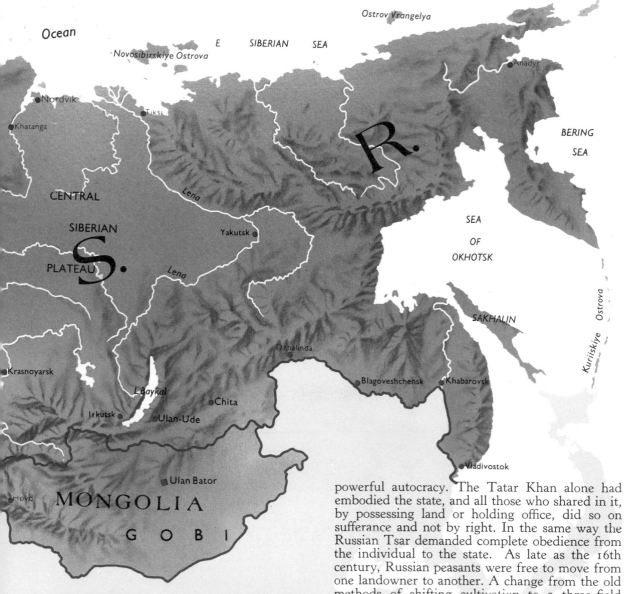

VEGETATION

Ice
Permanent ice field

Tundra
Moss and lichen

Conifer Forest
Pine, spruce, larch

Broadleaf Forest
Deciduous

Temperate
Arable, broadleaf, grass

Mediterranean
Citrus, olive, agave

Subtropical
Dry and wet evergreen

Steppe
Short grass

Savanna
Grass and scrub

Semi Desert
Cactus, sparse shrub and grass

Desert
No vegetation

Marsh and Swamp

Salt
Salt lake, marsh

■ Capital Cities
● Major Towns

∙ Towns
Small town village

―― Country Borders

── Borders
Provinces, states

Ivan the Terrible (1533-84), who captured Kazan and Astrakhan from the Tatars, so opening up new trade routes to Persia and India. Muscovite traders and settlers crossed the Urals into Siberia, which by 1697 held 150,000 Russians and 125,000 native peoples. By 1763 settlements had sprung up on the Pacific coast and early in the 19th century Russians even reached Alaska (which was later sold to the United States). The present population of Siberia —about 30,000,000—is overwhelmingly of European Russian descent.

The Tatars had profoundly influenced Muscovite military organization, the tax collection system, criminal law and diplomatic protocol, but above all they gave a strong impetus to the development of a powerful autocracy. The Tatar Khan alone had embodied the state, and all those who shared in it, by possessing land or holding office, did so on sufferance and not by right. In the same way the Russian Tsar demanded complete obedience from the individual to the state. As late as the 16th century, Russian peasants were free to move from one landowner to another. A change from the old methods of shifting cultivation to a three-field rotation system, however, increased the peasants' obligations. The landowners needed cheap labour to profit from the growing urban corn markets, and in 1649 autocracy and serfdom became absolute. Peasants could no longer escape by moving to the frontier regions. This ruthless system gradually weakened the structure of the community. Despite emancipation in 1861, exploitation of the peasants continued and grievances accumulated, while industrialization created a proletariat in the cities with similar cause for resentment. The 1917 revolution led by the Bolsheviks brought the final collapse of Tsarist Russia.

The Union of Soviet Socialist Republics was created in 1923 to provide a cohesive multi-

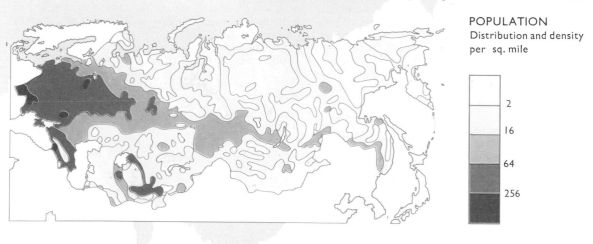

POPULATION
Distribution and density per sq. mile

2
16
64
256

RAINFALL
Average annual rainfall in inches

10 20 40 60 80 100

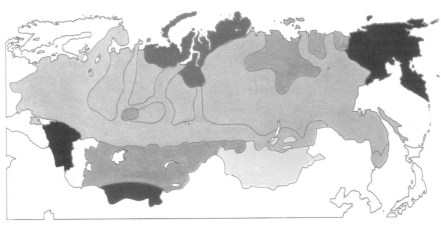

Slavic

Turkic

Mongolian

Samoyed

Palaeo-Asiatic

Iranian

Caucasian

Other

LANGUAGE
Distribution of major languages

national structure for Russia's imperial territories, which by now stretched from Poland to the Pacific, and from Persia and China to the Arctic. It is a federation of many varied nations based on a single political structure, and consists of 11 republics (SSRs) with numerous subsidiary 'autonomous republics' (ASSRs) and 'autonomous regions'.

Since 1917 three major developments have taken place in the Soviet Union, two of which are direct results of socialist policy, the other reflecting world economic and technological trends. These are, first, a crash programme of industrialization, second, the collectivization of agriculture, both dating from 1928. The third is a more general tendency which has brought improvements in several different areas: transport facilities, comminications media, medicare and education. These processes have led to greater population mobility and cultural interpenetration.

Nonetheless, there remains a great variety of nationalities and cultures within the Soviet Union. In the far north and the Chukchee peninsula, many small native groups continue to work in traditional occupations. Typically, a section of each ethnic group engages in hunting at sea, for seals and walrus, while another section lives entirely in the tundra or forest interior, herding reindeer, hunting and fishing in the rivers. Some, like the Yakuts and the Evenki, also herd cattle and horses.

Below the northern zone, Siberia is covered by dense taiga forest, cut by the huge rivers which flow into the Arctic Ocean. In the south there are dry steppes interspersed with upland forest and mountain chains which cut the whole area off from Mongolia. It is in these areas that most of the native population—Buryats, Evenki, Tuvinians, Altaians—live. Their economies are mainly rural, with collectivized herding now supplemented by substantial grain agriculture.

The northern peoples of the Soviet Union have not suffered the blows to their traditional economy experienced by Canadian and Alaskan native peoples. This is largely because in the planned economy of the Soviet Union prices can be adjusted to make local enterprises viable. Yet the organization of the local economy has changed greatly: all huntsmen are in collectives, and so are reindeer herders, fishermen, and fur farmers. Even if they still lead a nomadic existence, these people return to permanent towns within the collectives, where the children live while at school. It is important to realise that by the 1920s these people, who were once far more numerous, were on the way to dying out completely from disease and demoralization.

South-west of Siberia, the Caucasus can be divided into two sections, Trans-Caucasia and the northern Cis-Caucasia. After 1918 the three culturally distinct republics of Georgia, Armenia and Azerbaijan joined together to form a united Trans-Caucasian republic and it was not until 1924 that the Soviet gained full control over the region. For a time the republics had run their own foreign and trade affairs, and even now the commercial reputation of Georgians within the Soviet Union is very high. In Azerbaijan the development of industry and oil refineries at Baku has led to an urbanization of the population, and in general the peoples of Trans-Caucasia are materially better off than in almost any other part of the Soviet Union.

In the north Caucasian region there is a be wildering complex of different peoples and languages. Many of these groups lived in almost complete isolation in mountain villages well into the Soviet period. More recently some have been given land in the valleys, while others have moved to make national units where previously they lived scattered amongst different language groups. Some groups, such as the Kalmuk, were moved from their homeland into exile by the Soviet government and are only now being allowed to return. Yet others disappeared altogether, either destroyed in reprisal for open defiance, or scattered to different points of exile.

Central Asia ranges from the wide steppes of Kazakhstan in the north, to the oases and fertile lands of Tashkent, Samarkand and Bukhara in the centre, and the deserts and great mountain ranges of the Pamirs, Tyan-Shan and Altay ringing the area to the east and south. Here the native peoples differed from one another not so much along ethnic or linguistic boundaries as by the economies which were adapted to the various geographical regions. Thus the Kazakh and Kirghiz mostly had a mixed nomadic pastoral economy in the mountainous steppes, with herds of sheep, cattle, goats, horses and camels. At the other extreme were the Uzbek, the most urbanized people of central Asia, who are traditionally masters of textile manufacture, carpet-making and metal-work, and also had an intensive agricultural economy

The region had a certain cultural unity in that virtually all these people were Muslims. This enabled them to resist Russian colonization with a series of rebellions in the late 19th and early 20th centuries. Central Asia was also one of the areas of the Soviet Union most resistant to collectivization, the emancipation of women, and the great influx of settlers in the Soviet period. Ultimately, however, the leaders of the different groups fell out and some of the most rebellious tribes of Kirghiz emigrated to Afghanistan and China.

The Mongolian People's Republic, previously known as Outer Mongolia, lies to the south-east of the Soviet Union. It forms a vast pastureland sloping from the Altay and Tyan Shan mountains in the west through the Khangai and Khentei hills down to the Gobi desert, which is its border with China. Almost all of this area is settled by Mongolians, except for some Kazakh in the far west, and Buryats and Evenki in the north.

An independent socialist country, formed after a revolution in 1921, Mongolia was part of the Manchu-Chinese Empire before 1911, but Chinese influence in the country has gradually been superseded by Russian. Mongolia has its own international representation at the United Nations, but such matters as exports and imports, education, and the fundamental policies of the Revolutionary Party are kept very much under the control of the Soviets. The Mongolians call this relationship *akh-düü* (older brother-younger brother).

Nomadic pastoralism with sheep, cattle, horses, goats and camels was formerly almost the only occupation, but now at least half the population, which has doubled this century, is engaged in urban pursuits—industry, administration, transport, education. The economy has been collectivized along the lines of the Soviet Union, but this was not completed until the late 1950s.

The Soviet government has a clear policy towards the 'nationalities'. Immediately after 1917 and during the civil war of 1918-21 the Bolsheviks sought support in every area of the old empire and national and ethnic minorities were encouraged to follow socialist policies consistent with 'democratic centralism'. Local languages were supported for use in general literacy and educational programmes. The Arabic script used for Turkish languages like Azerbaijani, Kazakh, Tadj and Tatar was replaced by Latin and some 50 or more small minority groups received a specially devised written language. Later on, Russian increasingly became the primary language of education and administration, and Cyrillic script replaced Latin in all but the Georgian and Armenian republics.

Today policy varies according to the status of the group. Some peoples, for example, the Yakuts, Buryats and Tadjik, are reckoned to be socialist 'nations', while others, like the Nentsi, Chukchee and Evenki are 'on their way'. These groups are given priority in the administrative structure, with schools conducted in the national language and radio programmes on ethnic themes. Smaller peoples like the Eskimos and Lapps will keep some national culture, but need the Russian language in order to absorb socialist culture. Lastly, some tiny groups are being assimilated: for example, the Nganasans, the Kets, the Yukaghirs and the Aleuts.

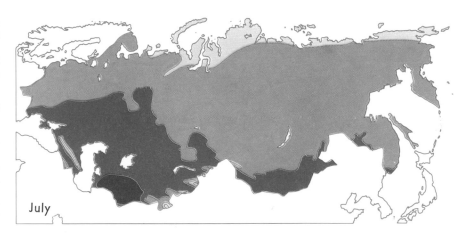

July

TEMPERATURE

Actual surface temperature in centigrade

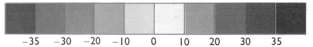

−35 −30 −20 −10 0 10 20 30 35

January

The Soviet Union faces certain problems in dealing with its nationalities which are peculiar to itself. For example, because the rural population may not move to the cities without special permission, the world-wide phenomenon of shanty towns is avoided; but conversely, there are the problems of underemployment in collective farms, and of the production of too many well-trained people by the education system. Another factor is the unwillingness of native peoples to go into industry or mechanized jobs where employment does exist. They prefer, if they leave the land at all, to become teachers, doctors, writers, administrators.

Although the Soviet government has always been highly distrustful of nationalist and separatist movements, and has punished them severely, there is no evidence that belonging to one of the nationalities is a disadvantage in the 1970s. In areas such as Tadzhikstan and Uzbekistan, where there is a national government, it is a positive advantage since national cadres are encouraged to run the administration. Nevertheless, the fact that Russians are in the majority nearly everywhere, and that the administration is directed by the Communist Party by means of a hierarchy based in Moscow, means in effect that a national policy which diverges from the central line has no chance at all.

Soviet Union
Karelians, Baltic Peoples, Russians, Ukrainians, Cossacks

Russian Expansion

- ■ Borders in 1505
- ■ Borders in 1725
- ▓ Present Soviet borders

Karelians
pop: 150,000

The Karelians extend from eastern Finland to the glacial lake-ridden plains north of Lake Ladoga to the White Sea. They are related to their neighbours the Finns and the Estonians and, like them, have suffered regular incursions, war and annexation. While the western half of Karelia is now in Finland, the eastern half has been formed into the Karelian autonomous republic.

The mediaeval source of Karelian wealth was the ·fur trade, but supplies were exhausted centuries ago and the economy now hinges on game and fish and trading. During the past century the vast timber resources of the area have been exploited, and this has led to the suppression of the semi-nomadic slash-and-burn farming techniques of the more northerly Karelians.

In the north, long trips often lasting many months, to trade buttons, needles, cotton and clothes with the Finns, were not uncommon. Many of the Finnish epics such as the *Kalevala* were the product of such travels. Elaborate rituals for marriage and death (often accompanied by poetry or singing) and strong animistic beliefs underlying the outward Orthodox faith were especially characteristic of Karelian society.

Baltic Peoples
pop: 5,200,000

The SSRS of Lithuania, Latvia and Estonia were independent countries before coming under Soviet rule in 1946. Together with that part of the Russian SFSR around Kaliningrad, they are the home of Poles, Finns, Belorussians, Russians, Jews and Ukrainians, as well as the indigenous peoples.

Estonia is inhabited by an Ugro-Finnish people who came originally from east of the Urals. They are closely related linguistically to the Finns and Hungarians. The indigenous peoples of Latvia and Lithuania are of Balto-Slavonic descent and their languages belong to the Indo-Germanic group.

Throughout the region, an ancient farming and fishing peasantry has been subjected to a two-fold process of sudden change. Firstly they have been extensively industrialized over a very short period; secondly they have undergone full collectivization. Now large-scale mechanized farms, some owned collectively and some by the state, dominate the agricultural sector. About 10 per cent of the people make their living from the sea, directly as sailors and fishermen or indirectly as cannery workers or in the docks.

Russians
pop: 130,000,000

The Russians are a Slavic people who originated in the Carpathian mountains, from where they began their expansion eastwards in the 5th century AD, eventually spreading from eastern Europe to the Pacific Ocean, north to the Arctic tundra and south into the central Asian steppe.

The Russian SFSR is by far the largest of the 15 republics in the Soviet Union and contains more than half the population. Russians are also the largest minority in most other republics: more than 12,000,000 Russians live elsewhere.

Before the revolution, most Russians were peasants, tilling their landlord's estates without mechanized implements. Rural areas suffered from acute overpopulation, and most peasants lacked sufficient land to provide for their families. Today the standard of living is still lower in the country than in the towns, but starvation and undernourishment are no longer major problems.

There are now two types of farm — the collective farm *(kolkhoz)* and the state farm *(sovkhoz)*. The collective farm is a community of farmers, often formed from a number of villages. Legally the land belongs to the state and is leased to the collective; there are no fixed wages, so a peasant's income will depend on his type of work and the productivity of the farm. The state farms are fewer, but much larger, the

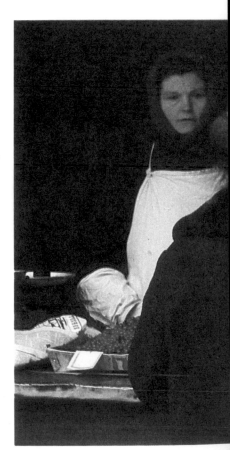

peasants are state employees and have fixed wages.

The position of women has changed drastically. Since Mongol times women had occupied a purely servile position; now women work in offices, schools, hospitals and even heavy industry. As nearly every woman goes out to work, the state takes care of the children in crèches, nurseries and schools.

Although villagers may not move to the cities without special permission, the RSFSR has still experienced considerable urbanization. Moscow, with a population of 7,000,000, is the centre of a massive industrial complex and the hub of the Soviet Union's distribution system.

Ukrainians
pop: 41,000,000
North of the Black Sea lies the agriculturally rich steppe land of the Ukraine, which since the revolution has also become an important industrial area. The Ukrainian SSR is second only to the Russian SFSR in population. However, as a direct result of Soviet policy, many Ukrainians live as far afield as the Far Eastern regions of the USSR, which they have colonized since the revolution.

With its rich *chernozem* soils, the Ukraine became known as the 'breadbasket of Europe', and remains to this day the richest grain producing area of the Soviet Union. It has long been collectivized, grain production lending itself to this structure. The Soviet created a system of *kolkhoz* (collective farms), some of which were later amalgamated into much larger *sovkhoz* (state farms).

Despite centuries of foreign rule the Ukrainian people have successfully resisted assimilation. Today Ukrainian continues to be the spoken language of the vast majority of the population, but there are a number of distinct ethnic groupings. These include the Lemky, the Boiky, the Volhynians and the Hutoule.

Cossacks
pop: not available
Cossacks are the people of the steppes, the vast rolling plains of the south-west, which now provide much of the Soviet Union's grain crops. In the past they were hard-living, horse-riding, plundering peoples who, though of Russian stock and not a separate ethnic group, were nevertheless distinctive for their habits and lifestyle.

There are two divisions of Cossacks in the steppes: the Siberian and the Ural Cossacks. The Siberian Cossacks came into the country together with other Russian settlers from south-east European Russia. They were organized as irregular light cavalry, whose duty it was to maintain order and to guard the frontier.

The ranks of the Cossacks were swelled by dissidents, deserters and escaped serfs, as well as adventurers from local tribes, who formed the nucleus of the Ural Cossacks. The common aim was to create a free and independent lifestyle far from any government.

The various Cossack groups were named according to the areas from which they came. Together they formed Russia's military élite, and were often used to suppress uprisings of other groups. However during the revolution and the subsequent civil war their loyalties were divided. Under Soviet rule they no longer have separate administrative areas.

Redcurrants on sale at a Leningrad market

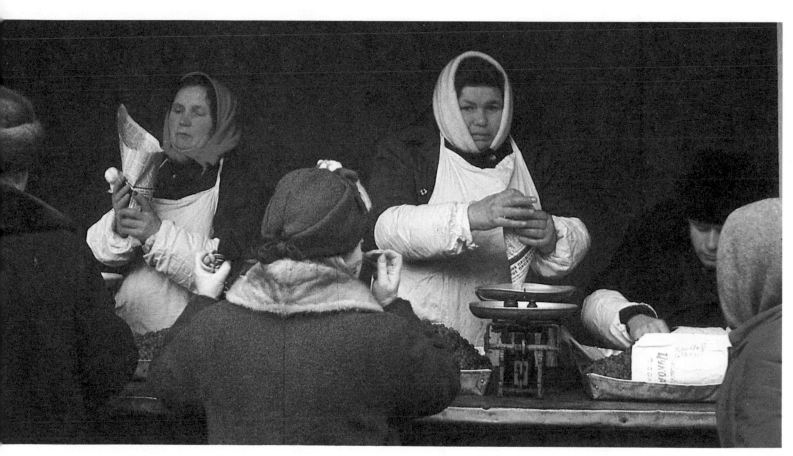

Map labels:

ARCTIC OCEAN
90° 100° 110° 120°
Sev. Zemlya
70°
60°
50°
40°
30°
70°
Kara Sea
BYRRANGA MTS
Nordvik
Novaya Zemlya
Dikson
Khatanga
LAPPLAND
Murmansk
Yamal Peninsula
Ust-Port
PUTORANA PLATEAU
Kotuy
Noril'sk
Olenek
Beloye More (White Sea)
Arctic Circle
Salekhard
Gulf of Ob
CENTRAL
Arkhangel'sk
KOMI
NENTSI
SIBERIAN
Sev. Dvina
Ob
WEST
Lower Tunguska
Yenisey
Kotlas
Syktyvkar
SIBERIAN
PLATEAU
KET
Stony Tunguska
Kirov
PLATEAU
MARI
Kama
Perm
Nizhniy Tagil
Ob
Angara
Kazan
Sverdlovsk
KHANTI-MANSI
BASHKIR
URAL
Irtysh
Tomsk
Krasnoyarsk
Kuybyshev
Ufa
Chelyabinsk
Petropavlovsk
Novosibirsk
EASTERN SAYAN
Omsk

Through the use of irrigation and the vast Kuybyshev reservoir, agriculture flourishes and the area is specially renowned for grain and melons. The original tribal economy of mixed farming and herding continues on a small scale, as do the traditional crafts of leatherwork, weaving, metalwork and ceramics.

Komi
pop: 500,000

The Komi, who are related to the Mari, have a distinguished tradition of oral epics and other folk literature. They live in and around the Komi autonomous republic in the extreme north of European Russia, and speak their own Uralic language. The winters are cold and the summers cool, so that agriculture is scarcely feasible except for rye and potatoes in the south.

Instead the vegetation of barren tundra, bogs and dense taiga over a vast area allows an economy of hunting, fishing, lumbering and reindeer herding. Transport was traditionally by boat along the many rivers but following the improvement of railway links since 1940 the exploitation of natural deposits of coal, gas and other minerals has developed along with the lumber industry.

Mari
pop: 500,000

The Mari, or Cheremis, have their own autonomous republic (capital Yoshkar Ola) by the river Volga, in an area which is thought to have been the original home of the Finno-Ugric tribes. They are closely related to the Komi, but while the latter migrated northwards and lived in isolation, the Mari survived both contact with the Bulgars and the fierce struggles between Tatars and Russians.

The climate of the region is cold in winter, since influxes of arctic air can lower still further the already severe continental temperature. The summer, however, is fairly warm and the flood-plain meadows along the Volga and Vyatka rivers allow good husbandry and agriculture, the main crops including oats, rye, barley, potatoes, flax and vegetables. Since the revolution the rural Mari have been organized into collective farms

Tatars
pop: 5,000,000

The Tatars, or Tartars, are probably the most dispersed of all the native peoples of the Soviet Union. Though there is now an autonomous Tatar republic with its capital at Kazan on the river Volga, more than half the Tatars live elsewhere, some as far afield as Romania, Turkey and even China. They are descendants of the Golden Horde, the 13th century Mongol army which so terrorized mediaeval Europe that they were believed to be named after Tartarus in hell.

The Golden Horde had broken up by the 15th century into several groups, of which the most important were the Tatars of Kazan. Since they were in the direct line of the eastern expansion of the Russian state of Moscow, the Tatar *khans* (rulers) of Kazan found themselves at war with Moscow for a century before Ivan the Terrible captured Kazan in 1552. However, from that period until the revolution in 1917 the Russians resorted to a cycle of excessive repression alternating with appeasement

as dangerous revolts broke out.

Since the Tatars had become Sunni Muslims in the 14th century, this repression by Christian Moscow often took a religious form. During the late 19th century revolutionary feelings found expression in the emergence of religious leaders. By this stage the Tatar people had developed a high rate of literacy and a well-developed national culture which was to form the nucleus of their new republic in 1920. After the Second World War, all the Crimean Tatars were exiled from their homeland for alleged collaboration with the Germans, and many have still not been allowed to return.

In spite of harsh winters and hot dry summers, the Tatar SSR is well endowed with natural resources. The huge Volga river, passing through rolling plains between the Volga hills and the Ural mountains, carries heavy cargo and passenger traffic from the Caspian Sea through a canal right into Moscow, and the area's development since 1943 as the centre of the Soviet Union's oil industry has led to the rapid expansion of industrial cities.

Territory of Golden Horde, 14th century

(kolkhoz), while the industries related to timber processing and machine building have become very important.

Bashkir
pop: 1,000,000

The Bashkir live mainly in the Bashkir SSR, a land of dense coniferous forests in the eastern foothills of the Urals, coming down to open steppe interspersed with deciduous woods towards the river Volga in the west. The climate is continental with extremes of temperature. The capital, Ufa, was founded by the Russians soon after the area passed into their hands at the fall of the Tatar capital in 1552 and it was from there that they began to colonize the area and dispossess the people.

Like other Turkic tribes the Bashkir were originally pastoral nomads, but by the 19th century colonial pressure forced them to settle and take up agriculture to such an extent that it has become more important than herding. Even before the revolution the Bashkir were living in fixed houses made of earth, logs and sun-baked bricks. The names of the patrilineal clans have been preserved, but their function has long since died out and social life is organized round the collectives. Bee keeping is one distinctive popular tradition which has continued.

Nentsi
pop: 29,000

The Nentsi (previously known as Samoyeds) live scattered throughout the forest and tundra of north-west Siberia. Their economy is based on reindeer herding, which provides them with transport, draught animals, meat and skins. Coastal Nentsi also hunt seals and whales; those further inland fish for sturgeon and salmon, and hunt deer, geese, foxes, and ermine.

The Nentsi are composed of scattered nomadic patrilineal clans, whose pastures and traditional hunting grounds were owned by the clans. After the revolution the clan areas were collectivized and the Nentsi partly settled; each group of families is directed where to herd the reindeer in its charge. Many traditional artefacts have been modernized, such as the

Nentsi wigwams which are now covered with tarpaulin rather than fur and birch bark, although most have not been replaced by wooden houses.

Khanti-Mansi
pop: 29,000

The Khanti (21,000) and Mansi (8,000) are two closely related Finno-Ugric peoples occupying a swampy plain of tundra and taiga (coniferous forest) on the river Ob. They moved north from their original homeland on the steppes due to pressure from the Tatars and Russians, and changed from horse-breeding steppe nomads to nomadic hunters, fishermen and reindeer herders.

The traditional semi-nomadic life cycle alternated between hunting in winter and returning to small settlements by the rivers to fish in summer. After the revolution hunting and fishing were collectivized, and settlement size has greatly increased. Some Khanti and Mansi groups are becoming Russianized and others are merging with the Ket, but a core of Khanti people still

retain their own distinctive view of the world. Shamanistic practices co-exist with nominal Christianity.

Ket
pop: 1,200

The Ket language is unique in Siberia, differing sharply from the surrounding Turkic, Samoyedic and Tungusic languages. It is thought that the Kets originally came from far south of their present home. They live in close association with the long-established Russian population; they border on the Evenki in the east and the Selkups in the west.

The Kets first came under Russian protection in 1607. Their basic occupation was hunting, chiefly for squirrel, but also for Siberian ferret, ermine, fox, sable, wild reindeer, elk and polar fox. Bear hunting had a strictly religious significance.

Today almost the entire Ket population of Turukhansk and Yartsevo are united in collective farms, with guns and steel traps replacing bows and arrows for hunting.

The kindergarten of a
Khanti-Mansi collective

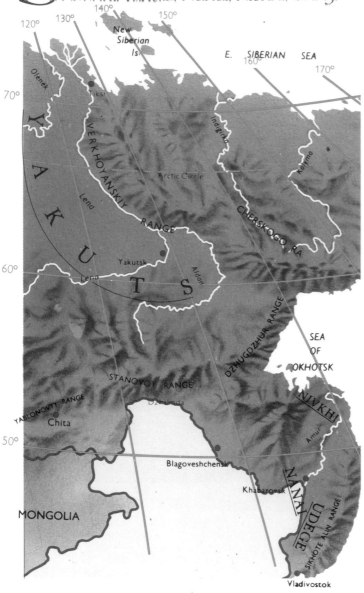

Distribution of Evenki

Evenki
pop: 25,000

The Evenki, or Tungus, inhabit a vast area from the Sea of Okhotsk across the central Siberian plateau almost to the river Ob, also penetrating into Manchuria and China. Their territory is criss-crossed with trails, cleared and marked by generations of hunters.

The Evenki who inhabit the taiga, marshes and tundra of northern Siberia live by hunting squirrel, sable, fox, weasel, stoat, lynx, elk, wild reindeer, wapiti (red deer) and wild goats, supplemented by herding reindeer. Other groups in the grasslands and wooded valleys of southern Siberia rear horses and cattle, and practise some agriculture. Across the entire area, except near the Pacific Ocean, the climate is continental.

During the winter, fur-bearing animals were hunted with guns, traps and dogs. In early spring the Evenki moved to new places to hunt wapiti and elk, which they chased on short, wide, wooden skis, covered with fur for a better grip. The men sometimes used a long birchwood tube which gave a cry like the challenge of a male in the rutting season to attract wapiti or elk. In the autumn the Evenki hunted squirrel, which some groups considered the main hunt of the year because of the price the pelts fetched.

The Evenki had several kinds of dwelling: bark-covered tipis for the summer, birch bark dwellings for use during travel, solid log houses for winter, and tipis covered with tanned skins for travel or for winter use. Although they lived in the forest, the Evenki had contact with other peoples of Siberia for hundreds of years. They paid a tribute of valuable furs either to the Chinese or the Russians from the 17th century.

In the early 19th century, Russian hunters arrived from the west and depleted the game in many regions. At the same time the new settlers cut down the nut-bearing cedar groves for building materials and fire wood. The Evenki population, at least in eastern Siberia, fell dramatically during this period.

In 1930, an Evenki national region within the Russian SFSR was set up to collectivize the economy. At first simple productive unions were established in which Evenki put their reindeer while they were away hunting. At this stage the deer remained in private hands and were only looked after collectively. By 1939 collectivization was fully developed, with the establishment of large permanent settlements of wooden houses from which the hunting groups of 3-4 men set forth, taking birch bark tipis for temporary use. In the south, however, the emphasis has been on agriculture and vegetable growing and herding.

Yakuts
pop: 296,000

The Yakuts are the largest group of native peoples in the Soviet Far East and have their own autonomous republic, whose capital is Yakutsk, in the north-east corner of the Soviet Union. The climate is extreme, with hot summers even in the far north and winter temperatures among the coldest on earth (—43°C in the capital).

The Russian conquest of Yakut lands was spearheaded by the Cossacks, who in 1632 built a fortified post at Yakutsk and imposed the fur tax or *yasak* on the native people. In the 19th century political deportees introduced education and Christianity, while under socialism the Yakuts' traditional role as hunters, trappers and traders has been modified by collectivization. Efforts to settle Yakut reindeer herders caused great friction and bloodshed until Moscow recognized the necessity for a semi-nomadic life in this region—reindeer are the main source of meat.

Yakut costume is no longer elaborately embroidered, but fur and skin are still the best protection in such an extreme climate. The traditional wooden houses, with their carved eaves and window frames, are being replaced in the towns by multi-storied apartment blocks, but flat-roofed log huts, insulated with mud on the outside, are still found in the country. Yakutiya's rich mineral resources have brought an influx of thousands of Russian managerial staff, and by 1970 they outnumbered the native population.

Nanai
pop: 10,000

The Nanai, who live on the far eastern border of the Soviet Union and China in the Amur river basin, are of Paleo-Asiatic stock. They are basically hunters and fishermen rather than reindeer herders. In their national area they are vastly outnumbered by more than 1,000,000 Russians who have settled in their area since 1888.

Nanai clothing and footwear used to be fashioned from cured fish-skin (which looks rather like fine canvas) and furs. In summer they lived in tents or bark-covered huts; in winter in log-frame huts sunk half into the ground. Collectivization has replaced these with larger log houses and has introduced a written language, grain and vegetable farming, bee keeping, animal husbandry and secondary industry (at Komsomol'sk-na-Amure). About 60 per cent of all Nanai are still engaged in collective farming, specializing in fishing.

Nivkhi
pop: 4,400

The Nivkhi, or Gilyak, of the lower Amur basin and the northern part of Sakhalin Island are one of the most ancient peoples of the Soviet Far East. They are considered to be the direct descendants of the original neolithic population of the area. Their language has the peculiarity of using different sets of numerals according to whether one is counting long objects like sticks, small round objects, large round objects, flat objects, paired objects, animals or men.

They are traditionally a fishing and sea-hunting people who, like the Nanai, wore clothes made of tough fish-skin as well as animal skin and birch bark. Clans were patrilineal and took their wives not from the same clan to whom they gave their women, as among the neighbouring Evenki and Manchu, but to a third clan, and common membership of a clan was thus declared by saying 'We have a common father-in-law and a common son-in-law'.

The dead of the clan were celebrated in the Bear Festival which lasted several days and involved the ritual killing of a bear. Skulls of all bears killed, whether in ritual or in hunting, were kept in a clan storehouse.

During the 19th century the Nivkhi were exploited by Russian, Japanese and American traders and adventurers, and succumbed readily to disease and cultural degradation. The break-up of the old Nivkhi social organization was accelerated and, by the time their territory had been used for several years as a battleground during the civil war which followed the revolution, considerable reconstruction was needed.

Traditional economic activities were collectivized, and cattle breeding and agriculture (previously considered sinful) were introduced. Extensive drives were made to persuade the people to accept improved medical facilities and their health greatly improved. Collectivization met with strong resistance, especially the policy of resettlement in collective farm villages, and some Nivkhi still live along the Rybnovsk coast in small isolated fishing camps accessible on land only by sleigh. About two-thirds of the Nivkhi are still rural, but

many of them now live in Russian-style log cabins instead of mud huts. Most inland Nivkhi now wear Russian clothes, but those on Sakhalin Island still prefer reindeer- and fish-skin clothing.

Udege
pop: 1,600

One of the smallest groups of native peoples inhabiting the Soviet Far East, the Udege speak a Manchu-Tungusic language. They became subjects of Imperial Russia in 1860, having been previously under Chinese domination. Trading contact with China continued, however, and contributed to the reduction in the native population. Owing to the high level of bridewealth *(kalym)*, many bachelor Udege were unable to marry, especially as Chinese traders often paid 400-500 silver roubles for a Udege woman, or acquired one in payment of debt.

Fishing took second place to hunting in the Udege economy. The southern Ussuri Udege (Tazy) practised some agriculture, and wild ginseng was sold to Chinese traders. Since the revolution all Udege have been collectivized and have developed agriculture as well as hunting and fishing.

Winter in Yakutsk

Yukaghir

pop: 600

The Yukaghir have been readily assimilated by the Yakuts and Evenki, and their numbers have declined constantly over the last three centuries. However, a Yukaghir legend tells that they were once as numerous as the stars in the black polar night, and the northern lights were regarded by the Yakuts as the reflection of Yukaghir camp fires.

The early Yukaghir were hunters and fishermen, who learned reindeer breeding from neighbouring Evenki tribes. Traps, cross-bows and later guns were used for hunting wild reindeer, elk, sable, foxes, ermine, squirrels and birds. The principal diet was reindeer meat and fish, which they caught with bone hooks and horse-hair nets bought from the Yakuts, supplemented by berries. The Russians introduced tea, bread, flour, sugar and tobacco. Transport was almost entirely by dogsled, reindeer, raft or canoe.

The Yukaghir winter dwelling was a yurt of the Yakut type with a flat log roof covered with bark and earth. Conical reindeer-skin tents were used in the summer. Since 1929, when the first Yukaghir soviet was formed, they have moved towards settlement in Russian log houses, a little cultivation and collective fishing, fur hunting and reindeer breeding.

Eskimos

pop: not available

Eskimos, or Yugyt, formerly occupied the Arctic coast of the Soviet Union in considerable numbers, but in the course of time they were either assimilated or driven out by the Chukchee. The latest Soviet census figures include them with the Chukchee. Far greater numbers live along the Arctic coast of America from Alaska to Labrador and in Greenland (a total of 64,000), a vast population compared to their Soviet relatives.

Before contact, the Eskimos lived by hunting walrus, whales and seal with harpoons fitted with bone and stone tips. Much of their equipment was made from these animals, including sleds, shoes, thimbles and needles of walrus tusk, and clothing made from seal skin. There were also simple pottery and wooden implements, but no iron artifacts.

In the latter half of the 19th century whale hunting declined because of over-killing by American whalers, which frequently resulted in famine among the Eskimos. When a whale was killed, however, it supplied an entire village with meat and blubber for a year.

Chukchee

pop: 14,000

The Chukchee are a Paleo-Asiatic people, closely related to the Asiatic Eskimo, who live in the most remote north-eastern corner of the Soviet Union on the tundra by the Bering and East Siberian Seas. They are divided into inland reindeer herders and coastal seal hunters. The coastal Chukchee traded the leather, tusks and other products of seals and walrus with their neighbours the Russians, Yakuts and Koryaks, as well as with the reindeer-herding half of their own community.

Although they lived by the sea the Chukchee caught very few fish. Since the revolution, however, fishing has become more efficient with the introduction of motor boats, radios and modern harpoons. Coastal Chukchee now live in villages built of wood with centralized social amenities.

The inland Chukchee once managed very large reindeer herds using extraordinarily archaic techniques. For example, any reindeer breaking free of the herd was chased by a Chukchee rather than herding dogs, and deer had to be caught by lasso whenever it was necessary to harness them.

Herding was nomadic with separate summer (coastal) and winter (inland) pastures. Tipi houses were made of deer hide and wooden poles which were easily transported by sledge. The most extended social group was a union of 15-20 herding camps, each of which comprised three or four households. Travelling together, such herding camps consisted of families related to each other through the men. Few Chukchee had more than one permanent wife, but nearly all men made temporary marriages in which they could share the wives of a group of cousins or close relatives.

Divorce was easy and frequent.

Because of their isolation the revolution affected the Chukchee only in the 1930s with the collectivization of reindeer herding. Each collective farm now includes both herdsmen and sea hunters and the old trade between them is now a natural process of redistribution within the collective.

Koryak
pop: 7,500

The Koryak language is closely related to that of the Chukchee, who are their nearest neighbours. The two have become so mingled in some places that they are not always easy to distinguish. There are more similarities between the reindeer-breeding groups of the two peoples than between the reindeer-breeding and coastal groups of the same people.

The Koryak live in the Koryak national okrug of the Kamchatka peninsula. The land and vegetation vary from rock and taiga to swamp and tundra, but are always harsh and can support only a sparse population. The name Koryak means 'reindeer people' in their own language and reindeer herding is their main economic activity. Some men formerly owned as many as 10,000 reindeer which were looked after by poor Koryak who had few or none. As among the Chukchee, herding was done without dogs, by running with a leather lasso. Sledges were often pulled not by dogs but by reindeer.

Among the Koryak on the coast, reindeer herding was combined with sea hunting. The huntsmen drove on to the ice in large parties with dog-sledges and returned the next day with their kill. In early summer, when there was open water between ice floes, they also hunted in skin boats. They caught fish with barriers made of woven sticks and are even said to have hunted whales with nets made of leather, using large rocks as sinkers.

The necessities of daily life were mostly taken from animals. As well as food, whales provided blubber for oil lamps, and the skins of many animals were used for clothing. Hunting was confined to men, but women supplemented the diet by collecting edible grasses and berries, as well as roots.

The civil war following the revolution raged for some time around Koryak territory and did a great deal of damage. Soviet rule was established only in 1923, after which the slow process of collectivization began. The opposition of the Koryak was based both on traditionalist grounds and on practical decisions dictated by the reindeer economy. Use of pasture has been rationalized and is now allotted to collectives, which send out brigades of herdsmen to follow the reindeer while remaining based in permanent villages. Reindeer-skin tents or semi-dugout huts set in the earth and supported by a framework of logs have been replaced by modern villages with a greater range of civic amenities.

Eskimos drag in a harpooned seal

of livelihood is agriculture and sheep herding, although many now work in the busy ports along the Black Sea coast.

Although originally Christian, the Abkhaz accepted Islam in the last decades of the 17th century and came under Russian dominance in 1863. Polygyny, an old custom among the Abkhaz, is dying out due to the enforcement of Soviet marriage conventions, and collectivization has modified their traditional farming practices.

Osset
pop: 488,000

The Osset are of special interest as descendants of the ancient Scythian tribes, who preserve many features of the old Persian language (mixed with later Caucasian influence) as well as of pre-Islamic Persian religion. Their autonomous national area, with its capital at Tskhinvali, is located in the central Caucasus, within the Georgian SSR, where they live mainly by farming and sheep herding.

Osset traditions give their place of origin in the region of the Don. Most are Orthodox Christian with a minority of Sunni Muslims, a religious pattern that occurs frequently in the Caucasus.

Both Christians and Muslims however, have largely preserved their earlier beliefs. Present-day folklore confirms much of the account of Scythian religion given by the Greek traveller Herodotus in the 5th century BC. At funerals an epic speech is recited describing the dead man's journey on horseback to the world of the warrior-heroes called Narts. His soul is interrogated at a bridge over a river, and only if he has led a righteous life can he cross without the bridge breaking under him.

Chechen
pop: 600,000

The Chechen are a Caucasian people, who live mostly in the Chechen-Ingush ASSR (capital, Grozny) in a land which plummets from the bare icy summit of Mount Tebulos, at 14,741 feet, through alpine meadows, then forest, down to the broad valleys of the Terek and Sunzha rivers, the rolling Noghay steppes and the Caspian shore.

Throughout the 18th and 19th centuries the Chechen resisted the expanding Russians and earned a reputation for being hospitable but proud and quick to seek revenge. Their emphasis on honour resembles that of some Mediterranean cultures, and vendetta was widespread—the aggrieved man would wrap himself in a white woollen shroud and, carrying a coin to pay a priest for the funeral, would set out in search of his victim. Murder was avenged with death unless the guilty man grew his hair long and the wronged man agreed to shave him.

In common with other Caucasian peoples including the neighbouring Persian-speaking Osset, from whom the stories are believed to have spread, the Chechen have epic poems about heroes called Narts. The interweaving of languages and traditions in the Caucasus is very complex and the stories have been adapted in each locality. The Chechen tell of the exploits of the hero Orhustoj on their territory, and point to a well made magically by the hoof of Soska-Solsa's horse, from which no-one will drink.

Daghestanis
pop: 1,365,000

The Daghestanis are the peoples and tribes of the mountains of Daghestan in the north-eastern Caucasus. Linguistically the term Daghestani is reserved for languages belonging to the eastern group of the Caucasian family, but in fact the area includes groups who speak Turkic languages. Among the speakers of Caucasian languages, strictly speaking only the Kurins are true Lesghians, but this term is used for the entire group of proto-Caucasians living in Daghestan. Most of the inhabitants of the area are Muslim.

The more important groups recorded in the 1970 Soviet census include the Avars, who at 396,000 are the strongest and most numerous Daghestani tribe, and live in central Daghestan, from its northernmost part to the main ridge. The Avars played an important part in the pre-Russian history of Daghestan and consequently their language, which has several dialects, became the

Cherkess
pop: 420,000

According to legend, the Cherkess were at one time a powerful pastoral people, occupying an extensive area north of the Caucasus. They were then forced into the mountains and came to overrun the Kabardians. In 1777 the Russians drove the remaining Cherkess further south, and finally conquered them completely. A large number of Cherkess, Abkhaz and all the Ubykhs migrated to Asia Minor, Syria and the Balkans.

The Cherkess are divided into the western Cherkess, occupying the north-west Caucasian range, and the Kabardians, or eastern Cherkess, who live in the north-central Caucasians. The western Cherkess follow Orthodox Christianity; the Kabardians are Sunni Muslims. All Cherkess were Christian before the Islamic conversions in the 18th century.

Cherkess tribes are named after their particular economic speciality. Horse breeding (the Abadzekhs), forestry (the Beselenians), bee keeping (the Medovei) and trading (the Natukhadz) were the main Cherkess occupations before collectivization, when agriculture became more important.

Abkhaz
pop: 83,000

The Abkhaz inhabit the northern Caucasian mountain range, and are famous for the number of healthy centenarians in their population. Their main source common means of intercourse over a considerable part of north-west and west Daghestan.

The Kumyks live in the north-eastern part of Daghestan on the lower course of the Terek river; they number about 189,000. The Muslim Kumyk are now more settled than their Azerbaijan and other Turkic neighbours, but still breed cattle. They also fish and have become cultivators since the revolution. Socially they used to be divided into two classes: the peasants or 'black bone' and the nobility or 'white bone', a system often found among Turkic and Mongol nomads.

Georgians
pop: 3,250,000

Georgia is an area of fertile valleys where the rugged Caucasus mountains meet the Black Sea. The Georgians were converted to Christianity in 349 AD and have survived as a distinct group despite repeated invasions by Mongols, Turks and Persians since their golden age in the 12th century. An alliance with Russia resulted in 1921 in the absorption of Georgia into the Soviet Union. Sheep herding and farming are the main occupations; cash crops include tea, grapes and citrus fruits; the most important traditional craft was silversmithing.

The Georgians were formed originally of a number of tribes, with several linguistic and cultural differences. Today the boundaries of administrative areas tend to coincide with those of the former regions. Distinctive groups in the west include the Mengrelians, Ajars, Gurians, Imeretians, Lechkhumians, Rachuelians and Syanians. In the eastern mountains live the Khevsurs and Khaketians, in central Georgia the Kartlians and in the south the Meshkians, perhaps one of the first people to enter the area.

Despite this extraordinary diversity, all Georgians believe they have a common origin. Customary hospitality towards guests and, in the past, the tradition of swearing brotherhood with friends from distant areas, contributed to social cohesion. Today, with increased urbanization—one-third of all Georgians now live in the capital, Tbilisi—the regional differences are dwindling and the Georgian language is becoming more uniform.

Armenians
pop: 3,560,000

Once an independent country with a recorded history of over 2,000 years, Armenia is now a socialist republic of the Soviet Union. It lies between the Black and Caspian Seas along the borders of both Iran and Turkey. Many Armenians, however, now live in other parts of the Soviet Union, having (like the Ukrainians) been offered the opportunity to help colonize Siberia, thus diluting their presence in their own SSR whose capital is Yerevan. Of Indo-Germanic origin, the Armenians were dominated by the Ottoman Empire for many years. Their culture accordingly has been influenced by Turkey, though retaining its own language, alphabet, art form and literature.

Armenians maintain their religious identity (they once formed an island of Orthodox Christianity in a sea of Islam) and a spirit of free enterprise in a system which is both atheist and socialist. Such eccentricity is tolerated in Moscow because the Armenians strongly support the régime, and have contributed many men to the ranks of the 'old guard' political leaders.

Although the region is geographically inhospitable, the rich Ararat plain on which Yerevan is situated produces a wide range of agriculture produce. Collective farms with their modern settlements have replaced many of the villages—clusters of stone or mud-brick houses with flat roofs—but in the more mountainous regions, small vineyards and orchards cling to the slopes. Here the traditional way of life persists, including festivals for Palm Sunday, Ascension Day, the pre-Christian festival *dryndez* in early summer, and the 'water holiday' of August.

The introduction of hydroelectric projects, mining and light industry is largely restricted to urban centres.

Kalmuk
pop: 137,000

The Kalmuk are a Mongol people who live in the Kalmuk ASSR, far to the west of other Mongol groups on the lower reaches of the Volga, north-west of the Caspian Sea. Their name is derived from Turkish and signifies that many of them refused at first to change their Mongolian Buddhism and shamanism for the Islamic religion of their neighbours. Their language is mutually intelligible with Buryat.

Throughout history the Kalmuk have been outsiders: in order to avoid wars between Mongol khans they were forced to move far westwards. They entered their present home in the early 17th century, soon after the Russian destruction of the Tatar and other khanates which had previously controlled the area, but before the Russians had turned their attention to colonizing it.

The Kalmuk led a typical nomadic life, herding cattle, horses and sheep and living in yurts made of felt stretched over a lattice framework. However, they found their new home rather poorer than the fully grassed steppes further east, since much of it is semi-desert. The constant search for new pasture was urgent in this land of light soil and low rainfall.

The herds owned by princes often followed a different route from those of commoners and had exclusive rights to the more favourable pastures along river banks and the melting snowline. Princes and commoners were held to correspond respectively to white and black 'bones', or patrilineages. There was also a third class, of Buddhist lamas, though a great deal of pre-Buddhist shamanism survived in Kalmuk rituals. In the modern Soviet Union only the black bone survives.

The present Kalmuk ASSR (capital, Elista) hardly touches on the Volga river and is still oriented largely towards the rolling steppe-desert. Industry is of minor importance and the economy is based on livestock with some agriculture and fishing. After the Second World War the Kalmuk were accused of collaboration with the Germans and deported to central Asia; their republic was abolished. They returned in the late 1950s when the republic was restored. Since then the population has started to recover from its decline during the years of exile.

Turkmen

pop: 1,525,000

The Turkmen SSR stretches from the Caspian Sea to the borders of Afghanistan. Turkmen are also found in north-east Iran and in neighbouring parts of Afghanistan. Until quite recently all Turkmen lived in dome-shaped tents and made seasonal migrations on the borders of the Kara Kum (Black Sand) desert. The Turkmen in Russia maintained political independence despite occasional nominal acceptance of settled suzerains. Such independence meant freedom from taxation, conscription and manipulative government officials.

Turkmen social organization was based on a hierarchy of named patrilineal descent groups. All individuals who traced their descent from a particular ancestor lived in a region owned corporately by that descent group. Under military threat they would unite with several other similar groups linked by more distant ancestry. In this way, though usually living in scattered nomadic camps, the Turkmen could form large enough fighting units to meet most of the military expeditions a sedentary ruler might send against them. Otherwise they would retreat quickly into the inhospitable regions closer to the centre of Kara Kum, beyond the range of their attackers.

As the nomadic life lost its political advantage most Turkmen became sedentary, but some still live part of the year in tents, making short migrations to find grazing for their flocks of sheep and goats. Only a very few in the Soviet Union are still fully nomadic but in other countries the traditional way of life continues largely unchanged. In the Soviet Union stock breeding, though still a major occupation, is generally no longer nomadic, and the Turkmen have taken to agriculture raising especially wheat, barley and cotton.

In more arid regions, however, Turkmen are generally very conservative and have continued their traditional practice of livestock production and marginal agriculture dependent on the irregular rainfall. All Turkmen continue to make their famous rugs, which are an important element in the economy.

Turkmen society is based on patrilineages. Three generations may live together, sons taking wives to live with them in their father's house until they are 30-40 years old at which point they move away to form their own extended family. Daughters are married off young in exchange for a bridewealth which may be 10 camels or 100 sheep, or the cash equivalent, and women generally occupy a very subservient position.

The Turkmen are strict Muslims of the Sunni sect and even within the Soviet Union observe both daily prayers and Ramadan (the month of dawn to dusk fasting) very rigorously, despite official Soviet policy which seeks to reduce the importance of religion.

Karakalpak

pop: 236,000

The Karakalpak (meaning 'Black Cap') live almost entirely in the Karakalpak ASSR, which is administratively part of the Uzbek SSR. Their language is so close to Kazakh that it has often been considered a dialect and one mythical tradition

Distribution of Turkmen

makes these peoples the descendants of two brothers, an important way of expressing closeness in the absence of a common political structure or territory.

Like the Kazakh they were traditionally pastoral nomads who have taken to agriculture. Their territory extends from the vast shifting sands of the Kyzylkum desert to the marshes of the lower Syr Dar'ya, which are criss-crossed by numerous canals and water courses. It is here that rice is grown. Other agricultural crops include cotton, and there is a certain amount of light industry as well as fishing and oil refining on the Aral Sea. Other specialities include the breeding of musk-rats and silkworms. In the desert pastoralism continues, but it has been collectivized and made sedentary.

The old Turkic clan organization survived among the Karakalpak well into the 20th century. Clans were exogamous but not territorial since a clan comprised several nomadic villages or patrilineages. The relative powers of clans and patrilineages were balanced so that herds belonged to the

individual patrilineages or villages, though they were branded with signs belonging to the whole clan. The clan came into its own mainly in time of war, when the component villages would unite under the name of an illustrious patrilineal ancestor, which was used as a battle-cry.

Uzbek
pop: 9,200,000

The Uzbek SSR is located in the steppe catchment area of the Amu Dar'ya and Syr Dar'ya rivers. The capital, Tashkent, is the fourth largest city in the Soviet Union. The region is arid, with a dry continental climate and an inland drainage system. The Uzbek are Mongoloid in appearance but a mixed genetic type has been produced by generations of intermarriage with the Tadjik, who are of partly Mediterranean-Caucasoid stock.

Before the revolution the Uzbek were principally steppe nomads of the Hanafi Sunni Muslim sect. With the Tsarist expansion from the north and the British presence in India, many moved to independent

Afghanistan. A similar exodus occurred between 1924, by which time the last Uzbek freedom fighters *(basmachi)* had been suppressed, and the Second World War. In 1930 collectivization was underway and an extensive mechanized type of farming began with the concurrent development of necessary irrigation systems. Secondary industry was established in the Uzbek SSR during the Second World War, when many factories were transplanted from the more vulnerable Ukraine, bringing them closer to iron ore deposits at Magnitogorsk.

The nomadic Uzbek have been driven into the arid zones, where herding is now collectivized. Others are settled on the grain-producing *sovkhoz* state farms, where the Tadjik dominate agricultural organization. In the towns, Uzbek craftsmen work as silver and goldsmiths, leatherworkers, woodcarvers and rug-makers—the famous carpet-producing centre of Bukhara is located within the Uzbek SSR. Twice-weekly bazaars are a feature of both town and village life.

In clothing and diet, the rural Uzbek resemble their Tadjik neighbours. The men wear a turban cap, or *kola*, a long cotton skirt, baggy trousers and boots. Women wear a red and white head shawl *(chadar)* and high yoked dresses with long, full skirts. Diet reflects the Mongol influence, with unsugared green tea, noodle soup *(ash)*, ravioli *(ashak)* and meat dumplings *(mantu)*.

The general mixing of Uzbek and Tadjik has affected kin relationships in both groups. The basic terms of marriage will normally be those of the dominant group, usually the Tadjik in the east and south, and Uzbek in the west and north. Where the dominant group is Uzbek, Uzbek males will marry Tadjik females; *vice versa* where the Tadjik predominate. Most marriages take place within related lineages.

In addition to the usual square and rectangular domed houses made of mud bricks, the Uzbek build a distinctive type of house with individual rooms leading off from a long, covered porch, situated inside a walled compound. Nomadic Uzbek continue to use the yurt.

photograph:
A Turkmen encampment

Distribution of Uzbek

with an older tribal shamanism. The pre-Islamic mythical links between the tribes are often traced genealogically through the Biblical Japhet to either Noah or Adam.

Tadjik
pop: 7,155,000

The Tadjik are a mountain people living on the borders of the Soviet Union, Afghanistan and China, in the parallel valleys between the peaks and ridges of the Pamirs. An even larger number than in the Soviet Union live in Afghanistan, where at 5,000,000 they constitute one-third of the population, while an isolated 15,000 live on the western edge of the Chinese province of Sinkiang.

The Tadjik are a mixture of Mediterranean-Caucasoid with some Mongoloid stock, and adhere to the Sunni sect of the Muslim religion, though there are some Shi'ites in the more remote valleys. Their economy is based both on herding sheep, goats, cattle, camels and horses on natural upland pasturage, and on the cropping of wheat, barley and some mountainside irrigated crops. Cash crops include cotton and fruits.

The Tadjik language, which has several dialects, is closely related to Persian and the people are of special interest as an outpost, on the edge of a traditionally nomadic and pastoral area of Asia, of the old sedentary agricultural and gardening culture developed under irrigation thousands of years ago in Iran. With this economy, fairly large, dense population could be supported, provided there was peace and a political system which allowed widespread co-operation, since the land was arid and water scarce. It was from the Tadjik that the thinly scattered nomadic Turkic tribes such as the Turkmen, Kazakh, Kirghiz and Uzbek learned to grow crops as a secondary occupation in addition to herding.

Many of the Tadjik towns were important centres of trade on the routes between India, Persia and China, and the capital of the new Tadjik ASSR is the old town of Dushanbe, meaning Monday, and named after the day on which the bazaar was held. Many Tadjik

Kazakh
pop: 5,300,000

The Kazakh are found mainly in the Kazakh SSR, though about 500,000 live in the Sinkiang province of China and others in Afghanistan. They are still one of the most numerous of Turkic peoples but have declined in numbers since sedentarization during the course of this century. According to one etymology their name means 'freebooter' or 'having no masters'. Historically they have always been closely linked with the Karakalpak and the Kirghiz, with whom they share a common myth of origin, expressed in genealogical terms by saying that their founders were brothers.

The way of life was typically nomadic, with seasonal migrations to seek pasture for horses, cattle, sheep, goats and camels. Diet was based on milk and mutton, with horseflesh and fermented mare's milk *(kumiss)* as luxuries. As is common among nomadic Turkic tribes, dwellings were usually yurts made of felt stretched over collapsible wooden frames. However, the nomadic way of life was gradually curtailed by Russian encroachment, and especially during the 19th century the Kazakh began to take up agriculture around the borders of their territory.

This process has been intensified since the revolution; pastoralism though still a main occupation has been made sedentary, and the traditional mixed herds are maintained from permanent villages. At the time of the revolution some Kazakh fled to Sinkiang and Afghanistan, where the nomadic life persists. In the Soviet Union, with the opening up of virgin land for agriculture and the intensive development of industry, a large influx of Russian settlers with a high birth rate has made the Kazakh a minority in their own republic, where they constitute only one-third of the population.

With its capital at Alma-Ata, and stretching 1,200 miles from east to west, this vast area produces one-third of the total grain output of the Soviet Union through highly mechanized farming. In parts the rivers, which seep into the earth, are continuously depositing sand to make the huge Karakum and Kyzylkum deserts to which Kazakh nomadism was so well adapted. The most important river, the Syr Dar'ya, now has several dams for irrigation and flood control. Industries include especially the working of lead and copper in the east of the republic, and huge deposits of oil on the shores of the Caspian Sea.

The religion of the Kazakh is Islam, but this still co-exists

Distribution of Tadjik

have migrated to the towns, where the exploitation of the republic's mineral and hydroelectric wealth has created jobs in the chemical, building, mining and textile industries. However, these industries often loose their Tadjik workers during harvest times.

Kirghiz
pop: 1,455,000

The Kirghiz, like the Tadjik, live across the Soviet border with Afghanistan and China. They are of Turkic descent, modified by contact with their Mongol neighbours, and occupy the high plateau between the Hindu Kush, Pamir and Tyan Shan mountain chains.

The Kirghiz population extends throughout the Tadjik, Uzbek and Kirghiz SSRs. Like the Tadjik they live in yurts, felt covered frame tents, which provide moveable accommodation for whole families during the annual cycle of transhumant pastoralism. Besides sheep and goats, yaks, horses and bactrian camels are kept for milk and transport.

The Kirghiz have been settled on collective farms, the *sovkhov* and *kolkhoz*, but have continued their pastoral existence, trading at market towns such as Yarkand or Kashgar for agricultural supplies.

Seasonal activities are very marked as the Kirghiz summer is short, with only about 60 days when the ground is free from snow. As a result, this is the time when most social activities take place. During winter the family units, called *uy*, living in their individual yurts are separated from each other, trying to utilize the sparse exposed grassland in the shelter of the mountains. For these bitter months survival becomes a matter for the family unit alone. In summer the scattered *uy* group together to form larger settlements known as *aul*. During the summer months grass is manured, watered and then gathered for storage; felt is made for the yurts, and the pack animals are prepared for the long treks to collect grain and other household necessities.

Altai
pop: 56,000

The Altai are the Turkic-speaking population of the Altay mountains. They include the Altai Kizhi, the Telengits, the Telesy, the Teleuts (the southern Altai), the Kumandins, the Tubalars and the Chelkans (the northern Altai). They live in the area now designated as the Gorno-Altay autonomous oblast, being recognized by the Soviet government as an autonomous ethnic group.

The political and economic domination of the Altai by the Mongols reached a peak under Genghis Khan, whose descendants ruled them until the end of the 14th century. The Altai then remained subject to incursion by various Mongol groups until they were made Russian subjects at their own request in 1756. Before the revolution, the northern Altai retained their worship of the goddess of children, Umay or Mayene, but the southern Altai were converted to Islam.

Originally the Altai were nomadic or semi-nomadic pastoralists, herding mainly cattle. Barley was made into bread, their staple diet; hay-making supplemented natural pasturage. The Russians introduced both the scythe and the iron plough to the Altai, the latter replacing the *abyl* and *andazyn*, their hoe and wooden plough.

Inside a Kirghiz yurt

Distribution of Kirghiz

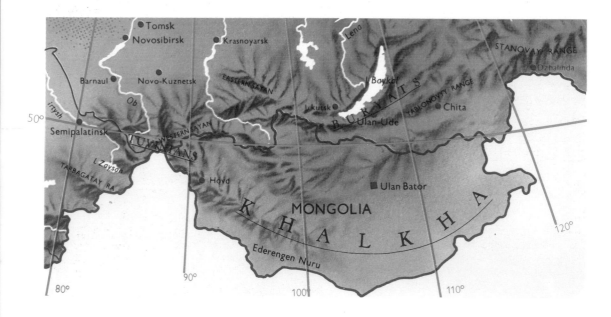

Tuvinians
pop: 140,000

Almost all Tuvinians now live in the Tuvin ASSR, which is part of the RSFSR. Their lands range from the moist Sayan mountains to the arid sandy wastes of northern Mongolia. Hunting and reindeer breeding were the main activities in the north-east, while modest agriculture was practised in the central and western regions. In the drier south the Tuvinians herded cattle, horses, camels and even yaks, moving seasonally in search of pasture.

Before the revolution, the basis of the Tuvinian economy was nomadic pastoralism practised under feudal lords who owned the pastures. Religion was lamaist Buddhist for the feudal lords and shamanistic among the peasants which, together with the feudal system, made socialist collective ownership difficult until the ruling classes were forcibly disenfranchised in 1931.

The remains of ancient irrigation systems indicate a previously agricultural economy, reintroduced by the Soviets together with pastoral collectives, which have state-guaranteed prices.

Buryats
pop: 315,000

The Buryats, a Mongoloid people, live in the vicinity of Lake Baikal on the frontier of the Soviet Union and Mongolia. Their economy is based on the sheep and the horse.

In the past, Buryat society was founded on the clan or lineage. A man's home, his political position, inheritance and status were determined to a large extent by his clan membership. People could not marry within their own lineage and marriages consequently formed the basis for alliances elsewhere. Weddings were often celebrated with elaborate feasting and ceremony and the bride would usually leave her own family to live with her husband and his lineage.

Converted to Tibetan lamaist Buddhism, the Buryats were the most northerly people to recognize the religious authority of the Dalai Lama. By the 19th century temples and monasteries were widespread, and the population supported a large number of monks. The Buddhist influence, however, has steadily declined since the revolution which has discouraged religion of all forms. Three Buryat national areas have been established, all located within the RSFSR.

Many of the old customs are now dying out and collectivization has altered much of the pastoral organization. Herds consist of cattle, horses, sheep, goats and, in the east, camels. Under the present system, the chairman and committee of the Buryat collective, which may have as many as 3,000 members and covers up to 40 square miles, allocate grazing areas for the various collectively owned herds, which are moved out of any areas in danger of over-grazing. Winter quarters for the animals include byres for the more delicate animals and fenced meadows for the horses and sheep.

Because of the need to move the herds between summer and winter pastures, Buryat families have several houses. The traditional felt tent yurt, still used by their neighbours the Mongols, has now gone out of use. A Buryat winter house is a solid wooden construction made of closely fitted logs, with moss in the outer chinks. Summer houses are scattered over distant pastures and each family may visit four or five of them during the season as they move with their herds.

Mongols
pop: 3,000,000

The present distribution of the Mongols of central Asia is the result of treaties between China and Russia finalized in the 18th century. These established guarded borders between Inner and Outer Mongolia and Outer Mongolia and Siberia. The Buryats and Kalmuks are full citizens of the Soviet Union; the Chakhar, Khorchin, Dagur and Torgut are subjects of the People's Republic of China; and the Khalkha and a few other inhabitants of what used to be called Outer Mongolia are now living in the Mongolian People's Republic.

Despite their incorporation into centralized states nearly all groups of Mongols retained until recently a way of life largely determined by the steppe environment. While Mongols on the borders of Tibet and the Buryats west of Lake Baikal took up some agriculture, the main Mongol groups were nomadic pastoralists, living in round felt-covered yurts and moving with their herds of horses, sheep, cattle and goats according to the seasons. Although thousands of miles apart the fact that the Mongols were nomadic meant that the different groups were always in contact.

The centre of Mongol culture today is the Mongolian People's Republic. In the early part of this century the country was the focus of various pan-Mongol movements, but the possibility of altering the borders agreed by the Mongols' huge neighbours, China and Russia, was

Mongol Expansion

■ c.1300
■ Origins

out of the question. In 1921, a revolution took place in what was then called Outer Mongolia, and since that time a transformation of society has slowly taken place, including the elimination of the aristocracy, of large private herds and of the power of the lamaist Buddhist monks. There has also been industrialization and the introduction of collective farms and western-type education.

Khalkha
pop: 900,000

The Khalkha are the central core of all the Mongolian peoples living in central Asia. They regard themselves as the carriers of Mongol culture—their language is the true Mongolian; other groups are held to speak variants or dialects. Today, the Kalkha form the majority in the only independent Mongolian state—the Mongolian People's Republic.

The Khalkha have been literate since the 12th century, possessing a code of laws, systems of messenger communication, knowledge of the major world religions and a literature which includes works of theology, philosophy and medicine. Yet their economy has been based almost exclusively on nomadic pastoralism: the extensive herding of sheep, horses, cattle, camels and goats. Other Mongolian peoples have combined this way of life with agriculture, but traditionally the Khalkha supplemented their economy only by hunting.

With the spread of Buddhism and the establishment of Manchu administration all over north Asia in the 17th century, patrilineal clans lost their political significance and people migrated within the territory of a *xošun*, a unit in the Manchu system. One lineage of princes, the Borjigin (the clan of Genghis Khan), provided the hereditary rulers of the *xošuns*, and were responsible for inviting eminent lamas from Tibet, founding monasteries, and administering the laws and messenger services. Yet they remained nomadic, living in yurts and following their herds.

Khalkha society contained two main subservient classes: those who owed services and dues to church and state, and the personal serfs of the princes, who were known as *xamjlaga*. Before the revolution in 1921 the extremes of wealth and poverty had been intensifying: the officials and high lamas had huge herds, while the poor were forced to serve most of their lives, herding for others or performing forced labour.

Since 1921 almost all the monasteries have been abolished and differences between rich and poor have been eradicated. The political influence of the Borjigin clan has disappeared. Today, political decisions are taken by the Mongolian People's Revolutionary Party and carried out by a central government.

Herding is now carried on by collectives, known as *negdel*. All *negdels* have central settlements, but the herdsmen live in scattered camps of 2-10 tents in the distant pastures of the *negdel* territory. Within the collectives people are allowed to keep small private herds, and the traditional crafts of felt-making, rope-making and leatherwork continue.

Herding sheep, Mongolia

India/South Central Asia

188

VEGETATION

	Ice Permanent ice field
	Tundra Moss and lichen
	Conifer Forest Pine, spruce, larch
	Broadleaf Forest Deciduous
	Temperate Arable, broadleaf, grass
	Mediterranean Citrus, olive, agave
	Subtropical Dry and wet evergreen
	Tropical 'Selva'
	Steppe Short grass
	Savanna Grass and scrub
	Semi Desert Cactus, sparse shrub and grass
	Desert No vegetation
	Marsh and Swamp
	Salt Salt lake, marsh
■	**Capital Cities**
•	**Major Towns**
•	**Towns** Small town village
───	**Country Borders**
───	**Borders** Provinces, states

South central Asia is a region of extreme contrasts, reflected in the topography, climate and the variety of indigenous cultures. The north is dominated by the three mountain ranges of the Karakoram, the Hindu Kush and the Himalayas, which between them contain 92 of the world's 94 highest peaks, including Mount Everest at 29,028 feet. Called the Great Snowy Range by the pre-colonial British, the mountains comprise the countries of Nepal and Bhutan, as well as parts of Afghanistan, Pakistan and India. To the south lies the vast lowland belt of the Thar and Indo-Gangetic plains, reaching from Pakistan in the west to Bangladesh in the east and dissected by the Indus and Ganges rivers. Still greater contrasts are found on the main Indian peninsula, between the Deccan plateau in the centre and the forested hills of the coastal belts. The large island of Sri Lanka completes the region.

As might be expected where the topography is so varied, the climate has no overall consistency. In some areas of Afghanistan annual rainfall is below 6 inches, but as much as 400 inches has been recorded in the Bay of Bengal, while in Sri Lanka and regions of the Indian west coast up to 200 inches is common. There are similar contrasts in temperature, with July temperatures below freezing in parts of the Himalayas, while on the Coromandel coast of south-east India and in the Thar and Indo-Gangetic plains they are above 30°C.

The dominant climatic feature is the monsoon which blows from the south and south-west from June to October, bringing heavy rains. Although generally welcomed by the farmer as bringing water for his crops, the monsoon can have disastrous results, causing both erosion and uncontrollable flooding. Yet the suffering and destruction brought by flooding, cyclones and erosion are minimal compared to the appalling consequences when the rains fail. Drought followed by famine in this heavily populated part of the world can take innumerable lives: in the last 25 years of the 19th century more than 15,000,000 people died in three consecutive droughts.

The monsoon rains and high temperatures have encouraged forest cover over huge tracts of India, Bangladesh and Sri Lanka. This varies from extreme tropical rain forests and mangrove swamp forest in Bangladesh to what is generally known as open jungle over much of the centre of the region. In Afghanistan and parts of Pakistan, where rainfall and temperatures are more moderate, a steppe vegetation of brush and grassland predominates. Only the Thar desert, in the Rajasthan state of north-west India, and parts of the mountain ranges are without natural vegetation of any kind.

South central Asia is the home of more than 750,000,000 people, with a great variety of religions, languages and cultural traits. Because of the natural mountain and water barriers, the heritage of these people was possibly less chaotic than that of their neighbours in the Middle East, western Asia, Russia or China. The earliest known settlement is believed to have been of forest-dwelling Australoid peoples, from whom some of the southern tribal peoples may be descended. Between the 2nd and 3rd millennia BC, the Dravidian civilization (related to the Sumerian of Mesopotamia) arose and was in turn replaced by an invasion of Aryan pastoralists, who entered India from the north-west and brought a lasting cultural influence that is still evident in the language of north India.

The Aryan civilization dominated the early history of the area until first the Persians conquered what is today Afghanistan, Pakistan and north and central India, and later Alexander the Great entered the Ganges valley. The greatest empire to be established in India and the surrounding countries was that of the Muslim Moguls. The successors and descendants of the Mongols and Tatars, they built an empire stretching from Afghanistan to Bangladesh at the start of the 16th century.

With their mixture of Arab, Turkish, Persian and Afghan cultures, the Moguls converted much of the population to Islam. South India, however, successfully resisted the invaders, and uprisings by the Marathas, a militant Hindu people from the Deccan plateau, hastened the empire's decline. With the Afghans also in revolt against the Moguls, the British pushed up from Bengal to become the dominant power in north India. For a century they ruled theoretically with Mogul consent until the old empire was abolished in 1857.

The British presence in the Indian sub-continent came as a result of economic rivalries between the British East India Company and the French, Portuguese and Dutch. Total economic dominance in the region was finally established by force of arms under the leadership of Clive in 1757, but India was officially a part of the British Empire for less than 100 years, from 1858 to 1947. The extraordinary wealth accruing to England from India during this colonial period led to fears of Russian expansion south and accounts for the British presence in Afghanistan during the 19th and early 20th centuries, which ended only after humiliating military defeats.

Nationalism in India developed under the leadership of Mahatma Gandhi between the two

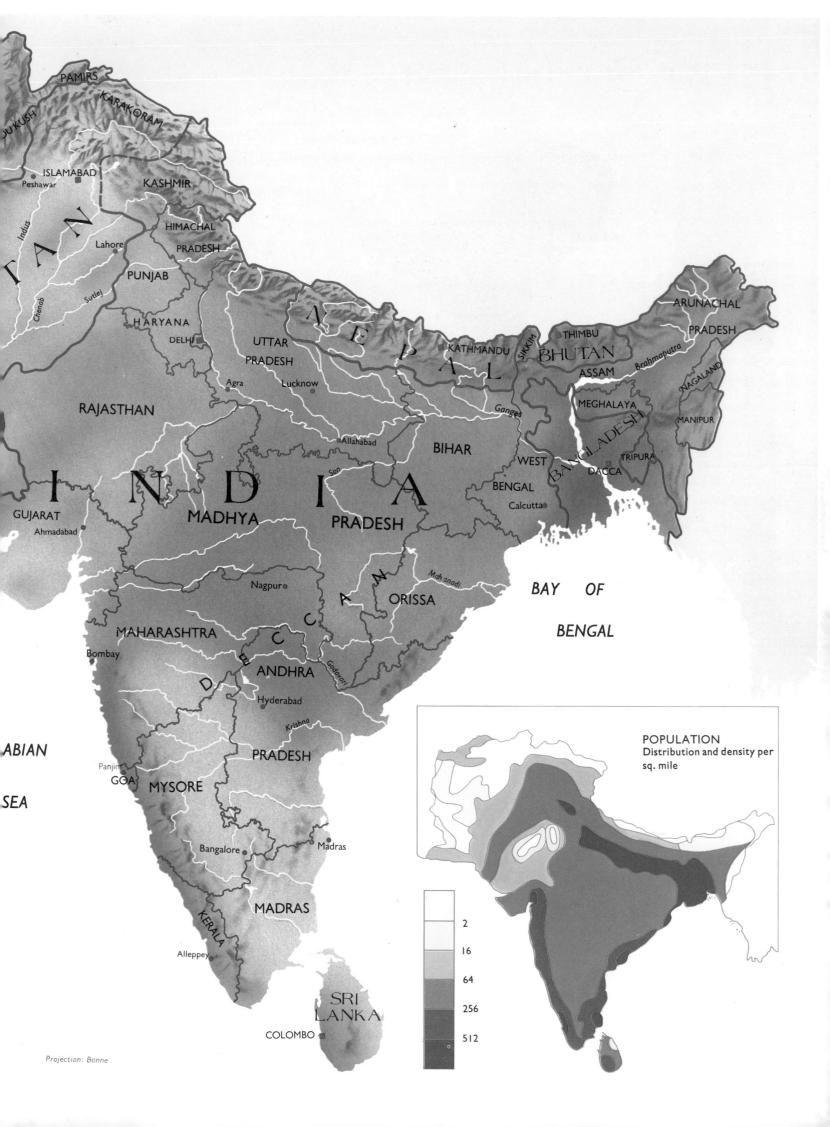

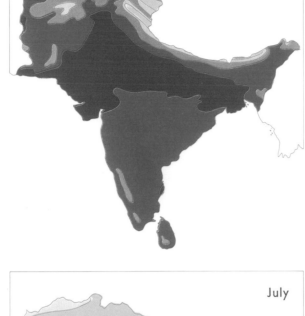

January

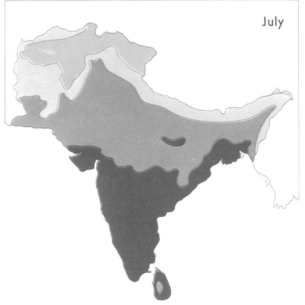

July

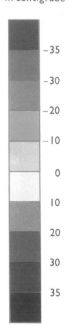

TEMPERATURE
Actual surface temperature in centigrade

- −35
- −30
- −20
- −10
- 0
- 10
- 20
- 30
- 35

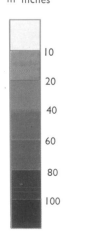

RAINFALL
Average annual rainfall in inches

- 10
- 20
- 40
- 60
- 80
- 100

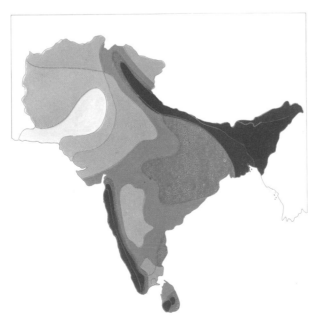

world wars; but the conflict of interest between his largely Hindu following and the Muslims under Muhammad Ali Jinnah flared into violence in 1946 and 1947 when the goal of independence was nearing realization. A mass reshuffle of the population, at an estimated cost of more than a million lives, accompanied independence and the formation of the two nation states of India and Pakistan in August 1947. Yet partition, which also divided Pakistan into East and West, did not exactly coincide with religious differences—more than 60,000,000 Muslims found themselves nationals of India, while more than 10,000,000 Hindus were citizens of East Pakistan. The problems of administration by West over East Pakistan led to further bloodshed and war in 1971 when the East, with support from India, fought and won independence as the state of Bangladesh.

The different civilizations dominating the region before British colonial rule left a religious heritage that is today marked by three major faiths—Hinduism, Islam and Buddhism—and by many smaller religions. The founder of Buddhism, Siddhartha Gautama, came from Bengal on the borders of Nepal, but it is now only in the Himalayan states and Sri Lanka that his teachings still hold sway in south central Asia. Parsees, Sikhs, Ismailis, Jains, Christians and many indigenous tribal peoples practise the bulk of the other minority religions found in the region.

The language groupings are no less varied than the religions. The largest group of more than 350,000,000 people speak Indo-Aryan languages. The most important of these is Hindi, the national language of India; the others are Urdu, Assamese, Punjabi and Bengali. Dravidian languages have a much older heritage and are still spoken over much of south India and in Sri Lanka; in Afghanistan and Pakistan Indo-European languages are the most important. Even older than the Dravidian languages are the unwritten Munda group, still spoken by some 6,000,000 tribal people in northeast India. All these linguistic and religious divisions overlap and it is difficult to relate them neatly to economic activities or to other cultural attributes.

A vast majority of the population is engaged in rural occupations; the overall figure is around 80 per cent, although in Nepal, Afghanistan and other Indian border states it can be as high as 90 per cent. There the mountainous terrain has suited a combination of agriculture with pastoral nomadism that can support only a low density of population. For the mass of south central Asia, however, an average density of more that 350 people per square mile means overcrowded villages, small landholdings and extensive rural poverty, barely alleviated by the introduction of higher yield seeds, increased mechanization, better fertilizers and advanced irrigation techniques. An increased birth rate, lower infant mortality, better medical conditions and longer life expectancy have all combined to reduce the impact of the 'green revolution'.

The bulk of all agricultural produce is used for subsistence, and on average only one-third of foodstuffs is sold. Farmers grow mostly low-cash grains like millet to ensure the family's survival, and far fewer high-risk but high-cash products like cotton or groundnuts. Despite this cautious approach to cash crops, India, Pakistan and Bangladesh have the world's largest jute industry and the second largest cotton industry; a major proportion of the world's supply of tea comes from Sri Lanka and India; and production of coffee, coconut and rubber is increasing.

Adaptation to differing rural economies and contrasting climates in south central Asia has meant that there are dramatic variations in village structures and types of habitat throughout the region. The nomads of Afghanistan and Pakistan live in portable, goat-hair tents or felt-covered yurts, while the villagers of the Gangetic plain live in permanent mud-brick settlements. In the former a community might consist of an extended family of two or three brothers, their children and grandchildren; in the latter several thousand people may live together.

The rapid growth of cities in south central Asia was a feature heralded by industrialization and British colonial policy. Although there is considerable poverty in the major cities, average incomes there are twice the national averages. They have all attracted massive migration from the land and in recent years the pattern of overcrowding, expanding slums and visible poverty has been repeated in Afghanistan, Pakistan, India and Bangladesh. The migration problem has meant, for example, that in the three largest towns of India —Bombay, Calcutta and Delhi—only 6,000,000 of the 18,000,000 inhabitants are indigenous; the other 12,000,000 form temporary or migrant populations that are somehow being absorbed into the urban structure. This massive influx of largely unskilled labour is supported mainly by cottage industries and only a limited number are employed in iron and steel or other heavy industrial development.

Throughout south central Asia different systems of social stratification determine the economic activities and social relationships of the people. In Afghanistan, for example, status is acquired at birth through an individual's membership of an ethnic or tribal group. The Pashtun are politically and economically dominant, with the Durrani, one of the Pashtun tribes, at the peak of the pyramid. At the bottom of the social ladder are the Mongol Hazara tribes, despised for their ethnic origins and their adherence to the Shi'i branch of Islam in a country which is predominantly Sunni.

In India social stratification is even more marked, yet its basis is neither directly religious nor tribal. It is dominated by the caste system which, in the past and to a great extent still today, determines the behaviour of individuals and their relationships to each other. The numerous castes of India overlap several main ritual categories *(varna)* of which the most important are the Brahman (priest); Kshatriya (warrior); Vaishya (merchant); Shudra (servant) and Harijan (untouchable). Each individual is born into one caste and cannot then change, nor normally marry anyone outside that caste.

Although the caste system is identified with a predominantly Hindu philosophy, other religious groups are also incorporated. In Sri Lanka, for example, a largely Buddhist population has a similar hierarchic system of stratification. Modern governments have made efforts to break down many of the differentials created by castes in the towns, since the system keeps such a large proportion of the population in non-competitive positions. In rural areas, however, the breakdown is far

slower and, despite Gandhi's attempts to abolish the system of 'untouchability' during the 1920s and 1930s and the provisions of the 1955 Untouchability Offences Act, discrimination has yet to be stamped out.

Outside the caste system there have been problems of tribal assimilation and administration. In the days of the Raj, the general tendency was to leave the tribes to their own devices, a policy criticized after independence as encouraging 'human zoos'. Today, despite the presence of a commissioner for scheduled castes and tribes, the different local authorities tackle their administration in very different ways. The government is far more tolerant of cultural diversity in the eastern hills than in central and southern India, where integration and modernization are considered more desirable. The end result is that most smaller tribes are losing their identities, while some larger groups, although adapting to the technological age, still manage to preserve their own language and other aspects of their cultural heritage.

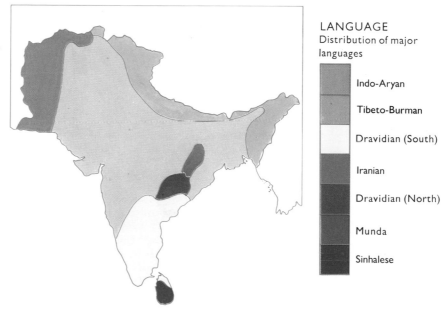

LANGUAGE
Distribution of major languages

- Indo-Aryan
- Tibeto-Burman
- Dravidian (South)
- Iranian
- Dravidian (North)
- Munda
- Sinhalese

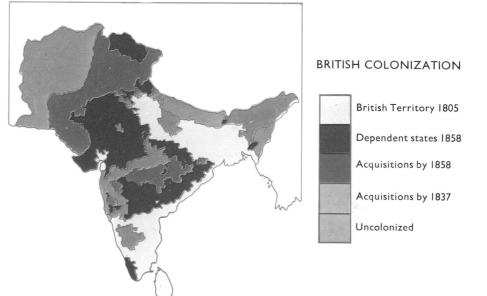

BRITISH COLONIZATION

- British Territory 1805
- Dependent states 1858
- Acquisitions by 1858
- Acquisitions by 1837
- Uncolonized

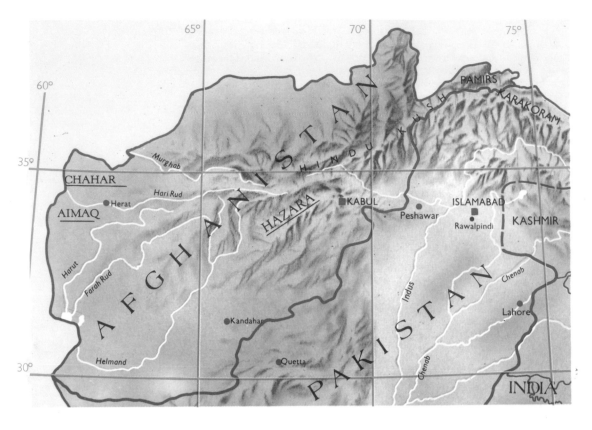

Afghanistan

pop: 19,811,000

The mountainous 'crossroads of Asia', Afghanistan is wedged between Iran, Pakistan, the Soviet Union and China. Most of the country is semi-desert and only 12 per cent of the land is cultivated. With scant mineral resources, most of the population are supported by a precarious animal husbandry.

There are many distinct groups including Pashtun, Tadjik, Hazara, Turkmen, Uzbek, Nuristani, Baluch and Kirghiz. The national language is Pashto, but about half the population speaks a Persian language, Dari. Until 1973 the country was one of the world's last monarchies but a republic was established that year in a bloodless coup.

Distribution of Pashtun

Pashtun

pop: 15,000,000

The Pashtun are perhaps the largest of all tribal societies. Since the 16th century they have occupied a vast territory which stretches from Iran, through Afghanistan and Pakistan, up to the Soviet Union. Their origins are uncertain, but in different areas they share the physical characteristics of their neighbours – Iranians in the west, Punjabis in the east, Turko-Mongols in the north and Baluch in the south. They have their own Pashto language.

The Pashtun have a wide range of lifestyles. The great majority are farmers who, except in the driest terrain, harvest two crops per year. They use traditional farming implements and extensive irrigation systems to produce wheat and barley in the spring, and maize, cotton, vegetables, melons and sometimes rice in the summer.

Vast stretches of the mountains and plains which cannot be cultivated are used by the 2-3,000,000 nomads. Some use camels to carry goods to special nomad bazaars in the mountains, or to take timber from the forests in the east of Afghanistan to the towns. There, many Pashtun work as tradesmen, craftsmen, businessmen and officials.

All true Pashtun are bound by the *Pakhtunwali*, an exacting code of honourable behaviour. It places great emphasis on the rule of vengeance, demanding retaliation for any wrong. It also requires hospitality to be given to all visitors and sanctuary to be granted to all who seek it. As a result of this code the Pashtun combine generosity with violence, particularly in disputes over women, money or land.

Such quarrels are traditionally settled by councils *(jirga)* in which all tribesmen have the right to participate. They are found at each level of the tribal system, which is based on the Pashtun belief in democracy and equality. There are over 50 tribes subdivided into sections and subsections down to the level of the local community. In the past, the equality of all Pashtun within each of these communities was ensured by the redistribution of land every few years – a practice known as *wesh*.

Today this system is breaking down outside the central areas of Pashtun territory. Chiefs *(khans)* have made successful efforts to increase their landed wealth and build small empires which are often formally recognized by the state. Usually, the only check on their power is the authority of religious leaders.

Chahar Aimaq

pop: 800,000

The Chahar Aimaq are a group of eight tribes who claim to have originated from as varied a past as Genghis Khan's Mongol army, Syrian Arabs

A Chahar Aimaq
camp, Afghanistan

and Persians. They form the predominant tribal grouping of the west Afghanistan provinces of Ghor and Herat, and many of them live today in the Iranian province of Khorasan. Dari and Farsi are the languages spoken.

The lands now inhabited by the tribes were allotted to them by the central powers of Persia and Afghanistan in the 19th and early 20th centuries. Some have settled in the fertile valleys of the Hari and Kashaf rivers, but many are still nomadic herdsmen. They graze their sheep and goats in the valleys and plains, sometimes entering permanent villages in the late summer.

The livestock provide milk, meat, and hair and wool for weaving tents and decorative carpets. The last are often an important source of income and increasingly form part of a woman's dowry. The Chahar Aimaq have always preferred to marry within their own tribe, but smaller tribes have sometimes been exogamous.

The basic social unit is the patrilineal nuclear family. Traditionally politics are centred on the *khan* or chief of each tribe, but in Iran the chief's power is now disappearing. Disputes are now settled by village courts and decisions made by councils.

Hazara
pop : 870,000

The homeland of the Hazara lies high in the western Hindu Kush mountains, in the part of east central Afghanistan known as Hazarajat. Access to their valleys is difficult in summer and impossible in winter. Since rainfall is meagre and erratic their survival depends upon the volume of water flowing down from the mountain rivers.

The history of the Hazara is uncertain; they are Mongoloid people who speak a dialect of Dari and it seems likely that they came to Afghanistan around 1300 AD. They live by a rather precarious agriculture, growing grain in the short summer and raising livestock. Pasture is sparse, so during the summer the sheep and goats are driven to temporary encampments where the grazing is lush and insect-free. Permanent villages consist of 30-100 single-family houses clustered around a water source. The houses are built of stone and mud, with stables to accommodate the animals during the winter. For six months of the year most villages are completely cut off and there is little to do but tend the livestock, surviving on stocks of food and fuel gathered and stored during the previous summer.

The Hazara do not form a politically united group; traditionally there were a number of tribal and regional divisions. Although these are no longer marked by hostilities, some differences remain. The number of Hazara is increasing and, despite the harshness of the environment, population density is high. Many Hazara have left their homeland and can be found in towns and villages elsewhere in Afghanistan, where they have low status: despised and denigrated by other Afghans, they are forced to take the most menial jobs, as porters, water carriers and refuse collectors.

This prejudice springs partly from religious differences: most Hazara are Muslims of the Shi'a sect, while the majority of Afghan Muslims are Sunni. Although the Shi'a sect is popular in Iran, in Afghanistan it is viewed as heretical. The Hazara are the largest and most notorious group of religious dissidents in the country, and with their Mongoloid features form an easily recognized target for discrimination.

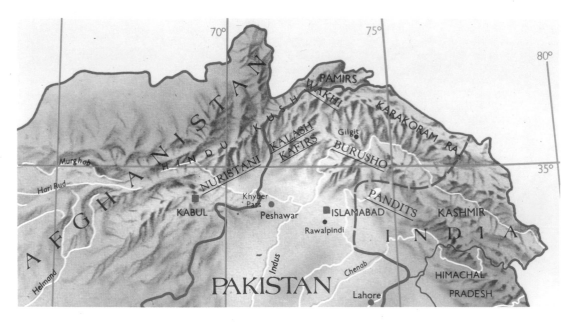

Nuristani
pop : 100,000

The home of the Nuristani is in north-east Afghanistan, on the southern slopes of the Hindu Kush mountains. They are related linguistically to the Kalash Kafirs across the border in Pakistan. Nuristani villages, which lie at a height of some 6,000 feet, are separated by deep narrow valleys and can usually be reached only on foot. Each is surrounded by trees, terraced fields and irrigation channels fed by the winter snows. The women are responsible for planting and harvesting the crops – mainly maize, millet, wheat and barley. The men are expected to care for the goat herds and make dairy produce, duties which entail spending at least 200 days away from home each year on the mountain pastures.

Each village is an economically and politically independent unit comprised of patrilineal clans. Only craftsmen stand outside the social system, which obliges a man to support his kinsmen in any dispute as well as providing support during economic difficulties. Every spring a number of young adult males are chosen by the elders of their own lineage to uphold village laws until the autumn. Their reward for these duties is the fines exacted from the lawbreakers. A second institution controlling village affairs is the all-male *du-vrai*. This has no fixed size or composition and is formed only when there is a major dispute in need of arbitration.

Before 1900 and their reluctant conversion to Islam by the Pashtun, men gained prestige as warriors or feast-givers. Today they rely on having several sons and owning a large number of goats to assert their status in a highly competitive society.

Kalash Kafirs
pop : 2,500

In three valleys in northern Pakistan at the eastern extremity of the Hindu Kush are 20 small permanent villages of Kalash Kafirs. They have survived waves of Buddhist, Hindu and Muslim influences and today maintain their own traditional religion although surrounded by Muslims. Their name Kafir is the Arabic word for unbelievers. Unlike their Nuristani neighbours in Afghanistan they have also resisted change imposed by central government. Isolation has helped them maintain their own language and a complex system of ritual and belief, but they are now being threatened by tourism and a new highway.

The Kalash Kafirs are farmers, with women doing the cultivation and men looking after the sheep, goats and cattle. Kalash villages are compact, with houses constructed from timber and stone, often with fine carvings on the wooden panels. Political structure is based on a system of patrilineal descent. Elders at the head of the lineages jointly direct a group of younger men *(roi)* who collect fines, direct public works and regulate the activities of the Muslim outsiders. Kalash religion is based on a belief in many gods with an overall creator called Dezau. Ritual life is dominated by spring and autumn festivals with animal sacrifices to the gods and spirits at shrines dotted throughout the valleys.

Wakhi
pop: not available

The Wakhi live in scattered communities in the mountains of three countries; they speak a dialect of Dari. Some have been integrated into the Tadjik population of the Soviet Union but many live along the Hunza valley of Pakistan and in the Wakhan corridor of north-east Afghanistan. Badakhshan

is believed to be their place of origin and it is here that in recent times they have become prey to the debilitating effects of opium. The Wakhi farm wheat and millet which they trade for livestock produce from their Kirghiz and Pashtun neighbours, but according to a recent UN report some 80 per cent of all Wakhi are opium-dependent and much of their energy is devoted to the cultivation or acquisition of that product.

Borusho
pop : 10,000

The Burusho live 8,000 feet up in the Karakoram mountains of north Pakistan. They have a precarious agricultural subsistence, utilizing terraces that stretch along the Hunza river valley. With water ingeniously tapped from high glaciers, they are able to grow sufficient millet, buckwheat and various fruits to enable them to survive the harsh winters, when they are totally isolated by snow and ice. Their myths tell that they originated from Alexander the Great's soldiers and, like many of their Nuristani and Wakhi neighbours, they have converted to Islam, most of them belonging to the Ismaili sect. They have remained independent partly through fighting prowess and partly through geographical isolation.

Pandits
pop : 100,000

The Pandits, sometimes known as Bhotta, regard themselves as the original inhabitants of the valley of Kashmir, and speak the Kashmiri language. Their spectacularly beautiful home is high in the Himalayas but its nearness to the borders of the Soviet Union, Pakistan and China has brought political turbulence for many decades. A literal translation of the word Pandit is 'scholar' and, in contrast to their more numerous Muslim neighbours, the Pandits are Hindu Brahmans and their society is divided into two groups, the priests and the workers.

With their high caste status, the Pandits have a tradition of landowning, administration, teaching and clerical work that has given them great influence not only in Kashmir but elsewhere in Indian administrations. The most famous Pandit was India's first prime minister, Jawaharlal Nehru.

The industriousness of the Pandits' Muslim neighbours in farming, fishing and trading activities has led to a decline in Pandit economic power in Kashmir and to a fall in the Pandit population over the past few decades.

Kalash Kafirs celebrate the spring, Pakistan

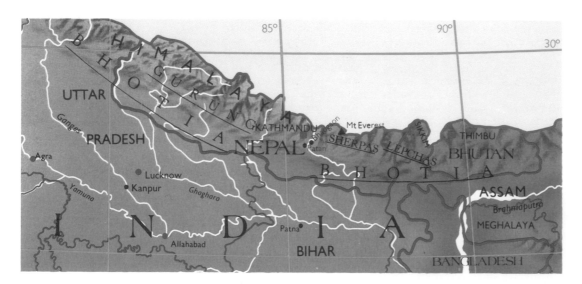

Bhotias
pop : 400,000

The Bhotias are Mongoloid mountain people whose homelands spread through the Himalayas from Himachal Pradesh to Bhutan and Arunachal Pradesh; they speak a number of Tibeto-Burman dialects and live by agriculture, animal husbandry and trade. For six months of the year, from April to October, they cultivate barley, buckwheat, potatoes and radishes. They also keep large herds of yaks, goats and sheep, which provide them with milk, meat, hair and wool, as well as carrying goods over the mountain passes.

Trade is a vital part of their economy. By acting as intermediaries between the arid Tibetan plateau and the fertile valleys in the foothills of the Himalayas, the Buddhist Bhotias have succeeded in acquiring far more wealth than the local high-caste Hindus. They spend the winter months in makeshift camps exchanging salt for grain.

Villages are the main sociopolitical units in Bhotia society. Within each village all householders are considered equal and civic tasks are taken in rotation. Because the men spend so much time making short expeditions for trade or taking the herds to high summer pastures, the women often assume responsibility for running the farms. This arrangement has promoted a high degree of sexual freedom and polyandry is widespread.

In recent years the prosperity of the Bhotias has been seriously affected by the closure of the Indo-Tibetan border and by improvements in communications between India and Nepal. The Bhotias no longer enjoy a monopoly of the trade in salt and the time is approaching when they may have to drift to the lower regions, which are already over-populated.

Nepal
pop: 13,006,000

The largest of the independent Himalayan states, Nepal extends for 500 miles along the central Himalayas. Bounded by Tibet in the north and India in the south, the country's population is composed of many different elements. In the lower foothill regions live some Hindu castes who have cultural and linguistic affinities with high-caste north Indians, and there are three main groups of Tibeto-Burman speakers. The Newars predominate in the Kathmandu region, combining Buddhist and Hindu elements in their culture; in the middle mountain ranges tribal groups such as the Gurungs, Magars, Tamangs, Rais and Limbus subsist by farming, and in the highest habitable regions live communities of Bhotias, growing and trading grain.

Gurungs
pop : 180,000

The main concentration and historic home of the Gurungs is in western Nepal, where they live as hill farmers in the middle ranges of the mountains. Most Gurungs depend for their subsistence on agriculture and the raising of livestock. They grow millet, maize and potatoes on the higher slopes and some rice and wheat on lower, irrigated fields. Villages are clusters of up to 100 thatched houses at altitudes of 3,500-5,000 feet; although they are permanent, there is some seasonal migration to favourable pastures.

Gurung society is divided into two sections of uneven rank, each in turn divided into hierarchical units. Although people of both major social strata are found in many villages, social intercourse between them is limited and intermarriage extremely rare. The religion, ideology and Tibeto-Burman language of the Gurungs are essentially unchanged from those of their tribal ancestors, despite their familiarity with Hindu culture.

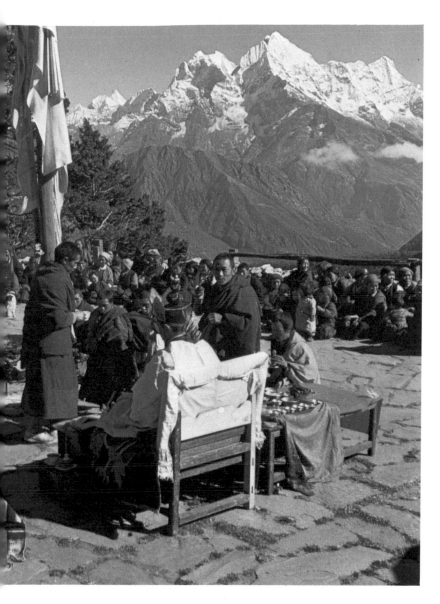

Sherpas

pop: 40,000

The Sherpas are the most famous of the Mongoloid people known as Bhotias who inhabit the Himalayas along the border between Nepal and Tibet. Speaking a Tibeto-Burman dialect, they live in Nepal, near the foot of Mount Everest. Here the inhabitants have adapted to the harsh climate and terrain by establishing a number of temporary settlements at a height of up to 16,000 feet. Permanent villages, where the Sherpas live for most of the year, are at a height of 12-13,000 feet, and surrounded by fields planted with barley, buckwheat, potatoes and radishes.

Within each village authority is delegated to elected officials who have clearly defined duties. These do not include the settlement of disputes, which are resolved through private mediation. The women are very independent. There is great sexual freedom among single people, and marriages are easily dissolved. Monogamy is the most usual form of marriage, but polygamy, particularly polyandry, is also common. Women who marry two brothers are performing a useful function by preventing the fragmentation of property.

Until the Chinese occupied Tibet in 1959, the Sherpas monopolized trade across the high Nangpa pass. They became prosperous by bartering rice, wheat and maize from their southern neighbours for Tibetan salt and wool. Now Sherpas rely largely on activities associated with tourism and mountaineering to maintain their standard of living.

photograph:
A fire ceremony held
by Sherpa monks, Nepal

Gurung men have a famous tradition of military service; many served as Gurkhas with the British army before Indian independence, and in many villages today up to 50 per cent of the eligible men are serving with either the Indian or the British army.

Newars

pop: 500,000

Although many of the Tibeto-Burman speaking peoples of the Himalayas are mountain dwellers, the Newars have always preferred to live in the deeper valleys and on flatter terrain. They are the most numerous of Nepalese city dwellers. The Newar civilization ruled in the heart of Nepal until the 18th century, when it was overthrown by invading Gurungs. No longer dominant in Nepalese politics, the Newars play an important role in the economy and administration of the country and are particularly influential in the three towns where they make up the majority of the population: namely Kathmandu, Patan and Bhadgaon.

Before they lost power to the Gurungs, the Newars had been Buddhist and had strong links with Tibet. Since then, Hinduism has also been adopted and today both religions are merged in Newar rituals and beliefs. The influence of Hinduism has not however affected Newar marriage traditions, which differ from those of other Nepalese peoples. Newar girls are symbolically married at the age of 7-9 and from then on form associations with men that can be easily terminated. Marriage with non-Newars is generally frowned upon.

Lepchas

pop: 30,000

The Lepchas were the original inhabitants of the Himalayan protectorate of Sikkim – a group of both shifting and irrigation cultivators whose influence in the area declined as waves of new immigrants entered the area after the 17th century. They now form 12 per cent of Sikkim's population, with smaller groups living in Nepal and West Bengal. Their language is part of the Tibeto-Burman group.

197

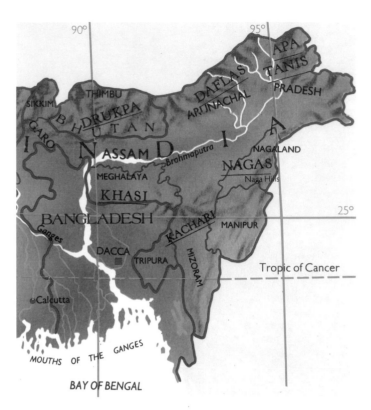

Bhutan
pop: 1,217,000

An Indian protectorate consisting largely of Himalayan mountains and valleys, Bhutan possesses only a few miles of flat land. Its inhabitants are mainly Drupkas, together with Nepalese immigrants who live in the south-western foothills. The Monpas, or Dakpas, live by shifting cultivation in the eastern forests, and a small group of Tibetan nomads practise yak rearing in the far north. Bhutan is characterized by its many monasteries, a legacy of Tibetan Buddhism.

Drukpa
pop: 400,000

The Drukpa are the largest distinct group in Bhutan. They are similar in culture, religion and language to their Tibetan neighbours and live by mixed farming in the central valleys. Their small hamlets among the rice fields and pastures are formed of substantial houses, each the home of an extended family, the basic social unit.

Drukpa society is traditionally hierarchical; until recently the lowest stratum was composed of slaves, descendants of Indian war captives who have now been emancipated. Above them are land-holding farmers, while the highest class consists of aristocratic landowners led by a hereditary monarch.

Daflas
pop: 16,000

The Daflas are mountain dwellers, a Mongoloid group living in the rugged uplands of Arunachal Pradesh; they speak a Tibeto-Burman language. The economy is based on slash-and-burn cultivation and animal husbandry, supplemented by hunting and fishing. Dafla settlements consist of clusters of longhouses, each housing 60-70 related people and forming the only effective political unit. With no organization above this level, feuding and raiding are frequent. There is competition for wealth and prestige, and formerly slavery was common. Under Indian administration many Dafla practices have been discontinued.

Apa Tanis
pop: 15,000

The seven large villages of the Apa Tanis lie between Assam and the borders of Tibet, concentrated in an area of less than 20 square miles of Arunachal Pradesh; they speak a Tibeto-Burman language. Irrigation allows them to grow rice and other crops intensively. Land is considered the source and essence of wealth: cultivated land is transferable private property. Apa Tani society is divided into landowners and landless commoners, with intermarriage forbidden. The unity of the tribe is maintained by elaborate ceremonial obligations; there are protracted feasts each year at which villages exchange ritual gifts.

Kachari
pop: 400,000

The Kachari live in Assam, in the part of the Bangla plains which projects into that province. They are found mainly in the Brahmaputra and Kachar valleys and in the surrounding hills. Although the Boda and Dimasa peoples are separate, both are regarded as Kachari and speak Tibeto-Burman languages. Many of them, particularly those living on the plains, have become Hindus and a few are Christians, but some traditional beliefs have been retained. Domestic oxen are thought to be a gift from the god of plenty, a symbol of wealth as well as a source of food and labour.

The Kachari have been partly assimilated into the Hindu caste structure of India. As cultivators they belong to the Koc sub-division. Their land is fertile but is plagued by flooding, which periodically results in loss of life and destruction of property and homes. Generally an irrigation system channels the monsoon rains to produce paddy rice.

Garo
pop: 280,000

The Garo live mainly in the hill region of western Assam, close to the border with Bangladesh, and speak a Tibeto-Burman language. At one time they lived by slash-and-burn cultivation, hunting and fishing. Now the Garo have begun to grow rice in paddy fields, but they still plant some crops on cleared forest and continue fishing. Ginger and cotton are grown as cash crops.

Villages consist of about 300 people living in small bamboo houses woven in intricate patterns. Each village is based on a kin group, a section of one of the exogamous matrilineages which make up the society. Property and status are inherited by daughters, one of whom is selected by her parents to live with her husband as their heirs in the family home.

Nagas
pop: 500,000

The Nagas are a group of Mongoloid tribes who live in a mountainous tract of country straddling the border between India and Burma; they speak a Tibeto-Burman language. Most Naga groups still practise slash-and-burn cultivation on the hill-slopes. One exception is the Angami, who long ago developed a system of irrigated rice-terraces. These terraces, which still allow the repeated cultivation of the same plots, are carved out of the hill-slopes over drops of thousands of feet and are

often reinforced by walls of pebbles and mud 15-20 feet thick. They are irrigated by a complex system of channels and aqueducts which collect the waters from every rivulet.

Whatever their method of cultivation, all Nagas live in large permanent villages, normally situated on the highest parts of hill ranges or spurs. The houses are built of broad wooden planks and decorated with carvings, trophies and fertility symbols. Naga villages were autonomous and heavily fortified in the days of warfare and head-hunting. Each contained a number of patrilineal exo-gamous clans, but while the Sema and some of the Konyak were ruled by hereditary chiefs, the remainder had a very democratic system.

The Nagas were sheltered from outside influences during the years of British administration. Even in the 1940s head-hunting was still practised in areas along the border. However, missionaries persuaded large numbers to convert to Christianity. By the time India won independence there were enough educated and politically-aware Nagas to demand that Nagaland should be a separate country. Guerrilla warfare soon broke out and only died down in 1962 when negotiations between the Nagas and the Indian government created the Indian state of Nagaland.

Enormous funds were injected into the new state, and economic conditions improved. Many young people are now literate in English, the official language, but are causing a social problem because they cannot find the jobs to which they aspire. They have begun to look to the past with considerable nostalgia.

Khasi
pop : 364,000

The Mongoloid Khasi are the major tribe inhabiting the mountainous region of Meghalaya; they speak a Mon-Khmer language. They live on a plateau at between 5,000 and 6,000 feet, which has the highest recorded rainfall in the world and is admirably suited to the cultivation of potatoes. This has been the Khasi's main crop since its introduction by the British in the mid-19th century. Two neighbouring sub-tribes are the Jaintias and the Wa.

In the 20th century the British administration opened the way for missionaries, who established schools, churches and hospitals. Many of the Khasi were converted to Christianity and today they have one of the highest literacy-rates in India. However, the traditional structure of their society has hardly changed since the days when they were shifting cultivators.

The Khasi are divided into a number of matrilineal clans, with land tenure based on the nuclear family. Property is passed on from mother to youngest daughter, who also serves as the family priestess. A man who marries a non-heiress is expected to set up his own household and work to acquire property. If he marries an heiress he lives in the house of his wife's parents, but has to leave the management of the property to her brother or maternal uncle.

Konyak women during the rice harvest, Nagaland

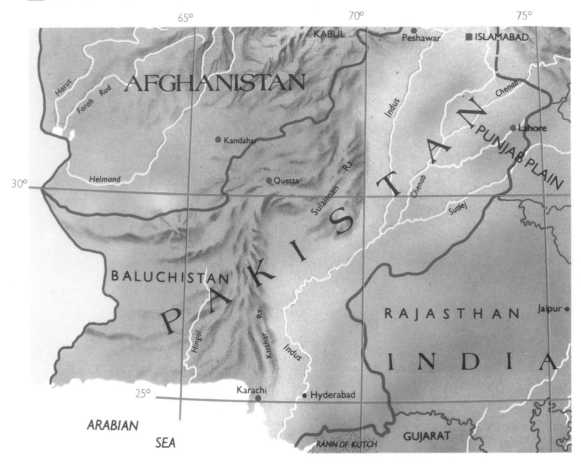

Pakistan

pop: 73,452,000

The original state of Pakistan was created in 1947 when India was partitioned and the largely Muslim areas of the north-east and north-west became independent. The 1,000 miles separating East and West Pakistan made its administration as one nation almost impossible and, amidst fierce fighting in 1971, East Pakistan seceded and became independent as Bangladesh.

Some 75 per cent of Pakistan's population are peasant cultivators. Ethnically they are a mixture of numerous peoples who entered the area over many centuries, including Aryans, Persians, Greeks, Pashtun and Moguls. Apart from Urdu, the official state language, which is spoken by only 8 per cent of the population, the main languages are Punjabi, Sindhi, Pashto, Baluchi and Brahui.

Sikhs

pop: 10,000,000

The Sikhs are neither a caste nor an ethnic group but a religious order, whose home is the Punjab. This is an area where Hinduism and Islam have confronted one another since the 10th century AD, but where attempts have also been made to harmonize the two religions. One such attempt in the 15th century resulted in the foundation of Sikhism: its adherents have gradually assumed the character of separate people.

All Sikhs revere a succession of gurus starting with Nanak, whose message has been preserved in a holy book known as the Granth. Nanak did not formulate a rigidly-defined doctrine, but he laid the foundations for a Sikh 'church' by arranging for his succession. The Sikhs subsequently created a theocratic state and in the 17th and 18th centuries became involved in armed conflict with the imperial Mogul power and surrounding Hindu states. By the end of the 18th century they had secured a large sovereign state whose independence came to an end after clashes with the British.

In 1947 the Punjab was divided by the partition of the sub-continent into India and Pakistan. The Sikhs around Lahore became the victims of Muslim persecution; they fled south across the border and with their co-religionists embarked on a political struggle to gain their own state in India. This was achieved in 1956.

The Sikhs form an easily recognizable community. Since they first formed a military as well as a religious order, all good Sikhs have worn the five *kakkas*: a steel bracelet, a wooden comb, short breeches, a small knife and uncut hair covered by a turban. The women's dress consists of a tunic and breeches.

Emotional ties between men are highly valued by the Sikhs. The women usually have to rely on their children, particularly their sons, for companionship. Membership of a party or faction which supports a man's interests at the village or even state level is considered of paramount importance, as is the creation of a wide circle of acquaintances.

Jats

pop: 8,000,000

In sheer numbers and power, the Punjabi speaking Jats are the dominant caste of northern

India. They are mostly found in the Punjab plain and adjacent areas between the Juana and Ganges rivers, which they claim as their traditional homeland. They are mostly peasant cultivators, growing wheat and sorghum, and keeping cows and buffalo for milk. Each of their villages is inhabited by the members of a single clan – the patrilineal descendants of a common male ancestor.

Jat women generally have more freedom than those in the higher castes. They are allowed to re-marry if widowed and they are not required always to wear a veil and remain secluded from men.

Most Jat villages consist of tightly-clustered houses connected by a series of narrow alleyways. The surrounding fields are largely owned by Jat families, each of which works its own specific plot. No village community is composed entirely of Jats: there are also Brahmans to act as family priests, carpenters to maintain the ploughs, water-carriers to deliver water twice daily from the village wells, and numerous other castes. Today almost every Jat in the Punjab is a Sikh.

Jains
pop : 3,000,000
One per cent of the total population of India are Jains. They live mainly in Gujarat, Maharashtra and Karnataka and follow a religion derived from Mahavisa, the last prophet of the faith, who was born in about 545BC. Like Buddhism, Jainism was a reform movement against the rigid caste system of Hindu society, but although Buddhists and Jains share a belief in reincarnation on the basis of accumulated merit and demerit, they differ on the rules governing behaviour in everyday life.

Jains must maintain a stringent observance of the sanctity of all forms of life, extending this to objects such as rocks and running water, not regarded as animate in most religions. Carried to its extreme, this precludes agriculture and Jains have found an alternative livelihood in commerce; the banking and finance sector of north-west India is dominated by Jains, who have strict rules of business conduct enjoined upon them by their religion. Despite the original aims of

the Jain movement, numerous castes and sub-castes still exist, similar in form and function to those of the Hindus.

Parsees
pop : 100,000
Descended from the Persian Zoroastrians, who escaped from Muslim influence to India in 785AD, the Parsees now live principally in and around Bombay and speak Hindi. Although few in number by comparison with other Indian communities the Parsees play a prominent role in Bombay society. The majority are prosperous members of the professions.

Many Parsees have become highly westernized through close contact with Europeans; however, this has not affected their religion, which remains central to Parsee life. Zoroastrianism involves concepts of purity and defilement; priests tend sacred fires and conduct rituals of purification which extend beyond humans to the natural world of the environment. At death the bodies of Parsees are exposed to vultures and the bones treated with lime and phosphorus to avoid defilement of the four elements.

A Pakistani spice trader

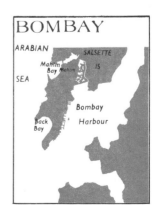

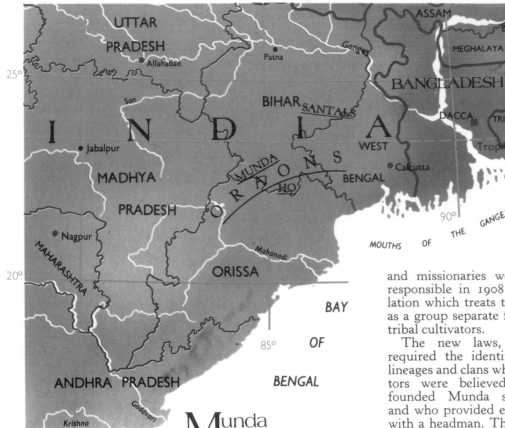

Bengal

🔴 Borders of Bengal, 1900
■ Present borders
of Bangladesh

photograph:
Bathing elephants in
the Ganges river

Munda
pop : 600,000

The Munda are one of several Mundari-speaking tribes who probably originated in central or south-east Asia and migrated to India before the Aryan invasion. Munda, which means 'man of wealth', or 'substantial cultivator', is a name first used by the British. The Munda call themselves Horoko, men.

In the past the Munda moved continually in a search for virgin lands or to escape from Hindu and Muslim landlords. When they were finally forced to settle, the tribe established villages on the Chotanagpur plateau. They now cultivate rice on the terraced hillsides and grow coarse dry rice, millet and pulses on the uplands; they also hunt small game and collect roots. Munda society is rigidly divided into castes; a clan council will drive out any villager who has eaten with or married a member of another caste.

The Munda have been involved in a struggle to retain their lands for 700 years. In the 18th century the claims of Hindu and Muslim landlords provoked a series of uprisings which were finally suppressed by the British. However, the efforts of British administrators and missionaries were finally responsible in 1908 for legislation which treats the Munda as a group separate from other tribal cultivators.

The new laws, however, required the identification of lineages and clans whose ancestors were believed to have founded Munda settlements and who provided each village with a headman. The holdings of these clans were recorded and those who did not belong to a main clan were assumed to be tenants. The imposition of this static system of land tenure has resulted in the impoverishment of the Munda. Unable to take over the remaining areas of forest, they have been forced repeatedly to divide their limited amount of land amongst an ever-increasing population. Many now work for the government, or as labourers in the Assam tea gardens.

Ho
pop : 500,000

Thought to have originated in South-East Asia, the Mundari-speaking Ho settled first in the Gangetic plain but were pushed out by Aryan invaders and later by Hindus and Muslims. They settled in the district of Singhbum in south Bihar about 500 years ago.

In the past they lived by hunting and gathering. Today lack of game in the forests means that hunting is little more than a pastime, passionately followed. However, the Ho still rely on collecting roots, mushrooms, berries, flowers and nuts to feed themselves for several months each year.

The Ho grow pulses, maize and millet in vegetable gardens, and rice in irrigated fields. In a good year they can produce enough cereals to feed them for five months, but they are generally poor cultivators. Formerly they invited Hindu castes into their villages to perform such tasks as herding, smithing and potting instead of acquiring the skills themselves.

In recent years the Ho villages have been threatened by the development of industries based on local mineral wealth, and many Ho have been forced by pressure of population on the land to turn to wage labour. The hereditary headmen and elders who traditionally controlled village affairs have found their authority undermined by Indian government attempts to set up elected village councils to carry out an extensive welfare programme.

Oraons
pop : 1,333,000

The Oraons, who speak a north Dravidian language, are the fourth largest tribe in India. They live in south Bihar and north Orissa in agricultural villages. They have much in common with their neighbours and there are non-Oraons living in most of their communities, either other tribesmen or Hindu occupational groups.

The young men live in bachelors' huts until marriage, and during their time there are divided into age grades with varying duties. This practice is dying out, a fact regretted by many older Oraons who stress the unifying effect of the experience upon a village composed of families of differing clan status.

Religious life owes much to traditional beliefs, but is overlaid with Hindu elements. Worship of Hindu deities is mixed with reverence of tribal spirits, and fire-walking takes place in some villages. During these ceremonies men walk barefoot over beds of glowing coals as a demonstration of faith or an act of thanksgiving; at the end their feet show no sign of burns or blisters, and during the ceremony the walkers indicate neither pain nor distress.

As communications improve and land competition increases, the Oraons are abandoning their agricultural life and with it much of their distinctive culture. Many of them now work in sawmills and tea plantations, and some have migrated to the cities.

Santals
pop : 3-5,000,000

Living in the central Indian plateau, the Santals are the second largest tribal grouping in the country; they speak a Mundari dialect. Originally shifting cultivators, they now live mainly in settled village communities practising plough agriculture either for themselves or as labourers for others. Each village consists of a row of small family dwellings; there is a headman and often a shaman.

It is common for tribal groups in India gradually to lose their own language, adopt the more general Hindi and assimilate into the national culture. Yet although some Santals have lost their language, the process of assimilation is being strongly resisted. The Santal way of life has little in common with that prescribed for Hindus – they emphasize drinking, dancing, meat-eating and general conviviality, and over time have built up a deep antipathy to the more stringent Hindus.

In 1855 the Santals revolted against the Hindus taking over their land. Since then relations have scarcely improved and recently there has been a revival of Santal language and culture in an effort to promote tribal pride and stop the spread of Hinduization. Despite the fact that 3,000,000 people speak Santal, their children can speak only Hindi at school.

Bengalis
pop : 130,000,000

The Bengalis live on one of the world's most fertile deltas, formed by the confluence of the Ganges and Brahmaputra rivers. The eastern part now constitutes the Muslim state of Bangladesh, where the vast majority of the population depend for their livelihood on agriculture and fishing. In contrast, Hindu West Bengal is the most industrialized state of India. Only a little more than half the population are engaged directly in agriculture, growing jute, pulses, oil seeds, maize, wheat, barley, sugar cane and vegetables as well as rice, which forms four-fifths of the total production.

The aboriginal settlers of the delta developed a decentralized society, adapted to their economic needs in an area where the land surface is constantly reforming because of alluvium deposited by the rivers. As a result, neither the Aryan nor the later Mogul invaders had much effect on society in Bengal, which remained on the periphery of their civilizations. However, Brahmanism spread to the region in the 5th century, and Islam was introduced during the Turko-Afghan conquest in the 13th century.

Before partition in 1947, Bangladesh and West Bengal formed an area of cultural unity, despite religious differences. Many Muslims crossed into Bangladesh, but even now 20 per cent of West Bengalis follow Islam. Economic differences are marked, however, and Calcutta, with a population of more than 7,000,000, is surrounded by India's greatest concentration of mines and industries.

Bangladesh
pop: 76,565,000

The state of Bangladesh arose in 1971 out of the ruins of Pakistan. The former country, created in 1947 as a homeland of Islam in the sub-continent, had always been an anomaly, bound together only by religion. The two countries were separated not only by 1,000 miles of Indian territory, but also by ethnic, social, linguistic and cultural differences. The Punjabis treated the East as little more than a colony, supplying the capital to develop industries in the West. Today Bangladesh is still beset by political and economic problems which are often aggravated by natural disasters such as floods. With only three cities, just 4 per cent of the population are urbanized; the rest are mostly peasant farmers or fishermen.

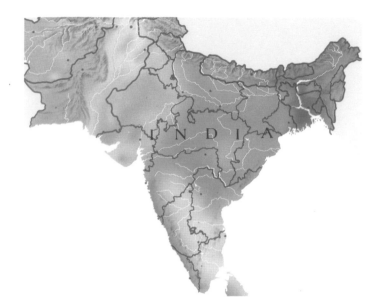

India
pop: 643,993,000

Both Mongoloid and Aryan elements can be discerned in the modern Indian population and the different languages indicate influences from peoples both east and west of the sub-continent. The original inhabitants may have been similar to the Veddoid peoples who now live as hunter gatherers and horticulturalists in many jungle regions. The tribal groups are generally outside the influence of Hinduism, a social as well as a religious system, which has done much to unify Indian society. There is a large minority of Muslims, as well as Sikhs, Buddhists, Jains, Parsees and Christians.

Rapid population increase and low food production mean that an estimated 20 per cent of all Indians live in a state of semi-starvation. Migration to the towns only exacerbates the government's problems: Uttar Pradesh, for example, the largest state in the nation, has only one industrial centre. Many migrant workers face severe hardship and are reduced to living in the streets.

Harijans
pop: 80,000,000

The Harijans – a term meaning 'children of god' – are the most under-privileged section of Indian society. Until Mahatma Gandhi took up their cause in the 1920s they were always referred to as 'Untouchables'. The higher castes carefully avoided contact with them, for their mere presence was considered to be polluting. They were not allowed to draw water from wells used by 'clean' castes and they were excluded from most public bathing places. They were prohibited from entering Hindu temples and denied access to nearby public roads.

Since independence in 1947, the Indian government has abolished Untouchability and made this sort of discrimination illegal. However, the new laws have had little effect in the villages, where 90 per cent of the Harijans live. They are still expected to do all the most despised forms of work, such as the emptying and cleaning of latrines and the removal and skinning of dead animals. The 'clean' castes refuse to accept cooked food or water from Harijans and will perform a simple act of cleansing after each contact.

Village lay-out reflects the Harijans' social position, for they commonly live in settlements separated from the main site by some open space and with their own water source. Harijans rarely own land, but often work for farmers in return for cash or grain. The Harijans dare not claim their legal rights because they do not wish to offend those on whom they are economically dependent. In many regions Harijans are still not permitted to adopt the lifestyle of the higher castes. Until quite recently they were forbidden in southern India to use sandals, umbrellas or silken cloth. In an attempt to gain self-respect in a society which despises them, many have rejected Hinduism to become Christians, Muslims, Sikhs or Buddhists.

In the cities, educated Harijans have gained respectable jobs. There are over 350,000 holding central government posts and a considerable number working as teachers or for local authorities. The constitution provides them with reserved seats in parliament and every government since independence has included one or two Harijan ministers. However, even those who are successful in the professional sense are rarely acceptable socially to other castes.

photograph:
A Hindu festival near Jaipur

India
Brahmans, Kshatriyas, Vaishyas, Shudras

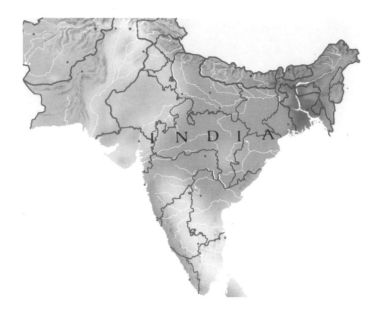

Brahmans
pop: not available

The Brahmans constitute the highest of the four classes or *varna* into which Indian society has been divided since the second millennium BC. Today the membership of a class is not as immediately significant to an Indian as the membership of a caste; there are more than 3,000 castes, each of which is usually associated with a particular occupation. However, the status of each caste ultimately depends on the extent to which its claims to belong to a particular *varna* are accepted.

In the ancient Hindu scripts the *varna* were also defined in terms of occupation: originally all Brahmans were priests. Material needs quickly forced them to find other means of earning a livelihood; today Brahmans dominate government and the professions, and Brahman priests are lower in social status than academics or landowners.

Priests are required to give the routine performance of rituals, and in the large temples they are exposed to pollution. This is of great significance to Brahmans, who are expected to be continually on their guard against anything which might affect their purity. In villages and small towns, particularly in south India, the Brahmans live apart from the other castes. Those who adhere strictly to tradition refuse to eat meat or drink alcohol, and reject food cooked in water by someone of a lower caste. Only in the cities are Brahmans beginning to eat with members of lower castes.

Each Brahman caste consists of numerous clan-like units known as *gotra,* believed to be descended from a mythical saint. No two persons with the same *gotra* name are allowed to marry. A Brahman may not even marry a girl from his mother's or maternal grandfather's group. Parents who, by providing a large dowry, enable their daughter to marry into a family with a higher social status acquire a more prestigious position within society themselves.

It is now possible for Brahmans to obtain a divorce, but the fate of a widow is still a hard one. She is required to sleep on a plank or the floor, wear only white clothes, and act as a general drudge for her deceased husband's family. She is regarded as someone who brings bad luck to all but her own children. It is not surprising that in the past many widows chose to bring honour to themselves by committing suicide on their husbands' funeral pyres: the act of *sati.*

Brahman boys are not considered to be true Brahmans until they have been invested with a cord known as the 'sacred thread'. This ceremony is regarded as a second birth, and is one which Kshatriya and Vaishya males also undergo. It gives them the right to read the sacred books, through which they learn the meaning of their daily ritual devotions. For a priest these begin before dawn and continue for most of the day. However, the majority of secular Brahmans spend only about 90 minutes each day on worship and ritual washing.

Kshatriyas
pop: not available

The Kshatriyas (warriors) were traditionally members of the ruling class, whose duty was to protect their subjects by means of good government during times of peace and by leading armies into battle during times of war. When the four classes or *varna* were becoming established in India, the Kshatriyas often claimed precedence over Brahmans; the followers of the historical Buddha had no doubt that as a Kshatriya he was a member of the highest social class.

The ideal Kshatriya should be easy to anger, always ready to defend his honour, brave in combat, magnanimous in victory and generous with his possessions. He is not expected to be as stringent about food, drink and ritual etiquette as the Brahmans. In the recent past the inhabitants of the princely states of Rajasthan were the greatest admirers of these qualities and, no matter what their caste, all took great pride in their warrior ancestry. They revelled in hunting and feasting, eating large quantities of meat and drinking much strong liquor. Courage in the face of danger was a quality which Kshatriya women were also expected to demonstrate.

Today, the older generation of Rajputs, the noble dynasty of the Kshatriya *varna,* still dress in warrior style with a long moustache and high turban, and carry a heavy wire-bound staff. They consider themselves to be rulers by birthright, and see it as their duty to preserve the hierarchical structure of society. This, however, has not prevented them from joining forces with martial tribal peoples to form politically powerful pressure groups. These propagate the view that Kshatriyas are bound to each other not by ties of caste, but by ideals. Princely Rajputs should not be bound by the sort of rules which prevent them from sharing meals with tribesmen.

Vaishyas
pop: not available

The Vaishyas are the third class, or *varna,* in the traditional division of Indian society. Ranked below the Brahmans and the Kshatriyas, but grouped with them as belonging to the 'twice-born', they have the full ritual status of Aryans and the right to wear the sacred thread.

In the past, the Vaishyas were described as farmers and more particularly as herders of the cattle to be sacrificed by the ritual specialists, the Brahmans. Gradually they entered the sphere of trading, and became dealers in metals, cloth, thread, jewellery and

spices; meanwhile, the Shudras were drawn increasingly to agriculture. In Buddhist times the Vaishyas organized themselves into powerful guilds and were patronized by kings because of their riches and influence.

Perhaps because of their humble status in relation to the Brahman class, wealthy Vaishyas have often inclined towards Buddhism and Jainism. However, many castes claiming Vaishya status tend to follow the Brahmanic model very closely. Wealthy trading castes such as the Agarwals of Bihar in north India and the Nagarths of Bangalore in south India follow the customs of the Brahmans, particularly in respect of marriage and ritual.

Vaishyas are found all over India. The most common caste occupations are those of banker, contractor, jeweller and grain merchant; there is a definite stigma attached to working on the land because of its association with the lower-caste Shudras. Those Vaishya castes that do practise agriculture consider such work as ploughing dishonourable and employ lower castes to do it.

Shudras
pop: not available

According to the ancient law-books, the duty of the Shudras was to serve the other three *varna*. On the basis of occupation they were divided into the 'pure' and 'excluded' castes, but were hardly distinguishable from the Untouchables. Shudras had few rights and little value was attached to their lives: a Brahman who killed a Shudra was punished as though he had killed a cat or dog.

In later ages the ranks of the Shudras were swollen by non-Aryans and by individuals and groups who had failed to conform to orthodox caste practices. Today a large part of the Indian population are Shudras, but their numbers vary greatly from region to region. In the Dravidian south, where there are few Kshatriyas, they form an overwhelming majority, but among the Pahan of the lower Himalayan hill regions they and the Untouchables constitute just 10 per cent of the population.

Shudras are no longer oppressed by the other three *varna*, and include prosperous farmers as well as more menial workers, but they are often involved in fierce rivalry for increased status. This has prevented the Shudra castes from assuming static positions within society, but it has also served to emphasize the superiority of the 'twice-born' castes. Items of dress and jewellery, and the style and decoration of their houses are all used to reflect Shudra status.

Today tribal peoples are in the process of becoming Shudras through their gradual integration into Hindu society. Few Indians actually describe them as Shudra but they realize that the tribal peoples are not to be treated as impure.

Republic Day parade, New Delhi

India
Bhils, Yanadi, Gonds, Baigas, Khonds, Gadabas, KondaReddis, Chenchu

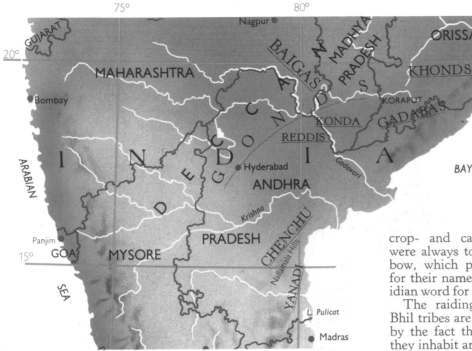

Distribution of Bhils

Bhils
pop : 3,500,000

The Bhils are scattered over a wide area of country from western Madhya Pradesh to Gujarat and Maharashtra. There are many sub-divisions of peoples who regard themselves as Bhils and, because of the extent of Hinduization among them, the population figure is only an estimate. Nonetheless, they are the third largest tribal group in India and, despite many sub-divisions, display enough indigenous characteristics to link them together as one people. Most now speak Bhili, a dialect of Hindi.

The Bhils are related to the Chenchu and Reddi tribes and their origin, like that of many south Indian peoples, is thought to be pre-Aryan and pre-Dravidian. Formerly they were hunters, fishermen and jungle gatherers, but Hinduization has meant that the skills they once showed at these occupations have all but disappeared.

As with many of their neighbours, there is a major division between the plains agriculturalists and those who still practise slash-and-burn cultivation in the hills. The latter are now in a minority, but their way of life is closest to what is known about the Bhils in the past. Until recently they had a reputation for being aggressive

crop- and cattle-raiders and were always to be seen with a bow, which perhaps accounts for their name since the Dravidian word for a bow is *vil*.

The raiding tactics of the Bhil tribes are partly explained by the fact that the hill areas they inhabit are not very fertile and, even with the addition of some food from jungle gathering, their economy is on the margin of subsistence. The Hinduized plains Bhils grow grains and vegetables, but are regarded as poor farmers and have not achieved high status in Hindu society. Many of the less successful plains Bhils look for work as labourers in neighbouring Hindu villages.

There is no overall social organization that incorporates all Bhils. There are exogamous clans which formerly were totemic and still have individual headmen, but these are local remnants of past Bhil society and the communities have little contact with each other. However, the Bhils have always had a special relationship with the princely caste of Rajputs and, although the present impoverished condition of the Bhils owes much to aggression from the Rajputs in the past, it was the Rajputs who gave the Bhils their cultivation techniques, language and those aspects of Hindu life that are part of Bhil society today.

Yanadi
pop : 200,000

Scattered throughout India are different groups of nomadic peoples who serve Hindu society as musicians, tinkers and handymen. The Yanadi are one of the largest of these semi-itinerant groups: being outside the caste system they are free

to undertake any sort of labour which seems convenient. They are to be found mainly in eastern Andhra Pradesh north of Madras, around Lake Pulicat; other groups live further north and as far to the south as Arcot. There are four sub-divisions of the Yanadi: the Reddi, Adavi, Kappala and Challa. All speak the Dravidian Teluga dialect.

The Yanadi practise a range of economic activities, but along the coast are best known as fishermen. They use nets and traps, selling their catch in local markets. Further inland, many Yanadi have taken up cultivation or are prepared to work in menial labouring jobs. Yanadi houses are designed for this unsettled lifestyle, tiny conical huts thatched to the ground with palmyra leaves. They are generally erected on the outskirts of large villages and towns in which their inhabitants are temporarily employed. With their scattered distribution and high degree of mobility, the Yanadi have no political leaders; decisions are made by family heads and occasional community councils.

Gonds
pop : 4,000,000

The Gonds form the largest tribal group in India. Less than half now speak their own unwritten Dravidian language; the rest have adopted the language of their Hindu neighbours. They are dispersed over the north-eastern corner of the Deccan plateau – hilly country which once contained large areas of forest.

The Gonds have always regarded agriculture as the most acceptable occupation. Some men become carpenters or blacksmiths, but all refuse to take up pottery or weaving as full-time occupations. Unlike their Telugu neighbours, they do not use artificial methods of irrigation. They grow rice where water collects naturally, but they usually cultivate millet, maize, wheat, pulses and oil-seeds. The more isolated groups still employ slash-and-burn techniques, but the majority now use wooden ploughs to prepare the land.

Today pressure of numbers is forcing many Gonds to claim and stay on one particular piece of land, but when their

homelands were sparsely populated they moved regularly in search of fertile ground. As a result, each of their villages was, and still is, a haphazard collection of houses, lightly built with timber and bamboo and thatched with grass.

The Gonds and their dynasties have appeared in recorded history for centuries. They have been subjected to many external influences but have succeeded in maintaining a social structure very different from that of Hindu society. There are no words or phrases in their language which imply deference to authority. However, the members of each village respect the family of the headman, whose post is hereditary and who is appointed at the foundation of each new settlement. His duty is to maintain a spirit of co-operation between the villagers and to end all disputes. Final authority is vested in an assembly of adult men; they can pass a sentence of banishment which is valid throughout Gond territory.

Many Gonds have kept their cultural distinctiveness despite increasing social interaction with Hindus. In some states they have gained representation in legislative assemblies and a few have become ministers. However, the great majority remain subsistence cultivators outside the Hindu caste system.

Baigas
pop: 145,000

The Baigas are one of the most populous of the slash-and-burn cultivating tribes living in the Gond areas of Madhya Pradesh. Although they are Hindi-speakers, using the Chattisgarhi dialect, and much of the population is now Hinduized, their elaborate system of social control backed by magic has helped to maintain their identity as a distinct tribal group.

The original technique of farming adopted by the Baigas was that of shifting cultivation, using iron hoes as their main tools. They believed that to use a plough was a sin and lacerated the breasts of Mother Earth, and that the result of disregarding such beliefs was to cause disease and even death. Similarly they believed that incest could cause both leprosy and blindness.

Today, however, while many Baigas retain these beliefs, others have adapted to economic pressures and use the ox and plough. Roots and wild fruits are gathered as a supplement to agriculture, but the Baigas believe that cultivation is overwhelmingly important and their magicians still seek to protect and encourage good crops by animal sacrifice to supernatural powers.

Khonds
pop: 170,000

The Khonds are shifting cultivators who occupy an extensive area of southern Orissa. Dravidian speakers, they are closely related to neighbouring tribes, especially the Kui. Some Khonds still practise slash-and-burn subsistence agriculture, but with government encouragement many have taken up rice growing on irrigated fields. Their villages are traditionally arranged as rows of family huts facing each other across a central clearing, and this pattern is still followed.

The Khonds came to public attention in the 19th century when it became known that human sacrifice was part of their religious system. The victims were sacrificed to the Earth God, in order to ensure fertility of the soil, and the method of execution, known as *meriah,* was reported as particularly brutal. The victim was crushed to death or suffocated in a pit, and part of the flesh was buried as an offering. Since the suppression of this ritual by the British, the Khonds have substituted a buffalo calf and traditional villages still have a sacrificial stone in the central clearing.

Gadabas
pop: 67,000

The Gadabas, who live in the Koraput plateau of Orissa and the adjoining hill region of Andhra Pradesh, are only one of a group of tribes speaking the ancient Mundari language. They practise shifting cultivation on the hill slopes and grow millet on permanent flat fields, as well as rice on carefully constructed terraces. They once supplemented their diet by hunting and fishing, but today

the only animal hunt is a tribal rite held during the spring festival.

The principal unit of their society is the village cluster, with two or more villages which are divided into several exogamous clans. The village headmen have only nominal authority and social position depends on ability and the possession of wealth. The latter imposes an obligation to provide feasts, the most elaborate of which are known as *gotrs.* These put the potentially dangerous spirits of the dead at rest, while preserving the ancestors' beneficial powers. They involve the erection of stone monuments, a ritual which is widespread among the societies of southern Asia.

Konda Reddis
pop: 35,000

Although the Konda Reddis, or Hill Reddis, now speak a Dravidian dialect known as Teluga, they are almost certainly Veddoid in origin. They live in the hills of Andhra Pradesh, above the Godavari river, and their way of life varies according to the degree of contact with neighbouring Hindus. The more remote groups still grow millet by slash-and-burn techniques, but shifting cultivation has been restricted by recent improvements in communication and the commercial exploitation of forests. Although some Reddis have adopted the plough most are losing their independence and becoming wage-earners.

Chenchu
pop. 18,000

One of the last groups of hunter-gatherers in India, the Veddoid Chenchu live in the Nallamala hills of Andhra Pradesh. Only a few hundred still follow the traditional way of life, depending for food entirely on the flora and fauna of the forest. In the past each group of kinsmen had hereditary rights over a particular tract of land and hunted and gathered within its boundaries. The Chenchu have gradually been deprived of most of their land by the surrounding Hindu population, and many have had to adapt to agriculture or wage-labour in order to survive.

**Distribution of
Dravidian-Speakers**

■ North & Central groups
■ South Dravidian groups

Dravidians
pop: 110,000,000

The Dravidians occupy the greater part of south India and constitute the second largest language group in the subcontinent. However, a certain amount of mystery surrounds their origins: so far they have not been connected with any other known language group and the manner of their arrival in south India is unknown.

The Dravidians do not constitute a homogeneous group. Languages of the Dravidian group are spoken by people of widely differing physical types and cultural patterns, ranging from hunter-gatherer forest dwellers to the sophisticated élite of Madras and Trivandrum. These languages, though not mutually understandable, conform to a common grammatical pattern and share a considerable amount of vocabulary. They are divided into southern, central and northern groups. The southern is the largest and includes Tamil, Kannadu and Malayalam, each with an extensive literature going back to the early centuries AD. The central group includes tribal languages such as those spoken by the Gonds and Oraons. Speakers of the northern group are scattered and few in number.

Discrimination against the lower strata of society, and especially against the Harijan castes, is exceptionally severe.

Until recently streets inhabited by Brahmans were barred to the polluting castes, and Harijans were unapproachable to an extent measured by numbers of paces. Recent legislation has mitigated such extreme discrimination, but a strongly developed caste consciousness remains a characteristic feature of Dravidian society.

Todas
pop: 1,100

The Dravidian-speaking Todas are a pastoralist people living in the Nilgiri hills, who migrate seasonally in search of pastureland. They subsist almost entirely on the dairy products of their buffalo, occasionally supplemented by gathered fruits and plants and bartered grain. Social organization is complex: there are exogamous clans forming two endogamous moieties. Polyandry is permitted, but one husband assumes paternity of all the children of each woman, thus determining inheritance.

Religious life is closely linked to pastoralism. If grazing land is restricted and the Todas are forced to turn to agriculture their culture will suffer considerable dislocation. Today, however, tourism is giving their society an economic boost and the population is now increasing steadily.

Badagas
pop: 100,000

Several of the tribes of south India live in symbiosis with one other. In the Nilgiri hills of Madras are three such groups, the Kotas, the Todas and the Badagas. The Badagas, who speak a Dravidian language, belong to an agricultural caste and are traditionally potato and rice farmers, owning only a few cattle. Today they also grow tea on small plantations. They live in separate villages from the Todas but rely on the buffaloes reared and herded by them for dairy produce and ploughing. The Badagas for their part provide the Todas with rice and potatoes. A further link in the relationship between the two groups is that the Badagas act for the less numerous Toda in the local Madras market. They sell Toda animals and produce, and

generally act as middlemen.

The third of the tribes in symbiosis are the Kotas, who are smiths and musicians and who live on the edges of Badaga villages, where they officiate at Badaga ceremonies. The Badagas regard them as untouchable, however, especially since the Kotas eat the flesh of cattle and buffaloes. Nonetheless, most Badaga ceremonies, particularly their funerals, are incomplete without Kota or Kurumba musicians. The Badagas worship many deities of the Hindu pantheon, especially Shiva and Rangaswami.

Nayars
pop: not available

The Nayars of the Malabar coast are a caste of Hindu landholders of high status and considerable wealth. In the past they formed a military aristo-

cracy and the men were away from home for long periods training and fighting. The Nayars are one of the few matrilineal groups in India, inheriting land, wealth, name and status through the mother.

Formerly all Nayars lived in extended family households known as *taravads*. They generally had 10–50 members, but surviving households consist of up to 200 people. The *taravad* consisted of all people born into it, and residence remained unchanged at marriage: a formal link between men and women of different *taravads* did not imply co-habitation and often was not consummated. After her marriage a woman was free to take lovers of her choice, all of whom continued to regard their own *taravad* as their home, and any children belonged automatically to the mother's lineage and *taravad*.

Today less than five per cent of Nayars live in *taravads*; for the rest, earned income and a sedentary life for men has led to conjugal units and some departures from the strict rule of matrilineal inheritance.

Irulars
pop : 100,000

The Irulars are widely distributed in southern India, with the biggest concentrations in the Nilgiri, Melagiri and Javadi hills. Originally they were semi-nomadic hunter-gatherers who supplemented their diet with occasional crops grown on cleared jungle plots. Slash-and-burn is now illegal and, although Irulars in the more inaccessible areas can still survive by hunting and gathering, most have turned to millet cultivation on permanent smallholdings. Trade is im-

portant to many Irular groups, while others work in tea and coffee plantations or as casual labourers for Hindu neighbours.

Irular society is divided into exogamous clans and cross-cousin marriage is preferred. In the past, political organization did not extend above the level of the hunting-gathering band, but there is now a headman presiding over each cluster of agricultural villages.

Although nominally Hindu, many Irulars, particularly the more remote, maintain traditional beliefs and practices. For others religion is a blend of old and new, reflecting their marginal position in Indian society. The Irulars are gradually being absorbed into the Hindu system as a Harijan caste, while remaining to some extent culturally distinct from the surrounding society.

Landscape near Madurai, south India

Tamils

pop: 21,500,000

Tamil refers both to a cultural group and to the oldest living language in India, which is spoken extensively in an area from Madras in south India to Sri Lanka. It has proved more resilient to the influence of Sanskrit and Indo-Aryan than any other Indian language. The Tamil people can be classified as the Tamil-speakers of the Indian state of Tamil Nadu and the 1,500,000 Hindu inhabitants of north Sri Lanka. The natural boundaries of Tamil Nadu with the Kaveri plain and delta as its centre make Tamil land a geographically, linguistically and culturally distinct region of India.

The caste differentiation among Indian Tamils is much the same as elsewhere in India, with Brahmans at the apex and Harijans at the base of the social hierarchy. Tamil villages have a geographical layout which strongly expresses this social order. There are usually three distinct blocks for the three main groups: Brahmans, non-Brahman castes and Harijans.

The majority of the Sri Lanka Tamils are Kodun, Tamil-speakers of high castes, many of whom have lived on the island for centuries and are Sri Lankan citizens. But many are low-caste Indian Tamils who have not all been granted citizenship and whose sense of grievance against the Sinhalese majority has led to recurrent

conflict. A little less than half the entire Sri Lankan Tamil population is concentrated in the small peninsula of Jaffna in the northernmost part of the island, with a density more than twice the overall national average. The scarcity of available land has led to a migration of Tamil youth to administrative centres in the towns of Sri Lanka, India and, during the colonial era, to British Malayan territories.

Tamil kinship ties are strong and, whenever possible, the migrants return to seek further employment in Sri Lanka. Such opportunities are not great and, with the potential for agricultural work so limited, the causes of conflict have been difficult to eradicate. The whole issue was aggravated in 1958 by attempts to legislate for the adoption of Sinhala as the official language in Tamil areas. This legislation was repealed after violence swept across the north of the island. India finally agreed to repatriate half a million Tamils from Sri Lanka. This policy has never been effectively implemented and, as long as they remain stateless, the troubles are likely to continue.

Sri Lanka

pop: 13,990,000

Sri Lanka is a small, fertile island with a mixed population, the result of succeeding invasions of its shores. The original inhabitants were probably the Vedda, a few of whom still live in the forests of the central highlands. By far the majority now are the Buddhist Sinhalese, descended from the Aryan and Dravidian migrations from India. There is also a community of Burghers whose forefathers were Dutch and Portuguese immigrants, an Arab group, and 2,500,000 Tamils. Considerable conflict between the Hindu Tamils and the Buddhist Sinhalese continues to the present day. The island won independence from the British in 1947.

Sinhalese

pop: 10,000,000

Nearly 75 per cent of the population of Sri Lanka are Sinhalese. They are named after a north Indian king known

as *Sinha*, or lion, and are thought to have come from north India to Sri Lanka as long as 2,500 years ago, replacing the indigenous Vedda tribes of the island. The Sinhalese became Buddhist soon after the 3rd century BC and ever since have remained the last stronghold of Theravada Buddhism in south Asia. Today, apart from a small Christian community, the Sinhalese are practically all Buddhist.

There is a major division in Sinhalese society. Most of the population regard themselves as belonging to either the 'low country' Sinhalese or the central highland Kandyans. The Kandyans are the more traditional: in the past they were always confronting Tamil or Chola invasions from the north. Low country Sinhalese integrated far more readily with successive European invasions.

There has been extensive intermarriage between some Sinhalese and immigrant groups, although rarely among Kandyans. As a consequence of intermarriage with Dutch and Portuguese immigrants in the 16th and 17th centuries, a substantial population known as Burghers live in the north of the island.

Long-standing tensions between the Sinhalese and their northern neighbours, the Tamils, were aggravated in the 19th century when the British developed a plantation economy on the island, with coffee, tea, coconut and rubber as the most successful products. The Sinhalese were agriculturalists, but not plantation workers, and so the British brought in cheap Tamil labour. Since independence in 1947, the Sinhalese have taken over many of the plantations and tea has become the island's main export crop. However, the cultivation of rice, coconut and cotton still forms the backbone of their subsistence economy and provides raw materials for the batik, textile and copra industries.

Despite their Buddhist beliefs, the Sinhalese have a system of about 25 castes, of which the Goyigama is the highest. This is the cultivator caste, to which a large proportion of Sinhalese belong, but the Goyigama claim descent from Sinhalese kings and

Ethnic divisions of Sri Lanka

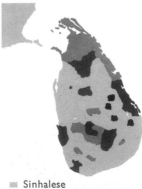

- Sinhalese
- Tamils
- Mixed
- Vedda

jealously protect their pure blood. High-caste Sinhalese prefer endogamous marriage so as to reinforce kinship ties, but many of the caste rules are becoming weaker in Sri Lanka's urban centres.

Karava
pop: 500,000

The Karava are an immigrant community but are generally regarded as part of the Sinhalese population of Sri Lanka. All that is certain about their origins is that they came from the mainland. The Karava were well established on the island by the time the Portuguese arrived in the 16th century, when many were converted from Buddhism to Christianity. They now extend over widely separated areas stretching from the coast of Southern Province to North-Western Province, and the majority depend on fishing for their livelihood.

In the south-west they use outrigger canoes known as *ora* for deep-sea fishing. The owner of each *ora* is usually the captain of a freelance three-man crew who obey him implicitly while they are at sea. The profit from the sale of the catch is then divided into five shares, two of which go to the owner. During the south-west monsoon, from May to September, when the *oras* have to go out to deeper waters, the owner takes half of the profit. Further north, catamarans are used, as well as seine nets along the beaches. However, all these traditional methods of fishing are in the process of being replaced by power-driven craft, a change partly sponsored by the government.

In the towns, where many Karava have gained wealth through trading enterprises and industry, or have reached important positions in government, there are obvious divisions between upper, middle and lower classes. In the coastal settlements and villages of the interior, class distinctions are less pronounced; and although the Karava community contains Buddhists and Roman Catholics, poor fishermen and wealthy merchants, it shows no tendency to split into sub-castes.

Vedda
pop: 500

The Vedda form part of a group of Veddoid peoples who were probably the original inhabitants of Sri Lanka and south India. Cave-dwelling hunter gatherers, they lived in communities of about five families with rights over a specific tract of land. Descent was matrilineal and a man lived with his wife's group.

Encroachment on their lands by Sinhalese cultivators has forced the Vedda to leave the forest and take up agriculture. Nonetheless, many traces of their former culture survive, most notably in religious belief. Ancestor and nature spirits, or *yakku*, are invoked and special veneration is accorded to two in particular, who are believed to control the other spirits and must sanction any assistance given to men.

Karava fishermen, Sri Lanka

China/East and South-East Asia

East and South-East Asia cover an enormous area stretching from Heilungkiang in north-east China to Indonesia in the south, and from Sinkiang in west China to the east coast of Japan. North of the Yangtze river, China has a dry, continental climate, but elsewhere the region is sub-tropical, with warm or hot weather all year round. The equator cuts through the islands of Sumatra and Borneo in the south.

The natural vegetation varies with altitude, climate and soils. Grass and scrub cover the loess plateau north of the Yangtze, with woodland scrub on the mountains beyond the Great Wall frontier and steppe grass where the land drops away northwards. In the far west, high mountains surround vast inland drainage basins where steppe and steppe-desert border the central deserts. East China, with mountains, hills and plains, is notable for its river basins and the range and intensity of its agricultural activity. Japan and Korea are mountainous, with a mixture of deciduous and evergreen forest; South-East Asia's vegetation is mostly sub-tropical and tropical rain forest. There are dry tropical forests in parts of Cambodia and southern Vietnam, and patches of monsoon forest in northern Vietnam, Burma and Thailand.

Some 80 per cent of China's estimated 850,000,000 people live by agriculture in the fertile eastern plains. The far south-west, which has only recently been fully integrated administratively with the remainder, is occupied by both Chinese and non-Chinese tribes—lowlanders such as the Tai and Chuang, and highlanders like the Hmong and Yao—whose political importance is enhanced by their location close to the national frontiers. Along the south coast are the speakers of dialects such as Cantonese and Shanghainese, to the north of whom are the native, Mandarin-speaking, Han Chinese majority, comprising some 70 per cent of the total. A Korean minority of 1,250,000 lives along the borders of North Korea.

Outside the main agricultural zones lie two other vast regions. To the north-west are Inner Mongolia and Sinkiang, the sparsely populated homelands of China's Mongol, Uighur and other minority nationalities. Here the plains and desert basins are most conducive to pastoralism and oasis agriculture. Further south are the high plateaux of Tsinghai and Tibet, homelands of Tibetan and related peoples. Here too, pastoralism predominates, with some high altitude agriculture possible in favourable locations.

Historically, these regions were subject to the ebb and flow of Chinese and 'barbarian' nomadic suzerainty and sovereignty. At times they produced dynasties of conquest, such as the Yuan (1260-1368) and the Ching (1644-1912), when first the Mongols and later the Manchus were themselves strong enough to subdue the Chinese. Today there is no doubt about the extent of China's sovereignty, the last major challenge having been the unsuccessful Tibetan rebellion in 1959, and the three major regions are being welded together by communications, the transfer of Han Chinese population, economic development and the integration of their minorities—some 1,500,000 Mongols, 6,000,000 Turkic-speaking Muslims (Uighurs, Kazakh and Kirghiz) and 2,000,000 Tibetans—into the life and culture of communist China.

The earliest known civilization in China had

emerged near the Huang Ho (Yellow) river in northern Honan as early as the second millennium BC. By 221 BC the Chin dynasty controlled a unified empire extending from Tibet to the Pacific coast—to this dynasty is attributed the construction of the Great Wall. Designed to protect the agricultural and relatively more civilized Chinese from raiding nomads, its span of 1,400 miles was completed by joining sections of wall already built by other northern states to that of the Chin.

The problems of keeping together such a huge territory in pre-industrial times would probably have been insuperable had not China managed on the whole to keep one step ahead of her neighbours in military, economic and organizational skills. By AD 1, China had a population of some 60,000,000 and distinctive aspects of government and society had already emerged. Administrative institutions requiring a large, salaried bureaucracy, and a social structure comprising officials and rich landowners on the one hand and peasant tax-payers on the other, had superseded the earlier system of hereditary aristocrats and commoners. Chinese society was based firmly on the family unit, a hierarchical, self-governing group which the state could administer simply by dealing with the family head. This system was fortified, as in much of South-East Asia, by ancestor worship: the propitiated spirits were thought to intercede with the gods to help create good conditions for crop growing, hunting, harvesting or warfare.

Many of the earliest Chinese beliefs were systematized by Confucius, born about 500 BC, who stressed the subject's duty to the ruler and the son's duty to his parents, emphasizing that the ruler should in return be benevolent and fatherly. Taoism emerged at the same time, largely as a reaction against Confucianism, stressing the need

VEGETATION

Ice	Permanent ice field
Conifer Forest	Pine, spruce, larch
Broadleaf Forest	Deciduous
Temperate	Arable, broadleaf, grass
Subtropical	Dry and wet evergreen
Tropical	'Selva'
Steppe	Short grass
Savanna	Grass and scrub
Semi Desert	Cactus, sparse shrub and grass
Desert	No vegetation
Marsh and Swamp	
Salt	Salt lake, marsh
■	**Capital Cities**
•	**Major Towns**
•	**Towns** Small town village
———	**Country Borders**
———	**Borders** Provinces, states

HEILUNGKIANG

MANCHURIA

- Harbin

KIRIN • Ch'ang-ch'un

INNER MONGOLIA

Shen-yang

LIAONING

HOPEH

PEKING

T'ien-ching

Lu-ta

HUANG HO

SHANSI

T'ai-yuan

SHANTUNG

Ch'ing-tao

KIANGSU

HONAN

NANKING

Hsi-an

SHENSI

HUPEH

Wuhan

Shanghai

CHEKIANG

Wenchou

KANSU

Lan-chou

Huang Ho

NINGSHIA HUI

C H I N A

SZECHWAN

Ch'eng-tu

Ch'ung-ch'ing

KIANGSI

FUKIEN

HUNAN

Ch'ang-sha

KWEICHOW

KWANGSI

CHUANG

KWANGTUNG

Canton

HONG KONG

K'un-ming

YUNNAN

Salween

V I E T N A M

HANOI

HAINAN

Chiang Mai

VIENTIANE

L A O S

Mekong

THAILAND

GOON

BANGKOK

CAMBODIA

PHNOM PENH

SAIGON

Gulf of Siam

HEILUNGKIANG

SEA OF JAPAN

HOKKAIDO

• Sapporo

Hakodate

• Aomori

JAPAN

HONSHU

TOKYO

Yokohama

N. KOREA

PYONGYANG

SOUL

S. KOREA

Pusan

Fukuoka

Kyoto

Kobe

Osaka

SHIKOKU

Kumamoto

KYUSHU

YELLOW SEA

E. CHINA SEA

T'AI-PEI

TAIWAN

SOUTH

CHINA

SEA

LUZON

QUEZON CITY

Manila

PHILIPPINES

MINDANAO

SULU SEA

MALAYSIA

SABAH

BRUNEI

CELEBES SEA

SARAWAK

Kuching

Balikpapan

BORNEO

SULAWESI

MOLUCCAS

MALAYA

KUALA LUMPUR

SINGAPORE

SUMATRA

Padang

Palembang

BANDA SEA

INDONESIA

JAVA SEA

TIMOR

DJAKARTA

Bogor

Surabaya

JAVA

BALI

POPULATION

Distribution and density per sq. mile

2   16   64   256   512

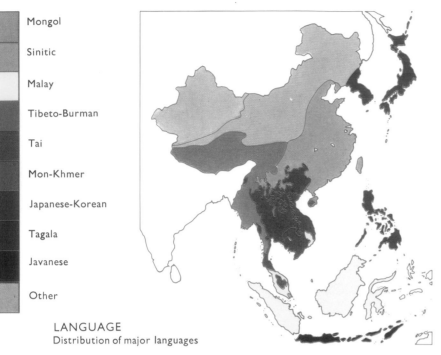

Mongol
Sinitic
Malay
Tibeto-Burman
Tai
Mon-Khmer
Japanese-Korean
Tagala
Javanese
Other

LANGUAGE
Distribution of major languages

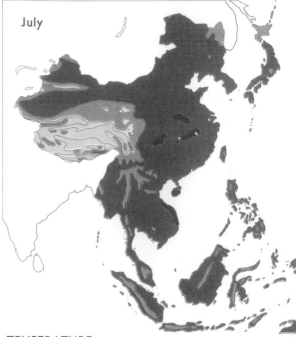

July

TEMPERATURE
Actual surface temperature in centigrade

to be in harmony with nature and the importance of not resisting the natural way. Buddhism too, which reached China and South-East Asia from India in the early centuries AD, was a major inspiration.

Another important factor in Chinese unity was the development of a writing system, employing characters including pictographs, ideographs and later compound forms of phonetics and significs. Although in modern times its complexity is an obstacle to widespread literacy, it has unique graphic and aesthetic qualities, and the historical continuity and cultural affinity symbolized by the script cannot be over-emphasized. It has the incomparable advantage that it can overcome differences of dialect and even more fundamental linguistic barriers, thus reducing the tendency, encouraged by phonetic writing systems, to split into separate national groups. Today China is the largest cohesive national grouping in the world, and this cohesiveness extends in a diluted form to the rest of East and South-East Asia.

Chinese culture, institutions, art and religion had a profound influence on Japan, Korea and Vietnam, all of which paid tribute to China for much of their history. Apart from an ideographic script, Japan's most notable inheritance was Buddhism, which arrived in the mid-6th century. Korea, though with its own language and alphabet, adopted a strict interpretation of Confucianism, which underpinned a rigidly stratified society. Vietnam inherited the Chinese script, literature and government system.

China's isolation from the rest of the world came to an abrupt end with the onslaught of European imperialism in the 19th century. Attracted by a potentially enormous market, but rebuffed by the emperor as barbarians, western powers forcibly demanded ports, whose operations they then controlled; it was during this period that Hong Kong was ceded to Britain. Like China, Japan at first resisted the intruders, but was forced to submit by an American fleet in 1854. Subsequently Japan embarked on a rapid programme of industrializa-

tion and by 1905 was strong enough to have inflicted military defeats on both China and Russia.

The events of the 20th century have forced China and Japan into opposite camps, a situation since mirrored by the division of Korea. With the collapse of the empire in 1912, China was plunged into civil war, resolved finally by the communist triumph of 1949. Meanwhile Japan's imperial expansion into Manchuria and South-East Asia led to defeat by the United States in the Second World War. Since then, Japan has been reconstructed on bourgeois democratic lines and industrialization and urbanization have been accelerated.

South-East Asia has had a far more varied historical experience than China, and has never been unified politically. The region is geographically fragmented, with some 60 per cent of the land area covered by forest, and numerous mountain ranges. The highest population densities are in Java and in the river valleys of the mainland: the Irrawaddy in Burma, the Menam in Thailand, and the Red River and the Mekong in Indo-China.

The earliest civilizations of South-East Asia date from the first centuries AD, and arose either in coastal areas bordering the great trade route between China and the East, or in the fertile inland riverine regions. Early migrants from the north brought with them the notion of a 'god-king', which encouraged the formation of individual states, as well as a material culture which included weaving and bronze casting. Some 2,000 years ago many distinct cultures had already emerged and these adapted to the influence of Indian and Chinese civilizations in much the same way that contemporary Europe and the Middle East were absorbing the cultural influence of Greece.

Subsequent waves of migration accelerated the process of state formation. Han Chinese pressures on minority peoples such as the Tai of south-central China forced them towards Yunnan, where many of them still live, and later down the rivers to the south. The modern state of Cambodia traces its direct descent from the kingdom of Angkor,

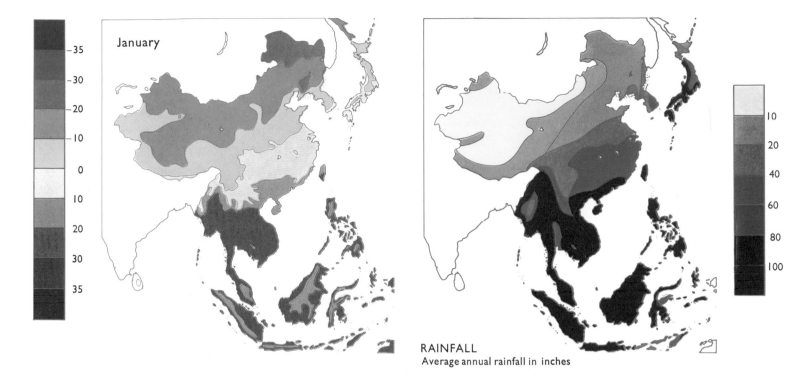

RAINFALL
Average annual rainfall in inches

conquered by the Khmer in 1431. Another movement from south China took the Annamese to the lowlands of Vietnam.

The art of South-East Asia, together with the languages and the literature, testifies both to the heterogeneity of its civilizations and to their dependence on imported ideas. The peoples of the region borrowed heavily from India, China and the Islamic world, and, in recent times, from the West. Most of South-East Asia came under Indian influence early in the Christian era and there is evidence of a wide variety of Indian cultural and religious traditions, although neither a caste system nor a priestly class ever developed. A curious form of Hinduism survives in Bali, and even today the tales of the Hindu epic, the *Mahabharata*, form the principle repertoire of Javanese shadow-puppet theatre. Java's temple-mountain Borobodur is an illustration of Mahayana Buddhist doctrines; by contrast, many of the buildings of Pagan, the Burmese empire which fell in the late 13th century, display an adherence to Theravada Buddhism which was to prevail throughout mainland South-East Asia, with the exception of Vietnam and the Malay peninsula, which is Muslim. Islam reached South-East Asia from India in the 14th century, but its impact was limited mainly to the islands.

European traders arrived in South-East Asia during the 16th century; before long they were operating throughout Indonesia and even as far as south China. Initially they came to buy spices, but by the 19th century, following the industrial revolution in Europe, they required both raw materials and markets for their own ever-increasing output. Colonization advanced rapidly—the British seized Malaya and Burma, the Dutch colonized Indonesia and finally the French conquered the whole Indo-Chinese peninsula except for Thailand. The United States inherited the Philippines from Spain after the Spanish-American war in 1898. The main colonial period ended with the Second World War, but political confusion in the area was perpetuated by American intervention on the mainland and war in Vietnam, which ended only in 1974.

Throughout South-East Asia, western words have entered the local languages and European literary, legal and political traditions have been imported. Westernization continues today: the loyalty of many South-East Asians has shifted away from the local village or traditional sovereign towards the nation state with its fixed borders and legal constitution. New demands are being made of governments once concerned more with spiritual than material ends. Economic progress, in the form of highways, improved standards of living, urbanization and industrial growth, is increasingly sought after, and the interests of the individual vie with a web of traditional custom which can tolerate no real personal freedom.

Yet throughout East and South-East Asia, with the exception of Japan, agriculture remains the dominant economy. Less than 15 per cent of the population live in towns; the rest are peasant cultivators, growing rice and other crops for subsistence and cash. With one-fourth of the world's total population, China is experiencing severe pressure on the available agricultural land, while the Indonesian government has been forced to encourage migration from Java elsewhere in the archipelago. The lowland areas of mainland South-East Asia are also facing a high rate of population increase: around 30 per 1,000 each year. The basic problem of food supplies grows ever greater, with the frequent danger of famine brought on by earthquakes and monsoon flooding.

In the post-colonial period, much may depend on the example of China's socialist development. Mao Tse-tung, the Chinese leader until his death in September 1976, encouraged a policy of 'putting the countryside first', and since 1958 China has sought to become industrialized without becoming urbanized. Continuing their ancient tradition of self-sufficiency, the Chinese hope to eradicate poverty, illiteracy, disease and corruption, while maintaining independence from foreign powers.

217

Wulumuchi, the capital, has a population of about 150,000. Uighurs make up about 80 per cent of the population of Sinkiang, the remainder being Kazakh (9 per cent), Chinese (5 per cent), and various nomadic tribes. Only a few of the Uighurs live by herding; the vast majority are farmers. It is a point of publicity with the Chinese government that the Uighurs enjoy the same civil and political status as any other citizens of the People's Republic of China, plus the right to speak their own language and practise their own religion. They speak a Turkic language and they are all Muslims.

Before 1949, the attempts of the Chinese administration to penetrate Uighur culture always met with resistance. However, since Chinese acceptance of Uighur national identity after 1949, relations have greatly improved. The area became an autonomous province in 1955, and the Uighur language is the official language of Sinkiang. Uighurs have since then been given leading posts in the administration. The Uighur language is used in the state sponsored schools; the legal system has incorporated some concepts based on Koranic teaching. The old feudal system of land tenure has been reformed and it is said that 102 mechanized farms have been set up on the 2,500,000 acres of land that have been reclaimed for agriculture since 1958.

Tibetans
pop: 4,000,000

Tibet, the highest plateau in the world, is inhabited by a variety of predominantly Mongoloid peoples. The inaccessibility of their homeland and its different climatic environments have helped produce a number of varying lifestyles. The primary distinction is between the two settled and nomadic peoples — known from ancient times as the Bopa and the Drokpa. In Kashmir, these peoples are known more commonly as Dards. Other groups, who may in fact represent the remainder of Tibet's aboriginal peoples, include the Monpa.

Throughout the country the tribes of pastoral herdsmen and the settled populations live side by side, exchanging goods by barter and trade – yak and *dzo* (half yak, half cow) products are the most important, with barley, wheat and a few vegetables. Despite the responsibilities of agriculture even the settled Tibetans are extremely mobile, moving house to suit herd movements.

Before the Chinese invasion of Tibet in 1959, polyandry, with several brothers sharing a single wife, was the most characteristic form of Tibetan marriage, although monogamy and polygyny were equally acceptable. Marriage contracts were strict. Whether married or single, women enjoyed an exceptionally independent status, often taking full responsibility for household affairs, trade and agriculture. While Tibetan society was everywhere patrilineal, traces survived of an ancient matrilineal descent system.

Radical changes have taken place since 1959, most notably in the destruction of the lamaist (Buddhist) hierarchy. In the past, large monasteries were supported by the peasant communities, and their wealth was considerable. After the invasion, many of the Buddhist leaders including their leader, the Dalai Lama, fled to India. Today Tibet is organized along communist lines, with emphasis on increasing crop yields by collectivist agriculture, and several local industries have been established.

Uighurs
pop: 4,000,000

The Uighurs are a recognized national minority living in the autonomous region of Sinkiang in the far west of China.

Chinese
pop: 850,000,000

A quarter of the world's population, the Chinese people inhabit a country divided into many distinctive geographical regions. The south of the country is sub-tropical and the north has a dry continental climate. The Yellow river and the Yangtze divide the country from east to west, and mountain ranges make further divisions. The diversity is such that the people's way of life could not be uniform. Crops and agricultural requirements vary from area to area and, among other factors, have a bearing on the lives of the people and the organization of their society.

Han Chinese Expansion

■ Chinese Empire, 100 BC

photograph:
A Chinese family

The Han majority have traditionally been the dominant group in China, but the most important feature common to all Chinese cultures is the written language. Although many mutually unintelligible spoken languages have developed from the common root, the non-phonetic script of the written language, which has remained fundamentally the same for 2,000 years, means that it is always possible to communicate through writing.

The Chinese are a notably hard-working people. Each member of China's population is required to make a contribution. Teachers, students and administrators are all called upon to do their share of manual work. It is an important part of the modern Chinese philosophy that, unlike in the past, all should understand and appreciate the life of the workers and peasants who make up the majority of China's population. To this end, on leaving school most young people begin work immediately in factories or in communes. No matter how brilliant young people may be at their studies, or however keen they may be to enter university, they are required to join the ranks of workers and peasants. All salaries are determined by the workers themselves at annual meetings, and men and women receive equal pay for equal work. Each work-place is governed by a revolutionary committee elected by fellow workers. A committee member who abuses his position can easily be removed from it by popular vote.

Although there is no shortage of workers, China has a massive food supply problem. In an effort to reduce population growth young people are urged to marry late – women at 26, men at 28. Birth control measures and abortions are free and sterilization is encouraged after the birth of a couple's second child.

China is a country which makes the maximum use of its own resources, the greatest of which is the Chinese population itself. For this reason, in contrast to the trend towards automation in the capitalist world, China maintains a fundamentally labour-intensive technology.

Manchuria

Manchus
pop: 2,420,000

Manchuria in the north-east of China is formed of forested hills, mountains, fertile plains and semi-arid grasslands. Various distinct cultural patterns have emerged in these different environments, and its rich resources have attracted migrations from east Siberia, the Mongolian plateau, the Korean peninsula and China.

Since 1954, this part of the People's Republic of China has been divided into the three provinces of Liaoning, Kirin and Heilungkiang. The Mongol inhabitants of western Manchuria became part of the Inner Mongolian autonomous region; a Yen-pien Korean autonomous district was created in eastern Kirin; and the Manchus themselves were fully integrated into China's political structure. Manchus now speak Mandarin Chinese and use Chinese written characters; the ancient Manchu language, which belongs to the Manchurian-Tungusic language group, is virtually extinct.

Manchurian tribes are mentioned in Chinese sources as early as 1000 BC. The following centuries saw constant warfare and conflicts between the settled Chinese agriculturalists and the nomadic and semi-nomadic tribesmen. In the 17th century, the tribal peoples of Manchuria were united by Nurhachi in his attempts to forge an empire. After his death, his son Abahai continued the task of expansion and adopted the name Manchu for all the people he brought together. As early as 1644, the Manchus, helped by dissident Chinese, established the Ching dynasty in China which was to last until 1912. The present day Manchus consider themselves the descendants of the 17th century invaders.

In the 19th and 20th centuries, political unrest in China caused large numbers of Chinese to emigrate to Manchuria. From depending on primitive self-sufficiency Manchuria became an important centre for international trade and attracted imperialist expansion from both Russia and Japan. Since 1949, the Communist government has brought change to Manchuria, beginning with land reforms. By 1949 all land had been redistributed among the peasants. From 1953-1957 Manchuria received the bulk of Chinese investment in the first five year plan and the area which used to be known as Manchuria is still the industrial heartland of China.

Koreans
pop: 52,832,000

The Koreans are the descendants of two peoples, the Chinese who spread along the coast of the Yellow Sea and the Mongoloid peoples who established a neolithic culture in the north of the peninsula. Since the defeat of Japan in 1945, their country has been divided between the communist north *(17,294,000)* and the capitalist south *(35,538,000)*. Society in the north has undergone radical change with the transition to collective farming, but traditional patterns continue in the southern countryside.

Less than a quarter of Korea is cultivable, and most families own only a hectare of land; little heavy machinery is employed. The main crops are rice, soya beans and maize. Houses have wooden walls and thatched roofs, with stone foundations forming a hypocaust which is used for cooking as well as heating. The floors are covered with oiled paper. Family life is communal, with little privacy for the individual. The house of the senior clan member will include an area where clan services and meetings can take place, and where ancestors are offered food and gifts on their memorial days and on special festivals.

Korea experiences sharply distinguished seasons. From December to February the temperature is rarely above freezing in the central and northern regions, and this is the time when repairs are made to tools and equipment. In March the paddy is filled and the barley and other winter crops are harvested. May brings the summer rains and in June the rice seedlings are transplanted to the flooded paddies, which must then be weeded constantly until the harvest at the end of October.

Traditional Korean culture sought to instill in all individuals a feeling for balance in dealing with the affairs of life. Courtesy, sincerity, loyalty and consensus were emphasized. Buddhism, which grew to great power during the Middle Ages, was supplanted around 1400 AD by the neo-Confucianism of the Sung Chinese philosophers. This was developed in Korea into a doctrine embracing everything from personal relationships to metaphysics, and produced a rigidly structured class system which proved a serious obstacle to modernization after the late 19th century. In North Korea

the communist leaders have opposed all traditional religions and in particular the authority of the elders.

Japanese

pop: 113,462,000

Japan consists of some 3,000 islands of which the four largest are Hokkaido, Honshu, Shikoku and Kyushu. The industrial heartland is centred on Honshu. Enjoying a temperate climate at the north-eastern end of the monsoon area, the Japanese are descended from a group known as the Yamato, which gradually asserted its supremacy over other warring tribes and clans during the first three to four centuries AD. The Yamato leaders are generally accepted as the ancestors of the Japanese imperial family.

For centuries Japan was dominated by the *shoguns,* the title under which families of generalissimos ruled Japan with unlimited power. In effect the emperor was a puppet figure until 1868, when Emperor Mutsuhito – who adopted the reign name Meiji – took control of the government and changed Japan from a little-known feudal agricultural country into a major industrial power. During the Meiji Emperor's reign the capital was transferred from Kyoto to Tokyo and Japan established an elected parliament and a constitutional monarchy. A new constitution was promulgated on November 3rd 1946, after Japan's defeat in the Second World War.

The country is poor in mineral resources and only a sixth of the land is cultivable, the rest being mountainous and barren. Nevertheless Japan ranks today as the world's third industrial power, with great economic potential. The dark side of this success lies in the country's pollution problems, which are among the world's worst.

The Japanese owe much of their culture to the Chinese, whose technology, arts and crafts came to Japan via Korea with the Buddhist expansion of the 6th century. Although Japan has been modernized and industrialized to a vast extent, the country has not become entirely westernized; it has retained its own tradi-

Street scene in Tokyo

tions of ancestral worship, honouring the family. Society is still male-oriented, but more women are entering commercial life. Paternalistic management is normal in commerce and industry, with emphasis laid on working in harmony for the common good. In religious life, Shintoism – an indigenous cult of nature and ancestor worship – and Buddhism predominate. Since the war a number of new religions have emerged, based on an amalgamation of Shinto, Buddhism, Taoism, Confucianism and Christianity.

Ainu

pop: 18,000

The Ainu live in Japan's northernmost island of Hokkaido, the Kuril Islands, and in some parts of Sakhalin. Their origins are still a matter of speculation, but their light skin and round dark eyes suggest they may be of Caucasoid stock. Archaeology indicates that the Ainu were living in north-east Hokkaido as early as 5000 BC, before the great Mongoloid expansion.

The Ainu are a deeply religious people and in the past worshipped fire, the sun, the wind, the stars, the ocean and particularly the bear. Once

they had large tribal areas, but with the expansion of Japanese government schemes the Ainu were herded into reservations and forced to eke out a living by working barren areas. Today there are less than 100 Ainu *kotan,* or villages.

The lives of the Ainu were strictly governed by a belief in the *kamui,* the invisible spirits of the natural world. Consequently every tree and plant, mountain and stream, bird and animal had its own spirit, as did the objects of the household and the fabric of their dwellings. The traditional Ainu house is the *chisei,* a thatched one-room dwelling made of grass, bullrushes and bark, with a window facing the sacred east and the door in the west wall.

Until the late 19th century, when the Japanese government prohibited the practice, all young girls were tattooed around the mouth as a sign of their marriageability. As increasing numbers of Japanese settled in Hokkaido the Ainu gradually mingled with the new society. Some anthropologists now consider that the Ainu have ceased to exist as a distinct ethnic group, and that of the 18,000 people categorized as Ainu only about 300 may be full-blooded.

221

along different lines.

Huadong commune may be a good example of the importance the Chinese place on self-reliance and diverse economic activity. Traditionally an area devoted almost exclusively to rice, the commune now also grows peanuts for the manufacture of oil, a large variety of vegetables and tropical fruits including the world-famous lichees, and has a thriving fish hatchery. The commune has experimented with winter wheat and mines much of its own coal. Even a machine-tool factory was built, which not only created employment for hundreds of workers but also made the commune more self-sufficient.

culturally productive and industrially advanced regions of imperial China.

Since then the greater transformation has been in industry, especially in the last twenty-five years. To the previous industry – coal and gold mining, small workshops, canning, and the assembly and packaging of consumer goods – have been added the large-scale manufacture of steel, ships, cement, textiles and electronic products. Hydro-electric power plants have been built, and nuclear ones are projected. Industrial production since 1952 has increased annually by over 15 per cent and the agricultural population is still

Cantonese
pop : 3,100,000

The inhabitants of Canton, capital of the sub-tropical Kwangtung province in south China, speak their own, non-Mandarin dialect. Pressure on land has at various times caused them to leave China and it is the Cantonese who form the majority of Chinese emigrants around the world.

Canton was the first Chinese port open to foreign trade. In the 16th century, British, Dutch and French traders followed Indians, Arabs and Persians who had made trading links earlier. Canton then became a centre for the production and export of porcelain, silk, embroideries, jade and ivory carvings, and fans.

In 1949, the communist revolution led by Mao Tse-tung brought a new government which sought to improve the life of the peasants (the vast majority of the population) by drastic measures of land reform. In Kwangtung, as in other provinces, hitherto landless peasant families were given land of their own. Later, households joined together to form mutual-aid teams.

Today the commune is the basic unit of Chinese society. It is responsible not only for agriculture but also for industry and trade, education, health and the militia. It is a new concept which brings together politics, the economy, social services, military affairs and culture. There is no typical commune, for all are self-governed and develop

Hakka
pop: 20,000,000

The Hakka are members of a distinct linguistic group who are supposed to have originated in north China in the Shantung peninsula and who, in the course of over 1,000 years, found their way to the south coast of China. It is thought that invasions from the north periodically drove them from their homeland. They settled in large numbers in south China and to this day have retained a certain distinct identity in terms of language, costume and some customs. Hakka are settled agriculturalists, known for their hard work.

Hakka are found in Fukien, Chekiang and also in Kwangsi, where they constitute 60 per cent of the population. In Taiwan in 1945, before the influx of mainlanders arrived, 16 per cent of the population was descended from Hakka stock. They are also a sizeable minority in Hong Kong.

Taiwanese
pop: 16,453,000

An island 120 miles off the south-eastern coast of China, Taiwan deserves the name Ilha Formosa (beautiful island) given to it by Portuguese merchants almost 400 years ago. It has high green mountains, and richly fertile plains which are amongst the world's most densely populated regions. By the end of the 19th century Taiwan had been made into one of the most agri-

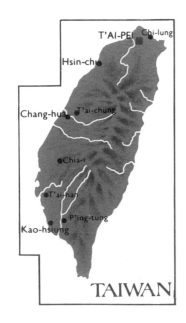

declining.

Most of Taiwan's population are Chinese, speaking seven major Chinese languages. They are composed of two groups: a sizeable number of Mandarin-speaking refugees who came from all parts of China after the communist revolution in 1949; and descendants of immigrants of the 16th to 19th centuries from a number of mainland provinces. There are four major aboriginal groups numbering about 250,000: the Ami, Atayal, Apayao and Paiwan. All are descendants of a number of peoples who came to Taiwan from Malaya and Polynesia, and have distinctive

languages with several dialects. They are partly autonomous, with an agricultural economy based on rice, corn and tropical roots. This is supplemented by hunting, rearing livestock, trade with the lowlands and a craft industry aimed at tourists. Settlements are of hamlet size, integrated by marriage and kinship ties.

Taiwan is controlled by remnants of the Chinese Nationalist Party, which fled to Taiwan after its defeat in the revolution. There are elections for district, county, municipal and provincial chiefs and assemblies, but the election issues are parochial and government is repressive. The

basis of political organization and power locally is embedded in farmers' associations, clan or surname associations, religious and other public works committees, cliques of bureaucrats and businessmen.

Tens of thousands of young Taiwanese men and women have climbed the educational ladder out of the island altogether and moved to the United States and Japan. Many of them have then voiced their criticisms of Taiwan's political régime and formed organizations to campaign for an independent Taiwanese nation. The People's Republic, however, continues to regard Taiwan as part of China.

Ploughing a rice
paddy, Canton

China, Macao, Hong Kong
Boat People

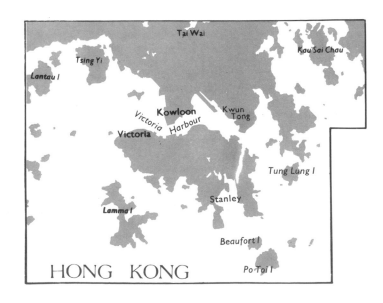

Macao
pop: 255,000

The importance of the tiny Portuguese province of Macao has for centuries far outweighed its size of six square miles. As early as 1557 Macao became established as the Portuguese base of the Far East and it was through Macao that the West was introduced to and acquired an appetite for many Chinese products, such as tea, porcelain, silk and rhubarb.

The region of China surrounding Macao is partly mountainous, partly low-lying; the hills are almost completely barren, the low ground fertile though prone to flooding. Macao itself has for years been devoid of agriculture since all cultivable land is used for building. All foods other than fish have to be imported, mostly from China. During the 19th century, economic hardship in China drove many people off the land and through Macao. A large number remained and took up service trades connected with the port. In the middle of the 20th century the major influx of immigrants arrived as a result of the political upheaval on the mainland. Today Macao is a predominantly Chinese community with 245,000 Chinese and about 8,000 Portuguese. With so much available labour, industries, notably clothing, have flourished. Trade in gold, and gold smuggling, are also important. In addition, Macao earns a considerable income from the large number of tourists, particularly from Hong Kong, who find its comparative peace and ever-open casinos a constant attraction.

Boat People
pop: 11,000

The junks and sampans which pack the harbour of Hong Kong are owned and manned almost exclusively by Chinese Boat People. For those who live on board, their home is also their main capital investment. There are 5-6,000 fishing vessels, but only in the larger boats – some of which stay at sea for two weeks at a time and require 30 or more able-bodied hands, both men and women – is it necessary to employ non-family members to complete the crew. Most frequently, the father is the captain, the family is the crew.

On the larger junks, the men of the family are expected to stay as crewmen. Intermarriage with landspeople is rare and when a man takes a wife she becomes a crew member, and their young children learn to help with fishing operations as soon as they are strong enough. Smaller boats usually house a married couple and their unmarried children. Women work harder than men; for not only do they take charge of cooking and cleaning, washing and looking after the children, they also help with the fishing.

Many fishing villages appear to have been founded by Boat People. If the fisherman prospered, they came ashore and built a temple. When landsmen came to settle they did so because they could make a living by providing services to the Boat People. Beyond these economic ties landsmen and Boat People have little in common.

Hong Kong
pop: 4,497,000

The Crown Colony of Hong Kong comprises the island of Hong Kong, the peninsula of Kowloon, both ceded to the British in the 19th century, and the New Territories on lease from China until 1995. The vast majority of the population are Chinese, highly concentrated in one or another of the huge conurbations which now stretch the full distance along the northern shore of Hong Kong island and cover virtually the whole of the

Junks in Hong Kong harbour

Kowloon peninsula. There are minorities of Britons, Americans, Indians, Bangalees and many other nationalities.

Until the late 1940s most of the Chinese immigrants came from the neighbouring and relatively accessible parts of Kwangtung, or from Canton, the capital city. Since then Hong Kong's dramatic growth in population has been due more to immigration than to natural increase, spectacular though the latter has been in the 20th century.

The accession of the People's Government in China in 1949 brought great changes to Hong Kong, not least the closing of the border with the mainland. As a result, by the 1970s, more than half the population had actually been born in the Colony and most have never visited their ancestral homes in China.

The revolution also brought an influx of Nationalist army refugees, private individuals, businessmen with their capital and sometimes their workers too. Other Chinese languages, especially Mandarin (the national language used in all schools in China), and the Shanghai dialect were heard increasingly in the streets.

One of the first acts of the new government in Peking was to curtail international trade sharply. Virtually overnight, the entrepôt business which had created Hong Kong and maintained it for more than a century was destroyed. Yet almost immediately Hong Kong was back in business and trading – but this time in its own products. The next 25 years witnessed an industrial revolution. Hong Kong now exports its own manufactured goods – glassware, ships, textiles, electronic goods, cameras, watches, wigs, plastic products, toys, textiles, handbags, shoes and machinery – to all parts of the globe, and in the whole of Asia its standard of living is second only to that of Japan. In terms of diet, it is one of the highest in the world.

Primary school education is now universal; some 2,000,000 people have been re-housed; there is a cheap and efficient public transport system; excellent telephone service and medical system. Side by side with these achievements are continuing corruption, prostitution, child labour, drug addiction and the lack of an elected government.

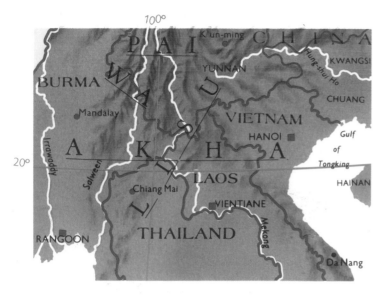

photograph:
A Yao village in Laos

Pai

pop: 700,000

The Pai – pronounced *bai* – are the largest concentrated minority group in the province of Yunnan in south-west China. The majority live in the Tali Pai autonomous ch'ou (a ch'ou is smaller than a province but larger than a county). A lake plateau over 7,000 feet above sea level, the Tali plain has a warm climate with ample, reliable rainfall, and is especially suitable for rice cultivation, which constitutes the principal occupation of the Pai.

Most other national minorities in south-western China have lived until recently by slash-and-burn agriculture and hunting. That the Pai are close to the Han Chinese in their preference for rice cultivation has undoubtedly contributed to reasonably harmonious relations, despite a period of massive Han Chinese immigration. The basic lifestyle of the two nationalities was sufficiently similar to allow close contact and intermarriage. In spite of this the Pai have retained distinct cultural attributes, which are most conspicuous in their language, religious beliefs, marriage customs and dress.

Until the transformation of social institutions under the communist government, Pai marriages were arranged, with the help of a marriage broker, for girls at about 17 years and boys at about 20. The parties to the marriage did not usually meet beforehand. Pai women traditionally enjoyed a higher status in the family than their Han Chinese counterparts. They were not subjected to foot-binding and never suffered from a greater value being placed on male children.

Since 1950, when communist troops entered Tali, the Chinese have promoted a policy of autonomous government for recognized national minorities within the People's Republic. Nonetheless, the Pai have experienced a socialist transformation and the movement to set up the people's communes. The spread of education, particularly literacy in Chinese (since Pai is not a written language); the improvement in communications through the mass media; and the opportunity for travel and work elsewhere will all contribute to the integration of the Pai with the Chinese.

Wa

pop: 400,000

The Wa inhabit a wide region of highland savanna in the border zone between Burma and China; they speak a Mon-Khmer language. The densely populated areas where they live in fortified villages of 200-400 houses are characterized by continual warfare.

The main crops grown are maize, buckwheat and beans on the upper mountain slopes, and rice on the lower. However, difficult physical conditions make famine a frequent occurrence. Opium is cultivated in exhausted soils where staple crops will not grow. Since the opium trade has always been controlled by Shan and Panthay Muslim merchants, it has been a source of economic indebtedness rather than profit.

Headhunting is a regular part of the agricultural year. A captured head is transformed into a kind of pseudo-ancestor of the captor and as such is considered able to increase the fertility of the crops. Heads are usually taken from within Wa country as they are apparently ritually powerful only if taken from groups within the same economic sphere.

The Wa have their own blacksmiths and make their own tools as well as guns, bullets and powder. They import salt, cattle, which are sometimes stolen, and some rice from the lowlands.

Endemic warfare and economic crises, however, mean that the Wa's future survival depends on a considerable transformation of their conditions and a more advantageous integration into the larger regional economy.

Lisu

pop: 500,000

Slash-and-burn cultivators of dry hill rice, the Lisu live in mountain villages widely scattered over south-west China, Burma and Thailand. They speak a Tibeto-Burman language and are organized into a number of patrilineal clans.

years or so. A wide variety of crops are grown, including the tobacco which all Akha, however young, smoke constantly. The most valuable product is raw opium. Domestic animals roam free and cattle, buffalo and horses are herded for occasional trading.

The Akha shun contact with the national majorities and remain relatively isolated in self-governing communities. Their appearance is distinctive: the women wear elaborate head dresses, breastbands and leggings decorated with silver coins and beads; the men wear their hair short with a long strand at the back, said to prevent evil spirits entering their heads.

Yao
pop: 1,000,000

About three-quarters of all Yao speakers live in China, mostly in the southern provinces. The remainder are scattered through northern Vietnam (about 180,000), Laos (about 5,000), and Thailand (about 16,000). A few hundred live in the Shan state of Burma. This population distribution represents many centuries of southwards migration due partly to a desire to escape the old imperial Chinese administration, and partly to the search for new land.

Yao villages are usually found in the hills. In Thailand, the villages average around 15 households, but in China settlements of over 500 houses have been reported. Chopping down and burning areas of the forest outside villages, the Yao plant clearings with dry hill rice to meet their subsistence needs, and other crops – opium, maize, cotton, tobacco and vegetables – either for sale or for their own use.

The basic unit of Yao society is the extended family. Most Yao houses have several rooms where the individual family groups sleep, but all members share a large common hearth and eat together. The head of the household is usually the eldest male and his authority over household members is absolute so long as they remain under his roof. The Yao worship many gods and spirits, and all the ancestors of lineage members.

They worship a multitude of ancestral and other spirits.

The Lisu build wooden houses directly on the ground or bamboo houses raised on stilts. Roofs are thatched with grass. Inside, the fireplace in the main room is the social centre of the house. The household's ritual centre is an altar to the ancestral spirits on the wall opposite the door.

Akha
pop: 120,000

The Akha have spread from their ancient homelands in Tibet to China's inhospitable Yunnan district and into Burma, Laos, Thailand and Vietnam. Wherever they go they take their own language, customs, music and traditions.

The bamboo and thatch villages are built and maintained in accordance with many rituals to placate the capricious spirits. A new entrance gate is built each year, with carved wooden birds to give warning of evil spirits and fertility figures to ensure many children. The shaman, *tumo,* mediates with the village guardian spirit, *Ioka,* and officiates over the many ceremonies to celebrate the rice crop and honour the ancestors.

As the Akha practise slash-and-burn cultivation the village has to be moved every five

Distribution of Yao

Andaman Islands
pop: 630

It is not known for certain where the Andaman Islanders come from. Only two peoples share their physical features – very dark skin, tightly curled hair and unusually small stature: the Semang of the Malay peninsula, and the Aeta of the northern Philippines. These scattered peoples are the last of the Negritos who once inhabited many parts of South-East Asia.

Having lived in complete isolation for thousands of years, the Andaman Islanders have developed several different cultures and languages. All, however, are hunters and gatherers, living off the resources of forest and sea. Two tribes predominate today, the Jarawa in the interior of South Andaman and the Onga of Little Andaman.

The Andaman Islanders are among the very few peoples of the world who do not make fire themselves – they rely instead on forest fires created by lightning during the frequent tropical storms. Domestic fires are carefully tended for cooking and for frightening away the evil spirits of the forest. The islanders live in large com-munal beehive huts of woven palm leaves; these huts are the centre of daily ceremonial life for several families.

Burmese
pop: 31,501,000

Formerly a province of British India, Burma became independent in 1948. The majority Burmans (22,650,000) have since faced both civil war and insurrection by left wing groups and ethnic minorities. Many of these struggles are a legacy of the past, when the Burmans subdued neighbouring hill tribes and were themselves invaded by Shan, Tai and Chinese.

Although the Burmans are the political, economic and religious leaders of Burma, they now occupy less than half of the country. This is a result of their preference for wet rice cultivation in the arable flood plains of the Irrawaddy and Chindwin rivers, and their avoidance of the hill areas where shifting cultivation is practised.

Burman farmers live in villages clustered along thoroughfares or on high land. The whole family, even the aged, goes out into the fields to work each day. Houses are built entirely of wood and usually have only one room. The mats for sleeping are therefore stacked away during the day. Food is prepared and eaten on the floor and it is considered grossly impolite not to remove footwear on entering a home. Almost all houses have a statue of Buddha (the Burmans are Theravada Buddhists) alongside shrines for the *nats*, or spirits.

Burmese folk Buddhism is concerned to help people find the 'golden road' to happiness, in other words the best and wisest way to live. The splendour and opulence of many religious buildings contrasts sharply with the simple possessions of the peasant farmers. Some pagodas are masterpieces of classical Burmese architecture.

Chin
pop: 400,000

The Chin hill people live in a pan-shaped area of Burma, south of Mawlaik, including the Arakan Yoma. Peoples of the same southern Mongoloid group in Assam and Bangladesh are known as Kuki. Mainly hunter-gatherers, they also keep domestic animals and grow some hill rice, maize and millet. Spices, vegetables and tobacco are grown in jungle clearings.

Villages usually consist of one clan divided into several lineages; descent is patrilineal. The northern Chin have an elaborate material culture, manufacturing pottery, mats and iron goods for trade; their society is stratified. The southern Chin culture is based on subsistence, with limited trade; they have no social stratification.

Kachin
pop: 550,000

The Kachin are hill peoples who live to the north-east of Burma, along the Chinese and Indian frontiers. They have their own state and have spilled over into the Mang-shih plains in China, and into eastern Assam. In Assam they are known as the Singpho, and in China as the Chingp'a, descendants of hill bandits. They speak their own Tibeto-

Burman language.

The various Kachin groups distinguish their origins and status by the great variations in their customs and culture, costume and ornament. They have been much influenced by their Shan neighbours, and are adherents of Buddhism as well as their own ancient beliefs. Most Kachin are shifting cultivators of rice, and grow supplementary harvests of maize, seasame, millet and tobacco. They are also expert cattlemen and hunters. Villages are often built on hills; houses are scattered, with no obvious plan apart from a good siting for defence and water supply.

Shan
pop: 2,000,000

The Shan are Tai speakers, related to the Ahom of Assam in the west, as well as to the numerous Tai of China in the north and those of Laos and Thailand in the east. The Shan are generally regarded as a hill people, although the most populated Shan areas are the low river valleys of Burma. They are able agriculturalists and cultivate many crops, including potatoes, tea, coffee and fruit, as well as rice.

The Salween river flows throughout the length of the Shan plateau and its mountain banks form a natural barrier resulting in differences of names, dialects and customs of neighbouring tribes. Consequently, the Shan have more cultural similarities with the Tai than with the Burmans. The majority of the Shan follow the conservative Theravada school of Buddhism.

Karen
pop: 2,000,000

The Karen inhabit the rugged uplands which divide Burma and Thailand and are notable amongst the hill peoples for the care with which they cultivate their lands. Most slash-and-burn cultivators move their villages every few years, but the Karen are unusually stable. They maintain the fertility of the soil by clearing their gardens according to a cyclical system. Through mixing with their lowland neighbours, they have also learnt to build terraced and irrigated fields, but dry hill rice remains their staple and they grow no cash crops. Some individuals supplement their incomes by driving elephants

for timber companies.

In Burma, many Sgaw Karen took advantage of British rule to gain education and work as teachers, pastors, doctors and minor government officials; since independence a movement for Karen autonomy has been a potent force. In Thailand, however, the Pwo Karen have remained in their hill communities. The village remains the largest political unit, normally consisting of 15-25 houses built close together and enclosed by stockade, with no main thoroughfare or central meeting place.

Houses are constructed of bamboo, thatched with grass and raised several feet off the ground by wooden supports. Each is inhabited by a married couple with their unmarried children. Marriage is monogamous and remarkably stable; young men choose their own brides but require parental permission.

The matrilineage is an important ritual unit among the Pwo Karen; members tend to build their houses close together and, if they move to other villages, must return periodically for the ritual feeding of the ancestral spirit, or *bgha*. The socio-religious leader of the village, however, inherits his position through the male line, and is responsible for dealing with the most powerful spirits on behalf of all the villagers. Together with the village elders, he also wields power in secular matters.

Padaung
pop: 30,000

The Padaung, or Kayah, are a sub-group of the Karen. Their main crop is rice, grown on the hillsides above the Salween river and in valley paddy fields. Other crops include cotton, tobacco, vegetables and fruit; the Padaung also keep cattle. They are basically Buddhists, with a strong animist tradition. Villages, some with pagodas and monasteries, are independent communities ruled by a headman and elders.

The word *padaung* means 'brass wearer', and many Padaung women still wear brass rings. Up to 24 neck rings may be worn by mature women, stretching the neck up and forward.

photograph:
Shan poppy farmer, Burma

Distribution of Tai-Speakers

Tai

pop: 62,000,000

Tai is the name of a group of languages, spoken in South-East Asia, which are as diverse as the Romance languages of Europe. The great majority of all Tai-speakers (nearly 40,000,000) live in Thailand, the next largest grouping (10,000,000) occupy parts of south and south-west China, and there are more than a million Tai-speakers in north and north-east Burma, Laos and northern Vietnam.

Tai peoples are mostly settled cultivators growing many kinds of rice in irrigated fields. They have a recognizable stratum of religious and metaphysical beliefs – for instance, in a multiple personal soul and in anthropomorphic spirts: spirits of the dead, spirits of the natural world and spirits of the political world. The last are guardian or locality spirits identified with different sections and hierarchical levels of Tai society.

Most Tai peoples have long adopted the southern form of Buddhism known as Theravada Buddhism (distinct from northern, Mahayana Buddhism found in Tibet, Mongolia and China). Whether in southern China, even after the Communist revolution, or in Burma, Laos and Thailand, Tai peasant villagers are likely to have built and rebuilt over the centuries a Buddhist temple in which the majority of their young men are temporarily ordained as Buddhist monks.

Tai society, especially at the village level, is characterized by local communities knit together by overlapping networks of exchange relationships between households, frequently focused on locality spirit cults and the village temple. Some communities cooperate in maintaining irrigation systems and in certain field tasks such as planting and harvesting rice. Tai households also raise some livestock, including cattle, water buffalo and pigs. Fishing, gathering of forest products, some hunting, and several manufacturing activities, notably basketry and weaving, are other common economic pursuits.

There are several autonomous Tai areas within China. The autonomous Tai area of Hsishuang (or Sipsong) Panna in southern Yunnan province on the Chinese border with Laos was still basically a feudal area until 1949, with peasants owing up to 70 per cent of their production to landlords. By 1955 it had the first multinational autonomous government in an area with a large minority Tai population. By 1963 some 30 per cent and by 1975 90 per cent of officials and representatives at all levels were members of the non-Chinese (non-Han) and mainly Tai minority. Land reform was carried out peaceably in 1955.

Where there were very few roads or industries in 1949, by 1975 there were copper, iron, and manganese mining industries, and some 300 mining areas managed by the autonomous area itself, or by lower level organizations such as people's communes. Consequently, there is now a sizeable sector of Tai in the Chinese working class.

Thais

pop: 43,736,000

The majority people of Thailand are related to many millions of Tai-speakers beyond their borders, including the Shan of north-east Burma, the Lao of Laos, the Tai of north-east Vietnam and

photograph:
House on the Mae Khlong
river, Thailand

the Tai and Nung people of China's Yunnan province. Other Tai speakers are to be found in Kwangsi and Kweichow. The people of north-east Thailand belong mainly to the Lao populations on the other side of the Mekong river.

The Thais share broadly the same religion, Theravada Buddhism, with neighbouring Burma and Cambodia, with which they have a history of hostile contact. Culturally they have least in common with their Malayan, Vietnamese and Han Chinese neighbours. The large Chinese-speaking minority within Thailand, however, is economically and politically integrated. By contrast, racial and cultural discrimination exists against the hill-dwelling minorities of the north and a Muslim community of over a million in the far south.

Thailand is known as the granary of South-East Asia, the largest rice exporter in the world. Until recently, 90 per cent of the population were peasant small-holders with less than 10 acres. As agriculture becomes more capital-intensive, however, and land acquires a higher exchange value, peasant cultivators have tended to lose their land, which is becoming concentrated in the hands of a wealthy élite.

Consequently there has been a significant growth of a Thai industrial and agricultural wage-earning, working class. Where formerly the mass of of the population could satisfy the bulk of their own subsistence needs, there is now a large number of unemployed or chronically underemployed workers. Trade unionism and student activism have emerged as new forces in Thailand's political affairs.

Hmong
pop: 1,600,000

The Hmong, or Meo, live traditionally in central and southern China; they speak a Meo-Yao language. At the end of the 19th century, many were driven further southwards by the majority Han Chinese, and Hmong are found today in Laos, Thailand, northern Vietnam and Burma. They have all become hill-farmers, cultivating rice by the slash-and-burn method; they also grow opium.

The Hmong lifestyle has been best preserved in Laos, where population has become concentrated in the Xieng Khouang province. The Hmong of Laos form two main dialect groups: the Green Hmong and the White Hmong. These names are based on traditional dress colours, though the White Hmong dialect is also spoken by a third group, the Striped-Sleeved Hmong.

These three groups are organized into 15 or 16 patrilineal clans, whose names and ritual observances are given in a common myth concerning the foundation of the clan. Women become members of their husbands' clans under the direct authority of the heads of the individual households.

A Hmong village may contain as many as 70-80 households, though the average seems to be around 10; a network of trails connect the villages for trade and ritual purposes. Each clan is represented by its head, who is a member of the council of elders, and the village headman acts as negotiator with the Laos authorities. Xieng Khouang province is sufficiently populated to have chiefs of districts and sub-districts as well as headmen.

Hmong men often take more than one wife, but the first is regarded as the senior. Each wife is responsible for her own children, poultry and vegetable garden. Most girls marry at the age of 14-16, and divorce is rare. The household is the basic unit of social, political and economic life.

The Hmong are constantly worried by the threat of disease and sudden death, owing to the extreme variability of temperature in the mountains and their inadequate diet. They think of themselves as constant prey to the whims of the spirit world whose fickleness the village shaman tries to control. In a trance a shaman is deemed to mediate with malevolent spirits and to divine the future. Mythology and beliefs about death are often expressed in terms of journeys. Animal sacrifice is central to the ritual of Hmong religion.

Vietnam, Laos, Cambodia
Vietnamese, Laotians, Montagnards, Cambodians, Jarai, Cham

States of Indo-China, 14th century

1. Annam
2. Champa
3. Khmer Empire

Vietnamese
pop: 47,101,000

Most of Vietnam lies in the tropical monsoon zone, except for the Hong (Red) river delta in the north. The two deltas of the Hong and the Mekong in the south are of great economic importance to the country, providing rich agricultural soils. The population – about 90 per cent of which is Annamese – is concentrated in the lowlands. The remaining 10 per cent are Tai-speakers (1,000,000), Hmong (400,000), and Tho and Nung tribesmen in the hills. There are about 800,000 Chinese, mostly in the south.

In 1954 an agreement between the communist Vietminh and the French high command divided Vietnam into two countries. American intervention in South Vietnam was followed by years of fighting before the country was unified in April 1976, under the communist government of former North Vietnam.

The French, Japanese and Americans have all left their mark on the contemporary Annamese. Their culture, however, was most deeply influenced by the Chinese, who ruled the old kingdom from 112 BC to 939 AD. It was they who gave the name of Annam to the kingdom of Dai-coviet,

which had first been formed in northern Vietnam.

Most Annamese practise a mixture of Confucianism, Taoism, and Buddhism. Some are Roman Catholics and new indigenous religions include Cao Dai (1919) and Hoa Hoa (1939). Houses usually have an altar where ritual ceremonies are held to honour dead ancestors.

Most Annamese villages are enclosed by a bamboo fence which gives some protection against bandits. The Annamese village is a self-contained community, dealing with its own internal domestic disputes and problems. In areas likely to experience flooding villages are built on stilts.

The Annamese are wet rice cultivators, using human labour with more intensity and irrigating their fields on a larger scale than elsewhere in South-East Asia. Each village has its own specialist craft, such as wood carving, weaving, basketry or lacquerwork, which is organized communally. War has altered the population map of Vietnam, but the most prosperous and powerful Annamese societies are still around the fertile deltas of the Hong (Red) river in the north and the Mekong in the south. Others, who once lived in the delta regions, now live and work among the hill tribes and grow sweet potatoes, taro and other root crops.

Laotians
pop: 455,000

Surrounded by its larger neighbours, China, Vietnam, Cambodia, Thailand and Burma, Laos is a small land-locked country. Most of the population can be described as Lao, but the official estimates distinguish four principal linguistic groups in the country: Lao-Lu or valley Lao; Lao-Tai or tribal Tai; Lao Theng or Mon-Khmer; and Lao-Soung or Meo or Man. All these are sub-divided into further mutually unintelligible dialects.

Urban areas in Laos consist of the administrative capital Vientiane, the royal capital Luang Prabang and four or five other large towns. The urban population is predominantly Lao with many Chinese, Vietnamese and Europeans.

Western influence in town life has been massive, with large numbers of foreign personnel and vast sums of money entering the country during the Vietnam War.

The majority of the population lives in the lowlands and valleys of the Mekong in the west and central region of the country. Apart from the language differences the people are also divided by variations in religion and custom. The valley communities live in villages of between 50 and 2,000 people close to roads and rivers. More than 50 per cent of the lowland people are involved in wet-rice cultivation. Hill peoples, who practise shifting cultivation, move around in smaller groupings.

Lao villages are mostly self-sufficient, although salt must usually be imported. Rice is the staple food, supplemented by vegetables, fruit and fish. Pigs, chickens and ducks are also kept. Water buffaloes are bred for ploughing and oxen for pulling carts, but neither is normally killed for food except on ceremonial or ritual occasions. Both animals are considered repositories of wealth.

The official religion is Theravada Buddhism, and every young Lao man is expected to spend at least three months as a novice or a monk. Before that he is regarded as immature. However, much of the population also practise spirit worship, recognizing a multitude of nature spirits as well as spirits of the ancestors.

Montagnards
pop: 800,000

The term Montagnards, meaning highlanders, is a relatively recent French designation for the tribal peoples who live on the plateaux of southern Vietnam and in neighbouring Laos and Cambodia. Very different from the Vietnamese who live in the river valleys and coastal plains, the Montagnards are internally differentiated by culture, social organization and language, speaking various dialects of Mon-Khmer, Meo-Yao and Malayo-Polynesian.

The Montagnards are shifting agriculturalists, using the slash-and-burn method; a few live lower down the hills and in the highland marshes where they practise irrigated rice cultivation. Staple foods of the Montagnards are rice, maize and millet, supplemented by wild and cultivated fruits, vegetables and game.

The household, with its male head, is the basic economic unit and the centre for the ritual occasions of birth, marriage and death. Each household is a part of the village group, led by a headman, with communal ownership of land and hunting rights. Several villages may combine for offensive or defensive purposes under the temporary leadership of a warlord.

Cambodians
pop: 7,887,000

In the south-west part of the peninsula, Cambodia is part of the area formerly known as Indo-China. The capital city is Phnom Penh, situated at the confluence of the Mekong, Basak and Sap rivers. Most of the urban population lives in the central lowland region.

Cambodia is a country of unique ethnic homogeneity in South-East Asia: Khmer stock make up 90 per cent of the population. There are also about 350,000 Chinese, who are the country's entrepreneurs and merchants; 90,000 Vietnamese Cham-Malays; a group of Malayo-Polynesian and Austro-Asian hill tribes numbering about 50,000 who live in the eastern highland region; about 30,000 Tai and 5,000 or so French. Since 1975, after the overthrow of the pro-American régime, the country has been controlled by the communist Khmer Rouge.

The name Khmer is believed to be a Chinese transcription of the word *bhnam,* meaning mountain. However, their land is mainly flat, and the Khmer have traditionally lived beside the main waterways of the Mekong and the Tonle Sap. Although the soil of Cambodia is not very fertile, one-third of the plains are flooded each year during the rainy season, allowing sufficient rice cultivation to feed the peasant population.

Most Khmer live in villages of one-storey houses, built on posts with the floor some six feet above the ground. The walls are made of wood, bamboo or palm leaves, with shingle or thatch roofs. The household unit is generally a nuclear family of parents and their children, perhaps with one relative. Formerly, villages might disperse within a few years, as one by one each family moved to another community. This was facilitated by the bilateral descent system, which maintained links of kinship and property among the many different villages.

Khmer society was stratified into six categories – royalty, Brahmans, Buddhist monks, officials, commoners and slaves – with a certain mobility between the classes. Each class had its own ritual practice, some rituals concerning only a small group of people: those connected with childbirth, for example, or associated with local spirits or cultivation, were usually attended only by close relatives.

The Khmer followed Theravada Buddhism, celebrating all the anniversaries of the Bhudda's birth, enlightenment and death, his first sermon, the anniversary of the four miracles the beginning and end of the rainy retreat, and the presentation of robes to monks. Villages and hamlets were grouped into districts, each supporting a monastery, which was the centre of Khmer community life. An elected committee of *achars,* men well-versed in ritual traditions and dogma, was entrusted to handle community and monastery funds.

Since the communist revolution of 1975, the monasteries are no longer educational centres, as compulsory primary education in secular schools has been introduced. As with so many other areas of life in Cambodia it is difficult to ascertain in full the impact of the new government; but there can be little doubt that Buddhism is still a powerful force in Khmer society.

Jarai
pop: 200,000

The Jarai inhabit the Dar Lac plateau in the southern part of the central highlands of Vietnam; their territory overlaps into parts of north-eastern Cambodia. The Jarai are the largest – after the Rhadé – of the Cham sub-groups living in the highlands of Vietnam. Although the Jarai have a capital at Pleiku, they are nearly all farmers.

The Jarai are one of the largest matrilineal groups in South-East Asia, but are unlike the others in that they are upland shifting cultivators who have only recently begun to practise wet rice farming. Work is shared between sexes, but each has defined tasks.

The Jarai live in villages of longhouses built along a north-south axis on hardwood stilts or piles of logs, usually on a ridge or hill with access to a river or stream. Each house has its own garden, divided into family units. Most villages, perhaps with as many as 60 longhouses, consist of several matrilineages. Others, no bigger than a hamlet, comprise a single matrilineage. The Jarai worship a pantheon of spirits, some of which are ancestral spirits, while others are spirits of the forest, the mountains, rivers and other water places.

Cham
pop: 20,000

The Cham live in villages in the foothills of the Vietnamese highlands and along the banks of the Mekong river in Cambodia. A widely scattered people, the Cham are the remnants of the Champa civilization which was one of the earliest Hindu-influenced states of Indo-China. Their descent system is matrilineal.

Today most of the Cham in Cambodia are Muslims, and their mosques resemble Khmer temples. They have assimilated with Malays, and their culture is distinct from that of the Buddhist Khmers in Cambodia.

The Cham of Vietnam practise a religion in which both Hindu and animist elements are recognisable. The farmers in particular are devotees of the rice goddess who ensures the fertility of their crops. Spirit and ancestor worship are also prevalent. Cham villages are devoid of vegetation, for it is feared that trees can exert a harmful influence on dwellings. Today many of the Vietnamese Cham have become fully Vietnamese, and even those remaining identifiably Cham show a strong Vietnamese influence.

Philippines
Filipinos, Isneg, Ifugao, Kalinga, Moros, Tasaday

photograph:
Young Tasaday boy,
Mindanao

Filipinos
pop: 43,705,000

Inhabiting 26 of the 7,000 Philippine islands the Filipinos have many racial and linguistic ties with the populations of Indonesia and Malaysia, and are Mongoloid in origin. Although lowland Filipinos, who form the great majority of the population, speak several Malayo-Polynesian languages, they share a basically common culture influenced by a long period of Spanish rule.

The Filipinos are a people of extreme diversity. The sophisticated urban élite of Manila, living in splendour and luxury reminiscent of the 19th century European aristocracy, have little in common with the subsistence farmers of the countryside apart from devout Roman Catholicism and certain basic social values. In the southern islands, moreover, there is an important Muslim minority, while many of the mountain people of the northern Philippines have scarcely been touched by either Christianity or Islam. Less than a generation ago several were headhunters with an ideology and life-style totally different from that of the lowland peasantry.

In the towns and villages of the open plains, Filipino Christian culture is relatively uniform from north to south, although members of each language group have stereo-types for the other groups. Thus the Ilocanos are believed to be hard-working, the Tagalogs intensely nationalistic and the Visayans prone to open displays of affluence.

The traditional pattern of social organization has the nuclear family as a basic unit within a larger family group. In the large extended family the Filipino is related equally to his father's and to his mother's kinsmen. There is no clan organization and no group in which descent is solely matrilineal or patrilineal.

Status among Filipinos is mainly dependent on wealth, which is still largely synonymous with ownership of land, for the cultivation of rice, maize, sugar cane and tobacco supports about 60 per cent of the population. The expansion of the cultivated area has so far kept pace with population growth, and the Philippines are one of the few Asian countries where there is, as yet, no serious overcrowding. Manufacturing now generates nearly 20 per cent of the national income.

Isneg
pop: 1,000

The Isneg of the northernmost Cordillera mountain range practise a shifting, slash-and-burn economy based on dry rice, which they supplement by vegetables introduced by traders. They are neither weavers nor potters and have to barter for the ceramic jars necessary for a marriage settlement. Families are widely scattered, but will co-operate over certain activities.

Women have a high social and economic importance: although men predominate in political affairs, a number of women hold positions of considerable influence. New ideas and methods have been accommodated alongside traditional values, but so far physical isolation and an inhospitable climate have protected the Isneg from government attempts to develop their territory.

Ifugao
pop: 70,000

The Ifugao of north Luzon still use the extensive and skilfully constructed rice terraces built by their ancestors long ago. The walls reach 50 feet in height and irrigation is by an elaborate system of pipes and ducts. The Ifugao also practise slash-and-burn cultivation on the hill-sides.

Villages have no headmen, and households rarely combine for joint activities. Disagreements are settled by fines or, if more serious, by revenge killings. Headhunting is no longer practised but blood feuds are frequent and will lie dormant until the offended kin are strong enough to attack.

Many young people have now received education from state and missionary schools, and a system of elected governments has been established. Other western influences can be seen as western clothes replace the traditional striped cloths, ritual carvers export their work and villagers leave to become wage earners.

Kalinga
pop: 40,000

The Kalinga's reputation for being fierce and dangerous warriors has kept them remarkably isolated from other tribesmen in the highlands of Luzon. They occupy an area of hills, steep mountain sides and deep canyons watered by rapid streams. Here some of the Kalinga have hewn terraced slopes for rice paddies, although most still practise slash-and-burn cultivation. Animal husbandry, the preparation of alcoholic beverages from sugar cane, weaving, pottery and the manufacture of iron implements for war and commerce have been Kalinga activities for centuries.

In the rugged north, villages are normally small, with 6-30 houses, but in the broader valleys to the south villages of 250 houses are not uncommon. The Kalinga's basic social unit is composed of brothers, sisters and their descendants down to great-grandchildren; spouses are included in the group. Members are obliged to support each other in all disputes and conflicts, so villages may suddenly split into warring factions. Men can gain authority by acting as intermediaries in disputes, and by committing violent acts to intimidate rivals.

The Kalinga believe in a single creator god to whom they appeal directly through verbal invocations. Women act as mediators between humans and the world of spirits. Much of the medium's task is the diagnosis and curing of disease.

Moros
pop: 1,775,000

The word Moro was first used by the Spaniards in the 16th century to describe the Filipino Muslims. Today it is applied to nine distinct ethno-linguistic groups scattered throughout the Philippines, all of whom practise Islam. The five largest are the Maguindanao, the Maranao, the Tausug, the Samal and the Yakan. The Tausug were the first to be converted and consequently consider themselves superior to other Moros. Political power is exercised by sultans.

The sea-faring Tausug and Samal live in villages built on stilts over the sea or among mangrove swamps. The Manguindanao cultivate rice, corn and tobacco; the Maranao grow rice and herd carabuo water buffalo; the Yakan, who formerly grew rice, now cultivate fruit. All Moros are known for their multi-coloured weaving and brightly painted boats.

Tasaday
pop: 25

The Tasaday, who were first contacted in 1971, may have been isolated in the forest of the Tiruray highlands, south Mindanao, for more than 500 years. There are few signs that they have ever numbered more than 30. They use stone tools, and live mostly in cave dwellings reached by vine ropes, although some have now built wooden platforms and shelters.

They have no leader. Sex roles are strongly defined, the men gathering food and the women looking after the children. Diet consists of wild yams and some 200 species of wild flowers and plants; grubs, lizards, snakes, crabs and other small animals are also eaten. The Tasaday seem to have no ceremonies associated with birth or marriage. Their language is similar to that of the nearby Blit.

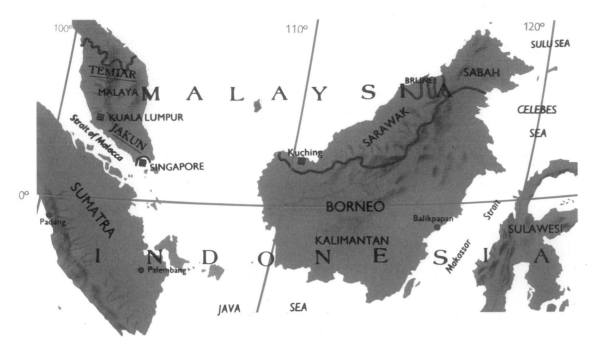

Malays

pop: 12,395,000

The federation of Malaysia is composed of two regions: West Malaysia on the Malay peninsula and East Malaysia made up of Sabah and Sarawak on the island of Borneo. Its establishment as a political entity in 1963 represents the unification of territories formerly under British rule.

Malaysia remains a member of the Commonwealth of Nations and is a federal constitutional democracy. As the world's largest producer of tin it is one of the richest countries of the area. The population is predominantly Malay, with aboriginal, Chinese, Indian and Pakistani minorities.

The first Malays may have been the proto-Malays, who originally came from south China; with some admixture of coastal Chinese and Indians these formed the modern deutero-Malay.

Islam was substantially modified by the time it reached Malaya and has assimilated animistic beliefs which existed before its arrival. Nonetheless, the religion proved of crucial importance in the development of Malay society and attitudes, which involve monotheism, prayer, fasting, payment of tithes, pilgrimages to Mecca, and taboos on eating pork and drinking spirits. Ceremonies and feasts are held to celebrate events in the rice-growing year, the Muslim calendar and stages of the life-cycle.

The spheres of loyalty for a Malay are his family, relatives and other Malays. Many members of the same village will in fact be relatives or connected by marriage, so that the village constitutes a kind of extended family. Villagers claim that they are all of the same social class, as 'all Muslims are brothers', and respect is due to those with special knowledge, experience or wisdom, rather than those with wealth.

Women take no part in Malay ceremonials; they do all the household chores and a great deal of hard agricultural work, and can be divorced by their husbands without consent. Yet women have considerable power in the household, hold property rights and exercise decisive influence over economic affairs.

Much of the peninsula is now a landscape of tin-mines, rubber trees, small towns and coconut plantations, but despite urbanization, the Malays are still overwhelmingly rural, with villages strung out along river valleys. They grow rice for subsistence and, on the whole, rely on rubber or fish for cash. However, differences in wealth are increasing and the relatively stable village life is being changed by the switch to a money economy.

Temiar

pop: 5,000

The Temiar, known to the Malays as Sakai, live along the rivers in the northernmost interior of Malaya. Some Temiar women have married Malays, but hill Temiar have had little contact with the outside world. In the past all contact with neighbours was conducted by hereditary officers, whose powers have now been assumed by government-appointed headmen.

Nuclear families own the cultivation and gathering rights over a specific area of land; hill rice, millet, maize and pumpkins are grown to supplement fruit and roots from the jungle. Most Temiar live in groups of up to 60 people, in communal longhouses raised some 20 feet from the ground. Sleeping compartments for each family lead off from a central corridor.

Jakun

pop: 14,000

The Jakun are the aboriginal Malays, who probably came from across the Straits of Malacca, and may be related to the Sakai of Sumatra. The Jakun think of themselves as belonging to sub-groups such

as the Orang Darat (land people) or Orang Laut (sea gypsies). Living on the upper reaches of rivers in Pahang, Selangor and Johor, the Jakun comprise about 30 per cent of all the Malayan aborigines.

Traditionally the Jakun are hunter-gatherers, but in some areas they have taken to cultivating rice or manioc root. In many regions they even follow a Malay way of life as rubber planters and cattlemen. Jakun live in split-bamboo and planking houses raised high on stilts, which can easily be dismantled to escape strangers, disease or misfortune.

Singapore
pop: 2,297,000

Singapore Island and 50 other islets make up the republic of Singapore, an independent city state founded in 1819. Dominating the Strait of Malacca, which leads from the Indian Ocean to the South China Sea, it is the largest port in South-East Asia and the fourth largest port in the world.

Some 70 per cent of the land is less than 50 feet above sea level and, although much of the soil is extremely infertile a quarter of the total area is devoted to agriculture. Most of the 20,000 registered farms produce vegetables, fruit and livestock for the local markets. Rubber and coconuts are also cultivated.

The four official languages, namely Chinese, English, Malay and Tamil—reflect the diverse nature of Singapore's population. Chinese form 76 per cent, Malays 15 per cent and Indians 7 per cent. Within these groups, however, are further sub-divisions of peoples speaking mutually incomprehensible dialects. Singapore's economy is run by an urban population engaged in trade, finance and industry, and 20 per cent of the total gross domestic product comes from the manufacturing sector.

Bajau
pop: 50,000

The Bajau are found throughout the vast area of sea and islands stretching more than 4,000 miles from Burma to New Guinea. Traditionally the pirates and 'sea gypsies' of the region, they live on boat clusters or in villages of stilt houses built over marshes or estuaries. The men wear colourful head-dresses of handwoven cloth, each group having its own characteristic cloth patterns. Their sturdy sea-going vessels, or *praus*, are readily distinguishable amongst the shipping of the archipelago.

Though they can no longer remember their place of origin, or come together from their widely separated settlements, the Bajau still share a common language, an old form of Malay. Their society has always been egalitarian, with no slave class, and they have avoided becoming vassals of other kingdoms. As Muslims the Bajau are bound by both Islamic *shari'ah* and *adat* customary law.

Not all Bajau earn their living at sea. Many have adapted to cultivation, while others are now labourers on rubber estates and coconut plantations, or work as loggers for timber companies.

Bajau boats in the Sulu Sea, Philippines

Borneo
Dayak, Dusun, Iban

Borneo
pop: 6,000,000

The third largest island in the world, Borneo is now divided between Malaysia, Indonesia and Brunei. The southern part, called Kalimantan, forms 73 per cent of the total area of the island and belongs to Indonesia. In the north, Sabah and Sarawak are part of the federation of Malaysia. Brunei, also on the north coast, is a British protectorate.

In Kalimantan (4,100,000), which is divided into four provinces, there is a division of peoples between the coasts and the inland areas. Chinese and Muslim Malays form the majority of the population in the coastal regions, while in the interior there live a variety of Dayak tribes practising shifting agriculture. On the southern shore there are tin deposits; rubber and coffee are cultivated as cash crops.

In the north, Sabah (660,000) and Sarawak (980,000) are characterized by a multitude of ethnic groups. It is estimated that without counting minor tribal peoples there are 25 different peoples in Sarawak and 26 in Sabah. In Sabah, 30 per cent of the population are Dusun, 22 per cent Chinese, 10 per cent Bajau, and 5 per cent Muruts. Other indigenous peoples make up about 20 per cent of the population. The Bajau are divided into the settled cultivators of the north coast, and the seafarers of the east coast; most of them are Muslims. The remainder of the population are Malays, Indonesians, Filipinos, Indians, Pakistanis, Europeans and Eurasians.

Chinese – over half of whom are Hakka speakers – form a third of all Sarawak's population. The Iban or Sea Dayak form the largest indigenous group; they speak Austronesian languages, and practise shifting cultivation. Malays form less than 20 per cent of the population and are mostly indigenous peoples who adopted Islam and the Malay way of life about 500 years ago. The Land Dayaks, less than 10 per cent, speak five dialects and practise a traditional religion. The Melanaus, most of whom are Muslims, comprise about 5 per cent. The heaviest concentration of population is in the south-west.

Although only a tiny proportion of the land in Sabah and Sarawak is under cultivation, most of the population depend on agriculture for their livelihood. Others are engaged in forestry, fishing and mining. In economic terms these territories lag behind West Malaysia. Brunei (136,000), however, has an economy based on oil production, giving it one of the highest standards of living in South-East Asia. This Islamic sultanate is divided in two geographically by Sarawak.

Dayak
pop: 362,000

The term Dayak – Malay for 'up-country' – describes the groups of non-Muslim peoples on the island of Borneo. It was first used as a derogatory term by Dutch and British settlers but is now being adopted by the people themselves.

Dayak groups trace their origins and cultural identities from such dispersed areas outside Borneo as Sumatra and mainland South-East Asia. Their beliefs, economies, social structures and languages are quite different. They now span many political borders; the Iban, Land Dayak, Karen and Kenyah are all found in both Sarawak and Kalimantan. They live under widely differing conditions: the sago-producing Melanau of Sarawak inhabit the swampy coastal belt where the majority of the Malay fishing community live, while the Punan, Bukitan, Ukit and Bukat are nomadic hunters in the remote jungle regions. Other groups include the Dusun, Kelabit, Murut, Maloh and Ma'anyan. Languages are Malayo-Polynesian.

Most groups live in longhouses, a collection of family apartments raised on stilts and reached by a log ladder. Government policy has tried to encourage single dwellings and stop the practice of slash-and-burn cultivation but many Dayak still grow their hill (or swamp) rice by that method. Protein is obtained from fish and wild game, killed with a blowpipe. The variability in price of their main cash crop, rubber, has meant an increasing migration away from the villages to seek work in logging, construction or the oilfields.

Young people now take advantage of the state and missionary schools and sometimes go into business in the towns. Hospitals and clinics have brought western medicine to the Dayak; they often operate alongside the shamans. The village headmen and leaders have the task of mediating between the traditional life of the village and the government's policies.

Many Dayak believe in the spiritual properties of the paddy field and the significance of dreams and bird omens. The introduction of Christianity, however, has brought significant modifications to the elaborate marriage and death rituals, and feasting of the ancestor spirits. Headhunting continued until recently but, along with many other aspects of traditional Dayak life, is gradually dying out. The Dayak groups are losing their separate identities and in time will probably merge with one another.

Dusun
pop: 200,000

The Dusun of northern Borneo include several linguistically-related farming groups, including the Kiau, the Rungus, the Tegas, the Ranau and the Tambunan. As the Dusun of the coastal regions have intermarried extensively with the Malays, the range of physical types is varied.

On the flat coastal plains of western Sabah, the Dusun practise a form of irrigated wet rice cultivation using buffaloes and ploughs. Inland they grow dry hill rice, using the slash-and-burn method. Dusun often trade with the coastal Bajau, exchanging agricultural produce for seafood. Domestic animals such as pigs and chickens are kept for ritual sacrifice, and some are sold or bartered. Cattle and buffaloes are indices of wealth.

The cultural diversity of the Dusun is evident in a wide range of settlement patterns and dwellings. The inland villages usually consist of longhouses on stilts. Towards the coast separate family houses are more common, normally clustered into hamlets. All Dusun groups reckon their kinship relations bilaterally through both males and females. The domestic family is the basic social and economic unit, farming its own lands, producing for its own needs and supplying the bridewealth when the men marry.

The Muslim Dusun of the coast and the urbanized Christian Dusun still mix with the Dusun of the interior where many tribesmen follow the traditional way of life, although teeth filing and headhunting are no longer practised. Of particular significance are the hosts of malevolent spirits (*rogon* or *ragun*), who delight in causing human suffering and sickness. Male and female spirit mediums summon familiars and guardian spirits to assist in recovering the lost souls of sick people.

Iban
pop : 260,000

The Iban, once known as the Sea Dayak, mostly inhabit the interior upland areas of Sarawak and west Kalimantan, Borneo. According to Iban folklore, their origins can be traced from as far as the Middle East and Sumatra. Within Borneo the most important migration route followed the great Kapuas river in Kalimantan; this route accounts for the broad settlement of Iban culture in Borneo. Other Dayak groups including the Kantu, Desa and Katungau still live in the Kapuas region and show strong cultural affinities with the Iban.

Most Iban live in longhouses set on ironwood posts, containing several family apartments, or *bilek*. Located usually on a river bank, the longhouse is entered by climbing a narrow, notched log. Up to 400 people may live together, but each separate *bilek* family has a strong sense of independence and individuality, and marriages are generally monogamous. Each longhouse has a headman, or *tuai rumah*, who leads a council of elders.

In common with other interior Borneo groups the Iban are mostly shifting cultivators, although a few grow swamp rice in down-river areas. During the cultivation of hill rice, the Iban move to small, temporary longhouses, *dampa*.

Punan Dayak school-girl, Borneo

Indonesians

pop: 135,913,000

The largest nation in South-East Asia, Indonesia is an archipelago of more than 13,600 islands extending from Sumatra to Irian Jaya, the western half of New Guinea. Many of the islands have few inhabitants, and Java, with the three largest cities, has more than half the entire population. Nearly all Indonesians are Muslims, but Buddhism and Hinduism have many adherents. Some 250 Malay-Polynesian languages are spoken. A large Chinese minority of some three million dominates Indonesia's commercial life. Oil and rubber are the most valuable natural resources, with tin, bauxite and nickel also important for the national economy.

Sumatra

pop: 20,900,000

Sumatra is one of the largest islands in Indonesia. There are high temperatures all the year round, and the west monsoon brings heavy rain to southern Sumatra from December to February. From June to August, the east monsoon winds from Australia bring dry air.

The major cities are Medan in the north-east of the island and Palembang in the south-east. Both have between 500,000 and 600,000 inhabitants. Agricultural activity is concentrated in the estate section of north-east Sumatra. Around Medan large plantations produce coffee, tobacco, palm oil, kapok, tea and rubber. None of these products is indigenous to the area.

The peoples of Sumatra, speaking between them 15 Malayo-Polynesian languages, which are further sub-divided into dialects, comprise the strict Muslims of the northern plains; the Batak in the hilly areas of the north; Malay peoples in the east, where the Indonesian language developed; and the matrilineal Menangkabau, who are also strict Muslims, in the west.

Menangkabau

pop: 3,000,000

The Menangkabau inhabit the valleys of Sumatra's tropical highlands. Most live in hamlets and villages varying from a few to several hundred houses, closely grouped according to clan membership. Villagers cultivate terraced rice fields, many of which are irrigated. They work fixed or shifting-plot gardens in river valleys and on mountain slopes, growing chilli peppers, cloves, cassava, bananas and other subsistence and cash crops.

Once controlling their own kingdom, the Menangkabau practise a form of patronage in which poorer highland families attach themselves to wealthier landlords and become a part of the latter's village. Although the highland Menangkabau have a matrilineal social structure, they are also strongly Islamic. Marriage is arranged by senior lineage members.

Leadership of a hamlet is inherited matrilineally by men, but lineage property is owned in common. Some property is also owned by individuals, usually the proceeds of trade, or of salaries in the case of civil servants. This property is inherited patrilineally. With two conflicting kinds of inheritance there are often disputes over distribution of a deceased clan member's property.

Batak

pop: 2,500,000

The Batak are a collection of seven main related groups whose legendary home is Lake Toba in central Sumatra. They practise rotation farming

The Hindu temple of
Besakih, Bali

based on rice and live in
communal, boat-shaped houses.
Despite recent dispersal each
district of autonomous village
communities still has a rajah
who is head of the patrilineage.

About 80 per cent of the
largest group, the Toba, are
Christian; the Mandailing are
Muslim. Belief in taboos and
numerology also regulates
many aspects of life. Western
secular education is gradually
changing this and an increasing
number of Batak are entering
the business world.

Javanese
pop: 77,000,000
Java, the fourth largest island
in the Greater Sundas, is
culturally, politically and
economically the most important island in Indonesia. It has
been inhabited for at least a

million years, as was indicated
by the discovery of Java Man,
an early form of *Homo erectus*;
other fossil remains bear wit-
ness to this continuity. The
ancestors of the Javanese were
Malayo-Polynesians, who probably introduced the wet rice
agricultural techniques to the
eastern islands.

Three major linguistic groups
live on the island. The
Sundanese inhabit the western
region and were originally
associated with the Prijangan
highlands; the Madurese in the
north come from the offshore
island of Madura; the majority
Javanese are located mainly in
eastern and central Java. There
has been much intermarriage
between these groups. Minority
peoples, classified together with
the Javanese, are the Badui
and the Tenggerese: both
groups have prolonged their

distinctiveness by conserving
and maintaining traditional
religious beliefs.

Islam swept into South-East
Asia during the 14th and 15th
centuries, and is followed with
varying degrees of orthodoxy
by the Javanese. In the centre
of the island, however, once
the heart of the Javanese
kingdom of Mataram, a culture
exhibiting both Hindu and
Buddhist elements has persisted since the 8th century.

Java has a stratified society,
divided between the nobility
(ndara) and administrators
(priyayi), and the peasantry
(wong cilik) with their village
headmen *(lurah)*. Villagers are
grouped to the needs of estate
agriculture and a multitude of
smallholdings. The landless
tend to gravitate towards the
towns and add to the ranks of
the urban poor.

Bali, Timor, Sulawesi, Moluccas
Balinese, Toradja, Moluccans

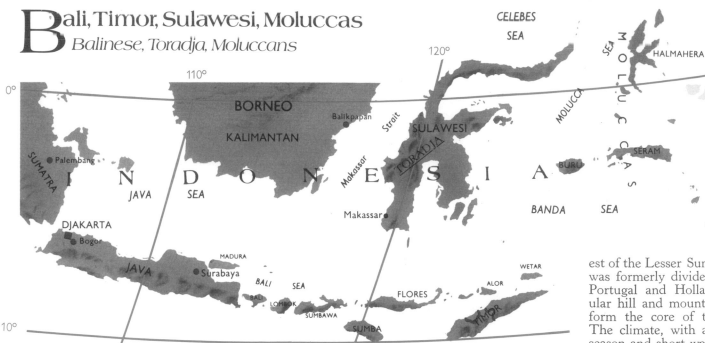

Balinese
pop: 2,150,000

The mountainous island of Bali is some 90 miles across and 50 miles from north to south. The basic culture and ancestral stock came from Java, just one mile away across the Selat Bali strait. The Balinese live predominantly in communities called *desa*, each having a temple dedicated to its founding ancestor. Every community also has a temple dedicated to the *subak*, the irrigation co-operative which ensures that the rice terraces are all fed with sufficient water.

Co-operation is fundamental to the Balinese way of life. The basic unit of society is the patriarchal family group, in which each member traces descent from the same father, grandfather or even great-grandfather. This group lives together in a walled courtyard enclosing living quarters and the household shrine. The village community is the next level of organization; every villager has equal obligations to the community and rights to its prosperity.

It is the *subak* which binds villages together most strongly. Every important task is carried out under its supervision – canal repairs, rice planting, water distribution – as are the village ceremonies. Groups of villagers, known as *banjars*, organize weddings, funerals and the ritual dances. The range of Balinese dance themes is extensive, from fire dances to animal dances.

Balinese men do most of the work in the fields, with assistance from the women and older children, especially at harvest time. The women tend the animals and run the markets, as well as preparing temple feasts. Cock-fighting is the main Balinese sport and has ritual significance, for the spilling of a cock's blood sates the thirst of evil spirits.

Balinese religion is based on Hinduism, which was brought to the island some 800 years ago, combined with native beliefs and ancestor worship. Life is seen as a perpetual contest between the supernatural forces of good and evil. There is a constant need to appease evil forces and to seek the blessings of gods, particularly Ida Sang Hyang Widhi Wasa, god of creation.

The Hindu caste system has never been followed rigidly, but Balinese society is divided into four classes: peasants *(Sudra)*, merchants and soldiers *(Wesia)*, nobles *(Satria)* and priests *(Brahman)*. The difference between the classes is emphasized by language: the higher castes use a courtesy language to address their superiors, while a common language is spoken between equals and when addressing people of a lower rank. Malay is used to communicate with other Indonesians outside Bali.

Timor
pop: 570,000

The island of Timor, the largest of the Lesser Sunda group, was formerly divided between Portugal and Holland. Irregular hill and mountain ranges form the core of the island. The climate, with a long dry season and short wet season is not conducive to successful agriculture.

The aboriginal peoples are mainly mountain dwellers, practising shifting agriculture; they were displaced from the more favoured areas of the island by later Indonesian-Malay arrivals. Most of the commerce is controlled by Chinese and other Asian immigrants.

Sulawesi
pop: 6,817,000

The island of Sulawesi is part of the territory of Indonesia. Ujung Pandang, with some 600,000 people, is the most important city. It functions as a metropolitan area rather than a provincial city and contains major government, business and financial offices.

For its size the island has a remarkably long coast, fringed with coral reefs and with three large gulfs on the north, east and south. Ranges of mountains cut by deep rift valleys form the land mass. There is great ethnic variety on the island: many Malayo-Polynesian languages are spoken and many religions practised including Islam and Christianity.

Toradja
pop: 50,000

Toradja is the general name for the people living in the interior of the Indonesian island of Sulawesi. They have little contact with the outside world, and until the end of the last century were practically unknown to the West. They have developed a striking and sophisticated culture with elaborate

ancestor worship and a rich mythology. Today about half the Toradja are Christians, converted by missionaries from the Dutch Christian Reform Church just before the First World War.

Until quite recently Toradja society had a rigid class system, with a nobility, commoners and slave labourers. On penalty of death, a woman of noble status could not marry below her class, nor could a common woman marry a slave. A woman of the lowest class, however could marry a commoner or a nobleman, though her children would belong to her own class and not to the father's.

Diet among the Toradja is largely vegetarian, rice being the staple food. Other crops include maize, yams, manioc and peanuts, with coffee a valuable export crop. The most important domestic animal is the water buffalo which, like the pig, dog and chicken, is a sacrificial animal: ritual slaughter is most common at funeral feasts, when large numbers may be killed. Buffaloes are status symbols among the Toradja, each social class owning a certain type of animal.

Moluccans
pop: 1,010,000

Between Sulawesi in the west and New Guinea in the east, the Moluccans occupy a transitional zone where the flora and fauna of southern Asia merge with those characteristic of Australasia. Sago extracted from the palm trunk is the most important staple, along with taro, manioc, sweet potatoes and yams. These crops, together with bananas and plantain, are generally cultivated in mixed gardens prepared by the slash-and-burn method.

The region has had a varied history of contact with both South-East Asia and Melanesia. Moluccan culture owes much to the Indianized kingdoms of Java and Sumatra and was also affected by the Portuguese and Dutch pursuit of the spice trade. Of the tribal people of the north and central Moluccas, only a few isolated groups remain and are fast being assimilated into a wider Moluccan creole culture, and into the Indonesian economy. Small bands of nomadic hunters known as Togutil survive on Halmahera, however, and on Seram and Buru, where the groups are more settled. There the clan is the most important unit of organization, although political systems among the Wemale and Alune peoples of west Seram formerly involved groupings above the clan level.

Many of the non-tribal Moluccans are Muslims, but on Seram and Ambon there are large Christian protestant communities, usually termed Ambonese, who were converted by the Dutch. Their creole culture is a blend of colonial and indigenous elements in which a dialect of Malay has superseded the use of local Malayo-Polynesian languages.

Rotinese walk home from the fields, Timor

Australasia/Pacific

The vast area of Australasia and Oceania encompasses sharp contrasts as well as continuities, ranging from the harsh deserts of central Australia, where only scattered Aborigine tribes learned to survive, to the myriad islands of Polynesia, teeming with nature's products. The region can be divided into three major areas: the Australian continent; the island of New Guinea, including the western half now known as Irian Jaya, and the other islands of Melanesia; and Polynesia-Micronesia. European colonization and settlement cross-cuts these major cultural zones.

In Australia there is definite evidence of human settlement from 40,000 years ago at Keilor in Victoria and from 32,000 years ago at Lake Mungo in New South Wales. Until some 8,000 years ago the Sahul shelf linked Australia to New Guinea by land; archaeological sites of comparable antiquity to those in Australia have been discovered at Kosipe in Papua (26,000 years old) and at Kuk in the Western Highlands Province (30,000 years old). These early inhabitants must have arrived from the land masses of South-East Asia, using sea-going craft to migrate between islands.

The settlement of Polynesia and Micronesia is much more recent, dating to no more than 4,000 years ago, and resulting probably from sea journeys made by populations of mixed ancestry from the south China coast or some other part of South-East Asia. Great controversy has surrounded these migrations. Were they planned or accidental? Polynesians were excellent navigators and could build canoes to hold as many as 100 people; but current opinion holds that much of the colonization of the islands must have occurred through accidental voyages rather than purposeful journeys of discovery. Settlement dates from the mid-2nd millennium BC have been deduced for Saipan in western Micronesia; 1,000 BC for New Caledonia

VEGETATION

- **Conifer Forest** Pine, spruce, larch
- **Broadleaf Forest** Deciduous
- **Temperate** Arable, broadleaf, grass
- **Mediterranean** Citrus, olive, agave
- **Subtropical** Dry and wet evergreen
- **Tropical** 'Selva'
- **Prairie** Long grass
- **Savanna** Grass and scrub
- **Semi Desert** Cactus, sparse shrub and grass
- **Desert** No vegetation

- **Marsh and Swamp**
- **Salt** Salt lake, marsh

- ■ **Capital Cities**
- • **Major Towns**
- • **Towns** Small town village
- — **Country Borders**
- — **Borders** Provinces, states

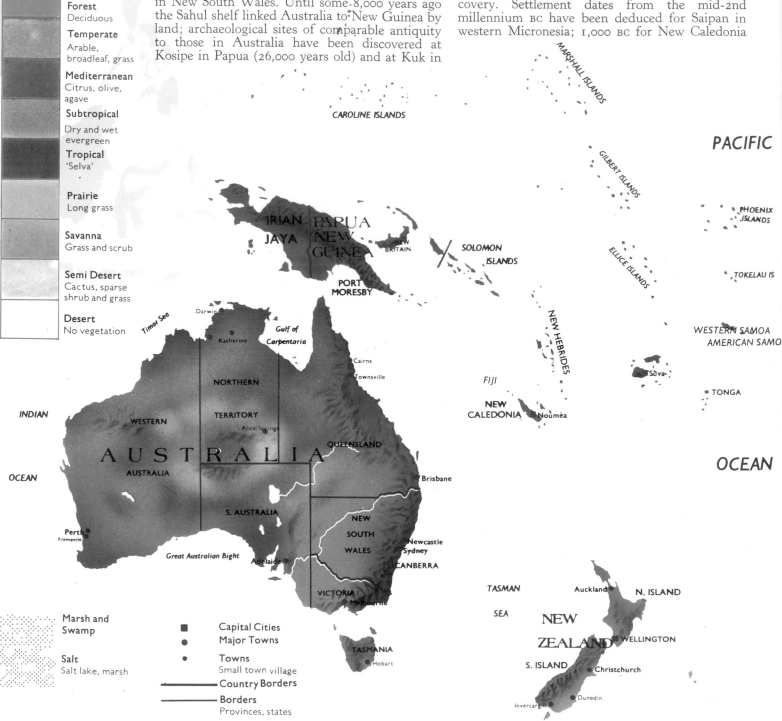

244

and Fiji, and more than 2,000 years ago for Tonga and Samoa. In eastern Polynesia the Marquesas group was settled by about AD 300.

The peoples who arrived in these places shared physical characteristics deriving both from Asians and from darker-skinned Melanesians. Asian traits are most in evidence in Micronesia; in Fiji and Tonga, Melanesian and Polynesian elements intermingle. In these two places archaeologists have also found examples of decorated pottery ware known as Lapita, which spread throughout the south-west Pacific. The producers of Lapita ware were probably the direct ancestors of contemporary Polynesian peoples. Artefact assemblages indicate a separate and unbroken history for Samoa, and also suggest links between the Marquesas and Easter Island, Hawaii and Tahiti. New Zealand was settled by the 9th century AD; the Maori people may have arrived via the Cook Islands.

Polynesian cultures developed from their initial settlement along remarkably similar lines. Their most salient characteristic is the consistent use of hereditary rank as a basis for political authority, leading in the larger islands to highly stratified societies with grades of chiefship and kingship accompanied by politico-military centralization of power. Rank, based on kinship seniority, is bolstered by the idea of *mana*, supernatural force possessed by chiefs.

Melanesian societies present quite a different picture. They are on the whole smaller-scale (except in the highlands of Papua New Guinea) and are less marked by systematic use of ranking principles, although forms of chiefship directly parallel to those of Polynesia are found in Papua, notably in the Purari, Mekeo and Trobriand Islands areas. Their languages are also more diverse than those of Polynesia. The predominant form of political structure is based on the 'big men', who achieve their position largely by persuasive powers, hard work and manipulation of wealth, in the form of goods such as shells and pigs. Leadership is thus a personal creation and not inherent in the kinship structure.

Polynesian, Micronesian and many coastal languages of Melanesia are related as members of an ancient and wide-flung stock of languages known as Malayo-Polynesian or Austronesian, and including the languages of Madagascar, far to the west of Oceania. Speakers of Austronesian arrived on the coasts of New Guinea, probably from eastern Melanesia, at roughly the same time as parts of Polynesia were being settled, and were ancestral to the present population—for example, the Tolai people in New Britain and the Motuans in Papua. In the interior of New Guinea, where settlement is very ancient, large linguistic groups have been discovered among non-Austronesian speakers—for example, the east New Guinea highlands group, which includes almost all the languages spoken by more than 750,000 highlanders. These highlands languages have probably been established for some 10,000 years, or have developed in that period from ancestral forms. Agriculture also began early in the highlands, possibly 9,000 years ago.

Australian Aboriginal languages are mostly related to one another (85 per cent show some genetic correspondence) and not to other Pacific language areas. Aboriginal culture and art forms are also highly distinctive. The Aborigines had a vast knowledge of their habitats and utilized them with skill and endurance to survive as hunters and gatherers. They did not, as New Guinean peoples did, make the transition to agriculture, and it was

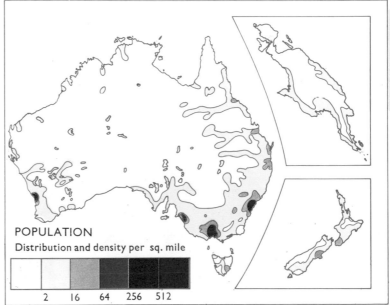

POPULATION

Distribution and density per sq. mile

2	16	64	256	512	

Easter Island

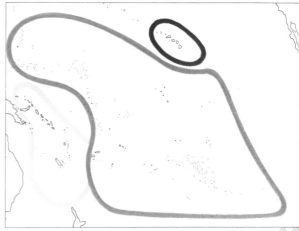

245

TEMPERATURE

Actual surface temperature
in centigrade

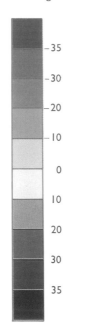

-35
-30
-20
-10
0
10
20
30
35

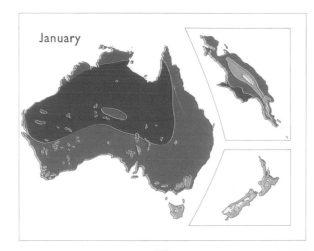

January

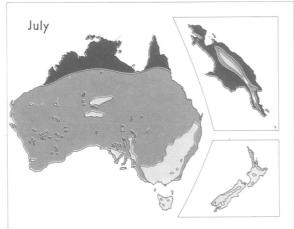

July

RAINFALL

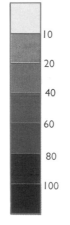

10
20
40
60
80
100

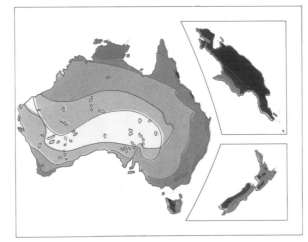

LANGUAGE

Distribution of major
languages

Indo-European

Aborigine

Papuan

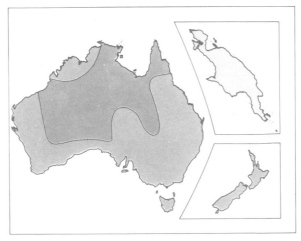

this lack of obvious claims to land and of a settled way of life that made them so vulnerable to competition from European settlers in Australia during the 19th century.

European exploration of the Pacific began with the search for *Terra Australis Incognita*, a fabled southern continent. Spanish and Portuguese explorers, including Magellan, Mendana, de Quiros and Torres, sailed in galleons via America across Oceania and back to Europe in the 16th century; but these adventures ended soon after the death of King Philip II in 1598. Dutch ships took over, seeking to extend the trading contacts of the Dutch East India Company; the names of Van Diemen and Tasman became identified with the area. Malayan traders arrived in their *praus* on the north-west shores of Australia from 1700, seeking the trepang sea-slug also known as *bêche-de-mer*. In the 18th century British and French sailors, such as Byron, Wallis, Carteret, Bougainville and Cook, completed much of the work of exploration.

Serious colonization then began. The era of invasion of the Pacific by Europeans from 1767-1840 (later in Papua New Guinea) has rightly been described by one historian, Alan Moorehead, as a time of 'the fatal impact'. Diseases such as smallpox, influenza, measles, tuberculosis, dysentery, syphilis and gonorrhoea swept through populations quite lacking in resistance. Firearms and alcohol caused yet more destruction. Massacres and mass abductions by labour recruiters occurred, especially up to the expansion of plantation agriculture in 1850. Mining also increased from that date, and in New Caledonia French convicts, Vietnamese, Javanese and Japanese were all brought in as labourers. Indian workers were brought to Fiji.

Missionaries also began operating everywhere. Soon the entire Australasian and Pacific area was carved up between the British, Dutch, French and German powers. In the Second World War the Pacific became an amphitheatre for mass conflict and has since been exposed to nuclear testing and forced resettlement. Most recently a giant copper mine has radically altered conditions of life in the North Solomons (formerly Bougainville) Province of Papua New Guinea. Under the combined weight of such influences, traditional social structures and values have in many places crumbled or re-appeared in the distorted forms which outsiders identify as 'cargo cults'.

Cargo cults are local movements for social change, often with strong apocalyptic and messianic overtones. At their centre is usually a charismatic leader or prophet, who crystallizes his people's desire for the wealth and power possessed by incoming Europeans and who purports to know how to secure this power. A situation in which people are subjected to colonial control coupled with missionary influence provides fertile ground for the development of such movements. People often think that the outsiders are withholding secrets, for instance by removing from the Bible certain pages in which the 'true' names of God and Jesus appear. If they could discover these names, they would have access to the white men's power.

Christian and traditional ideas coalesce: for example, the notion that Christ 'saved the world' produces a local idea that human sacrifice may again be necessary if society is to be redeemed. Strong cult leaders, such as Yali in Madang Province, preach messages of overall social reform and innovation as well as 'cargo' ideas. Indeed their movements may, as time goes on, take on the character of political associations for development, such as the Palian and Tommy Kabu movements of Manus and Purari respectively.

At early stages of contact Europeans themselves were sometimes thought of as alien deities or as returning ancestors. In coastal areas of Papua New Guinea, such as New Britain, New Ireland and the North Solomons (Bougainville), such early contact from the 1870s onwards brought much bitterness as these 'gods' proved less than generous, and deep-rooted frustrations led to a continuous repetition of cargo cults aimed at securing equality with the Europeans.

Less complicated versions of the cult sprang up sporadically in the New Guinea highlands from the early 1940s onwards, after the late entry of Europeans with their powerful guns and plentiful supplies of glittering shell valuables brought up from the coast for trade. People thought they could secure large quantities of such shells by cult actions, supplicating their ancestors or by attracting the white men's planes to land on makeshift air-strips constructed for the purpose.

Similar practices re-emerged in the 1970s with a belief that ancestors, returning as 'wind people', would convert piles of stones and rubbish secured in red boxes into cash, provided that appropriate sacrifices were made and taboos observed. Cult promotors took in 'subscriptions' of pork and money from supporters, but the cults rapidly disintegrated when the money was not forthcoming. Modern Papua New Guineans often strongly oppose cargo cults themselves and are critical of outsiders who too readily label indigenous associations or practices as cargo cults.

The two major settler countries, Australia and New Zealand, now play an important role in the Pacific through monetary aid, provision of experts, direct administration in a few places, supply of training facilities, and as a source of wage-earning opportunities for migrants. The European populations of these two countries are relatively prosperous. Australia is economically the richer of the two, with vast mineral resources in addition to its ranching and general manufacturing industries. New Zealand is quieter, cooler, and with a stronger dairying and sheep-farming tradition.

New Zealand has taken in considerable numbers of Polynesian migrants, who mix easily with their fellow-Polynesian Maoris. Australia's main ties are with Papua New Guinea, but relations with Indonesia are also important. The official foreign policy of both Australia and Papua New Guinea in 1977 was to maintain good relations with the Indonesian Republic.

The post-independence period for Pacific nations is one of reassessment and reconstruction, their leaders attempting to build on whatever material advantages and improvements have accrued from the colonial period, and at the same time attempting to mould their countries in ways distinctive to their own traditions and needs. The Maori and Aborigine populations in New Zealand and Australia are not in such a favoured position. Maoris, however, play an increasing part in New Zealand politics, and Aborigines are beginning to make some progress in reasserting their rights to the ancient lands in which they lived, like other Oceanic people, for millennia before the white men came.

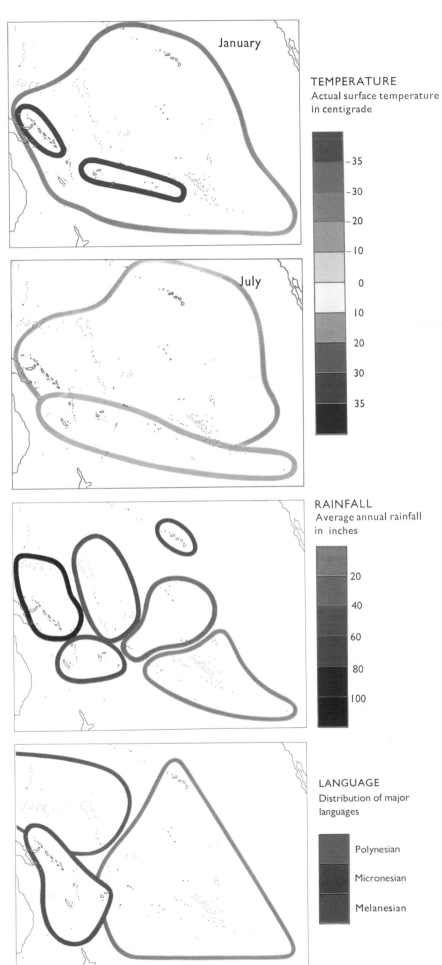

TEMPERATURE
Actual surface temperature
in centigrade

- 35
- 30
- 20
- 10
  0
  10
  20
  30
  35

RAINFALL
Average annual rainfall
in inches

20
40
60
80
100

LANGUAGE
Distribution of major
languages

Polynesian

Micronesian

Melanesian

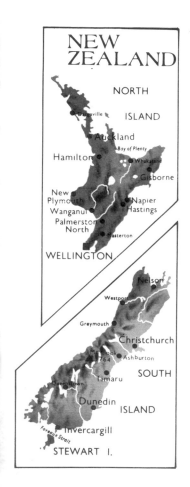

farms. The north and east coasts are generally well-watered, but in central and western Australia droughts are often a problem, rain sometimes not falling for up to three years at a time, and bushfires are not uncommon. However, the sheer size of land holdings, often measured in thousands of square miles, tends to minimize the effects of local disasters.

There are minor cultural differences between the city dwellers, who have access to social facilities comparable to those in Europe, and the farm-

Australians
pop: 14,160,000

Australia is a vast, mainly rural country of sheep farms and cattle stations, whose fertile coastal area attracts the bulk of the population. However, four out of five Australians live in towns, and many have never seen the 'outback': less than 6 per cent derive their living directly from the land.

The population is predominantly European in origin, being of British (85 per cent), Italian, Greek, Dutch and German origin, with increasing numbers of Turks and Lebanese. There are small communities of Australian-born Chinese, a legacy from the gold rush days, and a tiny percentage of other South-East Asians, Indians and Japanese.

The indigenous Aborigines (c. 107,000) have mostly left or been driven off their traditional homelands and now live outside towns, at missions or on cattle stations where many are employed as stockmen. Some have migrated into the cities, where they tend to remain in small suburban enclaves.

Secondary industry employs about a quarter of the population and state capitals service an extensive hinterland of dairy, sheep, wheat and cattle

ing or mining communities, who preserve some of the pioneer qualities of the early Australians. Cultural ties with Great Britain are responsible for a steady pilgrimage of Australians to London.

Aborigines
pop: 107,000

The Australian Aborigines are generally thought to have migrated from South-East Asia and show physical characteristics consistent with this view. With the arrival of British settlers, many were driven away from the more fertile areas into the arid interior. The southern groups suffered worst, many dying in subsequent tribal hostilities or as a result of the change to a desert environment. Alcohol and imported disease took a disastrous toll, and by the mid-20th century the population had shrunk from about 300,000 to 67,000. This trend has now been reversed, but the social pressures remain severe.

Previously the Aborigines had evolved a lifestyle well suited to the environments they inhabited. Food was obtained by hunting and gathering—they did not domesticate ani-

mals or plant crops—and there was a wide range of stone tools and efficient weapons.

A highly complicated social structure still exists. Tribes are divided into local groups, clans and up to eight sections. A kinship system defines all relationships and there are strict marriage rules. Each tribe believes in spiritual ancestors who created the people and their physical and natural world in the 'dreamtime' long ago. Their religion consists of a body of mythology, songs, sacred sites and objects, and a rich visual art and elaborate ceremonies which represent their belief in and reliance upon these ancestors. Adolescents undergo ordeals during initiation.

While some groups have maintained their traditions, detribalized Aborigines live on mission stations, on the fringes of country towns or on pastoral properties, where they have to accept alien white rule. Politically, however, the Aborigines are becoming much more active, and their land claims and political aspirations now have to be considered seriously by the Australian government.

New Zealanders
pop: 3,203,000

The first European to reach New Zealand (known to the indigenous Maoris as Aotearoa) was James Cook, who arrived in the Endeavour in 1796. Following him came increasing numbers of traders, mainly from Australia, seeking timber, flax, sealskin, whale oil and other local products. By 1839 small coastal communities had been established on both the North and South Islands. In 1840 the Maori leaders signed the treaty of Waitangi, ceding sovereignty to Britain; a government was established along the lines of the British parliament and the rate of immigration accelerated.

The settlers soon realized that the land, though fearsomely rugged in most areas, had great potential for those prepared to clear the hills for farming. There, and on the rolling plains of the south-east, conditions were ideal for rearing sheep and cattle. Today pastoral and agricultural products are New Zealand's major exports—the total flock exceeds

60,000,000—although the soil must often be treated with imported fertilizer for successful cultivation.

Most New Zealanders still regard farming as the mainstay of the community, but the population is highly urbanized, with more than 70 per cent living in towns. Mechanization in the farming industry and an increasing demand for workers in the metropolitan centres of Auckland, Wellington, Christchurch and Dunedin have stimulated this drift from the countryside. In recent years, New Zealand has also drawn increasing numbers of migrant workers from Polynesia, but racial tensions remain muted despite a total Polynesian population of around 250,000. There are also small Indian and Chinese minorities. Cities are characterized by suburban sprawl: high-density, multistorey housing is uncommon. There are no urban slums, nor are there conspicuous displays of wealth in housing style; instead a homogeneous exterior and a consistently high level of material prosperity are evident.

Maori
pop: 236,000

Recent study has cast increasing doubt on the long-accepted view that the principal ancestors of the Maori people arrived at New Zealand in a fleet of seven or eight canoes about the year 1350 AD. A gradual development from initial settlement around the 9th century seems more likely. The early hunting and fishing culture called Moa Hunter (from the large flightless bird, the moa, now extinct) is often described as Archaic Maori; it was succeeded by the agricultural economy of Classical Maori culture.

The first evidence of the staple sweet potato comes from the early 14th century; the plant was probably introduced by chance voyagers. The classical period also saw the beginning of widespread warfare and the construction of defensive settlements. The continual warfare can be connected with population pressures on agricultural land. Tribal and subtribal boundaries were frequently disputed in battle.

The basic kin and economic

unit was the *whanau*, or extended family of an elder, his wife or wives, unmarried children, and some married children with grandchildren. Several *whanau* descended from a common ancestor made a *hapu*, or sub-tribe, which, if large, could occupy a whole village. In time of war a number of *hapu* would retreat from the open agricultural settlements to a defensive position such as a fortified hill village. Village activities focused around a central courtyard, or *marae*, and the meeting house beside it. These were the sites for communal discussion, ceremonial welcome, funeral addresses and much other day to day activity.

The authority of chiefs, elders and priestly experts was strengthened by the notions of *mana* and *tapu*. *Mana* was a person's effective power and increased with rank. Though linked to political status and dependent on practical success, *mana* was sometimes seen as an abstract property which had to be protected from pollution. *Tapu* involved laws which limited contact between the powerful and pure and the relatively impure and demeaning. Chiefs also possessed great *tapu* restricting their contact with common people and things. *Tapu* lay over religious sites and regulated key activities such as the planting of the sweet potato. It could also be

used to impose a closed season on hunting or fishing. Breaking a *tapu* would lead to spiritual attack, sickness and perhaps death.

From the beginning of the 19th century contact with Europeans, initially whalers, traders and missionaries, increased steadily. The introduction of the musket gave new scope for destruction in intertribal warfare. With this, disrupted food production and European diseases, the population fell rapidly. In 1840 Maori chiefs signed the treaty of Waitangi, recognizing British sovereignty, but friction between the settlers and the Maori led to further wars during the 1860s. From the basis of missionary Christianity a number of Maori prophetic movements arose. One of the longest lasting has been the Ratana Church, a movement begun in 1918, which has been involved in national politics. This century there has been a resurgence both in the Maori population and of interest in the traditional culture.

Massive movement to towns and cities has brought new problems, although voluntary associations such as culture clubs, sports clubs, Maori missions, welfare leagues and Maori councils try to provide a new focus for the urban workers. Rural *marae* are still visited and some urban *marae* have been constructed.

Australian beach boys, Sydney

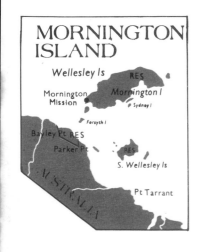

MORNINGTON ISLAND

Murngin
pop: 3,000

Several Aborigine groups who live in the northern and eastern parts of Arnhem Land and share a similar culture have been given the collective name of Murngin. Each of the groups speaks a dialect of the tribal language, but most individual Murngin can speak several dialects of the region.

The men hunt many animals and catch fish; women gather plants and shell-fish. During the dry season, the Murngin move frequently as food is scarce, but in the rainy season the bands settle and build semi-permanent shelters. The basic unit for hunting and warfare is the patrilineal clan, consisting of up to 50 people who share the same name, dialect and .totemic waterhole. The clan has inalienable rights over its territory.

Each tribe is divided into two moieties, and an individual's position in society is determined by a kinship and age grade system, the most important stage of puberty being marked by a rigorous initiation ceremony for boys. Clans join together for all ceremonies, which facilitates marriage as a Murngin must marry someone from a clan in the opposite moiety. Girls are betrothed young and join their husband's clan. Many men have more than one wife.

Since European intervention the Murngin have abandoned their elaborate personal adornment for clothing and some have become labourers. Traditional life is changing but less drastically than in other areas of Australia.

Gulf Aborigines
pop: 1,500

Aboriginal population densities are higher on the coasts and islands of the Gulf of Carpentaria than in the inland regions and deserts of Australia. This is because coastal and island Aborigines can obtain food from the sea as well as by hunting and gathering on land. Fishing is of great importance. Modern boats have replaced bark and dugout canoes and rafts, but spears and fish-traps are still used alongside nets and lines. Dugongs (sea cows), turtles, salmon and particularly the dulnho (a bream-like fish) are caught and divided in accordance with strict taboos and complex tribal rules.

The Gulf Aborigines have a prodigious knowledge of the environment on which their survival depends. Each edible plant and animal is classified according to its source and use. Among the Groote Eylandt Aborigines, for example, *wur-adjidja* denotes creatures of the air, *jinungwangba* of the land, *augwalja* of the sea and *ega* refers to trees and plants.

Each tribe is divided into two moieties, made up of inter-related clans. Each of these has its own ancestral myths and totemic creatures from the spirit world or 'dreamtime', a timeless age which is used to explain every aspect of life. These creatures and culture heroes are represented in bark paintings and as decorations on didgeridoos (musical instruments). The Wanindiljaugwa of Groote Eylandt are renowned for this art form.

Dances and songs are learned from 'dreamtime' through men talking in their sleep and are jealously guarded until they can be performed in ceremonies with rival clans. Amongst the leeward and windward factions of the Lardil of Mornington Island these ceremonies are highly competitive and often include ritual fights, when the boomerang may be used.

Western life is affecting all the Gulf Aborigines, especially as mining companies are taking much of their land. Some are becoming labourers and stockmen, others are employed in the mines. On the islands, however, traditions and mythologies are as well preserved as anywhere in Australia.

Wikmungkan
pop: 800

The Wikmungkan are one of the many tribes of Cape York whose name begins with the prefix 'wik', which means language or speech. As is common with hunters and gatherers, every aspect of their traditional life is closely related to their environment. They believe that the animals they hunt were originally created by human clan ancestors, who made kangaroos and other species. Emu meat is a delicacy reserved for older people; the feathers are used for personal decoration. Gathering and distributing honey is considered very important and is subject to strict taboos: a father cannot accept honey from his sons.

A complex marriage and kinship system operates. The people are divided into patri-clans, each with its mythological stories of totems. A man should marry his mother's younger brother's daughter or equivalent relative. Relations with this brother are formal and food must be presented to him indirectly, but the mother's elder brother's property can be freely borrowed.

Most of the Wikmungkan live on a mission. Some work in the bauxite mine at Weipa; others are stockmen or commercial fishermen. They are adapting to the cash economy, and although their traditions are endangered by further mining, they have so far maintained their clan dances.

Walbiri
pop: 1,400

The Walbiri are one of the largest aboriginal groups in the Northern Territories of Australia. Divided into four major tribes called Yalpari, Waneiga,

Walmalla and Ngalia, they occupy the arid regions north and north-east of Alice Springs. They share a collective pride in their identity and consider other Aborigines inferior. Now that many Walbiri work in other territories, they tend to dominate the host tribe and assimilate its members. The Walbiri have a reputation as fighters which protects them from retaliation.

Each of the clans shares a totemic being which exists in 'dreamtime' and resides in a particular place in their territory. Since most Walbiri now live on government settlements or cattle stations and not in their totemic area, a re-organization of general community relations has been necessary. In the past there was no need for a secular government; leaders emerged for the organization of such events as Gajari or the Big Sunday cycle of celebrations.

Europeans tend to put English-speaking Walbiri in positions of authority, although these intermediaries try to maintain their traditional roles in tribal matters. Walbiri society is basically patrilineal with sub-sections and age groups and a highly complex system of kin bonds. These rights and duties are translated into a modern idiom; a young mine worker, for example, will help an old man who cannot work.

Aranda
pop: 300

The Aranda live in the semi-arid steppe lands east of the desert region of Western Australia. In normal seasons there is plenty of game for the men to hunt and plant life for the women to gather. They have developed intricate social and cultural institutions.

Each group had inalienable rights and an emotional attachment to its territory, focused on the 'big place' where their particular totemic creature resides. Rituals performed there re-enact the creature's experiences in 'dreamtime', with songs and drama. Invitations to such ceremonies are sent to other groups living along the routes of the mythical ancestor's wanderings.

In the past, local groups of the Aranda developed their own dialects of the language, and

some of them were traditionally hostile. Aranda marriages were based on clan ties and on an eight-class kin group system, which was regulated by social obligations. Relationships were governed by traditional rules and denoted by kin and class names. Today, detribalization and education in government and mission schools has resulted in a confusion of values.

Jigalong
pop: 500

The aboriginal group known as Jigalong is of fairly recent formation, drawing its members from the Njijabali, Mand-jildjara and Gadudjara tribes. They migrated west from the Gibson desert in Western Australia to the mission centre of Jigalong, 1,250 miles north-east of Perth, where they rapidly acquired a taste for tea, sugar, flour and alcohol.

Jigalong settlement, which came into being in 1907 as a small maintenance camp for a supposedly rabbit-proof fence, has stimulated intercourse between tribes. Kinship ties are still very strong, and living standards have been improved by government medical aid, schooling and food supplies, and the establishment of a Jigalong Aboriginal council.

Aborigine performing a *corroboree* dance

Irian Jaya
Dani, Asmat, Jalé

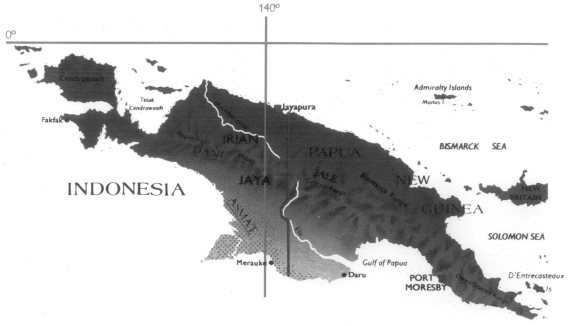

Irian Jaya

pop: 923,000

Irian Jaya is the current name for the western half of New Guinea. 'Irian' itself is a Biak word meaning 'hot land'. Well-known and populous tribes in or near the highland areas are the Dani of the Balim Valley, the Jalé and the Kapauku. The Asmat of Merauke near the south coast were renowned both as artists and headhunters, and resemble culturally the Marind-Anim and neighbouring peoples of Western Province in Papua New Guinea. Coastal areas have experienced contact with Malayan traders for two centuries, and Malayan is known as a *lingua franca*. The present administrative capital is Jayapura in the north.

The Dutch took permanent possession of the island in 1814. Development was slow until more than a century later, when a struggle over the country emerged between Holland and Indonesia, after Indonesia gained its own independence in 1945. In the last years of their control the Dutch built up both an economic infrastructure and an indigenous élite, but they were too late to prevent an Indonesian takeover, consolidated later by the 1969 act of 'free choice' *(PePeRa)* in which the people's representatives voted to become part of the Indonesian Republic.

Irian Jaya rebels, however, have opposed Indonesian control and a movement to 'free West Papua' still exists, although it is not strong. The area is difficult to settle, but the Indonesians have sent a number of migrants and also derive income from copper, nickel, petroleum, fishing and timber industries run by American, European and Japanese consortia. The area seems likely to remain part of Indonesia.

Dani

pop: 75,000

The Dani live in the precipitous Balim valley of Irian Jaya, some 5,000 feet above sea level. Their small villages, housing 2-5 families, are usually rectangular and surrounded by a wooden fence. At the end opposite the entrance is the men's house which, though only 10 feet high, has an upper storey for sleeping. The kitchens are a continuous longhouse and stretch along one side of the fence, opposite the women's round houses.

Around the village are the gardens, intersected by drainage channels. Sweet potato is almost the only vegetable grown and forms the Dani's staple diet; pork and green vegetables are eaten at celebrations. The men do the heavy work, such as clearing the land and digging the ditches; the women do the planting, weeding and general fetching and carrying.

The Dani's possessions are very limited. Their tools are stone axes, bone knives and digging sticks. The men wear only penis gourds; the women wear skirts plaited from orchid fibres. Nets hanging from their foreheads and down their backs are used for carrying crops and babies.

The various Dani festivals punctuate the steady rhythm of their life. The most important festival is the *mauwe*, which takes place only once every few years. On this occasion the boys are initiated into manhood, marriages are arranged and old debts and quarrels are settled. Ordinary work comes to a standstill and hundreds of pigs are killed, cooked in a pit full of hot stones and then eaten. Since pigs are the chief repository of wealth, this ceremony also serves to maintain the egalitarian nature of their society.

Until recently, open warfare was a fairly common occurrence in the Balim valley and watchtowers were a prominent feature of the landscape. A dead

photograph:
Asmat men's house, Irian Jaya

A marriage is accompanied by exchanges of wealth and carried out with mock gloom and reluctance on the part of the young couple. Kinship groups are linked to their neighbours by mutual adoption, a ritual rebirth of selected adults as members of the other group. Substitute sons may be offered after a killing to avoid retribution. When a man dies his wives and relatives squirm in the mud to display anguish and cover their scent from his ghost. Ancestors are revered and the men use their highly polished skulls as head rests when sleeping. Enemy skulls, from which the brains have been removed and eaten, are used as trophy ornaments and must be contemplated by the boys for some days during initiation.

Despite efforts by missionaries and the Indonesian government to stop headhunting raids in remote areas, they are still carried out in the full traditional manner.

Jalé
pop: 10,000

The Jalé live in the remote Snow mountains of the central highlands of New Guinea. They were not contacted by the outside world until 1961 and their lifestyle remains essentially unchanged. Jalé territory is generally open hilly country and villages, consisting of 20-100 homes, are located on ridges for easy defence. Near the settlements are gardens, in which sweet potato is the major crop, but taro, yam, banana and sugar-cane are also grown. Pigs are a measure of wealth as well as a source of food.

Inter-village wars break out when a man has a grievance which cannot be settled by the usual negotiations and exchange of pigs. The villages will send out bands of warriors to the battlefield and a series of 'shoot and run' encounters occur. If an enemy is killed a great effort is made to capture his body. If he had no immediate kin connections with the killers, the body will be cooked in an earth oven and the meat distributed throughout the village. The Jalé do not regard this cannibalism as a religious experience, but merely as a supplement to their diet.

warrior, it was thought, could not rest in peace until he was avenged by the killing of an enemy, so each killing required a counter-killing. The battles followed strict rules and, while hundreds of warriors might take part, only a few men might be wounded or killed. If the numbers killed on each side were equal the matter was considered settled. The last serious outbreak of fighting was in 1968, since when the Indonesian government and missionaries have brought warfare almost to an end. This change has had a profound effect on the role of men in Dani society, as there are no alternative activities bestowing such prestige into which their energies can be channelled.

Asmat
pop: 30,300

The Asmat live in scattered villages along rivers in the mangrove swamps of Irian Jaya.

Their material culture and livelihood is based on the surrounding woods, which provide timber for houses, weapons, canoes and paddles. The main source of food is sago starch, supplemented by fish, which the women catch.

The sago tree is identified with the human body and fertility rites emphasize its life-giving female aspects. Cutting down the sago tree is symbolically linked with ritual headhunting. In legend a culture hero is said to have built the first *yeu*, or men's house. Ancestors' skulls, masks and drums are stored in these houses and women are only allowed to enter for the ceremonial festivals. The *yeu* is built between the village and the river and used as a lookout and defence against enemy raiding parties.

Apart from birth and marriage, which are treated as secular matters, all aspects of life have a religious significance.

Papua New Guinea
Huli, Melpa, Fore, Anga, Goilala

Papua New Guinea

pop : 2,865,000 (1977)

Papua New Guinea comprises the western half of New Guinea plus a large number of adjacent islands, including Manus, New Ireland and New Britain.

The cultures of Papua New Guinea are rich, complex and diverse, but show an underlying unity. Most of the coastal peoples are Austronesian-speakers with seafaring origins. The highland peoples, who inhabit the valleys and hills of the central mountains, were not discovered by Europeans until the 1930s. They have developed intensive cultivation of sweet potatoes and other crops such as bananas and sugar cane. They also keep large herds of pigs, used in elaborate ceremonial exchanges along with shell wealth and nowadays cash. Coastal people grow taro, yams, coconuts, banana varieties and many other crops.

Cash crops are coffee and tea in the highlands, and copra, cocoa, rubber and palm oil on the coast. An expatriate-dominated plantation economy is gradually being replaced by indigenous enterprise. The country's capital city is Port Moresby, situated in the traditional area of the Motu people on the southern coast of Papua.

Huli

pop: 30,000

The Huli live in the basin of the Tagari river in the southern highlands of New Guinea. There are no nuclear villages and houses are spread out across parishes. Gardens and political units are marked with deep ditches which also provide drainage and defence.

As in other New Guinea societies, the men live separately from the women and even prepare their own food. Young bachelors are segregated for several years in order to ensure their physical growth; men fear the polluting effect of menstruation. Women's domestic duties involve cultivating sweet potatoes and other tubers and rearing pigs for ceremonial feasts. The men gather wild food and hunt small game and birds, whose feathers are considered symbols of the forest's purity and are used as badges of sexual potency.

Men usually remain chaste until marriage in their mid-20s. Girls marry from the age of 12 onwards but will be divorced if barren; large families are encouraged by polygyny. Population density has increased considerably since the 1950s and problems of land shortage are likely to emerge soon, even though many Huli have migrated in search of cash income.

Melpa

pop: 60,000

The Melpa occupy the head of the Wahgi valley, near Mount Hagen in the central highlands of Papua New Guinea. They live in small settlements of related clansmen and their wives. The men live separately from the women, fearing their strength might be sapped by pollution, especially during menstruation.

Women's houses have separate stalls for the pigs as well as a living and sleeping area for themselves and their children. Girls remain with their mothers until their marriage; boys move to the men's house at the age of 10. The women tend individual gardens where the staple crop of sweet potatoes is grown. Taro, yams, sugar cane, bananas, greens and the maize, cabbages and cassava introduced by Europeans are grown in other gardens.

Each clan has a magnificently laid out ceremonial ground, adjacent to a cemetery or cult place where sacred stones are buried. The grounds are focal points for public discussions and ceremonial gift exchanges. These occasions are presided over by 'big men' who obtain their rank primarily by prominence in exchange, displays of oratorical skill and manipulation of social relations.

Before warfare was abolished by the Australian administration, a complex network of combatants and allies was established which still operates today. Each tribe had a traditional major enemy, or might join with another tribe against a common enemy. No compensation for killing would be paid between enemies and the defeated tribe might be permanently displaced from its land. Compensation for loss of life would be paid only to allies. Battles were usually formal occasions, with lines of spearmen supported by bowmen.

Payment of compensation took place during ceremonies which, along with special wealth exchanges, are known as *moka*. These have become more competitive since the element of warfare has been removed. Dressed in elaborate finery, donors present large numbers of pigs, pearl shells and nowadays cash to the recipients. The latter are obliged to make returns later. Exchanges can go on indefinitely without final defeat being necessary.

Fore

pop: 14,000

The Fore-speaking people of Papua New Guinea live among the mountains south of the Ramu-Purari divide in the Eastern Highlands Province. Despite recent economic development they still clear the forest for gardens where they produce sweet potatoes by slash-and-burn. Apart from tubers they now grow corn, cabbages and tomatoes and their diet is supplemented by domesticated pigs, and game.

Traditionally the Fore lived in small hamlets which would combine for defence, since mutually destructive wars were part of normal social life. The large houses used by the men were separated from the women's quarters by a cooking area with ovens for ceremonial feasts. Leaders or 'big men' proved their worth by being aggressive fighters, expert orators and efficient organizers of ceremonial food exchanges.

In 1952 an Australian government post was set up; warfare was suppressed but internal suspicions and tensions have increased. The Fore adopted Christianity and planted cash crops but are now curtailing social activities and moving away from the areas near to government roads, as they believe enemy sorcerers are responsible for *kuru,* a debilitating neurological disease. Women and children were the main victims and since the peak of 3.6 per cent deaths among women in the early 1960s, the banning of cannibalism, in which they were the principal participants, has reduced the death rate. It is currently thought that this is because the micro-organisms which cause *kuru* were transmitted through consumption of the brains of *kuru* victims.

Anga
pop: 12,000

The Anga (sometimes referred to as the Kukukuku) live in the north-east of the Owen Stanley ranges in Papua New Guinea, some 4-5,000 feet above sea level. A short, stocky people, they have a reputation for being ferocious warriors.

Anga villages, built on easily defended spurs, contain up to a dozen houses and are surrounded by bamboo palisades some 20 feet high. The houses themselves are circular or oval, with conical, bamboo, grass or pandanus thatched roofs. A low entrance and entry walkway prevents surprise attacks.

The Anga engage in slash-and-burn cultivation of sweet potatoes, sugar cane, and to a lesser extent taro, yams and bananas. Maize, cabbage and tomatoes have recently been introduced.

Goilala
pop : 28,750

The people of the Goilala subdistrict live in the high ranges of the south-east chain of mountains which divides the island of New Guinea. They are within the state of Papua New Guinea. The district was pacified by the Australian administration in the 1930s and Catholic missions now provide schools, trading stores and dispensaries.

The women's houses are built in parallel rows on either side of a ridge, with the more elaborate men's houses at each end to protect them. The forest is cleared for gardens which the women tend, growing sweet potatoes and other root crops. A stock of smoked nuts from the pandanus tree would be eaten if an enemy destroyed the garden. Domestic pigs are kept by the women,

Several hundred pigs are slaughtered at ceremonial feasts, when more than 1,000 guests, including enemies, gather in a large dance village. Men dress in their finest feathers and imitate the heroes of old.

The Goilala gained a reputation for being one of the most warlike peoples of Papua New Guinea. At least one member of each small tribe would die every year, sometimes at the hand of a fellow tribesman. The bodies of enemies were sometimes eaten, as a gesture of contempt and in celebration of victory. Since this part of their traditional life has been banned, the men pour their energies into the pig feasts at which gestures of violence between hosts and guests are allowed as a ritually contained demonstration of aggression.

Melpa warriors,
Papua New Guinea

255

Papua New Guinea
Arapesh, Sepik River People, Abelam, Manus, Tolai, Kilenge

Arapesh
pop : 23,500

The mountain Arapesh inhabit an infertile strip of land in the Prince Alexander mountains of Papua New Guinea; other Arapesh live in the plains and coastal areas. Men and women work together in some of the basic tasks, but ceremonial and spiritual life focuses upon the differences between the sexes.

On the one hand are men, yams and the male blood of penile incision; on the other are women and the female blood of menstruation and childbirth. Good blood is associated with parental sexuality, observance of taboos and the avoidance of aggression; bad blood is linked with aggressive sexuality, death and failure to observe taboos.

Young males must undergo two stages of initiation into the men's cult. The ceremonies involve segregation, stinging with nettles, a ritual meal of blood, penile incision and, eventually, the showing of sacred wooden flutes and instruction in how to play them.

Menstruation is regarded as a dangerous time. A menstruating girl must sit in a special hut outside the village and fast. She is rubbed with stinging nettles in order to make her strong and her breasts large. Girls menstruating for the first time are also scarified by their mother's brother.

Although self-sufficient in the basics of life such as food, clothing and shelter, the Arapesh trade fairly widely outside their own lands. The government requirement to pay annual taxes in cash, however, has meant that many young men now go to work on plantations in distant parts of Papua New Guinea. Many mountain Arapesh have now also settled in the Cape Hoskins area of New Britain as smallholders working small commercial farms of oil palm trees.

Sepik River People
pop: 297,000

The Sepik river rises near the border of Irian Jaya and Papua New Guinea, and flows more than 1,000 miles to the sea near Wewak, on the north coast of Papua New Guinea. The indigenous peoples are predominantly village dwellers, divided into totemic and kinship groups. Cash crops grown include rice and coffee, with yams, sago, coconut, betelnut and certain varieties of fruit and vegetables providing the main subsistence crops. Fish and pigs are an important part of the diet.

Villages consist of thatched houses built on stilts in the wetter areas to avoid floods. Each village is dominated by a *haus tambaran,* which is the artistic and ritual centre. Hostility between adjoining communities is a common feature which used to result in regular head-hunting parties.

There is no system of hereditary chiefs; tribal leaders emerge by political, economic, oratorical or martial abilities. The yam and spirit cults, found throughout the Sepik area, give senior men a monopoly of supernatural knowledge with which they can dominate their juniors. These cults act as secret societies, from which women are excluded. Women who stumble upon the men's secrets are no longer killed, as would have once happened in some parts of the highlands, but only sworn to secrecy.

Abelam
pop: 30,500

The Abelam are subsistence farmers who live in the middle plains of Papua New Guinea's Sepik river. They are best known for their yam cults, their skill at carving and the remarkable spirit houses they build, known as *haus tambaran.* Little is known of their origins as factual history goes back only three or four generations.

The Abelam base most of their social, working and spiritual lives upon a strict sexual division of activities. Men and women may work together on clearing the bush, but the women grow the household's food, prepare sago, rear pigs, fetch firewood, cook and care for children, while the men concentrate on growing yams, building and hunting.

To ensure good yields, yams require constant tending and an elaborate series of male rituals surrounds their cultivation. Magical procedures are observed in small huts in the yam gardens and, until recently, men growing the crops had to abstain completely from sex and eating meat during the growing season. Women are excluded from the yam gardens.

The basic aim of each man is to grow larger tubers than his rivals, and the cult climaxes in the harvest festival. Each man decorates his finest yams with painted designs and woven masks and, after displaying them, he must exchange them with a partner. A tally is kept of the lengths of the vegetables and those men who give longer yams than they receive gain greatly in prestige.

The women have their own rituals. At the time of a girl's first menstruation a scarification rite is performed by the women, marking the girl's breasts, stomach and upper arms while she is held by her mother's brother. Afterwards, the women dance on the men's dance ground. The following day the girl emerges profusely decorated and with her head shaven, to begin the months which celebrate her new womanhood. She does no work, but visits the households of her own and neighbouring villages where she is entertained and given the finest food. At the end of this period she will marry.

Decisions were traditionally taken by consensus and at first the Abelam refused to recognize headmen appointed by the Australian administration after the Second World War. Now, however, there are four well-established local government councils in the area, made up of representatives elected from the villages. The councils have initiated development projects, cleared dirt roads, opened trade stores and marketing co-operatives and introduced new crops such as dry rice and coffee.

Manus
pop: 30,000

The Manus inhabit Manus Province of Papua New Guinea which comprises the Admiralty Islands. The people around Bunai on Manus Island, including those of Peri village, are known as Titan and number some 2,000. Until the first impact of western government policies in 1912, the Manus maintained a highly structured social and economic life.

Wealth was based on fish, dugong and turtles, which they caught from spacious outrigger canoes. All Manus, even children, were expert in manoeuvering these vessels around the Melanesian islands. They traded for food with the other islands, using discs of shell and dog's teeth (the currency of the Admiralty Islands) to buy pots from Mbuke, carved beads from Rambutchon, war charms from Pak and fishing nets and tools from Baluan and Lou.

Villages were organized into patrilineal clans under a hereditary leader, although kinship ties traced through women were also important in daily life. Each person through his clan membership had a right to perform a particular task and believed himself to be protected by the spirit of a deceased relative, called 'Sir Ghost'. The skull of this person would be preserved and, providing any contravention of ritual taboo was admitted to him in public, it would be forgiven. Personal mishaps would be blamed on the ineffectiveness of this guardian spirit and the skull would then be destroyed.

Manus society was held together by a network of financial marriage arrangements and the debts incurred by obligatory exchanges of wealth. These would take place during ceremonies to celebrate birth, ear-piercing, puberty, betrothal, pregnancy and death.

Gifts distributed by American soldiers during the Second World War gave rise to a cargo cult called the Noise, and the people flung their old goods into the sea. When it was realized that nothing could be expected from this, they adopted the New Way under the leadership of a gifted outsider called Paliau. They abandoned their sea villages and accepted a council and elected leaders in place of kinship ties; women were officially given equality and the burden of huge feasts was removed.

The young Manus who go to mainland Papua New Guinea for education are now returning home to form a new social and intellectual élite and are remoulding Manus society.

Tolai
pop: 80,000

The Melanesian Tolai live on the Gazelle peninsula of New Britain, off the northern coast of Papua New Guinea; their language is Kuanua. Formerly they practised shifting cultivation of taro, yams and sweet potatoes in gardens which the men cleared and the women tended. The men hunted small wild animals to supplement the diet and spent much of their time protecting the village from attack or carrying out raids on enemy groups. Blood feuds were a frequent result of insults or suspected sorcery.

Traditional society was based on principles of matrilineal descent and on personal prestige. All Tolai belong to one of the two matrilineal moieties further divided into clans and localized landholding matrilineages, headed by established leaders. These 'big men' are respected for their ability to arrange ceremonial exchanges of pigs and other goods, the number of wives they can support, their knowledge of tribal affairs and nowadays for their business enterprises.

There was previously a complex trading system between the islands which was regulated by customs and taboo; *tambu* or shell money is still used in ritual transactions. Other aspects of Tolai life suffered from the intrusion of traders, colonists and missionaries. Copra plantations were developed using native labour, and nearly 40 per cent of the land was alienated.

The Australian administration which followed after 1918 commandeered even more land, and further encouraged the people to move from subsistence crops to copra production and later cocoa grown for cash. The Tolai showed a natural facility for trading and many became wealthy, even by European standards. By the 1920s many already lived in European-style houses and bought steel tools, guns, ammunition and tinned foods.

Gradually the mutual hostility between groups has been replaced by a sense of national identity and the Tolai, now the best educated people of the Bismarck archipelago, are playing an influential part in political life. The national government is already buying back the alienated land, but a rapidly increasing population means the problem is urgent.

Kilenge
pop: 4,000

The Kilenge are a Melanesian group who inhabit the coastal regions of western New Britain. Their main source of food is grown in individual gardens and includes sweet potatoes, yams, taro, bananas, manioc and sugar cane. Wild pigs are hunted and domestic pigs kept for ceremonial purposes. Coconut palm is the only cash crop.

Artists and craftsmen have a valued place in society but are not excused from everyday tasks. Each adult has to work one day a week on government-introduced schemes to improve the village. The work teams are led by elected government councillors who may also be traditional 'big men' or heads of kin groups.

'Big men' organize the ceremonial festivals. Formerly these occasions were the focus of artistic expression in dancing and mask making. Secret cults restricted to the men involved dances in sacred masks which the women were forbidden to see on pain of death.

The decrease in infant mortality since the introduction of western medicine has meant a sharp rise in the population. The young men are leaving the villages to find paid work in more developed areas. This means families have to cope with an increasing demand on the working capacities of the middle-aged and on local food and trade resources to feed their younger children.

Melanesia
Trobriand Islands, Dobuans, Solomon Islands, Siuai, Tikopia

pre-eminent role.

Since 1962 the tourist trade has boomed. Charter tours, often operated by people who went to the Trobriand Islands during the Second World War, now cater for up to 3,000 visitors a year. Local carvings have become popular and their sale is one of the main sources of income along with copra.

Trobriand Islands
pop: 15,000

The Trobriand Islands are politically part of Papua New Guinea. The inhabitants live in circular villages of up to 200 people. Each household owns both major and minor gardens in which yams and taro are grown in accordance with magical rituals. Some of each man's yearly produce must be contributed to his sister's husband and yam houses are built and filled each year for the families of prominent men by their brothers-in-law, as a mark of respect. Pigs are eaten on special occasions and their meat plays a prominent part in gift ceremonies.

The *kula*, an elaborate ceremonial exchange system, links many of the islands off the eastern tip of Papua New Guinea. This is primarily an exchange of necklaces for arm-shells, purely for prestige, but in the past the 'argonauts' who set sail for remote islands to complete the complex transactions also traded in stone axes, pottery, feathers and foodstuffs. The search for suitable shells is now carried out in government trawlers as well as the traditional canoes. Although the ritual *kula* still operates, trading stores and regular shipping have diminished the ordinary trade aspect.

Trobriand society is matrilineal and there are high ranking members as well as commoners. Spirits are believed to reincarnate themselves through a woman of their former matrilineal group. The public denial of the man's part in procreation seems intended to appease these spirits, who are thought jealously to guard their own

Dobuans
pop: 26,000

Dobu or Goulvain is a small island located at the centre of the D'Entrecasteaux group. Dobuan is the most widely spoken language in the group and is used in radio broadcasts from Alotau in Milne Bay Province on the mainland. As Dobu itself has little fertile land and pigs can no longer be kept, most people live on the more fertile islands. The staple diet of yam is produced on available hill slopes by slash-and-burn methods.

The most striking feature of traditional Dobuan society is its combination of tracing descent matrilineally with a custom whereby husband and wife live alternately in each other's villages. Whichever spouse is currently the outsider in the village of residence is at a psychological disadvantage, and tension is common within the nuclear family.

Despite governmental encouragement to grow more varied crops and improve the commercial fishing facilities, advancement has been slow. Many Dobuans have abandoned subsistence agriculture for work on coconut plantations, or in teaching, nursing or trade.

Solomon Islands
pop: 190,000

The Solomon Islands, off the east coast of New Guinea, have been divided into two political units. Buka and Bougainville are part of independent Papua New Guinea. The islands from Choiseul to Santa Cruz, including Santa Isabel, the New Georgia group, Guadalcanal, Malaita and San Cristobal, formed a self-governing British protectorate before independence in 1978.

More than 70 different languages and dialects are spoken in the Solomons and there are two main cultural influences: Melanesian (which is predominant) and Polynesian. Islanders live in small scattered communities and practise shifting cultivation on the hill slopes, growing various staple foods of root crops and fruit. In coastal regions fishing was traditionally men's work; the women collected shell fish. Produce was traded and the teeth of porpoises or fruit bats used as currency. Pigs are reared by the Melanesian people for ceremonial purposes and rock oyster shells are still used on the southern islands in wealth exchanges.

Although social life has changed little, there is a danger of commercial interests upsetting the balance of natural resources. Copra is an important cash crop, and fishing ventures are run by Japanese companies. There are eight local councils who are acquiring more responsibility for agricultural development, education and general administration. The islanders are concerned that each of the four main centres should develop equally but it has been difficult to maintain each community's cultural inheritance while deve-

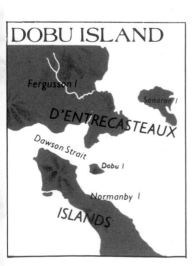

loping economic and political independence. Efforts are being made to ensure that the new educated élite are versed in local traditions.

Siuai

pop : 5,000

The Siuai of the North Solomons Province in Papua New Guinea live on the central plains of the Buin river. They are gardeners, growing taro, sweet potatoes, coconut and areca nut palm; the men also hunt small wild animals. Every household keeps some pigs which are ritually exchanged for shell money and pots to demonstrate wealth and status. Ceremonies are accompanied by feasting, dancing, singing, speech making and music played on various instruments. They are sponsored by 'big-men', who compete directly for prestige, especially in the dramatic *muminai* exchanges.

With the abolition of warfare by the Australian government villages of pile houses were introduced, but most Siuai still live in scattered hamlets, sited for defence. Marriage is subject to strict taboos within the matrilineal kin group, but polygyny is practised by the wealthier men and large families are much desired. Men and women live separately; the men's longhouses, which the boys join after initiation, are built near the main roads.

The Siuai maintain the belief that *kapunas* (spirits) are responsible for every aspect of life, both material and spiritual, but traditional culture has been disrupted by the introduction of Christianity. The Siuai were always suspicious of strangers, even other Motuna-speaking people, so adaptation to imposed administrative systems has been particularly difficult. Although the authority of the *mumi*, the important men, has been officially transferred to government appointed chiefs, they are still highly regarded.

Tikopia

pop : 1,050

The Tikopia form an outlying branch of Polynesian culture located geographically within Melanesia. The island is to the south-east of the Santa Cruz group, in the political jurisdiction of the Solomon Islands, and was probably settled from Samoa. Strong European influences were late in arriving. The chiefs continued their rule under a British protectorate and a Christian mission was established only in 1911.

The island is an extinct volcanic crater of about six square miles, its centre occupied by a lake. The chief crops are taro, yams, breadfruit, coconuts, sago and bananas, together with other fruits. Land title is held from the chiefs, *ariki*, but land can be considered the property of a lineage, shared out directly by its households. Though descent through the male line is strongly stressed, women also share in the distribution of land.

The basic kinship unit is the household of parents and children. The lineage, averaging about 40 members, comprises a number of households related by descent in the male line from a common male ancestor. Several lineages, mainly of the same descent but including some adopted and some incorporated by warfare, compose the four clans.

Each clan was linked to one of the principal gods, in turn associated with one of the main crops, yam, coconut, taro and breadfruit. Thus the senior clan Kafika was the clan of the supreme god Kafika and ritually responsible for the yam, called 'the body of Kafika'. Through their chiefs and elders the clans took part in an annual island-wide ritual, 'the work of the gods', to promote crop growth and fishing successes.

In 1956 it was claimed that the Tikopia were entirely converted to Christianity. Though the traditional religious role of the chiefs had been undermined, their authority has survived. Now, increasing numbers of Tikopia have visited other islands and there are overseas settlements such as that of plantation workers in the Russell Islands.

Palm-leaf house, Solomon Islands

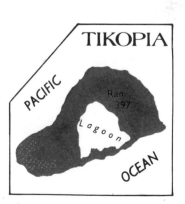

Melanesia
Melanesians, New Hebrides, Nambas, New Caledonia, Fijians

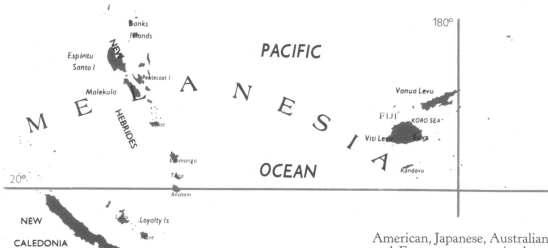

Melanesians

pop : 4,300,000

The islands of Melanesia span a distance of 2,000 miles across the south-west Pacific. They vary from small coral atolls to the third largest island in the world, New Guinea. Other large groups include the Solomons, New Hebrides and New Caledonia.

The Melanesians show a considerable diversity of physical type. Some are short in stature, with dark skin and frizzy hair; others are taller and more pale skinned. Some of the earlier inhabitants appear to have been pushed into less hospitable interior regions by waves of succeeding migrants. In colonial times there has been further immigration by alien populations, particularly in Fiji, where Indians, descendants of plantation labourers, now out-number the original Fijians.

The old way of life now exists only in isolated areas. Coconut palm, which is of paramount economic import-ance to coastal Melanesians, is the mainstay of life. The milk and flesh is eaten, the shells serve as utensils, the trunks provide building material and the fronds are woven for roof-ing, mats, baskets and clothes. Slash-and-burn cultivation is carried out with steel axes, spades, bush knives and wood-en digging and weeding sticks. Pigs are slaughtered and eaten during ritual feasts and cere-monies. Traditional craft objects are now increasingly being made for export and direct sale to tourists.

The indigenous people's land is officially protected but in the more accessible areas American, Japanese, Australian and European companies have exploited timber and mineral resources and destroyed the supplies of sandalwood, seals and whales. In parts of New Guinea, New Caledonia and the Solomons, plantations of copra, coffee and cocoa, or mining of copper and nickel, dominate the economy.

Melanesians are still partly dependent on external help for education, agricultural equip-ment and medicine. Young people are drawn away from their villages to wage employ-ment in the ports, where they gather in shanty towns and slums. Although the death rate, particularly amongst infants, has been reduced by western medicine, there has been a general decline in health due to the poor diet in these areas.

The abrupt mixture of two alien cultures has had a disas-trous effect on the Melanesians. Initially two-thirds of the population were killed by raiders and disease. In areas visited by American troops during the Second World War there has been a widespread development of cargo cults. The people threw away their own goods and worshipped western gods in the expectation of endless wealth that would come across the sea from a mythical benefactor. However, many of these cult activities have been replaced by develop-ment orientated political and economic movements.

New Hebrides

pop : 98,000

The New Hebrides consist of 12 main islands in Melanesia including Espíritu Santo, the largest, Tana, Efate, Pentecost, Malekula and Ambrim. They are under the general control of an Anglo-French condominium but each government retains responsibility for its own nationals. In the interior yams are grown and traditional cere-monies and arts flourish. The young tend to leave the villages for the coastal towns.

Coconut palm, always a mainstay of life, has become the major cash crop, followed by beef production, coffee and cocoa. Foreign settlers occupy a good deal of land. Experience of the American Army during the Second World War led to a cargo cult movement led by John Frum in the island of Tana. In recent years, the Nagriamel movement, based on Santo, has demanded inde-pendence for the islands.

Nambas

pop : 250

The Big and Small Nambas (Mbotgote) live at opposite ends of the island of Malekula in the New Hebrides; they grow yams and other vegetables by the slash-and-burn method. *Namba* is the word for the penis wrapper, whose relative size distinguishes these two tribes. Both have complex hierarchical fraternities; and in the case of the Small Nambas, a similar system exists for the women, who are typically excluded from the men's rituals and undergo the removal of their two front teeth on marriage.

The centre of male social life is the *nakamal*, or men's house, where *kava* drinking (a narcotic beverage derived from the root of *Piper methysticum*), graded initiation and, in the past, institutionalized homo-sexuality took place. Until the early 1900s cannibalism also featured in the ritual life of these two tribes.

Pigs are slaughtered during circumcision rituals for young men (which take place at about 17 years of age) and at ritual elevations from one level to another of the secret Nimangi society. Each ceremony is ac-companied by singing, dancing and drumming. The drums represent the ancestors, who are commemorated among the Small Nambas by carefully modelled clay figures incor-porating the actual skull of the deceased. The dancing signi-fies the initiate's rebirth into a new peer group in which he

assumes a new identity.

Many of the traditions of the Big Nambas have been lost as a result of migration to the coast, where conversion to Christianity has been necessary in order to acquire land or wives from the coastal Christian tribes. The Small Nambas, who live in the southern part of the island, have maintained their indigenous culture to a much greater extent.

New Caledonia
pop : 146,000

New Caledonia, disovered by James Cook in 1774, is today a French colony, the largest and most urbanized of the South Pacific islands. The population is a mixture of indigenous Melanesians, Europeans (mainly French), Indochinese, Javanese, Chinese and Japanese, the latter groups brought in originally as cheap labour. New Caledonia was particularly attractive to Europeans because of its mineral resources—iron and chrome, together with one of the most important nickel deposits in the world.

Friction between the indigenous Melanesians and cattle-raising European settlers has been rife, particularly as only

6 per cent of the land is arable. Coffee, coconut and timber are important cash crops and exports, but most of the Melanesians are subsistence farmers, growing yams, taro, manioc, maize and rice, and living in small rural villages.

Fijians
pop : 590,000

The 804 islands of Fiji lie on the eastern border of Melanesia. Many are coral atolls but they also include a number of high volcanic islands. The capital, Suva, is on the largest high island, Viti Levu. The indigenous Fijians (250,000) are outnumbered by Indians (295,000) descendants of those introduced in the colonial period as plantation labourers.

The indigenous Fijians seem to represent a fusion of Melanesian and Polynesian stocks. Probably first settled by the ancestors of the Polynesians around 1500 BC, the islands were Melanesianized a few centuries later by a new influx of people coming by way of the Solomon Islands. Later contacts with their western Polynesian neighbours further complicated the situation.

Trading and mission stations

were established in Fiji by the 1830s. Early contacts brought European diseases, reducing the local population. In 1858 the islands were ceded to Britain by King Cakobau, the chief of Bau. The colonial administration ended in 1970 when Fiji became an independent dominion of the Commonwealth. The term 'Fijian' has been used since then to cover all the inhabitants of the islands.

Most of the present population are engaged in agriculture. The Indian sector continues to play a major role in the cultivation of sugar, Fiji's most important export. With the small Chinese population, they also dominate the commercial life of Suva. In recent years, the indigenous Fijians have been moving in greater numbers to the Suva area, but the majority remain rural villagers.

The traditional food crops of taro and yams are still grown; coconuts are produced commercially on a large scale and their oil exported in a semi-refined state. Also important are bananas, rice, cocoa, maize and tobacco. Timber and animal husbandry are other sources of income and some gold is still mined.

Big Nambas in a Nimangi ceremony, Malekula

Micronesia

Micronesians, Mariana Islands, Caroline Islands, Marshall Islands, Gilbert Islands

Micronesians

pop: 120,000

The 2,000 small islands scattered across the Pacific Ocean between the Philippines and Hawaii include the Marianas, Carolines, Gilberts, Marshalls and Nauru. They are collectively known as Micronesia, but their inhabitants have little in common.

There are more than 11 mutually unintelligible languages and considerable physical variations can be seen even within single cultural groups. Peoples of the western islands have affinities with island South-East Asians; those of the eastern islands with Polynesians. Voyagers came from these areas in single outrigger canoes bringing their own culture and crops. They settled on the high volcanic islands such as the Carolines and Marianas.

Traditional communities vary from 50 to 500 people. Inter-island trade has never been highly developed, so each island depends on its own resources, from which tools, utensils, clothing, body adornments, housing and canoes are made. Staple foods range from rice, yams and taro to breadfruit and pandanus. Farming land is scarce so there is a heavy dependence on the sea.

Most islanders build one-room family shelters with smaller cooking huts. Meeting houses vary. On Palau they are spacious rooms of carved timber, while Yapese men's houses are small and made of logs lashed together. The Gilbertese have large assembly places with high roofs of thick thatch; the Trukese have low roofs. The Marshallese have no community centres.

Each household functions as an economic unit for subsistence activities; there are various systems of kinship groupings for wider social activities. Adoption is commonly practised, to balance family size and strengthen inter-family ties. Each person is assigned a particular place in the community according to kinship, residence, sex and age.

A group's identity is expressed by its traditional rights and obligations. Among unilineal groups, members with common ancestors, whether traced through the male or female line, are led by the eldest male. Land is the principal foundation of power, and some societies have a landowning upper class and autocratic chiefs. Competition for social prestige is through gift exchanges at sumptuous feasts. Death is the only event universally marked by ritual ceremonies. Marriages are usually arranged, but premarital sex is approved of (except in the Gilbert Islands), providing incest, within each local definition, is avoided.

Each society has its own creation myths and beliefs in spirits of the dead, who interact with the living during rituals. Christianity has been accepted with little effect on traditional religious beliefs.

The islands of Micronesia have been ruled variously by Spain, Britain, Germany, America, Japan and Australia. The effects of such rule ranged from minor modifications to new economic structures. Colonial rule prohibited warfare and helped alleviate the devastating after-effects of typhoons and droughts. The United States took over all the islands held by the Japanese after the Second World War. Modernization of Micronesian society has since accelerated, particularly with regard to health, education and politics.

Following the example of Pacific societies to the south of the equator, Nauru led the way for Micronesia by declaring independence in 1968. A year later the Congress of Micronesia in the United States Trust Territory initiated negotiations for self-government. Even on islands used as military bases moves have been made towards ultimate independence.

Mariana Islands

pop : 14,500

The Mariana Islands are the northernmost group in Micronesia. The indigenous population, Chamorros, are noticeably different from other Micronesians, partly owing to three centuries of intense intermingling with immigrants during Spanish and subsequent régimes. They were converted to Catholicism by Jesuit priests aided by government militia and their traditional culture was suppressed. The Chamorros' staple diet is rice supple-

160°

PACIFIC OCEAN

MICRONESIA

CAROLINE ISLANDS

Mariana Islands

Eniwetok

Truk Is

Ponape

Bikini

Rongelap

Rongirik

Bikar

MARSHALL

Wotho

Ailuk

Wotje

ISLANDS

Kwajalein

Ujae

Maloelap

Aur

Namu

Ailinglapalap

Majuro

Arno

Jaluit

Mili

mented by fish, but Japanese colonists introduced sugar cane as the main export crop.

Because of their strategic military position, the Marianas were made a trust area under the United Nations after the Second World War. When the United States' controlling body was approached by the Congress of Micronesia to negotiate self-government, it insisted on separate talks with the Marianas, largely to secure Tinian Island as a military base. In 1975, however, both sides agreed to a commonwealth status, with the prospect of independence by 1981.

More than 85 per cent of the population live on the island of Saipan, where archaeological work has produced evidence of human occupation at least 3,500 years ago.

Caroline Islands
pop : 80,000

The inhabitants of the Caroline Islands are ethnically Micronesian. They fall into five main cultural and linguistic groups, within which customs and dialects vary between the larger volcanic islands and outlying coral atolls. The staple diet is breadfruit and fish, which is in copious supply and easily caught. Coconut palm is the main cash crop.

Disease has been controlled by western medicine but the people still suffer from frequent typhoons and breadfruit blight. The Carolines belong to the American-governed Trust Territories of the Pacific. Offi-

cial policy is to encourage ways of bringing money to the islands other than by industrialization, which rarely benefits the islanders themselves. There are 64 small-scale cooperatives in the Trust Territories, handling local manufacture and marketing activities.

Yap islander, Micronesia

Marshall Islands
pop : 25,500

The Marshall Islands are composed of two atoll chains, Ratak and Ralik, and form the easternmost group of Micronesia. The people show mixed Asian and Polynesian characteristics and also cultural affinities with Polynesians. Their religious beliefs, however, have been lost and the chiefs' authority undermined by the successive influences of missionaries and traders.

Subsistence dependence on fishing and coconut palm has been changed by the pressures of world trade. Social benefits donated by America to atone for the effects of bomb testings on Bikini Island have increased cultural breakdown and led to overpopulation. The anticipated independent government will inherit these difficulties.

Gilbert Islands
pop : 51,500

The 16 Gilbert Islands, which form an arc linking Micronesia with Polynesia, are infertile and poorly watered coral atolls. The people are of Micronesian origin, and they had a turbulent history before British rule came late in the 19th century. Today the Gilbertese live in villages, a system introduced by the British, rather than their traditional scattered settlements. They have a sparse diet of coconut, pandanus and breadfruit, supplemented by fish.

263

Polynesians

pop : 720,000

The people of Polynesia live on Pacific islands within the vast Polynesian triangle which has corners over 4,000 miles apart at New Zealand, Easter Island and Hawaii. There are also Polynesian 'outlier' islands in the neighbouring areas of Melanesia and Micronesia.

It seems most likely that the ancestors of the Polynesians were a maritime people of South-East Asian origin, whose voyages, commencing about 4000 BC, led to a progressive spread across the Pacific. Speakers of eastern Oceanic languages established themselves in Fiji about 1500 BC and it seems that it was from here that the proto-Polynesian colony of Tonga was established some 300 years later.

The spread to eastern Polynesia was probably through Samoa to the Marquesas, the latter becoming the centre for the initial dispersion to the eastern islands. Though some islands within the Polynesian triangle were settled later, the limits of the dispersion were reached by the 9th century AD. Arguments have been put forward for the colonization of Polynesia from the American continent, thus explaining the widespread presence of the sweet potato, a South American food plant, but the bulk of evidence overwhelmingly favours Asian origins.

Many similarities persisted throughout Polynesia, especially in physical types and language. However, there is a marked distinction between the western and eastern groups, connected partly with the early split, partly with Melanesian influence in the west. Though there have been internal developments in the social structures of the various islands, a hierarchy with successive chiefly ranks above the base of commoners is widespread. Chiefly authority was frequently connected with descent in the line of firstborn sons from a founding ancestor.

European contacts, from the late 18th century on, disrupted the traditional way of life. In a number of areas introduced diseases such as smallpox and measles had a devastating effect on the population. The activities of the missionaries undermined both the traditional religions themselves and the ritual authority of the chiefs. Dispossession of lands was not infrequent. In the 19th century, the Polynesian people found themselves within the framework of colonial government.

In the 20th century there has been a great recovery in the population, and migration to work in centres such as Tahiti or New Zealand has become common. Accompanying a revival of interest in traditional culture has been the increasing awareness of, and development of skills for, the contemporary economic and political situation.

Hawaiians

pop: 847,000

The Hawaiian Islands, lying in the northern corner of the Polynesian triangle, have been the 50th state of America since 1959. The population is composed of a large number of racial groups. Apart from the descendants of the original Hawaiians, there are white Americans, Chinese, Japanese, Filipinos, Koreans, Portuguese, Puerto Ricans and many others.

The islands were first settled in the early centuries of the Christian era, probably from the Marquesas. But this seems to have been followed in the 12th century AD by an influx of people from the Society Islands. The Hawaiians developed a highly stratified political system with strong contrasts drawn between the *ali'i*, the chiefly title holders with authority over life and land, and the commoners who worked the land. The topmost grades of chief were supreme and sacred, supposedly transcending political affairs.

It was from a slightly lower grade of chieftainship that the first Hawaiian king, Kamehameha I, emerged from the 1780s onwards. The founding of the kingdom of Hawaii in 1810 was the climax of a period of warfare and social upheaval; as in Tahiti, European arms played a major part in the creation of a new state. European influence increased as the chiefs co-operated with foreign commercial and agricultural interests.

In the 10 years after 1820, Calvinist missionaries gained indirect control of the political decisions on all eight inhabited islands, aided by princesses of the Hawaiian ruling family. American sugar-planters and exporters became the dominant economic group, while Chinese, Japanese, and Portuguese labourers were brought in to work the plantations. By 1898, when the United States annexed the islands, the native Hawaiians had almost entirely lost control of their lands and their culture was in an advanced state of dissolution.

Modern Hawaii is a complex

Map labels

Niihau
Kauai
Oahu
Honolulu
HAWAIIAN ISLANDS
Maui
Hawaii
Hilo

Palmyra I
LINE
ISLANDS
Fanning I
Christmas I

0°

GILBERT ISLANDS

POLYNESIA

ELLICE ISLANDS

TOKELAU IS

Wallis Is

Pago Pago
AMERICAN SAMOA

Vanua Levu

Vava'u Group

and cosmopolitan society. Tourism and the servicing of military installations are superseding the sugar industry in importance. In this so-called 'melting pot' of races, tensions between the different groups remain muted. There has been much debate on what form the fusion of cultures should take and on the rights of the native Hawaiian population.

Samoans
pop : 200,000

Geographically and politically the Samoan archipelago falls into two divisions, the large islands of Savaii and Upolu in the west *(157,000)*, and the much smaller Tauila and Manu'a group of American Samoa *(30,000)*. Upolu is the most populous and fertile of these islands. Apia, the capital and main port of Western Samoa lies on its northern coast.

The group is believed to have been settled from Tonga about 800 BC or earlier. Traditions also refer to hostile invasions from Fiji and subsequently Tonga—it is claimed that the Tongan invaders were eventually expelled, but a period of internal wars followed. When the Europeans arrived they found widespread warfare, involving disputes over rank and dominance.

In 1900 the islands were divided between the United States and Germany. After the First World War, German Samoa came under New Zealand control but since 1962 has been the independent state of Western Samoa. American Samoa, still administered by the US Department of the Interior, is comparitively wealthy, with much economic assistance from the United States. The relative poverty of Western Samoa is parallelled by its greater cultural stability.

Villages, formed from the association of extended families or *aiga*, can vary in population from 100 to 1,000. At various levels of the social structure there are *matai*, or title holders. These range from village household heads, to the leader of several branches of an extended family, to the head of an entire district. At the top of the system there are four paramount chiefly titles with influence throughout the islands.

Samoa is increasingly drawn into the world economy, whether through its migrant labourers, tourism, or its export trade in bananas, timber, copra and cocoa. Over the last century its culture has shown itself adaptable and relatively cohesive in the face of outside influences, especially in the western islands.

Marquesas Islands
pop: 5,600

The Marquesas cluster of volcanic islands in the north-eastern corner of French Polynesia is now thought to be a likely site for the earliest settlement of eastern Polynesia. There is evidence, such as the presence of pottery in archaeological sites of the 4th century AD, to connect the Marquesas with western Polynesia and even with Melanesia. Dates as early as 150 BC have been suggested for the contact. Subsequently the Marquesas became a centre for the early east Polynesian dispersal.

Pigs and chickens were apparently brought by the early settlers and these, with taro, bananas, coconuts and fish, were important items in the traditional Marquesan diet after the staple breadfruit. Modern villagers continue to rely heavily on these foods.

Tongans
pop : 107,000

The kingdom of Tonga is composed of some 150 islands in 2,000 square miles of ocean. They form three main groups and are largely made up of coral limestone. Nuku'alofa, in Tongatapu, is the only urbanized area, and the political and administrative centre. Tonga became completely independent of Britain in 1970.

Tonga was settled by the ancestors of the Polynesians in about the 12th century BC, probably from Fiji. With them came the decorated Lapita pottery which has been useful in identifying the migration routes. There has also been contact with the Melanesian peoples who later occupied Fiji, and some intermarriage. Tonga developed a society with a strong central chieftainship which has left its mark in the presence of monumental tombs. After the 15th century, this dissolved into a long period of warring rivalry. It was not until European influence was operating that a lasting centralized authority was again established under the Tongan King George I (Tupou).

About 80 per cent of Tongan men are farmers. The main food plants are yams, taro, sweet potatoes, manioc and sugar cane, with introduced fruits. Fish, chickens, pigs and tinned meat provide protein; large pigs are often reserved for ceremonial occasions. Cash crops include bananas and coconuts for copra.

Most Tongans live in small villages, but migration to the larger towns is increasing About one-fifth of the total population of the group now live in Nuku'alofa on Tongatapu. Many urban dwellers work for the government or in light industries such as furniture production, sawmills or bakeries. Home production of goods such as shell necklaces, baskets or bark cloth provides a source of exports and an incentive to the prosperous tourist trade.

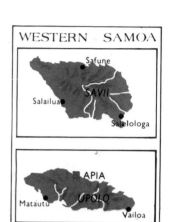

WESTERN SAMOA

Safune • SAVII • Salailua Salelologa

APIA • UPOLO • Matautu • Vailoa

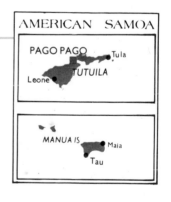

AMERICAN SAMOA

PAGO PAGO • Tula TUTUILA Leone •

MANUA IS • Maia • Tau

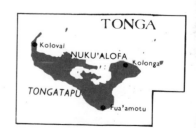

TONGA

• Koloval NUKU'ALOFA • Kolonga TONGATAPU • Fua'amotu

MARQUESAS IS
Nuku Hiva • Hiva Oa • Fatu Hiva

Caroline I

TUAMOTU
Rangiroa • Fakarava • Raroia
SOCIETY ISLANDS ARCHIPELAGO
Moorea • Tahiti • Anaa • Hao

140°

Cook Islands

pop : 21,000

The 15 islands of the Cook group lie in a band 770 miles long between Tonga and Samoa in the west and the Society Islands in the east. Of these, 10 are traditional centres of population: in the northern group of coral atolls, Pukapuka, Manihiki, Rakahanga and Tongareva (Penrhyn); in the southern group, largely high islands of volcanic origin, Rarotonga, Aitutaki, Mangaia, Atiu, Mitiaro and Mauke. Rarotonga, the largest island, is the centre of government, with more than half the population of the group.

The first settlers probably came from eastern Polynesia before 1050 AD, but archaeology and local tradition support the idea of further settlement, both from the Society group and from the Samoan area, around 1200 AD. Tradition also refers to voyages from Rarotonga to New Zealand. The first estab-

lished European presence came in the 1820s, with the arrival of Congregationalist missionaries. Since 1965 the Cook Islands have had their own government in free association with New Zealand. The prolonged treatment of the group as an administrative whole has tended to blur cultural and language differences between the islands.

Each island has one or more *ariki*, or principal chiefs, selected from chiefly lineages. First-born sons of the previous chief might usually have precedence but nowadays women may succeed to the titles. Formerly a rank of supreme authority, with control over life and land, the *ariki* are now forced increasingly into the position of advisors. However, some still wield a certain economic power with respect to the distribution of land. Ranking below the *ariki* are chiefs such as the *mataiapo* and *rangatira*, connected with lesser lineages and smaller land divisions.

Taro remains the staple root crop in most areas, but commercial citrus and pineapple production is now of major importance. Working opportunities remain limited, however, especially in the outer islands. Migration from these to Rarotonga and from there to New Zealand, in search of better employment and more varied living, has reached high levels. Some one-third of all Cook Islanders now live in New Zealand.

Tahitians

pop : 80,000

Tahiti is the principal island of the Windward group of the Society Islands. The town of Papeete is a centre for the whole of French Polynesia. It is a focus of territorial politics, communications, commerce and tourism.

The Society Islands were probably settled by Polynesians in about 500 AD. Little is known of the early history, but it seems that the group's early ritual and religious centre, on the island of Raiatea, was superseded by the military power of Tahiti. In the late 18th century, arriving Europans found a number of warring chieftancies. Some Europeans entered into these civil wars and it was with the aid of English firepower that the Tahitian chiefs Pomare the First and Second brought about the unification of the Society Islands under their control. Only after the population had been drastically reduced, in more than a decade of violent warfare, did the Tahitian state come into being with the collapse of resistance in 1815.

After a period of London Missionary Society activity, French influence began to grow in the 1830s. This led to the establishment of a protectorate in Tahiti in the next decade.

Under the influence of the missionaries district populations became concentrated into villages which became new political units, presided over by chiefs, with the backing of the central government. In the 1940s the election of village chiefs began. They are paid by the government and responsible for carrying out national policy; they also preside over village meetings.

Rural agriculture continues with copra and vanilla produc-

tion and the cultivation of food crops such as taro, sweet potatoes and bananas. However, many Tahitians have moved into the urban Papeete area and more are commuting into the town. Government spending in the late 1950s encouraged the growth of wage labour in such areas as construction, services and transport. Immigrants from the outer islands of the group have also swelled the population.

Pitcairn Islands

pop : 80

Sub-tropical Pitcairn is the tip of a volcano rising 1,000 feet above sea level, situated in mid-Pacific Ocean. The inhabitants are the offspring of mutineers from HMS *Bounty* and 12 Polynesian women whom they brought from Tahiti. After the mutiny in January 1790, led by Fletcher Christian, half the crew sailed to Pitcairn by way of Tahiti, where most of them remained. The nine mutineers who settled on Pitcairn hoped to avoid discovery and it was 18 years before a passing ship called in at the island.

The community today subsists on crops such as bread-

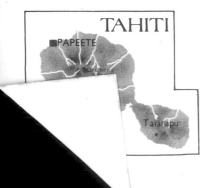

Night fishing in Tahiti

GAMBIER IS

Oeno

Pitcairn I

fruit, banana, coconut, taro, yam, sugar cane, beans, melons, pumpkins and arrowroot, grown in rich volcanic soils and supplemented by fish, poultry, goats, and occasional beef and other food from passing ships.

Several forays by the islanders into the outside world of Tahiti, Norfolk Island and New Zealand have not been successful, most returning to Pitcairn.

Easter Island
pop: 1,800

Easter Island is the most easterly outpost of Polynesia. It is perhaps best known for its massive stone statues, carved human figures, showing the top half of the body. These statues, up to 70 feet high, have provoked much speculation. It has been suggested that they are one of the signs of an island aristocracy of South American origin. However, the evidence from Easter Island overwhelmingly indicates strong cultural links with the rest of Polynesia. Settled about the 5th century AD, probably from the Marquesas, the limited set of seemingly unique features, such as the giant statuary or an embryonic writing, may reasonably be seen as internal developments of a culture isolated over a fairly long period.

Legend names Hotu Matua as the founding chief of Easter Island society. The ritual authority of chieftainship was held by the Miru tribe. If the sanctity of the high chief was always recognized, real political power came to lie in the hands of the warrior chiefs of the other tribes. Rivalry and warfare have marked the island's history, and there are traditions suggesting that the statues themselves were erected in competition with other tribes, as marks of power. Though the base of the warrior chiefs' power was military, they also had a religious role. The chief whose representative succeeded first in an annual ritual search for the egg of a certain seabird became, for a year, the Bird Man, representing a god. He was entitled to offerings from the whole island.

The 18th and early 19th centuries were a period of increasingly violent warfare. Legend tells how the 'Short Ears' fought the 'Long Ears' (aristocrats) and slew them, perhaps putting to an end the stonework in the quarries. But it was outside influences, the ravages of Peruvian slavers and the devastating introduction of smallpox, which ensured the almost total destruction of the culture. In 1888 the island came under the control of Chile and was largely turned over to a company of Scottish sheep breeders. The descendants of the last Easter Islanders, the impoverished agriculturalists and fishermen of today, have few links with the world of their ancestors.

Easter I

EASTER ISLAND

Glossary

Age grade. A group of people born within a specified period of time and forming an association within a given society.

Animism. Belief in spirits or souls, supernatural beings associated with objects or people.

Archaeology. The study of man's past, by reference to physical remains of skeletons and artifacts.

Band. A small, mobile group of hunter-gatherers, organised along the simplest lines and normally consisting of between 10 and 100 people.

Brideprice (Bridewealth). A payment of valued goods made by a man to the family of his wife. Bridewealth normally acts to legitimise a marriage and the subsequent children born within it, and often has wide-ranging implications for political and economic relations within the society.

Caste. A system of hierarchical social groups, often based on occupation. Membership is by birth, and each person must marry within their own group.

Clan. A group who are related by reason of common ancestors, from whom all members trace a real or fictive descent.

Cross-cousins. Children of a brother and sister are cross-cousins to each other. Where descent is traced through one parent, cross-cousins will be members of different social groups.

Dowry. Valued goods transferred from a woman's family to her husband or his family, upon marriage.

Ecosystem. The total system of organisms (including humans) and their environment.

Endogamy. Marriage within a defined group, with a prohibition on marrying anyone outside it.

Ethnocentrism. The belief that the practices and values of one's own group are exemplary and constitute a universal standard by which other societies may be judged.

Extended family. One which includes relatives other than those of the nuclear family.

Exogamy. Marriage outside a defined group, with a prohibition on marrying within it.

Horticulture. The cultivation of land without the use of the plough. Generally digging sticks and hoes are used to tend the soil.

Hunting-gathering. A form of subsistence relying solely upon naturally occurring vegetable products and hunted animals, birds and fish.

Initiation. The rituals surrounding a transition from one social category to another. Most usually associated with the acquisition of adult status.

Kinship. Social relationships implying either descent or marriage.

Lineage. A group who claim descent from a single ancestor, traced through either the male or female line. Smaller than a clan, which may consist of several lineages.

Matrilineage. A group who trace descent through the female line to a single ancestor or ancestress.

Monogamy. The practice of a man or woman taking only one spouse at a time.

Nuclear family. A married couple and their children.

Patrilineage. A group who claim descent through the male line from a single ancestor.

Pollution. Notion that contact with people of a certain status or condition, for example lower castes or menstruating women, can be spiritually defiling and require ritual cleansing.

Polyandry. The practice of having more than one husband at a time.

Polygamy. The practice of having more than one spouse at a time.

Polygyny. The practice of having more than one wife at a time.

Reciprocity. The obligation to provide aid, services or goods in return for aid, services or goods received.

Savanna. Tropical or sub-tropical region characterized by grassland with scattered trees.

Shaman. A religious specialist, with extraordinary supernatural powers and duties.

Totemism. A belief system identifying the founding ancestor of a clan or lineage with some aspect of the physical environment.

Transhumance. The seasonal movement of herding peoples between pastures.

Bibliography

Bacon E. E., Central Asians Under Russian Rule, 1966

Bawden C. R., The Modern History of Mongolia, 1968

Beauclair I., Tribal Cultures of South-East China, 1970

Birkett-Smith K. A. J., The Eskimos, 1959

Cameron N., China Today, 1974

Chowning A., An Introduction to the Peoples and Cultures of Melanesia (2nd ed.), 1977

Davidson B. R., Africa: History of a Continent, 1966

Davis J., People of the Mediterranean, 1977

Driver H. E., Indians of North America (2nd ed.), 1969

Duprée L., Afghanistan, 1973

Fisher W. B., The Middle East (5th ed.), 1963

Forde C. D. (ed.), African Worlds, 1954

Franklin S. H., The European Peasantry, 1968

Fürer-Haimendorf, C. von (ed.), Caste and Kin in Nepal, India and Ceylon, 1966

Gellner E. & Micaud C. A. (ed.), Arabs and Berbers, 1973

Gregory J. S., Russian Land, Soviet People, 1968

Grube E. J., The World of Islam, 1967

Harrison B., South-East Asia (3rd ed.), 1966

Heath D. B. & Adams R. N. (ed.), Contemporary Cultures and Societies of South America, 1965

Horowitz M., Peoples and Cultures of the Caribbean, 1971

Kunstadter P., South-East Asian Tribes, Minorities and Nations, 1967

Levin M. G. & Potapov L. P. (ed.), The Peoples of Siberia, 1964

Lévi-Strauss C., A World on the Wane, 1961

Maddock K., The Australian Aborigines, 1973

Mair L. P., African Societies, 1974

Maloney C., Peoples of South Asia, 1974

Ogilvie A. G., Europe and its Borderlands, 1957

Oliver D. L., The Pacific Islands, 1958

Pitt-Rivers J. (ed.), Mediterranean Countrymen, 1963

Steward J. H. & Faron L. C., Native Peoples of South America, 1959

Index

THE PHOTOGRAPHS

The photographs were reproduced by permission of the following agencies and their photographers
Title Page, Brian Culley, **The World of Man**, The Mansell Collection p.8, **North America**, William Albert Allard p 39, Ted Spiegel/Rapho p 41, Toby Molenaar p 43, Sigurd Bo Bojesen p 45, Adam Woolfitt/Susan Griggs p 48-49, Burt Glinn/Magnum p 53, 54-55, Jeffrey Fox/Susan Griggs p 57, **South America**, Brian Moser/ Disappearing World p 63, 64-65, Mike Andrews p 66-67, Jean Liedloff p 71, Reflejo/Susan Griggs p 72-73, Victor Englebert/Susan Griggs p 75, Bruno Barbey/Magnum p 84-85, John Hemming p 79, 81, Cornell Capa/ Magnum p 84-85, **Europe,** Daily Telegraph p 91, Bruno Barbey/Magnum p 94, Adam Woolfitt/Susan Griggs p 95, John Marmaras/Susan Griggs p 97, Elliott Erwitt/Magnum p 98-99, David Williamson p 101, Alan Hutchison p 102-103, John Bulmer p 107, Constantine Manos/John Hillelson p 108-109, **Middle East/North Africa,** John Bulmer p 115, Peter Fraenkel p 117, Foto Quilichi p 119, Peter Ibbotson/Robert Harding Ass. p 121, William Carter/Camera Press p 123, Tor Eigeland/Black Star p 124-125, 131, Daily Telegraph p 128-129, Bruno Barbey/Magnum p 132-133, **Africa,** Sarah Errington/Alan Hutchison p 141, Victor Engelbert/Susan Griggs p 143, André Singer/Disappearing World p 144-145, Christopher Hallpike p 147, Alan Hutchison p 151, Victor Engelbert/Susan Griggs p 152-153, S. Sassoon/Robert Harding Ass. p 156-157, M. Ricciardi/Virginia Fass p 159, James Barr/Syndication International p 161, Daniel Coulaud p 162-163, John Bulmer p 166-167 (Top), Brian Seed/John Hillelson p 166-167 (Bottom), **Soviet Union,** J. N. Reichel/Agence Top/Colorific p 172-173, Philip Lineton p 175, Howard Sochurek/John Hillelson p 177, Sigurd Bo Bojeson p 178-179, Roland Michaud/John Hillelson p 182-183, p 185, Brian Moser/Disappearing World p 187, **India/South Central Asia,** Josephine Powell p 192-193, Jay Myrdal p 194-195, Disappearing World/Granada TV p 196-197, C. von Fürer-Haimendorf p 199, Schuyler Jones p 200-201, R. Singh/John Hillelson p 203, Richard Waller/Ardea p 204-205, Marilyn Silverstone/ Magnum p 207, R. Singh/John Hillelson p 210-211, Bruno Barbey/Magnum p 213, **China/East and South Asia,** Donald McCullin/Sunday Times p 219, Bruno Barbey/Magnum p 221, Robert Harding Ass. p 222-223, Julian Cowan/Colorific p 224-225, Marc Riboud/Magnum p 226-227, M. Cowell/Transworld p 228-229, Bob Croxford p 230-231, John Launois/Black Star p 235, R. Singh/John Hillelson p 236-237, Victor Engelbert/Transworld p 239, Brian Culley p 240-241, James Fox p 243, **Australasia/Pacific,** Thomas Hopker/John Hillelson p 249, Photographic Library of Australia p 251, Malcolm Kirk p 252-253, Disappearing World/Granada TV p 255, David Moore/ Colorific p 258-259, Kal Müller/Susan Griggs p 261, F. J. Maroon/Louis Mercier p 623, Robert Lebeck/ Black Star p 267.